INTRODUCTION
RESEARCH
methods

INTRODUCTION TO
RESEARCH

methods

Robert B. Burns

SAGE Publications
London • Thousand Oaks • New Delhi

© 2000 Pearson Education Australia Pty Limited
First published 1990
Reprinted 1991
Second Edition 1994
Reprinted 1995
Third Edition 1997
Reprinted 1998
Fourth Edition 2000

Sage Publications International Edition 2000

SAGE Publications Ltd
6 Bonhill Street
London EC2A 4PU

SAGE Publications Inc
2455 Teller Road
Thousand Oaks, California 91320

SAGE Publications India Pvt Ltd
32, M-Block Market
Greater Kailash - I
New Delhi 110 048

British Library Cataloguing in Publication data

A catalogue record for this book is available from the British Library

ISBN 0 7619 6592 0 (hbk)
ISBN 0 7619 6593 9 (pbk)

Library of Congress catalog record available

Contents

Preface

Preface to the new expanded edition

Being asked to prepare an international edition is both exciting and a challenge. It is exciting because it means the continuation of a project that has been successful in its aims already—to provide a simple yet reasonably thorough basic grounding in the essential concepts and practical application of quantitative and qualitative research methods without too much mathematical notation and number manipulation, which many other texts appear to focus on and which make the subject a big turn off.

It is challenging because the request demands a response of further development. Therefore, in this edition I have introduced several additional topics. There are new chapters on regression and meta-analysis, both of which have been asked for by users of the text. Secondly, I have included a chapter which introduces the reader in simple terms to the role of effect size and power, both increasingly regarded as important alternatives to conventional significance testing in evaluating the results of investigations.

The ubiquity of statistical programs for the PC has encouraged me to include, at the end of each chapter covering statistical tests, a short set of instructions on how to use SPSS for data analysis for that statistical procedure and how to interpret the output. The choice of SPSS rather than any other program was based on the fact that it is the most popular statistical software used in the social sciences.

Little else has altered in the text but I hope the additional material will be to the liking of those who have used the text as teachers and students over the last decade.

R.B. Burns, Brunei, September 1999

Preface to the first edition

Education is a complex process and we know, even now, only a small part of how it operates and of the reciprocal interaction between the process and the pupils, teachers, parents and the many others involved. There are so many things we wish to know and the only safe way to produce knowledge in which we can put our faith is to conduct systematic research.

The overriding purpose of this book is to provide a basic understanding of the main techniques, concepts and paradigms for conducting research in education in both quantitative and qualitative modes.

Methodology and statistics have been integrated into one text, since neither is much use without the other. By the end of the book, the student should be able to evaluate the research of others, define a problem, formulate hypotheses about the problem, design and carry out a valid and reliable study of the problem, apply the correct statistics, discuss the results and implications, and write it all up in a sensible and logical manner.

Experience has shown that many students and teachers are reluctant to study this area as it is seen as mathematical and the milieu of experts. This book attempts to demystify the role of experts and dispel such fears and negative attitudes by the logical sequencing of material and by using simple examples and practice exercises employing only basic arithmetic. It is hoped that even the mathematically inept will enjoy and understand the material. What is a very complex array of concepts, designs and statistics has been presented in everyday language, and questions for self-testing current understanding (STQs) are presented within the text as well as at the ends of most chapters.

The text is addressed to a wide variety of students, but primarily to those in pre-service and in-service teacher education courses. It would also be suitable for any social science and para-medical course needing an introductory text in the area. The book can be used in class or in conditions of minimum support in distance education, as reference to previous material is deliberately made throughout the text since this distributed repetition improves retention, understanding and transfer.

The text organisation encourages students to proceed through the book, chapter by chapter, rather than dipping in here and there; for as students master the material in one chapter, they are providing a basis for the understanding of future material.

I am grateful to the Literary Executor of the late Sir Ronald A. Fisher, FRS, to Dr Frank Yates, FRS, and the Longman Group Ltd, London, for permission to reprint Tables III, IV and VI from their book *Statistical Tables for Biological, Agricultural and Medical Research* (6th edition, 1974).

Finally, I wish all those who use the text 'good luck' in their studies. Many of your predecessors have contributed to the viewpoints and thinking that characterise this text. To them I owe a debt of gratitude. I am particularly indebted to Shelley and Caroline who produced such a splendid manuscript out of my hieroglyphics.

Finally, to my family, who endured patiently the long periods of selfish devotion I spent on the production of this text, I am profoundly grateful for their support.

R.B. Burns
Perth, Western Australia

PART 1
GENERAL ORIENTATION

Contrasting perspectives

1
one

Introduction

Research is a systematic investigation to find answers to a problem. Research in professional social science areas, like research in other subjects, has generally followed the traditional objective scientific method. Since the 1960s, however, a strong move towards a more qualitative, naturalistic and subjective approach has left social science research divided between two competing methods: the scientific empirical tradition, and the naturalistic phenomenological mode.

In the scientific method, quantitative research methods are employed in an attempt to establish general laws or principles. Such a scientific approach is often termed *nomothetic* and assumes social reality is objective and external to the individual.

The naturalistic approach to research emphasises the importance of the subjective experience of individuals, with a focus on qualitative analysis. Social reality is regarded as a creation of individual consciousness, with meaning and the evaluation of events seen as a personal and subjective construction. Such a focus on the individual case rather than general law-making is termed an *ideographic* approach.

Each of these two perspectives on the study of human behaviour has profound implications for the way in which research is conducted.

The traditional scientific approach

This approach has been the conventional approach to research in all areas of investigation. The methods and purposes of scientific inquiry have been moulded by countless generations of scientists who have collectively built a foundation of premises and beliefs, including an assumption of the validity of the utility of empiricism. This assumption holds that data must yield proof or strong confirmation, in probability terms, of a theory or hypothesis in a research setting. Scientists ultimately aim to formulate laws to account for the happenings in the world around them, thus giving them a firm basis for prediction and control. The assumptions built into this scientific approach constitute a particular model of research incorporating objectivity, reliability, generality and reductionism. 'Truth' within this paradigm tends to be fixed and singular; reflective of a causal and factual view of reality.

The uncritical acceptance of this approach has led to its assimilation within research to the point where measurement and control have been seen as the central locus of investigative endeavours. The term *positivism* has been applied to this conventional approach to research which incorporates methods and principles of natural science for the study of human behaviour. It is understandable how this occurred, for what was seen as the alternative—namely, lay person's intuition, subjective judgement and common sense—provides, in most cases, information and theories which are neither common, in that they are generally agreed upon, nor make 'sense', in that they are rational. We are well aware that many of our everyday observations and opinions are distorted in the very act of being made through subjective bias and prejudice. We stereotype others on scanty evidence and generalise conclusions well beyond any valid range of generalisation. Human beings function on a folklore of unjustified assumptions about behaviour and woolly armchair philosophising. Every day, for example, teachers, parents, politicians and the media make unjustified assertions on often important issues, such as:

'Boys are better than girls at mathematics.'
'Too much TV watching ruins children's eyesight.'
'Memorising poetry improves the memory.'
'Corporal punishment never did me any harm.'
'Compulsory conscription for all young people would develop their character and national spirit.'
'Permissive parents produce children who end up in court.'

and so on. Additionally, we are confronted daily with claims by so-called experts; claims that have consequences in daily living. Those who can evaluate such claims are better able to separate good solutions from current fads.

However, in order to understand these topics and find real and valid evidence, traditional social science research holds that only a systematic, quantitative approach to generating and testing ideas is adequate. Too often, decisions are made by parents, schools, civil servants, professionals in the helping services, and local and central government on important social issues on the basis of expediency, preconception, personal ideology and bias, and not on the basis of the true facts.

The difference between the lay person and the scientific researcher is that the latter employs objective, systematic investigation with analysis of data in order to discern *what actually is the case* rather than a patchwork of likes and dislikes, rules of thumb, analogy and prejudice, half-truths and old wives' tales. For example, it seemed self-evident that punishment must be the most effective way to stop certain unwanted behaviours until Skinner demonstrated the greater effectiveness of extinction in conjunction with positive reinforcement.

STQ1

Write down in your notebook a couple of sentences explaining why research has tended to adopt a systematic approach to the study of human behaviour/human issues.

Methods of knowing

There are four general ways of knowing, according to Kerlinger (1986):

1 **Method of tenacity**. Here one holds to the truth because one knows it to be true. The more frequent the repetition of the 'truth', the more the enhancement of the validity of it. It is self-evident then, and people will cling to such beliefs. For example, even in the face of contrary evidence some people believe that all communists are spies.

2 **Method of authority**. A thing must be true if it is in the Bible, or the prime minister says it, or a teacher said so. The method of authority is not always unsound but we never know when it is or isn't. But we lack individual resources to investigate everything, so the presumed competence of authority offers advantages.

3 **Method of intuition** (*a priori* method). This claims that reason is the criterion of truth. It 'stands to reason' that learning difficult subjects must build moral character. But whose reason is to carry the judgement, if two eminent persons using rational processes reach different conclusions?

4 **Method of science**. This method has one characteristic none of the other methods has—that is, self-correction. The checks verify and control the scientist's activities and conclusions. Even if a hypothesis seems to have support, the scientist will also test alternative hypotheses. Knowledge is attained through a controlled systematic process because science ultimately appeals to evidence; hypotheses are subjected to test. None of the other ideas, opinions, theories and methods above provide any procedure for establishing the superiority of one belief over another. Science is not just a body of knowledge but a logic of inquiry, for generating, replenishing and correcting knowledge.

Characteristics of the scientific approach

The scientific method has specific characteristics. These characteristics, while necessary to distinguish science, are not limited to the realm of science. Each of the characteristics could also exist outside of science; however, science could not exist without these characteristics. The four most important characteristics of science are **control**, **operational definition**, **replication** and **hypothesis testing**.

Control

Control is perhaps the single most important element in scientific methodology because it enables the scientist to identify the causes of his or her observations. Experiments are conducted in an attempt to answer certain questions. They represent attempts to identify why something happens, what causes some event, or under what conditions an event does occur. Control is necessary in order to provide unambiguous answers to such questions.

To answer questions in education and social science we have to eliminate the simultaneous influence of many variables to isolate the cause of an effect. Controlled inquiry is an absolutely essential process because without it the cause of an effect could not be isolated. The observed effect could be due to any one or a combination of the uncontrolled variables. Here is an example:

> In order to test the hypothesis that anagrams formed from unfamiliar words are harder to solve than those formed from familiar words, several variables other than the one we are interested in (i.e. familiarity) must be controlled or else the results may be due to the unmeasured effects of these too. For example, all the words must be of equal length because length will influence solution time, and all the subjects must be equally unpractised or equally expert at solving anagrams, or else practice will have a major effect.

Operational definition

Operational definition means that terms must be defined by the steps or operations used to measure them. Such a procedure is necessary to eliminate confusion in meaning and communication. Consider the statement, 'Anxiety causes students to score poorly in tests'. One might ask, 'What is meant by anxiety?'. Stating that *anxiety* refers to being tense or some other such term only adds to the confusion. However, stating that anxiety refers to a score over a criterion level on an anxiety scale enables others to realise what you mean by anxiety. Stating an operational definition forces one to identify the empirical referents, or terms. In this manner, ambiguity is minimised. Again, *introversion* might be defined as a score on a particular personality scale, *hunger* as so many hours since last fed, and *social class* as defined by father's occupation.

Replication

To be replicable, the data obtained in an experiment must be reliable; that is, the same result must be found if the study is repeated. That science has such a requirement is quite obvious, since it is attempting to obtain knowledge about the world. If observations are not repeatable, our descriptions and explanations are likewise unreliable and therefore useless.

Hypothesis testing

The lay person uses theories and concepts in a loose fashion, often accepting ludicrous explanations for human behaviour. For instance, 'Being ill is a punishment for being sinful'; 'An economic depression may be attributed to Asian immigrants'. On the other hand, the scientific researcher would systematically create a hypothesis and subject it to an empirical test.

The lay person tests a 'hypothesis' in a selective fashion by choosing evidence to fit the hypothesis. He or she may believe that male students have long hair. The lay person will verify this belief by noting a large number of instances of it. He or she will, however, fail to notice exceptions. The more sophisticated researcher who is aware of this tendency will test the relationship systematically in the field or in the laboratory.

The best known of the critics of 'pseudo-science' is Karl Popper, who tells how, as a young man in Vienna, he knew the psychiatrist Adler:

> . . . I reported to him a case which to me did not seem particularly Adlerian, but in which he found no difficulty analysing the terms of his theory of inferiority feelings, although he had not even seen the child. Slightly shocked, I asked him how he could be so sure. 'Because of my thousand-fold experience', he replied; whereupon I could not help saying, 'And with this new case, I suppose your experience has become thousand-and-one-fold'. (Popper 1957, p. 35).

Without rules which could be followed by any trained observer for operationalising 'inferiority complex', observations of the concept are not observations in a scientific sense because there are no checks on what is and what is not an instance of the concept.

Science is a 'public' method, open to all who learn its methods, and a similar observation of the same subject using the same operationalised concept should give the same result. Where reliance is placed, argues Popper, on the 'private' opinion of the expert (such as Adler) without strict rules of observation, the test of any hypothesis linking 'inferiority complex' to another concept is unsatisfactory.

Science, logic and Popper

The general approach that scientific knowledge is the only valid form of knowledge is called *positivism*. The Positivists (often associated with the beliefs of the French philosopher Comte) emphasised the role of discrete and distinct steps on the path to knowledge as the best way of discovering things. Positivists were very hostile to the supposed existence of things that can neither be seen nor heard. The philosophy of Behaviourism that arose in psychology, as exemplified by Watson and Skinner, was an example of this sort of thinking. Thus, in studying human behaviour, beliefs, feelings, introspections and the like were not regarded as valid phenomena that could be investigated within the ambit of a scientific study of behaviour. However, most definitions of science and methods of scientific inquiry may only be valid for the natural sciences. They are less valid when applied to the human sciences due to the ability of humans to reflect on their own behaviour.

Popper proposed in his account of the logic of scientific discovery that theories should be 'falsifiable'. Falsifiability for him is the criterion which distinguishes science from pseudo-science (of which Freudianism, Marxism and astrology are his chief examples). Falsifiability is the doctrine that hypotheses should be submitted to rigorous testing in an attempt to show they are wrong. Science proceeds by refuting hypotheses, by making new observations which, when analysed, reject the hypothesis which prompted them. Scientists should not look for confirming instances of their conjectures or hypotheses—confirmations are often too easy to find—but submit their hypotheses to the most rigorous test which can be found. Popper's complaint against Marxism, among other doctrines, was that Marxists look for confirming instances and ignore or overlook events and observations which might disprove their theories. Adler, of course, was looking for confirming instances of his theory of inferiority complexes and not seeking to test and risk the refutation of his hypothesis, as Popper argued science should.

Research cannot study propositions that cannot be tested. Metaphysical statements cannot be tested, e.g. 'People are poor and starving because God wills it'. As Popper (1963) argues, 'Every genuine test of a theory is an attempt to falsify it or refute it' (p. 36). Freud's psychoanalytic theories are inadequate because they cannot be tested.

Science is based on the form of logic known as deduction. The basic syllogism is:

All Ps are Q.
This is a P.
Therefore this is Q.

An example of this pattern is:

All IQ tests are invalid.
This in an IQ test.
Therefore this test is invalid.

If the premises are true, then so too are the conclusions. The problem is that the universal generalisation involved in the first proposition, i.e. all Ps are Qs, is difficult to prove in many cases. For example, it would be difficult to prove the generalisations that all Liberal Party members voted Liberal in the last election, or that all Christians believe in God. But the generalisation is perhaps good or strong enough, even though there may well be just one individual Liberal or Christian who, for a very specific reason, does not fit the generalisation.

Karl Popper therefore suggests on this basis that the generalisation is good enough that we treat it as a hypothesis, thus avoiding the problem of whether we can ever know whether the universal statement is true or not. If we accept the statement as the hypothesis we can say that we predict the conclusion that follows from it. If our prediction is congruent with what actually occurs, the hypothesis is confirmed. It does not prove the hypothesis is true. If we find that the prediction is erroneous then we can conclude that the universal statement is false. Thus scientific reasoning is based on deduction, and a scientific hypothesis is one that can be proved to be false. What the true scientist must try to do is refute the hypothesis, test the ideas to destruction and then only if the hypothesis stands up can it be accepted as currently supported. Of course, later experiments might well find evidence to refute it. These points will be taken up later when we deal with hypothesis formation and testing in chapters 7, 13,14, 15 and 16.

The converse approach is *induction,* in which individual facts are pulled together in clusters to form manageable sets of generalisations which act as theories. Some scientists prefer to start with gathering data. When enough have been obtained, patterns of explanation or theory are feasible. There is a vital weakness in this inductive method. The flaw is the impossibility of unbiased observation of the basic events/facts. Each observer perceives and interprets what they see in subtly different ways from any other observer, with past experience, expectation and personality all influencing the construing of the event.

The inductive and deductive approaches are only different ways of approaching the same goal, and are not as clearly demarcated as the division would suggest. Skinner's work on reinforcement and learning is an inductive approach commencing with a database which was then employed in constructing theoretical principles. Festinger's theory of cognitive dissonance is a deductive theory.

STQ2

Summarise the main characteristics of the scientific approach. How does this approach differ from a common sense approach?

STQ3

Briefly explain the difference between induction and deduction.

Strengths of the scientific approach

The main strengths lie in precision and control. Control is achieved through the sampling and design; precision through quantitative and reliable measurement. Another strength is that experimentation leads to statements about causation, since the systematic manipulation of a variable can be shown to have a direct causal effect on another when other variables have been eliminated or controlled.

Furthermore, hypotheses are tested through a deductive approach and the use of quantitative data permits statistical analysis. In total, the method provides answers which have a much firmer basis than the lay person's common sense or intuition or opinion.

Limitations of the scientific approach

Huge problems are faced by the researcher in education and behavioural science since human beings are far more complex than the inert matter that is studied in physical sciences. This arises because humans are not only acted on by a plethora of environmental forces, but can interpret and respond to these forces in an active way. A classroom may seem in all respects to be a standard context for all who are there, yet some students may react differently from others to the teacher, to the content of the lesson, and to many other subtle elements impinging on them. We cannot predict how a particular child will respond as the varying perceptions and interpretations of the environment subtly alter his or her responses. The educational or social science researcher cannot operate in the sort of controlled environment available to the physical scientist with formal laboratory techniques and rigid control of conditions.

Many researchers are concerned that the scientific quantitative approach denigrates human individuality and ability to think. Its mechanistic ethos tends to exclude notions of freedom, choice and moral responsibility. Quantification can become an end in itself rather than a humane endeavour seeking to explore the human condition. It fails to take account of people's unique ability to interpret their experiences, construct their own meanings and act on these.

It leads to the assumption that facts are true and the same for all people all the time. Quantitative research often produces banal and trivial findings of little consequence due to the restriction on and the controlling of variables. This produces a synthetic puppet show rather than a rich dynamic mélange of human behaviours; an artificial situation, the results of which have no bearing on real life.

It is worth noting that a scientific approach cannot be totally objective, since subjectively it is involved in the very choice of a problem as worthy of investigation and in the interpretation of the results.

STQ4

1   Examine some recent newspapers and select two claims that are not accompanied by supporting evidence. Indicate briefly how support might be obtained.
2   How does the scientific approach differ from the commonsense approach to problem-solving?
3   Why are only testable ideas of worth in science?
4   Scientific study is empirical and objective. What is meant by this statement?

The qualitative approach

Despite the inestimable contributions brought forward through the employment of the scientific method in research, the approach also fostered a naive faith in the substantiality and ultimacy of facts.

While, traditionally, scientific beliefs may have continued unquestioned for a substantial period, the human element has become recognised increasingly as a critical and determining factor in the definition of truth and knowledge. Since human judgement is so profoundly a part of every human act, the supposed objectivity of science is, in fact, a delusion. Although there is evidence of researchers in the early part of the twentieth century using methods other than those from the dominant tradition, as in the use of ethnographic methods by Malinowski (1922), it was the decade of the 1970s that saw an increasing advocacy for the acceptance of the naturalistic methods in educational research.

The epistemological underpinnings of the quantitative motif 'hold that there exist definable and quantifiable "social facts"' (Rist 1975, p. 18). This viewpoint stands in opposition to the qualitative position that reality cannot be subsumed within numerical classification. Qualitative research places stress on the validity of multiple meaning structures and holistic analysis, as opposed to the criteria of reliability and statistical compartmentalisation of quantitative research.

After an initial period of clarification concerning the features of each paradigm, there emerged by the end of the 1970s a situation of détente wherein scholars began to agree that *both* approaches are needed, since no one methodology can answer all questions and provide insights on all issues. There is more than one gate to the kingdom of knowledge. Each gate offers a different perspective, but no one perspective exhausts the realm of 'reality'—whatever that may be. This change in direction can also be seen in Cronbach's (1975) wise observation that 'the time has come to exorcise the null hypothesis . . . there *are* more things in heaven and earth than are dreamt of in our hypotheses, and our observations should be open to them' (p. 124).

Qualitative evaluators frequently find themselves having to defend their methods because of the resistance posed by researchers who are ideologically committed to quantitative methods. The latter assume, out of context, that quantitative research, more rigorous than most qualitative methods, must therefore be the best method to use in all research situations. Quantitative researchers expect the qualitative researcher to demonstrate the validity and reliability of claims, to demonstrate the generality of findings—in short, to meet the same criteria as quantitative research.

What is often not understood is that the criteria that one considers appropriate for quantitative scientific work in education and social science are not those that are necessarily appropriate for work that rests on different assumptions, that uses different methods, and that appeals to different forms of understanding.

Qualitative forms of investigation tend to be based on a recognition of the importance of the subjective, experiential 'lifeworld' of human beings. Such reflection is the province of phenomenology. The phenomenological field of educational action embraces the host of personal meanings that are derived from the context of direct experiencing. Perceptions and interpretations of reality are linked with these meaning structures. Thus, the 'reality' of a given educational setting may be seen not as a fixed and stable entity but as a type of variable that might be discerned only through an analysis of these multiple forms of understanding. Qualitative methodologies provide avenues that can lead to the discovery of these deeper levels of meaning.

The task of the qualitative methodologist is to capture what people say and do as a product of how they interpret the complexity of their world, to understand events from the viewpoints of the participants. It is the lifeworld of the participants that constitutes the investigative field. 'Truth' within this context is bound to humanistic caprices. Thus, conventional attempts to emphasise the imperatives of science place unrealistic constraints on research.

It has been emphasised that much of the rationale for the qualitative approach rests within the criterion of meaning. Eisner (1979) describes this emerging form of research as being considerably relevant, since there can be 'little meaning, impact or quality in an event isolated from the context in which it is found' (pp. 14–15). The distinctive insights made possible through this form of research constitute one of the primary advantages of the approach. Qualitative research has made educators and other social scientists realise that reality should never be taken for granted, given that attention must be paid to the multiple realities and socially constructed meanings that exist within every social context, e.g. classroom, hospital ward, workplace.

At the heart of the conflict between these two streams of thought is a fundamental disagreement about the simplification of reality that provides the posture of the scientific method. It is precisely this fragmentation or compartmentalised style of evaluation which qualitatively-oriented researchers argue leads to distortions of reality and, as a consequence, necessitates a holistic or contextual model of research.

Eisner (1979) explains that, essentially, qualitative methods are concerned with processes rather than consequences, with organic wholeness rather than independent variables, and with meanings rather than behavioural statistics. Interest is directed towards context-bound conclusions that could potentially point the way to new policies and educational decisions, rather than towards 'scientific' generalisations that may be of little use at the coal face. Gone are the days 'when the answer to every research problem' could be found through the administration of a standardised test to experimental and control groups. Science has lost its aura of eliteness and sacredness, which in the past has prevented researchers from questioning its assumptions.

The basic problem in terms of contemporary interests is that the use of qualitative methods in evaluation is only just beginning, due in part to the fact that so many researchers and evaluators have been educated solely in the use of quantitative techniques. As a result, many people now engaged in qualitative research have had to learn how to do it themselves. Although a large body of cumulative research has not yet been developed, a body of methodological guidelines has now emerged, which helps to provide direction for action-oriented investigations.

Several interrelated approaches are used in qualitative educational and social science research, such as action research, case studies, and ethnography. These will be explored in depth in chapters 23–28 of this book. These approaches tend to be characterised by being context specific, collaborative and interventionist. Ethnography provides the major guidelines in methodology for qualitative research (chapter 23).

Limitations of the qualitative approach

The problem of adequate validity and reliability is a major criticism placed by quantitative researchers on qualitative methods. Because of the subjective nature of qualitative data and its origin in single contexts, it is difficult to apply conventional standards of reliability and validity. Contexts, situations, events, conditions and interactions cannot be replicated to any extent nor can generalisations be made to a wider context than the one studied with any confidence. These problems will be addressed later in the appropriate chapters. Basically, the richness, individuality and subjective nature of a participant's perspective and understanding are not amenable to the usual scientific criteria. This does not, however, make such understandings any less real or valid for that participant, and their explanatory function for that person's behaviour is highly predictive.

Perhaps one of the major limitations of qualitative research and evaluation is the time required for data collection, analysis and interpretation. There is a critical need for the researcher to spend a considerable amount of time in the research setting in order to examine, holistically and aggregately, the interactions, reactions and activities of subjects. In addition, Parlett (1975) notes that because of the intimacy of participant–observer relationships within the setting there is no doubt that the researcher's mere presence will have profound reactive effects on the subjects of the study. Concomitantly, the promise of anonymity, which often serves as the basis for trust, in concert with the requirement of authenticity, makes the qualitative evaluator's task particularly difficult in terms of the preparation and presentation of results. Possible bias, from the viewpoints of both researcher and participants, must also be identified and elucidated.

Rist (1975) also notes that:

> The variable of time may be viewed as a handicap; should one attempt to replicate findings accumulated for nearly three years, a comparable length of time would again be necessary for the adequate observation of a similar group. Similarly, there is no guarantee that the replication could be of an identical social context . . . Perhaps the most that is feasible is to achieve a high degree of similarity and to recognise that absolute reproduction is impossible (p. 94).

These problems and issues may well illustrate reasons for the sometimes defensive reactions of more traditionally-oriented researchers when encountering alternative conceptions and methodologies.

Strengths of the qualitative approach

The promise of qualitative investigation can be seen in Barton and Lazarsfeld's (1969) statement that 'like the nets of deep-sea explorers, qualitative studies may pull up unexpected and striking things for us to gaze on' (p. 166). Unlike many of the traditional, more narrow approaches to the examination of educational experience, the qualitative mode of inquiry is characterised by methodological eclecticism, a hypothesis-free orientation and an implicit acceptance of the natural scheme of things. Because of the need for the researcher to maintain close association with both participants and activities within the setting, the researcher gains an insider's view of the field. This proximity to the field often allows the evaluator to see (and document) the qualities of social and educational interaction too often missed by the scientific, more positivistic inquiries. Such propinquity can reveal subtleties and complexities that could go undetected through the use of more standardised measures.

Qualitative descriptions can play the important role of suggesting possible relationship(s), causes, effects, and even dynamic processes in school settings. Qualitative methods can highlight subtleties in pupil behaviour and response, illuminate reasons for action and provide in-depth information on teacher interpretations and teaching style. By pointing to alternative conceptions of our activities, by giving us new horizons against which we can value our curricular structures, and by showing the determinate limits of our accepted procedures, qualitative methods allow us to see that things could be other than they are. Similar illuminations can be made in other professional areas too.

Since qualitative reports are not presented as statistical summations, but rather in a more descriptive, narrative style, this type of research might be of particular benefit to the practitioner. Ordinary teachers, social workers, nurses etc., who may not have knowledge of sophisticated measurement techniques, could turn to qualitative reports in order to examine forms of knowledge that might otherwise be unavailable, thereby gaining new insight concerning their endeavours. The close connection between qualitative research and teaching might also inspire teachers themselves to become involved in research so that research in future could become more of a team effort. In this manner, the results of studies might lead more expediently into new decisions for action. Qualitative approaches certainly do not provide easy, quick answers to the complex issues that confront us. But they *do* offer a viable alternative.

Even though a strong contrast has deliberately been made in the preceding pages to emphasise the different approaches and philosophical rationales, the practice of dichotomising and polarising social science research into quantitative and qualitative modes is overdone and misleading. It suggests only serious and rigorous researchers will use quantitative methods and that only such designs are capable of producing legitimate research. In practice, many researchers will use both approaches as appropriate within one investigation. It is up to the researcher to choose specific methodologies that will enable a clear understanding of the topic to emerge. Qualitative research has often been described as not being empirical. This is false. The term empirical has nothing to do with numbers or the manipulation of variables, but refers to whether phenomenon are capable of being found in the real world and assessed by means of the senses. Since both quantitative and qualitative research are concerned with observation and recording of the real world they are both clearly empirical. All social science research is empirical, but by contrast philosophy is not. The contrast that can be supported is the dichotomy between naturalistic research and experimental research.

The role of computers in data analysis

Over the past decade the computer industry has expanded immensely with the development of faster and more efficient computers and programs which are readily accessible to people who are not technically trained. An important development has been in the area of *canned* and *packaged* statistical programs. These packages consist of sets of computer programs designed for a variety of statistical techniques. The programs are relatively simple to use, depending on the requirements of the particular package, and allow a person to do very complex computer analyses.

Many of these packages contain a wide variety of data-editing capabilities and statistical procedures, any of which can be applied to the user's data by a few standard commands. Some of the more commonly used packages on university campuses are the Statistical Package for the Social Sciences (SPSS), the Statistical Analysis System (SAS), Systat, BMDP, Epistat or Statgraphics. These programs will perform all the statistical operations and tests described in this book, as well as more advanced multivariate tests. Most of these statistical packages, although originally designed for mainframe computers, are now available in PC versions for Windows. NUD*IST offers a qualitative content analysis package for verbal material.

The programs have made many statistical procedures more feasible for research purposes, and have greatly reduced the time necessary to perform the procedures. In addition, the accuracy of such computations is greatly improved, since calculations done by hand often result in mistakes or crude answers, especially when the number of observations is large. With the availability of computers and packaged programs, the statistical analysis of relatively large data sets is technically as easy as that of small ones, which is desirable since larger samples usually provide more information than smaller samples.

Knowing how to run a statistical package program does not imply that a proper analysis will be done. A good background in statistics is necessary in order to know which program to run, which options to choose in that program, and how to construct valid conclusions based on the program's output. The main purpose of this text is to provide such a background. The 'garbage in-garbage out' principle applies here as elsewhere.

A range of considerations govern the appropriateness of any statistical test for a particular study. The major considerations involve assumptions about the distribution of the data, types of hypotheses used, research design employed and the level of the data. The application of SPSS provides many of the basic statistical procedures taught in this text.

STQ5

Read the following statement:

> If research shows something which I know from my experience to be wrong, then the research is faulty. If research proves what I know already, what is the point of it?

How would you treat such a comment? Is experience bound to be right, and research wrong?

References

Barton, A. & Lazarsfeld, P. (1969), 'Some functions of qualitative analysis', in *Issues in Participant Observation*, eds G. Macall & J. Simmons, Addison-Wesley, Reading.

Cronbach, L.J. (1975), 'Beyond the two disciplines of scientific psychology', *American Psychologist*, 30, pp. 116–26.

Eisner, E. (1979), 'Recent developments in educational research affecting art education', *Art Education* 32, pp. 12–15.

Kerlinger, F (1986), *Foundations of Behavioral Research*, Holt, New York.

Malinowski, B. (1922), *Argonauts of the West Pacific*, Routledge, London.

Parlett, M. (1975), 'Evaluating innovations in teaching', in *Curriculum Design*, (eds) J. Greenwald & R. West, Croom Helm, London.

Popper, K. (1957), *The Poverty of Historicism*, Routledge, London.

Popper, K. (1963), *Conjectures and Refutations*, Routledge, London.

Rist, R.C. (1975), 'Ethnographic techniques and the study of an urban school', *Urban Education* 10, pp. 86–108.

Further reading: Quantitative research

Adams, G.R. & Schvaneveldt, J. (1985), *Understanding Research Methods*, Longman, New York.
Keeves, J.P. (1988), *Educational Research Methodology and Measurement*, Pergamon Press, Oxford.
Mohsin, S.M. (1984), *Research Methods in the Behavioural Sciences*, Orient Longman, Calcutta.

Further reading: Qualitative research

Burgess, R. (ed.) (1985), *Strategies of Educational Research: Qualitative Methods*, Falmer Press, London.
Burgess, R. (ed.) (1985), *Issues in Educational Research: Qualitative Methods*, Falmer Press, London.
Denzin, N. & Lincoln, Y. (eds) (1998), *The Handbook of Qualitative Research*, vols 1–3, Sage, London.
Erickson, F. (1986), 'Qualitative methods in research in teaching', in *Handbook of Research on Teaching*, (ed.) M. Wittrock, 3rd edn, Macmillan, New York.
Finch, J. (1986), *Research & Policy: The Uses of Qualitative Methods in Social and Educational Research*, Falmer Press, London.
Glesne, C. & Peshkin, A. (1992), *Becoming Qualitative Researchers*, Longman, New York.
Jacob, E. (1987), 'Qualitative research traditions: A review.' *Review of Educational Research*, 57(1), pp. 1–50.
Sherman, R. & Webb, R. (1988), *Qualitative Research in Education: Focus and Methods*, Falmer Press, London.
Shipman, M. (ed.) (1985), *Educational Research Principles, Policies & Practices*, Falmer Press, London.
Smith, J.K. & Heshusius, L. (1986), 'Closing down the conversation: The end of the quantitative–qualitative debate', *Educational Researcher*, 15(1), pp. 4–13.
Tashakkori, A. & Teddlie C. (1998), *Mixed Methodology*, Sage, London.
Taylor, S.J. & Bogdan, R. (1984), *Qualitative Research Methods: The Search for Meanings*, 2nd edn, John Wiley, New York.

Further reading: Computer packages

Cramer, D. (1998), *Fundamental Statistics for Social Research: Using SPSS for Windows*, Routledge, London.
Foster, J. (1998), *Data Analysis Using SPSS for Windows: A Beginners Guide*, Sage, London.
Gahan, C. & Hannibal, M. (1998), *Doing Qualitative Research Using QSR NUD*IST*, Sage, London.

Ethics of research

2
two

Ethical principles, rules and conventions distinguish socially acceptable behaviour from that which is considered socially unacceptable. However, in social science research a few workers consider their work beyond scrutiny, presumably guided by a disinterested virtue which justifies any means to attain hoped for ends. In education, numerous children have been forced to learn nonsense syllables, native children have been taken from their natural mothers and brought up as though a member of another culture, many left-handed children have been forced to write with their right hands. Most children at some time are unwittingly involved in questionable experiments in teaching methods or medical procedures, and all of us have at some time felt obliged to complete some meaningless questionnaire.

Of course, some researchers feel that ethical rules or guidelines that attempt to define limits may be too rigid, limiting the effectiveness of research and denying research into aspects of human behaviour where knowledge would be valuable.

Ethical problems can relate to both the subject matter of the research as well as to its methods and procedures, and can go well beyond courtesy or etiquette regarding appropriate treatment of persons in a free society. Social scientists have often been criticised for lack of concern over the welfare of their subjects. The researcher often misinforms subjects about the nature of the investigation, and/or exposes them to embarrassing or emotionally painful experiences. Many subjects may feel obliged to volunteer for a variety of reasons. Professionals also feel troubled by ethical issues. It was found in a survey by the British Psychological Society that the two major areas of dilemma for members were confidentiality and research. Issues reported in this latter area included unethical procedures, informed consent, harm to participants, deception, and deliberate falsification of results.

Voluntary participation

The problem with volunteers is that they are not likely to be a random sample of the population. They tend to be better educated, of a higher social class, more intelligent, more social, less conforming and possess a higher need for approval than non-volunteers. This means that the external validity (the confidence to generalise to the population) is reduced.

Ethical requirements about volunteering can therefore act in direct opposition to the methodological requirements of good research. Some volunteers may not be as free to choose as the researcher may think. Much educational and social science research is conducted on students at school or university. Most will agree to participate, but often do so because they may believe that some undesired effect on their marks, report or references will occur if they do not. They may be free but do not feel so. Many parents may also be in this same circumstance, agreeing to their child's or their own participation for fear of possible consequences.

The following are examples of experiment recruitment practices that may raise ethical questions:

- subjects who are inmates of prisons who participate in anticipation of more favourable treatment;

- members of a university class who participate in order to meet a course requirement;

- unemployed persons who are offered a financial reward.

Involuntary participation

In naturalistic covert observation the observed person is usually unaware of their participation. This is not objectionable when unobtrusive observations are made and each observation is simply one more in a frequency count, such as children's playground behaviour. However, in other observation studies private lives can be invaded, such as studies on bystander intervention.

Informed consent

This is the most fundamental ethical principle that is involved. Participants must understand the nature and purpose of the research and must consent to participate without coercion. Many researchers have their potential participant sign an informed consent form which describes the purpose of the research, its procedures, risks and discomforts, its benefits and the right to withdraw. This makes the situation clear and provides a degree of proof that the person was informed and consented to take part.

Participants who are explicitly or implicitly coerced to get involved, such as prison inmates for more beneficial treatment or students for money or points towards unit assessment, are not assumed to have consented voluntarily. Lecturers and professors are in a position of power over students and even though they are not explicitly abusing it and actually threatening retribution on those who don't offer to participate, their request for volunteers from a unit they are teaching is implicitly a demand. Unfortunately, it is easy to get people to sign such forms due to inherent trust in scientific leaders and the 'man in the white coat', as well as a willingness to accept what authority figures say. 'It must be OK, it is a reputable university—they would never do anything shonkey'.

Deception

The primary justification for deception is that knowledge of the purpose of the investigation might contaminate results; subjects who are unaware of the real purpose will behave more naturally. Yet it is basically unethical in human relationships. Moreover, just being in an experiment even without a specific purpose can alter behaviour, so deception may not work as expected. Informed consent does lead to non-random samples as it implies voluntary involvement.

There are some situations where you would not wish to disclose the purpose of the study, or even that a study is proceeding, e.g. observation of play in preschool children, participant observation in a delinquent gang, etc. Active deception includes misrepresenting the purpose of the study, use of placebos, false diagnoses, false promises. Passive deception includes secret recording of behaviour, concealed observation, use of personality tests where the participant is unaware of the rationale. While deception is a well used tactic in social psychology and some ethnographic activities, a deceived subject may feel they have been part of an elaborate hoax, lose self-esteem and develop negative attitudes to research. Milgram's 1974 study on obedience is a classic deception study in which subjects were deceived into thinking that they were administering electric shocks to another participant.

Milgram's experiment also produced considerable stress as well as deception. Most deception is produced in studies on emotion, motivation, social behaviour and ethnography. There is little deception in memory and intellectual studies, although even here deception which does not harm the subject can be used, such as telling a subject they are reading newspaper stories in a study of readability when it is actually examining memory errors.

Some deception is somewhat innocuous, such as participants being told the baby is a male and others that it is female and then asked to describe the baby's personality and behaviour. The use of a placebo is deceptive but usually not harmful. Some students may be told their experimental rats are bright.

Other studies are more dangerous in their effect on human behaviour, for instance Rosenthal and Jacobsen's (1968) 'self fulfilling prophecy' studies, in which teachers were told of the degree of talent to expect from children in their classes. Subsequent performance did improve for those who at random were indicated as those who should 'bloom'. What about those who by chance were allocated to the group not expected to perform? Were their life chances lowered as a result of expectation fuelled by the teachers in the experiment? A number of studies have been similar to Milgram's and involved serious stress for participants, such as overhearing what was thought to be an authentic epileptic seizure. In this case the dependent variable was the speed or occurrence of reporting the seizure. Or in studies to assess the effects of different types of feedback providing false feedback which causes loss of self-esteem or anxiety. Researchers should be honest and open. Deception is seldom warranted.

Role-playing

Role-playing has been used as a means of avoiding deception. Subjects are fully informed about the investigation and then asked to act as though they were subject to a particular treatment condition. It is assumed that they understand they are not part of a real situation. This relies heavily on the subject's ability to role-play the required role adroitly. The Stanford Prison study (Zimbardo & Ruch 1973) showed that subjects role-playing guards and prisoners could become immersed in a role even when they knew the experimental nature of the situation. This study had to be stopped after six days of a planned fourteen days as the student prison guards became brutal and sadistic, while the student prisoners developed passive dependency. However, it is argued conversely that subjects who are fully informed of the experiment will produce results different from those produced by uninformed subjects. Other approaches have been to forewarn subjects that some of the experiments they might be asked to take part in may involve deception and only then ask for them to volunteer.

Debriefing

In a debriefing session you inform the subjects about the nature of the study, any deception and why it was necessary. You must restore the subject's self-esteem and trust in the motives of researchers. The debriefing should include the following:

- disclosure as to the purpose of the experiment, interviews, questionnaires, etc.;

- description of deception and why used;

- an attempt to make the research appear scientifically respectable and important.

- you may wish to allow subjects to view later experimental sessions showing another subject being deceived so that they fully realise what happened.

Privacy and confidentiality

Confidentiality involves a clear understanding between researcher and participant concerning the use to be made of the data provided. It is extremely important to ensure that responses to personal questions, scores on tests, etc. are confidential and anonymous so that the reader of the research would be unable to deduce the identity of the individual. Individual data can be quoted by referring to participant 'X' or 'Y', etc. Subjects must be informed that confidentiality will be maintained and feel confident of the researcher's commitment to that or else many potential subjects will refuse to take part.

The right to privacy is an important right enshrined now in international (UN Declaration of Human Rights) and national legislation, particularly in respect of information held by government departments, banks, etc. Individuals should decide what aspects of their personal lives, attitudes, habits, eccentricities, fears and guilt are to be communicated to others. In education and psychology, the use of concealed observers, one-way mirrors, concealed microphones and video cameras are formidable threats to privacy. This does not mean that personal and private behaviour cannot be observed ethically; it can, provided that the subjects volunteer to participate with full knowledge of the purposes and procedures involved. The general strategy for protecting privacy is to use codes to represent individuals and separate the coding key from the raw data.

Right to discontinue

Ethical research practice respects this right. It is an important safeguard. It is often used by those completing questionnaires or interviews when they refuse to respond to an item. It is more difficult in a captive group in an experimental situation; there are subtle forces at play between a researcher and a subject that make it difficult for the participant to discontinue.

Experimenter obligations

Researchers make several implicit contracts with their subjects. For example, if the subjects agree to be present at a specific time and place then the researcher must also. If the researcher has promised to send a summary of results to the subjects then that must be done. The researcher must not run overtime as many subjects may have made arrangements to fit round the time requirement already notified.

Publication of findings

Researchers should be open with their results, allowing disinterested colleagues to vet the research and its implications, because no one wants newspapers to seize on half-truths, misinterpreting information and making unnecessary waves, particularly if the issue affects people's lives. Nor does anyone want politicians and bureaucrats rushing off to create new policy before verification and replication among the academic community.

Education and social science research on such matters as racial differences, immigration policy, selection of specific populations for special programs, sexual behaviour, etc. will always stir up controversy, so that the most responsible researchers should announce their findings and implications with great qualification and caution. Remember it is always difficult to prevent unqualified persons from using research findings for their own discriminatory and abusive ends.

Stress

Some studies involve providing subjects with unfavourable feedback about their personalities or abilities in order to assess the effect on their self-concept or self-esteem.

This can produce psychological stress. Not all mental stress involves deception. Induced loss of self-esteem, exposure to aggressive film sequences, discomfort in sensory deprivation experiments, embarrassing feedback—all cause stress. Physical discomfort can be caused in studies investigating noise levels and sleep deprivation.

Intervention studies

These studies often involve willing participation, for example, working with parents at home to improve parental stimulation and to show the effect on child learning and intellectual performance. Ethical issues arise in selecting one group to be given special treatment, particularly if it endows the participants with some beneficial ability. Other interventions that examine the effect of an independent variable on a dependent behavioural variable which are of questionable ethics include raising the level of aggression in young children by showing them violent videos.

Conclusion

All in all it looks fairly difficult to conduct much research without running into ethical arguments. Codes of ethics have been developed by many professions which deal with human subjects. The most comprehensive and credible code of ethics is that issued by the American Psychological Association (1992). This has become a major standard and model for researchers in the social sciences. The British Psychological Society, which is the other major worldwide association of psychologists, also has a Code of Conduct (BPS 1993).

The Australian Association for Research in Education has recently published an annotated bibliography on ethics in educational research which has general application to research across the behavioural and social sciences. This bibliography can be accessed at *http://www.swin.edu.au/aare/welcome.html*.

Generally such codes include the following requirements:

- that risks to participants are minimised by procedures which do not expose subjects to risks;

- that risks to participants are outweighed by the anticipated benefits of the research;

- that the rights and welfare of participants are protected. The research should avoid unnecessary psychological harm or discomfort to the subjects;

- participation should be voluntary;

- the subject has the right to know the nature, purposes and duration of the study, i.e. informed consent. Participants should sign an informed consent form which outlines the study, who is conducting it, for what purpose, and how it is to be carried out; also providing assurances of confidentiality and voluntary participation. The participant should sign, acknowledging that they freely consent to participate. Should the subject be below the age of consent or incapacitated due to age, illness or disability, a parent, guardian or responsible agent must sign.

- the subject should be free to withdraw at any time without penalty;

- information obtained is confidential;

- participants are debriefed after the study.

You should find out the rules and procedures which govern ethical approval at your institution and take early steps to fulfil the requirements. It is difficult to cover all eventualities; however, the above principles provide a framework. Do not deceive, coerce, breach privacy and confidentiality for your own ambition, prestige or ego.

STQ6

1 If it is inappropriate to explain the reason for the research to the subjects before data collection, which of the following should the experimenter do?
  a   Inform them anyway since cooperation is vital.
  b   Not disclose any information.
  c   Tell the subjects they will be informed at the end of the experiment.
2 Because in the school setting it is essential to have cooperation of parents, teachers, students and administrators, which of the following must the researcher do?
  a   Ask the school principal to explain the research to all involved.
  b   Devise a plan to gain whole school cooperation.
  c   Work only where immediate cooperation is available.
3 If a student drops out of a research project which of the following should be done?
  a   The student should be required to provide a substitute.
  b   The student's personal records should be amended to note the fact.
  c   Nothing should be done.
4 In meeting with a school principal explain what steps you will tell him or her you are taking to protect the rights of the teachers and students in an experiment (e.g. give details of the research, right to privacy, who is involved, right to withdraw, no penalties for refusal to take part etc.)
5 Suppose you have conducted a study in which students have been given false scores on a maths test in order to see if this information has any effect on a subsequent similar test. Describe your procedures at the end of the experiment. (Design a program to explain why deception is necessary. Meet each student individually and show test papers with correct scores. Offer to give another similar test so they can be sure of real performance level etc.)
6 Discuss the contention that the ends never justifies the means where research with humans is concerned.

summary

Ethical problems are likely to occur in social science research since human subjects are involved. Researchers must be aware of ethical considerations involved in voluntary and non-voluntary participation, deception, informed consent, privacy and confidentiality, the right to discontinue, and obligations of the experimenter.

Codes of conduct issued by major professional associations in the social sciences attempt to raise awareness of these issues and provide guidelines for ethical behaviour.

References

American Psychological Association (1992), 'Ethical principles in the conduct of research with human participants', *American Psychologist*, vol. 47.

British Psychological Society (BPS) (1993), *Code of Conduct: Ethical Principles and Guidelines*, Leicester, BPS.

Milgram, S. (1974), *Obedience to Authority*, Harper Row, New York.

Rosenthal, R. & Jacobsen, L. (1968), *Pygmalion in the Classroom*, Holt, New York.

Zimbardo, P. & Ruch, F. (1973), *Psychology and Life*, Scott Foresman, New York.

Further reading

Australian Association for Research in Education (1998), *Ethics in Educational Research: Annotated Bibliography*, ed. K. Halasa. AARE, Coldstream, Victoria.

Burgess, R. (1989), *The Ethics of Educational Research*, Falmer Press, London.

Clark, J. (1995), Ethical and Political Issues in Qualitative Research from a Philosophical Point of View. Paper presented at the annual meeting of the American Educational Research Association, San Fransisco.

Doig, S. (1994), The Placement of Teacher Voice in Educational Research, Paper presented at the AARE conference, Newcastle.

Evans, T. & Jakupec, V. (1996), 'Research ethics in open and distance education', *Distance Education*, vol. 17, no. 1, pp. 15–22.

Jenkins, D. (1993), 'An adversary's account of SAFARI's ethics of case study', in *Controversies in Classroom Research*, ed. M. Hammersley, Open University Press, Milton Keynes.

Kimmel, A. (1988), *Ethics and Values in Applied Social Research*, Sage, Beverly Hills.

Mohr, M.M. (1996), Ethics and Standards for Teacher Research. Paper delivered at American Educational Research Association conference, New York.

Osbourne, B. (1995), Indigenous Education: Is There a Place for Non-indigenous Researchers? Paper delivered at AARE conference.

Thompson, A. (1992), 'The ethics and politics of evaluation', *Issues in Educational Research*, vol. 2, no. 1.

Wadeley, A. (1991), *Ethics in Research and Practice*, British Psychological Society, Leicester.

Finding a problem to investigate

In undertaking research in the behavioural sciences, the first problem is to find a problem to investigate. This statement may seem so self-contradictory and self-evident that it underestimates the difficulties that investigators have in doing just this.

Research starts with a problem; with a problematic situation. There is first a vague situation in which ideas are unclear, doubts are raised and the thinker is perplexed. The indeterminacy, however, must ultimately be removed. Initially, a researcher may often have only a general and diffuse notion of a particular problem, but sooner or later they have to have a fairly clear idea of what the problem is. Otherwise they can hardly get very far in solving it. Though this statement seems self-evident, one of the most difficult things to do, apparently, is to state one's research problem clearly and fully. You must know what you are trying to find out. When you finally know this, the problem is heading towards a solution.

As with most undertakings, the success of research depends largely on the care taken with the preliminary preparations. Much thought should be given to the problem beforehand, resolving it into crucial questions and then designing a study later on to answer the questions.

Novice researchers are surprised to find that this initial stage often takes up a considerable amount of the total time invested in a research project. However, research is impossible until a problem is recognised, thought through, and formulated in a feasible manner.

The difficulty is not due to a shortage of researchable problems in education. In fact, there are so many that researchers usually have trouble choosing among them. The main difficulty is that a problem must be selected and a question formulated early, when the beginner's understanding of how to do research is more limited. In addition, uncertainties about the nature of research problems, the isolation of a problem, the criteria for acceptability, and how to solve the problem often seem overwhelming. Even experienced researchers usually find it necessary to make several attempts before they arrive at a research problem that meets generally accepted criteria. The first attempt at formulation may, on closer examination, be found to be unfeasible or not worth doing. Skill in doing research is to a large extent a matter of making wise choices about what to investigate.

How do I find a research problem?

Though there are no set rules for locating a problem, there are three important sources of problems—experience, from theory, and related literature.

Experience

A researcher must first of all decide on the general subject of investigation. Such choices are necessarily *very personal* but should lead to an area that holds deep interest or about which there is a real curiosity. Otherwise, the motivation to complete the research may be difficult to sustain. The researcher's own knowledge, experience, and circumstances usually determine these choices.

For example, on a daily basis teachers make decisions about the probable effects of educational practices on pupil behaviour. For instance, primary teachers may question the effectiveness of their methods of teaching maths, or any of several other well-known methods, in order to decide what is the most effective approach to use. Secondary social studies teachers might wish to find out whether teaching about the problems of Third World countries changes students' attitudes to such countries and their inhabitants.

Observations of certain relationships for which adequate explanation does not exist are another source of problems for investigation. A teacher may notice a decrease in self-esteem in students at certain times. To investigate this the teacher can formulate various tentative explanations, then proceed to test them empirically. This investigation may not only solve the immediate problem but also make some small contribution to an understanding of how self-esteem is affected by classroom influences.

Similarly, there are decisions to be made about practices that have become routine in various professional areas—for example, penalties for lateness—which are based mainly on tradition or authority, with little or no support from scientific research. Why not evaluate some of these practices? Are there alternatives that would be more effective for the purpose intended than those now being used?

Thus everyday experiences can yield worthwhile problems for investigation and, in fact, most of the research ideas developed by beginning researchers tend to come from their personal experiences. Such studies can often be justified on the basis of their contribution to the improvement of professional practice, and are more meaningful to novice researchers than those derived from theory.

STQ7

From your everyday experience in your own professional areas as teacher or student, try to isolate a problem suitable for investigation.

Theory

There are many theories in behavioural science that are popular theories rather than scientific ones. These need to be tested by a variety of specific hypotheses to see in what ways/contexts/conditions they may or may not hold. In this way, research contributes to theory generation. For example, we are now aware that differences in performance between boys and girls in specific school subjects such as reading, maths and science—once believed in folklore theory to be innate sex differences—are in fact a function of such variables as social expectation, conditioning, self-esteem and individual attribution. In another example, failure to follow 'instructions' written on medical and social benefits leaflets is not due to unwillingness, but often to the material being written at too high a level for clients, i.e. a readability problem.

Review of literature

The review of literature is normally undertaken in two stages. The first stage involves a general overview of the relevant area using *secondary sources*, such as general textbooks which include relevant topics and literature reviews. Once the problem has been isolated, a more specific and structured review involving *primary sources* of salient research can be undertaken, using, for example, journal articles.

The preliminary review of the literature concentrates on more general texts and on existing reviews of previous research which summarise the state of knowledge in a particular area. Secondary sources, such as textbooks and reviews, are useful because they combine knowledge from many primary sources into a single publication. A good textbook, for example, combines the work of many other persons and simplifies or eliminates much of the technical material which is not of interest to the general reader, thus providing a quick and relatively easy method of obtaining a good overall understanding of the field.

The review of the literature can help in limiting the individual's research problem and in defining it more clearly. Many attempted studies are doomed to failure before the student starts because the problem has not been limited to an area small enough and sufficiently specific to work with satisfactorily. It is far better in research to select a limited problem and treat it well than to attempt the study of a broad general problem and do it poorly. Many students also commit themselves to a research problem before they have thought it out adequately. A fuzzy or poorly defined problem can sometimes result in the student collecting data and then learning that the data cannot be applied

Where do I begin?

to the problem the student wishes to attack. Before starting a review of the literature, the student should do sufficient background reading from secondary sources to permit a tentative outline of the research problem. The review of the literature will give the student the knowledge needed to convert the tentative research problem to a detailed and concise plan of action.

Reviews of previous research are a fertile source of research problems. Many research reviews suggest extensions of the research topic and new questions are raised frequently as old ones are answered. Many existing studies need replicating with different samples, for example, in cross-cultural modes.

Reviews of research literature

If students can locate a recent review of literature related to their research topic, they can get a useful overview with little effort. The quality of such reviews varies, however, and students should look at reviews critically before accepting the conclusions of the reviewer.

The desirability of replicating previous studies to confirm the findings can be shown through a literature review. As indicated in chapter 1, one major characteristic of the scientific method is that results should be replicable. Repeating a study is profitable, as confirming results provides further evidence of the validity of the findings. Disconfirmation of the previous findings is just as valuable and leads to further studies to elucidate the inconsistencies and contradictions. Reviewing literature with a critical eye will also reveal gaps in the organised knowledge of an area.

Suppose, for example, you were concerned with the general problem of the effect of personality on school attainment. The initial review would have shown that a number of theories of personality exist, that a number of relevant measures of personality and attainment are available, that the problem has been attacked from a number of different perspectives and that a number of hypotheses are in vogue. It will have shown that relationships between measures appear to vary depending on age, sex, type of schooling and so on of the children who were studied. Similarly in research on reading, the review will have shown that, amongst other factors, past research has considered the effect of intelligence, sex, impaired hearing, dyslexia, lack of sensory experience and the efficacy of different reading schemes.

Once this initial review has been completed it is useful to write a summary of the material sampled, outlining the major theories, salient studies and their results. Such a synthesis not only helps to clarify the major issues in the mind of the researcher but provides a foundation for further readings. At this stage a decision is made, if one has not been made already, about which particular aspect of the wider problem will be studied further. To take the personality example again, you may have become intrigued by the possibility that different cultural backgrounds could affect the manner in which personality relates to school attainment.

Once a feasible problem has been isolated, *a more detailed* review of pertinent literature is required in order to guide and inform the current study and provide an introduction in the research project report. This review concentrates mainly on *primary source materials*, research reports written by the original researcher.

This detailed review differs in a number of ways from the reading program of secondary sources often used to locate a tentative research project. First, such a review is much more extensive and thorough because it is aimed at obtaining a detailed knowledge of the topic being studied, while the reading program is aimed at obtaining enough general knowledge and insight to recognise problems in the selected area.

In the process of detailed review of the literature, the student should not only learn what work has been done but should also be alert to research possibilities that have been overlooked. The unique experience and background of an individual may make it possible to see a facet of the problem that other research workers have not seen. Such new viewpoints are likely to occur most frequently in areas where little research has been done, but even in well-researched areas, someone occasionally thinks of an approach that is unique and creative.

A detailed review of the literature can also provide insight into the methods, measures, subjects, and approaches used by other research workers and can thus lead to significant improvement of the design. A mistake made by many graduate students when reading research reports is to give little attention to anything but the results reported. Very often, a study that has little to contribute by way of results can help a great deal by suggesting methods and useful approaches. For example, discussions of the various measures used can help the student decide which of these measures would be best suited for her or his own research. A sampling problem discussed by one research worker can help other research workers in the field avoid the same difficulties.

The authors of research articles often include specific suggestions and recommendations for persons planning further research in the field. These suggestions should be considered very carefully because they represent the insights gained by the research worker after experience in the problem area. Specific research topics are often suggested that are particularly useful in helping the student delimit the research problem.

However, even if one has a considerable interest in the topic, a realistic appraisal of the following points should still be undertaken:

a The problem must be able to be researched, i.e. dealt with empirically. Testable hypotheses must be capable of being generated (see chapter 7).

b The researcher must be able to gain access to the samples, materials and other resources needed. If the data cannot be gathered because of lack of permission from schools, teachers, parents, administrators, etc., then another problem must be located. Other reasons such as time and money, and availability of test instruments also must be considered.

c The problem when solved should have spin-offs for developing theory and/or application to real-life educational contexts. Research that is trivial has little to contribute to real educational problems. Luckily few of these sort of studies get off the ground, as professionals, administrators and project supervisors in education, health and social work, etc., have little tolerance for the self-indulgent pastimes of naive researchers.

STQ8

Explain the purpose of an initial review using secondary sources.

Scope of the review

Perhaps the greatest difficulty encountered by the student in carrying out a review of the literature is deciding what should and should not be read. Unfortunately, there is no pat formula that can help the student make this decision. Obviously, the student should read all studies that are closely related to the research problem. Relatively new research areas usually lack an organised body of source information to provide a general background and thus require a fairly broad review.

For example, suppose a student wants to do research on the causes of 'teacher burnout'. Because widespread interest in teacher burnout is fairly new, they should probably read most of the studies in the broad area of 'burnout', even if the studies are not closely related to this topic. For instance, an article that discusses ways to train teachers to cope with stress, although only peripheral to the causes of teacher burnout, should be checked. Also, studies that deal with the causes of burnout in other similar professional groups, such as nurses and social workers, should be reviewed. In new research areas, such as the causes of teacher burnout, students may find no more than two or three studies that are very close to their topic. Thus a broader search is necessary.

A useful way to produce a logical and systematic account is to:

- start with the most recent studies in the area and gradually work backwards. This cuts down the reading as recent articles will most likely contain the findings, methods and ideas of earlier pieces of research.

- always read the abstract (summary) first, as this will help you decide whether the article is relevant and save time working through an article that will not have any bearing on your research.

- organise the large amount of material you will gather during the review. Record each piece of information on a bibliography card. The bibliography card should carry the author's name, date of publication, the title of the book or name of journal; it should also contain a brief summary of the salient details of the research including the page numbers, title of the article, details of the sample, techniques of measurement and summary of results. The author's main conclusions and any weaknesses in them will also be recorded together with additional references gained from the article. And, of course, if the research is one of the major ones in the field of study, further notes on additional cards or in a notebook will also be taken. An example of a completed bibliography card is shown in Figure 3.1. Do not put more than one article on each file card.

- refer to the *Current Index to Journals in Education* (CIJE)—the most productive source for the majority of students studying education. Therefore its format is advantageous to use when permitted. Most of the references will come from the subject index of CIJE, and articles listed by subject give the title of the book or article before the author's name. For your bibliography card, the author's name (last name first) should be listed before the title. This change is necessary because it is much more convenient for you to maintain your notecard file in alphabetical order by author, and the bibliography as prepared for your thesis normally will be listed in this order. It is advisable to print the author's name; misspelled names are a common source of errors and are difficult to detect when proofreading.

All this facilitates the typing of the references/bibliography. Students should check the rules in effect at their institution concerning acceptable format for the bibliography section of the thesis or dissertation.

FIGURE 3.1 *Example of completed bibliography card*

HADDON, F.A. and LYTTON, H. (1968)   BRITISH JOURNAL OF EDUCATIONAL PSYCHOLOGY, 38, 171–180

'Teaching approach and the development of divergent thinking abilities in primary schools'

SAMPLE:	211 11–12 year-olds from 4 schools, two designated 'informal' and two designated 'formal' by college of education lectures. Schools matched for socio-economic background. Mean Verbal Reasoning quotient 101.
MEASURES:	Verbal Reasoning—Moray House. 3 verbal and 3 non-verbal divergent thinking tests adapted from MTCT. Sociometric test (given in appendix).
RESULTS:	Children in informal schools significantly superior in divergent thinking abilities. Divergent children more popular in informal schools.
COMMENTS:	Sample size of schools very small and unrepresentative. Terms 'informal' and 'formal' open to different interpretation.

In more thoroughly explored areas, where research activity has extended over a longer period of time and much of the early work is covered in secondary sources such as textbooks, the student can usually develop adequate insight into the field by reading only those studies that are reasonably close to the research topic. In these more thoroughly explored areas, much greater depth is available, and the student can cover a narrower topic range to a greater depth.

Checking preliminary sources

Preliminary sources are references, such as indexes and abstracts, that identify and locate research articles and other primary sources of information. In education the most useful sources are *Resources in Education* (RIE), *Current Index to Journals in Education* (CIJE), *Psychological Abstracts*, and *Education Index*. These sources are organised by subject. Therefore, it is necessary that the research worker identify key words related to the topic so that they may be looked up in the index to locate sources of information related to the topic. For example, let us say that you wish to search *Education Index* for studies of changes in racial attitudes in children in relation to the number of migrant pupils in primary schools. Your first step in reviewing the literature would be to make a list of key words that relate to this study. Your first list might include the following: attitude, attitude change, integration, prejudice, race relations, racial prejudice, segregation, minority groups and immigrants. This preliminary list of key words will almost certainly be incomplete and will be changed when the actual search of *Education Index* begins. It does, however, provide a starting point, and as many possible key words as you can think of should be listed in order to reduce the likelihood of important studies being overlooked. The *Education Index* provides no abstract, only a list as shown in Figure 3.2.

FIGURE 3.2 *An example of an entry from the Education Index*

Research skills
Research mentor: a tool to aid in the training of scientific investigators / David Weiner and Judith Weiner *British Journal of Educational Technology*, Vol.27, no.1: Jan 96 pp.5–14.

What counts as 'better' practice? Supporting students in improving their practice by drawing out their value dimensions / Kath Green *Educational Action Research*, Vol.5, no.1: 97 pp.31–41.

Whose project is it anyway? / Gerry Urwin *Journal of Further and Higher Education*, Vol.20, no.3: Autumn 96 pp.94–103.

Research tools
Pestalozzi: de nouveaux outils pour la recherche / Michel Soetard *Paedogogica Historica*, Vol.32, no.3: 96 pp.739–745.

Research utilisation
Banking on education and the uses of research: a critique of: World Bank priorities and strategies for education / Jon Lauglo *International Journal of Educational Development*, Vol.16, no.3: Jul 96 pp.221–233.

Cooperation and competition: the creation of ecosystems of innovation / Piero Formica and Jay Mitra *Industry and Higher Education*, Vol.10, no.3: Jun 96 pp.151–159.

The cooperative research centres programme: an Australian initiative to link research to commercialization / Greg Tegart *Industry and Higher Education*, Vol.10, no.3: May 96 pp.160–169.

Creating data in practitioner research / Tony Brown *Teaching and Higher Eduction*, Vol.12, no.3: May 96 pp.261–270.

A systematic method for undertaking a manual search is to create a checklist to narrow down the volumes that contain articles, etc. that need to be read. A checklist for a study looking at the relationships between the provision of careers education at school and adolescent unemployment might look like Figure 3.3 below. This works well with *Education Index* which provides titles of articles listed under each key word.

FIGURE 3.3 *Example of a checklist*

Education index

Key words	Vol 23	Vol 24	Vol 25	Vol 26	Vol 27
adolescents	✔	✔	✔	✔	✔
vocational choice		✔	✔		✔
careers education	✔			✔	✔
vocational education	✔		✔	✔	
careers counselling			✔	✔	
vocational counselling				✔	✔
adolescent un-employment rates	✔		✔		

Psychological Abstracts provide a list of numbers under each key word in the index volume. These numbers should then be located in the correct volume. Here, a brief abstract will be provided of each article. This abstract is much more useful than the brief biographical data found in *Education Index* as the abstract helps a researcher to decide whether a journal article is of value to them or not. Any potentially useful article title should be written on a library index card. The amassing of these cards will help when the actual articles are being looked for and will provide a basis for the reference section of the thesis or article under production.

ERIC, an acronym for the Educational Resources Information Centre, was initiated in 1965 by the US Office of Education to transmit the findings of current educational researchers to teachers, administrators, researchers, and the public. Two very useful preliminary sources are published by ERIC. These are *Resources in Education* (RIE) and *Current Index to Journals in Education* (CIJE). Although ERIC abstracts some of the same documents as *Education Index* and *Psychological Abstracts*, it includes many documents not abstracted by these services. For example, RIE provides abstracts of papers presented at education conferences, progress reports of ongoing research studies, studies sponsored by federal research programs, and final reports of projects conducted by local agencies such as school districts, which are not likely to appear in education journals. Thus, ERIC will be valuable to the student in providing an overview of the most current research being done in education. In contrast, many of the studies currently referenced in *Education Index* and *Psychological Abstracts* were completed several years previously because of the time lag between completion of the study, publication in a journal, and abstracting by the service.

The CIJE indexes around 800 education journals and journals in related fields and includes more than 1000 articles each month. It contains a subject index, an author index, and a main entry section. Using the key terms related to the research problem derived from the ERIC Thesaurus, the subject index is searched first. The EJ numbers of relevant references are noted, and then looked up in the main entry section where the abstracts of research articles are found.

If you wish to obtain the full document that is abstracted in the entry, you can order it through the ERIC Document Reproduction Service. A reproduction service price is listed in the document resumé for each document. If you need an RIE document as quickly as possible, it can be ordered by computer using the ORBIT or DIALOG systems, which are available through most university libraries. An example is shown in Figure 3.4.

ERIC includes **AskERIC**, an electronic question answering service on the Internet (**askeric@ericir.syr.edu**). In addition, ERIC has sixteen separate clearing houses (the list in Figure 3.5 shows major ones) which abstract and index documents in specific subject areas. Should one of the clearing houses listed below cover an area in which you propose to conduct research it would pay to contact it.

RIE requires a search using key terms in the subject index. Each reference listed under a key term has an ED number at the end. The researcher then looks up this number in the document resumés section and will find an abstract and other biographical

---

FIGURE 3.4 *Sample record*

The position of the key fields are shown in the following sample record:

CH	AN	EJ330143 IR514912
	TI	VCRs Silently Take over the Classroom
	AU	Reider, William L.
JN	PY	TechTrends, V30 n8 p14–18 Nov–Dec 1985
	AV	Available from: UMI
	LA	Language: English
	DT	Document Type: JOURNAL ARTICLE: (080); POSITION PAPER (120): PROJECT DESCRIPTION (141)
	JA	Journal Announcement: CIJMAY86
	TA	Target Audience: Practitioners
	AB	Discusses the rapid growth of video cassette recorder (VCR) use in schools; compares ways in which VCRs, audiovisual materials, and micro-computers are used in classrooms; and suggests reasons for the dramatic increase in VCR use. The successful implementation of VRC technology in the Baltimore Country School System (Maryland) is described. (MBR)
	DE	Descriptors: Adoption (Ideas); * Audiovisual Aids; * Educational Trends; Financial Support; Futures (of Society); * Micro-computers; Teacher Role; * Videotape Cassettes; *Videotape Recorders.
	ID	Identifiers: * Baltimore Country Public Schools MD; Standardisation.

FIGURE 3.5 *ERIC clearing houses*

ERIC Clearinghouse on Elementary & Early Childhood Education
University of Illinois
805 West Pennsylvania Avenue
Urbana, IL 61801-4897
(217) 333-1386
(800) 583-4135

ERIC Clearinghouse on Reading & Communication Skills
SRC, Indiana University
2805 East 10th Street, Suite 150
Bloomington, IN 47408-2698
(812) 855-5847

ERIC Clearinghouse on Teaching & Teacher Education
AACTE
One Dupont Circle, NW, Suite 610
Washington, DC 20036-1186
(202) 293-2450
FAX (202) 457-8095
(800) 882-9229

ERIC Clearinghouse on Assessment & Evaluation
Catholic University
Department of Education
O'Boyle Hall
Washington, DC 20064

ERIC Clearinghouse on Education Management
University of Oregon
1787 Agate Street
Eugene, OR 97403-5207
(503) 346-2334
FAX (503) 346-2334
(800) 438-8841

ERIC Clearinghouse on Counselling & Student Services
University of North Carolina-Greensboro
School of Education
Curry Building
Greensboro, NC 27412-5001
(800) 414-9769

ERIC Clearinghouse on Disabilities & Gifted Education
Council for Exceptional Children
1920 Association Drive
Reston, VA 22091-1589
(703) 264-9474
(800) 328-0272

FIGURE 3.5 *Continued*

ERIC Clearinghouse on Information & Technology
Syracuse University
Huntington Hall, Rm 030
800 University Avenue
Syracuse, NY 13244-2340
(315) 443-3640
(800) 464 9107

ERIC Clearinghouse on Higher Education
George Washington University
One Dupont Circle, NW, Suite 630
Washington, DC 20036-1183
(202) 296-2597
(800) 773-3742

ERIC Clearinghouse on Science, Math & Environmental Education
Ohio State University
1929 Kenny Road
Columbus, OH 43210-1080
(614) 292-6717

ERIC Clearinghouse on Adult, Career & Vocational Education
CETE/Ohio State University
1929 Kenny Road
Columbus, OH 43210-1090
(614) 292-4353
(800) 848-4815

information. The CIJE works in the same way. Should the researcher want a hard copy of the full document it can be ordered from the source listed in the abstract entry.

If you discover a controversial article or theory and want to find out what later authors thought of it or what successive researchers have discovered in relation to it you can use the Social Science Citation Index (SSCI). Later works are located by looking up the key author and seeing in which later studies the work has been mentioned.

Review of Education Research

This journal provides critical integrative reviews of research literature bearing on important topics and issues. Such reviews provide an excellent basis for a literature search.

Dissertation Abstracts International

This is a monthly compilation of doctoral dissertations, many of which have never been published. Each issue contains a keyword title index which lists titles and page numbers on which the abstract appears.

A more complete description of the ERIC System and how to use it can be found in the booklet *ERIC: What It Can Do for You, How to Use It,* which is available in many libraries.

Psychological Abstracts

Another valuable preliminary source for research workers in education is *Psychological Abstracts*. This reference is published monthly by the American Psychological Association and contains abstracts of articles appearing in over 850 journals and other sources in psychology and related areas. Every issue of *Psychological Abstracts* has sixteen sections, each covering a different area of psychology. In addition to including abstracts, the monthly issues also include brief subject and author indexes. Table 3.1 lists some major sources of research literature in education and social science.

Test sources

In conducting research, a test or measuring device is often required. *Buros's Mental Measurement Yearbooks* are the major reference sources that list and critically review tests. These books are specifically designed to assist users in education, psychology and industry to make more intelligent use of standardised tests. Each yearbook is arranged in the same pattern and is meant to supplement rather than supersede the earlier volumes. Tests are grouped by subject, and descriptions of each test are followed by critical reviews and references to studies in which the test has been used. Each volume has cross-references to reviews, excerpts, and bibliographic references in earlier volumes. The volumes include aptitude and achievement tests in various subject areas, personality and vocational tests, and intelligence tests. Complete information is provided for each test, including cost and ordering instructions. *Tests in Print III* serves as an index and supplement to the first eight *Mental Measurement Yearbooks*. Buros also organises the material in the *Mental Measurement Yearbooks* into specialised monographs on tests of personality, reading, intelligence, vocational and business skills, English, foreign languages, mathematics, science, and social studies. The *Psychological Test Bulletin* published by ACER twice per year includes independent test reviews, research reports, articles on testing, Australian norms and information on new tests.

Conducting a computer search

Most researchers now use computers to search for sources rather than undertake a manual search. Computer searches remove the time-consuming activity of making detailed notes and summarising research articles, as a printout of abstracts is usually available. This printout can usually be obtained immediately at the terminal where you are conducting the search. It can be expensive if the search is extensive, as you will have to pay for online time. Most of the major indexes and abstracts are on computer databases. To carry out a successful online computer search a selection of essential key terms is required. Then combinations of key terms are used to produce references by employing '*and*' and '*or*'.

For example to obtain references for a study that is to investigate the self-concepts of beginning secondary school teachers you might require the following combination:

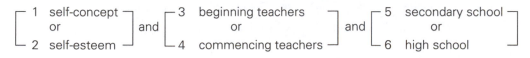

TABLE 3.1 *Sources of related literature in education and social science*

Applied Social Sciences Index and Abstracts	Titles, authors, journal citations and abstracts of journal articles in applied social science.
Business Education Index	Combined subject–author index of articles on business education.
Business Periodical Index	Titles, authors and journal citations of journal articles in the business field.
Contents Pages in Education	Copies of journal contents pages with master index of authors and subjects in each issue.
Current Index to Journals in Education (CIJE)	Titles, authors, and journal citations of journal articles related to education, with annotations where needed. Classification by subject, by author, and by journal. No abstracts.
Child Development Abstracts and Bibliography	Abstracts of journal articles in child development.
DATRIX II	Computerised sorting system for finding relevant dissertations listed in *Dissertation Abstracts International.*
DIALOG	Computerised search system for most education indexes and abstracts.
Dissertation Abstracts International	Abstracts of doctoral dissertations in the United States and Canada.
Education Index	Titles, authors, and journal citations of journal articles related to education. Indexed by subject and title. No abstracts.
Encyclopaedia of Educational Research	Summaries and evaluations of research in education, published at the end of each decade.
Exceptional Child Education Resources	Abstracts of journal articles in special education.
Mental Measurements Yearbooks	Information and evaluations of commercially available tests.
Psychological Abstracts	Abstracts of journal articles in psychology.
Resources in Education (RIE)	Abstracts of research reports and other documents acquired by ERIC clearing houses.
Review of Educational Research	Before June 1970: Review of research in selected topics in education in a three-year cycle. Beginning June 1970: Unsolicited reviews on various topics in each issue.
Social Sciences Citation Index	Bibliographic information for cited authors and topics.
Sociological Abstracts	Subject, author and source indexes plus abstracts.
Tests in Print III	Index and supplement to the first seven Mental Measurements Yearbooks.
Thesaurus of ERIC Descriptors	System for classifying and indexing ERIC documents.

We are asking the computer for any references that includes any combination of each pairing, such as 1 or 2 and 3 or 4 and 5 or 6. *Or* connections increase the number of references selected while *and* connections reduce the number selected.

Where can you have a computer search conducted?

Many universities and colleges have terminals that link them to one of the information retrieval systems such as the Lockheed DIALOG system, or the SDC/ORBIT system. You should visit the reference section of your library and see if a terminal is available.

Searching computer databases is similar to manually searching the printed indexes, as keywords are used to define the topic in both cases. A computer search is usually quicker and more efficient than a manual search, allowing improved access through title word searching in addition to searching indexing terms.

Ten different computer networks are available (DIALOG, AUSINET, AUSTRALIS, INFOLINE, STN, WILSONLINE, MEDLINE, ORBIT, BRS, ESA/IRS) offering a total of over 250 databases. Three networks (AUSINET, AUSTRALIS, MEDLINE) are located in Australia and lower fees are charged for these. Many databases are now on CD-ROM (e.g. ERIC, PsychLit) and are held by university libraries.

Writing the review

Writing a review of the literature is not an easy matter. You must do three things:

- describe the work which has been done, being critical where necessary;
- summarise the main facts and conclusions which emerge, synthesising to produce main themes, directions, contradictions etc.; and
- point out those areas of the field which are still inadequately covered.

Further reading

Brown, J., Sitts, M. & Yarborough, J. (1975), *ERIC: What It Can Do For You. How To Use It.* Syracuse, ERIC Clearinghouse on Information Services.

Buros, O. (ed.) (1978), *Mental Measurements Yearbooks*, 8th edn, University Nebraska Press, Lincoln.

Cooper H. (1998), *Synthesising Research: A Guide for Literature Reviews*, Sage, London.

Fink, A. (1998), *Conducting Research Literature Reviews*, Sage, London.

Hart, C. (1998), *Doing a Literature Review*, Open University, Milton Keynes.

Mann, L. & Sabatino, D. (1980), *Reviews of Special Education*, JSE Press, Philadelphia.

Mitchell, J.V. (1983), *Tests in Print III: An Index to Test Reviews and the Literature on Specific Tests*, University of Nebraska Press, Lincoln, NE.

Mitzel, H. (ed.) (1982), *Encyclopedia of Educational Research*, 5th edn, Glencoe, New York.

Thesaurus of ERIC Descriptors (1980), Onyx Press, Phoenix.

PART 2
QUANTITATIVE METHODS

Research in the quantitative tradition follows a linear sequence, as shown in the figure below. This section of the book covers the elements in this sequence.

Linear squence in quantitative research

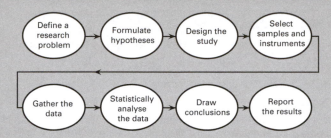

part 2 | quantitative methods

4

Descriptive statistics

The *descriptive* aspect of statistics allows researchers to summarise large quantities of data using measures that are easily understood by an observer. It would always be possible, of course, simply to present a long list of measurements for each characteristic observed. In a study of ages at leaving school, for example, we might just present the reader with a listing of the ages of all students leaving school within the past year in a particular state, or in a study of sex offenders, the sex of persons convicted of child abuse in 1998. This kind of detail, however, is not easy to assess—the reader simply gets bogged down in numbers. Instead of presenting all observations we could use one of several statistical measures that would summarise, for example, the typical age at leaving school in the collection of data. This would be much more meaningful to most people than the complete listing.

Thus descriptive statistics consist of graphical and numerical techniques for summarising data, i.e. reducing a large mass of data to simpler, more understandable terms.

Inferential statistics

Other statistical methods, termed *inferential*, consist of procedures for making generalisations about characteristics of a population based on information obtained from a sample taken from that population.

Over the last couple of decades, social scientists have increasingly recognised the power of inferential statistical methods. Hence, a discussion of statistical inference occupies a large portion of this textbook. The basic inferential procedures of estimation and hypothesis testing are explained in chapters 6 and 7.

Overall we can say that statistics consist of a set of methods and rules for organising and interpreting data. By common usage, statistics means facts and figures. In our approach it means techniques and procedures for analysing data.

Measures of central tendency

We often wish to summarise an entire distribution by a single, central score. Such a score is called a measure of central tendency. Three measures of central tendency are commonly used to express this central point of a distribution: the **mean**, the **median** and the **mode**.

The mean

By far the most common measure of central tendency in educational research is the arithmetic mean. The mean (M) is simply the sum of all the scores (ΣX) divided by the number of scores (N) or

$$M = \frac{\Sigma X}{N}$$

This is what most people think of as the average.

The mean is responsive to the exact position of each score in the distribution. Change any score and you change the value of the mean. The mean may be thought of as the balance point in a distribution. If we imagine a seesaw consisting of a fulcrum and a board, the scores are like bricks spread along the board. The mean corresponds to the fulcrum when it is in balance. Move one of the bricks to another position and the balance point will change (see Figure 4.1). In fact, the sum of negative deviations from the mean is equal to the sum of the positive deviations from the mean. This zero sum is the reason why measures other than actual deviations or range from the mean have to be used to measure the dispersal or spread of scores round the mean.

The mean is the only measure that reflects the influence of all scores in the distribution. If a constant is added to or subtracted from every score in the distribution, the mean will also increase or decrease respectively by this constant. If every score in a distribution is multiplied or divided by a constant, the mean will alter to reflect its multiplication or division by the constant.

The median

The word *median* means 'middle item'. Thus, when we have a series of scores which contain an extreme value or values, it would be sensible to arrange them in rank order

FIGURE 4.1 *Mean as balance point*

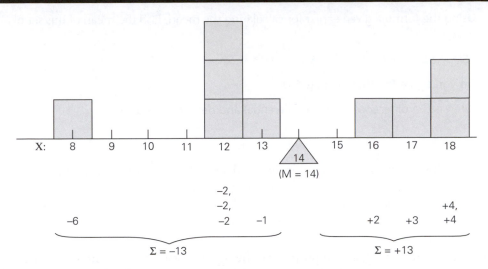

so that the highest value is at the top of the list, and the remaining scores are placed in descending order of magnitude with the score of least value at the bottom of the list. The median value will be the central value.

For example, if we have a series of nine scores, there will be four scores above the median and four below. This is illustrated as follows:

16   6   11   24   17   4   19   9   20

Arranged in order of magnitude these scores become:

24   20   19   17   16   11   9   6   4

median value

In our example we had a set of odd numbers which made the calculation of the median easy. Suppose, however, we had been faced with an even set of numbers. This time there would not be a central value, but a pair of central values. No real difficulty is presented here, for the median is to be found halfway between these two values.

Let us put the following numbers in rank order and find the median score:

16   29   20   9   34   10   23   12   15   22

In rank order these numbers appear as follows:

34   29   23   22   20   16   15   12   10   9

$$\text{median} = \frac{20 + 16}{2} = 18$$

STQ9

1   Using the formula given earlier for calculating the mean, find the mean of this set of data.

98   59   61   57   56   60   62   58   60   59

Do you agree that the mean is 63?

2   What is the difference between inferential and descriptive statistics?

Look at this mean of 63 in relation to the data and comment on what you notice. Hopefully you realised that the mean was larger than any of the other scores except the extreme score. This example of having one number much greater in value than the other numbers presents a real problem, for it renders the mean untypical, unrealistic and unrepresentative.

The median has the desirable property of being insensitive to extreme scores. In the distribution of scores of 66, 70, 72, 76, 80 and 96, the median of the distribution would remain exactly the same if the lowest score were 1 rather than 66, or the highest score were 1223 rather than 96. The mean, on the other hand, would differ widely with these other scores. Figure 4.2 shows the effect of extreme scores. The mean of 20.3 is hardly representative. It would not matter in this case if the extreme score were 1000, the median would remain the same at 11.50.

FIGURE 4.2 *Unrepresentative mean*

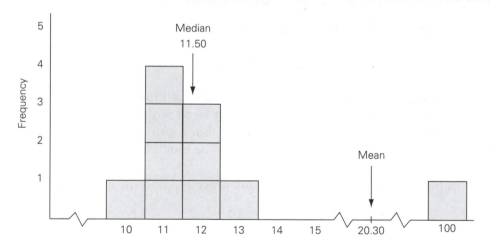

However, using the median often severely limits any statistical tests that can be used to analyse the data further, since the median is an element of ordinal or ranked data, whereas the mean is a major feature of interval data (chapter 8).

The mode

The third measure of central tendency is the mode, or modal score, which is the most frequently occurring value in a set of scores. It is a typical result, a common or fashionable one (à la mode), but not necessarily a mathematically sophisticated one. The mode in the following example is 24, since four people obtained that score on a test:

23   28   20   (24)   9   (24)   (24)   21   18   19   (24)

The mode is easy to obtain. However there may be more than one mode in a distribution. In a rectangular distribution where every score is the same, every score shares the honour.

The mode lacks the precision of the other two measures and can be misleading. It is rarely used in educational research.

Comparison of mean, median and mode

The choice between the mean and the median as a measure of central tendency depends very much of the shape of the distribution. The median, as shown earlier, is not affected by 'extreme' values as it only takes into account the rank order of observations. The mean, on the other hand, is affected by extremely large or small values as it specifically takes the values of the observations into account, not just their rank order.

Distributions with extreme values at one end are said to be skewed. A classic example is income, since there are only a few very high incomes but many low ones. Suppose we sample ten individuals from a neighbourhood, and find their yearly incomes (in thousands of dollars) to be:

25   25   25   25   40   40   40   50   50   1000

The median income for this sample is $40 000, and this value reflects the income of the typical individual. The mean income for this sample, however, is

25 + 25 + 25 + 25 + 40 + 40 + 40 + 50 + 50 + 1000 = 130 or $130 000.

A politician who wants to demonstrate that their neighbourhood has prospered might, quite honestly, use these data to claim that the average (mean) income is $130 000. If, on the other hand, they wished to plead for financial aid for the local school, they might say, with equal honesty, that the typical (median) income is only $40 000. There is no single 'correct' way to find an 'average' in this situation, but it is obviously important to know which measure of central tendency is being used. In general, if a distribution is substantially skewed—that is, when the bulk of observations are clustered together but a few have much higher or much lower values—then the median is usually preferred to the mean.

It is always best from an analytic viewpoint to use the mean wherever possible. Many of the summary measures used in descriptive statistics can be and are used in more complex analyses. The mean, which is calculated arithmetically, is mathematically much easier to manipulate than the median, which is found by ordering. Secondly, much of the data used in research derives from samples and from sampling procedures. Any sampling procedure leads to 'sampling errors' for a particular statistic, i.e. we can only estimate the mean or median income or age in a given population within certain limits of error. Sampling theory shows that this error or 'uncertainty' is less for the mean than for the median. Thus for most purposes we find that the mean is used in preference to the median, except when the distributions are substantially skewed.

STQ10

Why should the mean be used rather than the median or mode?

Measures of dispersal or variability

Averages or measures of central tendency are a useful way of describing one characteristic of a frequency distribution. But reducing a large set of data to one statistic can lead to a serious loss of information. Consider the three distributions below. Both mean and median are equal for each distribution, i.e. = 10, but a second characteristic differs quite markedly in each:

a	8	9	10	11	12
b	10	10	10	10	10
c	1	5	10	15	19

What other characteristic beside central tendency would seem necessary to describe it?

It is the variability of scores around the mean that is required, and we need to know how to measure this variability. This provides another way of summarising and comparing different sets of data. The notion of variability lies at the heart of the study of individual and group differences. It is the variability of individuals that forms the focus of research. We need some way to describe it. It has by now, even with brief acquaintance, become obvious to you that we can actually calculate a mean, median and mode for a set of scores even if they have variability or not. If all subjects in a test receive the same score, i.e. no variability, then the mean, median and mode will all be the same, and the same as this score. On the other hand, if there is considerable variation, our three measures of central tendency provide us with no indication of its extent. But what they can do is provide us with reference points against which variability can be assessed.

Range

One method of considering variability is to calculate the range between the lowest and the highest scores. This is not a very good method, however, since the range is considerably influenced by extreme scores.

Variance

The shortcoming of the range as a measure of variability is that it reflects the values of only two scores in the entire sample. A better measure of variability would incorporate every score in the distribution rather than just two scores. One might think that the variability could be measured by the average difference between the various scores and the mean, M, by:

$$\frac{\sum(\text{score} - M)}{N}$$

This hypothetical measure is unworkable, however, because some of the scores are greater than the mean and some are smaller, so that the numerator is a sum of both positive and negative terms. (In fact, it turns out that the sum of the positive terms equals the sum of the negative terms, so that the expression shown above always equals zero.)

The solution to this problem is simply to square all the terms in the numerator, thus making them all positive. The resulting measure of variability is called the variance (V):

$$V = \frac{\sum(X - M)^2}{N}$$

Variance is the average squared deviation from the mean, that is, the sum of the squared deviations from the mean divided by the number of scores. The sum of $(X - M)^2$ can also be written as SS which stands for the Sum of Squares or sum of squared deviations from the mean.

$$\text{Variance} = \frac{SS}{N} \text{ where } SS = (X - M)^2 \text{ or } (\sum X^2) - \frac{(\sum X)^2}{N}$$

This is the formula for population data.

The calculation of the variance is shown in Table 4.1. As the table shows, the variance is obtained by subtracting the mean (M, which equals 8) from each score, squaring each result, adding all the squared terms, and dividing the resulting sum by the total number of scores (N, which equals 10), yielding a value of 4.4.

Because deviations from the mean are squared, the variance is expressed in units different from the scores themselves. If our dependent variable were a distance measured in centimetres, the variance would be expressed in square centimetres. It is more convenient to have a measure of variability which can be added to or subtracted from the mean. Such a measure ought to be expressed in the same units as the original scores. To accomplish this end, we employ another measure of variability, the standard deviation.

Standard deviation

This is the most important measure of dispersal. It is often symbolised as 'σ' or 'SD'. Some researchers use σ with population and SD with samples. It reflects the amount of spread that the scores exhibit around some central tendency measure, usually the mean. The standard deviation is derived from the variance (V); it is obtained by taking the square root of the variance.

TABLE 4.1 *Calculating variance*

Score	Score – mean	(Score – mean)^2	
8	8 – 8 = 0	0^2 = 0	$\dfrac{44}{10}$ = 4.4
11	11 – 8 = 3	3^2 = 9	
6	6 – 8 = –2	$(–2)^2$ = 4	
7	7 – 8 = –1	$(–1)^2$ = 1	
5	5 – 8 = –3	$(–3)^2$ = 9	
9	9 – 8 = 1	1^2 = 1	
5	5 – 8 = –3	$(–3)^2$ = 9	
9	9 – 8 = 1	1^2 = 1	
9	9 – 8 = 1	1^2 = 1	
11	11 – 8 = 3	3^2 = 9	

Thus,

$$\sigma \text{ or SD} = \sqrt{V}$$

$$\sigma = \sqrt{\frac{SS}{N}} \text{ or } \sqrt{\frac{\Sigma(X - M)^2}{N}} \text{ or } \sqrt{\frac{(\Sigma X^2) - \frac{(\Sigma X)^2}{N}}{N}}$$

In our example in Table 4.1, SD is about 2.1, the square root of the variance which is 4.4.

Here is another example. Imagine our data is 15, 12, 9, 10 and 14.

a Obtain the mean of the values (M = 12).
b Calculate the differences of the values from the mean (3; 0; 3; 2; 2).
c Obtain the squares of these differences (9; 0; 9; 4; 4).
d Find the sum of the squares of the differences (26).
e Divide by the number of items 26/5 = 5.2. This is the variance.
f Obtain the square root of the variance, which is the standard deviation = 2.3.
   The formula for obtaining the standard deviation is:

$$\sigma = \sqrt{\frac{\Sigma(X - M)^2}{N}} \qquad \text{i.e. in our example} = \sqrt{\frac{26}{5}} = 2.3$$

If we are concerned only with finding the standard deviation as a measure of dispersion of the sample, this formula will suffice, but if we want to gain some idea of the variability of the population from which the sample was taken, then N – 1 should be used as the denominator for greater accuracy,

$$\text{sample variance} = \frac{SS}{N - 1} \text{ or } \frac{\Sigma X^2 - \frac{(\Sigma X)^2}{N}}{N - 1}$$

$$\text{sample standard deviation} = \sqrt{\frac{SS}{N - 1}} \text{ or } \sqrt{\frac{\Sigma X^2 - \frac{(\Sigma X)^2}{N}}{N - 1}}$$

When calculating population data, always use N as the denominator. When calculating variance or standard deviation of a sample use N – 1 as the denominator. Thus:

$$\sigma = \sqrt{\frac{\Sigma(X - M)^2}{N - 1}} = \sqrt{\frac{26}{4}} = 2.55$$

We use N – 1 rather than N when working with samples in order to produce an unbiased estimate of the population standard deviation. Due to chance factors in drawing a sample from a population, we know that the sample is unlikely to be the same as the population in terms of mean or standard deviation. However if the sample mean is an unbiased estimate there is an equal likelihood that it will fall above or below the population mean. If it is biased it will always tend to fall below the population parameter.

Let us take a population of only four scores: 2, 2, 4, and 4. The mean is 3. Since all the deviations are equal to 1 the variance and standard deviation is also 1. If you select a sample of two scores from the population, only four samples are possible. These are listed in the table below. The table also shows the sample variance using both N and N – 1 as the denominator. If we use N for the sample variance the four values add up to 2, so the average sample variance is .5. This underestimates the population variance which we know is 1. Using N – 1, the four values add up to 4, giving an average sample variance of 1. This is exactly the same as the population variance. Thus using N results in a biased measure.

Sample score	1st score	2nd SS	Sample variance using N – 1	Sample variance using N	Sample variance
1	2	2	0	0	0
2	2	4	2	2	1
3	4	2	2	2	1
4	4	4	0	0	0

N – 1 will provide a better estimate of the population SD. As you will realise, as sample N gets larger and the difference between size of sample and size of population becomes much reduced, the difference between dividing by N or N – 1 becomes negligible. Purely by chance, a sample may include an extreme case. But the larger the size of that sample, the less the effect of an extreme case on the average. If a sample of three persons includes an exceptionally short person, the average height will be unusually far from the population mean. In a sample of 3000, one exceptionally short person will not affect the average very markedly. However, as you will see, research generally involves samples which are considerably smaller than the population from which they are drawn. Hence the use of N – 1 as denominator is strongly advised.

This formula,

$$\sigma = \sqrt{\frac{\Sigma(X - M)^2}{N - 1}}$$

works well if M is a whole number, but so often it is not and causes unwieldy computations with deviations that are not whole numbers going to perhaps two decimal places. Then you have the problem of having to square such awkward numbers. Inaccuracy is often introduced here by rounding, so a formula more convenient to use is:

$$\sigma = \sqrt{\frac{\sum X^2 - \frac{(\sum X)^2}{N}}{N-1}}$$

where $\sum X^2$ is the sum of the squared raw scores and $(\sum X)^2$ is the sum of the raw scores squared.

This formula is mathematically equivalent to the first formula above. Let us check that we do get the same answer.

X	X²
15	225
12	144
9	81
10	100
14	196
ΣX = 60	**ΣX² = 746**

$$\sigma = \sqrt{\frac{746 - \frac{60^2}{5}}{4}}$$

$$\sigma = \sqrt{\frac{746 - 720}{4}} = \sqrt{\frac{26}{4}}$$

$$\sigma = 2.55$$

This formula too must employ $N - 1$ as the denominator when used with samples.

Figure 4.3 shows two different standard deviations—one with a clustered appearance, the other with scores well spread out illustrating clearly the relationship of spread to standard deviation.

Generally, the larger the σ, the greater the dispersal of scores; the smaller the σ, the smaller the spread of scores, i.e. increases in proportion to the spread of the scores around M as the marker point. But measures of central tendency tell us nothing about the standard deviation and vice versa. Like the mean, the standard deviation should be used with caution with highly skewed data, since the squaring of an extreme score would carry a disproportionate weight. It is therefore recommended where M is also appropriate.

Adding a constant to every score does not change a standard deviation. This is because each score still remains at the same distance from other scores as it did before, and the mean simply increases by the constant too. Therefore deviations from the mean remain the same. However, multiplying each score by a constant causes the standard deviation to be multiplied by that constant as each distance between scores is also multiplied by the same constant. For example, given three scores 10, 12 and 14 with a mean of 12 we

FIGURE 4.3 *Two distributions with same M but different SDs*

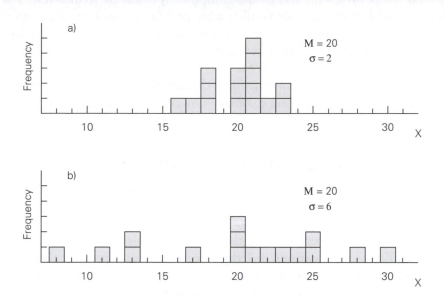

can multiply by 3 and obtain 30, 36 and 42 with a mean of 36. The deviation of each score from the mean has increased three times and so will the standard deviation.

So in describing an array of data, researchers typically present two descriptive statistics: the mean and the standard deviation. Although there are other measures of central tendency and dispersion, these are the most useful for descriptive purposes. Variance is used extensively, as we shall see, in inferential statistics.

Statistical software packages for the computer

Since computers and software packages for statistical analysis are so prevalent that everyone has access to 'statistics', it has become more important than ever before to teach the correct use of statistics. Using computing power should go hand-in-hand with—not replace—statistical reasoning, the correct selection of a statistical test, careful evaluation of the underlying assumptions, and cautious interpretation of results. It is my hope that this book stresses these aspects more completely and understandably than most other statistics texts. It is, in fact, the development and implementation of new statistical software that made me realise just how important it is that we teach the concepts of statistics well. When a microcomputer can be used to perform complicated analyses, statistical instruction that does not cover such topics is behind the times.

The book therefore shows how to use a computer program to undertake most of the statistical tests discussed and how to interpret the printout of results. There are many widely used packages of statistical software available today. Almost any one of them will be able to perform all the operations discussed in this text. In particular, I have given examples of how to use SPSS for many of the statistical procedures, as this program is perhaps the one in most common use. In each chapter where data analysis is conducted you will find a section on the use of the computer for that particular test. For the convenience of readers who are not familiar with, or who do not have access to SPSS, sufficient detailed information is given to enable calculations to be done by hand or with an electronic calculator. Most other statistics packages will do the job just as well and operate in very similar fashion to SPSS.

It must be emphasised that the information is the bare minimum to get you started. To become a skilled user will require you to obtain a more detailed handbook on the use of SPSS.

Labelling variables and their values

The first task in using a statistical program is to label the variables and place or input your obtained data into their respective variable columns. You should create your variable names before you input any data. With SPSS it is necessary not only to label each variable with an abbreviated name that is a reasonable guide to what it is—for example, 'qualif' for qualifications or 'ethgp' for ethnic group—but also label the variable in full, and where coding is involved for various categories of the variable include this in order to make your print-out of results clear, since the full names will be printed there. Below is an example of the procedure used to create your variables before you enter any data.

In this example, imagine you are going to create a column for data relating to qualification level of some teachers. The teachers answered a questionnaire that asked them to indicate their highest qualification. They were given five qualifications to choose from which would be coded 1 through to 5.

Example procedure

1 Select the column you wish to label with a variable. This is usually the first free column from the left in the data editor window. To select the column make sure your cursor or the active cell which is framed in bold is in that column.
2 Click on *Data* from the menu bar to produce a drop-down menu.
3 On the drop down menu, select *Define Variable* which opens the *Define Variable* dialogue box.
4 Variable Label: Variables can have a label of up to eight characters in length, so *var00001* (the SPSS default label) which is to represent the qualifications of the teachers will be abbreviated to '*qualif*' by typing in '*qualif*' which will delete the highlighted default name '*var00001*' in the *Variable Name*: box.
5 Next click on the *Label* button to display the *Define Labels* box.
6 In the *Variable Label* box, type the full variable name 'qualification'.
7 In the *Value* space type the figure '1', and in the V*alue label* space type 'Certificate'.
8 Select *Add* which puts 1.00 = 'certificate' in the bottom box.
   Repeat this procedure for the remaining four values of 2 for 'diploma', 3 for 'bachelors degree', 4 for 'masters degree' and 5 for 'Ph.D'.

9. When all the coding is complete, select *Continue,* then *OK*. The first column is now labelled *'qualif'* and is ready for data entry. Your output will now show the full names and related coding.

Using SPSS for descriptive statistics

Percentages and frequencies

1 Click on *Statistics* on the menu bar.
2 From the drop-down menu select *Summarize,* then click on *Frequencies.* This opens the *Frequencies* dialogue box.
3 Highlight the variables for which you wish to generate descriptive statistics and use the arrow button to place them in the *Variable[s]:* box.
4 Select *Statistics,* which brings the *Frequencies statistics* box into display.
5 In the *Dispersion area* click *Minimum* and *Maximum*.
6 Choose *Continue,* then *OK* to obtain output similar to that shown below in Table 4.2.

TABLE 4. 2 *Example of table produced by the frequency procedure*

Drink preference

		Frequency	Per cent	Valid per cent	Cumulative per cent
Valid	Fizzie	22	26.2	26.2	26.2
	Bubbly	31	36.9	36.9	63.1
	Pepco	31	36.9	36.9	100.0
	Total	84	100.0	100.0	
Total		84	100.0		

How to interpret the output in Table 4.2

- The table gives us frequencies and percentages for the drink preferences of a group of students.
- Column 1: The value labels are listed: 'fizzie', 'bubbly', etc.
- Column 2: The frequency of each of the categories is presented. Thus there are thirty-one cases who chose 'bubbly'.
- Column 3: The percentage of cases in each category for the sample as a whole is displayed. This includes any values that you may have defined as missing values (there are none in this example). Thus 26.2 per cent of the cases in the sample chose 'fizzie'.
- Column 4: The percentage of cases in each category for the sample excluding any missing values is presented. Since there were no values defined as missing in our example, columns 4 and 5 are identical in this instance.
- Column 5: The cumulative percentage excluding any missing values is found in the final column of numbers. Thus 63.1 per cent of the cases chose 'bubbly' and 'fizzie' combined.

How to report the results in Table 4.2

Table 4.2 presents most of the main features of these data. Depending on your purpose you would discuss certain noteworthy percentages and frequencies. Don't try to report all of the SPSS output since there is an excess of detail. Avoid SPSS-specific terms, like 'valid percent' as it has little meaning for those readers not *au fait* with SPSS.

Using SPSS graphs

The presentation of data in the form of a chart such as a bar chart, pie chart or histogram aids understanding and brings out salient features of a mass of figures in a visual summary form.

For example, to create a pie chart:

1 Click *Graphs* then select *Pie*.
2 Click *Summaries For Groups of Cases*.
3 Select *Define* and in the *Define Pie Summaries for Groups of Cases* box, highlight the variable of interest to you and move it to the *Define Slices* box.
4 Click *OK* and the chart will be displayed.
5 To add percentages to the slices double click on the chart to select it for editing.
6 Select *Chart* then *Options*.
7 In the pie chart *Options* box click next to percents in the *Labels* box.
8 Select *Format* then click on the down arrow next to *Position* and select *Numbers inside, Text outside*.
9 Choose *Continue* and then *OK* to display the edited pie chart.

FIGURE 4.4 *Example of a pie chart*

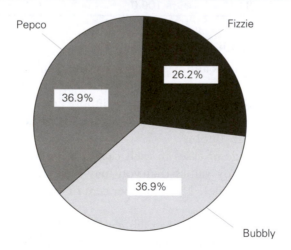

Descriptive statistics

1 Click on *Statistics* to display a drop-down menu.
2 From this menu, select *Summarize,* then *Explore* to obtain the *Explore* dialogue box.

3 Transfer to the Dependent list box, by clicking and highlighting those variables for which you wish to obtain the descriptive statistics.

4 In the *Display* box choose *Statistics*.

5 Click on the *Statistics* button which will bring the *Explore:Statistics* dialogue box into view.

6 Make sure *Descriptives* is chosen. Select *Continue* and then *OK* to produce output similar to that shown in Table 4.3.

If you wish to compute descriptive statistics for a quantitative variable within levels of a qualitative variable, for example, age for men and women separately, after step 3 above place the qualitative variable into the *FactorList* box.

TABLE 4.3 *Example of descriptive statistics produced by the explore procedure*

	Gender			Statistic	Std error
STATS	Female	Mean		45.1429	1.4842
		95% confidence interval for mean	Lower Bound	42.1455	
			Upper Bound	48.1402	
		5% trimmed mean		44.9418	
		Median		44.0000	
		Variance		92.516	
		Std deviation		9.6185	
		Minimum		29.00	
		Maximum		65.00	
		Range		36.00	
		Interquartile range		14.2500	
		Skewness		.225	.365
		Kurtosis		−.610	.717
	Male	Mean		42.8571	1.5365
		95% confidence interval for mean	Lower Bound	39.7542	
			Upper Bound	45.9601	
		5% trimmed mean		42.9444	
		Median		44.0000	
		Variance		99.150	
		Std deviation		9.9574	
		Minimum		25.00	
		Maximum		59.00	
		Range		34.00	
		Interquartile range		15.5000	

TABLE 4.3 *Continued*

	Gender			Statistic	Std error
		Skewness		−.121	.365
		Kurtosis		−.987	.717
SELFCONC	Female	Mean		44.0476	1.4293
		95% confidence interval for mean	Lower Bound	41.1611	
			Upper Bound	46.9342	
		5% trimmed mean		44.0423	
		Median		45.0000	
		Variance		85.803	
		Std deviation		9.2630	
		Minimum		26.00	
		Maximum		62.00	
		Range		36.00	
		Interquartile range		10.0000	
		Skewness		.067	.365
		Kurtosis		−.290	.717
	Male	Mean		39.3333	1.9226
		95% confidence interval for mean	Lower Bound	35.4505	
			Upper Bound	43.2161	
		5% trimmed mean		40.0556	
		Median		40.0000	
		Variance		155.252	
		Std deviation		12.4600	
		Minimum		7.00	
		Maximum		58.00	
		Range		51.00	
		Interquartile range		12.7500	
		Skewness		−.620	.365
		Kurtosis		.590	.717

How to interpret the output in Table 4.3

- The output provides information about the scores on a statistics test and self-concept scores for males and females.
- The top table simply reveals the number of cases and whether there is any missing data.

- Valid cases are the number of cases which have been included in the analysis. In our example it equals the number of scores.
- Missing cases are the number of scores which have been disregarded for the purposes of the analysis. SPSS permits you to identify particular values of a variable as 'missing'. If the computer comes across these for a particular variable they will be disregarded for analysis purposes.
- The important statistics lie in the bottom sub-table; that is, the mean, median and standard deviation. For example, the mean female statistics score was 45.12, the median was 44.00 and the standard deviation was 9.62 (rounded).

How to report the output in Table 4.3

- While SPSS reports this data to four decimal places, two decimal places are usually more than enough for most social science, psychological and educational data. Measurement in social science is less accurate than that in the physical sciences, so the use of more than two decimal places is overkill and infers a precision that is not warranted.
- For the median and mode it is better to report values as a whole number (e.g. 6) rather than with decimals (6.00). However, if the decimal places are anything other than .00 this should be reported, since it indicates that the median or mode does not correspond to any actual scores.
- The table is largely self-explanatory.
- There are many other statistical values that have been calculated such as *95% confidence intervals, skewness, variance, range, maximum and minimum score,* and *standard error.* They would be quoted if the occasion warranted it. You would not report all the measures displayed but reproduce those of interest in a more simplified form, omitting some of the clutter of detail. Charts and diagrams such as histograms, pie charts and box plots could also be produced where necessary to clarify the results as shown below, and to aid understanding and clarity of presentation of information. These visual aids are located under Graphs in the menu bar.

Creating a box plot

A box plot can present a clear visual expression of a set of data and can be used instead of histograms and bar charts.

1 Click *Graphs* then *Boxplot* to produce the *Boxplot* dialogue box.
2 Select *Simple* then click on *Summaries for Groups of Cases*.
3 Select *Define* to display the *Define Simple Boxplot; Summaries* box.
4 Choose your quantitative variable(s) by highlighting and clicking the arrow button to transfer to the variable box.
5 Choose your qualitative variable and move it to the *Category Axis* box.
6 Finally select *OK* and the box plot is displayed.

The box plot shows the maximum and minimum scores using horizontal lines, while the mean is depicted as a horizontal line within the interquartile range, which is shaded.

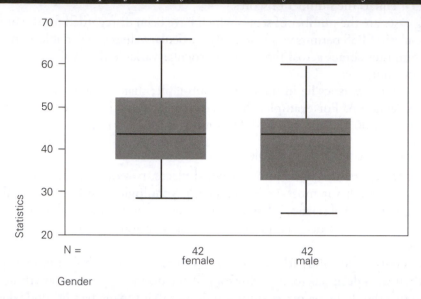

STQ11*

1. Calculate M and σ for the following sample distributions:

   a   2   4   6   8   10

   b   10   9   8   7   6   5   4   3   2

   c   2   6   12   20   50

   d   Which has the largest σ and why?

2. If you are told that one score in a distribution has a value of 8.0 and σ = 0, which of the following is true?

   a   The M cannot be calculated.

   b   All scores are identical.

   c   N cannot be known.

   d   The distribution is skewed.

3. Calculate the σ of the following scores:

     8   10   11   12   12   14   16   18

   a   Now subtract 3 from each of the scores and recalculate. What has happened?

   b   Now multiply each original score by 2, and recalculate σ. What has happened in this case?

4. Under what circumstances is the mean a poor choice as a measure of central tendency?

5. When is the median likely to be the best choice of central tendency measure?

6. Find the variance and standard deviation of the following sample scores.

   a   1, 9, 8, 5, 7

   b   1, 6, 4, 3, 8, 7, 6

*Answers on p. 594.

Measuring relative performance

Standard scores

Sometimes we need to compare different individuals on a particular test, and there are occasions when a number of different assessment instruments are given to individuals or groups (for example, in vocational guidance, educational assessment and research studies) and comparisons are made about a person's performance on these tests on the basis of the raw scores. This is not an informed or sensible procedure, but it is one that is often erroneously applied. You may have a school report which shows that you were better at English than you were at history, judged solely on raw scores. Let us look at this more carefully.

Take, for example, a student who obtains 60 marks in a mathematics examination and 50 marks in an English examination. Is the student more able in mathematics than in English? At first sight, yes: the mark is higher in mathematics, but since these are different subjects it may be that one teacher is an 'easier' marker than the other. Thus we need to look at how the group as a whole performs in these examinations. To do this, we can take each mark (X) away from the mean mark (M) from the group or subject. Now, if the mean in mathematics was 40 marks and in English 60 marks, then within this group the student is above average in mathematics and below average in English—which more or less answers our original question.

But, what if the mean mark is 55 in mathematics and 45 in English? The student is now 5 marks above average in each subject, but we cannot necessarily regard these differences of 5 marks above average as being equivalent because the variations in the marks, i.e. the standard deviation, may differ between the groups. Thus, some teachers may give marks over a limited range and others over a much wider range—the latter is often the case in mathematics.

Assume that the standard deviation of mathematics marks for all examinees is 10 marks, and that of English 5 marks; then there would be a wider spread of marks in mathematics than in English and the overall distribution of marks in the two subjects might well be as shown in Figure 4.6 below. The effect of the different spreads of marks is that in mathematics a mark of 60 is quite close to the mean of 55, while a mark of 50 in English is comparatively much further away from the mean of 45.

FIGURE 4.6 *Distribution of marks in mathematics and English examinations*

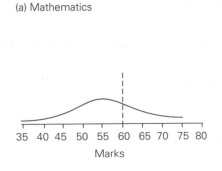

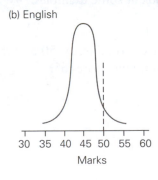

Thus, comparing 'raw' scores can be misleading; they have to be put into context. The characteristic of the distribution from which they came must be taken into account. This is done by calculating new 'scores' from the 'raw' data, to create a common scale.

We often have to use common scales in many other fields besides education. For instance, temperature, length, weight etc. There are so many different scales in each, we cannot compare, say, two different temperatures, each measured on a different scale, and produce a meaningful comparison unless we can turn one into terms of the other or convert both to a common scale. Many of us who have been brought up on °F can only understand the implication of a temperature reported in °C by converting it into °F. The best way to compare a length measured in yards and a length in the old Biblical cubits would be to convert the latter into yards, or both into metric units. Now, we hope you see the problem. It is totally erroneous in test measurement to add and average marks obtained from different distributions which have different means and SDs. If this is done, it is akin to adding °F to °C or yards to metres. Test results should only be combined when:

- they are from a common scale;

- they have been converted to a common scale; or

- they are all converted into the M and σ of one of the existing distributions.

When an entire distribution is standardised the individual standard score is in the same relative position to the other standard scores as the raw score was originally. A standard score is a transformed score that provides information of its location in a distribution.

A standardised distribution is composed of standardised scores that result in a predetermined value for M and standard deviation regardless of their values in the raw score distribution. Standardised scores do not alter the rank order of performance; the highest scoring person in raw score terms will still maintain that position though the numerical value of the score may change.

The most common standard scale in test measurement is known as the Z score. Such Z scores take account of both M and σ of the distribution. The formula is:

$$Z = \frac{\text{Score} - \text{Mean}}{\text{SD of distribution}} = \frac{X - M}{\sigma}$$

The mean of the Z score distribution is always 0 and the σ is always 1.

Let us look at some examples.

EXAMPLE 1

The mean score on a test is 50 and the standard deviation is 10. What is the standard score for John who scores 65?

$$Z = \frac{X - M}{SD}$$

$$Z = \frac{65 - 50}{10} = 1.5$$

John's score is 1.5 standard deviations above the mean. It can be represented diagrammatically as shown in Figure 4.7.

Scores can, of course, have negative Z values. All those scores below the mean have negative Z values; all those above the mean have positive Z values.

FIGURE 4.7 *Standard score diagram of Example 1*

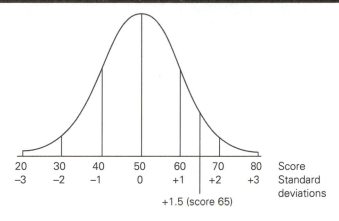

| Score | 20 | 30 | 40 | 50 | 60 | 70 | 80 |
| Standard deviations | −3 | −2 | −1 | 0 | +1 | +2 | +3 |

+1.5 (score 65)

EXAMPLE 2

As part of an apprenticeship selection assessment, school leavers are required to take three tests consisting of Test 1 (numeracy), Test 2 (literacy) and Test 3 (general knowledge).

Given the following results for Candidate R, and assuming normal distribution of results, on which of the three tests does that individual do best?

TABLE 4.4 *Numeracy, literacy and general knowledge scores*

	Raw score	Mean	Standard deviation
Test 1 Numeracy	87	75	12
Test 2 Literacy	16	13	2
Test 3 General Knowledge	31	34	10

1 Calculate Z for numeracy test:

$$Z = \frac{X - M}{SD} = \frac{87 - 75}{12} = +1$$

2 Calculate Z for literacy test:

$$Z = \frac{X - M}{SD} = \frac{16 - 13}{2} = +1.5$$

3 Calculate Z for general knowledge test:

$$Z = \frac{X - M}{SD} = \frac{31 - 34}{10} = -0.3$$

Candidate R achieves better results on the literacy test than on the numeracy or the general knowledge tests, in as much as her Z score shows that she is further above average for Test 2. Candidate R's results can be represented diagrammatically (Figure 4.8).

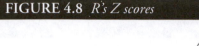

FIGURE 4.8 *R's Z scores*

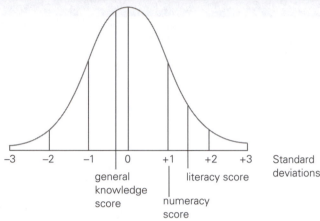

You can probably detect the source of the major disadvantage in adding and averaging raw scores from the above example. It lies in the size of the σ of each distribution. If you do badly in a test with a small σ, it will not affect you as much as doing poorly in a test with a large σ. In raw score terms, this latter situation implies a larger loss of marks, whereas your position relative to others in the group might be very similar in both cases. The converse applies too. Doing well in a test with a large σ will be a better boost to raw score average than a similar relative position in a test with a small σ. Tests with large σ carry more weight in the summation and averaging of raw scores than tests with small σ because there is a greater range of marks around M in the former. Z scores provide a standard unit of relative worth; for example, +1Z above the mean in any test is always a position only exceeded by 16 per cent of the population, provided the distribution is normal.

T scores and deviation IQs are other forms of standard scores. T scores have a mean of 50 and a standard deviation of 10, while deviation IQs have a mean of 100 and a standard deviation of 15. Standard scores combine all the information needed to evaluate a raw score into a single value that specifies a location within a normal distribution.

Stanines are formed by dividing the normal curve into nine equal intervals along the baseline. Rather than provide a score, a stanine provides a grade from 1 to 9. Within each grade are a set percentage of scores in the following sequence from the left-hand extreme end of the normal curve to the extreme right-hand end: 4%, 8%, 12%, 16%, 20%, 16%, 12%, 8%, 4%.

How SPSS computes Z scores

1 Click *Statistics*, then *Summarize*, and then *Descriptives*.
2 Select your chosen variable(s) and move them to the *Variables Text* box.

3 Select *Save Standardised Values* as variables.

4 Click *OK*.

For each of your scores the Z score will be calculated and placed in a separate column in your data window at the end of your data. This new 'variable' will be lost unless you save your data before ending the session.

As well as using Explore, you can obtain a range of descriptive statistics from Descriptives. These include the mean, sum, standard deviation, range, standard error of the mean, maximum and minimum score, and skewness.

STQ12*

1 If a student received a Z score of 0, one would know that this student's raw score was
   a below
   b above
   c equal to
   the mean.

2 Below are listed the scores made by five students on maths and spelling tests. The maths test had a mean of 30 and a standard deviation of 3. The spelling test had a mean of 45 and a standard deviation of 5. For each, say whether the student did better on the maths or the spelling test, or did equally well on both:

	John	Hui	Rachel	Chris	Zola
MATHS	36	33	27	33	36
SPELLING	35	55	40	45	55

3 A student was told that she had made a Z score of +1.5 on a test where the mean was 82 and the standard deviation was 6. What raw score did this student obtain?

4 What IQs are represented by the following standard scores?
   (mean = 100, σ = 15) (a) Z = 2 (b) Z = –1 (c) Z = 1.5 (d) Z = –0.66
   (e) Z = 0

5 What information does a Z score provide?

6 Given a mean of 45 and a standard deviation of 5, find the Z scores of the following:
   47, 39, 56
   and the raw scores of the following:
   +1, –3.0, + 2.8

7 Why is it possible to compare scores from different distributions after each distribution is transformed into Z scores?

8 Distribution A has a M = 20 and SD = 7 while distribution B has a M = 23 and SD = 2. In which distribution will a raw score of 27 have higher standing?

9 A population has a mean of 37 and a standard deviation of 2. If it is transformed into a distribution with a mean of 100 and a standard deviation of 20, what values will the following scores have: 35, 36, 37, 38 and 39?

10 Given scores of 2, 4, 6, 10 and 13 in a distribution with a mean of 7 and a standard deviation of 4, transform these scores into a distribution with a mean of 50 and a standard deviation of 20.

*Answers on p. 594.

summary

The purpose of central tendency is to determine the single value that best represents the entire distribution of scores. The three measures of central tendency are the mean, median and mode. The mean is the arithmetical average and is the preferred measure of central tendency. The mode is the most frequently occurring score. The median is the value that divides the distribution exactly in half. It is preferred when the distribution has a few extreme scores that distort the mean.

Variability is measured by the variance and standard deviation. The variance is the mean of the sum of the squared deviations from the mean. The standard deviation is the square root of the variance and is the basis of many other statistical operations.

In calculating the variance and standard deviation of sample statistics it is preferable to use a denominator of N − 1 to correct for bias in sampling. The larger the spread of scores round the mean, the larger the standard deviation.

Adding a constant to each score does not change the standard deviation. Multiplying each score by a constant causes the standard deviation to be multiplied by that constant.

In order to compare or combine scores from different distributions it is necessary to standardise the distributions to a single scale. The Z score is the most common standard score with a mean of 0 and standard deviation of 1. Any scores in a distribution can be transformed into a Z score that specifies an exact location within the distribution.

The sign of the Z score indicates whether the score is above or below the mean and the magnitude specifies the number of standard deviations between the score and the mean. When a entire distribution is transformed into Z scores the Z score distribution will have the same shape as the original distribution.

Frequency distributions

So far, we have considered data only in terms of its central tendency and its dispersal or scatter. If we plot the data we have obtained from any of our previous observations, we would find a host of differently shaped curves when the graph lines were drawn. These graphs are often called frequency distributions. The X-axis, or base line, supplies values of the scores with lowest values placed to the left and increasing values to the right. Every possible score should be capable of being located unambiguously somewhere along the X-axis. In frequency distribution, the vertical, or Y-axis, represents the frequency of occurrences, i.e. values of N.

These many differently shaped frequency distributions can be classified as normal or skewed. Normal distributions are symmetrical, affected only by random influences—i.e. influences that are just as likely to make a score larger than the mean as to make it smaller—and will tend to balance out, as the most frequently found scores are located in the middle of the range with extreme scores becoming progressively rarer (see Figure 5.1).

Skewed frequency distributions are biased by factors that tend to push scores one way more than another (see Figures 5.2 and 5.3). The direction of skewedness is named after the direction in which the longer tail is pointing. Imagine Figures 5.2 and 5.3 were the distributions of scores of two end-of-year examinations. What reasons could you suggest might have caused the skewedness in each case?

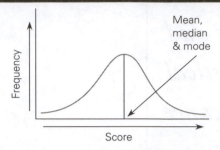

FIGURE 5.1 *Normal distribution (Gaussian curve)*

FIGURE 5.2 *Negatively skewed distribution*

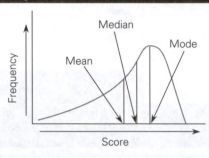

FIGURE 5.3 *Positively skewed distribution*

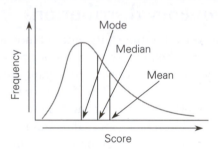

Some of our suggestions are:

For Figure 5.2   An easy examination; marking too easy; students working hard; a well-motivated and/or generally intelligent set of students, etc.

For Figure 5.3   A hard paper; severe marking; inadequate learning and revision by most; poor motivation; incompetent teaching, etc.

The normal distribution has been so thoroughly studied that the proportion of the area under the curve that lies between the central (mean) value and any Z score is known. Table 5.1 (p. 73) gives these proportions which have tremendously important applications. There are three such proportions of area that you should learn. These are:

between $+1\sigma$ and -1σ from the mean = 68% approx.
between $+2\sigma$ and -2σ from the mean = 95% approx.
between $+3\sigma$ and -3σ from the mean = 99.9% approx.

Since the area under the curve represents the total number of cases plotted, the particular percentages quoted above can be translated into the percentage of cases lying within the designated areas.

Table 5.1 is a very important table as it enables research workers to determine the area within any designated segment of the normal distribution curve, and by implication if we know the total number of cases plotted then we know the number of cases within that segment.

Turn to Table 5.1 now. For each Z score it shows the proportion of the area that lies between 0 (the mean) and Z. Since the normal distribution is symmetrical, the proportions for –Z are exactly the same as for +Z. If the area you are interested in extends on both sides of M (or 0) then it is necessary to add the two relevant areas together. Here are some examples for you to follow.

EXAMPLE 1

What proportion of the total area lies between 0 and 1.5σ? To find the answer look up 1.5σ in the Z column. Then look across to the next column. The answer is 43.32% (since the figures are given as proportions of 1).

EXAMPLE 2

What proportion of the total area lies *beyond* –2.3σ? Look up 2.3Z (forget the negative sign). It is 48.93%. But remember we want the area beyond; therefore the answer is 1.07%, i.e. 50.00% – 48.93%. Remember this table only covers one-half of the curve.

EXAMPLE 3

If one of the Z scores is positive and the other is negative, we find the proportion of the curve between them by adding values from column 2 in Table 5.1. What proportion of the curve lies between σ of –1.6 and σ of 0.5? Column 2 indicates that the proportion between Z = –1.6 and the mean is 0.4452, and from the mean to Z = +0.5 is 0.1915. Therefore, the proportion between Z = –1.6 and Z = +0.5 is 0.4452 + 0.1915, or 0.6367. This means that 63.67 per cent of the cases in a normal distribution will fall between these Z scores.

EXAMPLE 4

When we want the proportion of the normal curve falling between two Z scores with the same sign, we subtract the area for the smaller Z score from the area for the larger Z score. For example, let us find the proportion of cases between a Z of –0.68 and a Z of –0.98 in a normal distribution. Column 10 in Table 5.1 indicates that the area between the mean and a Z of 0.98 is 0.3365, while the area between the mean and a Z of 0.98 is 0.2517. Thus, the area between Z = 0.68 and Z = 0.98 is found by subtracting the area for the smaller Z score from the area for the larger Z score; in this case, 0.3365 – 0.2517 = 0.0848. We would expect 8.48 per cent of the cases in a normal distribution to fall between these Z score points.

Frequency distributions are then convenient ways of describing all the basic information contained in the measurement of any variable. They are charts or tables showing the frequency with which each of a number of values of a variable are observed.

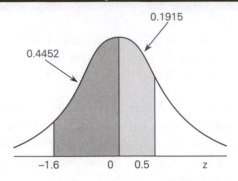

FIGURE 5.4 *Area under curve, Example 3*

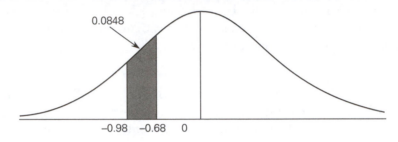

FIGURE 5.5 *Area under curve, Example 4*

More importantly, we often need to know the shape of a distribution to justify using one or another statistical technique. Many statistical tests should only be used if the data can be shown to be 'normally distributed' or only slightly deviated from a normal distribution. So the most important frequency distribution in our particular context is the normal distribution, or Gaussian curve (Figure 5.1).

Normal distribution

The normal curve is a mathematical abstraction. It is not associated with any event in the real world, just as circular objects do not exist simply because of a mathematical formula for the equation of the area of a circle. Again, just as the mathematical formula of a circle defines a family of circles, so too does the equation for the normal curve define a family of normal curves which differ in terms of their standard deviations and means. But in all other respects, members of this family have the same characteristics.

It is important to remember that our recorded observations tend to be discrete in practice rather than continuous, nor are they of infinite size. It is reasonable to speculate that no real variable is exactly normally distributed. This does not matter too much as it is the utility of the model that counts. Even variables that appear normally distributed in a large homogeneous population will fail to be so under other circumstances, particularly with a selected part of the population.

The real importance of the normal distribution for us is that it is the model for a distribution of sample statistics—in particular, sample means, as we shall see in chapter 6.

There is a family of normal distribution curves whose shapes depend on the mean and standard deviation of the distribution. However, they all retain the same mathematical characteristics. Figure 5.6 illustrates this.

FIGURE 5.6 *Different normal distribution curves*

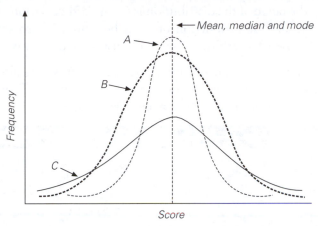

The normal distribution curve is the theoretical distribution of chance or random occurrences, and is thus centrally related to probability. Normal distribution curves possess some notable characteristics which are always present; otherwise normality would not exist. Figure 5.7 depicts these constants.

FIGURE 5.7 *The shape and important characteristics of the normal, or Gaussian, distribution*

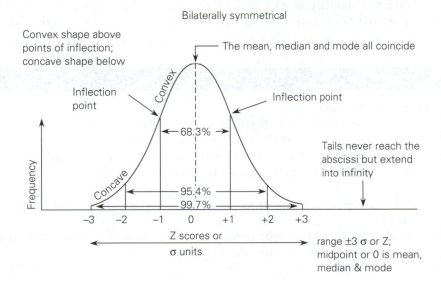

The following points should carefully be noted:

1 The distribution is bilaterally symmetrical and bell-shaped.
2 The mean, median and mode all coincide. This is the only situation where this congruence occurs.
3 The tails of the curve never quite reach the X-axis but continue outwards to infinity, yet simultaneously get progressively and infinitely closer to the axis.
4 In practical terms, the range of the distribution is 6 standard deviation units, i.e. 3 on each side of the mean. The proportion of cases beyond ±3 is so small that it is common practice to use ±3 as arbitrary limits in illustrative diagrams.

If we know the σ of any normal distribution, we can assign scores along the X-axis corresponding to the Z scores we have been using so far. For example, Figure 5.8 depicts a normal distribution with a mean of 50 and a standard deviation of 10.

FIGURE 5.8

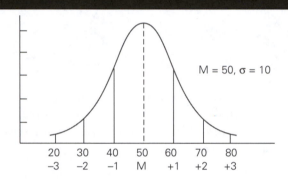

M = 50, σ = 10

20	30	40	50	60	70	80
−3	−2	−1	M	+1	+2	+3

As you see, for every unit of Z the score increases or decreases by 10 marks, i.e. +1Z is 10 marks higher than M since we regard the Z as a standard deviation unit. Most standardised published tests of intelligence, aptitude, and attitude are standardised to give a mean of 100 and a standard deviation of 15, i.e. a child who scores an IQ of 130 is two standard deviations above the mean, and referring to Table 5.1, we note that this score is only bettered by approximately 2.5 per cent of the child population of this age.

STQ13*

Use Table 5.1 (p. 73) to help you.
1 a What proportion of the total area lies between 0 and +2.6Z?
   b What proportion of the total area lies between ±1.8Z?
   c What proportion of the total area lies between −1.96Z and +1.96Z?
   d With a normal distribution involving 20 000 cases, how many lie beyond +2.65 Z?
   e Can you explain in simple terms why the median and mode coincide with the mean?
   f Now check the approximate percentages given earlier for areas between ±1σ, ±2σ and ±3σ by referring to Table 5.1.

(continued)

part 2 | quantitative methods

TABLE 5.1 *Fractional parts of the total area (taken as 10 000) under the Normal Probability Curve, corresponding to distances on the baseline between the mean and successive points laid off the mean in units of Standard Deviation. Example: Between the mean, and a point 1.3, σ is found 40.32% of the entire area under the curve.*

Z	.00	.01	.02	.03	.04	.05	.06	.07	.08	.09
0.0	0000	0040	0080	0120	0160	0199	0239	0279	0319	0359
0.1	0398	0438	0478	0517	0557	0596	0636	0675	0714	0753
0.2	0793	0832	0871	0910	0948	0987	1026	1064	1103	1141
0.3	1179	1217	1255	1293	1331	1368	1406	1443	1480	1517
0.4	1554	1591	1628	1664	1700	1736	1772	1808	1844	1879
0.5	1915	1950	1985	2019	2054	2088	2123	2157	2190	2224
0.6	2257	2291	2324	2357	2389	2422	2454	2486	2517	2549
0.7	2580	2611	2642	2673	2704	2734	2764	2794	2823	2852
0.8	2881	2910	2939	2967	2995	3023	3051	3078	3106	3133
0.9	3159	3186	3212	3238	3264	3290	3315	3340	3365	3389
1.0	3413	3438	3461	3485	3508	3531	3554	3577	3599	3621
1.1	3643	3665	3686	3708	3729	3749	3770	3790	3810	3830
1.2	3849	3869	3888	3907	3925	3944	3962	3980	3997	4015
1.3	4032	4049	4066	4082	4099	4115	4131	4147	4162	4177
1.4	4192	4207	4222	4236	4251	4265	4279	4292	4306	4319
1.5	4332	4345	4357	4370	4383	4394	4406	4418	4429	4441
1.6	4452	4463	4474	4484	4495	4505	4515	4525	4535	4545
1.7	4554	4564	4573	4582	4591	4599	4608	4616	4625	4633
1.8	4641	4649	4656	4664	4671	4678	4686	4693	4699	4706
1.9	4713	4719	4726	4732	4738	4744	4750	4756	4761	4767
2.0	4772	4780	4783	4788	4793	4798	4803	4808	4812	4817
2.1	4821	4826	4830	4834	4838	4842	4846	4850	4855	4857
2.2	4861	4864	4868	4871	4875	4878	4881	4884	4887	4890
2.3	4893	4896	4898	4901	4904	4906	4909	4911	4913	4916
2.4	4918	4920	4922	4925	4927	4929	4931	4932	4934	4936
2.5	4938	4940	4941	4943	4945	4946	4948	4949	4951	4952
2.6	4953	4955	4956	4957	4959	4960	4961	4962	4963	4964
2.7	4965	4966	4967	4968	4969	4970	4971	4972	4973	4974
2.8	4974	4975	4976	4977	4977	4978	4979	4979	4980	4981
2.9	4981	4982	4982	4983	4984	4985	4985	4986	4986	
3.0	4986.5		4987.4		4988.2		4988.9		4989.7	
3.1	4990.3		4991.0		4991.6		4992.1		4992.6	
3.2	4993.129									
3.3	4995.166									
3.4	4996.631									
3.5	4997.674									
3.6	4998.409									
3.7	4998.922									
3.8	4999.277									
3.9	4999.519									
4.0	4999.683									
4.5	4999.966									
5.0	4999.997133									

(continued)

2 A set of scores is normally distributed with M = 100 and σ = 15. What percentage of scores lie:

a between M and –1σ?

b between M and +2σ?

c between –1.5σ and +0.8σ?

3 Using the same distribution as in question 2 above and knowing that 10 000 scores are plotted, how many subjects scored:

a between +3σ?

b between M and +1σ?

c above +3σ?

d over a score of 115?

e below 85?

4 a In a normal distribution of IQ scores where the mean is 100 and σ = 15, what percentage of children fall between 85 and 120?

b In a normal distribution where the mean is 70 and σ = 5, what percentage of the area falls between 66 and 76?

c In a normal distribution where the mean is 500 and σ = 100, what percentage of the cases could be expected to fall between 625 and 725?

5 On a classroom test, the mean was found to be 62 and the standard deviation 5. The teacher gave the top 10 per cent of the group an A. What was the minimum score needed to get an A? Assume a normal distribution.

6 A teacher wishes to identify the middle 50 per cent of a group on a test where the distribution is known to be normal.

a What Z-score range would include the middle 50 per cent?

b If the mean is 60 and the standard deviation 9, what raw scores would set off the middle 50 per cent?

*Answers on p. 595.

Probability

Probability can best be defined as the likelihood of something happening. Probability is usually given the symbol of 'p' and can be thought of as the percentage of occurrences of a particular event to be expected in the long run. For example, a fair dice will produce in the long run a '5' on 1/6, or 16.66 per cent of all rolls because each of the six sides is equally likely to come up on each roll.

STQ14

A roulette wheel has thirty-six numbers on it. On average, how many times would we expect any number to occur in 360 spins? In thirty-six spins?

In the first case you should have answered ten, and in the second case the answer is one. On average, over a large number of spins, we might expect each number to occur one time in every thirty-six spins. This fact is reflected in the odds given by a casino to gamblers against the bets on a number. If gamblers bet on a number which wins, they receive thirty-five times the size of their bet. In other words, the casino knows that the odds against the number coming up by chance are 35 to 1. The probability of any number's occurrence in any one spin is 1/36 or 0.028.

There is a second likelihood; that of a thing *not* occurring. This is q; p + q must equal 100%, because a thing does or does not happen. It is more usual to express p in decimal form, i.e. 1.00 rather than 100%, and 0.50 rather than 50%.

So, probability can be given a numerical value ranging from 1 to 0. The probability value of 1 means absolute certainty of an event or outcome, as when we predict heads when tossing a double-headed coin. The probability value of 0 implies the absolute impossibility of an event, such as obtaining tails on tossing a double-headed coin. Most events, of course, are more or less probable, less than certain, but more than impossible, and hence have a value less than 1 but greater than 0.

$$\text{Probability of A} = \frac{\text{number of outcomes classified as A}}{\text{total number of possible outcomes}}$$

It is possible, if not very probable, that we can get a very long run of heads by chance alone, we argue, but at some point we have to draw the line and start to believe in foul play rather than chance. At what point would you definitely believe the coin to be biased? What is the probability of getting such a run of heads by chance alone? Look at Table 5.2.

Here are the actual probabilities of getting a run of heads for each size of run.

TABLE 5.2

Toss	1st	2nd	3rd	4th	5th
Probability	**.500**	**.250**	**.125**	**.063**	**.031**
No. of times likely to occur by chance in 100	50 in 100	25 in 100	12.5 in 100	6.3 in 100	3.1 in 100
Toss	6th	7th	8th	9th	10th
Probability	.016	.008	.004	.002	.001
No. of times likely to occur by chance in 100	1.6 in 100	0.8 in 100	0.4 in 100	0.2 in 100	0.1 in 100

You probably notice that on the first toss the probability is 0.5, i.e. a 50/50 chance of obtaining heads or tails. For succeeding heads, the probability is half the preceding probability level. These probability levels are based on the assumption that only chance factors are operating, i.e. the coin is symmetrical, uniform and is not double-headed! Thus, the coin has no tendency whatsoever to fall more often on one side rather than another; there are absolutely even chances of heads and tails.

Look at Figure 5.9. It is a normal distribution curve with the three standard deviations above and below the mean marked as you saw earlier. In addition, the approximate p level of each point is added. At M there is a probability 0.5; at +1σ from M, the probability of obtaining a score by chance at that point is 0.16; a score occurs by chance at −2σ and +2σ with a probability of 0.023 and so on. In other words, as with our penny tossing, the rarer the combination of H/T—or the rarer the score—the lower the probability level and the nearer to the tails of the distribution the event is placed. The greater the deviation of the score from the mean, the less frequently it is likely to occur.

Do you notice any similarity between the p values and the areas contained within the curve beyond the point? Refer to Table 5.1 to refresh your memory. Since 68 per cent of the area or scores lie between ±1σ from the mean, then 32 per cent of the area or scores must lie beyond those points. Thus, the probability of drawing a score at random from the normal distribution at or below +1σ is 0.16 (16 per cent); at or below −1σ is also 0.16.

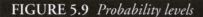

FIGURE 5.9 *Probability levels*

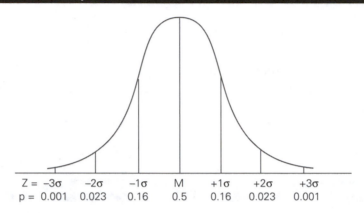

Z =	−3σ	−2σ	−1σ	M	+1σ	+2σ	+3σ
p =	0.001	0.023	0.16	0.5	0.16	0.023	0.001

Similarly, a score at +2σ or −2σ has a probability of 0.023 because approximately 95 per cent of all cases lie between +2σ and −2σ, hence the probability of obtaining a score with such a deviation from M is 1.0 − 0.95 (100% − 95%) = 0.05 (5%). This 0.05 covers both tails of the curve so must be halved when considering only one side of the distribution. The 0.05 therefore reduces to 0.025 for a score at +2σ and 0.025 for a score at −2σ. The slight difference between the theoretical probability of 0.023 and the approximation of 0.025 we have just worked out exists because the 95% limits are not ±2σ exactly but ±1.96. You can check this for yourself in Table 5.1. The whole number ±2σ is easier to remember as a major defining point on the normal ± curve than ±1.96σ, though as we become more confident in dealing with the normal curve and significance tables these other less convenient-to-remember numbers will begin to take root.

Statistical significance

By now you should have grasped the principles that:

- the normal distribution curve depicts the distribution of chance occurrences round a mean;

- some occurrences occur more frequently by chance than other occurrences; and
- each occurrence can be assigned a probability value, i.e. the likelihood of its occurring by chance.

In evaluating research results, we need to know whether the results might be expected fairly frequently on a chance basis, or whether it is a rare chance event, with a consequent low probability. Remember some of our coin tossing exploits. You found that an unbroken line of seven heads on tossing the same coin repeatedly was quite a rare event (Table 5.2).

But how far must an outcome be away from the expected? How infrequent must it be, or how far removed from the mean of a normal distribution before we say that although it *can* occur by chance occasionally, the fact that we have obtained this outcome in a 'one-off' research study implies that this is *not* a chance variation, but is due to our systematic manipulation of the independent variable.

Now that we are able to allocate probability levels to all points or scores on the normal distribution curve, the next step is to decide at what level of probability we believe a result is more than likely due to the experiment than to chance, always remembering that *every outcome is possible* on a chance basis, even if the odds are as high as those required for winning lotto.

The educational researcher is particularly interested in the probability of a particular sample result occurring by chance. He or she wants to know the odds against a chance occurrence. If the odds against occurrence by chance are greater than a certain figure, the educational researcher decides that the result is statistically significant. In practice, he or she focuses attention on certain fixed probability levels, which you repeatedly encounter in education research reports. These specify the probability of a chance occurrence of findings for a sample. The highest probability generally considered is $p = 0.05$ or 5 occurrences by chance in 100; the odds against this chance occurrence are 95:5 or 19:1. A lower level set is often $p = 0.01$ or 1 occurrence by chance in 100; the odds against this chance occurrence are 99:1. And an even lower level is $p = 0.001$ or 1 occurrence by chance in 1000; the odds against chances are 999:1. In general, the *lower* the probability of a chance result (low p value), the more confidence the researcher has in the results.

The three p values of 0.05, 0.01 and 0.001 are *conventionally* accepted as the major thresholds for decisions about statistical significance. But why have research workers picked on these levels? The problem is not unlike that facing the gambler playing roulette who has to decide whether to maximise possible profits on a single number (odds of 35:1 against) or to opt for less by betting on, say, all red numbers as opposed to black numbers (odds of 1:1, or evens). In a scientific manner, we generally opt for high odds, to minimise the possibility of claiming a significant result when the result is likely a chance one. The error of drawing a false conclusion that a relationship exists between variables is more serious than the error of failing to uncover some actual relation. So the minimum level usually acceptable is the 0.05 or 5% level. But remember that even here results will occur by chance five times in a hundred. By saying our result is significant at the 0.05 level, we are saying it is very unlikely to be due to chance, though that suspicion must always be in the back of our minds. That is why even more rigorous levels of 0.01 and 0.001 are also employed. At both these levels, chance results are even more unlikely. Hence we can be more confident in rejecting the view that chance has caused the result and assume that the result is statistically significant. But even here chance does still operate on rare occasions and we do not know on which! So statistical analysis of research results can never definitely prove a hypothesis, only support it at certain levels of probability (see chapter 7).

STQ15*

What does $p < 0.01$ and $p < 0.001$ imply?
*Answer on p. 595.

The probabilities of a chance occurrence of greater than 0.05 are usually designated 'not statistically significant' or, 'NS'.

STQ16

Can you now explain to yourself why such results are regarded as not statistically significant?

You may also encounter another form of expressing statistical significance, in that probability may be expressed as a percentage which is termed a significance level; for example, $p < 0.01$ becomes the 1% significance level.

FIGURE 5.10 *Selected significance or confidence levels*

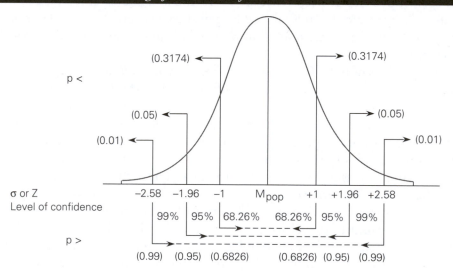

Try to complete the table below yourself.

Level	Probability limits	Frequency of a chance occurrence	Significance levels	Odds against a chance occurrence
NS	$p > 0.05$			
Low	$p < 0.05$			19:1
High	$p < 0.01$		1%	
High	$p < 0.001$	1 in 1000		

* A completed table is on p. 596.

Selecting a level of significance

So far we have not tackled the question of why we would be prepared to risk one level of probability rather than another. How small should the significance level be—that is, how small should the probability of an event be—before we reject the possibility of it having occurred by chance?

There is no simple answer. It is up to you to decide what odds you are prepared to accept when deciding whether the results of your research are significant (i.e. significantly greater than chance). This decision may involve political, social, educational, philosophic and economic considerations as well as statistical ones.

In order to answer this question, we must consider the consequences of the decision to act as though the event had or had not occurred. A somewhat fanciful Russian roulette example might make this point clear. Assume that you are presented with a box of 200 pistols, exactly ten of which you know to be loaded, and you are allowed to take one of them out. The probability that this pistol is loaded is, thus, 10/200, or 0.05. Would you act as if it were loaded or as if it were not?

In deciding, you would take into account not only the probability that the gun is loaded but also the consequences of your acting as if it were loaded. If you were asked whether you would be willing to hold the gun to your head and pull the trigger, you would act as though it were loaded. On the other hand, if you were asked whether you would be willing to use it to defend yourself in a duel, you would act as though it were not loaded. This approach is perfectly rational. Though the probability is the same in both cases, the consequences are not. Thus, to answer our question, we must consider the consequences of accepting or rejecting the null hypothesis.

Again, imagine you were an educational psychologist testing whether a new reading scheme might help backward children, and you carried out an experiment in which you compared the progress of a group of such children using your new scheme against the progress of a similar control group using traditional methods. Suppose you found a difference in reading improvement scores between the two groups in favour of the new scheme. Suppose the probability that this could have occurred by chance was 10 per cent (i.e. a 10-in-100 or a 1-in-10 probability that there were only random differences rather than a significant difference caused by the reading scheme). Would you accept that the difference was significant and introduce the new reading scheme, and at what cost in terms of materials and teacher training?

These examples bring home the fact that choosing a significant level is always a matter of deciding what odds you are prepared to accept in a particular situation that your results are due to chance. In the case of the reading scheme, no child would probably suffer all that much if it was all due to chance after all, so, as long as it was not too expensive you would probably go ahead and introduce the new scheme.

On the other hand, you might feel more doubtful about introducing a powerful drug with nasty side effects if there was a 1-in-20 chance that it was doing no good at all; although you might accept these odds if it were the only hope of saving people's lives. I don't think any of us would fly in a plane with a 1-in-100 chance of crashing!

In education (possibly because it is felt that nothing too terrible can happen as a result of accepting a result as significant), it is a convention to accept that odds of either 1 in 100 (i.e. 1%) or 5 in 100 (i.e. 5%) are adequate grounds for rejecting the null hypothesis that the results are random, and consequently accepting the experimental hypothesis. They are reasonable gambles for most situations (Figure 5.10).

So by now I hope you can detect the analogy between gambling and hypothesis testing. By setting a particular significance level, the researcher is gambling that chance results can be distinguished from genuine ones. If the level is set too high, i.e. a very low probability value, then the researcher may decide that a difference is a chance result when it is in fact a genuine one. If it is set too low, the researcher may be in danger of accepting a result which is really a chance effect.

The selection of a particular level of significance should be performed before the research data is analysed, just as anyone who bets on the horses must do so before the race is run. You can't go and place your bet after the race. But it is so easy to make it into a significant result by rounding up, or by retrospectively reducing the required significance level, or by stating that the result 'approached significance'. If we go around manipulating the research after the event to suit our wishful thinking, there is no reason to do the experiment in the first place, and we might just as well believe anything we want to believe.

Note: We are solely concerned here with the concept of statistical significance. What may be highly significant statistically may be of no educational significance whatsoever and vice versa!

summary

The probability of a particular event A is the number of outcomes classified as A divided by the total number of possible outcomes. All probability problems can be restated as a proportion problem, e.g. the probability of selecting a king from a deck of cards is equivalent to stating the proportion of the deck that consists of kings.

The normal distribution is a distribution of chance occurrences in which the mean, median and mode coincide. Areas between points under the curve can be determined and can be converted to proportions of the number of scores plotted.

For frequency distributions, probability can be answered by determining proportions of areas, e.g. the probability of selecting an individual with an IQ greater than 108 is equivalent to the proportion of the whole population that consists of IQs over 108.

With a Z score and the normal distribution table you can find probability values associated with any value of X. The table only shows positive Z scores, but since the distribution is symmetrical the probability values also apply to the half of the distribution that is below the mean.

Two accepted conventional cut-off or criterion points are used to indicate that if an event occurs beyond these points in probability terms then the event is most likely not to be due to chance or random fluctuation. These points or significance levels are the 5% and 1% levels.

Sampling and standard error of the mean

6
six

Why sample?

We could not carry out everyday life and business if we did not employ sampling in our decisions. The food purchaser examines the fruit on display and, using this as a sample, decides whether to buy or not. The official consumer survey behaves likewise with certain goods, a sample of which are tested. A teacher samples the increase in learning among his or her students by an examination which usually only tests a part of that learning. Many of our decisions are based on sampling—possibly inadequate sampling in some cases.

We are all guilty on many occasions of making generalisations about groups of people, or making inferences about individuals based on very limited experience or knowledge of them. We might meet one member of a group, say a Welshman who can sing, and this causes us to attribute such vocal ability to all natives of that country. One student once said to me, 'I don't like Norwegians; I met one once'. Likewise, we read in newspapers that 'people have no moral values now', or that 'politicians are corrupt'. Such generalisation is invalid, yet generalisation is necessary in research.

The educational researcher is not just interested in the students chosen for a particular survey; they are interested in students in general. They hope to demonstrate that the results obtained would be true for other groups of students.

The concept of sampling involves taking a portion of the population, making observations on this smaller group and then generalising the findings to the large population. Generalisation is a necessary scientific procedure, since rarely is it possible to study all members of a defined population.

Population and sample

When you are wearing your researcher's hat, always remember that a population is a complete set of all those things (people, numbers, societies, bacteria, etc.) which completely satisfy some specification; for example, all colour-blind male secondary school pupils. In this context, the population is not a demographic concept.

As the total number of potential units for observation, it can have relatively few units (e.g. all the students in the social science faculty); a large number of units (all Australian teachers); or an infinite number of units (e.g. all the possible outcomes obtained by tossing a coin an infinite number of times). So a *population* is an entire group of people or objects or events which all have at least one characteristic in common, and must be defined specifically and unambiguously.

The first task in sampling is to identify and define precisely the population to be sampled. If we are studying immigrant children we must define the 'population' of immigrant children: what ages are included by the term 'children'; what countries are implied by 'immigrant'; whether we refer to migration from one's place of birth or merely migration from a former place of residence, and so on. Careful attention must be given to the precise limits of the population, whether or not to include individuals whose position is marginal. For example, in defining a population of primary school children, does one exclude children from private schools? children attending special schools for the handicapped? children outside the normal age-range of primary school who happen to be at primary schools? and so on.

A sample is any part of a population regardless of whether it is representative or not. The concept of representativeness is not implicit in the concept of a sample. One of our great concerns in this current chapter will be to distinguish between samples which are in some sense representative of a population and those which are not, and to demonstrate ways of drawing samples that will be representative.

The major task in sampling is to select a sample from the defined population by an appropriate technique that ensures the sample is representative of the population and as far as possible not biased in any way. Since we can rarely test the defined population, our only hope of making any generalisation from the sample is if the latter is a replica of that population reflecting accurately the proportion or relative frequency of relevant characteristics in the defined population.

The key word in the sample population relationship is representativeness. We cannot make any valid generalisation about the population from which the sample was drawn unless the sample is representative. But representative in terms of what?—weight? IQ? political persuasion? cleanliness? The answer is that the sample must be representative in terms of those variables which are known to be related to the characteristics we wish to study. The size of the sample is important too, as we shall see, but it will suffice for now to remember from our Welshman who could sing, and from the student who disliked his one Norwegian contact, that we are on very dangerous ground trying to generalise from a sample of one. Usually, the smaller the sample, the lower the accuracy. However, size is less important than representativeness. There is a famous example of a sample of ten million voters supposedly representative of the electorate in the USA to poll voting intentions for the presidential election in 1936. The forecast, despite the sample size, was disastrously inaccurate because the sample was contacted by telephone. Telephone ownership biased the sample in favour of the middle class, who were mainly Republican. The Republican candidate went to bed on the eve of polling day contented with the prospects of an overwhelming victory. He awoke to find that his Democratic opponent was to be the new president!

A measure descriptive of a population characteristic is termed a *parameter*; the measure descriptive of an attribute of a sample is called a *statistic*. A sample may need to be re-labelled a 'population' if its function changes. Of course, if this happens the relevant statistic then becomes the parameter. An example may help to make this clearer. We might define a population as 'all nine-year-old children in Australia'. A sample of this population could be any smaller group less than the total—say, nine-year-old children attending one particular school. On the other hand, the focus of our research interest might change from the population as a whole to this one school. We might want to investigate certain characteristics of the children in this school in order to aid decisions about the curriculum of the school. In this case, our population is redefined as 'all nine-year-old children attending the school' and samples of this population are now defined as any smaller group of children in the school.

The function of a statistic is to give us some idea of the probable value of the corresponding parameter. In statisticians' jargon, we say the statistic *estimates* the parameter, since we rarely know the parameter or measure of the whole population (see Figure 6.1).

FIGURE 6.1 *Population and sample relationships*

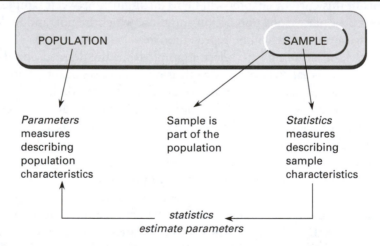

STQ18*

A research worker interested in studying ego strength among 12-year-old males found that the average ego strength level in a selected group from the Gas Works High School was higher than that of all the 12-year-old males in the city.

part 2 | quantitative methods

Name:

a   the statistic
b   the population
c   the sample
d   the parameter.

*Answers on p. 596.

STQ19

Educationists have few lists they can use and the tendency is to grab whatever sample is handy; often whatever group they are lecturing to, or schools where they have a good relationship with the principal (opportunity sampling). As a result, much research is carried out on captive groups of pupils and students, who are a biased sample of the general population. Can you think of the ways in which they are biased?

Techniques of sampling

In order to draw representative samples from which valid generalisations can be made to the population, a number of techniques are available. These techniques are, of course, the ideal. Few researchers, apart from government bodies, have the resources and time to obtain truly representative samples. For most research, investigators often have to make do with whatever subjects they can gain access to. Generalisations from such samples are not valid and the results only relate to the subjects from whom they were derived. This lack of representative samples is a deficiency in many research studies and should be noted in any research project write-up or evaluation of a research paper.

The random sample

Once the population has been carefully defined, a representative sample can be drawn. Random sampling is that method of drawing a sample so that:

- each member of the population has an equal chance of being selected; and
- the selection of one subject is independent of the selection of any other.

This will become clear by the following example. Suppose the population in which we are interested was the first-year group of a ten-form entry secondary school, but of the total population of 300 children we could only test one-third, i.e. 100. Since the population is clearly defined, it can, in principle, be listed, i.e. a list including each child's name or code number. This list is called the sampling frame. One method of drawing the random sample is to write each name or code number onto a slip of paper then shuffle the slips in a container. The slips are drawn out at random. At this stage there are two possibilities open. We can either replace the slip once it has been drawn or we can retain it and continue drawing slips from the remainder until the required sample size of 100 is obtained. This latter procedure is preferred statistically and does obviously alter the chances of being selected as the sampling proceeds, i.e. at the commencement in our example the first name has a 1-in-300 chance, but the last choice has a 1-in-201 chance.

For drawing large samples this manual technique would be rather laborious, so the alternative is to use a random number table (see Table 6.1). This consists of blocks of numbers in random order. The table can be entered at any point and can be worked through horizontally or vertically. In our example, each member of the population would be given a three-figure number from 001 to 300. Selection of the random sample of 100 takes place by entering the table and selecting three-digit numbers as they occur. Repetitions or numbers outside the population range are disregarded. For example, commencing with the left-hand column and working down, taking the first three numbers in each group, the numbers drawn run as follows:

201, 221, 162, 045, 036, 017, 275.

This method can be speeded up by the use of computers which select at random. By *random* we are implying 'without bias' and the sample is drawn unit by unit, with all members of the population having an equal chance of selection. Results may be generalised to the population but even a random selection is never a completely accurate reflection of the population from which it was drawn. There is always some sampling error and the generalisation is an inference, not a certainty, because the sample can never be exactly the same as the population.

Random sampling can be 'staged'; that is, a sample of schools from a population of schools (Stage 1), then a sample of children from each selected school (Stage 2). There can be more than two stages but this is dealt with later under cluster sampling.

STQ20

Try this exercise to prove to yourself that sampling error does occur even with random sampling. In Table 6.2, there are ten columns. In each column, you are going to list ten single digit numbers drawn at random from Table 6.1. (The first column is done for you.)

To draw these random samples, write the numbers 1–15 on separate slips of paper representing the rows of Table 6.1, and 1–10 on separate slips of paper representing the columns of Table 6.1. Place each set of slips in a separate box and shuffle them around. Draw out one slip from the first box and one from the second. The number of the first slip locates the row for your first random numbers and the second slip locates its column. Take the first number in the set of four in the table you have located. Thus, if the numbers you draw first are 15 and 2, your first random number will be 3. After drawing each slip replace it in its box. Continue the drawing process until you have selected all the random numbers you need. When you have drawn the remaining nine samples of ten random numbers, compute the arithmetic mean for each column.

(continued)

TABLE 6.1 *Random sampling numbers*

2017	4228	2317	5966	3861	0210	8610	5155	9252	4425
7449	0449	0304	1033	5370	1154	4863	9460	9449	5738
9470	4931	3867	2342	2965	4088	7871	3718	4864	0657
2215	7815	6984	3252	3254	1512	5402	0137	3837	1293
9329	1218	2730	3055	9187	5057	5851	4936	1253	9640
4504	7797	3614	9945	5925	6985	0383	5187	8556	2237
4491	9949	8939	9460	4849	0677	6472	5926	0851	2557
1623	9102	1996	4759	8965	2784	3092	6337	2624	2366
0450	6504	6565	8242	7051	5501	6147	8883	9934	8237
3270	1772	9361	6626	2471	2277	8833	1778	0892	7349
0364	5907	4295	8139	0641	2081	9234	5190	3908	2142
6249	9000	6786	9348	3183	1907	6768	4903	2747	5203
6100	9586	9836	1403	4888	5107	3340	0686	2276	6857
8903	9049	2874	2104	0996	6045	2203	5280	0179	3381
0172	3385	5240	6007	0671	8927	1429	5524	8579	3196
2756	4979	3434	3222	6053	9117	3326	4470	9314	9970
4905	7448	1055	3525	2428	2022	3566	6634	2635	9123
4974	3725	9726	3394	4223	0128	5958	9269	0366	7382
2026	2243	8808	1985	0812	4765	6563	5607	9785	5679
4887	7796	4339	7693	0879	2218	5455	9375	9726	9077
0872	8746	7573	0011	2707	0520	3085	2221	0467	1913
9597	9862	1727	3142	6471	4622	3275	1932	2099	9485
3799	5731	7040	4655	4612	2432	3674	6920	7210	9593
0579	5837	8533	7518	8871	2344	5428	0048	9623	6654
5585	6342	0079	9122	2901	4139	5140	3665	2611	7832
6728	9625	6836	2472	0385	4924	0569	6486	0819	9121
8586	9478	3259	5182	8643	7384	4560	8957	0687	0815
4010	6009	0588	7844	6313	5825	3711	1847	7562	5221
9455	8948	9080	7780	2689	8744	2374	6620	2019	2652
1163	7777	2320	3362	6219	2903	9415	5637	1409	4716
6400	2604	5455	3857	9462	6840	2604	2425	0361	0120
5094	1323	7841	6058	1060	8846	3021	4598	7096	3689
6698	3796	4413	4505	3459	7585	4897	2719	1785	4851
6691	4283	6077	9091	6090	7962	5766	7228	0870	9603
3358	1218	0207	1940	2129	3945	9042	5884	8543	9567
5249	4016	7240	7305	5090	0204	9824	0530	2725	2088
7498	9399	7830	7947	9692	4558	4037	8976	8441	7468
5026	5430	0188	6957	5445	6988	2321	0569	9344	0532
4946	6189	3379	9684	2834	1935	2873	3959	5634	9707
1965	1344	7839	7388	6203	3600	2596	8676	6790	2168
6417	4767	8759	8140	7261	1400	2828	5586	2338	1615
1843	9737	6897	5656	5795	0188	1189	4807	4260	1192
6558	6087	5109	9661	1553	6681	668	4475	3701	2888
7990	3100	9114	8565	3175	4315	4593	6478	3453	8802
0723	0015	5905	1609	9442	2040	6376	6567	3411	9410
9008	1424	0151	9546	3032	3319	0014	1928	4051	9269
5382	6202	2182	3413	4103	1285	6530	0097	5630	1548
9817	2615	0450	7625	2033	5484	3931	2333	5964	9627
0891	1244	8240	3062	4550	6454	6517	8925	5944	9995
3721	4677	8487	6739	8554	9737	3341	1174	9050	2962

Each digit is an independent sample from a population in which the digits 0 to 9 are equally likely; that is, each has a probability of 0.1.

(continued)

Since, in Table 6.1, each number from 0–9 occurs an equal number of times, the population average (a parameter) must be the average of the sum of the numbers 0–9, i.e.

$$\frac{0+1+2+3+4+5+6+7+8+9}{10} = 4.50$$

TABLE 6.2 *Samples of random numbers*

1	2	3	4	5	6	7	8	9	10
9									
7									
6									
7									
3									
8									
4									
1									
3									
2									
50 = total									

$$\text{Average} \frac{50}{100} = 5.0$$

Now we can see if any sampling error has occurred in your random samples in Table 6.2. Are any of your sample means exactly 4.5? This is not likely, though many will be close to it. When we tried it, our sample averages ranged from 2.9 to 6.2, with 4.3 as the sample average closest to the population average. In other words, there is always some error. We shall see later how this error can be estimated. Now, compute the average of the ten sample averages. Hopefully, this average is a more accurate reflection of the population mean than most of the sample averages. This illustrates an important point that usually the larger the sample, the smaller the sampling error.

STQ21

Given a population of 100 pupils in a room, would the following constitute methods for selecting a random sample?
a   Enter the room and grab the nearest twenty children.
b   Open the door and take the first twenty children to emerge.
Do these procedures qualify as random sampling? Why or why not?

part 2 quantitative methods

Systematic sampling

If the defined population can be listed, then the sample can be drawn at fixed intervals from the list. In the earlier example on random sampling, we wanted to select 100 pupils from 300—a 1-in-3 ratio. In systematic sampling, a starting number between 1 and 3 is chosen randomly (for our 1-in-3 ratio) and selection continues by taking every third person from that starting number. So, if 3 was the starting number, successive selections would be 6, 9, 12, 18, etc. The selected starting number fixes which successive numbers are taken or not taken.

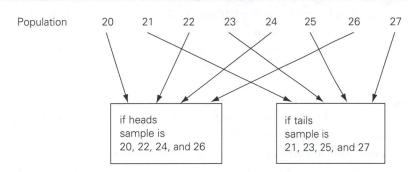

FIGURE 6.2 *Two possible samples resulting from a systematic sampling scheme*

Population 20 21 22 23 24 25 26 27

if heads
sample is
20, 22, 24, and 26

if tails
sample is
21, 23, 25, and 27

The major disadvantage of systematic sampling is where a periodic cycle exists in the sampling frame, or population list, which would bias the sample. For example, if all the school classes were twenty-five strong, with boys listed before girls, then a sampling interval of twenty-five would generate a sample all of the same sex. With lists of names, selecting those whose name begins with M may give a sample with too many Scots, while any other letter may result in too few Scots. Whether such bias matters depends on the topic. Date of birth, especially a number of dates spread evenly over the year, provides a sound basis for obtaining a representative sample which is easy to apply to school populations.

STQ22

If the number 2 was the starting point on a selection ratio of I to 5, what are the next four successive selections?

STQ23

There is a fundamental difference between random and systematic sampling. One of the conditions of random sampling is that the selection of one individual should be independent of the selection of another. Systematic sampling does not satisfy this condition. Can you explain why?

Stratified sampling

Stratified sampling adds an extra ingredient to random sampling by ensuring that groups or strata within the population are each sampled randomly.

It offers increased possibility of accuracy by ensuring all groups are represented in the sample in the same proportions as they are in the population.

We saw earlier that random sampling involves some degree of sampling error. One way to reduce this error and increase precision without increasing sample size is by employing prior information about characteristics of the population. This involves stratified sampling. Suppose we had a population of twenty persons—twelve men and eight women—and we wished to select a sample of ten containing six men and four women; we could select 1 in 2 from each sex or stratum. This will provide a better estimate because the right proportion from each stratum is obtained. There is always a risk with random sampling of getting a 'wild' sample of ten men. In this way, sampling error is reduced by stratification, for the sample cannot differ from the population with respect to the stratifying factor(s), so the distribution of sample means are not spread out as much as in a random sample. A stratum is fairly homogeneous with respect to the characteristic on which the stratum is based; therefore variance must be restricted and as a corollary sampling error reduced.

So in this design the researcher divides the population into layers or strata. The characteristics which define these strata are usually those variables which are known to relate to the characteristics(s) under study. Thus, a population can be divided on the basis of (say) social class membership, sex, level of intelligence, or level of anxiety, if these are known to be important. Having stratified the population, a simple random or systematic sample is drawn from each stratum.

The sampling of complete groups as units (cluster sampling)

All the previous methods have dealt with individual humans, or articles, or items. But one may experiment with a group as a unit, and indeed social psychologists and sociologists are predominantly interested in the group as such rather than the individuals composing it. There is no more difficulty in sampling a population of groups than individuals—and indeed there may be less. For instance, in educational research it is almost impossible to experiment on one or two children in a number of classes in a number of schools. The education service is not built to cope with such individual demands. So, educational research other than that carried out in laboratories (very little), or with individual students outside the class setting (not very common), samples groups or classes of students, even though the data is obtained on an individual basis.

Sampling of entire natural groups rather than individuals in this manner is called *cluster sampling*. It retains the principle of randomness and allows a research design within the scope of the individual researcher. Furthermore, lists of the whole population are not required but instead required only for the selected clusters.

Cluster sampling is of benefit to the researcher if the population is spread widely across a large geographic area.

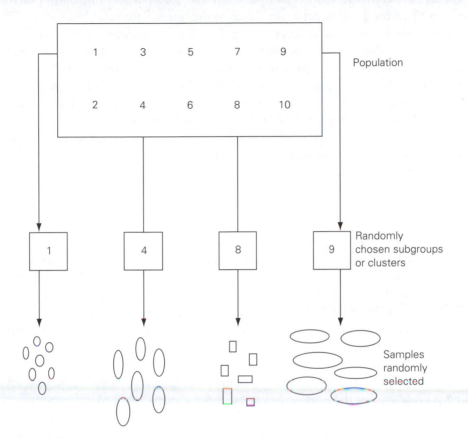

FIGURE 6.3 *Cluster sampling. Select subgroups then random sample*

In educational research, there is often a gap between sampling theory and practice because the designs are often unrealistic to use. Can you explain why random sampling of all the fourteen-year-old pupils in the state is unrealistic?

The efficiency of cluster sampling depends on the number and size of the clusters used. At one extreme, a large number of small groups could approach simple random sampling. At the other extreme, taking one large group such as a school at random, although more convenient, is likely to provide an unsatisfactory sample because of increased sampling error. The error is greatest when the clusters are large and homogeneous with respect to the variable under study. The term *homogeneous* in this context refers to groups whose members are very similar with respect to the characteristics one is studying. For example, there are dangers of taking the level of reading attainment in any one school as representative of the reading level for a whole area.

Primary schools are comprehensive in the sense that no academic selection procedure operates, so that theoretically each school can have an all-ability intake. In practice, they have a limited intake area, often restricted to the immediate neighbourhood. Thus, the school population tends to reflect the neighbourhood population in terms of social class membership. Suburban schools, therefore, could be 'over-populated' with middle-class children, and schools nearer the town or city centres over-populated with working-class or migrant children. In general, middle-class children score higher on intelligence tests and show higher standards of reading than working-class children. The classes in such schools will therefore tend to be homogeneous with respect to reading standards—the former will tend to have high reading standards; the latter will tend to have relatively low reading standards. Homogeneous groups are therefore not representative of the total population from which they are drawn, but only of those parts of it which are homogeneous in the same way.

Stage sampling

In the preceding section a distinction was drawn between simple random sampling of individuals, which in the practical situation may involve testing two or three children in each of a hundred schools, and cluster sampling, which describes the sampling of relatively few entire schools or classes, and usually has the disadvantage of a much greater error variance. A third possibility exists, intermediate between these two. It is possible to take a random sample of schools, and within each school a random sample of children.

Thus, a compromise may be obtained, which for the same size of sample avoids the virtually impossible rigour of a simple random sample, and at the same time ensures a wider representation than the sampling of entire groups.

This is *stage* sampling. A two-stage design would first take a random selection of schools, and within each school a random sample of children. A two-stage design could be used by a primary school survey to investigate the necessity for auxiliary help in such schools. Such a study could be concerned with classes rather than children, and therefore you would first select schools at random, and then select classes within these schools on a random basis. For larger studies, multi-stage designs can be introduced—regions within the state would be randomly selected; within these, districts would be randomly selected; within districts, schools would be randomly be selected; within schools, classes would be selected; within the classes, children would be selected, and so on. Such designs obviously lie beyond the resources of most individual researchers. But the great strength of such designs is that they permit accurate estimates of the sampling error. This is because at each stage the principle of *random selection* is maintained.

Opportunity sampling

This form of sampling involves considerable error but is often used because no other alternative is open to the research worker. This happens when, due to constraints of finance and even permission, research is carried out on conveniently accessible groups, such as students in one's own college, people living in your neighbourhood etc. There is no proper sampling involved and no possibility of generalisation to a wider population.

Students found in the library one afternoon, parents interviewed in a supermarket one morning, or teachers contacted at a union branch meeting are not likely to be representative of college students, parents, or teachers. Such samples are non-probability samples because the chance of selection is unknown.

Other opportunity samples involve volunteers, but we never know whether volunteers differ in some way from those who are not.

Opportunity sampling may produce biased samples, and therefore greater likelihood of error. The trouble is we can never know for certain because, strictly speaking, it is not possible to estimate the sampling error in such samples, though it is often done on the dubious assumption that any sample is one of the possible random samples that could have been selected. Opportunity samples are thus valuable in exploratory studies, but clearly the results cannot be generalised to any wider population. They should therefore be used only if the elements of the population of interest in the study cannot be found in any other way. It may be of interest to note that much 'opinion polling' is based on opportunity samples. This may help to explain why so much apparently contradictory evidence is collected by the market research agencies who carry it out.

Sample size

Size versus representativeness

In general, the larger the sample the better, simply because a large sample tends to have less error, as we found in the exercise using the table of random numbers. This is not to say that a large sample is sufficient to guarantee accuracy of results. Although for a given design an increase in sample size increases accuracy, it will not eliminate or reduce any bias in the selection procedure. We have already seen an example of this principle in the American presidential telephone survey mentioned at the beginning of this part of the chapter. As another example, if a 1-in-2 sample of the whole country consisted of one sex only, it would be large, but unrepresentative. Size is therefore less important than representativeness.

Non-response

In deciding size, account should also be taken of possible attrition of numbers; even the best designed projects lose about 10 per cent of their sample, depending on the nature of the study. This is particularly important in follow-up studies in which the same children are re-tested at a later date. There is always the likelihood that children have left the area between visits, but of equal importance is the level of school absenteeism. Losses of this order could seriously affect the representativeness of the sample and cause increased error. The children who stay away may have quite different characteristics from those who attend.

Completing Table 6.3 will provide a useful summary of the sampling designs which have been considered in the previous two sections. The type of sample is indicated in column 1. You should complete column 2, describing how each sample is drawn, and column 3, the advantages and disadvantages of each method. In completing column 3, keep in mind such things as representativeness, error, appropriateness and/or convenience to the researcher.

TABLE 6.3 *Summary of sampling techniques*

Column 1	Column 2	Column 3
Type of sample	**How sample is drawn**	**Advantages and disadvantages**
1 Simple Random		
2 Systematic		
3 Stratified		
4 Cluster		
5 Opportunity		

Sampling strategy in educational research

This is a set of suggestions, not of rules; a general guide, not a blueprint.

1 Define clearly the population about which you intend to generalise from your results.
2 Estimate roughly the size of sample required.
3 Consider the possibility of a simple random type sample. In most studies this will not be practicable, but if you are doing something like a postal survey on parental attitudes in a certain area with a complete sampling frame available, then it could be considered.
4 If simple random sampling is not practicable, decide if stratification would increase convenience or efficiency. For example, if testing attainment, the sample might profitably be broken down by school type, or social class.
5 If not using 4, then consider clusters selected on a random basis. Use several small clusters rather than a few large ones, or preferably a two-stage or multi-stage design which will cover a wider range of clusters for the same sample size.
6 If 5 is not possible, then the use of non-random samples must be considered. Such samples cannot be decried altogether; however the crucial problem is that it is not possible to make from the results themselves a theoretically satisfactory estimate of the sampling error which is always present, or to generalise to a presumed population.
7 Even an opportunity sample may yield information of considerable value, particularly in an exploratory study of an area previously under-researched or in

'case' or 'clinical' studies using a small number of individuals. The value of any conclusion from these types of study will depend on an intelligent assessment of how far the conditions have been satisfied for valid scientific generalisation. This is also an important point to take into consideration when reviewing research literature. Too many pieces of research in human behaviour are based on the behaviour of university students because they are an easily accessible 'captive' group.

STQ26*

1 Below are examples of the selection of samples. Decide for each which sampling technique was used.

   a Restricted to a 5 per cent sample of the total population, the researcher chose every twentieth person on the electoral register.

   b A social worker investigating juvenile delinquency and school attainment obtained her sample from children appearing at the juvenile court.

   c A research organisation took its sample from public schools and state schools so that the samples were exact replicas of the actual population.

2 Explain how you would acquire a random sample of first-year college students in a city with two colleges.

3 Explain why a random sample from a population in which certain subjects were inaccessible would be a contradiction in terms.

4 If, from an extremely large population, a very large number of samples were drawn randomly and their mean values calculated, which of the following statements are true?

   a The sample means would each be equal to the population mean.

   b The sample means would vary from the population mean only by chance.

   c The sample means, if averaged, would have a grand mean grossly different from the population mean.

   d The sample means would form a distribution whose standard deviation is equal to zero.

   e The sample means would be very different from each other if the sample sizes were very large.

5 Why is a stratified sample superior to a simple random sample?

6 In what context would a multi-stage cluster sample be particularly useful?

7 If a sample of psychologists were randomly selected from the *Yellow Pages* in a particular city would you have necessarily a representative sample?

*Answers on p. 596.

Standard error

The general difficulty of working with samples is that samples are generally not identical to the population from which they were drawn. The statistics collected from samples will therefore differ from the corresponding parameters for the population.

Furthermore, samples are not identical to each other. They are variable because they contain different individuals. Each sample from the same population will have a slightly different sample mean and standard deviation.

You probably remember an exercise we conducted when explaining random sampling procedures. You were asked to draw samples of ten numbers from the random number table and compute the means of each of these samples of ten numbers. (Turn back to p. 86 and refresh your memory.) Like us, you no doubt obtained a range of means round the 'true' mean of 4.5, and you became aware that despite random sampling procedures some chance or random error was involved. This is called *sampling error*. It is not error in the sense that it is wrong or incorrect; it is error in the sense that there is variation from the population parameters.

How can we tell which sample gives us the best estimate of the population parameter or best description of the population? Fortunately, all the possible samples from a population do fall into an orderly predictable pattern specified by the distribution of their sample means. The distribution of these sample means tends to be normal, provided the sample size is greater than 30. The fact that the distribution of sample means tends to normality should not be a surprise, as whenever you take a sample you expect the mean to be near to the population mean and the more samples you take, the greater the number that will be fairly close, while only a few will be grossly different. Thus they 'pile up' around the population mean. In fact, the mean of the distribution of sample means is equal to the population mean.

This sampling variability of the mean, which is the extent to which a mean can be expected to vary as different samples of the same size randomly selected from the same population, is expressed by its *standard error*. The standard error of any sample measure such as a mean is the standard deviation of the distribution of measures that would result if large numbers of different samples of the same size were randomly selected from the same population.

If this were the best of all possible research worlds there would be no random error. And if there were no random or chance variation or error, there would be no need for statistical tests of significance. The word *significance* would be meaningless, in fact. Any difference would always be a 'real' difference, the sort of difference we look for in an experiment. But such is never the case. There are *always* chance errors (and biased errors too), and in educational research they often contribute substantially to the total variance. Standard error is a measure against which the outcomes of experimental manipulations of the independent variable are checked to discern whether any difference between, say, two sample means is a 'real' one or simply one of those many relatively small differences that arise by chance as a function of sampling procedures.

It is possible to obtain the estimate of the amount of sampling error for a mean on the basis of only one sample. If we know the size of the sample and the standard deviation of scores in that sample, we can predict the standard deviation of sampling errors. This expected standard deviation of sampling errors is the standard error of the mean, often represented either by the symbol SE_m or as σ_m. In formula form it is written:

$$SE_m = \sqrt{\frac{\sigma}{N}}$$

The SE_m is much smaller than the σ because sampling means are not as spread out as the original scores. The equation makes it clear that as N increases so sampling error is reduced.

Sample size is critical in determining how well a sample represents the population. The larger the sample, the more representative it becomes. This is basic common sense. For example, a population of 1000 would be well represented with a sample of 990; a sample of 99 would be much less representative, even if randomly selected, and provide a greater sampling error.

Look at the hypothetical examples in Figure 6.4 and note how the SE_m changes with increasing sample size.

STQ27*

1   For each graph in Figure 6.4, what is the 95% probability limit of a mean of a sample of the size given, drawn at random?

2   Given a population of scores normally distributed with a mean of 100 and standard deviation of 16, what is the standard error you would expect on average between the population mean and sample mean for four scores and for sixty-four scores?

*Answers on p. 596.

Horowitz (1974) demonstrated this concept of the distribution of sample means by artificially generating a population of 1000 normally distributed scores so that the mean and standard deviation of the entire population would be known. This is almost never the case in actual research situations, of course. His 1000 scores ranged from 0 to 100 and had a mean of 50 and a standard deviation of 15.8. The scores were listed on 1000 slips of paper and placed in a container. Ninety-six students each drew samples of ten slips from the container, and calculated the mean. On each draw from the container, a slip was taken out, its number noted, and then replaced. The slips were mixed somewhat and another number was removed, and so on. After each student calculated the mean of the ten scores in her or his sample, Horowitz plotted the sampling distribution of these 96 means (Table 6.4). In Table 6.4 the intervals between which means might fall are on the left and the number of means falling within each interval is on the right. The distribution is almost perfectly symmetrical, with almost as many in any interval being a certain distance below the true mean of the population (50) as above it. Also, the mean of the 96 sample means (49.99) is quite close to the actual mean of the population (50.00).

But the main thing to note in Table 6.4 is the great variability among the sample means. Although each sample of ten was presumably random and not biased in any way, one sample had a mean of 37.8 while another had a mean of 62.3. Obviously, these are very disparate means, even though they were sampled from the same population. If you were doing an experiment and found two very different sample means like this and were trying to decide whether they came from the same underlying distribution or two different distributions, you might think that such a large difference would indicate that they come from different distributions. In other words, you would

FIGURE 6.4

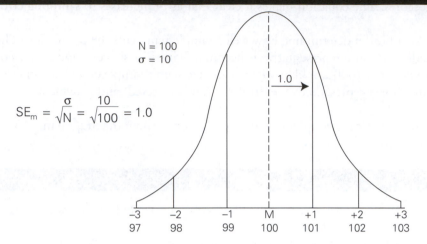

$$SE_m = \frac{\sigma}{\sqrt{N}} = \frac{10}{\sqrt{100}} = 1.0$$

N = 100
σ = 10

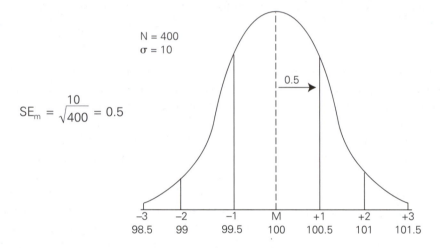

$$SE_m = \frac{10}{\sqrt{400}} = 0.5$$

N = 400
σ = 10

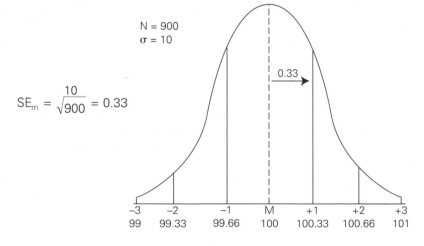

$$SE_m = \frac{10}{\sqrt{900}} = 0.33$$

N = 900
σ = 10

think that the experimental treatment produced scores reliably different (from a different distribution) than the control scores. Usually, this is a good rule—the larger the difference between means in the conditions, the more likely they are to be reliably different—but as we have seen here, even random sampling from a known distribution can produce sample means that differ greatly from each other and from the true population mean, which is known in this case. This is a lesson that should be kept in mind while pondering small differences between means. You can do a similar activity with SPSS (see page 103).

TABLE 6.4 *The distribution of sample means for the 96 samples taken by students in Horowitz class. Each sample mean was based on ten observations (after Horowitz 1974, Table 8.1)*

Interval	Frequency	
62.0–63.9	1	
60.0–61.9	1	
58.0–59.9	3	
56.0–57.9	7	
54.0–55.9	9	Mean of sample means = 49.99
52.0–53.9	12	Standard deviation of sample means
50.0–51.9	15	($SE_m = 5.01$)
48.0–49.9	15	
46.0–47.9	13	
44.0–45.9	9	
42.0–43.9	6	
40.0–41.9	3	
38.0–39.9	1	
36.0–37.9	1	
	96 samples	

Suppose we draw a random sample of 100 twelve-year-old children from the state school system. It would be difficult to measure the whole universe of 12-year-old children in the state for obvious reasons. We compute the mean and the standard deviation from a test we give the children and find these statistics to be M = 110: SD = 10. An important question we must now ask ourselves is, 'How accurate is this mean?'.

Or, if we were to draw a large number of random samples of 100 pupils from this same population, would the means of these samples be 110 or near 110? And, if they are near 110, how near? What we do, in effect, is to set up a *hypothetical distribution* of sample means, all computed from samples of 100 pupils each drawn from the parent population of 12-year-old pupils.

If we could compute the means of this population of means, or if we knew what it was, everything would be simple. But we do not know this value, and we are not able to know it since the possibilities of drawing different samples are so numerous. The best we can do is to *estimate it with our sample value or sample mean*. We simply say, in this case, let the sample mean equal the mean of the population mean—and hope we are right! Then we must calculate our standard error. The standard error is the measure of the dispersal of sample means.

A similar argument applies to the standard deviation of the whole population (of the original scores). We do not and probably never will know it. But we can estimate it. And we estimate it with the standard deviation computed from our sample. Again, we say in effect, let us assume that the standard deviation of the sample equals the standard deviation of the population. We know they are probably not the same value, but we also know, if the sampling has been random, that they are probably close. This is why the SE_m formula employs the standard deviation of the sample and not that of the unknown population.

Returning to our random sample of 100 12-year-olds with M 110 and SD 10, the SE_m =

$$\frac{10}{\sqrt{100}} = 1.00$$

This figure of 1.00 is the standard deviation of sampling means of random samples of 100 12-year-olds on that particular test. Now, how do we interpret it? Well, we know that if we had taken a large number of similar random samples and plotted their means, we would have produced a normal distribution. This normal distribution has a much narrower spread than that produced by the original raw scores. The mean of the population or the mean of all sample means will form the pivotal or central point on the baseline and the values for sample means will extend over the $\pm 3\sigma$ range as in any other normal distribution. The proportion of sample means found under any part of the curve can be found as before by reference to Table 5.1 on p. 73. In other words, the normal distribution of sample means is no different in characteristics from the normal distribution of raw scores. Do you remember the approximate percentages of scores found:

- between $\pm 1\sigma$?
- between $\pm 1.96\sigma$?
- between $\pm 2.58\sigma$?

Look at Table 5.1 if you are not sure.

The distribution of sample means follows the same pattern. A total of 68 per cent of all sample means from a defined population will fall between $\pm 1\sigma$ from the 'true' mean. Likewise, 95 per cent and 99 per cent of all sample means lie between $\pm 1.96\sigma$ and $\pm 2.58\sigma$ respectively, from the 'true' or population mean. The standard deviation of this distribution, let us repeat, is the standard error of the mean (SE_m).

The normal distribution of sample means provides again a theoretical probability distribution that acts as a mathematical model against which we can set our research findings. We are enabled to state the probability that a particular observation, in this instance, a sample mean, has occurred by chance. In other words, we are interpreting the probability of obtaining mean scores in this chapter in the same way as we interpreted the probability of obtaining individual scores in chapter 5.

Of course, we can only specify certain limits for the estimate of how far one sample mean, perhaps the only one we have and are ever likely to have, is close to the 'true' mean. We can never be certain.

EXAMPLE

How far away do we expect the true population mean to lie from a sample mean of 75 when the standard deviation of the sample is 18 and the size of the sample is 36?

$$SE_m = \frac{\sigma}{\sqrt{N}} = \frac{18}{\sqrt{36}} = 3$$

Therefore, the population mean has:

- a 68.26% chance of lying 75 ± 3, (M_s ±1 SE_m), or between 72 and 73;
- a 95% chance of lying 75 ± 1.96 × 3, (M_s ± 1.96 SE_m), or between 69.12 and 80.88;
- a 99% chance of lying 75 ± 2.58 × 3, (M_s ± 2.58 SE_m), or between 67.26 and 82.74;
- a 99.73% chance of lying 75 ± 3.00 × 3, (M_s ± 3.00 SE_m), or between 66 and 84.

It must be remembered that the mean of the population is a fixed value and does not vary. What the above confidence statements are saying is that the mean of the population is at a fixed but unknown point within a certain interval.

Look at the last confidence statement. Using the interval 66–84, we can conclude that there is only a 0.27% change (100 – 99.73%) that the population mean is at a distance greater than 9 (3 × SE_m) from the sample mean. Similar conclusions can be made about the other confidence statements.

It is never possible to find the exact value of a population mean from a sample mean. We can only estimate it by specifying an interval within which the population mean lies with a known degree of confidence or probability. As we know that the population mean is the average of all possible sample means, it is fairly obvious that we are on safe ground arguing that the population mean lies within +1.06 SE_m of our only known sample mean with a probability of 0.95.

Let us make a final return to our 100 12-year-old children, for whom with M = 110, σ = 10 the SE_m was 1.00. We can now calculate that 95% of all similar samples will have means that lie within ±1.96SE_m of 110, i.e. 1.96 × 1.00SE_m in either direction since 1.96 × 1.00 equals 1.96, the boundary scores for the 95% limits are 111.96 and 108.04.

STQ28*

Can you now calculate the boundary scores within which 99% of sample means will lie?
*Answer on p. 596.

The location of each sample mean in the distribution of sample means can be specified by a Z score just as a single score can be in a distribution of scores.

We can use the Z scores to find the probabilities for specific sample means and thereby determine which sample means are unlikely to be obtained from a particular population using the standard levels of significance.

Suppose we did obtain quite a number of other samples, most of whose means lay close to 110; but suddenly out of the blue we found one which was quite different—a mean of 114, in fact. We can calculate its Z score distance from the centre of the sampling distribution of means by the Z score formula:

$$Z = \frac{M - M_{pop}}{SE_m}$$

$$Z = \frac{114 - 110}{110} = \frac{4}{1.00} = 4.0$$

The probability of obtaining a sample M at this point is well beyond the 0.01 level, in fact, three times in 100 000.

This would be so rare a sample mean as to suggest that either it is a biased or non-random sample, or that the samples do not come from the same sampling distribution, i.e. they are from a different population of children; perhaps an older age group, for example.

STQ29*

1 Which sample size will provide the smallest SE_m assuming the same σ: 25, 100, 5 or 70?

2 A random sample of 290 10-year-old children were given a test of reading abilities with the intention of estimating the reading ability of all 10-year-old children; the mean was 104, standard deviation 5.67.
   a Calculate the standard error.
   b What limits does the population mean lie within at a 95% confidence level?
   c What limits does the population mean lie within at a 99% confidence level?

3 Evaluate each of the following hypothetical situations, in terms of whether the method of selecting the sample is appropriate for getting information about the population of interest. How would you improve the sample design?
   a A principal in a large high school is interested in student attitudes toward a proposed general achievement test to determine which students should graduate. She lists all of the first-period classes, assigning a number to each. Then, using a random number table, she chooses a class at random and interviews every student in that class about the proposed test.
   b An anthropology professor wanted to compare physical science majors with social science majors with respect to their attitudes toward premarital sex. She administered a questionnaire to her large class of Anthropology 437, Comparative Human Sexuality. She found no appreciable difference between her physical science and social science majors in their attitudes, so she concluded that the two student groups were about the same in their relative acceptance of premarital sex.

*Answers on p. 596.

part 2 | quantitative methods

Level	Interval range	Probability of sample mean lying within mean interval	Probability of sample lying outside interval
99%	$M_{pop} \pm 2.58\ SE_m$	0.99	0.01
95%	$M_{pop} \pm 1.96\ SE_m$	0.95	0.05
68.26%	$M_{pop} \pm 1.00\ SE_m$	0.6826	0.3174

TABLE 6.5 *Summary of selected confidence levels*

Using SPSS to produce random samples

It is very enlightening to discover how variable sample means, sample standard deviations, and sample standard errors of the mean can be, even when chosen randomly by computer from the same population.

You can see this for yourself by following this procedure:

1 Access the *Employment data* file or the *US General Social Survey* file that is provided on SPSS.

2 Choose an interval variable such as 'age' and select in sequence from the menu bar *Statistics,* then *Summarise* and finally *Descriptives* to obtain the mean, SD and SE_m for that variable. (Make sure these are selected in the *Options* box.)

3 Obtain a random sample by selecting *Data,* then choosing *Select Cases.*

4 Choose *Random Sample* of cases and click on the *Sample* button. Select *Approximately* and type in the sample size you want by typing in a percentage such as 25% or 33%.

5 Select *Continue* and highlight your chosen variable on which you already have obtained the population data at step 2 above.

6 Click *OK.* You will note that some of your cases now have a 45 degree angle line through them. These are the cases that are NOT selected for your sample.

7 To view results go to: *Statistics* then *Summarise* then *Descriptives.* Note the mean, SD and SE_m.

8 Repeat steps 3 to 7 three or four times to obtain the descriptive statistics of other random samples. The program will choose different samples each time, but you must retain the same percentage for selection so that you can compare the descriptive statistics.

9 After completing step 8, change the percentage selected and either type in a lower or higher figure and select several more samples at that level.

10 Print out your tables so that you can compare the statistics from the full number of cases with those derived from the different samples and two size levels.

How do these compare? Look particularly at the variation in means and SE_ms that occur in samples of the same and different sizes drawn randomly from the same population.

Descriptive statistics simplify and summarise data. Inferential statistics allow one to use sample data to make inferences about the population. Such generalisations are only valid if the sample is representative of the population. Random sampling helps to ensure that the sample is representative. The major types of random sampling are systematic sampling, cluster sampling and stratified sampling.

The distribution of sample means is normal if the population from which the samples are selected is normal and the size of the samples is thirty or more. The standard deviation of the distribution of sample means is the standard error of the mean and indicates how much error to expect if you are using a sample mean to estimate a population mean.

The formula is $SE_m = \frac{\sigma}{\sqrt{N}}$

The mean of the distribution of sample means is identical to the mean of the population.

Reference

Horowitz, L.M. (1974), *Elements of Statistics*, McGraw Hill, New York.

Hypothesis formation and testing

7

seven

Introduction

What is a hypothesis?

Chapter 3 described how research topics can arise and pointed out that the problem, still probably rather vague at this stage, has to be translated into precise operational hypotheses on which a research plan can be designed. This planning stage is possibly the most demanding and certainly the most important part of the research process.

The word *hypothesis* is generally used in a more restricted sense in research to refer to conjectures that can be used to explain observations. A hypothesis is a hunch, an educated guess which is advanced for the purpose of being tested. If research were limited to gathering facts, knowledge could not advance. Without some guiding idea or something to prove, every experiment would be fruitless, since we could not determine what was relevant and what was irrelevant. Try this everyday example of hypothesis formation. Suppose the only light you had on in the bedroom was the bedside table lamp. Suddenly it went off. You would no doubt ponder the reason for it. Try to think of several reasons; now and write them down. There could be a number, of course. I wrote:

- lamp bulb failure;
- plug fuse failure;
- main power fuse failure.

Whatever you wrote is an implied hypothesis—an educated guess. In practice you would test each one in turn until the cause was located. Let us imagine the cause was a fuse failure in the plug. The fact that the lights came on after I changed the fuse only lends support to the hypothesis. It does not prove it. The fault could have been caused by a temporary faulty connection which in turn caused the fuse to blow. In mending the fuse, I corrected the connection by chance as I caught the wire with my screwdriver unbeknown to me. 'Proved' carries the connotation of finality and certainty. Hypotheses are not proved by producing evidence congruent with the consequences; they are simply not disproved. On the other hand, if the observed facts do not confirm the prediction made on the basis of the hypothesis, then it is rejected conclusively. This distinguishes the scientific hypothesis from everyday speculation. A hypothesis must be capable of being tested and disproved.

This mode of accounting for problems is the characteristic pattern of scientific thinking. It possesses three essential steps:

1 The proposal of a hypothesis to account for a phenomenon.
2 The deduction from the hypothesis that certain phenomena should be observed in given circumstances.
3 The checking of this deduction by observation.

Let us look at an educational example. An educational researcher may have reasoned that deprived family background causes low reading attainment in children. He or she may have tried to produce empirical evidence that low family income and overcrowding are associated with poor reading attainment. If no such evidence was forthcoming then, as we have seen, the hypothesis must be decisively rejected. But if the predicted relationship was found, could the researcher conclude that the hypothesis was correct, i.e. that poor family background does cause low reading attainment? The answer must be 'no'. It might equally have been the case that a low level of school resources is also to blame. These alternative hypotheses will have other deducible consequences. For example, if lack of resources is related to reading backwardness, then improved resourcing should improve reading attainment among the children in these schools. To underline the main point again, the scientific process never leads to *certainty* in explanation, only to the rejection of existing hypotheses and the construction of new ones which stand up best to the test of empirical evidence.

How do we formulate hypotheses?

The formulation of hypotheses follows logically from the review of literature on the problem. But problems are not the only source of hypotheses. They are often derived from theory too, since theory guides research and provides predictions which need testing. Hypotheses are the working instruments of theory. But regardless of the source of the hypothesis it must meet one criterion. The hypothesis must be stated so that it is capable of being either confirmed or refuted. A hypothesis which cannot be tested does not belong to the realm of science. Consider the following hypothesis: 'Is a student's authoritarian behaviour directly related to his or her attitudes concerning punishment received from his or her parents?'. Although this statement of purpose is quite detailed, it conveys little information unless the meanings of *authoritarian behaviour*, *attitudes concerning punishment* and *received* are clearly defined. Even though these terms have meaning known to most individuals, they lack sufficient precision for use in scientific investigations.

The investigator can define the terms more specifically by using other terms, i.e. by substituting words about words. He or she may, for example, define *authoritarianism* by using phrases which include 'respect for order', 'stereotyped thinking', 'need for authority' and 'dependence'. The meaning is no clearer, however, unless each of these terms is further broken down into a description of states which can be directly observed. To avoid this dilemma of indefiniteness, the investigator can relate how authoritarianism will be measured. He or she can employ an operational definition in which a process is substituted for the conventional definitional description, i.e. by a score on a particular scale of authoritarianism.

If we want to study the relationship between childhood aggression and exposure to violent television programs, we need to define both the variables under study, i.e. aggression and television violence, operationally. The former might be simply a tally of the observed aggressive acts of children, such as hitting, kicking, biting others, damaging or destroying property. Or it might be based on an analysis of protective test material, i.e. aggressive feelings as revealed on the TAT (Thematic Apperception Test).

Another way to develop an operational definition of aggression would be to have a panel of judges watch a film of each child in a freeplay situation and then rate the child's aggressiveness on a seven-point scale. Or we could tell each child several stories about other children in frustrating situations and ask the child what he or she would do in each situation. We could then use the number of 'direct-attack' responses as a measure of aggressiveness. Another alternative would be to observe children as they play with a selection of toys we had previously classified as aggressive, such as guns, tanks and knives; or *non-aggressive*, such as trucks, tools and dolls. We could then measure the percentage of time that the child played with each type of toy. You can undoubtedly think of many other behaviours that would be an indication of a child's aggressiveness.

The defining of violent television programs may be somewhat harder to agree on. What constitutes violent television? Is the Saturday football or rugby match violent? Are Popeye cartoons violent? Is *The X-Files* violent? Are news and current affairs programs on the Middle East and Bosnia violent? Not everyone would agree on these.

The problem here is that there is a difference in precision between what the general public will accept in defining a term and what researchers will accept. An operational definition of the variable means that researchers must specify the operations they would go through to determine if a television program were violent and outline the specific steps they would take to classify television programs.

For example, if you were conducting our television experiment, you could operationalise the concept of a violent television program by showing each program to a randomly chosen group of 100 people and requiring that 75 per cent of them indicate a program is violent before you operationally define it as violent. Another alternative would be to devise a checklist with such items as, 'Is there physical contact of an aggressive nature?', 'Has an illegal act taken place?', 'Did one person act so as to make another feel inferior?'. Perhaps you would require that each program have at least five out of ten such items checked 'yes' in order for it to be considered violent.

A great many important educational questions require complex operational definitions. Do people whose mothers were affectionate make more successful primary teachers? Do students learn more from popular professors? Does a teacher's morale affect teaching style? Does anxiety cause low exam scores? Prior to doing an experiment to answer any of these questions, you would need operational definitions for the terms *affectionate, popular, morale, anxiety, successful, learn more*, etc.

STQ30

Try to formulate operational definitions of *affectionate, popular, morale,* and *anxiety*. How do you propose to measure such concepts?
1 How would you define and measure the variables underlined in the following?
    a Teachers who suffer *stress* are *less child centred* in their teaching method than teachers who are not so stressed.
    b *Stimulation at home* advances *language development in young children.*
    c Adolescents with *substance abuse problems* tend to come from *disrupted home* environments.

Research and operational hypotheses

Many research workers see a hierarchy of hypotheses in a research study, each hypothesis being a tighter and more testable statement than its predecessor. They often term the original hypothesis derived from the hazy problem as the *Research Hypothesis*. When this latter is re-expressed in operational terms it becomes the *Operational Hypothesis*.

As an example, suppose we have decided to investigate Eysenck's theory of personality in relation to academic attainment in tertiary students. The research hypothesis might read as follows: that extroversion and neuroticism are related to academic performance of students in higher education. This research hypothesis is still not in a form that can be tested; it needs to be operationalised, i.e. the phenomena referred to in it need to be defined in terms of observations that can be made.

In our research hypothesis about the relationship between personality and academic attainment, suppose that the measures used were the Eysenck Personality Inventory (the EPI), which is designed to measure the variables 'extroversion' and 'neuroticism', and degree result, which will give a measure of academic attainment.

STQ31

Write down now two operational hypotheses which could be derived from the research hypothesis.

In this instance, you could have postulated that 'Extroversion, as measured by the Eysenck Personality Inventory, will be significantly related to degree classification'. Or 'Neuroticism, as measured by the Eysenck Personality Inventory, will relate significantly with degree classification'.

Look at this sequence of hypothesis refinement moving from the general to the operational.

Problem or general hypothesis You expect some children to read better than others because they come from homes in which there are positive values and attitudes to education.

Research hypothesis Reading ability in nine-year-old children is related to parental attitudes towards education.

Operational hypothesis There is a significant relationship between reading ability for nine-year-old children living in a major city in NSW as measured by standardised reading test X and parental attitudes to education as measured by attitude test Y.

Criteria for judging hypotheses

1 Hypotheses should be stated clearly, in correct terminology, and operationally. General terms such as *personality, school attainment, self-esteem,* etc. should be avoided. The statement demands concise technical language and the definition of terms. More appropriate therefore are: 'Personality as measured by the Eysenck Personality Inventory'; 'School attainment as measured by English Progress Test E'; 'Self-esteem as measured by Coopersmith's SEI'. Such hypotheses as 'Creativity is a function of self-actualisation', and 'Democratic education enhances social learning', are too vague.

2 Hypotheses should be testable. Since hypotheses are predictors of the outcome of the study, an obvious necessity is that instruments should exist (or can be developed) which will provide valid and reliable measures of the variables involved.

3 Hypotheses should state differences or relationships between variables. A satisfactory hypothesis is one in which the expected relationship between the variables is made explicit.

These variables should be amenable to measurement, either directly or indirectly. For example, the following hypothesis *is* testable: 'Children who attend Sunday School show a better acquaintance with the Bible than those who do not', while the following hypothesis is *not* testable: 'Children who attend Sunday School show greater *moral fibre* than those who do not'. There is no valid test for 'moral fibre', while there are quite simple tests available to measure 'acquaintance with the Bible'.

4 Hypotheses should be limited in scope. Hypotheses of global significance are not required; those that are specific and relatively simple to test are preferable. It is, of course, possible to state a rather broad research hypothesis and derive a number of operational hypotheses from it.

5 Hypotheses should not be inconsistent with most known facts. All hypotheses should be grounded in past knowledge, i.e. the knowledge gained from a review of the literature. They obviously cannot be consistent with all known facts, since many studies give contradictory results. In these cases, the hypothesis may be formulated to resolve the

contradiction. For example, differences in the relationships found between personality and attainment in different age groups might be due to methodological errors or might be explained by a new hypothesis that the form of the relationship changes with age. There is also certainly room for the use of imagination in the extrapolation of known facts to new populations. But the hypothesis should not lead the cynical reader to say 'Whatever led you to expect that', or 'You made this one up after you collected the data'.

Unconfirmed hypothesis

But what if the hypothesis is not confirmed? Does this invalidate the prior literature? If the hypothesis is not confirmed then either the hypothesis is false or some error exists in its conception. Some of the previous information may have been erroneous, or other relevant information overlooked; the experimenter might have misinterpreted some previous literature or the experimental design might have been incorrect. When the experimenter discovers what he or she thinks is wrong, a new hypothesis is formulated and a different study conducted. Such is the continuous ongoing process of the scientific method. Even if a hypothesis is refuted, knowledge is advanced.

STQ32

Now consider the following examples in terms of the five criteria above. Look at each hypothesis and say whether it satisfies all the criteria. If it does not, say why not.

EXAMPLE 1

Among 15-year-old male school children, introverts, as measured by the Eysenck Personality Inventory, will gain significantly higher scores on a vigilance task involving the erasing of every 'e' on a typescript than extroverts.

EXAMPLE 2

Progressive teaching methods have led to a decline in academic standards in primary schools.

EXAMPLE 3

The introduction of politics into the curriculum of secondary schools will produce better citizens.

EXAMPLE 4

Anxious pupils do badly in school.

STQ33

1   Construct research and operational hypotheses for the following problems.
   a   Does 'learning how to learn' transfer to new situations?
   b   Does teacher feedback cause changes in student performance?
   c   Does group decision-making lead to less risk taking?

Hypothesis formation and testing

Two different ways of stating a hypothesis exist to match the two major approaches in research design:

- looking for differences between groups;
- looking for relationships between groups.

For example, a hypothesis which states that there is a difference between the performance of primary school boys and girls in reading skills is obviously a different hypothesis and requires different statistical measures from a hypothesis that states that there is a relationship between self-esteem and academic performance in secondary school pupils.

The null hypothesis

This brings us to the important point that in statistical analysis we do not actually test the operational hypothesis we are advancing but its logical opposite—the null hypothesis. In other words, we do not test the hypothesis that a statistically significant population correlation or difference does exist, but instead we test the hypothesis that there is no statistically significant population correlation or difference. Why do we do this?

The reason is based on simple logic. Suppose we hypothesise that there should be a difference between the mean scores of boys and girls on an arithmetic test with a range of marks from 0–20. This hypothesis would be satisfied by any difference in the mean scores from 0–20; the difference might be 3, 5, 17 or 19 marks—any of these would satisfy the hypothesis. We have only one value, zero, to deal with. We can then say that the null hypothesis is refuted if any difference occurs over and above zero.

This, of course, would be a valid statement to make about differences in the total population. In practice, we are generally dealing with a sample of data from the population which we use to estimate the population values of our variables. Any estimate of a population parameter involves sampling error, as we saw in chapter 6. So, what we are actually doing in stating a statistical null hypothesis is saying that there is no statistically significant difference between the mean values over and above the difference brought about by random sampling error. Statistical theory enables us to specify the limits of this sampling error around any estimated population value, including zero. We can thus set precise limits—significance levels—for the rejection of a null hypothesis. This is the basic principle on which all statistical tests are founded.

Setting aside the question of sampling error for a moment, supposing we are able to reject a null hypothesis. We can then confirm an alternative hypothesis that a difference does exist. This is, of course, the hypothesis that we are primarily interested in, but we now call it the *alternative hypothesis* to emphasise the point that we reach it via the null hypothesis and not the other way round.

The null hypothesis is thus a proposition which states essentially that there is no relationship or difference. When proposed, the null hypothesis is saying to you, 'You are wrong, there is no relationship (or difference); disprove me if you can'. The operational, or alternative, hypothesis is often designated H_1 and the null hypothesis as H_0.

The null hypothesis does *not* imply that there is no relationship or no difference, i.e. it does not mean absolute equality. It means that there is no relationship or difference greater than that due to chance or random fluctuation.

The null hypothesis is a succinct way to express the testing of obtained data against chance expectation. The null hypothesis is the chance expectation. The standard error expresses the null hypothesis since it is a measure of expected chance fluctuations around a mean of zero.

Hypothesis testing and significance

How do we know when the relationship or difference is large enough to exceed chance expectation? Well, we use the levels of significance (0.05, 0.01, 0.001) which we discussed in chapter 5. Tables exist for various statistical tests which tell us whether our results reach these levels or not. The sequence of hypothesis formulation is shown below:

General problem
↓
Research hypothesis
↓
Operational or experimental hypothesis
↓
Alternative hypothesis (H_1)
↓
Null hypothesis (H_0)

Operational or experimental (the alternative) hypotheses should be stated in a way similar to the following: 'That there is a significant relationship (difference) between . . . .'.

Null hypotheses should take the following form: 'That there is no significant relationship (difference) between . . . '.

By placing the term *significant* in the proposition, we are emphasising the fact that our test of the null hypothesis invokes the test against a stated and conventionally acceptable level of statistical significance. Only if such a defined level is reached can we discard the null hypothesis and accept the alternative one, always remembering that we are never proving a hypothesis, only testing it, and eventually rejecting it or accepting it at some level of probability. An example will add clarity.

Suppose an experiment tests the retention of lists of words under two conditions:

1 The lists are presented at a fixed pace determined by the experimenter.
2 The lists are perused at a rate determined by the subject attempting to memorise them—self-pacing.

The null hypothesis simply predicts that the two conditions, fixed and self-pacing, will not produce any real difference in list retention, i.e. differences are due only to sampling error. The experimental or operational hypothesis predicts the alternative—that the two conditions will produce a genuine difference in list retention.

These hypotheses cannot be tested simply by noting whether or not the retention mean scores are identical or different in the two experimental conditions. Different mean scores may be thought to support the experimental hypothesis, but a difference in mean scores might be due to chance sampling fluctuations alone. Conversely, identical mean scores might be thought to support the null hypothesis, but the identity might be a coincidental correspondence produced by variability of scores around two real and genuinely different levels of performance.

For such reasons, the null hypothesis says, 'The two conditions will not differ by an amount which is greater than that to be expected by chance alone'.

The experimental hypothesis says, 'The two conditions will differ by an amount which is greater than is to be expected by chance alone'.

In evaluating the null hypothesis, it is possible to work out the probability that an observed difference is due simply to chance, because we can use a theoretical sampling distribution.

So the procedure adopted for evaluating an experimental hypothesis is as follows:

1 Set up the null hypothesis, i.e. any observed difference between conditions is entirely attributable to chance fluctuations, i.e. random error.
2 Calculate the exact probability that the observed difference could have been derived by chance alone.
3 Fail to reject the null hypothesis if this probability is higher than a certain value (the level of significance). Reject the null hypothesis if a conventional level of significance is attained. The probability that random error alone produced a difference as large as the one we observed is sufficiently low that we reject this possibility, i.e. we reject the null hypothesis.
4 Accept the experimental hypothesis if the null hypothesis has been rejected. Reject the experimental hypothesis if the null hypothesis cannot be rejected.

Only the null hypothesis is sufficiently precise to permit us to compute the probabilities that are required to decide whether it is likely to be true or not. The null hypothesis states that exactly 100 per cent of the effect is random. In order to compute probabilities we need an exact hypothesis like this. Thus, we test directly the status of the more precise hypothesis and infer the status of the experimental hypothesis we are really interested in.

STQ34*

1   Formulate null hypotheses for the following experimental hypotheses:
     a   That there is a significant difference in the mean score on Raven's Progressive Matrices between male university students and male TAFE students;
     b   That there is a significant relationship between scores on Witkin's Embedded Figures Test and extroversion as measured by the EPI in MBA graduates.

(continued)

One-tailed and two-tailed hypotheses

There is one further point about the way an experimental hypothesis is formulated which has implications for the way in which you look up probabilities in statistical tables. This is whether the experimental hypothesis is unidirectional (known as one-tailed) or bi-directional (known as two-tailed), *tail* referring to the extremity of a distribution. A unidirectional hypothesis is one that, as its name implies, makes a prediction in one particular direction, e.g. that girls have a significantly higher standardised mean reading score than boys at age nine.

But there are some hypotheses which make a bi-directional prediction by predicting that the effect of an independent variable may go in either direction. In our example this would mean predicting that girls are significantly different from boys in standardised mean reading score at age nine, i.e. not predicting which way the difference will go.

It is obviously preferable to be able to give an explanation of human behaviour in terms of predicting behaviour in one direction, than to state vaguely that there will be an effect of some kind. However, there are times, particularly during the more exploratory phase of a research program, when you might just want to see whether a variable has any effect; for example, whether some teaching method has an effect, good or bad, on children learning basic skills.

One-tailed and two-tailed hypotheses also have implications for statistical analysis. This is in connection with the probabilities that the differences in scores in an experiment will occur randomly. The point is that, for a hypothesis which predicts a difference in only one direction, there is a specific probability that the difference will occur randomly by chance. But, if a hypothesis makes a prediction that a difference might occur in either direction, then the probability is divided equally at each tail. For example, the 5% level in a two-tailed test is split 2.5% at each tail beyond 1.96σ when N is large (Figure 7.1). But on a one-tailed test the 5% is all at one tail or one end.

Consider this example: Suppose we have a sample of 100 eleven-year-old children who have experienced discovery learning methods at primary school, and we want to find out whether this experience has affected their performance in arithmetic as assessed by an arithmetic test. Suppose further, that we are in the fortunate position of knowing the

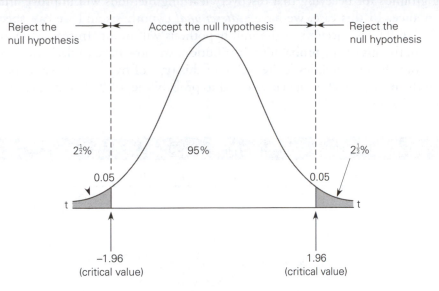

FIGURE 7.1 *Example: Testing the null hypothesis (two-tailed test)*

Reject the null hypothesis ——→ |← Accept the null hypothesis ——→|← Reject the null hypothesis

2½%   95%   2½%

0.05   0.05

t   t

−1.96   1.96
(critical value)   (critical value)

performance of all eleven-year-old children in the country on the arithmetic tests. We hypothesise that the mean score on the arithmetic test for the sample will differ from the population mean value. We decide to reject the null hypothesis at the $p < 0.01$ level. Our basic data are as follows:

Sample size = 100
Mean for population = 25
Mean for sample = 24
Standard deviation for sample = 3

Standard error $= \dfrac{3}{\sqrt{100}} = 0.3$

We can test the null hypothesis by seeing how many standard errors our observed sample mean value is from the population mean value. The value we obtain for this difference is:

$$\frac{25 - 24}{0.3} = 3.3$$

We know all values that are equal to, or exceed, 2.58 standard errors from the mean have a probability of occurrence by chance of $p = 0.01$. As our obtained value is 3.33 standard errors from the population mean, this means that at the $p < 0.01$ level the null hypothesis is rejected.

But now let us go a step further. You will notice that in our example we have not said whether the children's experience of discovery learning methods is likely to produce an improvement or a deterioration in their arithmetic attainment. We have simply said it will produce a difference; our hypothesis is *non-directional*. And to test it we used the areas at both ends of the normal distribution, a 'two-tailed' test. Supposing we have strong grounds for believing that discovery learning methods will improve arithmetic performance. In this case, we have a *directional* hypothesis and we can specify the direction in which rejection of the null hypothesis will occur. Instead of taking into account both tails of the probability distribution, we now have to deal with only one. To find out the probabilities for rejection of this type of hypothesis, we mark out the areas in the positive half of the curve equal to probabilities of 0.05 and 0.01. These are shown in Figure 7.2.

FIGURE 7.2 *One-tailed significance levels*

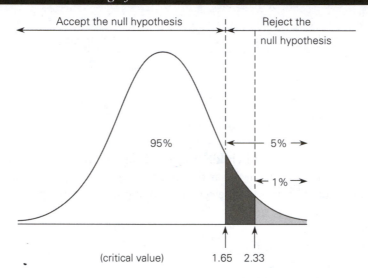

In this case, to reject the null hypothesis at the $p < 0.01$ level, we have to find a value that is greater than the population mean value by only 2.33 standard errors. Similarly, to reject the null hypothesis at the $p < 0.05$ level, our sample value needs to exceed a critical value of only 1.65 standard errors. Thus, our directional null hypothesis about the effect of discovery learning on arithmetic attainment is now even more strongly rejected. In other words, if we can confidently state the direction of a null hypothesis, we do not need such large observed differences to reject it at particular significance levels.

Type I and Type II errors

It should be clear from the above that stating a null hypothesis in a directional form loads the dice in favour of its rejection, i.e. we accept the experimental hypothesis on terms which are too easy. Can you see why? Most researchers commendably opt for caution by keeping the null hypothesis non-directional and consequently using a two-tailed significance test. Sometimes this caution may not be as admirable as it seems, for if we set the significance level too high there is always the danger we will accept a null hypothesis when it is false and reject the experimental hypothesis when

part 2 | quantitative methods

it is in fact true. This is termed a Type II error. The use of a one-tailed test pushes the problem the other way by making it easier to reject a false null hypothesis, but at the same time making it easier to gain erroneous support for a false experimental hypothesis. This is the Type I error. In choosing levels of significance and one- or two-tailed tests we are always balancing these two possible errors. Set the level too high and state a non-directional hypothesis and you maximise a Type II error; set the level too low and invoke a directional hypothesis and you will maximise a Type I error.

TABLE 7.1 *Type I and Type II errors*		
	Null hypothesis is actually	
Null hypothesis is	**True**	**False**
Accepted		Type II error
Rejected	Type I error	

STQ35*

1   Complete the following table:

P	*t*-value two-tailed	*t*-value one-tailed
0.05		1.65
0.01	2.58	Assume
0.001		N = 1000

2   What are the advantages and disadvantages of:
   a   one-tailed tests; and
   b   two-tailed tests?
3   A researcher predicts that a treatment will lower scores. If a one-tail test is used will the critical region be in the right- or left-hand tail as you look at it?
*Answers on p. 597.

summary

Hypothesis testing is an inferential procedure for using the limited data from a sample to draw a general conclusion about a population. The null hypothesis states that the treatment has not had any significant effect beyond that due to chance.

We set a level of significance that creates a critical level to distinguish chance from a statistically significant effect, usually at 0.05 (5% level) or 0.01 (1% level). Sample data that fall beyond the critical point in the tails of the distribution would imply that the effect is unlikely due to chance as it is a rare event on a chance basis. Consequently we assume that the effect is real and therefore the null hypothesis cannot be retained and must be rejected.

Directional tests may be used when the researcher predicts that a treatment effect will be in a particular direction, i.e. the outcome will be located entirely at one tail of the distribution. Directional tests should be used with caution as they may allow the rejection of the null hypothesis when experimental evidence is weak. It is always safer and never inappropriate to use a two-tail test.

A Type I error occurs when the null hypothesis is rejected although it is in fact true. A Type II error occurs when the null hypothesis is accepted when it is actually false.

Levels of
measurement

8
eight

The research data with which the quantitative approach deals are evaluated statistically. Much of the power of statistics results from the fact that numbers (unlike responses to a questionnaire, videotapes of social interactions in the classroom, or lists of words recalled by a subject in a memory experiment) can be manipulated with the rules of arithmetic. As a result, researchers prefer to use response measures that are in or can be converted to numerical form. Consider a hypothetical study of aggression and sex. The investigators who watched the subjects might rate their aggression in various situations (from, say, 'extremely aggressive' to 'extremely docile'), or they might count the number of aggressive acts (say, hitting or insulting another child) and so on. This operation of assigning numbers to observed events (usually, a subject's responses) is called *measurement*.

There are several levels of measurement that will concern us. They differ by the arithmetical operations that can be performed on them. The particular statistical technique that is appropriate for analysing a set of variables depends on the way in which those variables are measured.

Levels of measurement

We will refer to four distinct levels of measurement. These differ in the extent to which observations can be compared. From lowest to highest in the degrees to which comparisons can be made, the levels are **nominal**, **ordinal**, **interval** and **ratio**. It is important to understand clearly the distinction between these levels, since the use of inappropriate methods for the measurement levels of variables can lead to meaningless or incorrect results.

Nominal measurement

Nominal means *to name*; hence a nominal scale does not actually measure, but rather names. Observations are simply classified into categories with no necessary relationship existing between the categories. Nominal is the most primitive level of measurement, and only requires that one can distinguish two or more relevant categories and know the criteria for placing individuals or objects into one category or another. The relationship between the categories is that they are different from each other.

For example, when children in a poll are asked to name the television channel they watch most frequently, they might respond '7', '9', or '10'. These numbers serve only to group the responses into categories. They obviously cannot be subjected to any arithmetic operations. Again, marriage form would be measured on a nominal scale, with levels such as monogamy, polygyny, and polyandry. States of residence such as NSW, Victoria, etc. would be another example. Other common variables measured with nominal scales are religious affiliation, sex, race, occupation, method of teaching, and political party preference. Variables measured on nominal scales are referred to as nominal variables. Nominal variables are often called *qualitative*.

Names or labels can be used to identify the categories of a nominal variable, but those names do not represent different magnitudes of the variable. Bus route 10 is not twice as long as bus route 5. It is simply a labelling system; the numbers assigned to categories cannot be added, multiplied or divided. The major analytic procedure available for nominal data is chi square (χ^2).

Ordinal level of measurement

Ordinal measurement implies the ability to put data into rank order. Ordinal numbers convey more information, in that their relative magnitude is meaningful—not arbitrary, as in the case of a nominal scale. If pupils are asked to list the ten people they most admire, the number 1 can be assigned to the most admired person, 2 to the runner-up, and so on. The smaller the number assigned, the more the person is admired. Notice that no such statement can be made of television channels: Channel 7 is not more anything than Channel 9, just different from it.

Scores which are ordinally scaled cannot, however, be added or subtracted. The first two persons on the most admired list differ in position by one; so do the last two. Yet the individual who has done the ranking may admire the first person far more than the other nine, all of whom might be very similar in degree. In other words, given an ordinal scale, differences of one are not necessarily equal psychologically.

More often in educational research, ordinal scales consist of a collection of naturally ordered categories. To illustrate, social class may be classified into *upper*, *middle* and *working*; attitudes toward racial integration may be classified as *very favourable*, *favourable*, *neutral*, *unfavourable* or *very unfavourable*. The major analytic techniques for ordinal data are Wilcoxon, Mann-Whitney and rank order correlation.

Interval level of measurement

Scales in which equal differences between scores or intervals can be treated as equal units are called interval scales. IQ is a common variable which is usually treated as an interval scale.

Interval scales, in addition to incorporating orderings, have the property that there is a specific numerical distance between each pair of levels. Hence, we can compare values not only in terms of which is larger or older, but also in terms of how much larger or how much older. In interval scales, the distances between all adjacent levels are equal.

Examples of interval variables are the age of an individual, the birth rate of various ethnic groups, the population size of a city, the number of years of education one has completed and test scores. In each case, we can compare two values by identifying the following properties:

- Whether they are different (the nominal property).
- Which one possesses the greater magnitude (the ordinal property).
- The distance between them (the interval property).

For example, we can say that a sixty-year-old individual is of a different age to a twenty-year-old individual (nominally, they are labelled differently according to age); that one is older (an ordinal comparison); and that one is forty years older (an interval comparison). The whole range of parametric statistics is available for interval data.

Ratio level of measurement

Scores based on an interval scale allow subtraction and addition. But they do not necessarily allow multiplication and division. Consider the Centigrade scale of temperature. There is no doubt that the difference between 10 and 20 degrees Centigrade is equal to that between 30 and 40 degrees Centigrade. But can one say that 20 degrees Centigrade is twice as high a temperature as 10 degrees Centigrade? The answer is 'no', for the Centigrade scale of temperature is only an interval scale. Length and weight are *ratio scales* which allow statements such as '10 feet is one-fifth as long as 50 feet', or '15 pounds is three times as heavy as 5 pounds'. To make such statements, one needs a true zero point.

The four measurement levels may be viewed as forming a hierarchy. It is always possible to move downward in the hierarchy with respect to a specific measurement. In other words, any variable measured at the interval level may be treated as if it were ordinal or nominal, and an ordinal variable may be treated as a nominal variable.

For example, age is an interval variable. Since the various ages are also ordered, age could be treated as an ordinal variable, using ordered categories such as under 2, 2–3, 3–5, etc. Similarly, since we could artificially assign names to the values, we could even treat it as a nominal variable, with levels such as school age, working age and non-working age.

This fact is important because it implies that statistical procedures designed for variables measured at a certain level can also be used for variables measured at a higher level. A statistical procedure developed for ordinal variables, for example, can be used

FIGURE 8.1 *Higher order scales incorporate lower order scales*

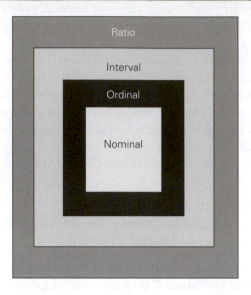

with interval variables as well, by using just the order characteristics of the numerical measurement. Normally, we would want to apply the statistical technique specifically appropriate for the actual scale of measurement (for example, interval level techniques for interval variables) since we then utilise the characteristic of the data to the fullest.

It is not possible to move in the other direction in the measurement hierarchy. If a variable is measured only on a nominal scale it is not possible to treat it on the ordinal level, since there is no natural ordering of the categories.

In general, it is important to try to measure variables at as high a level as possible, because more powerful statistical techniques can be used with higher level variables.

Levels of measurement and measures of central tendency

Fundamentally, the use of a particular 'average' is determined by the scale of measurement which can be assumed for the data. For data on a nominal scale there is no choice; the mode is the only appropriate measure. For ordinal scale data a choice is available and either the median or the mode may be appropriate, but the median is preferable for it retains more of the information contained in the data set by taking into account the rank order of the values.

As for data measured on interval or ratio scales, any of the measures may be used and the comparative merits of the mean and the median then become important.

A discrete variable consists of several categories. No value can exist between neighbouring categories. A discrete variable is typically restricted to whole countable numbers such as children in a family, despite the mythical 2.4 children per average family. School class size is in whole numbers. Similarly we code as a discrete variable whether a woman is pregnant or not using the codes of 1 and 0. We cannot have a value of 1.5 since it is impossible to be half-pregnant.

Continuous variables can have an infinite number of possible values that fall between any two values. The time taken to solve a problem could be 30 seconds for one person and 31 seconds for another. However, given sophisticated timing mechanisms it would be possible to measure many solution times between 30 and 31 seconds in milliseconds. Time is thus a continuous variable, as is length, weight and temperature. Our measurements are only limited by the limitations of our measuring instruments. So although a variable may appear to be discrete due to the way it is measured, we must always look behind the measurement and consider the variable itself. Any score on a continuous variable is an approximation of a theoretically infinitely precise scale.

For the most part, researchers in education and social science tend to treat most scales as though they are continuous—test scores may appear discrete but they are treated as a whole number approximation. For example, a test score of 50 is an approximation for all infinitesimal values between 49.5 and 50.5, just as by saying an event took place at 2.30 pm, or that we weigh 60.4 kg is an approximation for a far more exact time or weight. In general terms, we round up and down for convenience, assigning the observation to an interval.

STQ36*

1   What is the scale of measurement that is most appropriate for each of the following variables?
   a   Attitude toward legalisation of marijuana (*in favour, neutral, oppose*).
   b   Sex (*male, female*).
   c   Helen was born in 1968; Richard in 1975.
   d   Church affiliation (*Roman Catholic, Baptist, Methodist, . . .*).
   e   Political philosophy (*liberal, moderate, conservative*).
   f   The IQ of students.
   g   Highest degree obtained (*bachelor, master, doctorate*).
   h   Peter is the second most popular pupil in class.
   i   Average score in class test.
   j   Occupational status (*blue collar, white collar*).
   k   Numbering of houses along a road.
   l   Population size (*number of people*).
   m   Pass/fail split in a test.
   n   Annual income (*in dollars per year*).
   o   Time taken to solve anagrams.
   p   Aptitude scores.
2   Which of the following are continuous variables?
   a   Classification of emotional experience from facial expression.
   b   A measure of intellectual aptitude.
   c   Time taken to finish a test.

*Answers on p. 597.

A nominal scale labels observations so that they fall into different categories. These are only qualitative distinctions.

An ordinal scale involves ranking observations in terms of size or magnitude. Differences between ranks are not equal.

An interval scale reflects differences in magnitude between observations.

A ratio scale has a meaningful zero point and ratios of measurement reflect ratios of magnitude.

A discrete variable can only have a finite number of values between any two values. It typically consist of whole numbers. A continuous variable has an infinite number of values between any two values.

Variables

9

nine

The characteristics that are measured for each of the numbers of a sample are usually referred to as variables. A variable is a characteristic that can take on more than one value among members of a sample or population.

Examples of commonly used variables in educational research are sex (with values male and female); age at last birthday (with values 0, 1, 2, 3 and so on); religious persuasion (Baptist, Methodist, Roman Catholic, Unitarian and so forth); social status (upper class, middle class and working class); and exam results (say, measured in scores out of 100). To speak tautologically, a variable is something that varies. A variable must have a minimum of two values, but most are characterised by continuous values.

Independent and dependent variables

An experiment occurs when the environment is systematically manipulated in order to observe the effect of this manipulation on some behaviour.

The part of the environment that is manipulated is the *independent variable (IV)*. The particular behavioural effect of this manipulation is the *dependent variable (DV)*, i.e. what is measured.

[*IV* manipulated by researcher → measured change in *DV*]

The number of reinforcements given, the loudness of a tone, the inducement of a set are all *IVs*. *IVs* are selected on the basis that the experimenter thinks they will cause changes in behaviour. For instance, increasing the number of reinforcements for hand-raising should increase hand-raising behaviour; increasing noise levels should decrease attention to other signals.

The *DV* is that which is observed and recorded by the experimenter. It depends on the behaviour of the subject. The time taken to solve anagrams, the number of nonsense syllables recalled, the age at leaving school, could all be *DVs*.

For a variable to qualify as an *IV*, it must be manipulatable. The variable must be presented in at least two forms, even if this boils down to a presence versus absence type of variation.

The number of *IVs* the experimenter actually varies at will is small. In the main, most variables have to be taken at such levels as they occur in nature. Thus age, achievement and type of delinquency are not under the experimenter's control. He or she has to take existing groups which fall into these categories.

Presence versus absence

The *presence versus absence* technique for achieving variation is exactly what the name implies. One group of subjects receives the treatment condition and the other group does not. The two groups are then compared to see if the group that received the treatment condition differed from the group that did not. Figure 9.1 illustrates a hypothesis that uses two levels of the *IV*.

FIGURE 9.1 *Two levels of IV. Hypothesis: students who have completed a speed reading course will make significantly higher grades than students who have never taken such a course.*

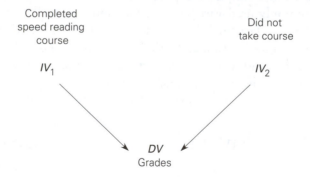

Instructions as an *IV*

So far, the manipulation of the *IV* has been discussed in terms of the manipulation of events. Another way variation can be introduced is by manipulating instructions. For example, in a memory experiment one group might be asked to rehearse the presented words in the period between learning and recall, while another group might be requested to think of other words which would remind them of the original words. There are two dangers inherent in the manipulation of instructions. Firstly, some subjects might be inattentive and not hear or understand the full set of instructions. Secondly, there is always the possibility of subtle intersubject variations in the interpretation of the instructional message. Both these dangers introduce uncontrolled variation or experimental error into the experiment.

The selection of the dependent variable

The experiment is conducted to answer the question, 'What is the effect of . . . ?', and to test the corresponding hypothesis, 'A certain change in X will result in a certain change in Y'. To accomplish this task, the experimenter has to select a *DV* that will be sensitive to, or be able to pick up, the influence exerted by the *IV*. If the *DV* has a limited range it is easy to reach the maximum or minimum values with minimal manipulation of the *IV*. Any further manipulation of the *IV* cannot be registered through changes in the *DV* since the latter's limits of movement have been reached already. When it is impossible to sink any lower on a scale, we have the 'floor effect'; similarly the impossibility of recording a higher score than maximum is the 'ceiling effect'. Unfortunately, there is no golden rule that will enable us to select the most sensitive *DV*. In any case, no *DV* will reveal sufficient variation if the variations or levels of the *IV* are insufficient in the first place.

The *DV* must also be operationally defined so that we are quite sure what we are measuring. Implicit in this too is that some accepted mode of measuring the *DV* exists. Many *DV*s in which educationalists are interested are hypothetical constructs, e.g. learning, intelligence, short-term memory, etc. These must be operationalised as observable and measurable behaviours that allow inference back to the construct. For example, it is impossible to study the learning process directly. If, on the other hand, a student sits down and studies certain material for an hour and then can answer questions they previously could not, we say learning has taken place. In this case, learning is inferred from an increase in performance.

The measures available to assess the *DV* must be reliable and valid. These two terms will be considered in detail later (chapter 22). For now it suffices to say that reliability is the consistency with which a result will repeat itself, all other things being equal. Validity implies that the measurement technique/instrument is actually assessing what it purports to measure.

STQ37

1 Differentiate between the *IV* and *DV* in a concise sentence.
2 In what ways is it possible to manipulate the *IV*?
3 What do you understand by the 'ceiling' and 'floor' effects?

Some examples of independent and dependent variables

Several hypotheses drawn from studies undertaken in a research methods course are listed below; the independent and dependent variables have been identified for each one.

Hypothesis 1 Under social reinforcement conditions, middle class children will learn significantly more than working class children.

    IV: Middle class versus working class.
    DV: Amount learned.

Hypothesis 2 Students who plan to pursue careers in marketing are more aggressive, less conforming, more independent and have a greater need for achievement than students who do not plan such careers.

    IV: Students who plan to pursue careers in marketing versus those who do not.
    DV: Aggressiveness, conformity, independence, need for achievement.

Hypothesis 3 Students with positive academic self-concepts will gain significantly higher grades than students with negative academic self-concepts.

    IV: Students with positive academic self-concepts and students with negative academic self-concepts.
    DV: Grades.

STQ38*

Identify the *IV* and *DV* in the following hypotheses:
1   Perceptions of the characteristics of the 'good' or effective teacher are in part determined by the perceiver's attitudes toward education.
2   In the elementary school age group, above-average height children are more often chosen as leaders by their classmates than are children below average height.
3   Test-wiseness affects test performance.
4   Working-class children will learn nonsense syllables slower than middle-class children.
5   Girls who follow science courses in Year 12 are more aggressive than girls following non-science courses.
6   The degree of illusion created by the Muller-Lyer illusion depends on whether it is presented vertically or horizontally.
7   Adults find it easier to remember a list of meaningful words than to remember a list of nonsense syllables.
8   Identify the *DV* and *IV* in the following:
    a   Noise affects efficiency of work.
    b   Time of day affects span of attention.
    c   Birth order affects individual personality.
    d   Performance is improved by practice.
*Answers on p. 597.

The moderator variable

The term *moderator variable* describes a special type of independent variable selected for study to determine if it affects the relationship between the primary independent variable and the dependent variables. The moderator variable is defined as *that factor which is measured, manipulated or selected by the experimenter to discover whether it modifies the relationship of the independent variable to an observed phenomenon.* The word *moderator* simply acknowledges the reason that this secondary independent variable has been singled out for study. If the experimenter is interested in studying the effect of independent variable X, and Y is altered by the level of a third factor Z, then Z can be in the analysis as a moderator variable.

Here is an example. First, suppose the researcher wants to compare the effectiveness of the discovery approach to teaching science to the effectiveness of the formal approach. Suppose further he or she suspects that, while one method may be more effective for average students, the other may have more effect for low IQ students. When all are tested together, the results of the two methods may appear to be the same, but when fast and slow students are separated, the two methods may have different results in each subgroup. If so, IQ level would be seen to moderate the relationship between *teaching approach* (the independent variable) and *effectiveness* (the dependent variable).

Because the situations in educational research investigations are usually quite complex, the inclusion of at least one moderator variable in a study is highly recommended. Often the nature of the relationship between X and Y remains poorly understood because of the researcher's failure to single out and measure vital moderator variables.

Some examples of moderator variables

Hypothesis Test scores and intelligence are more highly correlated for boys than for girls.

> *IV & DV*: Either test scores or intelligence may be considered the independent variable; the other, the dependent variable.

> *Moderator variable*: Sex (boys versus girls).

Hypothesis Adult attitudes to education are related to their socio-economic class.

> *IV & DV*: Attitudes to education and socio-economic class may be considered as either.

> *Moderator variables*: Here are some that ought to be considered:

- Whether they have school-age children or not.
- Level of their education.

Control variables

A control variable is a potential *IV* that is held constant during an experiment. It is not allowed to vary. For any one experiment, the list of control variables that it is desirable to control is large; far larger than can ever be accomplished in practice. The problem is that such variables have their potential effects on the *DV* so that it becomes impossible to separate those variations in the *DV* that are due to the *IV* and those that are due to other variables. The potential effects are unsystematic too, sometimes causing improvements and at other times deficits, so their influence is unmeasurable. Consider, for example, a simple experiment in which pupils are required to solve five-letter anagrams. Here one would want to control age, intelligence and previous experience with anagrams. Even time of day is important in affecting efficiency. Other variables such as motivation and interest can hardly be controlled though they will play an important part. The list could obviously be extended.

In practice, the experimenter will try to control as many of these salient factors as possible so that the effect of uncontrolled factors will be slight, relative to the effect of the *IV*. Most control variables are subject variables, i.e. variables that represent attributes vested in each subject and which they bring with them into the experimental context; for example, age, experience, social class, sex, motivation, expectation, etc. For example, if one group of subjects contains more intelligent people than another group, differences in performance may be due not to the *IV* but to the intelligence. When two variables are mixed up in this way, they are confounded with each other. Similarly, other control variables are context variable and they may confound the results; for example, task order, task content, noise instructions. If a varying amount of a tranquilliser is given to create different levels of anxiety, heavy doses may cause sleepiness so that performance on the *DV* is affected by an unknown combination of sleepiness and anxiety level. Specific methods of control such as randomisation elimination or equalising across groups will be dealt with in chapter 10.

Some examples of control variables

Control variables are not necessarily specified in the hypothesis. It is often necessary to read the methods section of a study to discover which variables have been treated as control variables. The examples below, however, specifically list at least one control variable in the hypothesis.

Hypothesis: First-born college students with an introverted personality get higher grades than their extroverted counterparts of equal intelligence, while no such differences are found among 'later borns'.

 Control variable: Intelligence

Hypothesis: Among boys there is a correlation between IQ and social maturity, while for girls in the same age group there is no correlation between these two variables.

 Control variable: Age

Hypothesis: Under social reinforcement conditions, middle-class children will learn significantly better than working-class children.

 Control variable: Reinforcement conditions

In each of the above, there are undoubtedly other variables, such as the subjects' relevant prior experiences or the noise level during treatment, which are not specified in the hypothesis but which must be controlled. Because they are controlled by routine design procedures, universal variables such as these are often not systematically labelled.

STQ39*

Check your ability to select *IV*, *DV* and control variables in the following:
1   A car manufacturer wants to know how bright brake lights should be in order to minimise the time required for the driver of the following vehicle to realise the car in front is stopping.
2   A behaviour therapist reinforces a patient by nodding, smiling and extra attention every time the patient says something positive about himself or herself and pays no attention (extinguishes) to negative verbal material about the patient.
3   A social psychologist tries to discover if male car drivers conform more to stop signs at crossroads than female car drivers.
4   With IQ held constant, children with perceptual motor training will perform better on hand–eye coordination tasks than children without this training.
*Answers on p. 598.

Intervening variables

All the variables so far discussed have been under the control of the experimenter. Each *IV* and control variable can be manipulated and each variation observed on the *DV*. However, what the experimenter may be trying to find out in some experiments is not necessarily concrete but hypothetical. The intervening variable is a hypothetical one whose effects are inferred from the effects of the *IV* on the *DV*. Significant effects suggest support for the hypothetical construct. Look at the following hypothesis.

Hypothesis 1   Pupils subject to high levels of criticism exhibit more aggressive acts than those not so criticised.

   IV: Criticised or not criticised.
   DV: Number of aggressive acts.
   Intervening variable: Frustration.

Frustration is an intervening variable because it links the criticism to the aggressive behaviour. For example, frustration occurs to create the link though it can only be inferred.

Hypothesis 2   Pupils given more positive feedback experiences will have more positive attitudes to others than pupils given fewer positive feedback experiences.

   IV: Number of positive feedback experiences.
   DV: Attitudes to others.
   Intervening variable: Self-esteem.
   Positive self-concept again links the *IV* and *DV*. It is a result of the *IV* and causes the *DV*.

The intervening variables can often be discovered by examining a hypothesis and asking the question, 'What is it about the independent variable that will cause the predicted outcome?'.

The combined variables

The relationship between the five types of variables described in this chapter is illustrated in Figure 9.2. Note that independent, moderator and control variables are inputs or causes, the first two being those that are studied, while control variables, the third, are neutralised or 'eliminated'. At the other end, dependent variables represent effects, while intervening variables are conceptualisations which intervene between operationally stated causes and operationally stated effects.

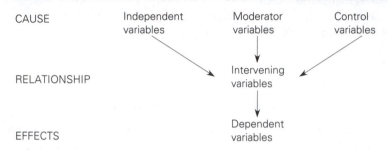

FIGURE 9.2 *Relationship between variable types*

STQ40*

Identify the various variables in the following:

1 Formal teachers are preferred by pupils who have convergent thinking style, while non-directive teachers are preferred by pupils who have a divergent thinking style.

2 In a research study, teachers are given feedback as to their in-class behaviour from (a) students, (b) supervisors, (c) both students and supervisors, (d) neither. Students' judgements are again obtained after ten weeks to determine if teachers given the different sources of feedback have shown differential change of behaviour in the direction advocated by the feedback. Differential outcomes are also considered in terms of years of teaching experience of each teacher.

3 In a research study, students considered to have a high level of test anxiety were divided into two groups: one receiving a behaviour modification program, the other not receiving any treatment. Results were measured on physiological indices just prior to sitting an exam.

4 Student female teachers are more likely to change their questioning techniques after having a microteaching experience than without having such an experience, while experienced female teachers are equally likely to maintain their existing technique either with or without microteaching.

5 With IQ held constant, students with perceptual-motor training will perform better on eye–hand coordination tasks than students without this training, while such differences will not appear among adults.

*Answers on p. 598.

summary

A variable is a measurable characteristic of a sample. Variables are the gears and cogs of an experiment. Their selection, control, manipulation and measurement is what makes an experiment run. The independent variable (*IV*) is manipulated and its effect is measured by changes in the dependent variable (*DV*). A moderator variable affects the relationship between the *IV* and *DV*. A control variable is held constant and an intervening variable is a hypothetical entity whose effects are inferred.

Research design and the control of error

10
ten

The purpose of research design is to minimise experimental error, thereby increasing the likelihood that an experiment will produce reliable results. Entire books have been written about experimental design. Here, we will cover only a sample of some common techniques used to improve the design of experiments. While this treatment is necessarily less complete than that of an entire text devoted to the subject, it should give you an understanding of the aims of designing an experiment, even though it will not give you all the techniques that could be used.

Experimental error

Experimental error occurs when a change in the *DV (dependent variable)* is produced by any variable other than the *IV (independent variable)*. What we are wholly interested in is the effect of the *IV* on the *DV*. When other variables that are causally related to the *DV* are confounded with the *IV*, they produce experimental error; they produce differences on the *DV* between the experimental conditions that add to or subtract from the difference that would have been produced by the *IV* alone. Experimental error covers up the effect you are interested in and can make it difficult or impossible to assess.

Let us imagine that we obtain some subjects, assign half to a formally taught educational psychology course and half to the same course taught by programmed instruction, and at the end of the term measure all subjects on an attainment test. There are a number of variables which, unless we are careful, may be confounded with the *IV*. One is time of day: one course may be taught in the middle of the morning, when students are alert; and the other at the very end of the day. Another is intelligence: students in one course may be brighter than those in the other. Since both of these variables are likely to affect the attainment score obtained at the end of the term, allowing either to be confounded with the *IV* is likely to result in experimental error.

There are two kinds of experimental errors: constant or systematic error and random error. An understanding of these kinds of errors and of ways to deal with them constitutes a fundamental basis of experimental reasoning.

- *Systematic* or *constant error* is an error or bias that favours the same experimental condition every time the experiment is repeated. Any error due to time of day would be a constant error, for whichever course is taught at the more favourable time of day is taught at that time for all subjects in that experimental condition.

  Constant error operates systematically so that it affects performance in one condition but not the other. The different manner and personality of the experimenter with the control group compared to those of the person handling the experimental group would affect each group in a different way. If, for instance, one group undertakes their experiment while sitting in a cold or noisy room but the other group is in more amenable surroundings, the results are likely to include effects from this variable. If one group has more practice than the other, this will produce improved performance and will be a constant error, provided practice is not designated as the independent variable.

- A *random error* is an error which, on repetitions of the experiment, sometimes favours one experimental condition and sometimes the other, on a chance basis. If subjects are assigned to conditions randomly, then any error resulting from differences in intelligence will be random error. Very often, the error from any particular source has both constant and random components. This would be true of the error produced by intelligence if the subjects volunteered for the conditions, and if the brighter subjects usually, but not always, chose the same experimental condition. We shall continue to consider just the pure cases of constant and random error, and it is perfectly legitimate to do so. But we do this with the understanding that the error from any particular source may involve these components in any proportions.

The effect of a constant or systematic error is to distort the results in a particular direction, so that an erroneous difference masks the affairs. The effect of a random error is not to distort the results in any particular direction, but to obscure them. In designing an experiment, controls are employed to eliminate as much error as possible and then randomisation is employed to ensure that the remaining error will be distributed at random. Controlling or randomising sources of constant error eliminates bias.

Sources of experimental error

There are four sources of experimental error: *sampling*, *assignment*, *conditions* and *measurement*. Experimental error can be introduced in sampling the subjects from the population, in assigning the subjects in the sample to the experimental conditions, in administering the experimental conditions and in measuring the *DV*. Error from any of these sources may be either constant or random.

We will leave measurement error in the *DV* (and its corollary reliability) to a later time (chapter 20) and discuss the first three sources now.

Error due to sampling

We have already considered sampling techniques in chapter 6. It was apparent from there, and also in discussing standard error, that random error is difficult to avoid, even with the best sampling techniques, and that systematic (constant) error is always a threat.

Error due to sampling could arise in the teaching method experiment above, if, as is usually the case, we did not test all the subjects in the population to which we wish to generalise the result, and if, as is also usually the case, the size of the experimental effect differs from subject to subject. Perhaps an educational psychology course taught by formal methods is of greater benefit to brighter students. Thus, while the true difference between the methods in the population as a whole might be a slight difference in favour of the formal method, the difference in a sample of bright students might be quite large, and in a sample of less bright students might be negligibly small. These discrepancies from the true difference constitute error. If the sampling procedure is random, sometimes bright students will be drawn and the error will be in one direction, and sometimes less bright students will be drawn and the error will be in the other direction. The error will be random. If subjects can volunteer and all bright students opt for the same teaching method, then constant error is introduced. The procedure of stratified sampling can be used to control sampling error too.

STQ41

Do you remember what a random sample is? Refer back to page 85 if you cannot recall.

Randomisation is the most important and basic of all control methods, providing control not only for known sources of variation but for unknown ones too. In fact, it is the only technique for dealing with the latter source. It is like an insurance policy, a precaution against disturbances that may or may not occur, and clearly stated procedures involving tossing coins and random number tables should be employed.

Error due to assignment

Error due to assignment could arise in the teaching method experiment above if subjects in the two conditions differed initially in intelligence, as they no doubt would. The observed difference at the end of the experiment would then be the true difference resulting from manipulating the *IV* plus or minus this initial difference. This error would be a constant error if the procedure for assigning subjects to conditions were in some way biased. Perhaps subjects were allowed to choose which course they would take, and brighter subjects tend to take the formally taught course. Such an error would always tend to favour the taught-course performance when a comparison is made. Control of experimental error due to assignment is affected by the subject allocation design of the experiment. There are three basic designs:

1 **between-subjects design**. Here we compare two or more samples, e.g. a control with an experimental group. Allocation to groups may or may not be randomised.
2 **within-subjects design**. We have only one group, which is tested twice or more in a 'before and after' research design.
3 **matched-subjects design** where the closeness of the matching produces two equivalent groups.

In almost all experiments, we have to make a decision whether to employ the same subjects in each condition or level of the *IV*, or to use different subjects for each condition.

Between-subjects design

There are some kinds of experiment in which it is very difficult to use the same people for all conditions. What about an experiment testing the relationship between sex and induced learned helplessness? There is simply no way (apart from a split-second sex change!) in which the same people can perform in both the male and female groups. So there have to be different people (men and women) in the two groups. This design is known as a between-subjects design because the comparison is between two independent groups or unrelated people.

There are other experiments too in which it is easier to use different people for the different experimental conditions. These include experiments involving very long tasks which would exhaust the patience and lower the motivation of subjects if the same people had to perform all the conditions. Another reason is that if you use different people you avoid the possibility of practice effects transferring from one task to another.

But individuals do differ markedly from each other. The only way to deal with this is to allocate the different people at random to the different experimental conditions. Here, *random* means that it is purely a matter of chance *which people* end up doing *which condition* or *level* of the *IV*. The reasoning is that if subjects are randomly allocated to experimental conditions on a chance basis, then people of different ages or abilities are just as likely to be found in all the experimental groups. For example, you might find that all the subjects who arrive first to volunteer for an experiment are the most highly motivated people who would tend to score more highly, quite regardless of experimental condition. So they should not be placed in the same group. It would be better to allocate alternate subjects as they arrived, or perhaps to toss a coin to decide which group each subject should be allocated to; in which case, unless your coin is biased, the allocation of subjects to groups should be truly random.

The groups should also be assigned their level of the *IV* by a random procedure, i.e. toss a coin to decide which group shall be the experimental one and which the control group. Random assignment exerts control by virtue of the fact that the variables to be controlled are distributed in approximately the same way in all groups. In this way, their influence is a constant across the groups, since they cannot produce any differential influence on the *DV*. Remember though, that bias can exist even after randomisation has been applied, since chance variation between groups will still occur. Do you recall the variation between means of randomly selected samples (chapter 6)?

Randomisation is the only method for the control of unknown variables. Other control techniques are only of value with known confounding variables. The principle is to randomise wherever and whenever possible, even when applying one of the other control techniques.

STQ42

1   Briefly outline what you see as the advantages and disadvantages of the between-subjects design.
2   How can we generally avoid error due to assignment?

FIGURE 10.1 *Independent randomised two group design*

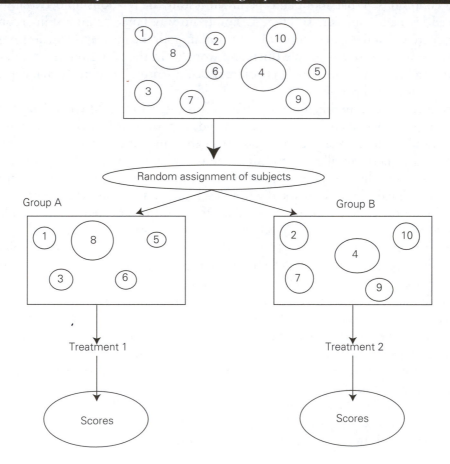

Inferential statistics for testing differences between two groups

In discussing hypothesis formation, it was noted that one major form of a hypothesis is that of stating that there are differences between two samples. This chapter will deal with tests for analysing data from two samples to determine whether there is a real difference between them, i.e. a difference greater than that due to chance, or whether it is a chance variation, i.e. the two sample means lie within the expected chance distribution of similar sample means from the same population at some level of probability.

There are three ways in which the difference comparisons can be made:

1 Between two independent groups—the between-subjects design.
2 Between the same group from one occasion to another—the within-subjects design.
3 Between two matched groups which are so similar that they can be regarded as the same group twice—the matched subjects design.

Each of these designs has statistical tests of differences appropriate to it, and according to whether the data is suitable for parametric or non-parametric statistical testing.

Within-subjects design

So far, we have presented exclusively the advantages of using different rather than the same subjects for all the experimental conditions, i.e. the between-subjects design.

STQ43

Can you list some of these advantages?

But, against all these advantages, there is one crucial disadvantage about using different subjects for each experimental condition. This is that there may be all sorts of individual differences in the way different subjects tackle the experimental task.

STQ44

What major individual differences affect the way different subjects tackle an experimental task? List as many as you can.

There are many. For instance, in a memory experiment some people might be more intelligent than others, some might think the experiment a bore, others that it would get them extra marks, some might not even be able to read the items, some might be old, some young, some take three minutes over each item, others four seconds, some might be anxious, and others might be thinking about the nightclub they are going to that night. Such variability might affect their ability to remember the items, from nil by a person who cannot read, to 100 per cent by an ambitious person who thinks they are going to get an A grade for their performance. The existence of all these other factors might mean that each subject's behaviour is being affected by variables which have nothing to do with the independent variable the experimenter is intending to manipulate.

An experimental design in which the same people are performing all the experimental conditions is the best method for eliminating such individual differences. This is known as a within-subjects design because the comparison is within the same set of subjects and so their scores are related. Anything peculiar to one individual (like high or low IQ or motivation) is then spread across all conditions. If a person is highly motivated when learning one list of words, thus inflating the scores for that condition, he or she will also tend to be well motivated when learning other lists of words, and so will inflate those scores as well. The point about using a same-subjects design is that any individual peculiarities get equalised out over all conditions. Note that they do not get removed; they simply form a constant on the results of each condition.

This is the ultimate way to minimise individual differences between subjects. A within-subjects design makes it more likely that any differences in performance discerned between levels of the independent variable are true differences.

One practical advantage of a within-subjects experiment is that fewer subjects are required. If N subjects are required to give you an adequate number of data for a within-subject experiment, then N × 2 are required for a two-level between-subjects experiment. There will also be times when the number of subjects available to you is limited, especially when the subjects must meet certain requirements. For example, you may need subjects with some disorder like a specific psychosis or colour-blindness or left-handedness. In such cases, you may not be able to find enough subjects who meet these requirements to use a between-subjects design, and you will need to rely on a within-subjects experiment.

Error from administration of experimental conditions

Since there are many practical and statistical advantages to using within-subjects designs, why should we ever use between-subjects designs? Unfortunately, the within-subjects design also carries some rather serious disadvantages.

The basic problem is that once subjects are exposed to one level of the independent variable, there is no way to change them back into the people they were prior to being exposed. The exposure has done something irreversible to the subject, whom we can no longer treat as a pure, uncontaminated, naive subject. How is the subject changed?

One way a subject can change is to learn. Suppose we wanted to know whether it takes someone longer to learn to type on a manual typewriter or an electric typewriter. We decide that because there are likely to be large individual differences in typing ability, we will use a within-subject design. We take ten subjects and find out how many hours they have to practise in order to type 30 words per minute on a manual typewriter. We then switch them to an electric typewriter and find out how many hours they have to practise to type 30 words per minute on that. We find that it takes them an average of forty-five hours of practice to reach criterion on the manual, compared with two hours on the electric. Can we conclude that the electric typewriter is that much easier to learn on? Obviously not.

During the first part of the experiment, in addition to learning the specific skill of using a manual typewriter, the subjects were also learning a general typing skill. The general skill is confounded with the specific skill. By the time the subjects typed on the electric typewriter, their general typing skill was undoubtedly at a higher level than when they started the experiment. Any time such an effect changes systematically across the trials, we must be careful to keep the effect of our independent variable from becoming confounded with it.

How can you get rid of this confounding effect? The answer is to *counterbalance* in order to control sequencing or order effects. Familiarity, practice, learning, motivational changes, fatigue, etc. may often influence performance quite markedly on the second task.

Counterbalancing

One way to minimise the effect of a systematic confounding variable like learning is to counterbalance the order in which you present the levels of the independent variable. One of the more frequently used techniques is called ABBA counterbalancing. If we call the manual typewriter 'A' and the electric typewriter 'B', then ABBA simply indicates the pattern in which subjects will learn typing. This pattern serves to counterbalance the confounding effects across the two levels of our independent variable.

An ABBA counterbalancing technique attempts to counterbalance order effects in a completely within-subject manner; the same subject gets both orders. Other counterbalancing techniques make order a between-subjects variable by counterbalancing order across subjects. In intra-group counterbalancing, groups of subjects are counter-balanced rather than each subject. So, for example, with two conditions (i.e. A and B) of the *IV*, half the subjects chosen at random receive sequence AB, and the other half receive BA. A completely randomised counterbalancing is possible too, with each subject receiving one of the sequences chosen by a random process. However, in all counterbalancing, you are making the assumption that the effect of having B follow A is just the reverse of the effect of having A follow B. This assumption is sometimes called *an assumption of symmetrical transfer*.

As we add more levels to our independent variable, we increase the complexity of a complete counterbalancing procedure. In a completely counterbalanced design, every level has to occur an equal number of times. Complete counterbalancing can become a monumental task when you have a large number of levels.

Counterbalancing will not remove an order effect. Hopefully, it will make it constant in both levels. Moreover, demand characteristics are likely to be a big problem in this design since taking several levels of the *IV* may allow a subject a greater chance of correctly guessing what the experiment is about or what the experimenter 'wants', whatever order the conditions are taken in.

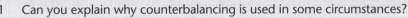

STQ45

1   Can you explain why counterbalancing is used in some circumstances?
2   What do you understand by the term 'order effects'? Can you name some order effects?

Matched-subjects design

This design gains the advantage of a between-subjects experiment yet avoids, like the within-subjects design, some of the problems of large individual differences between groups of subjects. At the same time, the order problems of the within-groups design are removed. *Matched pairs* simply means that an attempt is made to have the same kind of subjects undertake the experiment.

To do this, you match pairs of subjects on what seem to be important characteristics—sex, age, IQ, memorising ability, anxiety or whatever, depending on the experiment. The idea is that if IQ is important to performance then you have pairs of subjects at each IQ level, and one of each pair is allocated randomly to each group. This means that neither group should have a special advantage since they have equal ranges of IQ among their members.

A matched-pairs design can be treated as within-subjects design because the purpose of the matching is to end up with related pairs who are matched so closely that, on the characteristics relevant to the particular experiment, they are as near as possible the same person.

In the case of a within-subjects design, the related pairs are, of course, the same, performing under both experimental conditions.

You must match your groups on a variable that is highly correlated with the dependent variable. It is a waste of time for us to match two groups of runners on the basis of IQ scores. Fast feet are not related to quick minds! However, we could have had each subject run the 100 yards, then made up pairs of subjects: the two fastest, the two next fastest, and so on. We could then toss a coin to assign one member of each pair to each of the conditions. In this way, we know that the groups are somewhat equivalent in running speed prior to introducing the independent variable.

Subjects might be matched on intelligence if the experiment is a problem-solving one, on sex if the experiment is one on the effect of a particular film, on attitudes toward dating, and so forth. Matching on intelligence may not be of much help in a study of leadership because subjects who are perfectly matched on intelligence may be very poorly matched on leadership. Some measure more closely related to the *DV* of leadership, such as number of positions of leadership held in the past, would produce more relevant matching.

If a pre-test is necessary to obtain data on which the matching is to be based, such a pre-test must not contaminate the main experiment. For example, in a memory experiment, we find that matching on memory ability is the best variable, but the memory pre-test must not be similar to the task in the main experiment or else differential effects on subjects in terms of practice, learning, motivation, etc. will influence the experiment. Through matching, we decrease the probability of being wrong when we say that the *IV* caused a change in behaviour.

One disadvantage in doing matched-groups experiments is that it takes longer to match the groups, so that experiments sometimes require two sessions: one for the pre-test and one for the experiment itself. If you are planning to use many subjects anyway, the chances of getting large differences between groups using random assignment is quite small, and the problem of matching might not be worth the effort.

FIGURE 10.2 *Matched subjects with two groups*

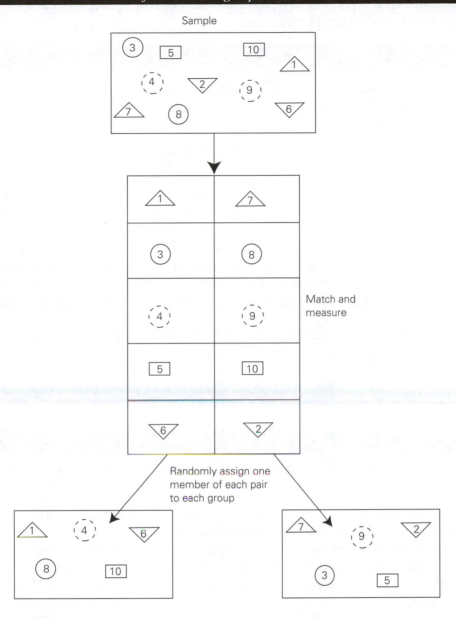

Matching causes the pool of potential subjects to be smaller, too. For example, we can hold constant across each experimental group by, say, sex by only using males, IQ by only using an IQ level, age by only having 21-year-olds, and ethnic group by only using Iranians, etc. But it would be difficult to locate sufficient numbers of male 21-year-old Iranian subjects with the same IQ. However, it is clear that experimental variation will not include any variation due to sex, or age, or ethnic group, or IQ variation, hence less of the variation is error variation.

Experimental error is considerably reduced because chance fluctuations in the performance on one person at two points in time tend to be smaller than the fluctuations of two people at the same point in time.

STQ46

List the advantages and disadvantages of the between-subjects, within-subjects and matched-subjects designs.

Standardising

This term can be applied in two ways. It can refer to the standardising of the experimental conditions, or the standardising of the marking or assessment of test instruments. It is the former which is to be considered briefly here. Standardising of the experimental conditions ensures that every subject undertakes the *IV* level applicable to himself or herself in the same conditions as everyone else. For example, think how the results of an experiment could be interpreted if some subjects had a longer time to complete the task, or were given different instructions, or suffered from noisy disturbances while undertaking the task. (Of course, experiments can be devised in which these variables could act as the *IV*.) These unstandardised conditions would be reflected in unknown ways in the *DV* variations, and would be impossible to disentangle from the real effects of the *IV*. So, for these types of variables, control of error is effected by holding them constant for all subjects.

Holding a variable constant ensures that it will produce no experimental error, for the obvious reason that variables which do not change cannot produce changes on any other variable.

STQ47

Can you write down a few variables that need to be held constant in most experiments?

It is now possible to see what each design and control technique achieves. In the between-subjects design, no subject variables are controlled. In the matched-pairs design, one or more between-subject variables (such as age, IQ, sex, social class) are controlled. In the within-subjects design, all between-subject variables are controlled, though the variables (on which a single person varies from time to time) such as fatigue and motivation, are not controlled.

In the between-subjects and matched-subjects designs, subject variables that have not been controlled are randomised by assigning the members of each pair randomly to conditions. In the within-subjects design, within-subject variables that are related to order of presentation, such as fatigue and adjustment to the experimental situation, can be counterbalanced with order of presentation. But the experimenter has no control over other within-subject variables, such as anxiety, and nature must be trusted to randomise these. The essential difference, then, between the three kinds of design is the degree to which they control error due to between-subject variables. Since between-subject variables usually contribute most to random error, this is an important difference. On this basis, the within-subjects design is to be preferred to the matched subjects, and the matched subjects to the independent subjects.

We have taken you through a number of considerations that you might take into account when designing an experiment. To summarise, firstly, there is the use of *systematic controls* to ensure that all variables except the *IV* are equalised across treatment groups. This may take the form of standardising experimental conditions and instructions, matching subjects, counterbalancing for order effects. The point is that the experimenter is trying to think about all possible variables which might affect the results, and then make sure that they are equalised across all the experimental treatments.

The second method is *randomisation*. When you deal with variables by randomly allocating subjects to treatments, or by randomising the order in which conditions are presented, you are really leaving it to chance that extraneous variables will be likely to be more or less equally distributed among all the experimental treatments. It may sound as if this is a 'weaker' method than controlling variables, but it is simply impossible to control for all possible extraneous variables, by counterbalancing subjects, settings, order, and so on, either for practical reasons or because the experimenter does not know which of all possible variables might be affecting subjects' behaviour. By randomising across conditions, the assumption is that all variables, except the *IV*, will be distributed so as to make the various treatment groups comparable.

STQ48

1 State one advantage and one disadvantage of the within-subjects design.
2 Imagine an experiment designed to test memory for categorised lists of words (e.g. words like *lion*, *tiger*, *bear* are all ANIMALS), as opposed to lists of uncategorised words. What sort of experimental design would you plan, and why?

Research design

A research design is essentially a plan or strategy aimed at enabling answers to be obtained to research questions. In its simplest form, an experiment has three characteristics:

1 An *IV* is manipulated.
2 All other variables except the *IV* are controlled.
3 The effect of the manipulation of the *IV* on the *DV* is measured.

To the extent that the experiment is inappropriately conceived and therefore inappropriately designed, solutions to research questions will not be attained. Unfortunately, research is, and has been, conducted using designs that are inappropriate. Here are several basic but sound designs.

Post-test comparison with randomised subjects

This design exerts a control over subject variables because subjects are randomly assigned to the two groups. Only the experimental group is exposed to the experimental treatment.

If the obtained means of the two groups are significantly different (i.e. more different than would be expected on the basis of chance alone), the experimenter can be reasonably confident that the experimental conditions are responsible for the observed result.

The main advantage of this design is randomisation, which assures statistical equivalence of the groups prior to the introduction of the independent variable. As the number of subjects is increased, the likelihood that randomisation will produce equivalent groups is increased. The post-test comparison with randomised subjects controls for the main effects of history, maturation, and pre-testing; because no pre-test is used, there can be no interaction effect of pre-test and X. This design is especially recommended for situations in which pre-test reactivity is likely to occur. It is also useful in studies in which a pre-test is either not possible, for example, in studies with kindergarten or primary grades, where it is impossible to administer a pre-test since the learning is not yet manifest. Another advantage of this design is that it can be extended to include more than two groups if necessary.

This design can be increased in sensitivity by matching subjects on relevant variables prior to random assignment to groups of members in each pair. A tossed coin can be used for the random allocation.

FIGURE 10.3 *Post-test comparison (randomised)*

Randomised subjects	IV ⟶	Post-test
Experimental group	X	Y
Control group	—	Y

Compare

Pre-test and post-test comparison design with randomised subjects

This design enables change to be measured. In this design, random assignment into experimental and control groups, plus previous matching if necessary, ensures both groups are equivalent.

FIGURE 10.4 *Pre-test and post-test comparison (randomised)*

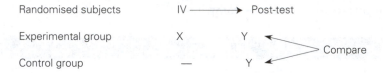

Random assignment	Pre-test	Treatment	Post-test	Compare
Control group	Y_1	⟶	Y_2	$Y_1 — Y_2$
				with
Experimental group	Y_1	⟶ X ⟶	Y_2	$Y_1 — Y_2$

Practice, learning, maturation and experimenter effects should be equally distributed in both groups, while matching and random assignment have ensured initial equality of the groups.

The average difference between the pre-test and post-test (Y_1–Y_2) is found for each group and then these average difference scores are compared in order to ascertain whether the experimental treatment produced a greater change than the control situation.

The significance of the difference in average changes (found when the average change for the control group is subtracted from the average change for the experimental group) is determined by an appropriate statistical test, such as the t-test.

The fact that the control group does not receive the experimental treatment does not mean that control subjects receive no experience at all. In research on teaching methods, the control group is generally taught by the traditional or usual procedure. In certain learning experiments, it is common practice to give the control group some kind of irrelevant activity between pre-test and post-test, while the experimental group is receiving specific training for the task. In an experiment on the effects of a particular drug, one would administer a placebo (such as a sugar pill) to the control group without letting them know that they were being treated differently from the experimental group.

The main concern in using the pre-test and post-test comparison design with randomised subjects is external validity. Although both experimental and control groups take the pre-test and may experience the sensitising effect, it can cause the experimental subjects to respond to the treatment in a particular way, just because of their increased sensitivity. The crucial question is: 'Would the effect of X on the experimental subjects be the same without the exposure to the pre-test?'. This problem has been particularly evident in studies of attitude change. When the first attitude scale is administered as the pre-test in a study, it can arouse interest or sensitise subjects to the issues of material included in the scale. Then re-test scores may reflect a component of this sensitisation.

Factorial designs

We have been considering so far the classical design in which an *IV* is manipulated with the effect measured on the *DV*. But in any research context, there can be a variety of variables interacting simultaneously. Such techniques as randomisation, matching, counterbalancing and standardisation have been discussed as ways of controlling the effects of variables. However, in some studies, the interaction effect is important. For example, particular teaching methods may have differential effects with pupils of different levels of IQ, so that Method A is effective with low IQ pupils and Method B with high IQ pupils. Similarly, changes in the *DV* may be effected by the interaction of sex, ethnic group, personality traits, family size, school size with the *IV*. By employing a factorial design, the effects of other variables (other *IV*s) can be determined. In essence, the researcher investigates the effect of the main *IV* at each level of one or more other attributes. This increases the precision of the findings and the validity and reliability of the research.

Factorial designs can be quite complex and the reader should consult more advanced texts for these.

Quasi-experimental designs

The goal of the experimenter is to use designs that provide full experimental control through the use of randomisation procedures. There are many situations in educational research in which it is not possible to conduct a true experiment. For instance, in research conducted in a classroom setting it may not be possible for the experimenter to assign subjects randomly to groups.

Non-randomised control group pre-test/post-test design

In a typical school situation, it is necessary to use groups as they are already organised into classes or other intact groups.

FIGURE 10.5 *Non-randomised design*

	Pre-test	IV	Post-test
Experimental group	Y_1	$\longrightarrow$ X $\longrightarrow$	Y_2
Control group	Y_1	$\longrightarrow$	Y_2

A researcher might conduct an experiment with the four parallel English classes of a high school. Because the classes meet at different times, subjects cannot be randomly assigned to treatments. However, the researcher can use a random procedure to determine which two sections will be *experimental* and which two will be *control*. Since both experimental and control groups take the same pre-tests and post-tests, and the experiment occupies the same time period for all subjects, it then follows that testing, instrumentation, maturation and mortality are not internal validity problems.

If the researcher teaches all four classes, history is not a problem. If the researcher only supervises the regular teachers who deliver the experimental and control treatments, differences among teachers can systematically influence results.

Another problem is the ceiling effect. Because no random allocation to groups occurs, the pre-test means can differ considerably. Thus any change measured on the post-test is constrained by how high one group scored initially.

For example, if the non-randomised control group pre-test/post-test design is used to compare the effects of two methods of maths instruction in which equivalent forms of a 100-item test are used as pre-test and post-test, and one group has a pre-test mean of 80 and the other a pre-test mean of 50, the ceiling effect would restrict the possible gain of the former more than the latter.

Demand characteristics

Researchers call the influence of an experimenter's expectations, or the subject's knowledge that an experiment is underway, *demand characteristics*. To the extent that the behaviour of research participants is controlled by demand characteristics instead of *IV*, experiments are invalid and cannot be generalised beyond the test situation.

A well-known example of a demand characteristic is the *Hawthorne effect*, named after the Western Electric Company plant where it was first observed. The company was interested in improving worker morale and productivity and conducted several experiments to improve the workers' environment (such as improved light, etc.). No matter what experimental manipulation was tried, worker productivity improved. The workers knew that they were in a 'special' group and therefore tried to do their best at all times. Thus, the demand characteristics were more important in determining the workers' productivity than the experimental manipulations.

The implication of this Hawthorne Effect can have a serious impact on educational experiments where, for example, the enthusiasm and interest of teachers and pupils engaged in an experiment on new teaching methods or new curricula content will produce results that show tremendous gains in performance. As the novelty wears off the Hawthorne Effect decreases. Therefore, studies should extend over a lengthy period of time when evaluating new methods and materials to ensure that the experimental effect is significant over time and not simply a manifestation of the Hawthorne Effect.

Orne (1962) has taken the position that volunteer subjects want to cooperate with the experimenter and be good subjects. To take such a position, the subject attempts to identify the hypothesis of the experiment from the available demand characteristics and acts in a manner that will support the hypothesis. Orne has gone to great lengths to demonstrate that subjects reveal tremendous persistence in this 'helping' behaviour. Orne found that subjects worked for five hours on summing two adjacent numbers presented on sheets of paper. Each sheet of paper contained 224 additions and the subject received 2000 sheets of paper. When subjects were questioned about their perseverance, they frequently hypothesised that the experiment was concerned with endurance.

Just knowing that one is being experimented on, and consequently observed, alters behaviour, regardless of one's attitudes or motivations about supporting or refuting the experimental hypothesis. Serving as a subject in an experiment is similar to being on stage or in front of a television camera. While in front of a television camera, most people do not act as they normally would, but produce behaviour that ranges from being silly to being stilted. Likewise, being in an experiment may generate behaviour that is more socially desirable, restrained, subdued or defiant. When such a tendency is coupled with behaviour controlled by the demand characteristics of an experiment, it is easy to see how results that are inaccurate can be produced.

Complete understanding of the behaviour of subjects in the experimental context is still lacking. All we can do at this point in time is to be aware of the problem, try to mitigate any possible negative attitudes by our interpersonal behaviour and rapport, and try not to use 'forced labour'.

Experimenter bias

Experimenters are not impersonal, anonymous people, all capable of identical observation and recording. Researchers too are human! They have attitudes, values, needs and motives which, try as they might, they cannot stop from contaminating their experiments. The researcher firstly has a motive for choosing and carrying out the particular study in the first place. He or she has certain expectations regarding the outcome. This is implicit if a sensible and critical review of previous work in the area has been carried out. The researcher would hence like to see their hypothesis confirmed. The experimenter, knowing about the hypothesis and projected outcome, is likely to provide unintended verbal and non-verbal cues which may be picked up by the subjects, thereby influencing their performances in the direction desired. Experimenters may themselves, therefore, be one of Orne's demand characteristics.

Attributes of the experimenter, such as age, sex, social class, ethnic group, warmth, dominance, need for social approval, etc., will to unknown degrees also influence the subjects' responses. The problem lies in the fact that these attributes have a different effect on each subject. It would be no problem if the influence of each attribute was identical for all subjects.

A further source of bias lies in the subjective interpretation of the obtained data. For example, the interpretation of the same twin study data on intelligence can be subject to wide divergence of opinion, which reflects the general philosophy of life of each person doing the interpreting.

But, as with subject bias, it is difficult to assess accurately experimenter bias or to find ways of eliminating it. Since experiments are generally conducted in social interaction contexts, all we can do at present is be aware of these sources of experimental error due to uncontrolled and possibly, in some cases, inherently uncontrollable variables.

STQ49

What do you feel are the main strengths and weaknesses of the experimental method?

STQ50

Consider an aspect of classroom behaviour in which you are interested, and think how you could investigate it with an experimental treatment, yet make it as 'real life' as possible.

summary

Research design tries to ensure that it is the manipulation of the *IV*, or the experimental effect, that produces the changes in the *DV* and not experimental error.

Experimental error can be systematic or random. The first distorts or biases results in a particular direction; the latter obscures results. Experimental error can result from sampling procedures, subject assignment, experimental conditions, measurement, experimenter bias and demand characteristics.

Reference

Orne, M. (1962), 'On the social psychology of the psychological experiment', *American Psychologist, 17*, 776–83.

Further reading

Rosenthal, R. (1966), *Experimenter Effects in Behavioural Research,* Appleton Century Crofts, New York.
Shaughnessy, J. & Zeichmeister, E. (1997), *Research Methods in Psychology,* McGraw Hill, Singapore.
Winer, B.J. (1971), *Statistical Principles in Experimental Design,* McGraw-Hill, New York.

part 2 | quantitative methods

Choosing statistical tests

11
eleven

There is a bewildering variety of statistical tests for almost every purpose. How do we pick an appropriate test from all those available? There is no hard-and-fast rule. Tests vary in the assumptions they make, their power, and the types of research design for which they are appropriate. The major considerations that influence the choice of test are reviewed below.

Parametric versus non-parametric tests

The functions of both kinds of test are identical. In both cases, an experimenter uses the tests to discover the probability that the results of the experiment occurred randomly by chance. On the basis of this, he or she can decide whether the chance probability is low enough to warrant rejecting the null hypothesis and accepting the experimental hypothesis. Which you use depends on whether your data satisfy the assumptions on which parametric tests are based.

Assumptions for parametric tests

Levels of measurement

Parametric tests require research data that can be treated as equal interval. So parametric tests should be restricted to 'naturally' numerical measures such as IQ scores, recall scores and reaction times. However, we often resort to allotting numbers to all sorts of scales and then assuming they are equal interval scales—for example, attitude scales—thereby allowing parametric procedures to be applied.

If the *DV* is ordinal (ranked) or nominal (categorical), then non-parametric tests are usually employed.

Distribution of scores

A second factor influencing the choice between parametric and non-parametric tests is the distribution of data. For a parametric test, data should be normally distributed or closely so. Extremely asymmetrical distributions should not be the basis for parametric testing.

Homogeneity of variance

The final assumption about the research data for use with parametric tests is that the amount of random, or error, variance should be equally distributed among the different experimental conditions. This goes back to the idea that all the variability due to variables which cannot be controlled should be equally distributed among experimental conditions by randomisation. The formal term for this is *homogeneity of variance*: the word 'homogeneity' simply indicates sameness; for example, that there should not be significantly different amounts of variance in the different conditions of the *IV*.

The normal procedure is for the experimenters to check for these three assumptions before using a parametric test. The point is that, if these theoretical assumptions are not met, then the probability you look for in a statistical table may not be the correct one. However, some statisticians have claimed that parametric tests are, in fact, relatively robust. This means that it is unlikely that the percentage probability will be very inaccurate unless your data do not meet the assumptions at all, i.e. are not on an interval scale and/or are distributed in a very asymmetrical fashion.

Tests which are appropriate for categorical data such as χ^2 or data in the form of ranks, such as the rank-order correlation *rho,* in general involve fewer assumptions than *t* or *F* tests. Many such tests do not specify conditions about the shape or character of the distribution of the population from which samples are drawn. Such tests are called *distribution free* or *non-parametric*.

In using distribution-free tests, we do not test hypotheses involving specific values of population parameters. This eliminates hypotheses involving values of M, σ or other descriptive parameters of population distributions.

Why use parametric tests?

By this time, you may wonder why, if all these complicated assumptions have to be met, one should ever use parametric tests at all. After all, non-parametric tests would give perfectly good estimates of the chance probabilities of obtaining experimental results. One major consideration needs to be taken into account—that of the power of the test.

The power of statistical tests

The term *power* refers to the sensitivity of a test; the extent to which it is likely to pick up any significant differences in scores which actually exist in the data. In this sense, the Wilcoxon is a less powerful test than the *t* test, because you are more likely to find a significant difference with a *t* test.

Parametric tests are considered to be more powerful because they not only take into account just the rank order of scores, but are also able to calculate variances. It has been argued, therefore, that parametric tests are more powerful than non-parametric tests at picking up significant differences.

We are less likely to reject a false null hypothesis with a non-parametric or distribution-free test than we are with a parametric test.

In testing statistical hypotheses where more than one test seems appropriate, we should choose the most powerful of the available tests.

However, there has been a lot of argument about this question of the relative power of tests among statisticians. Not all of them agree that parametric tests are much more powerful than non-parametric tests, and moreover, rank-ordering methods and equations for non-parametric tests are equally quicker and easier to compute.

Type of hypothesis

We saw in chapter 7 that hypotheses in educational research are very often tested from estimates of population differences on some variable; for example, whether children who attend pre-school play groups differ from children who did not attend play groups in social development on entry to infant school. But at other times, a hypothesis can state explicitly that one variable, say perceptual rigidity, is associated with another variability, say anxiety, among children. In general terms, therefore, we can distinguish two types of hypothesis in educational research:

• difference hypotheses between samples;
• hypotheses of association (or correlation) between variables.

Type of experimental design in hypotheses of differences

1 Using same subjects for different experimental conditions (within-subjects design) *or* using different subjects for different experimental conditions but making sure that the people in each condition are matched on some relevant criterion (matched-pairs design which can be treated statistically as if it were a within-subjects design).

The tests of statistical significance we apply to each type of hypothesis are different. In the case of different hypotheses, we employ a test of significance of the difference between two or more values of a statistic. On the other hand, in testing a hypothesis of association, we apply a statistical test of association or relationship between the variables.

2 Using different, non-matched subjects for each experimental condition (between-subjects design).

There are different statistical tests which should be used for within-subjects and between-subjects designs.

TABLE 11.1 *Relative merits of parametric and non-parametric tests*

Disadvantages	Advantages
Non-parametric tests	
1 Because non-parametric tests only look at the effects of single variables in isolation, they ignore a lot of the complexity of human behaviour.	They can be used for investigating the effects of single variables, and when your experimental data do not meet the three assumptions.
2 Because they make use of nominal data or rank ordering rather than exact calculations of variance, they may have slightly less power, in that they are less likely to pick up significant differences.	They are particularly useful when measurement is at only a nominal or ordinal level.
3	Most of the calculations are extremely easy and quick.
Parametric tests	
1 The experimental data have to meet the three assumptions of interval measurement, normal distribution, and homogeneity of variance.	They enable you to analyse interactions between two or more variables.
2 The mathematical calculations are somewhat more complicated.	They may be more 'powerful' at picking up significant differences.

Levels of data

The data may be nominal, ordinal, interval or ratio. The level of data obtained influences the choice of test.

To conclude therefore, in evaluating techniques of statistical analysis, you determine:

- Whether the statistics employed are appropriate for the type of data available.
- Whether the test employed is appropriate for the type of hypothesis being tested.
- Whether the test employed is suitable for the design.
- Whether the assumptions involved in the test are realistic.

Figure 11.1 is a guide to the selection of the correct statistical test.

Degrees of freedom

In using some statistical tables to evaluate the obtained statistic, we need to know the degrees of freedom for the particular sample rather than N. Why do we use degrees of freedom or 'df' as they are symbolised?

FIGURE 11.1 *Choosing your test flow chart*

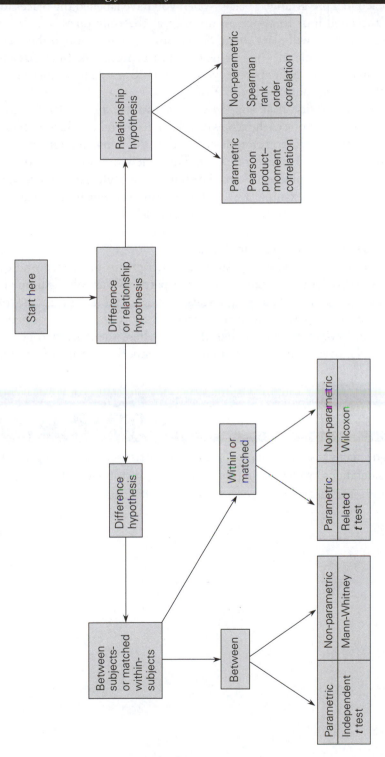

Imagine that you are holding a dinner party for twelve people. You wish to seat them round a table each in a pre-arranged place. When you have labelled the places for eleven of the guests, the twelfth or final person must sit at the only place left. We have no 'freedom' about where we will place them. So we can say that although there are twelve people (N) there are only eleven (N − 1) degrees of freedom. The final place is always determined, no matter how many people we are trying to seat. This principle applies in statistics, whether we are concerned with X or M.

Let us consider X and M first of all. Suppose we have a sample size N = 10. The mean value can be calculated and all but one of the scores can be altered to other values without altering the mean. One score's value is, however, determined by the remaining nine because of the necessity that their total scores sum to N × M. Thus one score is not free to vary, but is controlled by what the other nine values are. The number of degrees of freedom are one less than N, or N − 1. In another example if we had three numbers, which sum to 24 and hence a mean of 8, with two of the numbers known, for example 10 and 6, then the third is fixed, for example 8. If we alter the 10 to 11 and the 6 to 7 then we have determined that the third must be 6 if the ΣX and M are to remain the same.

In experiments with two groups of subjects, each group must lose one degree of freedom. To show this, let us return to our dinner party. We are old-fashioned enough to try to seat men and women in alternate seats round the table. In this case, once you had seated five men and five women, everyone would know where the last man and the last woman would have to sit. This is like the case where there are two groups of six subjects, N_1 and N_2. In fact, for each group there are only five degrees of freedom ($N_1 - 1$ and $N_2 - 1$).

summary

A range of considerations govern the appropriateness of any statistical test for a particular study. The major considerations involve assumptions about the distribution of the data, types of hypothesis used, research design employed and the level of the data.

Power and
effect size

12
twelve

So far in this book we have focused strongly on the concept of statistical significance and p values as being extremely important when interpreting conclusions from research. However, they can also be misused and can lead to misleading interpretations:

1 The play of chance can make it appear that a worthless treatment has in fact worked, causing the importance of minor findings to be inflated in the researcher's mind if they hit the threshold of significance.

2 Of more concern is the way important information is overlooked in studies that fall short of significance. It is almost as if a study that does not reach significance is worthless. In fact, most never get published and much interesting work and findings which could be the basis of further investigation are lost for ever. Thus, focusing too heavily on significance can have a major effect on the development of cumulative knowledge.

3 Dividing research findings into two categories—significant and not significant—is a gross oversimplification, since probability is a continuous scale. A rich data set reduced to a binary accept–reject statement may lead to false conclusions due to naturally occurring sampling error, even when using appropriate sampling methods in a rigorous way.

4 A vital yet often ignored question in statistical analysis is—are my findings of any real substance? We are usually asking one of three things:

- Is this a theoretically important issue?; or
- Is this issue one of social relevance?; or
- Will the results of this study actually help people?

While statistics can help to quantify the strength of the findings of the research, none of these questions are essentially statistical. This is due to confusion over the word 'significance', as it has a different meaning within statistics from that in normal daily use. This leads us frequently to imply and believe that even in a statistical context it also has the same implications as found in the normal sense of the word. However, by now you should have fully grasped the idea that statistical significance only means that you can be confident that your results are unlikely to be a random variation in samples (sampling error) but signify differences and relationships which rarely occur by chance, and that therefore the findings reflect real differences and relationships.

But it can happen, perhaps more frequently than we might suspect, that a statistically significant result has *little significance* whatsoever in the everyday sense. If we focus too much on statistical significance it can blind us to the dangers of exaggerating the importance of our findings.

Thus, researchers are now realising that there is more to the story of a research result than p < .05, or ns. This chapter will help you become sophisticated about other ways of interpreting research results. This sophistication means learning about three closely interrelated issues: power, effect size, and types of error.

Type I and Type II errors

You met these types of error earlier (see chapter 7). This kind of error is concerned with how conclusions from hypothesis testing can be incorrect. Error as a statistical concept is *not* about making mistakes in calculations, or even about using the wrong procedures. It *is* about how, even when we do everything properly, we can still be led to the wrong conclusion. Let us revise our understanding of Type I and Type II errors as they are vital to understanding why our conclusions about our results can be wrong.

Type I error

Suppose you conducted a study and set the significance level cut-off at a high probability level, say 20% or p = 0.2. This level would enable you to reject the null hypothesis very easily. If you conducted many studies like this you would often believe (about 20 per cent of the time) that you had support for the research hypothesis when you did not. This is called a Type I error. Even when we set the probability at .05 or .01 we can still sometimes make a Type I error because we will obtain a chance result at and beyond that level for 5 per cent or 1 per cent of the time, but we never know which occasion it is.

Imagine a study where stress management techniques have been taught to 100 teachers with the intention of reducing teacher absenteeism through stress-related health problems. Suppose the special instructions in reality made no difference. However, in doing the study the researchers just happened to pick a sample of 100 teachers to receive the instructions who were generally not the stressed-out sort anyway. This would lead to rejection of the null hypothesis and a conclusion that the special instructions do make a difference. This decision to reject the null hypothesis would be a mistake—a Type I error. (Note that the researchers could not know that they have made an error of this kind.) Type I errors are of serious concern to social scientists, who could construct entire theories and research programs, not to mention practical applications, based on a conclusion from hypothesis testing that is, in fact, mistaken.

Since researchers cannot tell when they have made a Type I error, what they can do is try to conduct studies so that the chance of making a Type I error is as small as possible. What is the chance of making a Type I error? It is the same as the significance level we set. If we set the significance level at $p < .05$ we are saying we will reject the null hypothesis if there is less than a 5 per cent (.05) chance that we could have obtained our result if the null hypothesis were true. When rejecting the null hypothesis in this way, we are still allowing up to 5 per cent chance that the null hypothesis is actually true. That is, we are allowing a 5 per cent chance of a Type I error. The problem is that we never know when our seemingly 'significant' result is simply due to sampling error. Because of this, and the fact that the significance level is the same as the chance of making a Type I error, the lower we set the significance level, the smaller the chance of a Type I error. Researchers who do not want to take a lot of risk set the significance level much lower than .05, such as $p < .01$ or $p < .001$. In this way, the result of a study has to be very extreme to lead to a conclusion to reject the null hypothesis.

The use of a .001 significance level is like buying insurance against making a Type I error. However, as when buying insurance, the better the protection, the higher the cost. What is the cost in setting the significance level at too extreme a level? It is the Type II error!!

Type II error

If you set a very stringent significance level, such as .001, there is a different kind of risk. You may conduct a study where in reality the research hypothesis is true, but the result does not come out extremely enough to reject the null hypothesis. Thus, the error you would make is in not rejecting the null hypothesis when the reality is that the null hypothesis is false (that the research hypothesis is true). This is the *Type II error*.

Consider again our study of teacher absence through stress. Suppose that, in reality, practising stress management does improve their attendance records. However, in conducting your particular study, the random sample that you selected to try this out on happened to include many teachers who were already too stressed to manage the stress reduction exercises properly. Even though your procedure may have helped somewhat, their attendance records may still be lower than the average of all teachers. The results would not be significant. The decision not to reject the null hypothesis would constitute a Type II error.

Type II errors especially concern social scientists who are interested in practical applications, because a Type II error could mean that a useful theory or practical procedure is not implemented. As with a Type I error, we never know when we have made a Type II error; however, we can try to conduct our studies so as to reduce the probability of making a Type II error. One way of buying insurance against a Type II error is to set a more lenient significance level, such as $p < .10$. In this way, even if a study results in only a very small difference, the results have a good chance of being significant. There is a cost to this insurance policy too—a Type I error. The trade-off between these two conflicting concerns usually is resolved by compromise, hence the standard 5 per cent and 1 per cent significance levels.

STQ51*

Briefly explain why protecting against one type of error increases the chance of making the other.
Answer on p. 599.

The power of a statistical test

Inferential statistics are designed to help you determine the validity of the null hypothesis. Consequently, you want your statistics to detect differences in your data that are inconsistent with the null hypothesis. *The power of a statistical test is its ability to detect these differences if the research hypothesis is true.* Put in statistical terms, power is the ability of a statistic to correctly reject the null hypothesis when it is false. (If the research hypothesis is false, we certainly do not want significant results—that would be a Type I error). A powerful statistic is more sensitive than a less powerful one to detect differences in your data.

The issue of the power of your statistical test is an important one. Rejection of the null hypothesis implies that your independent variable affected your dependent variable. Failure to reject the null hypothesis may lead you to abandon a potentially fruitful line of research. Consequently, you want to be reasonably sure your failure to reject the null hypothesis is not caused by a lack of power in your statistical test.

Now you may ask, 'If the research hypothesis is true in reality, won't the experiment necessarily give a significant result?'. Unfortunately the answer is no, because the effect of the independent variable on the particular representative sample that happens to be selected from the population may not be large enough to reject the null hypothesis. It might well be more effective on another random sample. This variation in effect is due to sampling error. Because we only usually conduct a study once and accept the result as common for all similar samples, we are blithely unaware of the true state of affairs. This is why meta-analysis (chapter 21) is becoming so important, as this technique enables the combination of replications of the same study—some successful and others unsuccessful in rebutting the null hypothesis—to find the overall general effect or trend. *The power of a statistical test is the probability of making a correct rejection of the null hypothesis when it is false.*

Statistical power is important for two reasons:

- Calculating power when planning a study helps determine how many participants you need.
- Understanding power is extremely important to anyone who reads research articles (for example, in making sense of results that are not significant, or results that are statistically but not practically significant).

EXAMPLE

Consider again our example of the effects of teaching stress management techniques to 100 teachers. In the hypothesis testing process, we compare two groups:

1 The experimental group: Teachers receiving stress management techniques
2 The control group: Teachers not receiving stress management techniques

The research hypothesis (one-tailed) is that the experimental group (Exp Gp) would record significantly higher attendance records than the control group (Con Gp). The null hypothesis is that the Exp Gp will not record significantly different attendance records from the Con Gp. The top distribution in Figure 12.1 shows the situation in which the research hypothesis is true. The bottom distribution shows the distribution for the Con Gp. Because we are interested in means of samples of 100 individuals, both distributions are distributions of means. The means are number of days in attendance.

FIGURE 12.1 *Comparison distributions*

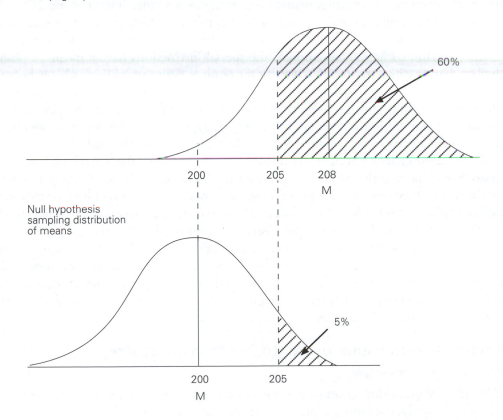

The bottom distribution is also the comparison distribution; the distribution of means that you would expect for both populations if the null hypothesis were true. The shaded part of the right tail of this bottom distribution is the area in which you would reject the null hypothesis if, as a result of your study, the mean of your sample was in this area. The shaded rejection area begins at 205 days of attendance (a Z score of 1.64), taking up 5 per cent of this comparison distribution (one-tailed test).

The top curve in the figure is the distribution of means for the Exp Gp. This is the distribution of means for the population receiving special instructions. If the null hypothesis is true, the distribution for Exp Gp would be the same as the distribution based on Con Gp, and would not be set off to the right as we have shown in Figure 12.1—the situation in which the research hypothesis is actually true (a statistically significant higher average attendance record). Specifically, the upper distribution of means is shown with a mean of 208 (whereas the comparison distribution's mean is only 200). This is to show that the population receiving the stress management techniques has, on the average, eight days higher annual attendance.

In this example, this upper distribution of means (from the researchers' prediction about Exp Gp) appears to the right of the comparison distribution. That is, the researchers obtained an increase in scores (8 points), so the mean of the upper distribution is to the right of the lower one. This picture tells us that there is a good chance that many means selected from this upper distribution will be to the right of the lower distribution to reject the null hypothesis. Our experimental mean is significant since it lies beyond 205. The power to reject is 60 per cent—the shaded area of the curve beyond 205. This study then had high power to produce a significant result when the research hypothesis was true.

In a situation where those who got the special instructions have a mean 15 points higher than teachers in general, a significant result is even more likely. This is because there is more of the top curve beyond the 5 per cent shaded area on the comparison distribution. In fact, the probability of obtaining a significant result (the power) for a mean of 15 points higher is 86 per cent. In any study, the bigger the difference we obtain between the means of the two populations, the more power in the study.

Overall, the general principle is that the less overlap between the two distributions, the more likely that a study will give a significant result. Two distributions might have little overlap, either because there is a large difference between their means or because they have so little variance (SD^2) that even with a small mean difference they do not overlap much.

The extent to which the two populations do not overlap is called the *effect size* because it is the extent to which the experimental manipulation has an effect of separating the two populations. That is, the larger the difference between the two population means, the greater the effect size; the smaller the variance within the two populations, the greater the effect size. The greater the effect size, the greater the power. We will be considering effect size in detail later in the chapter.

Factors that influence power (other than effect size)

Increasing sample size

The other major influence on power, besides effect size, is the number of people in the sample. Basically, the more people in the study, the more power. Sample size influences power because the larger the sample size, the smaller the standard deviation of the distribution of means. If the distributions have a smaller standard deviation, they are narrower and thus there is less overlap between them. If our teacher stress management example included 200 teachers instead of the 100 in the original example, the power moves up from 60 per cent to 85 per cent. With 500 participants in the study, power is 99 per cent.

In most practical cases, sample size is the main way to modify a study to bring it up to sufficient power. However, there is always a limit to what you can handle in terms of time and cost as well as the availability of more subjects.

The power of your statistical test increases with the size of your sample because larger samples provide more stable estimates of population parameters. In particular, the standard error of the means from your treatments will be lower, so the likely population means fall within narrower confidence limits. Consequently, it is easier to detect small differences in population means and thus to reject the null hypothesis when it is false.

Correlation causes a major problem with sample size. For example, even a small correlation can be statistically significant given a large enough sample. A correlation of 0.81 is needed to be statistically significant at the 5 per cent level with a sample size of 6. However, a sample size of 100 requires only a correlation of 0.20 to be statistically significant at the 5 per cent level. The squared correlation coefficient (sometimes called the coefficient of determination) indicates the proportion of the total variance shared by two variables (see p. 239). If the correlation is only 0.20, then $r^2 = 0.04$, i.e. the two variables only have 4 per cent of their variance in common. This is negligible, yet in a statistical sense it is significant, because of the large sample from which it was derived. In a similar but less dramatic way, you can see by inspecting the table of t (Table 13.1), that as sample size increases, so the t value needed for significance decreases.

What all this indicates is that if you include enough subjects, you could conceivably find statistical significance in even the most minute and trivial of relationships or differences. Consequently, your sample should be large enough to be sensitive to differences or relationships, but not so large as to produce significant but trivial results. Thus, sample size is the major factor which researchers can control to affect the power of the statistical analyses they use to analyse their experiments.

Increasing the predicted difference between population means—changing the design of a study

A researcher cannot just arbitrarily predict a bigger difference. In some cases, however, it is possible to change the way the study is done so that the researcher has reason to expect a larger mean difference. Consider again our example of the experiment about the impact of stress management techniques on teachers' attendance records. One way to increase the expected mean difference might be to make the techniques more elaborate—spending more time on workshop demonstrations and practice, and so forth. A disadvantage of this approach is that it can be difficult or costly.

The design of a study can increase the power to detect significant differences. For example, the use of repeated measures experiments keeps error variation generally smaller in repeated measures experiments than in independent designs because individual differences have been removed (see p. 140). The smaller error variation leads to an increased ability to detect small treatment effects in an experiment. And that is just what the power of a statistical analysis is—the ability to detect small treatment effects when they are present.

Decreasing the population standard deviation

It is possible to decrease the population standard deviation in a planned study in at least two ways. One way is to do the study using a population that is less diverse than the one originally planned. With the teacher stress example, you might only use teachers in a particular city school system rather than a wider sample. The disadvantage is that the results apply only to the more limited population.

Another way to decrease the population standard deviation is to use conditions of testing that are more stable, and measures that are more precise. For example, testing under a standardised situation or in a controlled laboratory setting usually produces smaller overall variation among scores in results (meaning a smaller standard deviation). Similarly, using tests with clear instructions and clear procedures for marking answers also reduces variation. When practical, rigour is an excellent way to increase power.

Using a less stringent level of significance

As we discussed earlier, the level of significance used should be the least stringent that reasonably protects against Type I error—normally, this will be .05. It is rare that much can be done to improve power in this way. Less extreme significance levels (such as .10) mean more power, and more extreme significance levels (.01 or .001) mean less power to produce significant differences. Less extreme means more power because when the significance level is not very extreme (such as .10), the rejection area for the null hypothesis is bigger. More extreme means less power because when the significance level is more extreme (such as .01), the rejection region is smaller.

Using a one-tailed test

Whether you use a one- or a two-tailed test depends on the logic of the hypothesis being studied and it is rare that you have much of a choice about this factor. A two-tailed test is less powerful than a one-tailed test. This can be easily demonstrated by looking at the critical values of t found in Table 13.1. At 20 degrees of freedom, the critical value at $p = 0.05$ for a one-tailed test is 1.73. For a two-tailed test, the critical value is 2.09. It is thus easier to reject the null hypothesis with the one-tailed test than with the two-tailed test. Using a two-tailed test makes it harder to get significance on any one tail. Thus, keeping everything else the same, power is less with a two-tailed test than with a one-tailed test.

Role of power when planning a study

Determining power is very important when planning a study. If the power of a planned study is low, this means that even if the research hypothesis is true, this study is not likely to give significant results in support of it (Type II error). The time and expense of carrying out the study would probably not be worthwhile. What is an acceptable level of power? Cohen (1992) suggests that ordinarily a study should have 80 per cent power to be worth conducting. Obviously, the more power the better, but costs of greater power, such as increasing sample size, often make even 80 per cent power beyond one's reach.

How can one increase the level of power of a planned study? The power of a planned study can, in principle, be increased by changing any of the factors summarised above and shown in Table 12.1 below.

TABLE 12.1 *Factors that influence power*

Feature of the study	Factor increasing power	Factor decreasing power
Effect size	Large effect size	Small effect size
Predicted difference between population means	Large differences	Small differences
Population standard deviation	Small population SD	Large population SD
Sample size (N)	Large N	Small N
Significance level (alpha)	Lenient (such as .05 or even .10)	Stringent (such as .01 or even .001)
One-tailed versus two-tailed test	One-tailed	Two-tailed

Importance of power in evaluating the results of a study

We have learned that a study with a larger effect size is more likely to come out significant. It also is possible for a study with a very small effect size to come out significant if the study has reasonable power due to other factors; especially a large sample size. Consider a study in which of all students in a region who take a particular test, a sample of 1000 who are all born under a specified star sign, say Gemini, are randomly selected. Suppose that their mean score is 152, compared to the mean 150 (SD = 20) for the entire population. This result would be significant at the .01 level. However, its effect size is a minuscule 0.1. That is, the significance test tells us that we can be quite confident that the population of students born under Gemini have significantly higher scores than the general population of students. The effect size (or just looking at the mean difference) makes it clear that this difference is not very important. The distributions of the two populations overlap so much that it would be of little use in any individual case to know under what star sign a person has been born.

The message here is that in evaluating a study you must consider first whether the result is statistically significant. If it is, and if the study has any potential practical implications, you must then *also* consider whether the effect size is sufficiently large to make the result useful or interesting. If the sample is small, you can assume that a significant result is probably also practically significant. If the sample size is very large, you must consider the effect size directly, as it is quite possible in such a case that the effect is too small to be useful.

Note that the implications are a bit of a paradox in light of what most people believe about sample size. Most people assume that the more people in the study, the more important the result. In a sense, just the reverse is the case. All other things being equal, if a study with only a few people manages to be significant, that significance must be due to a large effect size. A study with a large number of people in it that is statistically significant may or may not have a large effect size.

Because the business of inferential statistics is to allow you to decide whether or not to reject the null hypothesis, the issue of power is important. You want to be reasonably sure that your decision is correct. Failure to achieve statistical significance in your study (thus, not rejecting the null hypothesis) can be caused by many of the above factors. Your independent variable actually may have no effect, or your experiment may have been carried out so poorly that the effect was buried in error variance. Or, maybe your statistic simply was not powerful enough to detect the difference, or you did not use enough subjects.

STQ52*

What is the effect of each of the following on the power of a study?
a   A larger predicted difference between the means of the populations
b   A larger population standard deviation
c   A larger sample size
d   Using a more stringent significance level
e   Using a two-tailed instead of a one-tailed test.

Answers on p. 599.

Calculating statistical power

When planning a study, the main reason researchers calculate power is to help them decide how many people they need to include in the study. That is, since sample size is an important influence on power, a researcher wants to be sure to have enough subjects for the study to have fairly high power. To help researchers, statisticians such as Cohen (1988; 1992) and Keppel (1991) have prepared special tables that tell you how many participants you need in a study to have a high level of power, given a certain effect size. Simplified versions of such tables for each of the main hypothesis testing procedures you will be learning are provided in the relevant chapters of this text (see chapters 13, 14, 15, 16 and 19).

It is very important that you understand what power is about, especially understanding the factors that affect the power of a study and how to use power when planning a study and when making sense of a study you read. For all practical purposes, sample size is the primary factor that researchers can use to control power.

Effect size

What a statistically significant *t* test does *not* tell us is how large an effect the independent variable had. Measures of effect size are used to determine the strength of the relationship between the independent and dependent variables. That is, measures of effect size reflect how large the effect of an independent variable was.

From the discussion above, it is obvious that we need something other than an inferential statistics test to measure the size of the effect of an independent variable. What is needed to measure effect size is an indicator that reflects the strength of the relationship between the independent and the dependent variables that is *independent of sample size*. Several measures of effect size meet these criteria (Keppel 1991).

What is effect size?

This is the *degree* to which the phenomenon is present in the population. There are several ways of estimating effect size. The more frequent effect size estimates are:

- the standardised mean difference (*d*);
- correlation coefficients such as r and phi (see p. 263); and
- eta^2. This is a type of correlation known as the correlation ratio. It is used for determining the strength of association when there is a curvilinear rather than a linear relationship. For non-linear relationships in which the correlation is not equal to zero, eta^2 fits the points by a curved line.

Effect size conventions

It is difficult to know how big an effect to expect before we do a study. In fact, if we knew, we would not need to do the research. Cohen (1992) has come up with some effect size conventions based on the effects observed in many actual studies. These conventions at least tell us what to consider as small, medium, and large effects.

Cohen recommends that we should think of a 'small effect size' as about 0.2, and notes that with an effect size of 0.2 the populations of individuals overlap by about 85 per cent. This small effect size of 0.2 is, for example, the difference in height between 15- and 16-year-old girls, which is about a half-inch difference with a standard deviation of about 2.1 inches.

Cohen considers a medium effect size to be 0.5, which means an overlap of about 67 per cent. This is about the difference in heights between 14- and 18-year-old girls. Finally, he defines a large effect size as 0.8. This is only about 53 per cent overlap. It is about the difference in height between 13- and 18-year-old girls.

Consider another example. Most IQ tests have a standard deviation of 15 points. An experimental procedure that had a small effect size would mean an increase of 3.0 IQ points. (A difference of 3.0 IQ points between the mean of the population who go through the experimental procedure and the population that does not, divided by the population standard deviation of 15; 3.0 divided by 15 comes out to 0.2.) An experimental procedure with a medium effect size would increase IQ by 8 points. An experimental procedure with a large effect size would increase IQ by 12 points.

Cohen's conventions are extremely important to researchers because in most research situations it is quite difficult to know in advance how big an effect size to predict. (Without being able to predict an effect size, one cannot even look up the power on a table.) Sometimes researchers can base their predictions of effect size on previous research or theory. Also, sometimes a smallest effect size would matter for some practical purpose.

In most cases, researchers are studying something for the first time, and they can only make the vaguest guess about the amount of effect they expect. Cohen's conventions help researchers turn that vague guess into a number.

Estimating effect size

Standardised mean difference for two groups (usually experimental and control) or *d*

One commonly used measure of effect size in experimental research is called *d*. It is a ratio that measures the difference between the means for the levels of the independent variable relative to the within-group standard deviation. There are several alternative but mathematically equivalent formulae for computing *d* depending on the original statistic calculated for the significance test. The most common two for the independent *t* test (see p. 175) are :

$$d = \frac{M_{experimental} - M_{control}}{\text{pooled within group SD}}$$

or

$$d = t\sqrt{\frac{N_1 + N_2}{N_1 N_2}}$$

The pooled within group's SD $= \sqrt{\frac{(N_1 - 1)SD_2^1 + (N_2 - 1)SD_2^2}{N_1 + N_2 - 2}}$

For the paired sample test (see p. 198):

$$d = \frac{t}{\sqrt{N}}$$

As you already know, the standard deviation tells us approximately how far, on the average, scores vary from a group mean. It is a measure of the 'dispersal' of scores around a mean and, in the case of the within-group standard deviation, tells us about the degree of 'error' due to individual differences (i.e., how individuals vary in their responses).

The standard deviation serves as a useful measure by which we can assess a difference between means. The 'size' of the effect of the independent variable, in other words, is always in terms of the average dispersal of scores occurring in an experiment. If there is substantial within-group variability (i.e. the within-group standard deviation is large), then the difference between, for instance, two means must be greater to produce the same effect size than when there is little within-group variability (i.e. the standard deviation is small). Because effect sizes are presented in standard deviation units, they can be used to make meaningful comparisons of effect sizes across experiments using different dependent variables.

The conventional levels of effect size are used to interpret d values with each expressed in quantitative terms and regardless of sign, i.e.:

d of .80 = large effect
d of .50 = medium effect
d of .20 = small effect

Here is a simple example:

1 Compute mean for experimental group: $M = \dfrac{20 + 14 + 17 + 21}{4} = 18$

2 Compute mean for control group: $M = \dfrac{16 + 15 + 12 + 12 + 14 + 15}{6} = 14$

3 Compute pooled $SD^2 = 5.5$

4 Compute pooled $SD = \sqrt{5.5} = 2.34$

5 Compute $d = \dfrac{M_{experimental} - M_{control}}{2.34} = \dfrac{18 - 14}{2.34} = 1.71$

6 To interpret our value of $d = 1.71$, use the following classification of effect sizes:
　　$d = .20$ for a small effect size,
　　$d = .50$ for a medium effect size, and
　　$d = .80$ for a large effect size.

7 Because our value of d is larger than .80, we would conclude that the independent variable had a large effect on test performance.

We are only concerned with one population's SD, because in hypothesis testing we usually assume that both populations have the same or similar standard deviation.

In the teacher stress example in Figure 12.1 that we began with, the difference between the two population means is 8, and the standard deviation of the populations of individuals is 24. Thus, the effect size is:

$$\text{Effect size} = \frac{\text{Population M}_1 - \text{Population M}_2}{\text{Population SD}} \quad \frac{208 - 200}{48} = \frac{8}{24} = .33$$

If the mean difference had been 15 points and the population standard deviation was still 24, the effect size would be virtually doubled: 15/24, or .63. By dividing the difference between means by the standard deviation of the population of individuals, we standardise the difference between means in the same way that a Z score gives a standard for comparison to other scores—even scores on different scales.

STQ53*

Here is information about several different versions of a planned study, each involving a single sample. (This assumes the researcher can affect the population standard deviation and predicted mean by changing procedures.) Calculate the effect size for each study.

(continued)

| | Population 1 Control group | | Population 2 Experimental group |
	M	SD	M
a	90	4	91
b	90	4	92
c	90	4	94
d	90	4	86
e	90	2	91
f	90	1	91
g	90	2	92
h	90	2	94
i	90	2	86

Answers on p. 599.

Correlation coefficient method

r = Pearson product–moment correlation coefficient for the two groups. This is an effect size in itself and if this is not reported, it can be computed quite easily for most other statistical tests, basically by turning the statistic into a correlation. Once this is done, it makes it easy to assess the size of the effect.

For a t test

$$r = \sqrt{\frac{t_2}{t^2 + df}} \quad \text{or}$$

$r = \sqrt{\frac{Z}{N}}$ where Z is the Z value of the reported p-value and N is the sample size.

We can also turn a d into an r:

The relation between r and d is: $r = \sqrt{\dfrac{d}{\dfrac{d^2 + 1}{pq}}}$

where p is the proportion of cases in the first group and q = 1 – p

Again, we use the same effect size levels so that when r = 0, there is no difference between the two groups; if near ± 0.2 is small; near ± 0.5 is medium; while near ± 0.8 is large. Large effect sizes obtained under natural (less controlled) situations are more impressive than under strictly controlled situations.

For chi square

Other statistics can be turned into correlations too. A two-by-two chi square (see p. 221) can be turned into a correlation using r_{phi} in the following formula. r_{phi} is the Pearson r for frequency scores.

$$r_{phi} = \sqrt{\frac{\text{chi square}}{N}} \quad \text{where N is the number of subjects}$$

The result can be interpreted as though it were a correlation. It is always positive because chi square is always positive. If your chi square is larger than two-by-two, you can use the contingency coefficient instead. Here the formula is:

$$\text{contingency coefficient} = \sqrt{\frac{\text{chi square}}{\text{chi square} + N}}$$

It is feasible to interpret the contingency coefficient as though it were r, although they are not exactly parallel.

For the Mann-Whitney test

For non-parametric tests such as Mann-Whitney (see p. 189), an approximation has to be done to calculate a biserial correlation (see p. 260). One procedure is to determine the significance level for the Mann-Whitney and then look up what the value of the t test would be for that same significance level and sample size. For example, with U of 40 significant at the 5% level on a sample of 26, we consult the t table and find the value of t which would be significant at the 5% level on a sample of 26 (df = 24) The tabled value of t is 2.064. This value is then substituted into the formula:

$$r_{bis} = \sqrt{\frac{t_2}{t_2 + df}}$$

To compute the effect size from analysis of variance (ANOVA—see chapter 19), a correlation measure termed eta^2 is employed. This is analogous to a correlation but describes a curvilinear relationship rather than a linear one. It is used with the various forms of ANOVA because it is difficult to ascertain which of the independent variables is explaining the most variance.

To calculate eta^2 for any of the independent variables in an ANOVA the following formula is used:

$$eta^2 = \frac{(\text{treatment df})(\text{F ratio})}{(\text{treatment df})(\text{F ratio}) + \text{within df}}$$

Importance of effect size

- Measures of effect size can be used to summarise a series of experiments that have included the same independent variable or dependent variable (see chapter 21 on meta-analysis). This allows for a quantitative comparison of the outcomes across the series of experiments. For example, effect size can be used to find out whether a particular independent variable consistently had about the same amount of impact across the experiments, irrespective of sample sizes, different means and variances. This comparison is especially important in applied research examining the effectiveness of treatments such as an educational innovation or a new approach to psychotherapy.

- Measures of effect size provide information about the *amount* of impact an independent variable has had. Thus, they complement tests of statistical significance which give only *an indication of the presence or absence of an effect of an independent variable*. In this way, we can use measures of effect size to rank several independent variables within the same experiment as one indication of the relative importance of the independent variables.

  Within a particular study, our general knowledge of what is a small or a large effect size helps us evaluate the overall importance of a result. For example, a result may be significant but not very large; or a result that is not significant (perhaps due to a small sample) may have just as large an effect size as was found in another study (perhaps one with a larger sample) in which the result was significant.
- Effect size helps us calculate the sample size needed for a study with a particular level of power.

As noted above, an important development in statistics in recent years is a procedure called *meta-analysis* (chapter 21). This is a procedure that combines results from different studies—even results using different methods of measurement—to draw general conclusions. *When combining results, the crucial thing being combined is the effect sizes*. For example, a sociologist might be interested in the effects of ethnically mixed classrooms on prejudice, a topic on which there has been a large number of surveys. Using meta-analysis, the sociologist could combine the results of these surveys. This would provide an overall effect size. It also would tell the researcher how effect size differs for studies done in different countries or about prejudice towards different ethnic groups.

None of the important questions addressed using effect size can be answered using such statistics as *t* ratios, F ratios or p values obtained when inferential statistics tests are conducted. Nonetheless, measures of effect size and inferential statistics tests are complementary. For example, measures of effect size are more informative than are p values in helping researchers determine the substantive importance of experimental outcomes. At times, we want to know just how much of an 'effect' our treatment had, not just whether it reached a conventionally acceptable level of significance. Knowing the answer in terms of effect size may help us decide whether to actually implement this treatment in an applied setting. For example, the original work by Smith, Glass and Miller (1980) on psychotherapy outcome studies found an average effect size of r = 0.32. For those unaware of the meaning of effect size, the finding was viewed as confirmation of the failure of psychotherapy. However, an effect size of this magnitude is equivalent to increasing the success rate from 36 per cent to 66 per cent; an effect that is quite large and of course for those undergoing therapy, quite important. Table 12.2 provides increases in success rates for corresponding values of effect size 'r'.

Here is another example to show why one should not to discount small effect sizes. Consider the fact that studies have indicated there is a small positive effect in taking exercise to try to prevent stress-related illness. Considering the large number of people who are at risk for stress-related illness, the small positive effect of taking exercise could still have a beneficial impact on millions of people. In terms of the potential numbers of people who could benefit, the small beneficial effect of taking exercise would not be a small effect at all (particularly in a practical sense of medical fees and costs).

TABLE 12.2 *Success rate increases corresponding to 'r'*

Effect size 'r'	Success rate increased	
	From	**To**
	%	**%**
.10	45	55
.20	40	60
.30	35	65
.40	30	70
.50	25	75
.60	20	80
.70	15	85
.80	10	90
.90	5	95
1.00	0	100

Source: Based on Rosenthal & Rubin (1982), p. 168.

When an experiment is conducted to test predictions derived from a theory, however, the size of the effect of an independent variable is less critical. In this case we are usually content with knowing that the independent variable 'worked' as a theory said it should. In fact, as tests of a theory become more sophisticated, it is likely that small effects will be more critical. Inferential statistics tests are useful when experiments are conducted to test theories by confirming that an effect is present.

Sample size, power and effect size

As you read above, power refers to the probability of rejecting a null hypothesis when it is false and needs rejecting. For any statistical test, power is determined by three factors:

- the p level (the level of risk of drawing a spuriously positive conclusion);
- N, or the sample size; and
- *r*, or the effect size.

These three factors are so related that knowing two enables the determination of the third. Thus if you set 'p' and '*r*' in advance you can find out how big a sample must be to achieve these levels. Table 12.3 provides some information on determining sample size for various levels of effect with 'p' set at .05. For example, if you anticipate a small effect level based on a review of previous findings, say, r = .20, and you set decide to work with power = .8 or better, since this happens to be a strongly recommended level (Cohen 1988), Table 12.3 shows that you will need approximately 195 subjects.

STQ54*

You read a study in which the result is just barely significant at the .05 level. You then look at the size of the sample. If the sample is very large (rather than very small), how should this affect your interpretation of (a) the probability that the null hypothesis is actually true and (b) the practical importance of the result?
Answers on p. 599.

TABLE 12.3 *Sample sizes needed to detect various effects at p = .05 two-tailed*

Power	Effect sizes (r)						
	.10	**.20**	**.30**	**.40**	**.50**	**.60**	**.70**
.15	85	25	10	10	10	10	10
.20	125	35	15	10	10	10	10
.30	200	55	25	15	10	10	10
.40	300	75	35	20	15	10	10
.50	400	100	40	25	15	10	10
.60	500	125	55	30	20	15	10
.70	600	155	65	40	25	15	10
.80	800	195	85	45	30	20	15
.90	1000	260	115	60	40	25	15

Source: Based on Cohen (1988), p. 92.

summary

A Type I error occurs when the null hypothesis is rejected but the research hypothesis is actually false. A Type II error occurs when the null hypothesis is not rejected but the research hypothesis is actually true.

Power analysis and effect size estimation are two further procedures that social science researchers are now finding to be as valuable as significance testing in assessing experimental effects. The power of a statistical test is its ability to correctly reject the null hypothesis when it is false or the probability that it will yield a significant result if the research hypothesis is true. The power of your statistical test is affected by your chosen significance level, the size of your sample, effect size, whether you use a one-tailed or two-tailed test, and whether you use a repeated measure or independent design. The main practical ways to increase the power of a planned experiment are increasing effect size and sample size.

Measures of effect size reflect how large the effect of an independent variable is independent of sample size. The more frequent effect size estimates are:

- the standardised mean difference (*d*);
- correlation coefficients such as *r* and r_{phi}; and
- eta^2 for curvilinear rather than a linear relationship.

Effect size measures are essential for meta-analysis (see chapter 21).

References

Cohen, J. (1988), *Statistical Power Analysis for the Behavioural Sciences*, Laurence Erlbaum, New York.

Cohen, J. (1992), 'A power primer', *Psychological Bulletin*, 112, pp. 155–9.

Keppel, G. (1991), *Design and Analysis*, Englewood Cliffs, Prentice Hall.

Smith, M., Glass, G. & Miller, T. (1980), *The Benefits of Psychotherapy*, John Hopkins University, Baltimore.

Testing hypotheses of difference I: Independent groups design

13
thirteen

Statistical tests for independent groups
(between-subjects design)

Independent *t* test (parametric)

One of the two major types of hypothesis is one which is stated in difference terms, i.e. that there is a significant mean difference between the effects of different levels of the *IV*. This difference is essentially a difference between the two sample means. We want to know whether the difference between sample means is a real one or whether it could be reasonably attributed to chance, i.e. does the difference between the two sample means lie within the expected chance distribution of differences between the means of an infinite number of pairs of samples at some level of probability?

Standard error of the difference

Remember what we saw when we drew large numbers of samples when discussing random sampling (chapter 6) and standard error (chapter 6)? The means of the samples of a population distributed themselves normally around the 'true' population mean. Now, in the case of differences between sample means, we have the same principle applying. If we plot every difference between every possible pair of sample means, a normal distribution of differences between pairs of means is produced because on many occasions the differences will be nil or quite slight with larger differences occurring more rarely. We can calculate the σ of this distribution. It is called *the standard error of the difference between means*. It estimates the dispersal of these mean differences.

Suppose, for instance, that a random sample of male students produces a mean score of 52 on a creativity test while a random sample of female students attains a mean of 54. Does this difference reveal a real superiority on the part of females for this task? The answer depends on how this obtained difference of 2 in mean score would vary as further pairs of random samples are tested. Our obtained difference of 2 is only one value of a distribution of differences; a sampling distribution of the difference between means.

The standard deviation of this distribution is *the standard error of the difference between means*. This standard error depends on the sampling distribution or standard error of each of the two sample means. When each sample is selected independently of the other, the standard error of the difference between means is symbolised by SE_{diff}. It is expressed as:

$$SE_{diff} = \sqrt{SE_{m1}^2 + SE_{m2}^2}$$

The subscripts indicate sample mean 1 and sample mean 2 respectively. Since $SE_m = \sigma/\sqrt{N}$ then $SE_m^2 = \sigma^2/(N)$. We can then substitute into the SE_{diff} formula and obtain the following easier to compute formula, i.e.:

$$SE_{diff} = \sqrt{\frac{\sigma_1^2}{N_1} + \frac{\sigma_2^2}{N_2}}$$

the subscripts again referring to the first and second samples respectively. As with the standard error of the mean, a critical ratio is formed to find the deviation in standard error unit terms of the difference between the means. This ratio is called the *t* ratio.

$$t = \frac{M_1 - M_2}{SE_{diff}} \text{ or } \frac{M_1 - M_2}{\sqrt{\frac{\sigma_1^2}{N_1} + \frac{\sigma_2^2}{N_2}}}$$

The obtained *t* is compared to the tabled entry of *t* (Table 13.1) for the relevant *df* and level of significance. *df* in a *t* ratio is $(N - 1) + (N_2 - 1)$. If *t* is the *same as* or *greater than* the relevant tabled entry then the *t* is significant at that level of significance.

t distributions

In our outline of confidence intervals and limits, we used Table 5.1 to estimate, for example, that the 0.05 level of confidence is situated at ± 1.96 standard deviations or standard errors from the mean of the population (i.e. Z = 1.96). To find the exact limits in actual scores for a particular sample mean, we multiplied the calculated SE_m by 1.96.

Table 5.1 can only be used, of course, when the distribution of sample mean is normal. If the distribution is not normal, then the 0.05 level will not be located at a Z score of ± 1.96. As samples become smaller, their distributions become flatter and more spread out. These non-normal distributions are called *t* distributions.

The use of the *t* statistic requires that the data satisfy the homogeneity of variance assumption and that both sets of data are approximately normal. There is a family of *t* distribution which approximates to the normal distribution of Z. (Z cannot be used as the population SD is not known.) The shape of each *t* distribution depends on the sample *df* with *t* approaching normal distribution as *df* increases (see Figure 13.1). *t* values are determined by the level of confidence selected and size of *df*.

FIGURE 13.1

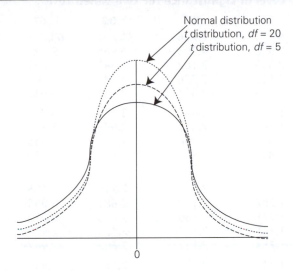

Normal distribution
t distribution, *df* = 20
t distribution, *df* = 5

0

Notice that there is a different *t* distribution for each size of sample (see Table 13.1). To obtain a confidence level for a *t* distribution within which 95 per cent of the theoretical sample means lie (i.e. the 0.05 level), we have to move further out in standard deviation units from the mean.

Suppose that the mean scores obtained in the creativity test above were derived from a sample of 200 men and 200 women with standard deviations respectively of 4 and 5. The research hypothesis is that there is a true sex difference in performance, the obtained difference of 2 between the means not being a random or chance sampling deviation. The computation in our example is as follows:

$$t = \frac{54 - 52}{\sqrt{\dfrac{4^2}{200} + \dfrac{5^2}{200}}} = \frac{2}{\sqrt{\dfrac{16}{200} + \dfrac{25}{200}}}$$

$$t = \frac{2}{\sqrt{0.08 + 0.125}} = \frac{2}{\sqrt{0.20}}$$

$$t = \frac{2}{.0444} = 4.54$$

This 4.54 is the obtained difference expressed in standard error units. From the *t* table (Table 13.1) with *df* = 400, we can see that there is much less than a 1% chance of differences in means of this magnitude arising from sampling error. The null hypothesis is therefore rejected and the difference in sample means accepted as a significant difference in performance on this creativity test between the sexes is supported quite strongly.

TABLE 13.1 *Critical values of t (between groups)*

df	Level of significance for one-tailed test					
	.10	.05	.025	.01	.005	.0005
	Level of significance for two-tailed test					
	.20	.10	.05	.02	.01	.001
1	3.078	6.314	12.706	31.821	63.657	636.619
2	1.886	2.920	4.303	6.965	9.925	31.598
3	1.638	2.353	3.182	4.541	5.841	12.941
4	1.533	2.132	2.776	3.747	4.604	8.610
5	1.476	2.015	2.571	3.365	4.032	6.859
6	1.440	1.943	2.447	3.143	3.707	5.959
7	1.415	1.895	2.365	2.998	3.499	5.405
8	1.397	1.860	2.306	2.896	3.355	5.041
9	1.383	1.833	2.262	2.821	3.250	4.781
10	1.372	1.812	2.228	2.764	3.169	4.587
11	1.363	1.796	2.201	2.718	3.106	4.437
12	1.356	1.782	2.179	2.681	3.055	4.318
13	1.350	1.771	2.160	2.650	3.012	4.221
14	1.345	1.761	2.145	2.624	2.977	4.140
15	1.341	1.753	2.131	2.602	2.947	4.073
16	1.337	1.746	2.120	2.583	2.921	4.015
17	1.333	1.740	2.110	2.567	2.898	3.965
18	1.330	1.734	2.101	2.552	2.878	3.922
19	1.328	1.729	2.093	2.539	2.861	3.883
20	1.325	1.725	2.086	2.528	2.845	3.850
21	1.323	1.721	2.080	2.518	2.831	3.819
22	1.321	1.717	2.074	2.508	2.819	3.792
23	1.319	1.714	2.069	2.500	2.807	3.767
24	1.318	1.711	2.064	2.492	2.797	3.745
25	1.316	1.708	2.060	2.485	2.787	3.725
26	1.315	1.706	2.056	2.479	2.779	3.707
27	1.314	1.703	2.052	2.473	2.771	3.690
28	1.313	1.701	2.048	2.467	2.763	3.674
29	1.311	1.699	2.045	2.462	2.756	3.659
30	1.310	1.697	2.042	2.457	2.750	3.646
40	1.303	1.684	2.021	2.423	2.704	3.551
60	1.296	1.671	2.000	2.390	2.660	3.460
120	1.289	1.658	1.980	2.358	2.617	3.373
∞	1.282	1.645	1.960	2.326	2.576	3.291

Source: Table III, Fisher & Yates, *Statistical Tables for Biological, Agricultural and Medical Research*, 6th edn, Addison Wesley Longman Ltd, London.

If you are comparing two means, the degree of freedom is the sum of the two samples minus 2, i.e. if one sample consists of 10 people and the other of 8, $df = 10 + 8 - 2 = 16$.

The table gives 'critical values'—the minimum value of *t* which is significant at the desired level. For example, with 19 degrees of freedom a *t* of 2.093 or larger is significant at the .05 level (two-tailed test); with 16 degrees of freedom you would need a *t* of 2.120 or larger. (Again you need to consider whether a one-tailed or a two-tailed test is appropriate.)

If your *df* is not represented in the left-hand column of the table take the next lowest figure, unless your sample size is well in excess of 120, in which case you may use the bottom row (∞, or infinity).

FIGURE 13.2 *The SE_diff shown on the normal distribution*

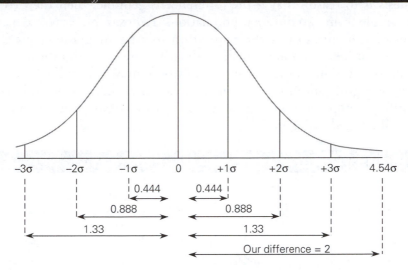

Let us look at the above result in a more visual way. The SE_{diff} is the estimate of the dispersal of all possible mean differences between an infinite number of similarly drawn pairs of samples. The $SE_{diff} = 0.444$. This is shown on the normal distribution above (Figure 13.2) which represents a population of differences M = 0, $\sigma = 0.444$ (the denominator in our example).

We would expect 95 per cent of sample mean differences to be between -0.888 and $+0.888$. Our difference of 2 is equal to 4.54σ, which is way beyond 3σ from the mean. Obviously something is happening here besides chance! It is, provided we have controlled other variables, *the experimental effect*.

The formula

$$SE_{diff} = \sqrt{\frac{\sigma_1^2}{N_1} + \frac{\sigma_2^2}{N_2}}$$

is unfortunately appropriate only when the samples are large and both groups are of approximately equal size. In some *t* test situations, the samples are small and of different sizes, and the way one must cope with this and compensate is by adopting this modified formula.

$$SE_{diff} = \sqrt{\frac{\sigma_1^2 + \sigma_2^2}{N_1 - 1 + N_2 - 1}\left(\frac{N_1 + N_2}{(N_1)(N_2)}\right)}$$

The σ^2 in the formula can be restated mathematically as $(\Sigma X^2 - (\Sigma X^2/N))$. Thus the total *t* formula for between-subjects design when samples are small, say 30 or less, is:

$$t = \frac{M_1 - M_2}{\sqrt{\frac{\left(\Sigma X_1^2 - \frac{(\Sigma X_1)^2}{N_1}\right) + \left(\Sigma X_2^2 - \frac{(\Sigma X_2)^2}{N_2}\right)}{(N_1 - 1) + (N_2 - 1)}\left(\frac{N_1 + N_2}{(N_1)(N_2)}\right)}}$$

One way of looking at the statistical inference of significance in a 'difference' hypothesis is to reason that if the difference is genuine, then the two groups are each a sample from two different populations. For example, if we take two random samples of students to test their speed on solving anagrams—one a sample of females, the other a sample of males—then if there is no significant difference in anagram solution times, they have probably been drawn from the same population. If there is a significant difference, then we can infer that female and male students form different populations as far as the ability to solve anagrams is concerned. This point is illustrated in Figure 13.3.

FIGURE 13.3 *Two samples from the same or different population*

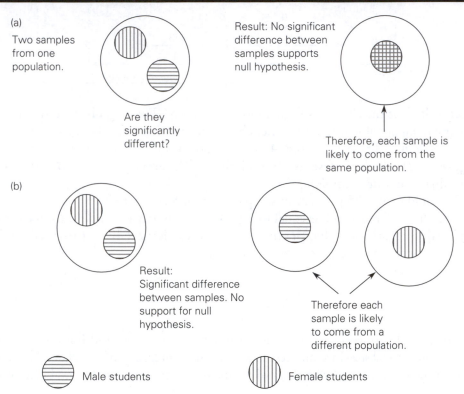

The following figures illustrate the influence of variability and what it is we are trying to determine in applying a *t* test. Both figures show a sample of seven from two populations with the same sample mean in both. The only difference is variability.

The first figure (Figure 13.4) shows each sample data clustered around the mean of that sample. Sample variability is small but the means are significantly different (in this case $t = 9.16$)

The second figure (Figure 13.5) shows that the two samples overlap and it is not easy to see a difference between the two samples. In fact all fourteen scores could have come from the same population. In this case $t = 1.18$ and we conclude that there is not sufficient evidence to reject the null hypothesis.

FIGURE 13.4

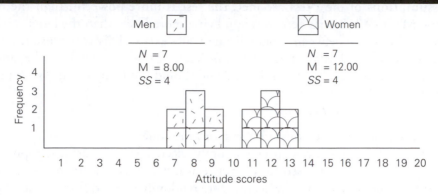

FIGURE 13.5

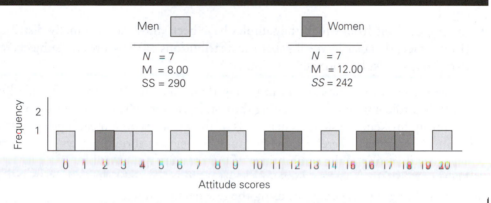

*Answers on p. 599.

STQ55*

1 If a near infinite number of pairs of samples were taken randomly from a population and the mean differences between each pair plotted on a graph, what would we term the standard deviation of these plotted differences? What would the average of these differences be?

2 An independent group experiment is carried out correctly and yields the following information:

	M	σ	N
Experimental	15.8	2.5	26
Control	17.6	2.0	21

What could you conclude?

3 The results in each of the two random groups of a two-tailed experiment are:

$M_1 - M_2 = 3$; $\sigma_1 = 4$; $\sigma_2 = 3$; $N = 25$ in each

Calculate t. Would you retain the null hypothesis at $p < 0.05$?

*Answers on p. 599.

Assumptions of the t test for the between-subjects design

If the assumptions of the t test are met, the test is more powerful than the non-parametric Mann-Whitney U test (p. 189), being more likely than the latter to show a significant difference between groups if one really exists. This is because the t test makes full use of interval data, while the Mann-Whitney test considers only the ranking of the subjects. However, the t test is invalid and should not be used if its assumptions are not met.

The assumptions of the t test are that:

- the measurements are made on an interval or ratio scale;
- the members of the sample have been randomly selected from the defined population; For example, if the test is used to test between fast and slow learners, the subjects representing the fast and the slow learners are randomly selected from the total pool of all fast and slow learners;
- the standard deviations of the scores for the two groups should be approximately equal;
- the populations from which the samples have been drawn are normally distributed. (In practice, this usually means that the distributions of the scores for subjects in the two groups must be normally distributed.)

These assumptions sound more imposing than they are. Within quite wide limits, they can be broken without invalidating the test. However, when assumptions of the test are seriously broken, the significance levels of the t test become meaningless or at least difficult to interpret. Therefore, the Mann-Whitney test should always be performed when more than one of the assumptions of the t test are questionable.

Here is another worked example of a t test, taking you right through from raw data derived in a memory experiment, using the raw data formula.

Twenty subjects are randomly assigned to two groups. Ten subjects learn lists of all-digit telephone numbers with background music and the other ten subjects learn lists of all-digit telephone numbers with no background music. Their recall scores are given in Table 13.2.

To calculate t we have to compare the means of the two groups of subjects. Let us look at the t test procedure step by step, using the data from our example. First, draw up a table of scores for each condition and find their squares (see Table 13.2).

The raw scores (X_1) in Condition A should be totalled (ΣX_1) and this total squared ($\Sigma X_1)^2$. Find the squares (X_1^2) of each of the raw scores and the sums of squares (ΣX_1^2). The mean will be calculated at this stage. Apply exactly the same procedure to the data in Condition B. You now have available the necessary information to find t.

Let us now apply these steps to the data in Table 13.2.

1 Sum the X_1 scores in Condition A and the X_2 scores in Condition B:
   $X_1 = 74$ $X_2 = 47$

2 Find the means of the scores in each condition:
   $M_1 = 7.4$ $M_2 = 4.7$

3 Square the total scores:
   $(\Sigma X_1)^2 = 74 \times 74 = 5476$ $(\Sigma X_2)^2 = 47 \times 47 = 2209$

4 Sum the squares in each condition:

$\Sigma X_1^2 = 588$ $\Sigma X_2^2 = 249$

5 We are now able to insert the values in the formula to obtain t:

$$t = \frac{M_1 - M_2}{\sqrt{\frac{\left(\Sigma X_1^2 - \frac{(\Sigma X_1)^2}{N_1}\right) + \left(\Sigma X_2^2 - \frac{(\Sigma X_2)^2}{N_2}\right)}{(N_1 - 1) + (N_2 - 1)}\left(\frac{N_1 + N_2}{(N_1)(N_2)}\right)}}$$

$$t = \frac{7.4 - 4.7}{\sqrt{\frac{\left(588 - \frac{5476}{10}\right) + \left(249 - \frac{2209}{10}\right)}{(9 + 9)}\left(\frac{10 + 10}{(10)(10)}\right)}}$$

$$t = \frac{7.4 - 4.7}{\sqrt{\frac{(588 \times 547.6 + 249 - 220.0)}{18} \times \frac{1}{5}}}$$

$$t = \frac{2.7}{\sqrt{3.806 \times 0.2}}$$

$$t = \frac{2.7}{.8725}$$

$$t = 3.09$$

TABLE 13.2 *Recall scores*

Background music Condition A		No background music Condition B	
Scores (X_1)	Squares (X_1^2)	Scores (X_2)	Squares (X_s^2)
11	121	3	9
6	36	2	4
7	49	8	64
4	16	5	25
10	100	5	25
9	81	6	36
8	64	3	9
6	36	6	36
7	49	4	16
5	36	5	25
$\Sigma X_1 = 74$ $[\Sigma X_1]^2 = 5476$ Mean: $M_1 = 7.4$	$\Sigma X_1^2 = 588$	$\Sigma X_2 = 47$ $[\Sigma X_2]^2 = 2209$ Mean: $M_2 = 4.7$	$\Sigma X_2^2 = 249$

Looking up the result for our example, we have a $t = 3.09$ with $df = N_1 + N_2 - 2 = 10 + 10 - 2 = 18$. Therefore, reading across the row for $df = 18$ (Table 13.1) we find that the value in the first column is smaller than the t which we have obtained. The tabulated values for 0.05 and 0.01 levels of significance are smaller than our value of t. Therefore our value of t is significant at the 0.01 level.

Hence the null hypothesis is not supported and the difference is significant ($p < .01$).

STQ56*

1   A researcher wishes to find out whether students of education are more empathetic than students of engineering. An empathy scale is applied to a random sample of each faculty. The results were:

Education	25	30	27	19	21	36	17	26	24
Engineering	20	17	15	27	18	24	19	16	29

   a   What is the null hypothesis?
   b   Is a one-tail or two-tail test appropriate?
   c   Apply an independent t test and make a statement about the status of the null hypothesis at the 5% level of confidence.

2   A researcher is studying comprehension skills in children of manual (M) and professional (P) parents. The data are as below.

'M' children	16	12	10	13	8	21	19	6
'P' children	15	10	23	26	12	9	18	14

   a   State the alternate and null hypothesis.
   b   Apply an independent t test and evaluate the results using the 5% level of significance.
   c   Did you use a one-tail or two-tail hypothesis? Explain your choice.
*Answers on p. 599–600.

Effect size and power for the t test for independent groups (means)

Effect size

Effect size for the t test for independent means is the difference between the population means divided by the standard deviation of the population of individuals. When using data from a completed study the effect size is estimated as the difference between the sample means divided by the pooled estimate of the population standard deviation (the square root of the pooled estimate of the population variance).

Stated as formulas:

$$\text{Effect size } (d) = \frac{\text{Population M}_1 - \text{Population M}_2}{\text{Population SD}}$$

$$\text{Estimated effect size } (d) = \frac{M_1 - M_2}{SD \text{ pooled}}$$

SPSS supplies all the information necessary to compute two effect size indices, d and eta^2. The mean difference is reported in the SPSS output, but the pooled standard deviation has to be calculated from the reported standard deviations for the two groups using the following formula, and substituted into the d equation to obtain the d index.

$$\text{Pooled with groups } SD = \sqrt{\frac{(N_1 - 1)SD_1^2 - (N_2 - 1)SD_2^2}{N_1 + N_2 - 2}}$$

However, it is easier to compute d using the following equation:

$$d = t\sqrt{\frac{N_1 + N_2}{N_1 N_2}}$$

A d can range in value from negative infinity to positive infinity. The value of 0 for d indicates that there are no differences in the means. As d diverges from 0, the effect size becomes larger. Regardless of sign, d values of .2, .5, and .8 traditionally represent small, medium, and large effect sizes respectively.

Eta^2 may be computed as an alternative to d. It too ranges in value from 0 to 1. It is interpreted as the proportion of variance of the test variable that is a function of the group variable. A value of 0 indicates that the difference in the mean scores is equal to 0, while a value of 1 indicates that there are differences between the sample means, but within each group there are no differences in the test scores (i.e. perfect replication). You can compute eta^2 using the following formula:

$$eta^2 = \frac{t^2}{t^2 + (N_1 + N_2 - 2)}$$

Power

Table 13.3 gives the approximate power for the .05 significance level for small, medium, and large effect sizes and one- or two-tailed tests.

Power is greatest when the participants in a study are divided into two equal groups. For example, an experiment with 10 people in the control group and 30 in the experimental group is much less powerful than one with 20 in both groups.

There is a practical problem in deriving power from tables when sample sizes are not equal. Like most power tables, Table 13.3 assumes equal numbers in each of the two groups. What do you do when your two samples have different numbers of people in them? It turns out that in terms of power, the *harmonic mean* of the two unequal sample sizes gives the equivalent sample harmonic mean size for what you would have with two equal samples. The harmonic mean sample size is given by the formula:

$$\text{Harmonic mean} = \frac{(2)(N_1)(N_2)}{N_1 + N_2}$$

Consider an extreme example in which there are 6 people in one group and 34 in the other. The harmonic mean comes out to about 10:

$$\frac{(2)(N_1)(N_2)}{N_1 + N_2} = \frac{(2)(6)(34)}{6 + 34} = \frac{408}{40} = 10.2$$

So, even though you have a total of 40 participants, the study has the power of one with equal sample sizes of only about 10 in each group. (This means that a study with a total of 20 participants divided equally would have had just as much power.) If the researcher is using the .05 level, two-tailed, and expects a large effect size, Table 13.3 indicates that this study would have a power of less than .39 (the figure for using 10 participants in each group). Suppose the researcher had been able to set up the study by dividing the 40 participants into 20 per group. That would have given the study a power of .69.

TABLE 13.3 *Approximate power for studies using the t test for independent means testing hypotheses at the .05 significance level*

Number of participants in each group	Small (.20)	Effect size Medium (.50)	Large (.80)
One-tailed test			
10	.11	29	.53
20	.15	.46	.80
30	.19	.61	.92
40	.22	.72	.97
50	.26	.80	.99
100	.41	.97	–
Two-tailed test			
10	.07	19	.39
20	.09	.33	.69
30	.12	.47	.86
40	.14	.60	.94
50	.17	.70	.98
100	.29	.94	–

Planning sample size

Table 13.4 gives the approximate number of participants needed for 80 per cent power for estimated small, medium, and large effect sizes using one- and two-tailed tests, all using the .05 significance level. Suppose you plan a study in which you expect a medium effect size and will use the .05 significance level, one-tailed. Based on Table 13.4 you will need 50 people in each group (100 in total) to have 80 per cent power. But if you conducted a study using the same significance level but could expect a large effect size, you would need only 20 people in each group (40 in total).

TABLE 13.4 *Approximate number of participants needed in each group (assuming equal sample sizes) for 80% power for the t test for independent means, testing hypotheses at the .05 significance level*

	Small (.20)	Effect size Medium (.50)	Large (.80)
One-tailed	310	50	20
Two-tailed	393	64	26

Using SSPS to compare two groups of independent (unrelated) samples

You need two columns of data in the Data window when you are going to calculate an independent *t* test. The first column represents the independent variable (grouping variable) usually 1's and 2's. The second column (*'var00002'*) consists of the scores of the dependent variable for *both* groups. The data are not kept separate for the two groups as we would have them in a raw data list. So each row is for a particular student and contains a code to designate which group they are in, and a score on the independent variable.

How to proceed

1 Select *Statistics* and choose *Compare Mean*s from the drop-down menu.
2 On the next drop-down menu click on *Independent-Samples T Test* to open *the Independent Samples T Test* dialogue box.
3 Select your dependent variable and click on the arrow button to place it into the *Test variables* box.
4 Select your independent variable and move it to the *Grouping Variable* area.
5 Choose *Define Groups.*
6 Type in the box beside Group 1 the coding for one category of your grouping variable.
7 Do the same with the other box beside Group 2.
8 Click on *Continue* and then *OK* to produce the output.

How to interpret the output in Table 13.5

- The table consists of two subtables. The top table summarises the descriptive statistics for the two groups (gender) on two dependent variables—attitudes to research scores and length of work experience scores. For example, the mean attitudes to research score for females is 47.52 with a standard deviation of 8.31.
- The bottom table displays the test statistics. The output for the independent groups *t* test on SPSS is somewhat confusing because there are two versions of the independent samples *t* test. Which one you should use depends on whether the (estimated) variances for the two groups of scores are significantly different or not.
- Read the columns under the heading 'Levene's test for equality of variances'. If the probability value is statistically significant then your variances are *unequal.* Otherwise they are equal.
- Levene's test for equality of variances in this case tells us that the variances for male and female groups are equal for the attitudes to research scores (significance = .08), but not so for the length of work experience scores because the significance value = 0.001 is highly significant.
- Finally look at the rest of the table. Look at the row for equal variances assumed for the attitudes to research scores and the equal variances not assumed for the length of work experience scores. The *t* value, its degrees of freedom and its probability are displayed in the output. For example, the *t* value for the length of work experience scores –3.010, which, with 70 degrees of freedom, has a two-tailed significance level of 0.004.

TABLE 13.5 *Example of independent t test output*

a   t test: Group Statistics

	Gender	N	Mean	Std Deviation	Std Error Mean
RESEARCH	Female	42	47.5238	8.3147	1.2830
	Male	42	46.7619	7.0531	1.0883
EXP	Female	42	13.1667	6.8107	1.0509
	Male	42	18.9524	10.4320	1.6097

b   Independent Samples Test

		Levene's test for equality of variances		t test for equality of means					95% confidence interval	
		F	Sig.	t	df	Sig. (2-tailed)	Mean difference	Std Error difference	lower	upper
RESEARCH	Equal variances assumed	3.101	.082	.453	82	.652	.7619	1.6824	-2.5849	4.1087
	Equal variances not assumed			.453	79.876	.652	.7619	1.6824	-2.5863	4.1101
EXP	Equal variances assumed	11.051	.001	-3.010	82	.003	-5.7857	1.9224	-9.6099	-1.9615
	Equal variances not assumed			-3.010	70.578	.004	-5.7857	1.9224	-9.6192	-1.9522

How to report the output in Table 13.5

You should state the results of this analysis like this: 'An independent-samples *t* test was conducted to evaluate the hypotheses that males and females differ significantly in their attitudes to research and in their length of work experience. The mean attitude to research score of females (M = 47.52, SD = 8.31) is not statistically significantly different (t = .453, df = 82, two-tailed p = .652) from that of male students (M = 46.76, SD= 7.05). The effect size is *d* = .02, implying virtually no effect at all'.

A similar statement indicating that the *t* test for unequal variances was used would be made for the length of work experience data but would emphasise in this case the statistical significance of the differences between the genders.

Many social scientists/psychologists are probably unaware of the existence of the unequal variance *t* test. If you have to use one, you should write: 'Because the variances for the two groups were significantly unequal (F = 11.05, p < 0.001), a test for unequal variances was used'.

Mann-Whitney U test (non-parametric)

The Mann-Whitney U test is used when testing for differences between two independent groups when the assumptions for the parametric *t* test cannot be met. For example, we might want to test whether the hearing of blind students is as acute as that of sighted students; or whether subjects told to learn a list of words by forming sentences linking the items have better recall than subjects given no specific instructions on how to learn the list. The test does not require equal numbers in the two conditions. It must, however, be possible to rank the scores produced by the subjects, i.e. the scale of measurement must be at least ordinal.

The mathematics of this test is based on the simple observation that if there is a real difference between scores in two samples then the scores in one sample should be generally larger than the scores in the other sample. Thus if all scores are ranked in order, the scores of one sample should be concentrated at one end, while the scores from the other sample are concentrated at the other end, as shown in Figure 13.6(a).

If no treatment effect exists, then scores from the two samples will be mixed randomly. The Mann-Whitney test ranks scores from the two samples into one ranking and then tests to determine whether there is a systematic clustering into two groups paralleling the samples.

It is based on the premise that a real difference in two treatments will cause the scores from one sample when placed in rank order to be located at one end of the distribution, while the ranked scores derived from the other condition will be at the other end of the distribution. If no real treatment effect exists then ranked scores from the two distributions will be randomised in the overall distribution. Figure 13.6(b) illustrates this.

By comparing our result for U with the table, we know whether our split in ranks is one that would occur less than 5 per cent of the time.

Let us imagine that we want to discover the effect of organisation on memory. The experiment will adopt a null hypothesis that it will not be significantly easier to

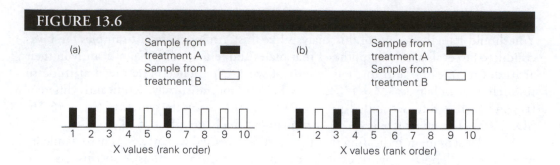

FIGURE 13.6

remember a set of words which are organised in categories than a set of words that has no organisation.

We allocate six subjects randomly to a group where they will learn material without the aid of organised categories, and allocate eight subjects to a group where they will. The effect of organisation on memory will be measured by the number of words each subject recalls (Table 13.6).

TABLE 13.6 *Calculation of the value of U (the Mann-Whitney statistic)*

Group I $N_1 = 6$	Condition 1 'non-category'	Rankings 1	Group 2 $N_2 = 8$	Condition 2 'category'	Rankings 2
1	13	4	7	21	14
2	14	5.5	8	16	8.5
3	12	3	9	10	1
4	18	11	10	15	7
5	16	8.5	11	11	2
6	19	12	12	14	5.5
			13	20	13
			14	17	10
		$T_I = 44.0$			$T_2 = 61.0$

1 Place all the scores in rank order, taking both groups together. Give 'rank 1' to the lowest score, 'rank 2' to the next lowest score, etc. Add the ranks for each group separately.

2 Use the following formula to find U_1.

$$U_1 = T_1 - \frac{N_1(N_1 + 1)}{2}$$

where
N_1 = number of group 1 subjects
N_2 = number of group 2 subjects
T_1 = rank total for group with smallest rank sum

$$U_1 = T_1 - \frac{N_1(N_1 + 1)}{2}$$

$$U_1 = 44.0 - \frac{6(6 + 1)}{2}$$

$$= 44.0 - \frac{42}{2}$$

$$= 44.0 - 21$$

$$= 23$$

Similarly,

$$U_2 = T_2 - \frac{N_2(N_2 + 1)}{2}$$

$$= 61 - \frac{8(8 + 1)}{2} = 25$$

The smaller of these two U values is used to test significance. The smaller this value the more significant it is.

3 Table 13.7 (1) to (4) gives you the critical values of U or U_1 at different levels of significance for one-tailed and two-tailed tests and different combinations of N_1 and N_2 for the groups of subjects. You have to locate the appropriate table from (1) to (4). In our case, as we have selected a significant level of $p < 0.05$ two-tailed, choose Table 13.7 (3) on p. 193; N_1 is shown on the top row and N_2 on the left-hand column. At the intersection of the appropriate N_1 column (in our case, 6) with the appropriate N_2 row (in our case, 8) you will find the critical two-tailed value of U = 8. Our smallest calculated U value is larger than this and therefore you can retain the null hypothesis and conclude that there is no significant difference in the scores due to the effect of the independent variable, i.e. the degree of organisation of the material.

In another example, a psychologist studying the manual dexterity of children recorded the amount of time in seconds required by each child to arrange blocks in a specified pattern. The data was as follows with scores ranked as though from one group:

Boys: Raw scores	23	18	29	42	21				$N_1 = 5 \; T_1 = 22$
Ranks	3	1	6	10	2				

Girls: Raw scores	37	56	39	34	26	104	48	25	$N_2 = 8 \; T_2 = 69$
Ranks	8	12	9	7	5	13	11	4	

The null hypotheses states that there is no significant difference between solution times for boys versus girls. For a two-tailed test with $p > 0.05$ with $N_1 = 5$ and $N_2 = 8$, the table gives a critical value of U = 6.

$$U_1 = T_1 - N_1 \frac{(N_1 + 1)}{2} \qquad\qquad U_2 = T_2 - N_2 \frac{(N_2 + 1)}{2}$$

$$U_1 = 7 \qquad\qquad\qquad\qquad U_2 = 33$$

	N_1 1	2	3	4	5	6	7	8	9	10	11	12	13	14	15	16	17	18	19	20
N_2																				
1	–	–	–	–	–	–	–	–	–	–	–	–	–	–	–	–	–	–	–	–
2	–	–	–	–	–	–	–	–	–	–	–	–	–	–	–	–	–	–	0	0
3	–	–	–	–	–	–	–	–	0	0	0	1	1	1	2	2	2	2	3	3
4	–	–	–	–	–	0	0	1	1	2	2	3	3	4	5	5	6	6	7	8
5	–	–	–	–	0	1	1	2	3	4	5	6	7	7	8	9	10	11	12	13
6	–	–	–	0	1	2	3	4	5	6	7	9	10	11	12	13	15	16	17	18
7	–	–	–	0	1	3	4	6	7	9	10	12	13	15	16	18	19	21	22	24
8	–	–	–	1	2	4	6	7	9	11	13	15	17	18	20	22	24	26	28	30
9	–	–	0	1	3	5	7	9	11	13	16	18	20	22	24	27	29	31	33	36
10	–	–	0	2	4	6	9	11	13	16	18	21	24	26	29	31	34	37	39	42
11	–	–	0	2	5	7	10	13	16	18	21	24	27	30	33	36	39	42	45	48
12	–	–	1	3	6	9	12	15	18	21	24	27	31	34	37	41	44	47	51	54
13	–	–	1	3	7	10	13	17	20	24	27	31	34	38	42	45	49	53	56	60
14	–	–	1	4	7	11	15	18	22	26	30	34	38	42	46	50	54	58	63	67
15	–	–	2	5	8	12	16	20	24	29	33	37	42	46	51	55	60	64	69	73
16	–	–	2	5	9	13	18	22	27	31	36	41	45	50	55	60	65	70	74	79
17	–	–	2	6	10	15	19	24	29	34	39	44	49	54	60	65	70	75	81	86
18	–	–	2	6	11	16	21	26	31	37	42	47	53	58	64	70	75	81	87	92
19	–	0	3	7	12	17	22	28	33	39	45	51	56	63	69	74	81	87	93	99
20	–	0	3	8	13	18	24	30	36	42	48	54	60	67	73	79	86	92	99	105

	N_1 1	2	3	4	5	6	7	8	9	10	11	12	13	14	15	16	17	18	19	20
N_2																				
1	–	–	–	–	–	–	–	–	–	–	–	–	–	–	–	–	–	–	–	–
2	–	–	–	–	–	–	–	–	–	–	–	0	0	0	0	0	0	0	1	1
3	–	–	–	–	–	–	0	0	1	1	1	2	2	2	3	3	4	4	4	5
4	–	–	–	–	0	1	1	2	3	3	4	5	5	6	7	7	8	9	9	10
5	–	–	–	0	1	2	3	4	5	6	7	8	9	10	11	12	13	14	15	16
6	–	–	–	1	2	3	4	6	7	8	9	11	12	13	15	16	18	19	20	22
7	–	–	0	1	3	4	6	7	9	11	12	14	16	17	19	21	23	24	26	28
8	–	–	0	2	4	6	7	9	11	13	15	17	20	22	24	26	28	30	32	34
9	–	–	1	3	5	7	9	11	14	16	18	21	23	26	28	31	33	36	38	40
10	–	–	1	3	6	8	11	13	16	19	22	24	27	30	33	36	38	41	44	47
11	–	–	1	4	7	9	12	15	18	22	25	28	31	34	37	41	44	47	50	53
12	–	–	2	5	8	11	14	17	21	24	28	31	35	38	42	46	49	53	56	60
13	–	0	2	5	9	12	16	20	23	27	31	35	39	43	47	51	55	59	63	67
14	–	0	2	6	10	13	17	22	26	30	34	38	43	47	51	56	60	65	69	73
15	–	0	3	7	11	15	19	24	28	33	37	42	47	51	56	61	66	70	75	80
16	–	0	3	7	12	16	21	26	31	36	41	46	51	56	61	66	71	76	82	87
17	–	0	4	8	13	18	23	28	33	38	44	49	55	60	66	71	77	82	88	93
18	–	0	4	9	14	19	24	30	36	41	47	53	59	65	70	76	82	88	94	100
19	–	1	4	9	15	20	26	32	38	44	50	56	63	69	75	82	88	94	101	107
20	–	1	5	10	16	22	28	34	40	47	53	60	67	73	80	87	93	100	107	114

TABLE 13.7 (3) Mann–Whitney U: one–tailed test at 0.025; two–tailed test at 0.05*

N₂ \ N₁	1	2	3	4	5	6	7	8	9	10	11	12	13	14	15	16	17	18	19	20
1	–	–	–	–	–	–	–	–	–	–	–	–	–	–	–	–	–	–	–	–
2	–	–	–	–	–	–	–	0	0	0	0	1	1	1	1	1	2	2	2	2
3	–	–	–	–	0	1	1	2	2	3	3	4	4	5	5	6	6	7	7	8
4	–	–	–	0	1	2	3	4	4	5	6	7	8	9	10	11	11	12	13	13
5	–	–	0	1	2	3	5	6	7	8	9	11	12	13	14	15	17	18	19	20
6	–	–	1	2	3	5	6	8	10	11	13	14	16	17	19	21	22	24	25	27
7	–	–	1	3	5	6	8	10	12	14	16	18	20	22	24	26	28	30	32	34
8	–	0	2	4	6	8	10	13	15	17	19	22	24	26	29	31	34	36	38	41
9	–	0	2	4	7	10	12	15	17	20	23	26	28	31	34	37	39	42	45	48
10	–	0	3	5	8	11	14	17	20	23	26	29	33	36	39	42	45	48	52	55
11	–	0	3	6	9	13	16	19	23	26	30	33	37	40	44	47	51	55	58	62
12	–	1	4	7	11	14	18	22	26	29	33	37	41	45	49	53	57	61	65	69
13	–	1	4	8	12	16	20	24	28	33	37	41	45	50	54	59	63	67	72	76
14	–	1	5	9	13	17	22	26	31	36	40	45	50	55	59	64	67	74	78	83
15	–	1	5	10	14	19	24	29	34	39	44	49	54	59	64	70	75	80	85	90
16	–	1	6	11	15	21	26	31	37	42	47	53	59	64	70	75	81	86	92	98
17	–	2	6	11	17	22	28	34	39	45	51	57	63	67	75	81	87	93	99	105
18	–	2	7	12	18	24	30	36	42	48	55	61	67	74	80	86	93	99	106	112
19	–	2	7	13	19	25	32	38	45	52	58	65	72	78	85	92	99	106	113	119
20	–	2	8	13	20	27	34	41	48	55	62	69	76	83	90	98	105	112	119	127

TABLE 13.7 (4) Mann–Whitney U: one–tailed test at 0.05; two–tailed test at 0.10*

N₂ \ N₁	1	2	3	4	5	6	7	8	9	10	11	12	13	14	15	16	17	18	19	20
1	–	–	–	–	–	–	–	–	–	–	–	–	–	–	–	–	–	–	–	–
2	–	–	–	–	0	0	0	1	1	1	1	2	2	2	3	3	3	4	4	4
3	–	–	0	0	1	2	2	3	3	4	5	5	6	7	7	8	9	9	10	11
4	–	–	0	1	2	3	4	5	6	7	8	9	10	11	12	14	15	16	17	18
5	–	0	1	2	4	5	6	8	9	11	12	13	15	16	18	19	20	22	23	25
6	–	0	2	3	5	7	8	10	12	14	16	17	19	21	23	25	26	28	30	32
7	–	0	2	4	6	8	11	13	15	17	19	21	24	26	28	30	33	35	37	39
8	–	1	3	5	8	10	13	15	18	20	23	26	28	31	33	36	39	41	44	47
9	–	1	3	6	9	12	15	18	21	24	27	30	33	36	39	42	45	48	51	54
10	–	1	4	7	11	14	17	20	24	27	31	34	37	41	44	48	51	55	58	62
11	–	1	5	8	12	16	19	23	27	31	34	38	42	46	50	54	57	61	65	69
12	–	2	5	9	13	17	21	26	30	34	38	42	47	51	55	60	64	68	72	77
13	–	2	6	10	15	19	24	28	33	37	42	47	51	56	61	65	70	75	80	84
14	–	2	7	11	16	21	26	31	36	41	46	51	56	61	66	71	77	82	87	92
15	–	3	7	12	18	23	28	33	39	44	50	55	61	66	72	77	83	88	94	100
16	–	3	8	14	19	25	30	36	42	48	54	60	65	71	77	83	89	95	101	107
17	–	3	9	15	20	26	33	39	45	51	57	64	70	77	83	89	96	102	109	115
18	–	4	9	16	22	28	35	41	48	55	61	68	75	82	88	95	102	109	116	123
19	0	4	10	17	23	30	37	44	51	58	65	72	80	87	94	101	109	116	123	130
20	0	4	11	18	25	32	39	47	54	62	69	77	84	92	100	107	115	123	130	138

Source: D. Auble, 'Extended tables for the Mann-Whitney statistic', in *Bulletin of the Institute of Educational Research,* Vol. 7, No. 2, Indiana University.

*Dashes in the body of the table indicate that no decision is possible at the stated level of significance.

As $U_1 = 7$ is the smaller of the two values it is used to compare within the tabled value of U. Because this is greater than the tabled value of 6, we fail to reject the null hypothesis. At the .05 level of significance the data does not provide sufficient evidence that there is a significant difference between boys and girls in manual dexterity.

STQ57*

1   Using random samples of 750 children, an investigator tested the hypothesis that children in Perth receive significantly less pocket money than children in Adelaide. Which one of the following tests should he apply?
   a t test for related samples.
   b   Z test.
   c   Mann-Whitney test.
   d t test for independent samples.
   In the hypothesis above, which one of the following procedures should the investigator use?
   a   A two-tailed test.
   b   A one-tailed test.
   c   Either a one-tailed or a two-tailed test.

2   What is the null hypothesis of the Mann-Whitney test?

3   Two random groups of pupils are used to determine whether a programmed textbook is worse than an ordinary textbook. The following data are the final test scores on a common examination.

Programmed text		57	78	45	33	52	58	28	76
Ordinary text	86	34	85	60	87	94	79	56	90

   Perform a Mann-Whitney U test and come to a conclusion using the 0.05 level.

4   Twenty six-letter words were presented on a screen to two groups of different subjects. For both groups, the words were all presented at a very fast level of exposure. For one group, the words were presented on the left-hand side of the screen; for the other group, the words were presented on the right-hand side of the screen. The experimenter was testing the effects of reading (left to right in our culture) on a subject's ability to recognise words at very fast levels of presentation. The results were as follows:
   Group 1 (left-hand side presentation): 18, 15, 17, 13, 11, 16, 10, 17.
   Group 2 (right-hand side presentation): 17, 13, 12, 16, 10, 15, 11, 13, 12.
   The level of significance chosen was $p < 0.05$. The experimental hypothesis stated that subjects given the words on the left-hand side of the screen would perform better. Use a Mann-Whitney U test.
   a   Why do we use a Mann-Whitney test in this experiment?
   b   Is the experimental hypothesis one-tailed or two-tailed?
   c   Can the experimental hypothesis be accepted at the $p < 0.05$ level of significance?

5   Children's tendency to stereotype according to traditional sex roles was observed. Two groups were drawn, one with mothers who had full-time paid employment

and one whose mothers did not work outside the home. The sex stereotyping scores and ranks are as follows:

Mothers with jobs $N_1 = 7$		Mothers with no jobs $N_2 = 9$	
Scores	Ranks	Scores	Ranks
17	1	19	2
32	7	63	12
39	9	78	15
27	4	29	5
58	10	35	8
25	3	59	11
31	6	77	14
		81	16
		68	13

Rank totals $T_1 = 40$ $T_2 = 96$

a What are the values of U_1 and U_2?

b What is the tabled value of U for this experiment at the 5% level (two-tailed test)?

c Is the result significant?

6 In a study of social assertiveness in preschool children, boys and girls are compared over a period in a day care centre. The data are:

Boys: 8, 17, 14, 21.

Girls: 18, 25, 23, 21, 34, 28, 32, 30, 13.

Test at the 0.05 level.

*Answers on p. 600.

Using SPSS for the Mann-Whitney test (non-parametric)

Computing an effect size statistic

SPSS does not report an effect size index for the Mann-Whitney test, but simple indices can be computed to communicate the size of the effect. For example, the difference in mean ranks between the two groups can serve as an effect size index.

Using SPSS with the Mann-Whitney U test

How to proceed

1 Click *Statistics* on the menu bar to reveal a drop-down menu on which you select *Non-parametric Tests*.

2 From the second drop-down menu, choose *2 Independent Samples* which opens the *Two-Independent Samples Tests* dialogue box.

3 Select your dependent variable and move it using the arrow button to the *Test Variable List* box.

4 Select your independent or group variable and place it in the *Grouping Variable* box.
5 Select *Define Groups.*
6 Type whatever codes you have used to define your categories of the independent variable into the Group boxes, e.g. '1' in the *Group 1* box and '2' in the *Group 2* box.
7 Select *Continue* and make sure that *Mann-Whitney U* is selected in the *Test Type* area.
8 Select *OK* to produce your output.

TABLE 13.8 *Example of Mann-Whitney U test output*

a *Ranks*

	Gender	N	Mean rank	Sum of ranks
HGHT	Female	42	23.21	975.00
	Male	42	61.79	2595.00
	Total	84		
RESEARCH	Female	42	43.50	1827.00
	Male	42	41.50	1743.00
	Total	84		
SELFCONC	Female	42	47.45	1993.00
	Male	42	37.55	1577.00
	Total	84		
STATS	Female	42	44.69	1877.00
	Male	42	40.31	1693.00
	Total	84		
SALNOW	Female	42	40.17	1687.00
	Male	42	44.83	1883.00
	Total	84		

b Test statistics [a]

	HGHT	RESEARCH	SELFCONC	STATS	SALNOW
Mann-Whitney U	72.000	840.000	674.000	790.000	784.000
Wilcoxon W	975.000	1743.000	1577.000	1693.000	1687.000
Z	−7.260	−.376	−1.862	−.824	−.878
Asymp. Sig. (2-tailed)	.000	.707	.063	.410	.380

a. Grouping variable: gender

The table displays data comparing males and females on five variables: height, attitudes to research, self-concept, statistics test score, and their current salary.

How to interpret the output in Table 13.8

• The focal data is in the top table where the average rank given to each group on each variable is located. For example, female height rank mean is 23.21, while the average rank given to male height is 61.79. This means that the heights for males tend to be larger than those for females, as the ranking is done from smallest person = rank 1 to tallest person = rank 84. The other variables can be interpreted in the same way.

- The lower table displays the important data, including the Mann-Whitney U and the significance levels. Significant differences occur for only for height, though self-concept level was only marginally short of reaching significance.

How to report the output in Table 13.8

We could report the results of this analysis as follows: 'The Mann-Whitney U test when applied to a number of variables found that only in the case of height was there a significant difference between males and females ($U = 72.0$, $p = .001$), with males being significantly taller'.

summary

The independent measures *t* test is used to draw inferences about mean differences between two populations or two treatment conditions. Two independent samples are randomly drawn, one for each treatment condition. The null hypothesis states that there is no significant difference between sample means. This often takes the form of an experimental and control group approach.

The Mann-Whitney test is the non-parametric equivalent of the independent *t* test. The rationale is that if differences between conditions are random then there should be a roughly equal sum of ranks in the two conditions.

14
fourteen

Statistical tests for two related groups and within-subjects design

The matched (or related) pairs *t* test (parametric)

The matched pairs or related *t* test is used when testing for significant differences between two samples which are 'related'. Examples of related samples are:

- When the same subjects are tested twice in a 'before and after' situation with an intervention such as a training session placed between the two occasions.
- When subjects in two groups are paired by selecting individuals who are as similar as possible with respect to other external variables which may influence the outcome of the research. Subjects might, for example, be matched for learning ability, sex, age and ethnicity.

For convenience, in the description of the test below it will be assumed that the scores are obtained from the same subject. However, if they were produced by different but matched subjects, this has no effect on the procedure.

Assumptions of the test

If the assumptions of the related groups *t* test are met, it is a more powerful test than the Wilcoxon signed-ranks test (p. 205); i.e. it is more likely than the Wilcoxon test to show a significant difference between the two conditions if one really exists. This is because the *t* test makes full use of interval data, while the Wilcoxon test considers only the ranking of the pairs. However, the *t* test is invalid and should not be used if its assumptions are not met.

The assumptions of the test are that:

- the measurements are made on an interval scale;
- the subjects have been randomly selected from the defined population;
- the standard deviation of the scores for the two samples should be approximately equal;
- the population from which the samples have been drawn is normally distributed. (This means in practice that the distribution of the scores for the subjects in each condition must be normally distributed.)

Within quite wide limits, the assumption can be broken without invalidating the test. However, when the assumptions of the test are broken, the power of the test is reduced so that the Wilcoxon test may well be as powerful, or more powerful. Therefore, the Wilcoxon test should be performed when the assumptions of the matched-pairs *t* test are clearly broken.

The principle of the *t* test for the within-subjects design is similar to that for the between-subjects design. One compares the actual difference that has been observed between the two sets of data with the estimate of the difference that could be expected by chance alone, i.e. the standard error of the difference. The standard error of the difference between the means for within subjects is symbolised S_D to distinguish it from the symbol SE_{diff} (used with the between-subjects *t* test).

Calculation of the standard error

The simplest way to calculate the standard error of the difference is known as the direct-difference method.

- Find the difference D between the two scores for each pair or each subject. If this difference is zero, the scores are the same for an individual under both conditions or for both members of the pair. The direction of any difference is indicated by its sign— if D is positive, then the first score is higher than the second score; if D is negative, then the second score is greater than the first score.
- Find the sum of all the D scores and divide the number of pairs in order to arrive at the mean difference, $\overline{D}$. In formula this is expressed as $\Sigma D / N$. An example of this is shown in Table 14.1. This is a within-subject design, but a matched-pairs calculation is exactly the same.

The mean difference is the numerator for the *t* test as shown in

$$t = \frac{\overline{D}}{S_{\overline{D}}}$$

where $S_{\overline{D}}$ = the standard error of the difference between two means when observations are paired.

TABLE 14.1 *Raw data for within-subjects t test*

Subject	Treatment 1	Treatment 2	Difference	D²
1	6	8	−2	4
2	10	14	−4	16
3	4	2	2	4
4	15	28	−3	9
5	5	8	−3	9
N = 5			$\Sigma D = -10$	$\Sigma D^2 = 42$
			$\overline{D} = -2$	

If you compare this with the between-subjects *t* test formula, you will notice that we have substituted $\overline{D}$ for $M_1 - M_2$ and $S_{\overline{D}}$ for SE_{diff}.

The denominator of the above formula SD is calculated from the following formula:

$$S_{\overline{D}} = \sqrt{\frac{\Sigma D^2 - \dfrac{(\Sigma D)^2}{N}}{N(N-1)}}$$

where: ΣD^2 = sum of the squared difference scores
$(\Sigma D)^2$ = sum of the difference scores squared
N   = number of pairs

Thus the full formula for *t* when the samples are correlated is:

$$t = \frac{\overline{D}}{\sqrt{\dfrac{\Sigma D^2 - \dfrac{(\Sigma D)^2}{N}}{N(N-1)}}}$$

Continuing with the example above, the D^2 value has already been computed, so:

$$S_{\overline{D}} = \sqrt{\frac{42 - \dfrac{(-10)^2}{5}}{5 \times 4}}$$

$$S_{\overline{D}} = \sqrt{1.1} = 1.05$$

$$t = \frac{-2}{1.05} = 1.90$$

Testing for significance

The difference in the obtained value of *t* can be looked up in Table 13.1, p. 178. The left-hand marginal column of Table 13.1 gives the degrees of freedom *df*, while the columns list the values of *t* which are significant at the different levels. If the value of *t* is larger than that listed in the table for the relevant *df*, then the result is significant at that level.

For this t test, the $df = N - 1$, where N is the number of pairs of observations. Thus, to look up the significance of a result, look down the df column until you find the relevant df, and read across to find the levels at which the obtained value of t is significant. If the exact df for your result is not tabulated, you must use the nearest, smaller df which does appear in the table.

Looking up the result for our example, we have a $t = 1.90$ with $df = N - 1 = 5 - 1 = 4$. Therefore, reading along the row for $df = 4$, we find that the values in columns 1 and 2 are larger than the obtained value of t, and our result is not significant at those levels. Column 2 lists the values of t which are significant at the 0.05 level with a one-tailed test, and at 0.1 level with a two-tailed test. The 0.05 level is the minimum level usually accepted for a significant result. If our experiment had involved a prediction of the direction of the difference, allowing a one-tailed test to be made, the result could be accepted as significant, but if no prediction had been made and a two-tailed test was therefore required, the result would have to be rejected as being not significant, and the null hypothesis retained.

STQ58*

Here are some raw data.

Subject	Before X	After Y	D	D^2
1	26	20	+ 6	36
2	17	27	–10	100
3	19	29	–10	100
4	13	33	–20	400
5	8	14	–6	36
			$\Sigma D = -40$	$\Sigma D^2 = 672$

1   Use the t table (Table 13.1, page 178) and decide whether the null hypothesis is retained or rejected in this example at the 0.05 level, two-tailed test.
2   What is the df when a matched-pairs design experiment is performed with a total of twenty subjects in all?
3   In a matched-group design with the following statistics, would you retain the null hypothesis using the 5% level of significance in a two-tailed test?
    $\overline{D} = 2.10$; $S_{\overline{D}} = 0.70$; N in each group = 18
4   To test the effects of organisation on recall, twelve out of twenty-four matched subjects were told to try and relate the forty words contained in a list. The other twelve subjects were not given this hint. After the first trial, the scores of the instructed subjects were 15, 12, 11, 16, 14, 11, 9, 15, 16, 12, 10, 15 (words recalled) and those of the naive subjects were 12, 13, 12, 13, 10, 13, 13, 12, 11, 14, 13, 12 (words recalled). Can you reject the null hypothesis at p < 0.01 (two-tailed)?
5   An investigator is interested in assessing the effect of a film on the attitudes of students toward a certain issue. A sample of six students is administered an attitude scale *before* and *after* viewing the film. The before-and-after scores are as follows (a high score reflects positive attitudes).

(continued)

Perform a two-tailed test at the 0.01 level and make a statement about the null hypothesis.

Before	20	15	23	17	19	11
After	25	19	24	15	26	10

6   The concept of sampling error underpins the whole subject of statistical testing. Can you explain why? Illustrate your answer by reference to two statistical tests.

7   A psychologist believes that relaxation can reduce the severity of asthma attacks in children. The researcher measures the severity of asthma attacks by the number of doses of medicine required. Then relaxation training is given. The week following training, the number of doses is again recorded. The data are reported below.

Subject	Before X	After Y	D	D^2
A	9	4	−5	25
B	4	1	−3	9
C	5	5	0	0
D	4	0	−4	16
E	5	1	−4	16
			sum of D = −16	sum of D^2 = 66

What conclusion could we reach about the effects of relaxation training using $p < .05$ two-tailed test?

8   A researcher wishes to examine the effect of hypnosis treatment on teenage smokers. A sample of four adolescent smokers records the average number of cigarettes smoked per day in the week prior to treatment. One month into the hypnosis treatment they record the average daily cigarette consumption over a week. The data are as follows:

Subject	Before	After
1	19	13
2	35	37
3	20	14
4	31	25

a   What is the mean D score?

b   What is the sum of D^2?

c   Test with a 5% level of significance and make a statement about the null hypothesis?

9   Consider the following experiment and then respond to the questions.
Subjects were given two equivalent sets of fifteen words to memorise under two conditions. The data from the study are shown below. Is the difference between conditions under which memorisation took place a significant effect?

Subject	Condition A	Condition B	Difference (D)	D^2
1	6	6	0	0
2	15	10	5	25
3	13	7	6	36
4	14	8	6	36
5	12	8	4	16
6	16	12	4	16
7	14	10	4	16
8	15	10	5	25
9	18	11	7	49
10	17	9	8	64
11	12	8	4	16
12	7	8	−1	1
13	15	8	7	49
	$M_A = 13.28$	$M_B = 8.85$	$\Sigma D = 59$	$\Sigma D^2 = 349$
			$(\Sigma D)^2 = 3481$	

    a   How many degrees of freedom are there?
    b   What is the value of t ?
    c   What is the critical value for t in the table given the appropriate number of df and a two-tailed test with $p < 0.01$?
    d   Is there a significant difference between the conditions?
10 a   For what sort of situation is the repeated measures design well suited?
    b   In what way is the matched subjects design similar to repeated measures design?
    c   What is the carry-over effect?
11 What happens to the critical value of t for a specific level of significance when df increases in value?
* Answers on p. 600.

Computing the effect size statistic for the parametric paired-samples t test

SPSS supplies all the information necessary to compute two types of effect size indices, d and eta^2. The d statistic may be computed using the following equations:

$$d = \frac{\text{mean}}{\text{SD}} \quad \text{or} \quad d = \frac{t}{\sqrt{N}}$$

where the mean and standard deviation are reported in the output under 'paired differences'.

The d statistic evaluates the degree that the mean of the difference scores deviates from 0 in standard deviation units. If d equals 0, the mean of the difference scores is equal to 0. As d diverges from 0, the effect size becomes larger. The value of d can range from negative infinity to positive infinity. Regardless of sign, *d* values of .2, .5, and .8 traditionally represent small, medium and large effect sizes, respectively.

An eta^2 may be computed as an alternative to *d*. This ranges in value from 0 to 1. A value of 0 indicates that the mean of the difference scores is equal to 0. In contrast, a value of 1 indicates that the difference scores in the sample are all the same non-zero value (perfect replication). Eta^2 can be computed as follows:

$$eta^2 = \frac{(N)(mean^2)}{(N)(mean^2) + (N - 1)(SD^2)}$$

$$or \quad = \frac{t^2}{t^2 + (N - 1)}$$

Traditionally, values of .01, .06 and .14 represent small, medium and large effect sizes respectively.

Using SPSS to compare two samples of correlated/related scores using the parametric paired samples *t* test

We will illustrate the computation of a paired samples *t* test with dummy data comparing the pre- and post-test scores of a group of social workers on an in-service course.

How to proceed

1 Choose *Statistics* to display a drop-down menu.
2 Select *Compare Means* to open a second drop-down menu from which you select *Paired Sample T Test*.
3 In the open *Paired-Samples T Test* dialogue box click on your first dependent variable which moves it to the *Current Selections* box as variable 1.
4 Select your other variable which puts it beside *Variable 2* in the *Current Selections* box.
5 Click on the arrow button to move both variables into the *Paired Variables* box.
6 Choose *OK* to produce the output.

TABLE 14.2 *Example of paired t test output*

a Paired samples statistics

		Mean	N	Std deviation	Std error mean
Pair 1	POST-TEST	47.1429	84	7.6727	.8372
	PRE-TEST	42.4048	84	9.7833	1.0674

b Paired samples correlations

		N	Correlation	Sig.
Pair 1	POST-TEST & PRE-TEST	84	.057	.607

c Paired samples test

		Paired differences					df	Sig. (2-tailed)
		Mean	Std deviation	Std error mean	95% confidence interval of the difference		t	
					Lower	Upper		
Pair 1	POST-TEST/ PRE-TEST	4.7381	12.0842	1.3185	2.1157	7.3605	3.594	83	.001

How to interpret the output in Table 14.2

- Three subtables are produced. The top table provides descriptive statistics. The average pre-test score was 42.41 with an SD of 9.78, while the mean post-test was 47.14, with an SD of 7.67.
- The second subtable displays a Pearson correlation between the two sets of scores.
- The bottom subtable provides the test statistics. The paired difference between these two mean scores is presented along with *t,* and the significance level and the standard error of this mean. The difference between the two means is 4.738 and the standard error of means for this sample size is 1.3185.
- The *t*-value of the difference between the sample means is 3.594, which has an exact two-tailed significance level of 0.001 with 83 degrees of freedom.

How to report the output in Table 14.2

The results could be reported as follows: 'A paired samples *t* test (N = 84) was conducted to evaluate whether test scores differed after an inservice course. The mean scores between pre- and post-tests differed significantly (*t* = 3.594, df = 83, p < .001) with the post-test mean being significantly higher then the pre-test mean.'

The calculated effect size (d) was .38, a small value.

Wilcoxon signed-ranks test (non-parametric)

This test is appropriate for a two-condition within-subject design, either when the same subjects perform under both conditions or when pairs of subjects are matched for a number of variables (sex, age, intelligence, motivation, etc.). The Wilcoxon test is used instead of a related *t* test if the differences between treatments can only be ranked in size, or if the data are quite skewed, or if there is clearly a difference in the variance of the groups, i.e. the assumptions for the related *t* test do not apply.

Rationale

The aim of the Wilcoxon signed ranks test is to compare the performance of the same subjects or matched pairs of subjects across two occasions or conditions, to determine whether there are significant differences between the scores from the two performances. The scores of *Occasion 2* or *Condition B* are subtracted from those of *Occasion 1* or *Condition A*, and the resulting differences given a plus (+), or, if negative, a minus (−) sign. The differences are then ranked in order of their absolute size; the smallest size difference is given a 1, the next in value is given a 2, and so on, up to the largest difference. The ranks are then added up separately for the pluses and minuses. The smaller total of ranks gives the value of T which can be looked up in the appropriate table for significance.

If there are only random differences, as stated by the null hypothesis, then there should be roughly equal numbers of high and low ranks for the plus and minus differences. If there is a preponderance of high ranks for one sign, this means that there are larger differences in one direction than would be expected by chance.

Step-by-step procedure to calculate the value of Wilcoxon T

TABLE 14.3 *Calculation of the value of T (the Wilcoxon statistic)*

Subject pair	Condition A Vocabulary of children at 'home'	Condition B Vocabulary of children at 'nursery'	D (A–B)	Ranks of D	Smaller signed sum
1	3	5	−2	5(−)	
2	4	5	−1	2(−)	
3	3	2	1	2(+)	+2
4	1	5	−4	8.5(−)	
5	4	1	1	2(+)	+2
6	2	5	−3	7(−)	
7	3	5	−2	5(−)	
8	4	4	0	omit tie	
9	1	5	−4	8.5(−)	
10	3	5	−2	5(−)	
					T = 4
					N = 9

1 Calculate the difference D between each pair of scores, assigning plus or minus signs.

See column D(A–B) in Table 14.3.

2 Rank the differences in order of their magnitude from the smallest (rank 1) to the largest. When ranking the differences, ignore signs.

See column 'Ranks of D' in Table 14.3.

3 Add together separately the ranks corresponding to the different signs. Since the total of ranks for the plus sign is smaller (4), the observed value of T = 4.

See column 'Ranks of D'. In brackets you will find the signs of the ranks corresponding to the signs of the differences. Observed value of T is 2 + 2 = 4. N = 10 − 1 = 9.

4 Count the number of pairs of subjects N (not counting ties).

5 Find the critical value of T for the selected level of significance. If the observed value of T is less than or equal to the critical value in Table 14.4, the null hypothesis can be rejected.

Selected level of significance is $p < 0.05$ (two-tailed). Since our observed value of $T = 4$ is less than the critical value of 6, the null hypothesis can be rejected.

a We arrived at our value of T by adding together the ranks with the plus (+) sign because their total is undoubtedly smaller than that of the ranks with the minus (−) sign. Sometimes the difference between the two totals is not obvious. If there is any doubt, the totals of the ranks for both plus and minus signs should be computed to see which is smallest.

b We reduced the number of pairs of subjects N from 10 to 9 in view of the tie which occurred between the scores of one pair.

Looking up significance in Table 14.4

Table 14.4 (p. 208) gives the level of significance of T for both a one-tailed test and a two-tailed test in the two top rows. In the left-hand column are the values of N.

In our example, there was no prediction of a direction, i.e. that there would be higher vocabulary scores for 'nursery' or 'home' children. Therefore you should use the levels of significance for a two-tailed hypothesis. Since the experimental hypothesis was tested at the $p < 0.05$ (two-tailed) level of significance, you select the appropriate column, and at the intersection with the N = 9 row, you will find the critical value of T, i.e. 6. Since the observed value of 4 is less than the critical value of T, you can reject the null hypothesis and conclude that there is a significant difference between the vocabulary scores in the two groups of matched subjects. *Note:* Remember that all this would also apply if the same subjects had performed under two conditions.

Suppose you had made a prediction in one direction, say, that children who went to nursery school (*Condition B*) would score higher on the vocabulary test. In this case, you could have used a one-tailed level of significance, in which the critical value for $p < 0.05$ would have been 8. The point is that for a one-tailed prediction T could have been larger—for example, 7—and would still have been significant at the $p < 0.05$ one-tailed level, although a T of 7 would not have been significant at the $p < 0.05$ two-tailed level. The actual observed value of 4 is smaller than 6, the critical value for a $p < 0.025$ one-tailed significance level. You would then have to look at the table of results to see whether the children in *Condition B* had in fact scored higher than the children in *Condition A* and that the results were significantly in the predicted direction.

Note that had a stricter criterion been applied, i.e. $p < 0.01$ for a one-tailed test or $p < 0.02$ for a two-tailed test, a T of 3 or less is required for significance. Our T is 4, so the result is not significant at these stricter levels of significance.

TABLE 14.4 *Critical values of T at various levels of probability (Wilcoxon)*

	Level of significance for one-tailed test					Level of significance for one-tailed test			
	0.05	0.25	0.01	0.005		0.05	0.025	0.01	0.005
	Level of significance for two-tailed test					Level of significance for two-tailed test			
N	0.10	0.05	0.02	0.01	N	0.10	0.05	0.02	0.01
5	1	–	–	–	28	130	117	102	92
6	2	1	–	–	29	141	127	111	100
7	4	2	0	–	30	152	137	120	109
8	6	4	2	0	31	163	148	130	118
9	8	6	3	2	32	175	159	141	128
10	11	8	5	3	33	188	171	151	138
11	14	11	7	5	34	201	183	162	149
12	17	14	10	7	35	214	195	174	160
13	21	17	13	10	36	228	208	186	171
14	26	21	16	13	37	242	222	198	183
15	30	25	20	16	38	256	235	211	195
16	36	30	24	19	39	271	250	224	208
17	41	35	28	23	40	287	264	238	221
18	47	40	33	28	41	303	279	252	234
19	54	46	38	32	42	319	295	267	248
20	60	52	43	37	43	336	311	281	262
21	68	59	49	43	44	353	327	297	277
22	75	66	56	49	45	371	344	313	292
23	83	73	62	55	46	389	361	329	307
24	92	81	69	61	47	408	379	345	323
25	101	90	77	68	48	427	397	362	339
26	110	98	85	76	49	446	415	380	356
27	120	107	93	84	50	466	434	398	373

Source: F. Wilcoxon, *Some Rapid Approximate Statistical Procedures*, American Cyanamid Co. 1949.

The symbol *T* denotes the small sum of ranks associated with differences that are all of the same sign. For any given N (number of subjects or pairs of subjects), the observed *T* is significant at a given level if it is *equal to or less than* the value shown in the table.

STQ59*

1 Twelve mothers were tested for their attitudes to pre-school education, before and after their own children attended a pre-school. Here is the data with high scores representing a positive attitudes:

Before	7	9	12	8	6	4	10	12	7	5	11	9
After	9	12	11	14	12	7	9	13	14	8	9	13

a What is the null hypothesis?
b Using the Wilcoxon, interpret the results at the 5% level with a two-tailed test.

part 2 | quantitative methods

2 A local school has made an intensive effort to increase parent attendance at the end of year parent evening. The data for each year group for last year and this year are as follows:

Year group	1994	1995	d	Rank of d
1	18	18	0	1.5
2	24	24	0	1.5
3	31	30	−1	3
4	28	24	−4	4
5	17	24	7	5
6	16	24	8	6
7	15	26	11	7.5
8	18	29	11	7.5
9	20	36	16	9
10	9	28	19	10

a What does the null hypothesis state?
b Why does N = 8?
c What is the critical value of T with N = 8 and p < .05?
d What is the calculated T?
e Do you reject or retain the null hypothesis? What do you conclude about the effectiveness of the campaign to get more parent attendance?

3 A doctor tested the effectiveness of a new allergy drug by measuring children's skin reaction before and after treatment. The difference scores for ten subjects were: 3, 46, 16, −2, 38, 14, 0, −8, 25 and 41.
Use Wilcoxon to test whether this data provides sufficient evidence to conclude that there has been a significant effect.

*Answers on p. 601.

Using SPSS for the Wilcoxon test (non-parametric)

Computing an effect size statistic

For the Wilcoxon test, the mean positive ranked difference score and the mean negative ranked difference score could be reported.

Using SPSS for the Wilcoxon test

1 Select *Statistics* and from the drop-down menu choose *Nonparametric Tests*.
2 Click on *2 Related Samples Test* in the second drop down window.
3 Highlight your two variables and place them in the *Current Selections* box.
4 Using the arrow button transfer them to the *Test Pairs List* box.
5 Make sure *Wilcoxon* is selected in the *Test Type* area.
6 Select *OK* to display the output.

TABLE 14.5 Example of Wilcoxon test output

a Descriptive statistics

	N	Mean	Std deviation	Minimum	Maximum
SALBEG	84	*****	$4412.79	$6000.00	$22000.00
SALNOW	84	*****	$12733.90	$25000.00	$75000.00

b Wilcoxon signed ranks test

		N	Mean rank	Sum of ranks
SALNOW	Negative ranks	0[a]	.00	.00
SALBEG	Positive ranks	84[b]	42.50	3570.00
	Ties	0[c]		
	Total	84		

a SALNOW < SALBEG
b SALNOW > SALBEG
c SALBEG = SALNOW

c Test statistics[a]

	SALNOW/SALBEG
Z	–7.963[b]
Asymp. Sig. (2-tailed)	.000

a Wilcoxon Signed Ranks Test
b Based on negative ranks

This table displays results comparing the starting salaries and current salaries of 84 persons in one organisation.

How to interpret the output in Table 14.5

- Three subtables are produced. The top one lists the descriptive statistics.
- The output in the middle subtable tells us that there are no cases where starting salary is higher than current salary, nor are there any ties, and that in all 84 cases current salary is higher than at commencement of job.
- In the bottom subtable, instead of using t tables, the computer uses a formula which relates to the standardised Z-distribution. The Z-value is –7.963 which has a two-tailed probability of 0.000. This means that the difference between the two variables is statistically highly significant.

How to report the output in Table 14.5

'A Wilcoxon test was conducted to evaluate whether 84 employees had significantly greater salaries now than when they commenced work. The results indicated a high statistically significant difference between commencement salary and current salary (Wilcoxon, Z = –7.963, p > 0.001).'

Comparison of the power of tests based on within-subjects and between-subjects designs

The formula used in calculating the standard error of the difference for within-subjects design provides a smaller standard error than does the formula used with between-subjects design. The lower standard error results in a more sensitive test of the significance of the difference between means, and increases the likelihood of rejection of the null hypothesis when it is false.

STQ60

Demonstrate this smaller standard error for the related *t* test, by recalculating the example in Table 14.3 by the between-subjects *t* test as though the sets of scores came from independent groups. What difference do you note? Why is the standard error now larger?

STQ61*

In a related *t* test, which of the following make it easier to reject the null hypothesis?
a   Increasing N
b   Decreasing N
c   Decreasing D
d   Using a one-tailed rather than a two-tailed test

*Answers on p. 601.

summary

In repeated measures or within-groups design a single sample of subjects is randomly selected and measurements repeated on this sample for both treatment conditions. This often takes the form of a before and after study. The null hypothesis states that there is no significant difference between conditions. The matched-pairs design employs two groups which are matched on a pair-by-pair basis, which can then be regarded as the same group tested twice.

The repeated measures design has the advantage of reducing error variance due to the removal of individual differences. This increases the possibility of detecting real effects from the experimental treatment. A problem is the likely presence of carry-over effects, such as practice and motivation. Counterbalancing should be used to prevent such order effects.

The Wilcoxon test is the non-parametric test for the within-groups design. It involves testing for significant differences between ranks in the two conditions.

Testing hypotheses of relationship I: Chi square

15
fifteen

We have seen how research data obtained to test hypotheses of difference are analysed. We now turn to research data obtained to test hypotheses of relationships and see how that is analysed.

Research on relationships is concerned with the association of variables; essentially how strongly variables are related to each other. In these situations there are a number of statistical techniques for analysing the data depending on the level of data. Three techniques will be considered:

1 Chi square for testing associations with nominal data.
2 Rank order correlation for testing relationships with ordinal data.
3 Product–moment correlation for testing relationships with interval data.

Chi-square rationale

Chi square is a simple non-parametric test of significance, suitable for nominal data where observations can be classified into discrete categories and treated as frequencies. Chi-square tests hypotheses about the independence (or alternatively the association) of frequency counts in various categories.

For example, the data may be the proportions of students preferring each one of three brands of low-calorie colas, or the proportion of students voting for particular candidates in an election for student union president. Categories of responses are set up, such as Brands A, B and C of colas or 'For and Against' in the election, and the number of individuals or events which fall into each category is recorded. In such a situation one can obtain nothing more than the frequency, or the number of times, that a particular category is chosen. This constitutes nominal data. With such data the only analysis possible is to determine whether the frequencies observed in the sample differ significantly from hypothesised frequencies. There are many educational and social science issues which involve nominal data for which chi square is a simple and appropriate means of analysis; for example, social class levels, academic subject categories, age groups, sex, voting preferences, pass–fail dichotomies, etc. The symbol is the Greek letter *chi* which is pronounced 'kye' to rhyme with 'sky', and written as χ^2.

The hypotheses for the chi-square test are H_0 where the variables are statistically independent, and H_1 where the variables are statistically dependent.

The formula is $\chi^2 = \Sigma \dfrac{(O - E)^2}{E}$ where

O = observed frequency—what is observed;
E = expected frequency; and
Σ = the summation over all the categories we are measuring.

There are two major uses of chi square (χ^2):

- As a goodness-of-fit test when it tells us how well an observed distribution fits a hypothesised or theoretical distribution; for example, in an essay exam are some questions chosen more than others?
- As a cross-tabulation between two categories, each of which can be divided into two or more subcategories; for example, preference for type of music (jazz, country and western, rock) against sex (male and female). The 2 × 2 contingency table is a special case of this and will be considered later.

But whichever of these uses chi square is put to, the general principle remains the same. In each case, one compares the observed proportions in a sample with the expected proportions and applies the chi-square test to determine whether a difference between observed and expected proportions is likely to be a function of sampling error (non-significant) or unlikely to be a function of sampling error (significant association).

STQ62

1   What level of measurement is used with chi square?
2   In the chi-square formula what do O and E represent?

Goodness-of-fit chi square

Here is an example of a goodness-of-fit chi square. Consider the question: are more children born in one season of the year than in another? To investigate this, we could start off by gathering some birth dates from a randomly selected sample of school pupils. Let's just suppose that we now have a total of 100 birth dates, and that we have defined the seasons so that each of spring, summer, autumn and winter has an equal number of days.

STQ63

How many birthdays out of the 100 would you expect by chance each season if season did not in fact have any influence?

We would expect an even distribution. That is 25 in each season. Now it might turn out that when we actually grouped the observed birth dates of the 100 pupils they were distributed thus:

Spring	Summer	Autumn	Winter
35	28	15	22

The question now would be, 'Is the fact that the observed frequencies are different from what we expected more likely due to chance, or does it more likely represent *actual population differences* in birth rate during the different seasons?'.

To arrive at an estimate of the probability that the observed frequency distribution is due to chance, the χ^2 test is applied. The chi-square test permits us to estimate the probability that observed frequencies differ from expected frequencies through chance alone.

If the null hypothesis is true, any departure from these frequencies would be the result of pure chance. But how far can a departure from these frequencies go before we can say that such a discrepancy would occur so infrequently on a chance basis that our observations are significantly different from those expected? Well, when χ^2 is computed it can be compared with its table value (Table 15.1) at the usual levels of significance to see if it reaches or exceeds them. If it does, the null hypothesis of chance variation is rejected.

STQ64

What are the two major conventional levels of significance we would employ?

STQ65

What two sets of data do we compare in a χ^2 test?

In calculating χ^2, we need to enter our observed and expected data into a table of cells. The cells are filled with the data on the lines of the following model:

$$
\begin{array}{|ll|}
\hline
O & E \\
 & \\
 & \\
 & \\
(O-E) & (O-E)^2 \\
\hline
\end{array}
$$

where   O = observed data
              E = expected data

We will now fill in the cells in our example by placing the observed and expected data into their respective cells and calculate $(O - E)$ and $(O - E)^2$.

Spring		Summer		Autumn		Winter	
35	25	28	25	15	25	22	25
10	100	3	9	10	100	3	9

$$\Sigma \frac{(O - E)^2}{E} = \frac{100}{25} + \frac{9}{25} + \frac{100}{25} + \frac{9}{25}$$
$$= 4 + 0.36 + 4 + 0.36$$
$$\chi^2 = 8.72$$

A relatively large chi square should indicate that the Es differed more from the Os than is likely by chance. As to how large a value for chi square is needed to reject the null hypothesis of no significant association between season and births, consult Table 15.1. To enter the table we need to know the *df*.

Degrees of freedom in a goodness-of-fit χ^2

STQ66

Do you recall what degrees of freedom (*df*) represent? Look back at p. 154 if you don't.

The number of observations free to vary in our example is 3 because once we have fixed the frequency of three categories, say spring, summer and autumn, the fourth has to be 22 to make the total 100. So the fourth category is fixed. The same principle holds true for any number of categories. The degrees of freedom in a goodness-of-fit test is one less than the number of categories $(k - 1)$.

STQ67

If we were dealing with preferences for five brands of a product, how many *df* would we have?

The final step is to refer to Table 15.1 in order to determine whether the obtained χ^2 value is statistically significant or not. Look at it now. The probability values along the top refer to the likelihood of the values of χ^2 listed in the columns below being reached or exceeded by chance. Our old friend *df* forms the left-hand column. In our example, it is entered with 3 *df*.

As is true with the *t*-table, if the χ^2 value calculated is equal to or greater than the value required for significance at a predetermined probability level for the *df*, then the null hypothesis of no real difference between the observed and expected frequencies is rejected at that level of significance. If the calculated χ^2 is smaller than the tabled value required for

TABLE 15.1 *Distribution of chi square*

df	0.1	0.05	0.02	0.01	0.001
1	2.706	3.841	5.412	6.635	10.827
2	4.605	5.991	7.824	9.210	13.815
3	6.251	7.815	9.837	11.345	16.266
4	7.779	9.488	11.668	13.277	18.467
5	9.236	11.070	13.388	15.086	20.515
6	10.645	12.592	15.033	16.812	22.457
7	12.071	4.067	16.622	18.475	24.322
8	13.362	15.507	18.168	20.090	26.125
9	14.684	16.919	19.679	21 666	27.877
10	15.987	18.307	21.161	23.209	29.588
11	17.251	19.675	22.618	24.725	31.264
12	18.549	21.026	24.054	26.217	32.909
13	19.812	22.362	25.472	27.688	34.528
14	21.064	23.685	26.873	29.141	36.123
15	22.307	34.996	28.259	30.578	37.697
16	23.542	26.296	29.633	32.000	39.252
17	24.769	27.587	30.995	33.409	40.790
18	25.989	28.869	32.346	34.805	42.312
19	27.204	30.144	33.687	36.191	43.820
20	28.412	31.410	35.020	37.566	45.315
21	29.615	32.671	36.343	38.932	46.797
22	30.813	33.924	37.659	40.289	48.268
23	32.007	35.172	38.968	41.638	49.728
24	33.196	36.415	40.270	42.980	51.179
25	34.382	37.652	41.566	44.314	52.620
26	35.563	38.885	42.856	45.642	54.052
27	36.741	40.113	44.140	46.963	55.476
28	37.916	41.337	45.419	48.278	56.893
29	39.087	42.557	46.693	49.588	58.302
30	40.256	43.773	47.692	50.892	59.703

Source: Table IV, Fisher & Yates, *Statistical Tables for Biological, Agricultural and Medical Research*, 6th edn, 1974, Addison Wesley Longman, London.

To use Table 15.1 you first compute the *df*—which is explained in the text—and locate the appropriate row. You then look across the table to see how large χ^2 needs to be in order to reach a desired level of significance. For example with 1 *df*, χ^2 must be at least 3.84 to be significant at the 5% level; with 10 *df* it must be at least 18.31.

significance at that level, then one may not reject the null hypothesis. Table 15.1 tells us that with 3 *df* a χ^2 value of at least 7.82 is necessary to reject the null hypothesis at the 0.05 level. The value of χ^2 in our example is 8.72. Since 8.72 is more than the value required for significance, we can reject the null hypothesis, and accept the alternative hypothesis that births are not randomly distributed through the year.

At this point, it is important to note the effect of the degrees of freedom on the significance of any calculated χ^2. In Table 15.1, it can be seen that the χ^2 required for significance at any given level gets larger as the number of degrees of freedom gets larger. For 2 *df* a χ^2 of 5.99 is needed for significance at the 5% level. With 3 *df* this χ^2 value increases to 7.82, to 11.07 for 5 *df* and to 43.77 for 30 *df*. Thus it is extremely important to know the correct number of *df* when attempting to interpret the significance of an obtained chi square.

STQ68*

1   Is an observed χ^2 of 14.6 with 5 *df* statistically significant at the 0.01 level?
2   Is an observed χ^2 value of 8.40 with 3 *df* statistically at the 0.05 level?
3   What is the critical value of χ^2 with 4 *df* at $p < 0.001$?

*Answers on p. 601.

Special correction for 1 *df*

The sampling distribution of χ^2, as represented in Table 15.1, is a continuous theoretical frequency curve. For situations where the number of degrees of freedom is 1, this continuous curve somewhat underestimates the actual probabilities. An adjustment is necessary to make the χ^2 probabilities in Table 15.1 more accurately approximate the actual probabilities of the discrete events. The appropriate adjustment is known as Yates' correction, which consists of subtracting 0.5 from the absolute difference between O and E for each category before squaring the difference. (The absolute difference between two numbers is the difference recorded as a positive number regardless of whether that difference is actually positive or negative.) The formula for χ^2 then becomes:

$$\chi^2 = \Sigma \frac{(|O - E| - 0.5)^2}{E}$$

For example, if in one cell O = 60 and E = 80 then (O – E) = 20. From this would be taken 0.5 so that (O – E) is corrected to 19.5 before squaring.

STQ69*

1   A random sample of teachers in a local authority were asked, 'Should the local council economise by cutting down the number of hours the town swimming pool is open?'. The results were:

Agree	Disagree	Indifferent
12	24	12

   a   What is the null hypothesis?
   b   What is the value of chi square?
   c   What are the degrees of freedom (*df*)?
   d   Is the value significant at the 0.05 level?
   e   What conclusion would be reached?

2   An investigator studying sex stereotypes in basic reading texts finds that there are 16 episodes in which Joe plays the role of leader and four in which Jane plays the role of leader. Could these proportions be a function of chance?

(continued)

3 A sample of 30 student voters were asked which of three candidates they planned to vote for student union president with the following results:

Candidate	Frequency
Smith	5
Jones	20
Brown	5

Test the null hypothesis that there is no difference in preference for any of the candidates.

4 A group of college students were shown a series of pictures illustrating a new clothing style. After viewing the pictures, each student was asked if they approved or disapproved of the style. Below are the data received from 54 students.

Approve   35
Disapprove   19

Compute the chi square for the above data.

Using p = 0.05 as your designated level for significance, use Table 15.1 to evaluate the chi square obtained. State the null hypothesis being tested. On the basis of the chi-square test, do you accept or reject the null hypothesis?

5 A researcher wished to examine children's preferences among four types of transportation. A sample of 90 children was randomly selected and asked which type they preferred. The following data were obtained:

Automobile	Bus	Train	Airplane
10	13	27	40

Compute the chi square for the above data.

6 Which of the following values of χ^2 is least likely to have occurred by chance?

a $\chi^2 = 6.55$ $df = 1$
b $\chi^2 = 10.50$ $df = 2$
c $\chi^2 = 8.75$ $df = 3$
d $\chi^2 = 12.31$ $df = 4$
e $\chi^2 = 14.79$ $df = 6$

7 A large department store reports the following incidence of shoplifting by children over three holiday periods:

Easter 50, Christmas 81, Winter 27.

Perform a χ^2 test and decide whether a significant difference exists among the holiday periods using p = 0.05.

8 A survey asked a random sample of teachers if they were in favour of corporal punishment in secondary schools. The results were:

Yes = 20   No = 60

Is this difference in response significantly different from the theoretical expectation?

*Answers on p. 601.

Chi-square test of the independence of categorical variables (cross classification)

We have just seen how to deal with categories divided on the basis of a single variable. However, another widely used application of the χ^2 procedure involves its use with data that are in the form of paired observations on two variables. That is, a sample of subjects is classified into categories on two variables and the question concerns the presence or absence of a relationship between the variables. For example, one might ask: 'Is there a relationship between the socioeconomic background of a child and his or her preference for extra-curricular activities at school? Is there a relationship between parental income level and attitudes toward some current education issue? Is there a difference in the extent of reported drug use among adolescents coming from different ethnic backgrounds?' The independence or the association of these variables can be determined by means of the chi-square test.

When data of these types are gathered, they are recorded in what is called a contingency table. The paired responses are categorised into cells organised by rows and columns. Let us consider whether there is an association between family size and religious persuasion. Here is the observed data from our survey.

	One child	Two children	Three or more children
Muslim	20	16	8
Protestant	40	22	10
Roman Catholic	12	36	42

STQ70

What is the null hypothesis for this table?

We hypothesised that there was no significant association between religious persuasion and the size of family.

It is now necessary to determine the expected frequency values for each of the cells in the contingency table. When the chi-square procedure is applied to a contingency table to test for independence of the row and column variables, there is no *a priori* basis for hypothesising the expected frequency distribution as there was in the χ^2 goodness-of-fit test. The expected frequencies in each cell are derived from the data themselves. These expected cell frequencies are those one would expect to get if the two variables were completely independent of each other and are derived from the row and column totals. To obtain the expected frequency we must first find the row totals and column totals and grand total. This is shown at the top of page 220.

	One child	Two children	Three or more children	Row total
Muslim	20$_a$	16$_b$	8	44
Protestant	40	22	10	72
Roman Catholic	12	36	42	90
Column Totals	72	74	60	Grand total 206

The expected frequency for each cell is calculated by multiplying the row total for that cell by the column total for that cell and then dividing by the grand total.

$$\text{Expected for cell 'a'} = \frac{44 \times 72}{206} = 15.40$$

$$\text{Expected for cell 'b'} = \frac{44 \times 74}{206} = 15.80$$

Now you work out the rest.

The expected frequencies have all been placed in the respective cells below. So now we must complete each cell by adding in $(O - E)$ and $(O - E)^2$. This has been done for you below.

	One child		Two children		Three or more children		Row total
Muslim	20	15.4	16	15.8	8	12.8	44
	4.6	21.1	0.2	0.04	4.8	23.0	
Protestant	40	25.2	22	25.9	10	21.0	72
	14.8	21.9	3.9	15.2	11	12.1	
Roman Catholic	12	31.5	36	32.3	42	26.2	90
	19.5	380.2	3.7	13.7	13.8	190.4	
	72		74		60		206

$$\chi^2 = \Sigma \frac{(O - E)^2}{E} = \frac{21.1}{15.4} + \frac{0.04}{15.8} + \ldots \frac{190.4}{26.2}$$
$$\chi^2 = 1.37 + 0.002 + 1.8 + 8.7 + 0.59 + 5.8 + 12.1 + 0.42 + 7.27$$
$$= 38.05$$

Degrees of freedom for contingency table

Recall that in any statistic the *df* are the number of values that are free to vary. The general rule is that the *df* for a contingency table equals the number of rows minus one, multiplied by the number of columns minus one:

$$df = (\text{rows} - 1) \times (\text{columns} - 1)$$

In our example with three rows and three columns we have:

$$(3 - 1) \times (3 - 1) = 4 \, df$$

part 2 | quantitative methods

STQ71

If we had a 3 × 4 table, how many would the *df* have been?

STQ72

Look up in Table 15.1 the intersection of 4 *df* and 0.05 level of significance. Is our value of 38.05 significant at the 0.05 level? Is it significant at the 0.01 level as well?

STQ73

Make a statement concerning the null hypothesis of this study.

Since our computed chi-square far exceeds the critical tabled values of 9.488 (0.05 level) and 13.277 (0.01 level), we are well justified in claiming that there is a significant association between family size and religious persuasion in our sample. We reject the null hypothesis that there is only a chance relationship, i.e. that both categories are independent.

2 × 2 contingency table

One of the most common uses of the chi-square test of the independence of categorical variables is with the 2 × 2 contingency table, in which there are two variables, each divided into two categories. Let use imagine our categories are 1) adult/adolescent, and 2) approve of abortion/don't approve. The χ^2 table would be as follows:

	Adolescent	Adult	
Approve of Abortion	120	18	138
Don't approve of Abortion	20	98	118
	140	116	256

(*df* = 1 always in a 2 × 2 table)

It is up to you now to work out E, (O − E) and (O − E)^2. Does Yates' correction mean anything to you? When you have done all this, calculate χ^2 and check for significance at the 0.05 and 0.01 levels. How many degrees of freedom are you to use? What is your conclusion about the results in terms of the null hypothesis? A completed table and interpretation of results will be found below for the cowardly.

	Adolescent		Adult		
Approve of Abortion	120 44.5	75.5 1936	18 44.5	62.53 1936	138
Don't Approve of Abortion	20 44.5	64.53 1936	98 44.5	53.5 1936	118
	140		116		256

χ^2 = 122.78 *df* = 1 (always in a 2 × 2 table!)

(Did you remember to use Yates' correction?!)

The result is extremely significant well beyond the 0.01 level. Hence the null hypothesis that there is only a chance association between age group and attitude to abortion is rejected for this sample. The two categories are not independent of each other for the sample considered.

Restrictions in the use of the chi square

1 It is important to remember that χ^2 is most appropriate for the analysis of data that are classified as frequency of occurrence within categories (nominal data). When the data are ordinal or interval, other tests of significance are usually preferred. It must be used on frequencies only, not on percentages.

2 When nominal data are arranged into categories for a chi-square analysis, these categories must be mutually exclusive categories, which means that each response can be classified into only one cell. This is true because a fundamental assumption in the use of the chi-square test is that each observation or frequency is independent of all others. Thus one could not obtain several responses or observations from the same individual and classify each as if it were independent of others. If this is done, the same individual is placed in several categories, which inflates the size of N, and may lead to the rejection of the null hypothesis when it should not be rejected.

3 Another restriction in the use of the chi-square test is that when there are multiple categories, larger samples are needed. If N is small and consequently the expected frequency in any cell is small, the sample statistic may not approximate the theoretical χ^2 distribution very closely. A rule-of-thumb which one may follow is that in a χ^2 analysis with 1 *df*, the expected frequency in all cells should at least equal or be greater than 5. When the number of *df* is greater than one, the expected frequency should be equal to or greater than 5 in at least 80 per cent of the cells. If this condition is not fulfilled, it may be necessary to omit one or more categories of one or both variables. Alternatively, we might combine categories, if it makes sense, so that we have the necessary expected frequencies in each cell. Neither of these alternatives is really desirable, since both involve a reduction in the amount of information available. If practically possible, we might obtain a larger sample so that the conditions are fulfilled for the original classification.

4 The χ^2 test is sensitive to difference but not direction of difference; it is inherently two-tailed. Only by inspection of the obtained data can the direction be determined.

Computing effect size and power

Effect size for the goodness of fit chi square

SPSS does not supply an effect size index for the goodness of fit chi square. However, one can be easily computed based on the reported statistics:

$$\text{effect size} = \frac{\text{chi square}}{(\text{total sample size across all categories})(\text{number of categories} - 1)}$$

part 2 | quantitative methods

The coefficient can range in value from 0 to 1. A value of 0 indicates that the sample proportions are exactly equal to the hypothesised proportions, while a value of 1 indicates that the sample proportions are as different as possible from the hypothesised proportions.

Effect size statistic for chi square tests of independence (contingency tables)

SPSS provides a number of indices that assess the strength of the relationship between row and column variables. They include the contingency coefficient, phi, Cramer's V, and lambda. The two indices usually used are phi and Cramer's V.

The phi coefficient for a 2 × 2 table is a special case of the Pearson product–moment correlation coefficient for a 2 × 2 contingency table. Because most social scientists have a reasonable understanding of the Pearson product–moment correlation coefficient, they are likely to feel comfortable using its derivative, the phi coefficient. Phi (ϕ) is the square root of chi square divided by the number of cases in the entire sample. In terms of a formula,

$$\text{phi} = \frac{\text{chi square}^2}{\sqrt{N}}$$

The phi coefficient has a minimum of 0 and a maximum of 1 and can be thought of as a correlation coefficient.

Cohen's (1988) conventions for the phi coefficient are that .10 is a small effect size, .30 is a medium effect size, and .50 is a large effect size. (These are exactly the same conventions as for a correlation coefficient.) With nominal data the sign of phi is not meaningful, and any negative phi values can be changed to positive values without affecting their meaning. If both the row and the column variables have more than two levels, phi can exceed 1 and, therefore, is hard to interpret. Cramer's V rescales phi in these circumstances so that it ranges between 0 and 1. It is calculated in the same way as the ordinary phi coefficient, except that instead of dividing by N, you divide by N times the degrees of freedom of the variable with the smaller number of categories. Here it is stated as a formula:

$$\text{Cramer's V} = \sqrt{\frac{\text{chi square}^2}{(N)(\text{df smaller})}}$$

Table 15.2 shows Cohen's (1988) effect size conventions for Cramer's V in which the smallest variable category is 2, 3, or 4. Note that when the smallest one is 2, with $df = 1$, the effect sizes are the same as those for the ordinary phi coefficient.

TABLE 15.2 *Cohen's conventions for Cramer's V*

Smallest dimension of contingency table	Effect size		
	Small	**Medium**	**Large**
2 (dfsmaller = 1)	.10	.30	.50
3 (dfsmaller = 2)	.07	.21	.35
4 (dfsmaller = 3)	.06	.17	.29

For 2 × 2, 2 × 3, and 3 × 2 tables, phi and Cramer's V are identical.

Power and needed sample size for chi-square test for independence (contingency tables)

Table 15.3 shows the approximate power at the .05 significance level for small, medium, and large effect sizes and total sample sizes of 25, 50, 100, and 200. Values are given for tables with 1, 2, 3, and 4 degrees of freedom. For example, consider the power of a planned 2×4 study (df = 3) of 50 people with an expected medium effect size (Cramer's V = .30), to be carried out using the .05 level. Using Table 15.3, this study would have a power of .40. This means that if the research hypothesis is in fact true, and there is a true medium effect size, there is about a 40% chance that the study will come out significant.

TABLE 15.3 *Approximate power for the chi-square test for independence for testing hypotheses at the .05 significance level*

Total *df*	Total N	Small (ϕ = .10)	Effect size Medium (ϕ = .30)	Large (ϕ = .50)
1	25	.08	.32	.70
	50	.11	.56	.94
	100	.17	.85	
	200	.29	.99	
2	25	.07	.25	.60
	50	.09	.46	.90
	100	.13	.77	
	200	.23	.97	
3	25	.07	.21	.54
	50	.08	.40	.86
	100	.12	.71	.99
	200	.19	.96	
4	25	.06	.19	.50
	50	.08	.36	.82
	100	.11	.66	.99
	200	.17	.94	

Table 15.4 indicates the approximate total number of participants needed for 80 per cent power with small, medium, and large effect sizes at the .05 significance level for chi-square tests of independence of 2, 3, 4, and 5 degrees of freedom. For example, suppose you are planning a study with a 3×3 *(df* = 4) contingency table. You expect a large effect size and will use the .05 significance level. According to the table, you would only need 48 participants.

TABLE 15.4 *Approximate number of subjects needed for 80 per cent power for the chi square test for independence for testing hypotheses at the .05 level of significance*

Total *df*	Small (ϕ = .10)	Effect size Medium (ϕ = .30)	Large (ϕ = .50)
1	785	87	26
2	964	107	39
3	1090	121	44
4	1194	133	48

Calculating chi square with SPSS

The goodness of fit chi square

We will illustrate the computation of a goodness of fit chi square using dummy data on rolling a dice with 42 people. Since the dice has six sides we expect that each number will turn up one-sixth of the time in the long run. We can test the observed numbers thrown against this chance expectation using the goodness of fit chi square.

How to proceed

1 Click on *Statistics* on the menu bar of the Applications window which produces a drop-down menu.
2 Select *Nonparametric Tests* from this drop-down menu to open a second drop-down menu.
3 Choose *Chi-square* which opens the *Chi-Square Test* dialogue box.
4 Select the variable that codes the three categories of agreement and then click on the arrow button which transfers this variable to the *Test Variable List:* box.
5 Select *OK*. The results of the analysis are then displayed like the dummy data below.

TABLE 15.5 *Example of chi square output*

a Diethrow

	Observed N	Expected N	Residual
1.00	12	14.0	–2.0
2.00	14	14.0	.0
3.00	20	14.0	6.0
4.00	16	14.0	2.0
5.00	10	14.0	–4.0
6.00	12	14.0	–2.0
Total	84		

b Test statistics

	DIETHROW
Chi square[a]	4.571
df	5
Asymp. sig.	.470

a. 0 cells (.0%) have expected frequencies less than 5. The minimum expected cell frequency is 14.0.

How to interpret the output

- The six possible outcomes of the die throw are listed vertically in the first column.
- The observed frequencies are presented in the second column.
- The expected frequencies of cases are displayed in the third column. These are all 14 since the expected frequency for each of the six faces on the dice with 84 throws is: $84 \div 6 = 14$

- The residual column displays the differences between the observed and expected frequencies.
- The value of chi square, its degrees of freedom and its significance are presented in the second box. Chi square is 4.571, its degrees of freedom are 5 (i.e. 6 – 1), and its significance level is 0.470.
- At the foot of the table a warning will appear about the number of cells with expected frequency less than 5.

Effect size

This is computed as:

$$\text{effect size} = \frac{\text{chi square}}{(\text{total sample size across all categories})(\text{number of categories} - 1)}$$

$$\frac{4.571}{(84)(5)} = 0.011$$

How to report the output

You should state: 'A goodness of fit chi square was conducted to determine whether a single throw of a dice by 84 subjects would produce a distribution not significantly different from that expected by chance to test whether the dice was biased. There was no statistically significant difference between the observed and expected frequencies (chi square = 4.571, *df* = 5, ns). This suggests that despite a visual impression that number 3 and number 5 occurred more and less frequently than expected respectively, the dice was not biased, that the variations were chance variations, and that in the long run each face will appear an approximately equal number of times. Effect size of 0.011 indicates that the observed frequencies hardly deviated from the expected frequencies.

Calculating chi square for the independence of categorical variables (contingency tables)

If you wish to calculate chi square with more than two categories in at least one variable then the procedure is basically the same. For example, you may wish to examine the relationship between 'gender' (coded 0 for female and 1 for male), and preference for three different brands of soft drink (labelled 'prefer', and coded 1 for Fizzie, 2 for Bubbly and 3 for Pepco).

The procedure is as follows:

1. Select *Statistics* to produce the drop-down menu of the various statistical processes.
2. Choose *Summarize* to obtain a second drop-down menu.
3. Select *Crosstabs*. This opens the *Crosstabs:* dialogue box.
4. Click on 'gender' and then the arrow button beside Row[s]: which transfers 'sex' into the *Rows* box.
5. Select 'drinkpre' and then the arrow button beside Column[s] which moves it to the *Columns* box.
6. Choose *Statistics* at the bottom of the *Crosstabs:* dialogue box. This opens the *Crosstabs: Statistics* dialogue box.

7 Select *Chi-square, phi* and *Cramer's V* in the *Nominal* data box.
8 Next click on *Continue*. This closes the *Crosstabs: Statistics* dialogue box.
9 Select *Cells*. This produces the *Crosstabs: Cell Display* dialogue box.
10 Choose *Expected* in the *Counts* box. (Observed should already be selected.)
11 Click on *Row* in the *Percentages* box.
12 Select *Continue*. This closes the *Crosstabs: Cell Display* dialogue box.
13 Finally select *OK*. The screen now displays the output shown in Table 15.6.

TABLE 15.6 *Example of output*

a Case processing summary

	Cases					
	Valid		Missing		Total	
	N	Per cent	N	Per cent	N	Per cent
Drink preference * gender	84	100.0%	0	.0%	84	100.0%

*b Drink preference * gender cross-tabulation*

			Gender		Total
			Female	Male	
Drink preference	Fizzie	Count	8	14	22
		Expected count	11.0	11.0	22.0
	Bubbly	Count	22	9	31
		Expected count	15.5	15.5	31.0
	Pepco	Count	12	19	31
		Expected count	15.5	15.5	31.0
Total		Count	42	42	84
		Expected count	42.0	42.0	84.0

c Chi-square tests

	Value	df	Asymp. Sig. (2-tailed)
Pearson chi square	8.669[a]	2	.013
Likelihood ratio	8.875	2	.012
Linear-by-linear	.019	1	.890
N of valid cases	84		

a 0 cells (.0%) have expected count less than 5. The minimum expected count is 11.00.

d Symmetric measures

		Value	Approx. Sig.
Nominal by nominal	Phi	.321	.013
	Cramer's V	.321	.013
N of valid cases		84	

How to Interpret the output

- Four subtables are produced. The top subtable lists the number of cases processed.
- The second subtable shows the observed and expected frequency of cases in each cell. The observed frequency (called count) is presented first, and the expected frequency (called expected count) appears second.
- The observed frequencies are always whole numbers so they should be easy to spot. The expected frequencies are always expressed to one decimal place so they are easily identified. Thus the first cell of the table (defined as 'female' and 'Fizzie') has an observed frequency of 8, but an expected frequency of 11.
- The next subtable displays the chi square value, its degrees of freedom and its significance level. Chi square is on the line labelled 'Pearson', after the person who developed this test. The chi square value is 8.669. Its degrees of freedom are 2 and its two-tailed probability is 0.013.
- The likelihood ratio test has similar properties to chi square and is an alternative. The linear-by-linear association test is inappropriate for qualitative variables.
- The final table reports phi and Cramer's V as measures of effect size, that is, 0.321.
- Also shown in the output is the warning about the minimum expected frequency of any cell in the table. If the minimum expected frequency is less than 5.0 then we should be wary of using chi square. If you expect small frequencies to occur it would be better to use the Fisher Exact Test which SPSS prints in the output in these circumstances.

Reporting the output in Table 15.6

You could write in this instance: 'A 2 x 3 contingency table analysis was conducted to determine whether there was an association between gender and preference among three types of soft drink. A significant relationship was present with chi square = 8.669, df = 2, p < .05, in that Bubbly was preferred more by females, while males preferred the other two drinks more than did the females. The effect size was .321, indicating a medium effect'.

Fisher's exact test

The chi square procedure computes Fisher's Exact Test for 2 x 2 tables when one or more of the four cells have an expected frequency of less than 5. The SPSS output then provides the significance level for both a one- and two-tail test. These are placed near the bottom of the normal chi square output window as the last two significance levels quoted.

STQ74*

1   A random sample of teachers were classified as class teacher, head of department, deputy principal, principal. They were asked if they would favour joining a union. The results were as follows:

	Class teachers	Head of Dept	Deputy Principal	Principal
Yes	230	46	20	4
No	40	14	20	8

Are these response differences significant at the 5% level? What is the hypothesis you will accept?

2   A sample of children was classified into those who took paper rounds out every evening and those who didn't. The teacher was then asked to indicate which children had failed to hand in homework at least once during the last month.

	Failure to hand in homework	Homework always handed in
Paper round	12	8
No paper round	6	19

Is the association between the categories significant at the 5% level?

3   A physical education instructor wished to determine preferences of boys and girls for three activities. She asked a sample of 40 boys and 30 girls to state their preferences. Here are the data she received:

	Basketball	Volleyball	Hockey
Boys	20	5	15
Girls	7	13	10

a   Compute the chi square for the above data.

b   Using p = 0.05 as your acceptable level for significance, evaluate the chi square obtained. Would you accept or reject the null hypothesis? If you reject it, what can be said regarding the preferences of boys and girls?

4   In a group of 100 boys, 30 are classified as good swimmers and of these, 20 show good personal adjustment. Of the poor swimmers, 30 show good personal adjustment. Is adjustment independent of swimming ability?

5   In an exam varying numbers of students passed after having been taught by one of three different methods. Is there an association between success and method of instruction?

	Method A	Method B	Method C
Pass	50	47	56
Fail	5	14	8

6   Let us assume you are interested in the relationship between smoking/non-smoking parents (i.e. one or both parents smoke or neither parent smokes) and adults. In order to test your view, you randomly select 200 adults between the ages of twenty-one and thirty, and assess whether they smoke and whether their parents smoked. The second question is whether the subject smokes. The hypothetical results for this experiment are presented on page 230. Do a chi-square test to determine whether the variables are related.

(continued)

	Subject	
	Smokes	**Does not smoke**
One or both parents smoked	70	40
Neither parent smoked	37	53

*Answers on p. 601.

summary

A chi-square test is a non-parametric technique of testing hypotheses about the form of a frequency distribution using nominal data. Two types of chi square tests are the goodness of fit test and the test for independence. The former compares how well the frequency distribution for a sample fitted with the frequency distribution predicted by the null hypothesis. The latter assesses relationships between two variables, with the null hypothesis stating that there is no relationship between the two variables. Rejecting the null hypothesis implies a relationship between the two variables. Both tests are based on the assumption that each observation is independent of the others, and that one observation cannot be classified in more than one category.

The chi square statistic is distorted when there are less than five observations in a cell and the test should not be performed if this situation exists. Yates correction should be employed in cross tabulations with $1\,df$.

Reference

Cohen, J. (1988), *Statistical Power Analysis for the Behavioural Sciences*, Laurence Erlbaum, New York.

Testing hypotheses of relationship II: Correlation

16
sixteen

Introduction

My dictionary defines *correlation* as 'the mutual relation of two or more things; the act or process of showing the existence of a relationship between things'.

You may note that the *relationship* is mutual or reciprocating and that we do not include in our concept of correlation any idea at all of the one thing being the cause and the other thing being the effect. We play safe. We merely say that we have discovered that two things are connected. Now, it may well be that one thing is a cause of another, but correlation does not delve that far down on its own.

In principle, correlation is different from any of the inferential statistics you have so far studied, because these techniques compare groups as groups, and not the individuals who compose them. Ask yourself, 'What happens to the individual in chi square?'. We throw him or her into a cell with a number of others and forget all about the individual. (Indeed, we like large numbers in chi-square cells in case the expected frequency is less than 5!) In *t* tests, we do not analyse the individual, but only the performance of the group to which he or she has been allocated—*t* tests cannot function with only one individual making up a 'group'.

Basically, however, all these techniques are 'difference' testings. All are quite practical: 'Are the persons in Group A (as a group) significantly better than those in Group B at doing something or other, etc.?'.

We are using the razor of difference to settle a question. But in relationship testing we are examining the strength of a connection between two characteristics which both belong to the same individual, or, at least, two variables with a common basis to them.

Many variables or events in nature are related to each other. As the sun sets, the temperature decreases; as children increase in age their size of vocabulary also increases; persons bright in one academic area tend to be bright in other areas. These relationships are correlations. If the river rises when it rains then the two events are said to have a positive correlation, i.e. when an increase in one variable coincides with an increase in another there exists the positive correlation. There is a negative correlation between altitude and air pressure, as an increase in altitude brings with it a decrease in pressure. In children there is a negative correlation between age and bed-wetting. A negative correlation thus occurs when an increase in one variable coincides with a decrease in another.

Most of you have tried to play the piano at some time. The movement of the hands over the keys also illustrates correlation. Imagine you are practising the scale of C major and both hands are commencing on C, an octave apart, to travel up the keyboard in unison. This is a positive correlation between the movements of the hands (or scores). If both my hands stay in the same position on the keyboard this is not a correlation since there is no movement (or scores) to calculate. Correlation is here a measure of mutual movement up and down a scale of scores.

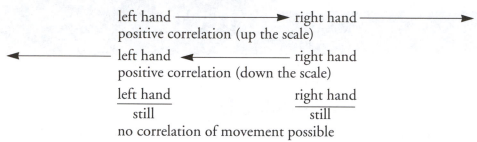

If you commence both hands on the same note and play the scale simultaneously in different directions, the right hand going up as the left hand travels down, then there is a negative correlation.

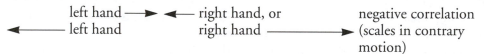

When the movements of my hands on the keyboard bear no systematic relationships in direction with each other then it is a zero correlation. But when the hands sometimes go in a systematic relationship with each other there is calculated a modest correlation, negative or positive as the case may be, i.e. when I am playing a piece of music. Now that we have some glimpse of what correlation is concerned with we will desert our piano practice and turn to drawing graphs.

The correlation coefficient

The main requirement of any research into the relationship between variables is that we should have observations arising from the same source. We can thus examine the extent to which scores on one variable are related to scores on another. Every additional pair of scores provides us with more information about the extent of their relationship. Obviously, if we were looking at data obtained from different groups of subjects we would have no information of this kind. We could only make comparisons between overall performance among the two groups on the two tests. We would have no means of telling how performance on the two tests is related.

Given that we have data from one sample of subjects on two variables such as locus of control and self-esteem, how can we describe the extent of their relationship? The simplest method is to plot the two sets of scores against one another in the form of a graph or scattergram. Consider a number of possibilities represented by Figure 16.1. Notice that each point on these graphs represents the intersection of subject scores on two variables.

In Figure 16.1 (a) and (b) all the points lie on a straight line. Each score is perfectly predictable from every other score because any change in one variable is accompanied by a proportional change in the other variable. In the first case, Figure 16.1 (a), increases in one variable are accompanied by proportional increases in the other variable. We call this perfect positive correlation.

A numerical index called the *coefficient of correlation* expresses the degree or magnitude of the relationship. The numerical index +1.00 is the highest possible value that the correlation coefficient assumes and it indicates a perfect relationship between the variables. The general symbol for correlation is 'r'. A perfect positive relationship ($r = +1.00$) indicates a direct relationship where each individual is as high or as low on one variable as he or she is on the other. In other words, each subject has the same z score on X as their z score on Y. In a perfect correlation all the dots in the scattergram can be connected with a single straight line. An example of a perfect positive relationship would be the heights of these subjects measured in inches and the heights of subjects measured in centimetres.

In the second case, Figure 16.1(b), increases in one variable are accompanied by proportional decreases in the other variable. We call this *perfect negative correlation*. An r of −1.00 indicates a perfect negative relationship. This means that the two variables bear an inverse relationship to each other, so that the highest z score on one variable is associated with the lowest z score on the other, and so forth. An example of a perfect negative relationship is that between the volume of a gas and the pressure applied when temperature is held constant. As pressure increases, the volume of the gas decreases. There is a perfect relationship between the radius and the circumference of a circle. But perfect correlations are not generally found among educational, social and psychological variables.

Since perfect positive and negative correlations are unlikely to be met within educational research, the sort of picture we are most likely to find is that of Figure 16.1 (c), (d) and (e). In (c) and (d) the points are scattered about a straight line in a roughly elliptical shape. Although there is a tendency for pairs of scores to go together, the prediction of one score from another is no longer perfect. We describe (c) as showing *positive* correlation and (d) as showing *negative* correlation. Now, finally look at (e) where we have the situation in which there is no discernible relation between the two sets of scores, for example, between IQ and shoe size.

As a positive relationship between variables becomes less close, the correlation coefficient assumes a value smaller than +1.00. Students with high intelligence tend to make high grades, but there are exceptions because of several factors other then intelligence that affect school grades. Although still positive, the correlation coefficient between these two variables is less than +1.00. Other variables may show a negative relationship that is less than perfect. In such cases the correlation coefficient would have a negative sign, but between 0 and −1.00. A negative relationship would be expected between the number of truancies among children and their scholastic performance.

FIGURE 16.1 *Scattergrams depict various degrees of correlation. When there is no relationship between the variables, the coefficient is 0.0*

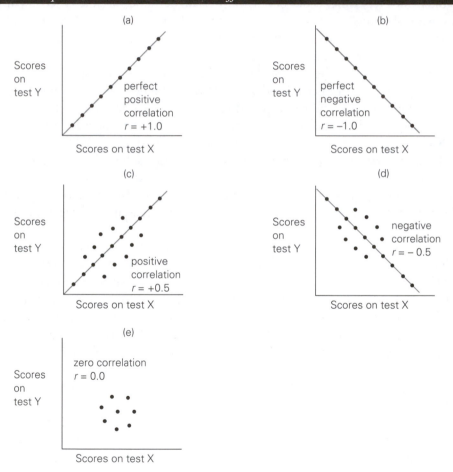

Thus, a correlation coefficient indicates both the direction and the strength of relationship between two variables. The direction of relationship is indicated by the sign (+ or −), and the strength of relationship is represented by the absolute size of the coefficient, i.e. how close it is to +1.00 or −1.00.

The following is a rough but useful guide to the degree of relationship indicated by the size of the coefficients (whether positive or negative).

0.90–1.00	Very high correlation	Very strong relationship
0.70–0.90	High correlation	Marked relationship
0.40–0.70	Moderate correlation	Substantial relationship
0.20–0.40	Low correlation	Weak relationship
Less than 0.20	Slight correlation	Relationship so small as to be negligible

STQ75

Below are the final examination scores in algebra and English for eight students. Draw a scatter diagram of these scores. Let the algebra scores be the X variable.

Student	A	B	C	D	E	F	G	H
Algebra scores	81	84	86	82	85	82	83	84
English scores	93	97	98	94	96	95	94	95

1 What is meant by a perfect positive correlation between two variables? A moderate positive correlation?

2 What is meant by a perfect negative correlation between two variables? A moderate negative correlation?

3 Does the scatter diagram you prepared dictate a positive or a negative correlation? Is it a perfect correlation?

Be careful never to confuse negative correlation with zero correlation. The latter simply means no correlation or relationship whatever between two sets of data, whereas a negative correlation is a definite relationship, the strength of which is indicated by its size. It is absolutely necessary to place the algebraic sign (+ or –) before the numerical value of the correlation as the interpretation of the correlation is affected by its positive or negative condition.

A correlation coefficient is not a direct measure of the percentage of relationship between two variables; however, its square is (see p. 239). One cannot say that a correlation of 0.90 is three times as close as a relationship of +0.30, but merely that it indicates a much stronger degree of relationship. It is a pure number that has no connection with the units in which the variables are measured. Correlations are usually expressed to two and often three places of decimals. There are a number of different correlation coefficients which can be calculated to express the strength of the relationship between two variables, depending on the level of data. All correlation coefficients, however, share in common the property that they range between +1.00 and –1.00.

The calculation of the Pearson correlation coefficient

While inspection of a scattergram furnishes some visual impression of the relationship between two sets of measures for a given group, a numerical index indicating precisely the degree of relationship is much more helpful. Several correlation indexes have been developed. The most widely used is the Pearson Product Movement.

This correlation is employed when both variables are expressed as interval data. This procedure was first proposed by the English statistician, Karl Pearson. Conceptually, the Pearson correlation coefficient is computed by

$$r = \frac{\text{the degree to which X and Y vary together}}{\text{the degree to which X and Y vary separately}} = \frac{\text{co-variability of X and Y}}{\text{variability of X and Y separately}}$$

The general formula is based on the Z score.

$$r_{XY} = \frac{\Sigma(ZX)(ZY)}{N}$$

EXAMPLE

Original mark X	List of Z scores for X ZX	Products of Z scores of X and Y (ZX)(ZY)	List of Z scores of Y ZY	Original mark Y
16	1.5	2.25	1.5	16
14	1.0	1.00	1.0	14
12	0.5	0.25	0.5	12
10	0	0	0	10
8	0.5	0.25	−0.5	8
6	−1.0	1.00	−1.0	6
4	−1.5	2.25	−1.5	4
M = 10		Sum of products = 7.00		M = 10

$$\textbf{Average product} = \frac{\textbf{7.00}}{\textbf{7.00}} = r_{XY} = \textbf{+1.00}$$

The scores for Test X and those for Test Y varied systematically to the highest degree, i.e. each person did precisely as well or as badly, on Y as on X, and so the r coefficient came out as +1.0 (the highest possible). With this degree of correlation one could have predicted a subject's score on X from his or her score on Y and saved oneself the trouble of testing him or her on X, or vice versa.

Look closely at the middle column in the above example—the products of ZX scores and ZY scores. Some people score a lot in this column and some score little—one subject scores zero. In other words, these subjects are each contributing quite different amounts to the sum of the cross-products (ZX × ZY). Why should they differ so much in their contributions when they all duplicate exactly their score on X and Y? Each person did precisely as well or as badly. The reason is seen in their Z score on X or on Y. Those people who had large Z scores, i.e. those people who were most different from their average colleagues, and who were consistently different (on Y as well as on X) contributed a high XY score in the middle column. (If you bet that you can pick the winner in both horse races you should be promised more winnings than if you bet only that you can pick the winner in one race, quite divorced from your ability to do so in any other.) In placing a 'doubles' bet with the bookmaker (and I hope you never will, for it is a tricky thing to pull off), you are claiming the ability to judge horse variations systematically. Next, let us look at the average person in the street—the scorer on the mean, here equalling 10. Now this individual contributes nothing to the pool because they do not vary one way or another, neither negatively or positively, so they contribute zero, even though he or she is consistent in non-variance. They are a little like the two hands on the piano keyboard which never move up or down.

Other formulas have been derived from the basic definitional formula. One of the most convenient allows us to work directly with the original raw scores without the necessity of finding the means and standard deviations. Here is the formula:

$$r_{XY} = \frac{N \sum XY - (\sum X)(\sum Y)}{\sqrt{[N \sum X^2 - (\sum X)^2][N \sum Y^2 - (\sum Y)^2]}}$$

where:
$\sum X$ = sum of the raw X scores
$\sum Y$ = sum of the raw Y scores
$\sum XY$ = sum of the products of each X multiplied by each Y
$\sum X^2$ = sum of the squares of each X score
$\sum Y^2$ = sum of the squares of each Y score
$(\sum X)^2$ = the square of the total sum of X scores
$(\sum Y)^2$ = the square of the total sum of Y scores
N = the number of paired scores

EXAMPLE: Computation of the correlation coefficient using raw scores

X	Y	XY	X²	Y²
20	14	280	400	196
26	10	260	676	100
17	8	136	289	64
14	2	28	196	4
8	6	48	64	36
85	40	752	1625	400

$\sum X$ = 85 $\sum Y$ = 40
$\sum XY$ = 752 $\sum X^2$ = 1625
$\sum Y^2$ = 400 $(\sum X)^2$ = 7225
$(\sum Y)^2$ = 1600 N = 5

$$r_{XY} = \frac{5 \times 752 - (85 \times 40)}{\sqrt{[5 \times 1625 - 7225][5 \times 400 - 1600]}}$$

$$r_{XY} = \frac{3760 - 3400}{\sqrt{900 \times 400}}$$

$$r_{XY} = \frac{360}{\sqrt{360\ 000}} = \frac{360}{600}$$

$$r_{XY} = +0.60$$

Interpreting the correlation coefficient

Let us imagine that you have followed the tortuous path of correlation without getting lost and are now the proud owner of a shiny new correlation coefficient of $r = +0.69$ between extroversion and social popularity—at least among the 50 students you managed to test at your school or college. Wonderful, but then what?

You have demonstrated a correlation that pertains to 50 people; fifty pairs of observations only. Even assuming that the fifty chosen were typical students, can we feel secure in concluding that a correlation between extroversion and popularity exists in general? If only because you are well inured to rhetorical questions by this time, you will allow that we cannot feel at all secure.

After all, you did not manage to test every student in the world. It is conceivable that if you had, the correlation might have been 0. Accidents do happen, and the 50 students observed might have displayed their correlation as a long-shot coincidence, not as an indication of any general rule. In other words, you have a choice: you must pick one of the following explanations for your obtained r.

- It happened because there really is a correlation out there, and it showed up in your sample.
- There really is not any general overall relationship between extroversion and popularity, but accidents do happen, especially when one tries to formulate a general rule about thousands of students (with more to follow) on the basis of only 50.

Can we ever conclude that our obtained (sample) r does reflect a population correlation?

An affirmative answer, which we would certainly enjoy having, depends on two factors:

1 the size of the correlation coefficient obtained,
2 the size of the sample.

We must also (as always) be able to assume, with some good reason, that the sample is a random one.

The need for these two factors should be clear. If a correlation coefficient is small, it could be merely an accident of sampling, and such an accident will be relatively likely if the sample is small. If either the correlation coefficient or the sample is very large, the probability of such an accident is reduced.

Now, in any population of X and Y scores, there is some degree of relationship between X and Y, even if the relationship is 0. And for every population correlation coefficient, there will be a range of sample correlation coefficients which will fall into a sampling distribution. The shape of this distribution is approximately Gaussian only when the population correlation coefficient is 0. When the population coefficient is other than 0, the sampling distribution is skewed. Usually though, it is the null hypothesis that $r = 0$ which we would like to reject. So, for any obtained sample value of r, we can ask, 'Assuming that population $r = 0$, what is the probability that this sample r came from the sampling distribution?'. If the probability is too small, less than 5 per cent or 1 per cent, we reject the null hypothesis and adopt instead the hypothesis that the population itself contains a correlation between X and Y. Table 16.2 (p. 241) shows that the critical value of r, whether for the 1 per cent or 5 per cent level, is related to the size of sample. It is not possible to interpret any correlation coefficient unless the value of N is known.

Compare your obtained value of r with the proper critical value in the table. If the obtained coefficient equals or exceeds the tabled value, the null hypothesis may be rejected at the level of risk chosen. We will do this for your hypothetical result in which N = 50 and r = +0.69. We find in Table 16.1 that a relationship *that* strong (or stronger) will occur less than 1 per cent of the time if H_0 is true, the critical value of r being 0.361, less than 0.69. So, you can generalise that extroversion and popularity are related to some unknown extent in the population. It is not possible, however, to use this procedure to infer the strength of the population correlation; you can merely infer its existence. It is possible to define the strength of a relationship in a more precise way, by means of the coefficient of determination.

This coefficient ($r^2 \times 100$) determines what percentage of the total variance of variable X is due to the variance of variable Y.

EXAMPLE

1 If the correlation (r) between variable X and variable Y = 0, then the coefficient of determination = $0^2 \times 100 = 0\%$ (see Figure 16.2).

FIGURE 16.2

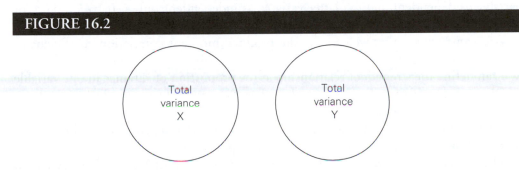

None of the factors accounting for variability is common to both variables.

2 If the correlation (r) between variable X and variable Y = 0.8, then the coefficient of determination = $0.8^2 \times 100 = 64\%$ of the factors accounting for variability are common to both variables (see Figure 16.3).

FIGURE 16.3

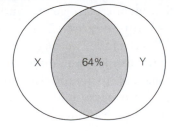

3 If the correlation (r) between variable X and variable Y = 1, then the coefficient of determination = $1^2 \times 100$ = 100%. One hundred per cent of the factors accounting for variability are common to both variables (see Figure 16.4).

FIGURE 16.4

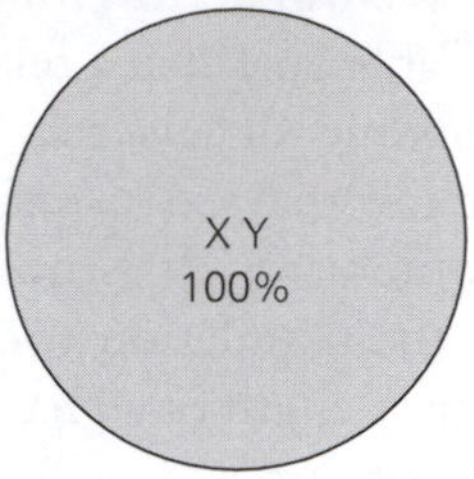

Now, let us bring the algebra to life by looking at a few examples. Imagine that we found a correlation of +0.73 between IQ scores and self concept scores. This means that $(0.73)^2$ = 0.53 or 53 per cent of the variance in the IQ scores is predictable from the variance in the self-concept scores. Similarly too, if we find an estimated correlation of +0.16 between desired age for leaving school and verbal fluency, this means that if we designate the former variable as dependent and the latter variable as independent only $(+0.16)^2$ = 0.03, or 3 per cent of the variance in desired age of leaving school is predicted from verbal fluency.

You can now see that we can use the product–moment correlation coefficient to interpret the strength of relationship between two variables in a much more precise way. We can define the strength of relationship as the proportion of variance in one variable which is predictable from variance in the other. We can go further and say now that a correlation of 0.71 is twice as strong as a correlation of 0.50 in the sense that the former correlation predicts twice the amount of the variance in a dependent variable than is predicted by the latter (50 per cent as against 25 per cent).

The variance interpretation of correlation emphasises the point that even with strongly correlated measures a substantial amount of variance in the dependent variable remains unaccounted for. It is well to bear this in mind when looking at correlations reported in research. Many researchers set their sights at finding statistically significant correlations, which simply means that the correlation is unlikely to have occurred by chance. When they come to draw causal inferences from their findings, however, the amount of variance they have actually explained by a significant correlation is very small indeed.

Take, for example, Entwistle's correlations (Entwistle 1972) between a number of personality characteristics and academic performance in higher education. The two largest correlations are −0.41 for 'neuroticism' among women students in polytechnics, and 0.39 for A-level grades among female students at colleges of education. It is notable that in the former case, only $(0.41)^2$ = 17% of the variance in academic performance is explained by neuroticism and in the latter case, 15 per cent. Such correlations are significant because N is large, yet personality factors are here explaining only a small part of the variance in academic performance.

TABLE 16.1 *Critical values of the Pearson product–moment correlation coefficient*

	Level of significance for one-tailed test				
	.05	.025	.01	.005	.0005
	Level of significance for two-tailed test				
$df = N - 2$	.10	.05	.02	.01	.001
1	.9877	.9969	.9995	.9999	1.0000
2	.9000	.9500	.9800	.9900	.9990
3	.8054	.8783	.9343	.9587	.9912
4	.7293	.8114	.8822	.9172	.9741
5	.6694	.7545	.8329	.8745	.9507
6	.6215	.7067	.7887	.8343	.9249
7	.5822	.6664	.7498	.7977	.8982
8	.5494	.6319	.7155	.7646	.8721
9	.5214	.6021	.6851	.7348	.8471
10	.4973	.5760	.6581	.7079	.8233
11	.4762	.5529	.6339	.6835	.8010
12	.4575	.5324	.6120	.6614	.7800
13	.4409	.5139	.5923	.6411	.7603
14	.4259	.4973	.5742	.6226	.7420
15	.4124	.4821	.5577	.6055	.7246
16	.4000	.4683	.5425	.5897	.7084
17	.3887	.4555	.5285	.5751	.6932
18	.3783	.4438	.5155	.5614	.6787
19	.3687	.4329	.5034	.5487	.6652
20	.3598	.4227	.4921	.5368	.6524
25	.3233	.3809	.4451	.4869	.5974
30	.2960	.3494	.4093	.4487	.5541
35	.2746	.3246	.3810	.4182	.5189
40	.2573	.3044	.3578	.3932	.4896
45	.2428	.2875	.3384	.3721	.4648
50	.2306	.2732	.3218	.3541	.4433
60	.2108	.2500	.2948	.3248	.4078
70	.1954	.2319	.2737	.3017	.3799
80	.1829	.2172	.2565	.2830	.3568
90	.1726	.2050	.2422	.2673	.3375
100	.1638	.1946	.2301	.2540	.3211

Source: Table VI, Fisher & Yates, *Statistical Tables for Biological, Agricultural and Medical Research*, 6th edn, 1974, Addison Wesley Longman, London.

For example, with a sample of 20, *df* = 18, and *r* must equal to at least .4438 to be significant at the .05 level (two-tailed test). With a sample of 12, *df* = 10, you need an *r* of at least .5760. If your *df* is not represented in the left-hand column of the table, take the next lowest figure.

In other words, there is a difference between statistically significant results and educationally significant ones. By educationally significant, I mean results that substantially increase our understanding of educational issues and problems. Since, in Entwistle's study, only 2.5 per cent of the variance in achievement is accounted for by neuroticism, we have not made a great deal of progress, despite its significance at the 5 per cent level, i.e. such relationships would only arise by chance in only 5 per cent of samples. It has been said that it is inappropriate to bother with *r*'s of 0.10, 0.20, and 0.30. With *r*'s of about 0.10 or less, this point is well taken. But with *r*'s of about 0.30, the point is not well taken. If an *r* of 0.30 is statistically significant, it may help the investigator later to find an important relationship—if he or she can clear up, say, the measurement problems. That is, the investigator might, by dropping a statistically significant *r* of 0.30, be losing a valuable lead for further hypotheses and subsequent research.

An example may help to drive this point home. Sears, Maccoby and Levin, in their large study of child-rearing practices, report a large number of correlations. Most are quite small, sometimes so small that one wonders whether they are of any value. Sears and his colleagues were measuring very complex variables and their measures were relatively crude (but not inept). They report, for instance, the correlation between an accepting tolerant attitude towards the child's dependent behaviour and being warm toward the child: to 0.37. This *r* is not high, true. But since it is based on an N of 379, it is statistically significant. Also, it reflects, very probably, an important relation. Other significant but low relations reported are between tolerant attitude toward dependent behaviour and gentleness in toilet training (to 0.30); low physical punishment (to 0.30); high self-esteem (to 0.39); and high esteem for husband (to 0.32). Such relations, though low, have the makings of important research findings and theory building.

STQ76*

1 Imagine some children had scores on two variables as follows:

Child	X	Y	X²	Y²	XY
A	4	9	16	81	36
B	1	4	1	16	4
C	3	1	9	1	3
D	6	7	36	49	42
E	5	3	25	9	15
F	4	2	16	4	8
N = 6	ΣX = 23	ΣY = 26	ΣX² = 103	ΣY² = 160	ΣXY = 108

$$r = \frac{N \sum XY - (\sum X)(\sum Y)}{\sqrt{[N \sum X^2 - (\sum X)^2][N \sum Y^2 - (\sum Y)^2]}}$$

Calculate *r* and make a sensible comment about the relationship of X and Y. Some calculation has already been done for you.

2 For the following set of data, the researcher has made this hypothesis: 'There is a relationship between the arithmetic scores and the English scores'. Compute the Pearson product–moment correlation coefficient for these data.

242

Student	A	B	C	D	E	F	G	H
Algebra scores	20	18	17	16	14	14	12	9
English scores	18	22	15	17	8	20	9	7

Does the hypothesis stated require a one-tailed or a two-tailed test of significance? Using Table 16.1, determine the magnitude of the *r* required for significance at the (a) 0.05 level, (b) at the 0.01 level.

State the null hypothesis being tested. Using p = 0.05 as your acceptable level for significance, would you accept or reject the null hypothesis?

3   For the following set of data, the researcher has made this hypothesis: 'There is a positive relationship between the spelling scores and the English scores'.

Compute the Pearson product–moment correlation coefficient for these data.

Student	A	B	C	D	E	F	G	H	I	J	K
Spelling scores	32	29	28	27	27	27	25	25	21	20	15
English scores	20	17	17	18	17	12	10	8	9	6	8

Does the hypothesis stated require a one-tailed or a two-tailed test of significance? Using Table 16.1, determine the magnitude of the *r* required for significance (a) at the 0.05 level, (b) at the 0.01 level.

State the null hypothesis being tested. If you designate p = 0.01 as your level of significance, would you accept or reject the null hypothesis?

4   If the world were fair would you expect a positive or negative correlation between hours spent studying and your final exam mark?

5   Data suggest that children from larger families have lower IQ than children from smaller families on average. Would this be a negative or positive relationship?

6   Compute Pearson's *r* for the following data:

x	y
2	9
1	10
3	6
0	8
4	2

7   A researcher obtains an *r* = –41 with N = 30. Using the 5% level, is this significant?

8   In a sample of 20 how large a correlation is needed for significance at .05 level?

9   As sample size increases the magnitude of the correlation necessary for significance decreases. Why?

10   On the next page are some data correlating children's reading test scores with their spelling scores.

(continued)

Subject	Reading		Spelling		
	X	X²	Y	Y²	(XY)
1	67	4489	65	4225	4355
2	72	5184	84	7056	6048
3	45	2025	51	2601	2295
4	58	3364	56	3136	3248
5	63	3969	67	4489	4221
6	39	1521	42	1764	1638
7	52	2704	50	2500	2600
sums = 396		23256	415	25771	24405
	sum of (X)² = 156816			sum of (Y)² = 172225	

a   What is the value of *r*?
b   What is the *df*?
c   Is r significant at p < .05?

*Answers on p. 602.

Rank order correlation (Spearman's rho)

This correlation is typically used when there are only a few cases (or subjects) involved and the data are ranked or can be ranked. There is no assumption that ranks are based on equal-interval measures, or that there is any measurement involved. The ranks are merely an indication that this person is first in this attribute or test, this person second, and so on. This correlation is usually designated as 'rho' to distinguish it from Pearson's '*r*'.

STQ77

What level of measurement is rho used on?

The formula for 'rho' is:

$$rho = 1 - \frac{6 \sum d^2}{N(N^2 - 1)}$$

where d is the difference between ranks for each pair of observations, and N is the number of pairs of observations. For example, if a subject is ranked first on one measure but only fifth on another, d = 1 − 5 = 4 and d^2 = 16.

Rank order correlation follows the same principles as outlined earlier; that is, it ranges from +1 to −1. It is very simple to use, but always remember to convert data into rank order. It also demonstrates very clearly the effect of changes in covariation between the two sets of data.

For example, (X and Y expressed in ranks):

(a)

X	Y	d	d²
1	1	0	0
2	2	0	0
3	3	0	0
4	4	0	0
5	5	0	0
			$\Sigma = 0$

$$\text{rho} = 1 - \frac{6 \times 0}{5 \times 24} = 1 - 0 = +1$$

i.e. perfect agreement in ranks.

(b)

X	Y	d	d²
1	5	−4	16
2	4	−2	4
3	3	0	0
4	2	2	4
5	1	4	16
			$\Sigma = 40$

$$\text{rho} = 1 - \frac{6 \times 40}{5 \times 24} = 1 - \frac{240}{120}$$

$$\text{rho} = 1 - 2 = -1$$

i.e. perfect inverse relationship.

(c)

X	Y	d	d²
1	1	0	0
3	2	1	1
5	3	2	4
4	4	0	0
2	5	−3	9
			$\Sigma = 14$

$$\text{rho} = 1 - \frac{6 \times 14}{5 \times 24} = 1 - \frac{84}{120}$$

$$\text{rho} = 1 - 0.7 = +0.3$$

i.e. a low positive relationship.

STQ78

Now you try switching the ranks around and notice how the correlation changes. The combination of the resulting rho with the visual impression of the rankings will bring home to you (if you do not fully comprehend already) what correlation reveals.

Here is a research example. We hypothesised that there would be a relationship between the order (or sequence) in which students finished an exam and their scores on the exam. The following example shows a hypothetical set of data designed to test this hypothesis.

Rank-order-correlation example

(a) Rank order of finishing test	(b) Score on exam	(c) Rank order on exam	(d) d (c – a)	(e) d²
1	20	1	0	0
2	24	3	1	1
3	23	2	1	1
4	25	4	0	0
5	29	7.5	2.5	6.25
6	28	6	0	0
7	30	9	2	4
8	32	10	2	4
9	27	5	4	16
10	29	7.5	2.5	6.25
				$\Sigma d^2 = 38.5$

The order in which the students finish the exam (column a) serves as one set of rankings. The test scores need to be ranked, however. The lowest score will be assigned the rank of 1, the next lowest a score of 2 etc., as has been done in column c of the data. Where two or more subjects have the same score the rank is calculated by averaging the ranks those subjects cover. In our example above, two candidates obtained 29. They were in seventh equal position, i.e. covering ranks 7 and 8. Hence, they are both ranked as 7.5.

Column d is the difference between the rankings in column a and c irrespective of + or – signs, since squaring them in column e eliminates these.

Using the sum of column e, the rank order correlation can be determined as follows:

$$\text{rho} = 1 - \frac{6 \times 38.5}{10 \times 99} = 1 - \frac{231.0}{990}$$
$$= 1 - 0.23 = +0.77$$

i.e. there is a strong relationship between the two rankings.

STQ79

Can you interpret this relationship? Use Table 16.3. What does it imply?

On page 247 is a further example which shows the scores of thirteen boys in a class of twenty-nine children on two variables—'verbal fluency' and 'desired age of leaving school'.

part 2 | quantitative methods

TABLE 16.2 *Critical values of rho (rank order correlation coefficient)*

	Level of significance for one-tailed test			
	0.05	0.025	0.01	0.005
	Level of significance for two-tailed test			
	0.10	0.05	0.02	0.01
5	0.900	1.000	1.000	—
6	0.829	0.886	0.943	1.000
7	0.714	0.786	0.893	0.929
8	0.643	0.738	0.833	0.881
9	0.600	0.683	0.783	0.883
10	0.564	0.648	0.746	0.794
12	0.506	0.591	0.712	0.777
14	0.456	0.544	0.645	0.715
16	0.425	0.506	0.601	0.665
18	0.399	0.475	0.564	0.625
20	0.377	0.450	0.534	0.591
22	0.359	0.428	0.508	0.562
24	0.343	0.409	0.485	0.537
26	0.329	0.392	0.465	0.515
28	0.317	0.377	0.448	0.496
30	0.306	0.364	0.432	0.478

Source: E.G. Olds, 'The 5% significance levels for sums of squares of rank differences and a correction' in *Annals of Mathematical Statistics*, Vol. 20, The Institute of Mathematical Statistics, 1949.

Boy	Desired age of leaving school	Verbal fluency	Rank	Rank		
	X	Y	X	Y	d	d^2
1	17	6	9	6.5	2.5	6.25
2	16	8	4.5	3.5	1	1
3	17	10	9	1	8	64
4	17	4	9	11	2	4
5	15	7	2.5	5	2.5	6.25
6	17	8	9	3.5	5.5	30.25
7	17	6	9	6.5	2.5	6.25
8	14	5	1	8.5	7.5	56.25
9	17	4	9	11	2	4
10	17	9	9	2	7	49
11	16	4	4.5	11	6.5	42.25
12	15	5	2.5	8.5	6	36
13	18	2	13	13	0	0
						$\Sigma d^2 = 305.5$

You can see from the columns X and Y again how we deal with the problem of 'tied ranks'. On verbal fluency Y, for example, two boys obtained a score of 8. These scores take up the ranks of 3 and 4 in the class. So that all ranks 1–13 will finally be taken up, we assign the average of these two ranks to each boy, i.e. 3.5. Similarly, seven boys had the score of 17 on the desired age of leaving school variable. These take up the ranks of 6–12 in the class, so we assign the average rank of 9 to each of them. Having converted each boy's score into a rank, we subtract one rank from another (ignoring the sign) to give the values in column d. We then square each of the d values and add them together to form d². We can now substitute values into our formula for rho:

$$\text{rho} = 1 - \frac{6 \times 305.5}{13 \times 168} = 1 - \frac{1833}{2184} = 1 - 0.84$$
$$= +0.16$$

This suggests barely any relation between these two variables in this sample of boys. That is to say, 'verbal fluency' and 'desired age of leaving school' show only a small positive correlation with each other.

While rho is only suitable for ranked (or ordinal) data, you will have realised that interval data can be used, provided it is first ranked. However, rho will always provide a lower estimate of correlation than *r* because the data is degraded, i.e. rho throws away information in changing interval data into ranks.

Interpretation of rho

As with *r*, the obtained value of rho must be compared with the critical values in Table 16.2, (p. 247). If the obtained rho equals or exceeds the tabled value, the null hypothesis is to be rejected at the level of significance chosen.

Problems and errors in interpreting a correlation coefficient

There are a number of problems and likely errors which must be avoided if the interpretation of the correlation is to be meaningful.

1 The inherent relationship of variables may differ from population to population. Among children between the ages of 10 and 16, physical prowess and chronological age are highly correlated. Among adults between the ages of 20 and 26, these two variables are not correlated. Among children, the variables *mental age* and *chronological age* are positively correlated; among the middle-aged, there is no correlation between these two variables; among the elderly they are somewhat negatively correlated.

Whenever correlation is computed from scores that do not represent the full range of the distribution, caution must be used in interpreting the correlation. For example, correlating the IQ scores of a group of university professors with their scores on creativity would produce a very different correlation than if a sample of the full IQ range of the population were used. A highly positive correlation obtained from a full range of scores can be obscured when data is limited to a limited range as in Figure 16.5 following. A zero correlation can be inflated to a positive one by restricting the range too as in Figure 16.6.

FIGURE 16.5

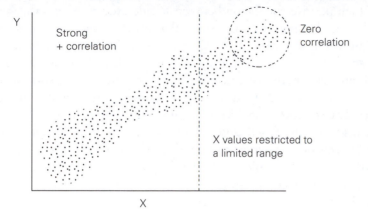

2 When a population is heterogeneous in the variables of concern, we expect to observe a higher correlation than when a population is homogeneous in these variables. For example, in a general population of male college students, we expect a positive correlation between height and success in basketball because the taller boys will tend to do better at the game. In a professional basketball team, we would not expect such a relationship. The members of a professional team are all tall and all very good at the game. In a group that is very homogeneous, we would not observe the correlation that exists in the population at large. This restriction in the sample is termed *attenuation*. A sample of university students would provide a very attenuated sample of IQ since they would all tend to have well above average IQs. A correlation of their IQs with their academic performance would produce a low positive correlation. Yet, throughout the whole population there is a high correlation since the whole range of IQ and performance levels is being employed.

FIGURE 16.6

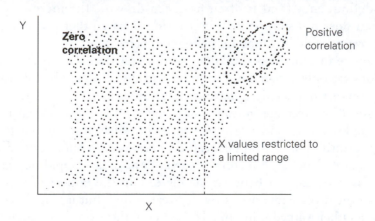

3 We may find a correlation between two variables, not because there is an intrinsic relationship between these variables, but because they are both related to a third variable. If there is a high positive correlation between seaside drownings and the sale of theatre tickets for the Pier Pavilion, we can predict that if ticket sales increase, so too will the number of drowning accidents. But while we can predict the likely occurrence of one event from another event, we cannot say that one event is the cause of the other. This statement cannot be over-emphasised, so easy is it to assume that two correlated conditions are causally related. Look back at our seaside drama. It is fairly obvious that drownings do not increase the sale of tickets, nor vice versa (unless the acts are so poor the patrons prefer to commit suicide by throwing themselves into the sea). A third variable, such as holiday fun or heatwaves encouraging more seaside trips, etc., are behind the relationship.

4 This leads on to a fourth problem hinted at in the introduction—that of falling into the seductive trap of assigning causality, i.e. that one variable causes the other.

Examine these persuasive communications:

a 'Buy an Apex Computer. Studies have proved that a relationship exists between computer use and grades. Get a computer now, and improve your marks.'

b 'Brown, your grades were poor this term. You have not been applying yourself, have you? The most successful students study at least nine hours a day. Now, if you apply yourself to your studies, I am sure you will do much better by the end of the school year!'

Can you detect the flaws in these arguments? In each case, there may be an undisputed fact of the relationships implied. Typewritten essays do tend to get better grades. Successful students often do study long hours. The flaws are not in the facts, but in the inferences of causation. Mere correlation does not imply causation. Good students are the ones who buy most of the computers, but they would do well anyway. The failing student may be stupid, or badly taught, or in the wrong kind of school, rather than lazy; a lot of study is done by bright students, but study is not the only requirement for good grades.

Illegitimate inferences of causation are often very subtle; they also become socially important when, for example, a high correlation is noted between poverty and delinquency of behaviour. If the conclusion is drawn that poor people naturally tend toward delinquency (and it often has been drawn), the mere existence of the correlation does not support that conclusion. Many other possible explanations besides poverty could be found for delinquent behaviour.

5 A final source of erroneous thinking about correlations lies in the fact that since correlations are only a mathematical index and therefore can be calculated between any two sets of data, it is apparent that some very high correlations, while mathematically correct, are in reality meaningless. It is easy to calculate correlations between trade statistics and social survey data in which, for example, there may be a very high positive correlation between the increase in church attendance and the increase in attendance at 'blue film' cinemas in an area of rapid population growth over the last ten years, or between the increase in the import of bananas and the increase in the divorce rate over a twenty-year period, but it would take an unusual theory or a rather warped mind to relate either of these two in a causal manner!

Effect size and power for correlation

Computing an effect size statistic

SPSS calculates the Pearson correlation coefficient, itself a measure of effect size. As with all effect size indices, there is no single acceptable answer to the question, 'What value indicates a strong relationship between two variables?'. What is large or small depends on the discipline within which the research question is being asked. However, for the behavioural sciences, Cohen's (1988) conventions for the correlation coefficient are .10 for a small effect size, .30 for a medium effect size, and .50 for a large effect size irrespective of sign.

Calculating power

Table 16.3 gives approximate power while Table 16.4 provides minimum sample size for 80 per cent power.

TABLE 16.3 *Approximate power of studies using the correlation coefficient 'r' for testing hypotheses at the .05 level of significance*

	Effect size		
	Small (r = .10)	Medium (r = .30)	Large (r = .50)
Two-tailed			
Total N:10	.06	.13	.33
20	.07	.25	.64
30	.08	.37	.83
40	.09	.48	.92
50	.11	.57	.97
100	.17	.86	1.00
One-tailed			
Total N:10	.08	.22	.46
20	.11	.37	.75
30	.13	.50	.90
40	.15	.60	.96
50	.17	.69	.98
100	.26	.92	1.00

TABLE 16.4 *Approximate number of participants needed for 80% power for a study using the correlation coefficient (r) for testing a hypothesis at the .05 significance level*

	Effect size		
	Small (r = .10)	Medium (r = .30)	Large (r = .50)
Two-tailed	783	85	28
One-tailed	617	68	22

Using SPSS to calculate Pearson's correlation and Spearman's rho

Pearson's correlation

We will illustrate the computation of Pearson's correlation with dummy data that list for 84 teachers their ages and length of work experience.

How to proceed

1 Click *Statistics* from the menu bar to display a drop-down menu.
2 From the drop-down menu, select *Correlate* which produces a smaller drop-down menu.
3 Choose *Bivariate*.
4 Select your variables and then click on the arrow button which places them in the *Variables* box. You can either select the two variables in two separate operations or drag the highlight down over the second variable using the mouse.
5 The Pearson option has already been pre-selected (i.e. it is a default option), so if only Pearson's correlation is required select *OK*; this closes the *Bivariate Correlations* dialogue box and produces output such as that shown in Table 16.6.
6 Should you wish, you can also obtain means and standard deviations by clicking *Options,* followed by those two items in the *Statistics* box.

   Additionally, you can create a scatterplot to visually represent the relationship. This would certainly enhance the results section. It also has the value of letting you see whether it is a linear or non-linear relationship. You should never report a correlation coefficient without examining the scattergram for problems such as curvilinear relationships.

   In a student project it should always be possible to include a scattergram of this sort. Unfortunately, journal articles and books tend to be restricted in the numbers they include because of economies of space and cost.

To produce a scatterplot

1 Click *Graph* and then *Scatter*.
2 *Simple* is the default mode and is already selected for you. Click on *Define*. (If you have a set of inter-correlations you click *Matrix* before *Define*.)
3 Move the two variables into the box by using the arrow button, then select *OK* to produce the graph.
4 With a correlation it does not really matter which variable represents the horizontal or X-axis (the abscissa), and which variable represents the vertical or Y-axis (the ordinate).

How to interpret the output in Table 16.5

- The variables on which the correlation was carried out are given both in the columns and in the rows. We have just two variables, so a 2×2 correlation matrix is generated.
- The printout gives the sequence of entries in the table, although in a vertical format.
- The correlation between age and work experience is +0.930.
- Ten pairs of scores were used to obtain the correlation coefficient.
- The exact significance level is given to three decimal places (p = .000). This is a highly significant level.

TABLE 16.5 *Correlations*

		AGE	EXP
Pearson correlation	AGE	1.000	.930*
	EXP	.930*	1.000
Sig. (2-tailed)	AGE		.000
	EXP	.000	
N	AGE	84	84
	EXP	84	84

* Correlation is significant at the 0.01 level (2-tailed).

FIGURE 16.7 *Scatterplot*

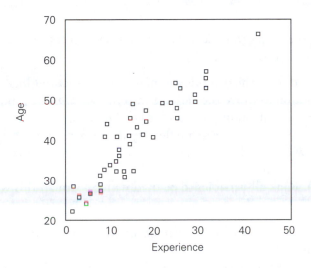

- Correlations are produced as a matrix. The diagonal of this matrix (from top left to bottom right) consists of the variable correlated with itself, which obviously gives a perfect correlation of 1.000. Obviously no significance level is quoted for this value.
- The values of the correlations are symmetrical around the diagonal from top right to bottom left in the matrix.
- The scattergram provides a strong visual demonstration of a strong positive correlation.

How to report the output in Table 16.5

- The correlation between age and work experience is +0.930. It is usual to round correlations to two decimal places, which would make it +0.93. This is quite precise enough for most measurements in the behavioural sciences.
- The exact significance level to three decimal places is 0.000. This means that the significance level is less than 0.001. It is better not to use a string of zeros as these are confusing. Alter the final zero to a 1 in these situations. In this case it means that the

significance level can be reported as being p < 0.001 even though the printout will quote it only at the 0.01 level under the table.

- It is customary to present the degrees of freedom rather than the number of cases when presenting correlations. Remember for correlation that the degrees of freedom are the number of cases minus 2, which makes them 8 for this correlation.
- In a report, you could write, 'There is a significant positive relationship between teacher age and length of work experience ($r = +0.93$, $df = 83$, $p < 0.001$). Teachers who are older have longer work experience'.

Spearman's rank order correlation

To demonstrate this statistic, a sample of ten employees provided length of work experience and current salary.

How to proceed

In order to correlate the scores in ranks rather than as raw scores, the scores have to be turned into ranks. To do this:

1 Select *Transform* and from the drop-down menu click on *Rank Cases.*
2 Select the arrow button to move the variable into the *Variables* text box.
3 Select the largest value button in the *Assign Rank 1* to area.
4 Click OK and a new variable is created reflecting the ranking of the original variable. This new variable will carry the same name as the original but is preceded by a letter 'r' to designate it as a ranked variable (e.g. 'age' will become 'rage'; 'salnow' will become 'rsalnow'). Rank all variables to be used with Spearman this way.

To produce Spearman's correlation

1 Select *Spearman* in the *Bivariate Correlations* dialogue box and de-select *Pearson,* which is the default statistic.
2 Select *OK* to close the *Bivariate Correlations* dialogue box and display the output like that shown in Table 16.6.

TABLE 16.6 *Correlations*

			RANK of SALNOW	RANK of EXPER
Spearman's rho	Correlation coefficient	RANK of SALNOW	1.000	–.006
		RANK of EXPER	–.006	1.000
	Sig. (2–tailed)	RANK of SALNOW		.987
		RANK of EXPER	.987	
	N	RANK of SALNOW	10	10
		RANK of EXPER	10	10

How to interpret the output in Table 16.6

- Spearman's rho is printed in a matrix form like that for Pearson.
- Spearman's correlation between the ranks for current salary and work experience is –0.006.
- The number of cases on which that correlation was based is 10 and is given by N (10) in the table.
- The exact significance level is given to three decimal places as .987.
- The degrees of freedom are the number of cases minus 2 which makes them 8.

How to report the output in Table 16.6

The correlation is reported to two decimal places as –0.01. The probability of achieving this correlation by chance is quite high (p = 0.987).

You could report this as follows: 'There is no statistically significant relationship between salary now and length of work experience (rho = –0.001, *df* = 8, p = 0.987). Length of work experience is therefore no guide to current salary as the relationship is random. Current salary must depend on a number of other variables not measured in this study'.

The *Bivariate Correlations* procedure allows you also to obtain Kendall's tau (see p. 258) and one-tailed tests of significance. There are a variety of scatterplots available. These can be edited in many ways. You should explore these.

STQ80*

1 A group of apprentices was given instruction in welding. A study was conducted to determine if the number of hours spent in practice was related to proficiency. Compute the rank order correlation for these data.

Apprentice	A	B	C	D	E	F	G	H	I	J	K	L
Hours of practice	24	23	19.5	18	17	16.5	16	15	14.5	14	13.5	10
Proficiency rating	75	83	98	80	74	69	71	69	59	62	70	54

Using Table 16.3, determine if the rho computed is significant. Use p = 0.01 as your designated level for significance. Would you accept or reject the null hypothesis?

2 A teacher was interested in knowing the extent to which her evaluation of her children's cooperativeness was related to their evaluation of themselves. She rated each child on cooperativeness, using a scale ranging from 1 for very *cooperative* to 10 for *uncooperative*. The children also rated themselves, using the same scale. Below are the data obtained for ten children. Compute the rank order correlation for this data.

Child	A	B	C	D	E	F	G	H	I	J
Teacher's rating	5	10	1	6	2	8	4	4	6	6
Child's self-rating	4	2	3	1	3	2	3	5	5	6

(continued)

Using Table 16.2 determine if the rho is significant. Use p = 0.05 as your designated level for significance. Would you accept or reject the null hypothesis?

3   In a painting competition, the various entries were ranked by two judges. To what extent do the judges agree? Interpret rho for significance at p = 0.05.

Entry	A	B	C	D	E	F	G	H	I	J
Judge X	5	2	6	8	1	7	4	9	3	10
Judge Y	1	7	6	10	4	5	3	8	2	9

4   Some pupils are asked to report the hours per week they spend watching TV. Their average academic grades are available. What is the relationship between the two? State your null hypothesis. Can the null hypothesis be rejected at p = 0.01?

Subject	1	2	3	4	5	6	7	8	9	10	11	12	13	14	15
Hrs/wk TV	0	25	14	9	20	9	15	30	25	17	25	3	11	12	7
Grade %	75	63	69	73	58	64	64	45	48	53	46	80	70	59	85

5   Here are some more fictitious data.

Student	Maths	Music	Difference between ranks (d)
1	3	6	3
2	1	5	4
3	4	3.5	0.5
4	5	2	3
5	6	1	5
6	7	7	0
7	2	3.5	1.5

a   What value is rho?
b   What is the critical value in the table for p < .05 two tailed test with N = 7?
c   Is the correlation significant?

*Answers on p. 602.

summary

Chi square and correlation assess relationships between variables. Chi square uses nominal data while correlation techniques mainly employ ordinal and interval data. Chi square assesses the goodness-of-fit of data to theoretical distributions and evaluates relationships between categories. Correlation techniques measure relationships but do not indicate cause and effect. The correlation coefficient varies between +1, a perfect relationship, and –1, a perfect inverse relationship. The more random the relationship, the closer the coefficient is to zero.

References

Cohen, J. (1988), *Statistical Power Analysis for the Behavioural Sciences*, Laurence Erlbaum, New York.

Entwistle, N. (1972), 'Personality & academic attainment', *British Journal of Education Psychology*, 42, pp. 137–51.

Sears, R., Maccoby, E. & Levine, H. (1957), *Patterns of Child Rearing*, Row Petersen, Evanston.

17
seventeen

A number of useful non-parametric correlation coefficients exist, as well as other valuable correlation techniques that aid the analysis of data.

Non-parametric correlation coefficients

Kendall's tau

This statistic can be used to correlate ranks such as rho, but has the advantage that it has a more normal sampling distribution than rho for samples under ten. The disadvantages are that it is harder to calculate than rho and it yields lower correlation coefficients than rho from the same data.

As an example, we might ask two teachers to rank four essays in terms of quality of expressive style. The rankings given are as follows:

Essay	a	b	c	d
Judge P	3	4	2	1
Judge Q	3	1	4	2

The order of the essays is then rearranged so that the first judge's ranks appear in numerical order.

Essay	d	c	a	b
Judge P	1	2	3	4
Judge Q	2	4	3	1

We are now in a position to determine the degree of correspondence between the two sets of judgements. We now determine how many pairs of rank in judge Q's set are in their natural order with respect to each other. We start by considering all possible pairs of ranks in which judge Q's rank 2, the farthest to the left, is in a natural order with the other ranks. The first pair, 2 and 4, has the correct order, so we assign a score of +1. The second pairing, 2 with 3, is also in the correct order, so it earns a +1. The third pairing, 2 and 1, is not in the natural order, so we assign −1 to this pairing. Thus for all pairs with rank 2 we total the scores as follows: +1 +1 −1 and obtain +1. We continue the process by looking at all pairings with the second rank from left, which is 4. Both pairings with 4 are not in a natural order (4 with 3, and 4 with 1), therefore the sum is −2. Finally, we consider the third rank from the left, which is 3. We only have one pairing here and that is in the wrong order, so we allocate a score of −1.

The total of all scores assigned is +1, −2 and −1, which gives an overall score of −2.

Now we need to determine what is the maximum possible total we could have obtained for the scores assigned to all the pairs in judge Q's ranking. The maximum possible would occur if both judges agreed on their rankings. This would place all judge Q's rankings in natural order. The maximum total then in the case of perfect agreement between P and Q would be four things taken two at a time, or 6.

$$\text{Kendalls' tau} = \frac{\text{actual total}}{\text{maximum possible total}} = \frac{-2}{6} = -0.33$$

That is, $r = -0.33$. This is the measure of agreement between the ranks assigned by judge P and those assigned by judge Q. One may think of tau as a function of the minimum number of inversions or interchanges between neighbours which is required to transform one ranking into the other. It is a sort of coefficient of disarray.

The actual formula for tau is $\dfrac{S}{1/2N(N-1)}$

where S = the actual total score of all pairing orders as calculated above (i.e. in our example, −2) and N = number of subjects ranked.

The effect of tied ranks is to change the denominator of the formula to:

$\sqrt{1/2N(N-1) - T_X}$ multiplied by $\sqrt{1/2N(N-1) - T_Y}$

where

$T_X = 1/2$ sum of $t(t-1)$ where t = no. of tied observation on X variable

and

$T_Y = 1/2$ sum of $t(t-1)$ where t = no. of tied observation on Y variable.

STQ81*

Calculate tau:

Subject	1	2	3	4	5	6	7
Rank X	1	2	3	4	5	6	7
Rank Y	1	2	4	5	3	6	7

*Answers on p. 603.

Point biserial correlation r_{pbis}

This is used when one of the variables is in the form of a continuous score and the other is a true dichotomy. For example, correlating sex with performance in school programs or on attitudes scales would require this statistic. It is a form of product–moment correlation, and its statistical significance can be determined by the tables used for the product–moment correlation.

One of the main uses of r_{pbis} is in item analysis of educational and psychological tests. The point biserial correlation of a test item with the total test score is used as an index of the discriminating power of the item. That is whether the individual item discriminates between high and low scorers on the test as a whole. The total test score of each individual from the X variable and the Y variable is the right and wrong scores on the item. A biserial correlation must be calculated for every item. An item that has a positive correlation with the total test score is discriminating between candidates in the same way as the overall test. An item that has a low positive or negative correlation is not discriminating between overall low and high scorers in the test in the same way as the whole test, and would not be included in the final version of the test.

Here is an example. Suppose we wished to correlate exam scores with the gender of the student. Gender is true dichotomy.

Student	Test score	Gender (male =1; female = 0)
	X	Y
A	60	0
B	56	0
C	51	0
D	58	0
E	49	1
F	48	0
G	55	1
H	45	1
I	47	1
J	55	0

The formula is:

$$r_{pbis} = \frac{M_p - M_q}{\sigma_x} \sqrt{pq} \quad \text{where}$$

M_p = mean score on X for group scoring 0 on Y

M_q = mean score on X for group scoring 1 on Y

p = proportion scoring 0 on Y

q = proportion scoring 1 on Y

o_x = standard deviation of all X scores

In our example:

$$M_p = 54.67; \ M_q = 49; \ p = .6; \ q = .4; \ o_x = 4.82.$$

$$r_{pbis} = \frac{54.67 - 49.00}{4.82} \sqrt{.24} = 0.58$$

STQ82*

Calculate r_{pbis} on the data below:

X	Y
0	1
1	1
2	0
4	1
5	1
6	0
7	0
8	0
8	1
9	0

*Answer on p. 603.

Tetrachoric correlation r_t

In a situation where both variables are in the form of dichotomies the tetrachoric correlation is used. Two examples are where passing or failing is correlated with the sex of the subjects, or where you are determining a relationship between leaving school or staying on at school after the compulsory years and the possession of some behavioural characteristic, such as smoking or not smoking. This statistic is sound when there are large numbers in the sample and when the dichotomies divide into almost equal groups. It has a large standard error.

As the observable data are dichotomous scores on both variables, the data are usually presented in a 2 × 2 table, with each individual placed in the cell that represents their two dichotomous scores. Here is an example:

Student	Attitude X (favourable = 1; unfavourable = 0)	Exam Y (pass = 1; fail = 0)
A	1	1
B	1	1
C	1	1
D	1	1
E	1	0
F	0	1
G	0	1
H	0	0
I	0	0
J	0	0

The steps to calculate r_t are:

1 Create 2 × 2 table

Attitude X

Achievement Y		0	1	
	1	2(a)	4(b)	6
	0	3(c)	1(d)	4
		5	5	10

2 Multiply a × d to get ad, and b × c to get bc. ad = 2 and bc = 12. When bc is greater than cd the correlation is positive; when bc is greater than ad the correlation is negative.

3 Divide the larger of the two products by the smaller. This gives us 6.

4 Enter the table below with bc/ad or ad/bc—whichever is larger—and read the corresponding value of r_t to the left of it. In our example we enter the table with a bc/ad ratio of 6 and find the tabled value to be 0.61.

STQ83*

Consider the following data and determine the r_t:

X

Y		0	1
	1	30	10
	0	4	16

*Answer on p. 603.

part 2 | quantitative methods

TABLE 17.1 *Tetrachoric correlations*

r_t	bc or ad / ad bc	r_t	bc or ad / ad bc	r_t	bc or ad / ad bc	r_t	bc or ad / ad bc
0	1.000	.26	1.941–1.993	.51	4.068–4.205	.76	11.513–12.177
.01	1.013–1.039	.27	1.994–2.048	.52	4.206–4.351	.77	12.178–12.905
.02	1.040–1.066	.28	2.049–2.105	.53	4.352–4.503	.78	12.906–13.707
.03	1.067–1.093	.29	2.106–2.164	.54	4.504–4.662	.79	13.708–14.592
.04	1.094–1.122	.30	2.165–2.225	.55	4.663–4.830	.80	14.593–15.574
.05	1.123–1.151	.31	2.226–2.288	.56	4.831–5.007	.81	15.575–16.670
.06	1.152–1.180	.32	2.289–2.353	.57	5.008–5.192	.82	16.671–17.899
.07	1.181–1.211	.33	2.354–2.421	.58	5.193–5.388	.83	17.900–19.287
.08	1.212–1.242	.34	2.422–2.491	.59	5.389–5.595	.84	19.288–20.865
.09	1.243–1.275	.35	2.492–2.563	.60	5.596–5.813	.85	20.866–22.674
.10	1.276–1.308	.36	2.564–2.638	.61	5.814–6.043	.86	22.675–24.766
.11	1.309–1.342	.37	2.639–2.716	.62	6.044–6.288	.87	24.767–27.212
.12	1.343–1.377	.38	2.717–2.797	.63	6.289–6.547	.88	27.213–30.105
.13	1.378–1.413	.39	2.798–2.881	.64	6.548–6.822	.89	30.106–33.577
.14	1.414–1.450	.40	2.882–2.968	.65	6.823–7.115	.90	33.578–37.815
.15	1.451–1.488	.41	2.969–3.059	.66	7.116–7.428	.91	37.816–43.096
.16	1.489–1.528	.42	3.060–3.153	.67	7.429–7.761	.92	43.097–49.846
.17	1.529–1.568	.43	3.154–3.251	.68	7.762–8.117	.93	49.847–58.758
.18	1.569–1.610	.44	3.252–3.353	.69	8.118–8.499	.94	58.759–71.035
.19	1.611–1.653	.45	3.354–3.460	.70	8.500–8.910	.95	71.036–88.964
.20	1.654–1.697	.46	3.461–3.571	.71	8.911–9.351	.96	88.965–117.479
.21	1.698–1.743	.47	3.572–3.687	.72	9.352–9.828	.97	117.480–169.503
.22	1.744–1.790	.48	3.688–3.808	.73	9.829–10.344	.98	169.504–292.864
.23	1.791–1.838	.49	3.809–3.935	.74	10.345–10.903	.99	292.865–923.687
.24	1.839–1.888	.50	3.936–4.067	.75	10.904–11.512	1.00	923.688– ∞
.25	1.889–1.940						

* If bc/ad is greater than 1, the value of r_t is read directly from this table. If ad/bc is greater than 1, the table is entered with ad/bc and the value of r_t is negative.

The phi coefficient

The phi coefficient is used when the two variables are both true dichotomies. As true dichotomies are rare in education, this statistic is rarely used. It is appropriate when correlation of responses is made between correct and incorrect answers to two test items, or between two yes/no or agree/disagree response type items on a test. Phi is related to chi square.

Here is an example:

Student	X Gender (male =1; female = 0)	Y Scholarship holder (yes = 1; no = 0)
A	1	1
B	0	0
C	0	1
D	0	0
E	1	1

(continued)

	X	Y
F	0	0
G	1	0
H	1	1
I	0	0
J	0	1
K	1	1
L	0	0

These data are then collated into a 2×2 table with cells labelled a, b, c, and d. Below is the 2×2 table for the above data:

$$
\begin{array}{c|c|c}
 & \multicolumn{2}{c}{X} \\
 & 0 & 1 \\
\hline
Y \quad 1 & 2(a) & 4(b) \\
\hline
0 & 5(c) & 1(d)
\end{array}
$$

$$
phi = \frac{ad - bc}{\sqrt{(a + b)(c + d)(a + c)(b + d)}} = +0.507
$$

The significance of phi can be tested by the following formula.

Chi square $= Nphi^2$ where $df = (r - 1)(c - 1)$ in the contingency table. This calculated value is then compared to the table value in the chi square table.

The contingency coefficient C

This coefficient is used when the variables are in the form of categories. As phi and the tetrachoric correlation coefficients cannot be used when there are more than two categories, the contingency coefficient is useful for multi-category variables like socioeconomic status, age groups, parental education levels, etc. It is closely related to chi square and can be calculated from chi square. It yields correlations close to Pearson's r. While chi square only indicates that there is a significant relationship, the contingency coefficient will assess the strength of the relationship. The formula is:

$$
C = \sqrt{\frac{chi\ square}{chi\ square + N}}
$$

Here is an example:

With a chi square of 9.78, an N of 50, and 2 *df* the result is significant at 1% level, so we can conclude that there is relationship between the two variables. To measure the strength of this relationship we substitute into the formula and obtain:

$$C = \sqrt{\frac{9.78}{9.78 + 50}} = +0.404$$

C never reaches +1.0 as its value depends on the number of cells in the chi square table. The maximum value in a 2×2 table is .707, in a 3×3 table is .816 and in a 4×4 is .866 and so on.

STQ85*

Match the statistic with the definition. (There is one statistic with no definition provided.)

a	Spearman's rho	i	Used when both variables can be split into artificial dichotomies at critical points
b	Product–moment correlation Pearson		
c	Kendall's tau	ii	Preferable to rho for N < 10
d	Tetrachoric correlation	iii	Is used with two true dichotomies
e	Phi coefficient	iv	Used in calculating inter-item correlations
f	Point biserial correlation		
g	Contingency coefficient	v	Smallest standard error of all correlations; both variables must be continuous
		vi	Used with ranks and also when number of cases is under 30

*Answers on p. 603.

Curvilinear relationships

All the correlation techniques described above assume the relationship is linear, i.e. a straight line best represents the relationship. However, the relationship may not be linear but curvilinear. For example, performance is related to anxiety, but at both low and high levels of anxiety performance must be low, since in the former low effort will result, and in the latter the high anxiety level can disrupt performance. Performance, then, is maximised somewhere in between, thus producing an inverted U-shaped graph. Other examples producing non-linear plots, as shown in Figure 17.1, are size of schools against number of schools, i.e. fewer, very small, and very large schools; or decreasing disturbed nights with increasing age of infant; or sudden increase in vocabulary, then tapering off with age in the young child.

FIGURE 17.1 *Curvilinear relationships*

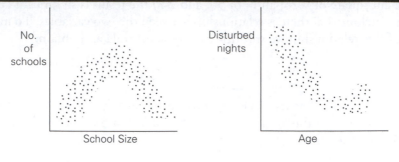

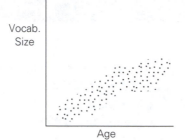

Multivariate correlation analysis

Previous chapters have assumed only one dependent variable. This is termed a univariate design. When two or more dependent variables are considered in a single analysis, we have a multivariate analysis.

Multivariate analyses allow the researcher to discount alternative explanations for a relationship that can arise when a survey/correlational design has been employed. You may be investigating people's self-assigned social class and whether they send their children to private schools. The relationship may well be strong, but a third variable such as income may be the determining factor, as income determines social class and also the ability to pay for private education.

Partial correlation

This is a valuable technique when you wish to eliminate the influence of a third variable on the correlation between two other variables. You may be studying the relationships between self-concept, racial attitudes and authoritarianism. The results show that self-concept is strongly related to the other two, as the less positive a person feels about themselves, the more intolerant they become of others, the more they feel threatened by others and the more they believe in coercive controls to protect the way they wish society to be organised; again all in an attempt to protect their threatened self-concepts. By partialling out self-concept, a 'truer' sense of the relationship between racial intolerance and authoritarianism is obtained.

Here is another example. Suppose a sociologist wants to know if the stress people experience in married life is related to how long they have been married. However, the researcher is aware that part of what causes an association between marital stress and marriage length is the fact that people who have been married longer are likely to have children, and having children could create marital stress. Simply calculating the correlation between marital stress and marriage length would be misleading. The researcher needs to determine the relationship between stress and length of marriage that would occur if everyone had the same number of children. To put it another way, the researcher wants somehow to subtract the information provided by number of children from the information provided by marital stress and length. Partial correlation accomplishes this.

In this case, the researcher would compute a partial correlation between marital stress and length of marriage, holding constant the number of children variable. While this is often described as 'partialling out' in research papers, other synonymous terms are 'holding constant', and 'controlling for'. Here the researcher is trying to remove the effect of family size to determine the relationship between length of marriage and marital stress. The actual statistic for partial correlation is called the partial correlation coefficient, which like most other correlations can take values between −1 to +1, and is thought of as an ordinary correlation between two variables, except that some third variable is being controlled for.

Partial correlation is often used to help sort out alternative theoretical explanations for the relations among variables. Suppose the sociologist found an ordinary correlation between marital stress and marriage length. The sociologist might want to use this result as support for a theory that the effect of time is to make people feel more stress in their marriage because their partners start taking them for granted. The sociologist would also be aware that another possible explanation for what is going on is that when people are married longer, they are likely to have more children, and having children might create stress in the marriage. If the correlation between stress and length is found, even after controlling for number of children, this alternative explanation about children is rendered unlikely.

Here is an actual research example. Baer (1991) was interested in verbal creativity (storytelling, poetry, and so on). Specifically, his study focused on whether verbal creativity is a single, general trait, or whether it is a group of individual abilities. In the past, researchers had found that creativity tests tended to correlate to a moderate degree with each other, and this was taken as evidence for the general, single trait of creativity. Baer, however, reasoned that the correlations among these tests may be due to factors, such as IQ, that enable students to do better on any kind of test. In one of his studies, Baer gave fifty adolescents several creativity tests, along with IQ and scholastic achievement tests. As was found in the previous studies, Baer discovered that there were moderate correlations among the creativity tests. Then Baer recalculated these correlations as partial correlations, holding constant scores on verbal IQ, reading achievement, math IQ, math achievement, and gender. (That is, all of these variables were partialled out at once.) In most cases, the partial correlations were considerably lower than the ordinary correlations. For example, the correlation between the story-task creativity test and the poetry-task creativity test went from an ordinary correlation of .23 to a partial correlation of −.01. Similarly, the correlation between poetry-task creativity and word-problem creativity went from .31 to .19.

The partial correlation is first computed by calculating Pearson's r for each pair of possible relationships. That is with three variables x, y, and z, we would calculate the correlations between xy, xz and yz. Possible relationships are illustrated in Figure 17.2.

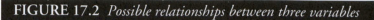

FIGURE 17.2 *Possible relationships between three variables*

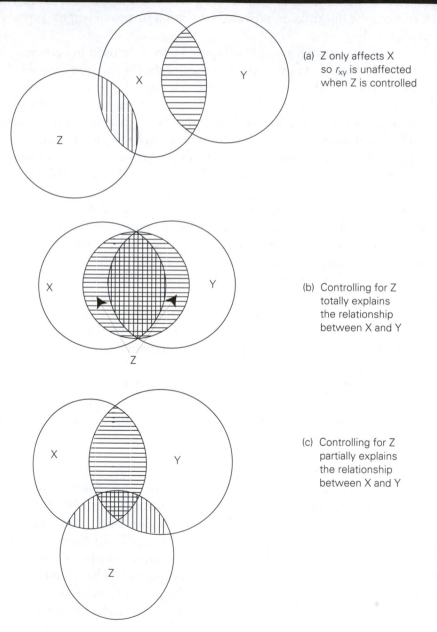

(a) Z only affects X so r_{xy} is unaffected when Z is controlled

(b) Controlling for Z totally explains the relationship between X and Y

(c) Controlling for Z partially explains the relationship between X and Y

In (a) z is only related to x, so the correlation between x and y is unaffected. In (b) all of the relationship between x and y is encapsulated by z. This would mean that the relationship between x and y when z is controlled is nil. The usual case is illustrated in (c), where a part of the relationship between x and y is explained by z. The partial correlation coefficient will be lower than the calculated one for xy. It is of course feasible to control any of the variables. The formula for the partial product moment correlation is:

$$r_{12.3} = \frac{r_{12} - r_{13}r_{23}}{\sqrt{(1 - r_{13}^2)(1 - r_{23}^2)}}$$

(in this case we are partialling out variable 3)

Suppose we have the following three variables:

1 = visual perception
2 = reading comprehension test score
3 = age

and the correlations for 200 primary school children are:

$r_{12} = +0.64$; $r_{13} = +0.80$; $r_{23} = +0.80$

Since children's reading and perceptual abilities increase with age, it seems appropriate to partial out the effect of age to determine the correlation of perception and reading with age removed.

$$r_{12.3} = \frac{.64 - (.80)(.80)}{\sqrt{(1 - .80^2)(1 - .80^2)}} = .00$$

With the effects of age removed, there is no relationship between perception and reading scores. It is totally random. The apparent relationship was caused by the effect of age in both variables. Significance is interpreted in the same way as r.

Computing an effect size statistic

The partial correlation is a type of Pearson correlation coefficient and can be interpreted in a similar manner. Like a bivariate correlation, a partial correlation can range in value from −1 to +1.

Calculating a partial correlation with SPSS

We will use dummy data to illustrate this. From a sample of 84 employees data was obtained on their age, their length of work experience and their current salary. A previous study had shown a high Pearson's r between length of work experience and current salary, but this could be an artefact of age, since age obviously impacts on both.

Pearson correlations were computed for the intercorrelation of three variables. These came out as:

age v. experience	=	0.930 p < .01
age v. salary	=	0.444 p < .01
experience v. salary	=	0.440 p < .01

Using these intercorrelations, a partial correlation was computed to 'hold constant' the variable of age.

How to proceed

1 Select *Statistics* and on the drop-down menu click on *Correlate*.
2 Next choose *Partial,* which brings the *Partial Correlations* box into view.
3 Select the variables that represent length of work experience and current salary and move them into the variables box by using the arrow button.
4 Select the age variable and move it into the *Controlling for* box.
5 Click the *Two tail* option in the *Test of Significance* box.
6 Choose *Options* and select *Zero-order correlations* in the *Statistics* box.
7 Click *Continue.*
8 Finally select *OK,* which produces output like Table 17.2 below.

TABLE 17.2 *Example of partial correlation printout*

Controlling for	AGE	
	EXP	**SALNOW**
EXP	1.0000	.0822
	(0)	(81)
	P= .	P= .460
SALNOW	.0822	1.000
	(81)	(0)
	P= .460	P= .

(Coefficient/(*df*)/2-tailed significance)
" . " is printed if a coefficient cannot be computed

How to interpret Table 17.2

- The output provides bivariate correlations between the two variables with age held constant.
- Each cell of the table includes the partial correlation coefficient, the degrees of freedom in parentheses and the p value.
- The partial correlation between length of work experience and current salary is 0.0822, *df* = 81, p = .460.

How to report the results

The partial correlation between current salary and length of work experience was computed holding age constant. The partial correlation of 0.08 indicates that current salary and length of work experience are randomly related. This strongly suggests that a wide variety of factors influence promotion rather than length of service itself. It also indicates that the original correlation of 0.44 was inflated by the effect of age, which impacts significantly on both variables.

STQ86*

1   Suppose we have correlated racism, self-esteem and neuroticism among secondary school pupils, but are aware that self-esteem may well underly racism and neuroticism. This suggests that the correlation between racism and neuroticism is false, simply because both are strongly related to self-esteem. Here are the data. Do you agree that the relationship between racism and neuroticism is a true one or simply the effect of both variables being related to self-esteem?
    r_{12} (racism v. neuroticism) = +0.50   N = 300
    r_{13} (racism v. self esteem) = +0.80
    r_{23} (neuroticism v. self esteem) = +0.60

2   A researcher correlates the income with attendance at religious services over one year. The correlation is +0.57. But when the researcher controls for the effects of age, the partial correlation falls to +0.14. Why has the size of the correlation fallen so much?

*Answers on p. 603.

Multiple correlation

If a researcher wishes to know the relationship between one variable and two or more other variables considered simultaneously, then multiple correlation is needed. The general formula is:

$$r_{12.3} = \sqrt{\frac{r_{12}^2 + r_{13}^2 - 2r_{12}r_{13}r_{23}}{1 - r_{23}^2}}$$

where $r_{1.23}$ is the multiple correlation between variable 1 and the combination of variables 2 and 3.

Suppose a university admissions officer is dissatisfied with selection procedures for undergraduate entry which rely on the applicant's tertiary entrance exam mark, and she wishes to find an additional measure that will enable a better prediction of future success to be made. The admissions officer decides on a personality measure, namely neuroticism. Data is obtained on 100 students in respect of:

1   first year undergraduate exam results
2   tertiary entrance exam mark
3   neuroticism

The following correlations are computed:

r_{12} = +0.50
r_{13} = −0.60
r_{23} = −0.20

substitute these values into the formula:

$$r_{12.3} = \sqrt{\frac{(0.50) + (-.60)^2 - 2(.50)(-.60)(-.20)}{1 - (-.20)^2}} = +0.71$$

This means that whereas the officer was able to attribute 25%, i.e. $(.50)^2$ of the variance in the first year exam to variance in the tertiary entrance exam, and 36%, i.e. $(-.60)^2$ of the variance in the examination results to student neuroticism on its own, by a combination of entrance results and neuroticism measures, 50.4%, i.e. $(.71)^2$ of the variance in the first-year exam can now be accounted for.

Factor analysis

This is a very popular and frequently used way of reducing a plethora of variables to a few factors; by grouping variables that are moderately or highly correlated with each other together to form a factor. It is an empirical way of reducing an unwieldy mass of variables into a manageable few. In studying the performance of students across the curriculum you would end up with a huge correlation matrix in which every subject's marks were correlated with those from every other subject. A factor analysis would show which groups of subjects were closely related and we may end up with three or four major factors, which in effect group similar disciplines together because performance is similar, such as a science group, a languages group, a social sciences group, or a practical subjects group.

Correlating the performance of athletes across a large number of events would also produce a large correlation matrix. Here, a factor analysis might show that some events were closely linked in terms of performance and three major factors might emerge in a factor analysis such as speed, endurance and strength, with each event lying within one of these factors. The aim is to see whether the original variables can be described by a much smaller number of factors. Factor analysis has been much used by Cattell, trying to determine the basic personality factors, and by many researchers attempting to provide construct validity for, among other things, intelligence tests. The mathematical basis of factor analysis is beyond the scope of this book and modern computer statistics programs carry out all the computations and produce the factor details without too much hassle.

summary

A variety of non-parametric correlation coefficients have been discussed in terms of their appropriate applications. Multivariate correlation techniques such as partial correlation, multiple correlation and factor analysis have been introduced briefly.

Reference

Baer, J. (1991), 'Generality of creativity across performance domains', *Creativity Research Journal*, 4, pp. 23–39.

Regression is a powerful tool for allowing the researcher to make *predictions* of the likely values of the dependent variable Y from known values of X (for example, when choosing the best applicant for a job on the basis of an aptitude or ability test, or predicting future university academic performance from a knowledge of HSC results). Regression is a widely used technique closely linked to Pearson's *r*, and shares many of the assumptions of *r* :

- the relationships should be linear; and
- the measurements must be in interval data.

Regression is an interesting phenomenon which is observed when there is a less than perfect relationship between two variables involved in prediction. In such a situation, it refers to the fact that the predicted score on a variable will be closer to the mean of the sample than is the predictor score. This is termed *regression to the mean*. For example, if one takes a number of students with high scores on a reasoning ability test, one will find that while most of these subjects are also above average on a mathematical ability test, most will be nearer to the average in the maths test than they were in the reasoning test. Similarly, students who score low in the first test will on the whole produce scores closer to the mean on the second test. Regression is always towards the mean of the second variable: that is, predicted Y scores are closer to the mean than the X scores.

This phenomenon was first described a century ago by Galton, who in his studies of heredity noticed that the children of exceptionally tall parents were tall, but on average not as tall as their parents, while those of 'short' parents tended on the whole not to be as short. The heights 'move' back, or regress, towards the population mean.

The accuracy of the prediction depends on the strength of the correlation between the two variables. Simple linear regression is concerned with finding the straight line on a scattergram that 'fits' the data best, i.e. as closely possible. This line is called the *line of best fit,* or the *regression line.* This line of best fit—a single line—will minimise the deviations from the line of all the dots in a scatter diagram and therefore make errors of prediction as small as possible. Some points will be above and some below, and a small proportion may actually be on it. The line of best fit is therefore the straight line about which the sum of the squared distances of the deviations of the scatter points (errors) is least or at a minimum. It is impossible to draw this line by hand or estimate it by eye. This is where regression comes in. Mathematical regression procedures permit the precise line of best fit to be calculated. Once we know this line, we can make a prediction of likely values of the dependent variable Y for particular values of the independent variable X.

Only two lines of best fit are perfectly related to the dots on a scatter graph (Figure 18.1a and b). These are where $r = +1.00$ and $r = -1.00$. We are able in these cases to make a perfect prediction of the dependent variable value if we know the independent variable value, as the line of best fit passes through all the points. For example, heights in inches are perfectly correlated with heights in centimetres. If we know a person's height in inches we can perfectly predict their height in centimetres.

When correlations between variables are less than perfect, predictions are good estimates rather than exact predictions. Prediction is less than perfect because there are exceptions to a consistent orderly relationship between the scores, so that the regression line will not pass through all the coordinate values used to determine the slope. But if we have a line of best fit we know that we can predict fairly closely with only a small range of error. The higher the correlation the more accurate our predictions.

FIGURE 18.1

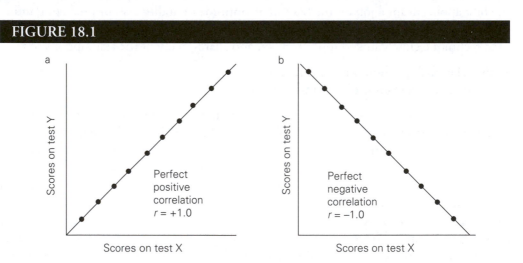

The slope of the regression line is a geometric representation of the coefficient of correlation, and is expressed as a ratio of the magnitude of the rise (if r is +) to the run, or as a ratio of the fall (if r is −) to the run, expressed in standard deviation units (see Figure 18.2).

part 2 | quantitative methods

FIGURE 18. 2

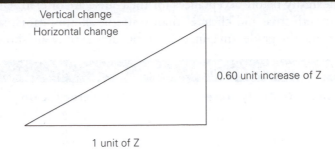

For example, if $r = +0.60$, for every Z unit increase (run) in X there is a 0.60Z unit increase in Y (see Figure 18.2).

Thus, predicted $Z_y = Z_x (r_{xy})$. For example, if we know that the correlation between reading test scores and spelling test scores is +0.7, we can predict that a student with a Z score of +2.0 in reading will have a Z score of (2.0)(0.7), or 1.4Z, in spelling. This formula can of course be used in either direction, so that we can predict reading Z scores from spelling Z scores. The correlation between X and Y is known as the standardised regression coefficient, which is symbolised by the Greek letter beta or β. So that a predicted $Z_y = Z_x(\beta)$ where β is the correlation coefficient.

FIGURE 18. 3

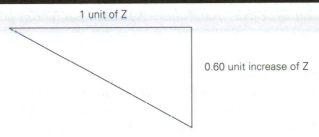

If $r = 0.60$, for every Z unit increase (run) in X, there is a 0.60Z unit decrease (fall) in Y (see Figure 18.3). So that, using the formula above, a student with Z score of -1.0 in reading will have a Z score of $(-1.0)(0.7) = -0.7Z$. The geometric relationship between the two legs of the triangle determines the slope of the hypotenuse (the regression line).

However, for practical purposes it is more convenient to use raw scores than Z scores.

EXAMPLE

Assume that research has shown that a simple test of manual dexterity is capable of distinguishing between the good and poor students in a word processing end-of-course test. Manual dexterity is a *predictor* variable, and input accuracy on the computer is the *criterion* variable. So it should be possible to predict which future students are likely to be the more accurate data input personnel from scores on this easily administered test of manual dexterity before acceptances for the course are offered. Using the test might be a lot more effective and cheaper than training all applicants, some of whom are unlikely to make the grade. Imaginary data for such a study are shown in Table 18.1.

TABLE 18.1 *Manual dexterity and input accuracy*	
Manual dexterity score	**Accuracy score**
56	17
19	6
78	23
92	22
16	9
23	10
29	13
60	20
50	16
35	19

The scattergram (see Figure 18.4) depicts the data above. Notice that the scores on the manual dexterity test form the horizontal dimension (X-axis), and the accuracy score is on the vertical dimension (Y-axis). In regression, in order to keep the number of formulae to the minimum:

- *the horizontal dimension (X-axis) should always be used to represent the variable from which the prediction is being made; and*
- *the vertical dimension (Y-axis) should always represent what is being predicted.*

It is clear from the scattergram that accuracy is fairly closely related to scores on the manual dexterity test. If we draw a straight line, *the regression line* or the *line of best fit,* as best we can through the points on the scattergram, this line could be used as a basis for making predictions about the most likely score on accuracy from the manual dexterity aptitude test score. In order to predict the most likely accuracy score corresponding to a score of 40 on the manual dexterity test, we can simply draw:

- a right angle from the score 40 on the horizontal axis (manual dexterity test score) to the regression line; and then
- a right angle from the vertical axis to meet this point. In this way we can find the accuracy score which best corresponds to a particular manual dexterity score (Figure 18.5).

Estimating from this scattergram and regression line, it appears that the best prediction from a manual dexterity score of 40 is an accuracy rate of about 14.

There is only one major problem with this procedure—the prediction depends on the particular line drawn through the points on the scattergram. Many different lines could be drawn. This eyeballing of a line of best fit is not desirable. It is preferable to have a method which is not subjective. So mathematical ways of determining the regression line have been developed. Fortunately, the computations are generally straightforward, and undertaken using SPSS.

part 2 | quantitative methods

FIGURE 18.4 *Eyeballing the line of best fit*

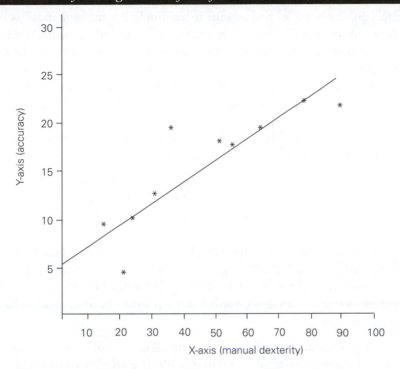

FIGURE 18.5 *Eyeballing the line of best fit*

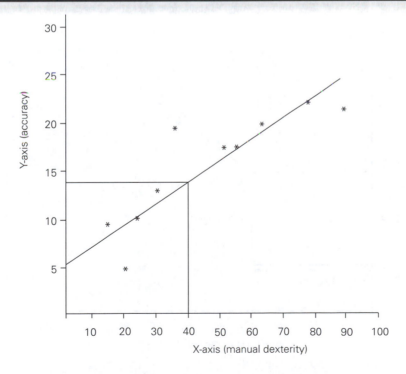

chapter 18 | prediction and simple linear regression

Theoretical background and regression equations

In order to establish an objective criterion, the regression line is mathematically calculated to gives the closest fit to the points on the scattergram. The procedure ensures that the sum of the deviations (d's) of the scattergram points from the regression line should be minimal.

Actually, the precise criterion is the sum of the *squared* deviations. This is known as the *least squares solution.* But it would be really tedious work drawing different regression lines, then calculating the sum of the squared deviations for each of these in order to decide which regression line has the smallest sum of squared deviations. Fortunately trial-and-error is not involved at all. The formulae for regression do all of that work for you.

In order to specify the regression line for any scattergram, you quantify two things:

1 The point at which the regression line cuts the vertical or Y-axis—this is a number of units of measurement from the zero point of the vertical axis. It can take a positive or negative value, denoting whether the vertical axis is cut above or below its zero point. It is normally denoted in regression as point *a,* or the *intercept.*

2 The *slope* of the regression line or, in other words, the gradient of the best-fitting line through the points on the scattergram. Just as with the correlation coefficient, this slope may be positive in the sense that it goes up from bottom left to top right, or it can be negative in that it goes downwards from top left to bottom right. The slope is designated by the letter *b.*

The intercept and slope are both shown in Figure 18.6. To work out the slope we have drawn a horizontal dashed line from X = 0 to X = 40 (length 40), and a vertical dashed

FIGURE 18. 6

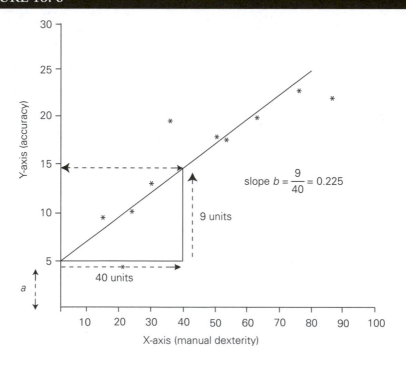

$$\text{slope } b = \frac{9}{40} = 0.225$$

part 2 | quantitative methods

line up to the regression line (length about 9 up the Y-axis). The slope *b* is the increase (+) or decrease (−) of the units produced (in this case +9), divided by the increase in the manual dexterity score (in this case 40), i.e. +0.225.

The slope is simply the number of units that the regression line moves up the vertical axis for each unit it moves along the horizontal axis. In other words, you mark a single step along the horizontal axis and work out how much increase this represents on the vertical axis. So, for example, if you read that the slope of a scattergram is 4.00, this means that for every increase of 1.00 on the horizontal axis (X-axis) there is an increase of 4.00 on the vertical axis (Y-axis). If there is a slope of −0.8 then this means that for every increase of 1 on the horizontal axis (X-axis) there is a decrease of 0.8 on the vertical axis (Y-axis).

In our example, for every increase of 1 in the manual dexterity score, there is an increase of 0.225 in the accuracy performance measure. We have estimated this value from the scattergram—it may not be exactly the answer that we would have obtained had we used mathematically more precise methods.

Regression equations

The regression line involves one awkward feature. As we have seen, all values really should be expressed in Z scores or standard deviation units. However, it is obviously more practical to use actual scores to determine the slope of the regression line. But because raw scores do not have the same means and standard deviations as Z scores, the prediction procedure has to make allowances for this by converting to a slope known as *b*, or the *raw score regression coefficient* (see below for the formula).

Fortunately, the application of two relatively simple formulae (see below) provides all the information we need to calculate the slope and the intercept. A third formula is used to make our predictions from the horizontal axis to the vertical axis.

EXAMPLE

Table 18.2 contains data on the relationship between anxiety scores and sociability scores for a group of ten individuals. Remember, it is important with regression to make the X scores the predictor variable; the Y scores are the criterion variable. N is the number of pairs of scores, i.e. 10.

The slope '*b*' of the regression line is given by several equivalent formulae.

When raw scores are many and/or large

$$b = \frac{\Sigma(X - M_X)(Y - M_Y)}{\Sigma(X - M)^2}$$

An alternative formula is: $b = \frac{SD_Y}{SD_X}(r)$

With small numbers, as above, a more convenient formula is :

$$b = \frac{\Sigma XY - \dfrac{\Sigma X \Sigma Y}{N}}{\Sigma X^2 - \dfrac{(\Sigma X)^2}{N}}$$

TABLE 18.2 *Important steps in calculating the regression equation*

Subject	Anxiety score X score	Sociability score Y score	X^2	XY
1	8	6	64	48
2	3	2	9	6
3	9	4	81	36
4	7	5	49	35
5	2	3	4	6
6	3	2	9	6
7	9	7	81	63
8	8	7	64	56
9	6	5	36	30
10	7	4	49	28
Sums	62	45	446	314

$$b = \frac{314 - \dfrac{2790}{10}}{446 - \dfrac{3844}{10}} = \frac{35}{61.6} = 0.568$$

This tells us that the slope of the regression line is positive—it moves upwards from bottom left to top right. Furthermore, for every unit one moves along the horizontal axis, the regression line moves 0.568 units *up* the vertical axis.

We can now substitute *b* in the following formula to get the cutting point or intercept (*a*) of the regression line on the vertical axis. *a* represents a constant factor of the value of Y when X equals zero:

$$a = \frac{\sum XY - b \sum X}{N}$$

$$a = \frac{45 - (3.522)}{10} = 4.148$$

This value for *a* is the point on the vertical axis (sociability) cut by the regression line. If one wishes to predict the most likely score for a particular score on the horizontal axis, one simply substitutes the appropriate values in the regression formula.

Thus if we wished to predict sociability for a score of 5 on anxiety, given that we know the slope (*b*) is 0.568 and the intercept is 4.148, we simply substitute these values in the formula:

Y (predicted score) = *a* (intercept) + [*b* (slope) x X (known score)]

Y = 4.148 + (0.568 x 5) = 6.988

This is the *best* prediction—it does not mean that individuals with a score of 5 on anxiety inevitably get a score of 6.988 (or rather 7.0) on sociability. It is just our most intelligent estimate. If in the future we have a person with an anxiety score of 5, we can say that they would in all probability obtain a sociability score of around 7.

When the relationship is negative, the regression equation for the line of best fit is:

$$Y = a - bX.$$

This implies that for every increment of X there will be a decrease in Y.

When the line of best fit intersects the horizontal axis, the intercept *a* will have a negative value. This is because it will cut the horizontal axis and when extended will intercept the vertical axis at a negative point, i.e. below the horizontal axis. In this situation:

$$Y = -a + bX.$$

The use of regression in prediction is a fraught issue, not because of the statistical methods but because of the characteristics of the data used. Our predictions are based on previously obtained data. For example, the data about anxiety and sociability are based on data already obtained. For future predictions based on this data, we are assuming the future sample is quite similar to the sample of our original data.

EXAMPLE

A private school charges a one-off registration fee of $2000, plus a fee for every semester of $1000. With this information the total cost of placing a student in the school for any number of semesters can be predicted.

$$\text{total cost} = \$2000 + \$1000 \text{ (no. of semesters)}, \text{ i.e.}$$

$$Y = a + bX$$

b is the slope that determines how much the Y variable will change when X is increased by one unit of $1000. *a* identifies the point where the line intercepts the Y axis; in this case *a* = $2000 since you pay this even if the student only attends for one semester. This is the base to which all semesters multiplied by a factor of 1000 are added.

For example, if a student attends for ten semesters, we obtain (see Figure 18.7):

$$Y = \$2000 + \$1000(10) = \$12\,000$$

Attendance for 16 semesters means $Y = \$2000 + \$1000(16) = \$18\,000$

STQ87*

Using the data in the table below:
1   Calculate *b* and *a*.
2   State the regression equation and use it to determine the best estimate of a students score on Y if they obtained 15 on X.

Student	X	Y
A	10	2
B	15	3
C	8	2
D	5	1.5
E	18	3.5

(continued)

F	12	2.5
G	6	2
H	16	3
I	17	4
J	12	3

Answers on p. 603.

A FURTHER EXAMPLE

Imagine a researcher who wants to know whether adolescents working part-time who put in extra hours tend to get on better in the organisation than others. The researcher finds out the average amount of time a group of twenty new adolescent part-time employees spend working extra hours. Several years later the researcher examines their hourly earnings which are taken as a measure of promotion. Assume the regression equation which is derived from an analysis of the raw data is $Y = 7.50 + 0.50X$. This line of best fit is shown in Figure 18.8. The intercept a is 7.50, i.e. $7.50 per hour; the regression coefficient (b) is 0.50, i.e. $0.50, meaning each extra hour worked per week has produced an extra $0.50 per week to the wage packet in terms of promotion. We can therefore calculate the likely income per hour of someone who puts in an extra seven hours per week as follows:

$$Y = 7.50 + (0.50)(7) = 11.00, \text{ i.e. } \$11.00$$

FIGURE 18.7

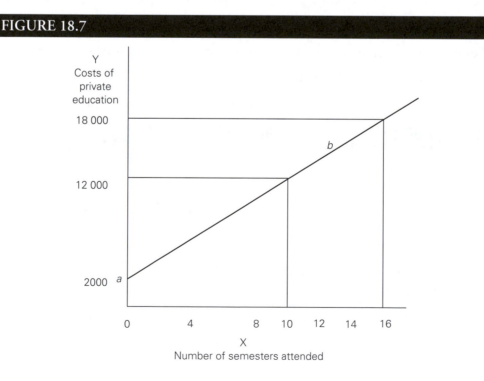

part 2 | quantitative methods

For someone who does an extra eight hours, the likely salary will be $11.50, i.e. an extra 0.50c for the further hour, and for 15 hours it predicts $15 per hour. For a person who does not do any extra hours the prediction is that the salary will have remained the same. Thus through regression we are able to show how Y changes for each additional increment of X, because the regression coefficient expresses how much more of Y you get for each extra increment of X. We can then predict the likely value of Y for given value of X (Figure 18.8).

FIGURE 18.8

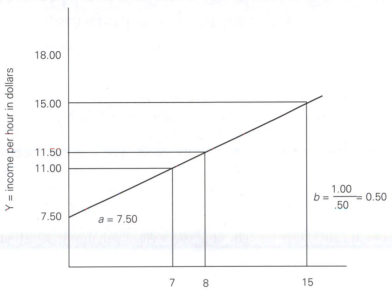

X = extra hours worked each week

STQ88*

Two regression equations have been developed for different predictions based on different samples of equal size. In one, $r = 0.69$, while in the other $r = 0.58$. In which situation will the most accurate predictions be made?

Answer on p. 603.

STQ89*

1 Using the equation $Y = -7 + 2X$ determine the values of Y for the following values of X:
   1, 3, 5, 10.

(continued)

2 The regression equation for the relationship between age and autonomy is:
   autonomy = 6.9643 + 0.6230 age.
   a   Explain what 6.9643 means.
   b   Explain what 0.6230 means.
   c   What is the likely level of autonomy of someone aged 18?
   d   What is the likely level of autonomy of someone aged 10?

Answers on p. 603.

Standard error: How accurate are the predicted score and the regression equations?

Predictions are never without some error unless the correlation is +1.0 or −1.0. The accuracy of the predicted score on the criterion is dependent on the closeness of the scattergram points to the regression line—the stronger the correlation between the variables the less error in the prediction. Visual inspection of the scattergram between two variables will give you an idea of the variability around the regression line and hence the precision of the estimated or predicted scores.

Statisticians however, prefer to calculate the standard error to indicate how certain one can be about aspects of regression such as the prediction, the intercept or cut-off points, and the slope. You remember that standard error is a standard deviation, except it applies to the distribution of *means* of samples rather than individual scores. It measures the average deviation of sample means from the mean of the sample means. The standard error of an estimate is best thought of as the average amount by which an estimate is likely to be wrong. Remember that whenever we use any characteristic of a sample as the basis for estimating the characteristic of a population, we are likely to be wrong to some extent.

Although the formulae for calculating the standard errors of the various aspects of the regression line are readily available, they add considerably to the computational labour involved in regression, so we recommend that you use a computer to relieve you of this computational chore.

The main standard errors involved in regression are:

- the one for the predicted (or estimated) value on the criterion (this is known as the standard error of the estimate of Y);
- the one for the slope of the regression line *(b);*
- the one for the intercept on the vertical axis (*a*).

We can use the calculated standard error to estimate the likely range within which the true value of the prediction, slope or intercept is likely to fall. The same confidence intervals (or significance levels) we have used before may be employed, depending on how confident we wish to be that we have included the true value. The interval is obviously going to be wider if you wish to be *very* confident rather than just confident. As you are aware, the 95 per cent confidence interval indicates the range of values within which the true value will fall 95 per cent of the time. That is, we are likely to be wrong only 5 per cent of times. The 99 per cent confidence interval deceases our likely error to 1 per cent. The argument is based on the assumption that for a single value of X there is a normal distribution of associated Y scores, as not all observed Y scores will exactly equal the predicted Y score. It is also assumed that for each of these sub-populations of Y scores, each Y mean falls on the regression line. This mean represents the predicted Y score for that value of X. This is displayed in Figure 18.9.

FIGURE 18.9

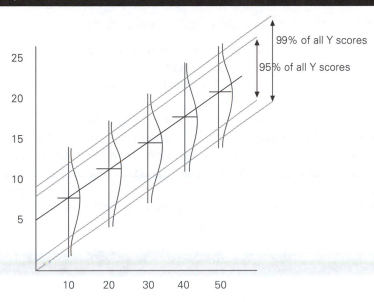

Because the correlation is not perfect—for any X score there is a range of scores which may be obtained on the Y variable—the range increasing as the correlation decreases. Thus in prediction it is important to obtain an estimate for the amount of variability in Y scores of persons who obtain the same X score. The variability of the Y distribution reflects error, and it is this error that is measured by the standard error of the estimate, which can be used as a measure of the accuracy of prediction.

The standard error of the estimate (SE_{est}) to estimate the prediction error of Y is:

$$SE_{esty} = sd_y \sqrt{1 - r^2}$$

As r increases the prediction error decreases.

When $r = +1.00$, $SE_{esty} = 0$.
When $r = 0.00$, $SE_{esty} = SD_y$.
When $r = 0.60$, $SE_{esty} = 0.80\ SD_y$.

The assumptions behind using the standard error of the estimate in this way are:

- the Y distributions for each value of X have the same variability; and
- for any value of X the associated Y scores are normally distributed.

If these assumptions are met, the normal curve table (Table 5.1, p. 73) can be used to set confidence limits around a predicted Y score. Based on this table, you can use the following as a rule of thumb. It is accurate enough for most purposes. Multiply the standard error by two (you probably remember that the actual tabled value for large groups is 1.96). This gives you the amount which you need to add and subtract from the estimated value to cut off the middle 95 per cent of the possible values—that is, the 95 per cent confidence interval. In other words, if the estimated value of the criterion (Y variable) is 6.00 and the standard error of this estimate is 0.26, then the 95 per cent confidence interval is:

6.00 plus or minus (2 × 0.26) = a 95% confidence interval of 5.48 to 6.52.

Thus it is almost certain that the person's score will actually fall in the range of 5.48 to 6.52, although the most likely value is 6.00.

Exactly the same applies to the other aspects of regression. If the slope is 2.00 with a standard error of 0.10, then the 95 per cent confidence interval is 2.00 plus or minus 2 × 0.10, which gives a confidence interval of 1.80 to 2.20.

The use of confidence intervals is not as common as it ought to be despite the fact that it gives us a realistic assessment of the precision of our estimates. Precise confidence intervals can be obtained by multiplying the standard error by the value of *t* from Table 5.1 (chapter 5) using the *df* row, corresponding to your number of pairs of scores minus 2 under the column for the 5 per cent significance level (i.e. if you have 10 pairs of scores then you would multiply by 2.31).

STQ90*

Given a correlation of +0.8 between distributions X and Y, a standard deviation of 3 for the Y scores, a score of 10 on X, and a regression equation of Y = 2.5X + 1.6:

1   Calculate the standard error of the estimate for Y and the 95 per cent confidence interval for the predicted Y score.
2   If the correlation is +0.3 recalculate the standard error of the estimate and the 95 per cent confidence interval.
3   Explain the difference between the two confidence intervals.

Answers on p. 604.

Advice

- Drawing the scattergram (see use of SPSS in chapter 16) will helpfully illuminate the trends in your data and strongly hint at the broad features of the regression calculations. It will also provide a visual check on your computations.
- These regression procedures assume that the dispersion of points is linear; that is, the scatter of points is the same around the whole length of the line of best fit. Where the amount of scatter around the line varies markedly at different points, the use of regression is questionable. If it looks like the regression line is curved or curvilinear, do not apply these numerical methods.

- In order to make predictions it is assumed that the individual or new group and the old group are both samples from the same population since we are predicting the Y score for the new individual/group on the basis of the data gathered from the original group.
- Regression is less accurate where one variable has a small range and the other has a large range.
- There are always two regression lines between two variables: that from which variable A is predicted from variable B, and that from which variable B is predicted from variable A. They almost invariably have different slopes. However, life is made simpler if we always have the predictor on the horizontal axis and the criterion to be predicted on the vertical axis. You need to be careful what you are trying to predict and from what.
- Finally, outliers affect the accuracy of prediction. Outliers are extreme values of Y or X. One extremely low or high value well away from the run of the other values distorts the prediction. Serious consideration has to be given to omitting the outlier from the calculation

Using SPSS for regression

Simple regression and a regression plot are illustrated with the data which relate length of work experience and age for eighty-four employees.

Remember, it is essential that the criterion or dependent variable (work experience in our example) is on the vertical axis (Y-axis) of a scatterplot, and the predictor or independent variable (age) is on the horizontal axis (X-axis).

How to proceed
1 Select *Statistics* and then *Regression* from the drop-down menu.
2 Choose *Linear* to open the *Linear Regression* dialogue box.
3 Click on the dependent variable and then the arrow button to place it in the *Dependent*: box.
4 Select the independent variable and with the arrow button move it into *Independent[s]* box
5 Select *Statistics* to obtain *the Linear Regression: Descriptives* dialogue box.
6 Choose *Descriptives* and ensure *Estimates* and *Model fit* are also selected.
7 Next choose *Continue* and finally *OK* to produce the output.

How to interpret the output in Table 18.3
As explained, with simple regression it is conventional to report the regression equation as a slope (*a*) and an intercept (*b*). SPSS does not quite follow this terminology, but all of the relevant information is located in fifth subtable. The output is far more complex and detailed than you require, but the following is what you need to take note of:

- Subtables a and b provide descriptive statistics and correlations. The latter in this dummy exercise is highly significant at +0.931.

TABLE 18.3 Regression

a Descriptive statistics

	Mean	Std deviation	N
EXP	16.0595	9.2272	84
AGE	40.9524	10.3504	84

b Correlations

		EXP	AGE
Pearson	EXP	1.000	.931
Correlation	AGE	.931	1.000
Sig.	EXP		.000
(1-tailed)	AGE	.000	
N	EXP	84	84
	AGE	84	84

c Model summary [a,b]

Model	Entered	Variables removed	R	R square	Adjusted R square	Std error of the estimate
1	AGE[c,d]		.931	.868	.868	3.3787

a Dependent variable: EXP

b Method: Enter

c Independent variables: (Constant), AGE

d All requested variables entered.

d ANOVA [a]

Model		Sum of squares	df	Mean square	F	Sig.
1	Regression	6130.609	1	6130.609	537.029	.000[b]
	Residual	936.094	82	11.416		
	Total	7066.702	83			

a Dependent variable: EXP

b Independent variables: (Constant), AGE

e Coefficients [a]

		Unstandardised coefficients		Standardised coefficients			95% confidence interval for B	
		B	Std Error	Beta	t	Sig.	Lower bound	Upper bound
1	(Constant)	−17.945	1.513		−11.861	.000	−20.955	−14.935
	AGE	.830	.036	.931	23.174	.000	.759	.902

a Dependent variable: EXP

- Subtable c provides R^2, which states in this case that 86.8 per cent of the variance in length of work experience is explained by the variance in age.
- Subtable e is the crucial one and displays the constant and beta.
- The intercept which we term *a* in the regression formula is referred to as the *constant* in SPSS. This is −17.945. As explained in the text, it is the point at which the regression line cuts the vertical (Y) axis. Since it is negative it implies the cut occurs below the X-axis.
- The unstandardised regression coefficient between the two variables is displayed under B as the second line and is .830.
- The 95 per cent confidence interval for B ranges from .759 to .902, i.e. based on this sample, and that for the constant or intercept ranges from −20.955 to −14.935. Since the regression is based on a sample and not the population, there is always a risk that the population regression coefficient is not the same as that in the population. The 95 per cent confidence intervals give the range within which you can be 95 per cent sure that the slope and the constant will lie. The 95 per cent confidence interval for the intercept is −20.955 to −14.935. This means that based on your sample, the intercept of the population is 95 per cent likely to lie within those ranges.
- The column headed Beta gives a value of .931. This is the Pearson correlation between the two variables. In other words, if you turn your scores into standard scores (Z-scores), the slope of the regression and the correlation coefficient are the same thing.

Regression scatterplot

The production and inspection of the scattergram of your two variables is warranted when doing regression. The provision of this scattergram in a report is also of benefit.
1 Select the *Graphs* option on the menu bar.
2 From the drop-down menu click on *Scatter*.
3 Since the *Simple option* is the default, select *Define*.
4 Move your dependent variable with the arrow button into the *Y Axis*: box.
5 Highlight your independent variable and transfer this to the *X Axis*: box.
6 Select *OK* and the scattergram will be displayed.
  To draw the regression line on the displayed chart:
1 Double click on the chart to select it for editing and maximise the size of the chart window.
2 In the *Chart Dialogue* box in the *Output navigator*, choose *Chart* and click on *Options*.
3 Select *Total* in the *Fit Line* box.
4 Select *OK*; the regression line is now displayed on the scatterplot.

How to interpret the scatterplot with regression line

- The regression line sloping from bottom right to top left indicates a positive relationship between the two variables.
- The points seem relatively close to this line which suggests that the beta weight (correlation) should be a large numerical value, and that the confidence interval for the slope should be relatively small. These are confirmed in the previous tables.

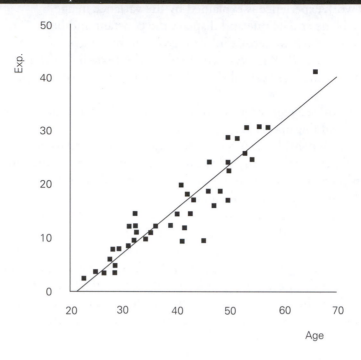

FIGURE 18.10 *Scatterplot*

How to report the results

You could write about the analysis as follows: 'A linear regression analysis was conducted to evaluate the prediction of length of work experience from age. The scatterplot for the two variables indicates that they are positively and strongly linearly related such that as age increases so does length of work experience.

The regression equation for predicting length of work experience is:

predicted length of work experience = −17.945 + .830 age

As hypothesised, there was strong relationship between the two variables. The correlation between the length of work experience and age was 0.931, p = .001. Approximately 87 per cent of the variance of length of work experience was accounted for by its linear relationship with age.'

Multiple regression

It may be that you have more than one predictor variable that you wish to use. If so, you will need multiple regression. However, multiple regression employs the same rationale, and the formula is a logical extension of the one for linear regression:

$$Y = a + b_1X_1 + b_2X_2 + b_3X_3 + \ldots \text{ etc.}$$

Multiple regression is about predicting a dependent variable on the basis of two or more predictor variables. A multiple regression prediction formula has a regression coefficient for each predictor variable. If you know a person's scores on the predictor variables, you multiply each predictor variable's score by that variable's regression coefficient. The. sum of these multiplications is the person's predicted score on the dependent variable. When working with Z scores, the regression coefficients are standardised regression coefficients, called beta weights. For example, with three independent variables the form of the prediction formula is as follows:

$$\text{predicted } Z_Y = (\beta_1)(Z_{X_1}) + (\beta_2)(Z_{X_2}) + (\beta_3)(Z_{X_3}) + \dots$$

As an example, we may be interested in the sources and amount of stress that teachers experience. This may be an effect of several variables in combination, such as class size, the amount of administration they do, length of experience, etc. The Z-score multiple regression prediction rule for this would be:

$$\text{predicted } Z_{Str} = (\beta_1)(Z_{\text{ class size}}) + (\beta_2)(Z_{\text{ admin hours}}) + (\beta_3)(Z_{\text{ length of exp.}})$$

Each of the betas is of course the respective correlation between stress and that variable. When working with raw scores, the standard formula is:

$$\text{predicted } Y = a + (b_1)(X_{\text{ class size}}) + (b_2)(X_{\text{ admin hours}}) + (b_3)(X_{\text{ length of exp.}})$$

Multiple correlation (designated R) is a measure of the correlation of one dependent variable with a combination of two or more predictor variables. In multiple regression, researchers can determine the statistical significance of both the overall multiple correlation coefficient, R, as well as for each beta individually. In most cases, however, if the overall R is not significant, the individual betas will not be tested for their significance. Yet, it is quite possible for the overall R to be significant, but for some of the individual betas not to be significant. For example, the overall significant correlation might be due to the strong influence of only one predictor variable, with the others having only a slight contribution.

Hierarchical and stepwise multiple regression

There are two forms of multiple regression: hierarchical and stepwise.

Hierarchical multiple regression

Sometimes researchers are interested in looking at the influence of several predictor variables in a sequential way. That is, they want to know what the correlation will be of the first predictor variable with the dependent variable, and then how much is added to the overall multiple correlation by including a second predictor variable, and then perhaps how much more is added by including a third predictor variable, and so on. This is known as hierarchical multiple regression.

In research using hierarchical multiple regression, the amount that each successive variable adds to the overall prediction usually is described in terms of an increase in R, the proportion of variance accounted for or explained.

Stepwise multiple regression

Often, especially in an exploratory study, a researcher may have measured many potential predictor variables and wants to pick out which ones make a useful contribution to the overall prediction. In the most common form of stepwise multiple regression, a computer program goes through a step-by-step procedure in which it first picks out the variable that has the highest correlation with the dependent variable. If this correlation is not significant the process stops, since even the best predictor is not of any use. If this correlation is significant, the process goes on to the next step. The next step is to pick out the predictor variable which, in combination with this first one, has the highest multiple R. The computer then checks this to see whether this combination is a significant improvement over the best single predictor variable alone. If it is not, the process stops. If it is a significant improvement, the program goes on to the next step.

The next step is to pick out which of the remaining predictor variables, when taken in combination with these first two, creates the highest multiple R. Then this combination is checked to see if it is a significant improvement in prediction over and above just the first two predictors. The process continues until either all the predictor variables are included, or the addition of any of the remaining ones does not give a significant improvement. Because this procedure proceeds one step at a time, it is called 'stepwise'. Here are the steps:

Step 1: Search all potential predictor variables and find the best bivariate correlation with the dependent variable.
Step 2: Test significance.
   If not significant
   STOP.
   If significant, include this variable in all further steps, and
   CONTINUE.
Step 3: Search all remaining potential predictor variables for the best single variable to combine with those already included for predicting the dependent variable.
   If no addition is significant
   STOP.
   If an addition is significant, include this variable in all further steps, and
   REPEAT STEP 3 TO SEARCH FOR THE NEXT BEST REMAINING PREDICTOR VARIABLE.

One caution about stepwise regression—the prediction formula that results is the best group of variables for predicting the dependent variable, *based on the sample studied*. However, it often happens that when the same variables are studied with a new sample, a somewhat different combination of variables turns out to be best.

Hierarchical and stepwise regression compared

Hierarchical and stepwise regression are similar in an important way. In both methods you are adding one variable at a time and checking whether the addition makes a significant improvement in the prediction. There is also a very important difference. In hierarchical regression the order of adding the predictor variables is based on some theory or plan, decided in advance by the researcher. In stepwise regression, there is no initial plan. The computer simply works out the best variables to add until adding more makes no additional contribution.

summary

If two variables are correlated, knowledge of the score in one can be used to predict the score in the other. The more scatter there is in a scatter diagram the less accurate the prediction, with prediction improving as the correlation coefficient approaches +1 and −1. The use of the line of best fit or regression line, which minimises the sum of the squared deviations, provides the best possible prediction. The relationship between the two variables must be linear. The regression line equation is $Y = a + bX$, where a is the intercept on the Y axis and b is the slope of the regression line. This regression equation that defines the line of best fit will only provide a prediction or estimate of likely Y values. The confidence interval round the prediction can be gauged using the standard error of the estimate.

Hierarchical regression is used in research that is based on theory or some substantial previous knowledge. Stepwise regression is useful in exploratory research where we do not know what to expect or in applied research where we are looking for the best predictive formula without caring about the theoretical meaning.

Analysis of variance (ANOVA)

19
nineteen

Analysis of variance (ANOVA) and *t* tests are two different ways of testing for mean differences. ANOVA has the tremendous advantage in that it can compare two or more treatment conditions, whereas *t* tests are limited to two treatment conditions.

ANOVA is a hypothesis testing procedure used to determine if mean differences exist for two or more samples or treatments. You are well aware by now that any samples chosen from a population are likely to differ simply due to sampling error. They will have slightly different means and standard deviations. The purpose of ANOVA is to decide whether the differences between samples is simply due to chance (sampling error) or whether there are systematic treatment effects that have caused scores in one group to be different from scores in other groups.

For example, suppose a psychologist investigated learning performance under three noise conditions: silence, background music and loud music. Three random samples of subjects are selected. The null hypothesis states that there is no statistically significant difference between the learning performance of the three groups. The alternative hypothesis states that different noise conditions significantly affect learning, i.e. that at least one group mean is significantly different from the other two. We have not provided specific alternative hypotheses as there are a number of different possibilities as to which group mean is different from the others, or whether all three are different from each other, although the researcher may well have a good idea as to the outcome, from intuition, commonsense or previous research literature, e.g. that performance is significantly better in the silent condition than at the other levels of noise.

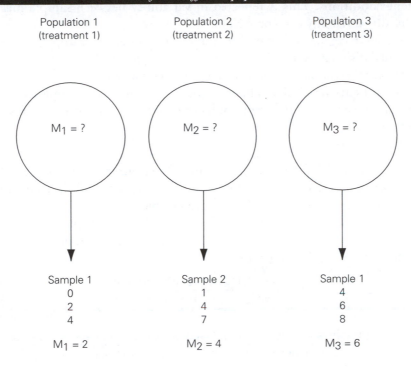

FIGURE 19.1 *Are these means from different populations?*

Population 1
(treatment 1)

Population 2
(treatment 2)

Population 3
(treatment 3)

$M_1 = ?$

$M_2 = ?$

$M_3 = ?$

Sample 1
0
2
4

$M_1 = 2$

Sample 2
1
4
7

$M_2 = 4$

Sample 1
4
6
8

$M_3 = 6$

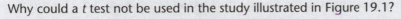

STQ91*

Why could a *t* test not be used in the study illustrated in Figure 19.1?

*Answer on p. 604.

Independent measures ANOVA

We will explain ANOVA with the help of an artificial experiment comparing learning performance under three different noise conditions The data are on page 297. The obvious characteristics of the score are that there are differences. Our aim is to measure this variability and to explain its source.

The first step is to determine total variability for the entire set of data. To do this we combine all scores from all samples to compute one general measure of variability. Having done this we break it apart into its separate components. Because we are going to analyse variability we obtain the name **analysis of variance** or **ANOVA** for this technique.

There are two basic components of this general variability between all subjects in the experiment.

1 **Between treatments variability.** This variability is due to the differences between treatment conditions. This is reflected in variability between sample means. The source of this variability can come from:
   - treatment effects, i.e. noise condition in our hypothetical example;
   - individual differences, i.e. the uniqueness of people; and
   - experimental error, i.e. uncontrolled and unknown causes.
2 **Within treatments variability.** There is variability within each sample as each person within a sample produced different results from others in that sample. This is due to:
   - individual differences; and
   - experimental error.

There can be no variability due to treatments effects within a treatment condition, as all members of the sample are treated exactly the same. Thus all differences within a treatment are chance and not systematic or predictable.

Once we have analysed the total variability into its basic components we simply compare them by computing a statistic called the F ratio. For the independent measures ANOVA that we are considering here:

$$F = \frac{\text{variability between treatments}}{\text{variability within treatments}}$$

or

$$F = \frac{\text{treatment effect} + \text{individual differences} + \text{experimental error}}{\text{individual differences} + \text{experimental error}}$$

The single difference between the numerator and the denominator is variability caused by the treatment effect. If the null hypothesis is true, then the numerator and the denominator are the same because there is no treatment effect. The F ratio then equals 1.

If the null hypothesis is false the treatment effect has some effect and the F ratio must be greater than 1.

The structure of the t and F statistic are very similar. t compares the actual differences between sample means with the differences expected by chance between sample means, as measured by the standard error of the mean. In the same way, F measures differences between samples as measured by the variability between them and differences expected by chance as measured by the within group variability. Because the denominator in the F ratio measures only uncontrolled and unexplained variability it is called the error term or residual. Because the numerator contains treatment effects as well as the same unsystematic variability of the error term, the difference in variability is due to the treatment. When the treatment effect is negligible, the denominator or error term is measuring approximately the same sources of variability as the numerator.

STQ92*

1 What does the denominator measure in the F ratio?
2 What happens to the value of the F ratio if the differences between treatments is increased?

part 2 | quantitative methods

3   When F = 1 what does this indicate about the variance in the numerator?
4   What value is expected on the average for the F ratio if the null hypothesis is true?

*Answers on p. 604.

Some new terminology

There is some special terminology used with ANOVA. Instead of using the term *independent variable*, the word *factor* is used. In our hypothetical experiment degree of noise is the factor. This experiment is a single factor experiment, but ANOVA can deal with more than one factor.

The term *level* is used for different values of the factor. In our experiment there are three levels of the factor. Levels are synonymous with treatments, conditions, samples or groups.

Because ANOVA can deal with several factors, each with a number of levels, an elaborate notational system is required to keep track of individual scores, degrees of freedom and totals.

The number of treatment conditions (groups) = k.
The number of scores in each treatment = n; each sample (treatment/condition) is identified by subscript e.g. n_2.
The total number of scores for the entire experiment = N.
The total sum of scores (sum of X) for each treatment or sample = T; each sample (treatment/condition) is identified by subscript, e.g. T_3.
The sum of all scores in the experiment (grand total) = G.

We also use M for each sample mean, the SS for each treatment condition or sample, and the sum of X^2 for the entire set of scores. SS is the sum of squared deviations from the mean (see p. 49).

All these symbols with their values are attached to the artificial data in the table below.

Treatment 1	Treatment 2	Treatment 3	
(IV or factor with three levels)			
Silence	Background noise	Loud noise	
0	4	1	
1	3	2	$X^2 = 106$
3	6	2	G = 30 (sum of all scores)
1	3	0	N = 15 (no. of subjects)
0	4	0	k = 3 (no. of treatments)
$T_1 = 5$	$T_2 = 20$	$T_3 = 5$	
$SS_1 = 6$	$SS_2 = 6$	$SS_3 = 4$	
$n_1 = 5$	$n_2 = 5$	$n_3 = 5$	
$M_1 = 1$	$M_2 = 4$	$M_3 = 1$	

(Note that these are three independent samples with n = 5 in each. The dependent variable is the number of problems solved correctly.)

The F ratio compares two variances, both computed from the sample data. The variance between treatments is the numerator, and the variance within treatments is the denominator. The variance is defined as:

$$\sigma^2 = \frac{SS}{df}$$

To compute the final F ratio, we need an SS and a df for each of the two variances. Thus the process of analysing variability will occur in two parts. Firstly, we will compute SS for the total experiment and analyse it into the two components, between and within. Secondly, we will calculate the df for each component.

Calculation of sums of squares (SS)

The total SS for the entire set of N scores is

$$SS = X^2 \frac{(\Sigma X)^2}{N}$$

To make this formula consistent with ANOVA terminology we substitute G for X. We therefore obtain for our experiment SS_{total}

$$= 106 - \frac{30^2}{15} = 46$$

Within treatments sum of squares SS_{within} is the sum of SS within each treatment group.

$$SS_{within} = SS_1 + SS_2 + SS_3 = 6 + 6 + 4 = 16$$

Between treatments sum of squares is the difference between the SS_{total} and SS_{within}, i.e.:

$$46 - 16 = 30$$

since both components of variability must add up to the total variability.

Should you wish to calculate it, the formula is:

$$SS_{between} = \frac{T^2}{n} - \frac{G^2}{N} = \frac{5^2}{5} + \frac{20^2}{5} + \frac{5^2}{5} - \frac{30^2}{15}$$
$$= 5 + 80 + 5 - 60 = 30$$

This is the same value we calculated above.

Calculation of degrees of freedom

Analysis of degrees of freedom follows the same pattern. First we find the total df and then partition this into the two components. Normally each df is obtained by counting the number of items that were used to calculate SS and then subtracting 1.

$$df_{total} \qquad = N - 1 = 14 \qquad \text{(lose 1 from whole experiment)}$$
$$df_{within} \qquad = N - k = 12 \qquad \text{(lose 1 from each treatment group)}$$
$$df_{between} \qquad = k - 1 = 2 \qquad \text{(lose 1 treatment)}$$

Of course $df_{total} = df_{within} + df_{between}$

Calculation of the variance

The final step in ANOVA is to compute the variance between treatments and the variance within treatments where variance

$$= \frac{SS}{df}$$

In ANOVA it is customary to use the term *mean square* or MS in place of variance, as variance is the mean of the SS or mean of the squared deviations from the mean.

$$MS_{between} = \frac{SS_{between}}{df_{between}} = \frac{30}{2} = 15$$

$$MS_{within} = \frac{SS_{within}}{df_{within}} = \frac{16}{12} = 1.33$$

FIGURE 19.2 *Structure and formulas for the independent measure ANOVA*

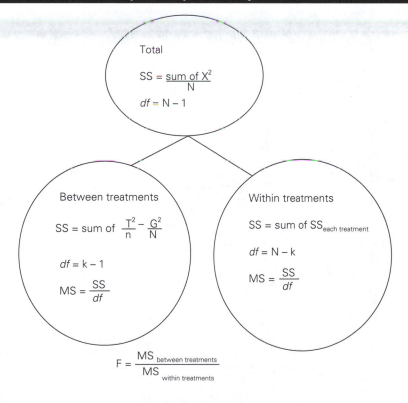

The F ratio

The F ratio compares these two variances.

In our experiment

$$F = \frac{MS_{between}}{MS_{within}} = \frac{15}{1.33} = 11.28$$

The obtained value of 11.28 indicates that the numerator of the F ratio is substantially bigger than the denominator. If you recall the conceptual structure of the F ratio you will understand that this indicates a strong effect from the treatments and could not be expected by chance. Degree of noise does appear to have a strong effect on learning performance. But is it statistically significant? To determine this we shall have to see how F is interpreted.

Distribution of F ratios

We have seen that F is constructed so that the numerator and denominator are measuring the same variance when the null hypothesis is true. F is expected to be around 1 in this situation. But how far does it have to be away before we can say there is a significant effect from the treatment?

To answer this question we need to look at the distribution of F. Like t, there is a whole family of F distribution which depend on the degrees of freedom. When graphed it follows the following typical shape (see Figure 19.3). All values are positive because variance is always positive. The values pile up around 1 and then taper off to the right. Part of an F table is depicted below (see Table 19.1).

FIGURE 19.3 *Graph of F distribution*

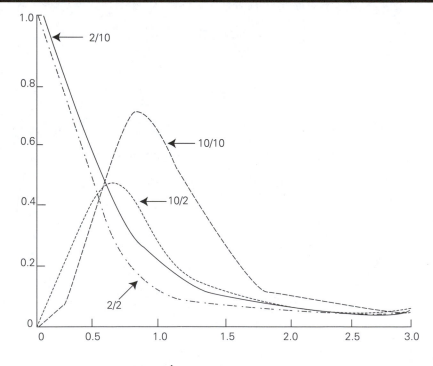

part 2 | quantitative methods

To investigate the significance of an obtained F you must know the *df* values used in the ratio and the level of significance being applied. The F table (for the full version see pp. 307–8), like the example above, has *df* values for the numerator printed across the top of the table and *df* values for the denominator are printed in a column on the left hand side. In our experiment we had a numerator *df* of 2 (3 – 1 conditions) and a denominator *df* of 12 (N – 3). This F ratio then has degrees of freedom equal to 2 and 12 and would be written as '*df* = 2, 12'. The numbers within the table provide critical cut-off points for .05 and .01 levels of significance.

TABLE 19.1 *Extract of F table*

Degrees of freedom: Denominator	Degrees of freedom: Numerator					
	1	2	3	4	5	6
10	4.96	4.10	3.71	3.48	3.33	3.22
	10.04	7.56	6.55	5.99	5.64	5.39
11	4.84	3.98	3.59	3.36	3.20	3.09
	9.65	7.20	6.22	5.67	5.32	5.07
12	4.75	3.88	3.49	3.26	3.11	3.00
	9.33	6.93	5.95	5.41	5.06	4.82
13	4.67	3.80	3.41	3.18	3.02	2.92
	9.07	6.70	5.74	5.20	4.86	4.62
14	4.60	3.74	3.34	3.11	2.96	2.85
	8.86	6.51	5.56	5.03	4.69	4.46
15	4.54	3.68	3.29	3.06	2.90	2.79
	8.68	6.36	5.42	4.89	4.56	4.32
16	4.49	3.63	3.24	3.01	2.85	2.74
	8.53	6.23	5.29	4.77	4.44	4.20
17	4.45	3.59	3.20	2.96	2.81	2.70
	8.40	6.11	5.18	4.67	4.34	4.10
18	4.41	3.55	3.16	2.93	2.77	2.66
	8.28	6.01	5.09	4.58	4.25	4.01

Source: Abridged from Table 18 of *Biometrika Tables for Statisticians,* vol. 1, eds E.S. Pearson and H.O. Hartley.

If you look at Table 19.1, with *df* = 2, 12, the tabled numbers are 3.88 (.05) and 6.93 (.01). In our experiment the obtained F was 11.28. This is well beyond the .01 level and therefore we can be confident in rejecting the null hypothesis and conclude that degree of noise does have a statistically significant effect on learning performance.

All parts of the ANOVA can be presented in a summary table form conventionally laid out as follows:

Source of variance	SS	df	MS	
Between treatments	30	2	15	F = 11.28
Within treatments	16	12	1.33	
Total	46	14		

However, we do not know between which treatment level or levels the significant differences exist. We need to perform a post hoc analysis using a Scheffe test.

STQ93*

1 As the difference between groups increases the F ratio:
   a decreases
   b increases
   c stays the same
   d cannot tell without calculating it

2 Which of the following is influenced by the observed differences between groups:
   a MS_{within}?
   b $MS_{between}$?
   c sum of N?
   d $N - k$?

3 Variance between groups is due to:
   a individual differences
   b error
   c random factors beyond researcher's control
   d experimental manipulation

4 The variance estimate derived from the variance of group means around the grand mean is called the:
   a MS_{within}
   b $MS_{between}$
   c F ratio
   d SE_m

5 If experimental manipulation has an effect on the dependent variable this will:
   a decrease the variance between group means
   b decrease the total variance
   c increase the variance between group means
   d increase the variance derived from the variation in scores within a group

6 A sum of squares divided by its *df* is called:
   a population mean
   b F ratio
   c sample mean
   d mean square

7 The null hypothesis is rejected if:
   a the F ratio is less than 1
   b the group means differ only as a function of chance
   c $MS_{between}$ divided by MS_{within} is zero
   d none of the above

*Answers on p. 604.

The Scheffe test

The Scheffe test is one of a number of post hoc tests that are used to determine where the significant difference(s) lie after the null hypothesis has been rejected in ANOVA. Other commonly used post hoc tests include Tukey's HSD test and Bonferroni. In rejecting the null hypothesis we are simply saying that there is at least one significant mean difference and there may be more. But we do not know between which means the difference(s) lie.

The Scheffe test uses an F ratio to test for a significant difference between any two treatment conditions. The numerator is the MS between treatments that is calculated using only the two treatments you wish to compare The denominator is the same MS within treatments that was used for the overall ANOVA. The safety factor of the Scheffe comes from the following:

- Although only two treatments are being compared, the Scheffe uses the value of k from the original experiment to compute df between treatments. Thus, df for the numerator of the F ratio is k − 1; and
- The critical value of the Scheffe F ratio is the same as was used to evaluate the F ratio from the overall ANOVA.

Thus the Scheffe requires that every post-test satisfies the criteria used for the overall ANOVA. The procedure is to start testing using the biggest mean difference and continue testing until a non-significant difference is produced.

For the above example we will test treatment 2 (background music) against treatment 1 (silence).

$$SS_{between} = \frac{T^2}{n} - \frac{G^2}{N} = \frac{5^2}{5} + \frac{20^2}{5} - \frac{30^2}{15} = 5 + 80 - 60 = 25$$

$$df_{between} = k - 3 = 2$$

$$MS_{between} = \frac{SS_{between}}{df_{between}} = \frac{25}{2} = 12.5$$

Scheffe uses MS_{within} which is 1.33

so the Scheffe F ratio $= \dfrac{MS_{between}}{MS_{within}} = \dfrac{12.5}{1.33} = 9.39$

With df 2 and 12 and $p < .05$, the critical value in the F table is 3.88; therefore this difference between silence and background music is significant. The difference between background music and noise would also be significant, but the difference between silence and noise is not likely to be significant.

STQ94

With two treatment conditions, is a post hoc test necessary when the null hypothesis is rejected?

We have calculated a very simple independent measures ANOVA as an example. ANOVAs with more than one factor and a variety of levels within each can require very complex calculations using computer programs. Few researchers would attempt ANOVA by hand. This example has been used purely to demonstrate the principles behind the technique.

STQ95*

1 Complete the following table:

Variance	SS	df	MS	F
Between groups	2.6	a	1.3	b
Within groups	c	27	d	
Total	170	e		

2 Interpret F by making a statement about whether to retain or reject the null hypothesis.

*Answers on p. 604.

STQ96*

Using the following data answer the questions below:

Treatment 1	Treatment 2	Treatment 3	
n = 10	n = 10	n = 10	N = 30
T = 10	T = 20	T = 30	G = 60
SS = 27	SS = 16	SS = 23	sum of X^2 = 206

1 Calculate SS_{total}, $SS_{between}$ and SS_{within}.
2 What is df_{total}, $df_{between}$ and df_{within}?
3 With the significance level set at 0.05, what is tabled F?
4 What is F in the above study? Is there a significant treatment effect?

*Answers on p. 604.

Repeated measures ANOVA

The ANOVA we have just considered was an independent group measure. The between group or repeated measures ANOVA is similar, although the denominator in the F ratio becomes the error term and does not include individual differences as the same subjects undertake all levels of the treatment factor.

You will remember that the F ratio = $\dfrac{\text{variance between treatments}}{\text{variance within treatments}}$

The error term is intended to produce a balanced equation if the treatment has had no effect, so in the repeated measures ANOVA the F ratio is:

$$F = \frac{\text{treatment effect } + \text{ experimental error}}{\text{experimental error}}$$

To obtain the error term we have to remove individual differences from the equation we used in the independent measures approach. This is done by computing the variance due to individual differences and subtracting it from the variance between treatments and also from the variance within treatments.

EXAMPLE

Here is an example worked through.

A teacher wishes to test the effectiveness of a behaviour modification technique in controlling the classroom behaviour of unruly children. Every time a child disrupts the class, they lose a play period. The number of outbursts are monitored at various periods to assess the effectiveness. The null hypothesis is that the behaviour modification program will have no significant effect. The alternative hypothesis states that there will be a significant difference without specifying between which time periods. We will use the 5 per cent level of significance.

The data are as follows:

Subject	Before treatment	One week after	One month after	Six months after	p
A	8	2	1	1	12
B	4	1	1	0	6
C	6	2	0	2	10
D	8	3	4	1	16

$$T_1 = 26 \quad\quad T_2 = 8 \quad\quad T_3 = 6 \quad\quad T_4 = 4$$
$$SS_1 = 11 \quad\quad SS_2 = 2 \quad\quad SS_3 = 9 \quad\quad SS_4 = 2$$
$$n = 4 \quad\quad k = 4 \quad\quad N = 16 \quad\quad X^2 = 222 \quad\quad G = 44$$

$$SS_{total} = X^2 - \frac{G^2}{N} = 222 - 121 = 101$$

$$SS_{between} = \frac{T^2}{n} - \frac{G^2}{N} = \frac{26^2}{4} + \frac{8^2}{4} + \frac{6^2}{4} + \frac{4^2}{4} - \frac{44^2}{16} = 77$$

$SS_{within} = 101 - 77 = 24$. This needs to be partitioned into between subjects SS and error SS.

$$SS_{between\ subjects} = \frac{p^2}{k} - \frac{G^2}{N} = \frac{12^2}{4} + \frac{6^2}{4} + \frac{10^2}{4} + \frac{16^2}{4} - \frac{44^2}{16} = 13$$

$SS_{error} = SS_{within\ treatments} - SS_{between\ subjects} = 24 - 13 = 11$
$df_{between\ treatments} = 3$ (4 groups − 1)
$df_{within\ treatments} = 12$ (each group − 1)
$df_{error} = 9$ (each testing occasion − 1 for each subject)

Finally we can compute the MS values and the F ratio. The repeated measures F ratio uses between treatments MS as the numerator and the MS error as denominator.

$$MS_{between\ treatments} = \frac{SS_{between\ treatments}}{df_{between\ treatments}} = \frac{77}{3} = 25.67$$

$$MS_{error} = \frac{SS_{error}}{df_{error}} = \frac{11}{9} = 1.22$$

$$F = \frac{MS_{between\ treatments}}{MS_{error}} = \frac{25.67}{1.22} = 21.04$$

The layout of the results table is as follows:

Source of variance	SS		df		MS	F
Between treatments	77		3		25.67	21.04
Within treatments	24		12			
Between subjects		13		3		
Error		11		9	1.22	
Total	101		15			

If you consult the F table on p. 308, F(3, 9) tabled value is 3.86. Our value of 21.04 is therefore significant at $p < .05$, and the null hypothesis can be rejected. However, we do not know between which treatments the significant differences lie and we would have to apply the Scheffe test as we did earlier. The only change in the Scheffe test is to substitute MS_{error} in place of MS within in the formula and use df_{error} in place of df_{within} when locating the critical value in the table.

STQ97

What sources contribute to within treatments and between treatments variability for a repeated measures design?

When the amount of individual differences may be great, a repeated measures ANOVA is more sensitive to treatment effects. Let's suppose we know how much variability is accounted for by the different components; for example:

treatment effect	10 units of variance
individual differences	1000 units of variance
experimental error	1 unit of variance

For the independent measures we get

$$F = \frac{treatment\ effect + individual\ differences + experimental\ error}{individual\ differences + experimental\ error}$$

$$F = \frac{10 + 1000 + 1}{1000 + 1} = \frac{1011}{1001} = 1.01$$

part 2 | quantitative methods

For the repeated measures we get

$$F = \frac{\text{treatment effect} + \text{experimental error}}{\text{experimental error}}$$

$$F = \frac{10 + 1}{1}$$

The repeated measures F is much larger because we have removed individual differences and so we are more likely to detect significant treatment effects which are no longer confused with individual differences.

TABLE 19.2 F table

Values of F at p < .01

df numerator

df denominator	1	2	3	4	5	6	7	8	10	12	24	∞
1	4052	5000	5403	5625	5764	5859	5928	5981	6056	6106	6235	6366
2	98.5	99.0	99.2	99.2	99.3	99.3	99.4	99.4	99.4	99.4	99.5	99.5
3	34.1	30.8	29.5	28.7	28.2	27.9	27.7	27.5	27.2	27.1	26.6	26.1
4	21.2	18.0	16.7	16.0	15.5	15.2	15.0	14.8	14.5	14.4	13.9	15.5
5	16.26	13.27	12.06	11.39	10.97	10.67	10.46	10.29	10.05	9.89	9.47	9.02
6	13.74	10.92	9.78	9.15	8.75	8.47	8.26	8.10	7.87	7.72	7.31	6.88
7	12.25	9.55	8.45	7.85	7.46	7.19	6.99	6.84	6.62	6.47	6.07	5.65
8	11.26	8.65	7.59	7.01	6.63	6.37	6.18	6.03	5.81	5.67	5.28	4.86
9	10.56	8.02	6.99	6.42	6.06	5.80	5.61	5.47	5.26	5.11	4.73	4.31
10	10.04	7.56	6.55	5.99	5.64	5.39	5.20	5.06	4.85	4.71	4.33	3.91
11	9.65	7.21	6.22	5.67	5.32	5.07	4.89	4.74	4.54	4.40	4.02	3.60
12	9.33	6.93	5.95	5.41	5.06	4.82	4.64	4.50	4.30	4.16	3.78	3.36
13	9.07	6.70	5.74	5.21	4.86	4.62	4.44	4.30	4.10	3.96	3.59	3.17
14	8.86	6.51	5.56	5.04	4.70	4.46	4.28	4.14	3.94	3.80	3.43	3.00
15	8.68	6.36	5.42	4.89	4.56	4.32	4.14	4.00	3.80	3.67	3.29	2.87
16	8.53	6.23	5.29	4.77	4.44	4.20	4.03	3.89	3.69	3.55	3.18	2.75
17	8.40	6.11	5.18	4.67	4.34	4.10	3.93	3.79	3.59	3.46	3.08	2.65
18	8.29	6.01	5.09	4.58	4.25	4.01	3.84	3.71	3.51	3.37	3.00	2.57
19	8.18	5.93	5.01	4.50	4.17	3.94	3.77	3.63	3.43	3.30	2.92	2.49
20	8.10	5.85	4.94	4.43	4.10	3.87	3.70	3.56	3.37	3.23	2.86	2.42
21	8.02	5.78	4.87	4.37	4.04	3.81	3.64	3.51	3.31	3.17	2.80	2.36
22	7.95	5.72	4.82	4.31	3.99	3.76	3.59	3.45	3.26	3.12	2.75	2.31
23	7.88	5.66	4.76	4.26	3.94	3.71	3.54	3.41	3.21	3.07	2.70	2.26
24	7.82	5.61	4.72	4.22	3.90	3.67	3.50	3.36	3.17	3.03	2.66	2.21
25	7.77	5.53	4.68	4.18	3.86	3.63	3.46	3.32	3.13	2.99	2.62	2.17
26	7.72	5.56	4.64	4.14	3.82	3.59	3.42	3.29	3.09	2.96	2.58	2.13
27	7.68	5.49	4.60	4.11	3.78	3.56	3.39	3.26	3.06	2.93	2.55	2.10
28	7.64	5.45	4.57	4.07	3.75	3.53	3.36	3.23	3.03	2.90	2.52	2.06
29	7.60	5.42	4.54	4.04	3.73	3.50	3.33	3.20	3.00	2.87	2.49	2.03
30	7.56	5.39	4.51	4.02	3.70	3.47	3.30	3.17	2.98	2.84	2.47	2.01
32	7.50	5.34	4.46	3.97	3.65	3.43	3.26	3.13	2.93	2.80	2.42	1.96
34	7.45	5.29	4.42	3.93	3.61	3.39	3.22	3.09	2.90	2.76	2.38	1.91
36	7.40	5.25	4.38	3.89	3.58	3.35	3.18	3.05	2.86	2.72	2.35	1.87
38	7.35	5.21	4.34	3.86	3.54	3.32	3.15	3.02	2.83	2.69	2.32	1.84
40	7.31	5.18	4.31	3.83	3.51	3.29	3.12	2.99	2.80	2.66	2.29	1.80
60	7.08	4.98	4.13	3.65	3.34	3.12	2.95	2.82	2.63	2.50	2.12	1.60
120	6.85	4.79	3.95	3.48	3.17	2.96	2.79	2.66	2.47	2.34	1.95	1.38
∞	6.63	4.61	3.78	3.32	3.02	2.80	2.64	2.51	2.32	2.18	1.79	1.00

TABLE 19.2 *Continued*

Values of F at p < .05

***df* numerator**

df denominator	1	2	3	4	5	6	7	8	10	12	24	∞
1	161.4	199.5	215.7	224.6	230.2	234.0	236.8	238.9	241.9	243.9	249.0	254.3
2	18.5	19.0	19.2	19.2	19.3	19.3	19.4	19.4	19.4	19.4	19.5	19.5
3	10.13	9.55	9.28	9.12	9.01	8.94	8.89	8.85	8.79	8.74	8.64	8.53
4	7.71	6.94	6.59	6.39	6.26	6.16	6.09	6.04	5.96	5.91	5.77	5.63
5	6.61	5.79	5.41	5.19	5.05	4.95	4.88	4.82	4.74	4.68	4.53	4.36
6	5.99	5.14	4.76	4.53	4.39	4.28	4.21	4.15	4.06	4.00	3.84	3.67
7	5.59	4.74	4.35	4.12	3.97	3.87	3.79	3.73	3.64	3.57	3.41	3.23
8	5.32	4.46	4.07	3.84	3.69	3.58	3.50	3.44	3.35	3.28	3.12	2.93
9	5.12	4.26	3.86	3.63	3.48	3.37	3.29	3.23	3.14	3.07	2.90	2.71
10	4.96	4.10	3.71	3.48	3.33	3.22	3.14	3.07	2.98	2.91	2.74	2.54
11	4.84	3.98	3.59	3.36	3.20	3.09	3.01	2.95	2.85	2.79	2.61	2.40
12	4.75	3.89	3.49	3.26	3.11	3.00	2.91	2.85	2.75	2.69	2.51	2.30
13	4.67	3.81	3.41	3.18	3.03	2.92	2.83	2.77	2.67	2.60	2.42	2.21
14	4.60	3.74	3.34	3.11	2.96	2.85	2.76	2.70	2.60	2.53	2.35	2.13
15	4.54	3.68	3.29	3.06	2.90	2.70	2.71	2.64	2.54	2.48	2.29	2.07
16	4.49	3.63	3.24	3.01	2.85	2.74	2.66	2.59	2.49	2.42	2.24	2.01
17	4.45	3.59	3.20	2.96	2.81	2.70	2.61	2.55	2.45	2.38	2.19	1.96
18	4.41	3.55	3.16	2.93	2.77	2.66	2.58	2.51	2.41	2.34	2.15	1.92
19	4.38	3.52	3.13	2.90	2.74	2.63	2.54	2.48	2.38	2.31	2.11	1.88
20	4.35	3.49	3.10	2.87	2.71	2.60	2.51	2.45	2.35	2.28	2.08	1.84
21	4.32	3.47	3.07	2.84	2.68	2.57	2.49	2.42	2.32	2.25	2.05	1.81
22	4.30	3.44	3.05	2.82	2.66	2.55	2.46	2.40	2.30	2.23	2.03	1.78
23	4.28	3.42	3.03	2.80	2.64	2.53	2.44	2.37	2.27	2.20	2.00	1.76
24	4.26	3.40	3.01	2.78	2.62	2.51	2.42	2.36	2.25	2.18	1.98	1.73
25	4.24	3.39	2.99	2.76	2.60	2.49	2.40	2.34	2.24	2.16	1.96	1.71
26	4.23	3.37	2.98	2.74	2.59	2.47	2.39	2.32	2.22	2.15	1.95	1.69
27	4.21	3.35	2.96	2.73	2.57	2.46	2.37	2.31	2.20	2.13	1.93	1.67
28	4.20	3.34	2.95	2.71	2.56	2.45	2.36	2.29	2.19	2.12	1.91	1.65
29	4.18	3.33	2.93	2.70	2.55	2.43	2.35	2.28	2.18	2.10	1.90	1.64
30	4.17	3.32	2.92	2.69	2.53	2.42	2.33	2.27	2.16	2.09	1.89	1.62
32	4.15	3.29	2.90	2.67	2.51	2.40	2.31	2.24	2.14	2.07	1.86	1.59
34	4.13	3.28	2.88	2.65	2.49	2.38	2.29	2.23	2.12	2.05	1.84	1.57
36	4.11	3.26	2.87	2.63	2.48	2.36	2.28	2.21	2.11	2.03	1.82	1.55
38	4.10	3.24	2.85	2.62	2.46	2.35	2.26	2.19	2.09	2.02	1.81	1.53
40	4.08	3.23	2.84	2.61	2.45	2.34	2.25	2.18	2.08	2.00	1.79	1.51
60	4.00	3.15	2.76	2.53	2.37	2.25	2.17	2.10	1.99	1.92	1.70	1.39
120	3.92	3.07	2.68	2.45	2.29	2.18	2.09	2.02	1.91	1.83	1.61	1.25
∞	3.84	3.00	2.60	2.37	2.21	2.10	2.01	1.94	1.83	1.75	1.52	1.00

Source: Abridged from Table 18 of *Biometrika Tables for Statisticians*, vol. 1, eds E.S. Pearson and H.O. Hartley.

Two factor ANOVA or two-way ANOVA

In some experiments there are two variables or factors that may interact. For example, the effect of anxiety on performance may depend on the level of self-esteem, with anxiety only having an effect when self-esteem is low. Again, verbal reinforcement may work well to produce a specified behaviour with middle-class children but not so well with working-class children, who respond better to tangible tokens of reinforcement. An interaction occurs when the effect of one independent variable on the dependent variable is not the same under all the conditions of the other dependent variable.

An interaction is often readily seen when depicted in a graph. The graphs below show a variety of possible interactions. However, it is only possible to assess whether they are statistically significant by testing them with ANOVA. An interaction is indicated when the graphed lines are not parallel. The dependent variable is usually placed on the vertical axis, while one of the independent variables forms the horizontal axis. The second independent variable is graphed.

The following graphs plotting achievement scores gained by boys and girls, under two different teaching methods, assist in understanding interaction. In Figure 19.4(a) there is no main effect for method as the means are both the same; however there is a main effect for sex, as girls do better under both methods. There is no interaction and the lines are parallel. In Figure 19.4(b) there is a main effect for sex as the girls' mean is above the boys' mean in both methods. There is also an interaction as the girls score higher with one method while the reverse is true for the boys.

FIGURE 19.4(a)

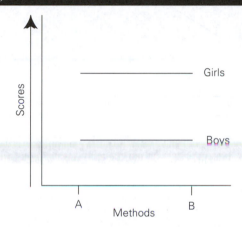

FIGURE 19.4(b)

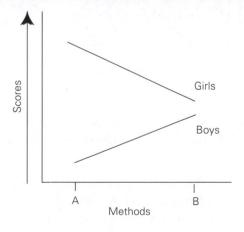

In Figure 19.4(c) there is a main effect for sex, as the girls' mean is higher than the boys' in each method. There is also an effect for method, with method B producing better results than method A, as well as an interaction with boys improving their scores on B more than girls. In Figure 19.4(d) there is neither a sex nor a method effect, as the boys' mean equals the girls' mean and the methods means are also equal. However, there is a strong interaction as boys do much better on B, while girls do much better on A. Remember in cases where lines are not parallel that only a statistical test will show whether there is a significant interaction present. Visual inspection is not adequate.

FIGURE 19.4(c)

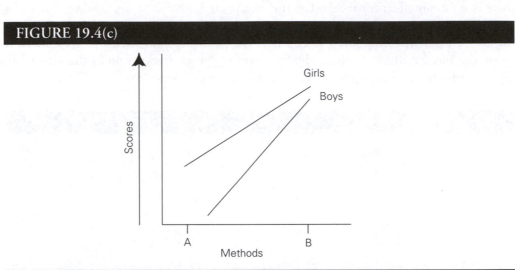

FIGURE 19.4(d)

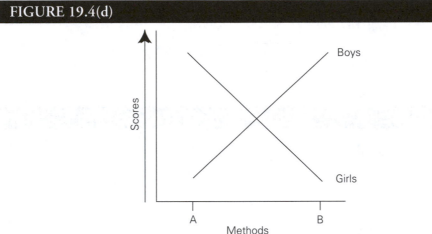

Since the between treatments variability is split between the two factors and the interaction (see Figure 19.5) the two factor or two-way ANOVA has three distinct hypotheses:

1 The main effect of factor A. The null hypothesis states that there are no statistically significant mean differences between levels of factor A.
2 The main effect for factor B. There is a similar null hypothesis for factor B.

3 The A × B interaction. The null hypothesis states that there is no statistically significant interaction. That is, the effect of either factor is independent of the levels of the other factor.

FIGURE 19.5 *Sources of variability*

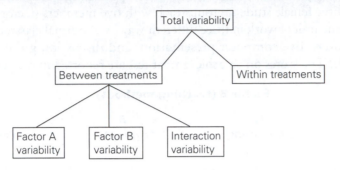

Three F ratios have to be tested each with the basic form of

$$F = \frac{\text{treatment effect} + \text{individual differences} + \text{experimental error}}{\text{individual differences} + \text{experimental error}}$$

The general format for a two-factor experiment is depicted below. The example has two levels of factor A and three levels of factor B. There could of course be any number of levels for each factor. Each cell corresponds with a particular treatment condition. It is possible to use either an independent measures or a repeated measures design in a two factor experiment. The example to be covered is an independent design. Calculations can become complicated and most ANOVAs of this sort will be performed on computer. It is unlikely you would ever attempt one manually.

		Factor B		
		Level B_1	Level B_2	Level B_3
	Level A_1	treatment cell A_1B_1	treatment cell A_1B_2	treatment cell A_1B_3
Factor A				
	Level A_2	treatment cell A_2B_1	treatment A_2B_2	treatment A_2B_3

To develop formulae for the two factor ANOVA we need:

G = sum of all the scores in the whole experiment
N = the number of scores in the whole experiment
p = the number of levels of factor A
q = the number of levels of factor B
n = the number of scores in each cell (treatment condition)

The total for each treatment condition specified by A and B and the relevant subscripts, e.g. A_2B_2, is the total of scores in that cell. In addition, A_1 refers to the total of all the scores in that treatment; B_1 refers to the total of all the scores in that treatment, and so on.

The general structure of the analysis of the two-way ANOVA is depicted in Figure 19.6. We will produce three between-treatment variances and one within-treatment variance. We will analyse the data in the table below, representing an experiment in which three male and three female student groups each with five members (factor A = gender) undertook the same unit of work in three different ways, viz. normal classroom teaching, individualised interactive computer presentation, and discussion group (factor B = teaching method). The scores on an achievement test are reported in the cells.

Factor B (teaching methods)

	B_1 (classroom)	B_2 (computer)	B_3 (discussion)
A_1 (female) $A_1 = 60$	1	7	3
	6	7	1
	1	11	1
	1	4	6
	1	6	4
	$A_1B_1 = 10$	$A_1B_2 = 35$	$A_1B_3 = 15$
	SS = 20	SS = 26	SS = 18
Factor A (gender)			
A_2 (male) $A_2 = 30$	0	0	0
	3	0	2
	7	0	0
	5	5	0
	5	0	3
	$A_2B_1 = 20$	$A_2B_2 = 5$	$A_2B_3 = 5$
	SS = 28	SS = 20	SS = 8
	$B_1 = 30$	$B_2 = 40$	$B_3 = 20$
	N = 30	G = 90	$X^2 = 520$

SS_{total} = sum of $X^2 - \dfrac{G^2}{N}$ = 520 − 270 = 250

SS_{within} = the sum of SS_{within} each treatment cell

= 20 + 26+ 18 + 28 + 20 + 8 = 120

$SS_{between}$ = sum of $\dfrac{(AB)^2}{n} - \dfrac{G^2}{N}$

$= \dfrac{10^2}{5} + \dfrac{35^2}{5} = \dfrac{15^2}{5} + \dfrac{20^2}{5} + \dfrac{5^2}{5} + \dfrac{5^2}{5} - \dfrac{90^2}{30} = 130$

Now we need to partition $SS_{between}$ of 130 into components relating to factors A and B, and interaction effects.

part 2 | quantitative methods

FIGURE 19.6 *Structure of two factor ANOVA*

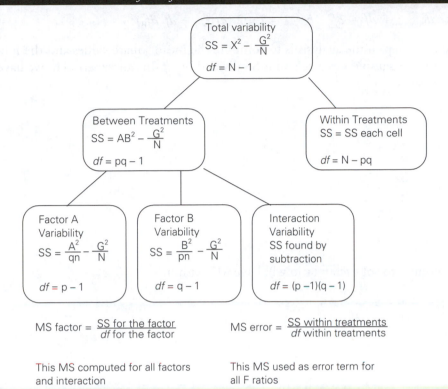

MS factor = $\dfrac{\text{SS for the factor}}{df \text{ for the factor}}$ MS error = $\dfrac{\text{SS within treatments}}{df \text{ within treatments}}$

This MS computed for all factors and interaction

This MS used as error term for all F ratios

Sums of squares

SS_A = the sum of $\dfrac{A^2}{qn} - \dfrac{G^2}{N} = \dfrac{60^2}{15} + \dfrac{30^2}{15} - \dfrac{90^2}{30} = 30$

SS_B = the sum of $\dfrac{B^2}{pn} - \dfrac{G^2}{N} = \dfrac{30^2}{10} + \dfrac{40^2}{10} + \dfrac{20^2}{10} - \dfrac{90^2}{30} = 20$

$SS_{A \times B}$ = $SS_{between} - SS_A - SS_B$

    = $130 - 30 - 20 = 80$

Degrees of freedom

$df_{total} = 30 - 1 = 29$

df_{within} = the sum of $(n - 1)$ or $N - pq = 24$

$df_{between} = 3 \times 2 - 1 = 5$

$df_A = p - 1 = 1$

$df_B = q - 1 = 2$

$df_{AxB} = df_{between} - df_A - df_B = 5 - 1 - 2 = 2 \; (df_{A \times B} = df_A df_B)$

The final step in the analysis is to compute the mean square values and the F ratios. The MS is the sample variance and is SS divided by *df*. In our experiment we have:

MS

$$\text{MS for A} = \frac{SS_A}{df_A} = \frac{30}{1} = 30$$

$$\text{MS for B} = \frac{SS_B}{df_B} = \frac{20}{2} = 10$$

$$\text{MS for A} \times \text{B} = \frac{SS_{A \times B}}{df_{A \times B}} = \frac{80}{2} = 40$$

The denominator of each F ratio will have MS within:

$$\text{MS}_{within} = \frac{SS_{within}}{df_{within}} = \frac{120}{24} = 5$$

F ratios

For factor A: $F = \dfrac{MS_A}{MS_{within}} = \dfrac{30}{5} = 6$

$df = 1, 24$
therefore F (1, 24) = 6.00

For factor B: $F = \dfrac{MS_B}{MS_{within}} = \dfrac{10}{5} = 2$

$df = 2, 24$
therefore F(2, 24) = 2.00

For factor A × B: $F = \dfrac{MS_{A \times B}}{MS_{within}} = \dfrac{40}{5} = 8.00$

$df = 2, 24$
therefore F(2, 24) = 8.00

Source of variance	SS	df	MS	F
Between treatments	130	5		
Factor A (sex)	30	1	30	6.00
Factor B (method)	20	2	10	2.00
A X B interaction	80	2	40	8.00
Within treatments	120	24	5	
Total		250	29	

The .05 tabled value (see p. 308) for F(1, 24) is 4.26 and for F(2, 24) is 3.40. Our conclusion is that:

- factor A, the sex of the subject, had a significant effect;
- factor B, method of presentation, did not have a significant effect; and
- the A × B interaction was significant, with males performing more poorly than females on two of the methods but better than females on the other. This is shown in Figure 19.7. You will remember that interactions are easier to see and understand if graphed.

FIGURE 19.7 *Graph of results*

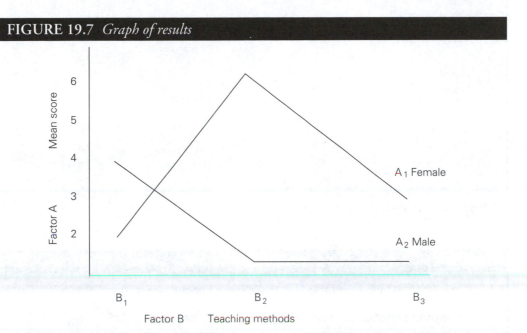

STQ98*

1 How does the F ratio for the repeated measures ANOVA differ from that of the one for the independent measures?
2 A study is conducted to ascertain the level of anxiety of the learner and the meaningfulness of the material on the speed of learning lists of words.
   a Between which two variables might the interaction effect be shown?
   b If a total of 60 subjects are equally distributed between the groups what F values are necessary for significance at the 5 per cent level?
3 In a two-way ANOVA, $SS_{between}$ is divided into three parts. Which of the following symbolises this?
   a $SS_{between} = SS_{A \times B} + SS_w + SS_t$
   b $SS_{between} = SS_A + SS_B + SS_w$
   c $SS_{between} = SS_{A \times B} + SS_A + SS_B$
   d $SS_{between} = SS_A + SS_w + SS_t$

*Answers on p. 604.

Calculate the following data using a two-way ANOVA and interpret F.

		Method of teaching	
		Directed learning B₁	Discovery learning B₂
		10	8
		11	9
English A₁		12	11
		14	13
		16	15
Home language			
		12	15
		15	16
Thai A₂		16	18
		17	19
		18	23

*Answers on p. 605.

1   Complete the following table and make some conclusions.

Source of variance	Sums of squares	df	MS	F
Between columns	13.5	1	a	1.32
Between rows	37.5	1	37.5	b
Columns by rows	c	1	73.5	7.21
Within groups	204	d	e	
Total	328.5	23		

2   The following data summarise the results of a two-factor independent measures experiment. Use ANOVA and evaluate the effects of factor A, factor B and the A x B interaction for the data below.

	Factor B		
	B₁	B₂	B₃
	n = 10	n = 10	n = 10
	AB = 0	AB = 10	AB = 20
A₁	X = 0	X = 1	X = 2
	SS = 30	SS = 40	SS = 50

Factor A			
	n = 10	n = 10	n = 10
	AB = 40	AB = 30	AB = 20
A$_2$	X = 4	X = 3	X = 2
	SS = 60	SS = 50	SS = 40
sum of X^2 = 610			

*Answers on p. 605.

Effect size and power for the analysis of variance

Effect size

Effect size for the analysis of variance is a little more complex than for a *t* test. With the *t* test, effect size is measured by taking the difference between the two means and dividing it by the standard deviation. In the analysis of variance, we can still divide by the standard deviation, but in analysis of variance we have more than two means, so it is not obvious just what is equivalent to the difference between the means to form the numerator required in calculating effect size.

Cohen suggests that in the analysis of variance, we should think of the effect size as the variation among the means. Specifically, he recommends using the standard deviation of the distribution of means. He defines the effect size for the analysis of variance as the standard deviation of the distribution of means divided by the standard deviation of the individuals.

With a bit of algebraic manipulation, it turns out that the effect size using estimated variances can be computed directly from knowing the F and the number of scores in each group. The formula is:

$$\text{Estimated effect size} = \frac{\sqrt{F}}{\sqrt{n}}$$

This formula is very helpful when evaluating the effect size of a completed study reported in a published research article. Cohen's conventions for effect size for analysis of variance, using the above formula, are .10 for a small effect, .25 for a medium effect, and .40 for a large effect size.

Actually, SPSS now computes an effect size statistic as part of its output for the one-way and general linear model procedure. This effect size is statistic partial eta^2 which ranges in value from 0 to 1. A value of 0 indicates that there are no differences between mean scores in the groups. A value of 1 indicates that there are differences between at least two of the means of the dependent variable and that there are no differences on the dependent variable scores within each group. Generally, partial eta^2 is interpreted as the proportion of the dependent variable that is related to the factor. Values of .01, .06 and .14 represent small, medium and large effect sizes respectively.

Partial eta^2 is computed for each main and interaction source and may be calculated using the equation over the page:

Partial eta^2 main or interaction source =

$$\frac{\text{Sum of squares}_{\text{main or interaction source}}}{\text{Sum of squares}_{\text{main or interaction source}} + \text{sum of squares}_{\text{error}}}$$

For two-factor or two multivariate ANOVA, the effect size is associated with Wilks' lambda (Λ), and this is usually quoted in research findings.

In general, partial eta^2 is interpreted as the proportion of variance of the dependent variable that is related to a particular main or interaction source excluding the other main and interaction sources.

Power

Table 19.3 shows the approximate power for the .05 significance level for small, medium, and large effect sizes; sample size of 10, 20, 30, 40, 50, and 100 per group; and three, four and five groups. These are the most common values of the various influences on power.

More detailed tables are provided in Cohen (1988, pp. 289–354).

TABLE 19.3 *Approximate power for studies using the analysis of variance testing hypotheses at the .05 significance level*

| | Effect size | | |
Participants per group (n)	Small (.10)	Medium (.25)	Large (.40)
Three groups ($df_{between} = 2$)			
10	.07	.20	.45
20	.09	.38	.78
30	.12	.55	.93
40	.15	.68	98
50	.18	.79	.99
100	.32	.98	
Four groups ($df_{between} = 3$)			
10	.07	.21	.51
20	.10	.43	.85
30	.13	.61	.96
40	.16	.76	.99
50	.19	.85	
100	.36	.99	
Five groups ($df_{between} = 4$)			
10	.07	.23	.56
20	.10	.47	.90
30	.13	.67	.98
40	.17	.81	
50	.21	.90	
100	.40		

part 2 | quantitative methods

For example, a planned study comparing five groups of 10 participants each, with an expected large effect size (.40) and using the .05 significance level, would have power of .56. This means that even if the research hypothesis is in fact true and has a large effect size, there is only a little greater than even chance (56 per cent) that the study will have a statistically significant outcome.

As we have noted in previous chapters, determining power is especially useful when interpreting the practical implication of a non-significant result. For example, suppose you have read a study using a one-way independent analysis of variance for four groups of 30 participants each, in which the researcher reports a non-significant result at the .05 level. Table 19.3 shows a power of only .13 for a small effect size. This suggests that even if such a small effect exists in the population, this study would be very unlikely to have had a statistically significant outcome. The table shows a power of .96 for a large effect size. This suggests that if a large effect existed in the population, it almost surely would have shown up in this study.

Planning sample size

Table 19.4 gives the approximate number of participants needed in each group for 80 per cent power at the .05 significance level for estimated small, medium, and large effect sizes for studies with three, four and five groups.

TABLE 19.4 *Approximate number of participants needed in each group (assuming equal sample sizes) for 80 per cent power for the one-way analysis of variance-testing hypotheses at the .05 significance level*

	Effect size		
	Small (.10)	**Medium (.25)**	**Large (.40)**
Threegroups ($df_{between} = 2$)	322	52	21
Fourgroups ($df_{between} = 3$)	274	45	18
Fivegroups ($df_{between} = 4$)	240	39	16

For example, suppose you are planning a study involving four groups and you expect a small effect size (and will use the .05 significance level). For 80 per cent power you would need 274 participants in each group, a total of 1096 in all. However, suppose you could adjust the research plan so that it was now reasonable to predict a large effect size (perhaps by using more accurate measures and a more powerful experimental manipulation). Now you would need only 18 in each of the four groups, for a total of 72.

Using SPSS for the one-way independent ANOVA

The computation of a one-way unrelated analysis of variance will be illustrated with dummy data for a study on the effect of different counselling techniques on stress scores.

How to proceed

1 Select *Statistics* and then *Compare Means* from the drop-down menu.
2 Select *One-Way ANOVA* to open the *One-Way ANOVA* dialogue box.

3   Choose your variable 'stress' and using the arrow button place it in *Dependent List*: box.
4   Select 'group' and use the arrow button to move it into the *Factor* box.
5   Click on *Post Hoc* and in the *Post Hoc Multiple Comparison* box select *Bonferroni, Scheffe* and *Tukey* if equal variances can be assumed. Choose *Dunnet C* if equal variances cannot be assumed.
6   Select *Continue* and then choose *Option* to gain access to the *One Way ANOVA Options* box, where you click on *Descriptives* and *Homogeneity of Variance*.
7   Select *continue*, then *OK* to produce the output like Table 19.5 on pp. 321–22.

How to interpret the output

- The top subtable provides the descriptive statistics. The important ones are the means, since once we have a significant result we need to have some awareness of where the significant differences between the means may lie.
- The second subtable suggests that there is a non-significant difference between the group variances; therefore homogeneity of variance can be accepted.
- The main ANOVA subtable appears next. This shows an $F (2, 27) = 9.722$, $p = .001$. The F ratio is the between groups mean square divided by the within groups mean square. It is statistically significant.
- This indicates that there is a significant difference in stress scores between the three treatment groups. However, it does not necessarily imply that all the means are significantly different from each other. In this case, visual inspection of subtable a may suggest that they are all significantly different. However, visual inspection is not scientific and post hoc tests must be run.
- Subtable d reports the results of various multiple comparison post hoc tests such as Scheffe and Tukey which determine between which groups the significant differences lie. (Normally only one post hoc test is used but several are shown for demonstration purposes only.)
- These tests indicate that the significance lies in the effectiveness of both counselling groups over the control but that there is no significant difference between the effectiveness of the two counselling modes.

Computing effect size

This can be calculated using the formula:
Partial eta^2 main or interaction source =

$$\frac{\text{Sum of squares}_{\text{main or interaction source}}}{\text{Sum of squares}_{\text{main or interaction source}} + \text{sum of squares}_{\text{error}}}$$

In our case, 'main' is the main effect, or between groups effect, while 'error' is the within groups effect:

$$\frac{294.467}{294.467 + 408.9} = 0.419$$

This is a strong effect size.

How to report the output in Table 19.5

We could report the results of the output as follows: 'The effect of the counselling conditions was significant overall (F(2,27) = 9.722, p < 0.001), and the effect size was strong at 0.419. However, post hoc tests indicate that the means for individual and group counselling groups did not differ significantly, but both differed significantly from the mean of the control group. This suggests that both methods of counselling are similarly effective in reducing stress level.'

Using SPSS for a one-way repeated measures ANOVA design

We will illustrate the computation of a one-way repeated measures analysis of variance with dummy data relating to six subjects who undertook a three-month weight reduction program. They were weighed on three occasions: at the start, midway, and at the end of the program. Thus we have a situation in which the same group produced three sets of scores.

How to analyse the data

1 Select *Statistics* from the menu bar.
2 On the displayed drop-down menu choose *General Linear Model* which opens another drop-down menu.
3 Click on *GLM Repeated Measures* to open the *GLM Repeated Measures Define Variable(s)* dialogue box.
4 In the *Within Subject Factor Name* text box type the factor name, e.g. time.
5 Type the number of levels of the within-subject variable in the *Number of Levels* box. In our case this is 3.
6 Click *Add.*
7 Select *Define* to open the *GML Repeated Measures* dialogue box.
8 Click on the three variables, i.e. occasions of weighing, and using the arrow button move them to the *Within-Subjects Variables* box.
9 Choose *Options* and highlight 'time' in the *Factors* and *Factor Interactions* box. Then use the arrow button to place it into the *Display Means for* box.
10 Click *Estimates for effect size* and *Descriptive statistics* in the *Display* box.
11 Select *Continue,* then *OK* to produce the output.

As it is essential to know the mean of each condition when you interpret the ANOVA output, included in the instructions above is the process to obtain the means and standard deviations for the three occasions of weighing.

You will find SPSS produces a massive amount of output for the repeated measures procedure. The output which is of most interest to us and reproduced in Table 19.6 is the descriptive statistics subtable, and the multivariate tests subtable.

TABLE 19.5 *Example of one-way ANOVA output.*

a Descriptives

	Counselling group	N	Mean	Std deviation	Std error	95% confidence interval for mean		Minimum	Maximum
						Lower bound	Upper bound		
Stress score	Individual counselling	10	12.8000	3.2249	1.0198	10.4930	15.1070	8.00	18.00
	Group counselling	10	14.4000	4.4020	1.3920	11.2510	17.5490	8.00	21.00
	Control	10	20.1000	3.9567	1.2512	17.2695	22.9305	14.00	25.00
	Total	30	15.7667	4.9248	.8991	13.9277	17.6056	8.00	25.00

b Test of homogeneity of variances

	Levene Statistic	df1	df2	Sig.
Stress score	.591	2	27	.561

c ANOVA

		Sum of squares	df	Mean square	F	Sig.
Stress score	Between groups	294.467	2	147.233	9.722	.001
	Within groups	408.900	27	15.144		
	Total	703.367	29			

d Multiple comparisons. Dependent variable: Stress score

	(I) counselling group	(J) counselling group	Mean difference (I-J)	Std error	Sig.	95% Confidence interval	
						Lower bound	Upper bound
Tukey HSD	Individual counselling	Group counselling	-1.6000	1.740	.633	-5.9151	2.7151
		Control	-7.3000*	1.740	.001	-11.6151	-2.9849
	Group counselling	Individual counselling	1.6000	1.740	.633	-2.7151	5.9151
		Control	-5.7000*	1.740	.008	-10.0151	-1.3849
	Control	Individual counselling	7.3000*	1.740	.001	2.9849	11.6151
		Group counselling	5.7000*	1.740	.008	1.3849	10.0151
Scheffe	Individual counselling	Group counselling	-1.6000	1.740	.660	-6.1076	2.9076
		Control	-7.3000*	1.740	.001	-11.8076	-2.7924
	Group counselling	Individual counselling	1.6000	1.740	.660	-2.9076	6.1076
		Control	-5.7000*	1.740	.011	-10.2076	-1.1924
	Control	Individual counselling	7.3000*	1.740	.001	2.7924	11.8076
		Group counselling	5.7000*	1.740	.011	1.1924	10.2076
Bonferroni	Individual counselling	Group counselling	-1.6000	1.740	1.000	-6.0422	2.8422
		Control	-7.3000*	1.740	.001	-11.7422	-2.8578
	Group counselling	Individual counselling	1.6000	1.740	1.000	-2.8422	6.0422
		Control	-5.7000*	1.740	.009	-10.1422	-1.2578
	Control	Individual counselling	7.3000*	1.740	.001	2.8578	11.7422
		Group counselling	5.7000*	1.740	.009	1.2578	10.1422
Dunnet C	Individual counselling	Group counselling	-1.6000	1.740		-6.4180	3.2180
		Control	-7.3000*	1.740		-11.8068	-2.7932
	Group counselling	Individual counselling	1.6000	1.740		-3.2180	6.4180
		Control	-5.7000*	1.740		-10.9259	-.4741
	Control	Individual counselling	7.3000*	1.740		2.7932	11.8068
		Group counselling	5.7000*	1.740		.4741	10.9259

* The mean difference is significant at the .05 level.

TABLE 19.6 *Example of repeated measures ANOVA output*

a Descriptive statistics

	Mean	Std Deviation	N
Endweight	59.8333	6.0800	6
Weight at halfway point	69.6667	4.2740	6
Start weight	79.0000	8.3427	6

b Multivariate tests [a]

Effect		Value	F	Hypothesis df	Error df	Sig.	Eta Squared	Noncent. Parameter	Observed Power[b]
TIME	Pillai's trace	.937	29.862[c]	2.000	4.000	.004	.937	59.724	.994
	Wilks' lambda	.063	29.862[c]	2.000	4.000	.004	.937	59.724	.994
	Hoteling's trace	14.931	29.862[c]	2.000	4.000	.004	.937	59.724	.994
	Roy's largest root	14.931	29.862[c]	2.000	4.000	.004	.937	59.724	.994

a Design: Intercept within subjects design: TIME

b Computed using alpha = .05

c Exact statistic

How to interpret the output in Table 19.6

- The three means and SDs are quoted in the top table.
- In the bottom table, we focus on Wilk's lambda as one way of interpreting the significance of the results. Wilk's lambda indicates a highly significant time effect with = .063, F (2, 4) = 29.862, p = .004. Eta^2 is .937 and observed power is .994.
- Since the F value is highly significant, we would conclude that there is a significant difference in the mean weights on the three occasions and that the program had a significant weight loss effect.
- In order to interpret the meaning of the ANOVA, you always need to consider the means of each of the three groups of scores. If you have three or more groups, you need to check where the significant differences lie between the pairs of groups. This can be done by conducting pairwise comparisons.

Performing pairwise comparisons

If ANOVA produces a significant result we need to determine which means differ from each other. You can do this by conducting a paired sample *t* test for every pairing (see p. 198). Table 19.7 details the paired sample results. This is an alternative to using a post hoc test like Scheffe.)

TABLE 19.7 *Paired samples test*

| | | Paired differences | | | | | | | |
| | | | | Std error mean | 95% confidence interval of the difference | | | | Sig. (2-tailed) |
		Mean	Std deviation		Lower	Upper	t	df	
Pair 1	endweight –weight at halfway point	–9.8333	5.0761	2.0723	–15.1604	–4.5063	–4.745	5	.005
Pair 2	endweight –start weight	–19.1667	5.4559	2.2274	–24.8923	–13.4411	–8.605	5	.000
Pair 3	weight at halfway point– start weight	–9.3333	4.5898	1.8738	–14.1501	–4.5166	–4.981	5	.004

How to interpret Table 19.7

• All the comparisons were highly significant with p < .005 as a minimum.

How to report the output

We could describe the results of this analysis in the following way: 'A one-way correlated analysis of variance showed a significant treatment effect from the weight reduction program for the three occasions of weight measurement (Wilks' lambda = .063, F (2, 4) = 29.862, p = .004. Eta squared is .937 and observed power is .994). The start mean was 79.0, the midpoint mean was 69.7, and the end of program mean was 59.8. Post hoc paired *t* tests between all three pairs suggested that there were highly significant differences between all pairings (p = 0.005 minimum). The results can be regarded as quite robust support for the effectiveness of the weight reduction program.

Using SPSS for a two-way ANOVA

This procedure will be explained using a dummy experiment to investigate whether there are differences in final test performance by male and female students using two different methods of learning statistics. The analysis will enable the investigator to determine whether there is a difference in the effectiveness in the two methods, whether there is a difference between the genders across both methods, and whether there is an interaction effect between methods and gender.

How to proceed

1 Select *Statistics,* then click on *General Linear Model.*
2 Choose *GLM-General Factorial.*

3 Select dependent variable, e.g. 'score', and move it to *Dependent variable* box with arrow button.
4 Click on the factors, e.g. gender and method, and move them to the *Fixed Factor(s)* box.
5 Select *Model* to obtain the *GLM-General Factorial Model* box.
6 Click *Custom.*
7 Select the factors in the *Factors and Covariates* box and move them to the *Model* box.
8 Ensure the default option *Interaction* is specified in the *Build Terms* box.
9 Click the arrow button and *Gender* Method* will appear in the *Model* box.
10 Ensure *Type III* is selected in the *Sums of squares* box.
11 Select *Continue,* then *Options.*
12 In the *Factors and Factor Interaction* box click on all the entries and move them using the arrow button to the *Display means* box.
13 In the *Diagnostics* box select *Homogeneity tests.*
14 In the *Display* box select *Descriptive statistics* and *Estimates of Effect size.*
15 Finally choose *Continue* and then *OK* to obtain the output.

TABLE 19.8 *Example of two-way ANOVA output*

a Descriptive statistics

	Gender	Learning method	Mean	Std deviation	N
Score on course test	Male	Computerised	20.8333	3.1885	6
		class teaching	13.6667	1.9664	6
		Total	17.2500	4.5151	12
	Female	Computerised	13.8333	1.7224	6
		class teaching	18.5000	1.8708	6
		Total	16.1667	2.9797	12
	Total	Computerised	17.3333	4.3970	12
		class teaching	16.0833	3.1176	12
		Total	16.7083	3.7819	24

b Levene's test of equality of error variances [a]

	F	df_1	df_2	Sig.
Score on course test	1.403	3	20	.271

Tests the null hypothesis that the error variance of the dependent variable is equal across groups.

a Design: Intercept + GENDER + METHOD + GENDER*METHOD

c Tests of between-subjects effects. Dependent variable: score on course test

Source	Type III sum of squares	df	Mean square	F	Sig.	Eta squared	Noncent. parameter	Observed power[a]
Corrected Model	226.458[b]	3	75.486	14.729	.000	.688	44.187	1.000
Intercept	6700.042	1	6700.042	1307.325	.000	.985	1307.325	1.000
GENDER	7.042	1	7.042	1.374	.255	.064	1.374	.201
METHOD	9.375	1	9.375	1.829	.191	.084	1.829	.251
GENDER * METHOD	210.042	1	210.042	40.984	.000	.672	40.984	1.000
Error	102.500	20	5.125					
Total	7029.000	24						
Corrected Total	328.958	23						

a Computed using alpha = .05

b R squared = .688 (Adjusted R squared = .642)

How to interpret the output

- We will focus on the descriptive statistics subtable a and the tests of between subjects effects subtable c.
- The descriptive statistics suggests that while the means between the two methods are very similar (17.33 v. 16.08), there were large gender differences between the methods, with males doing far better on computerised teaching and females on class teaching.
- The observations from the descriptive statistics are reflected in the analysis of between-subjects effects. Here, the main factors of gender and method do not produce significant differences, but the interaction between them is highly significant with $F(1, 20) = 40.98$, $p = .001$. These results were also reflected in the eta squared effect sizes and observed power which were only strong for the interaction effect.
- The interaction effect may be graphed as in Figure 19.8 (see p. 328) to demonstrate the interaction in a visual form by entering the graph mode of SPSS.

Using SPSS for multiple comparisons in ANOVA (post hoc comparisons)

Obtaining a significant F is only the start of interpreting the results. The important issue is to know exactly where significant differences lie between different conditions of the study. SPSS can conduct several *post hoc* procedures which are, as the name implies, applied after the data has been subjected to ANOVA. They all do slightly different things. The most often used techniques are the Scheffe and the Tukey methods. They compare each possible pairing of groups or conditions to determine exactly where the

FIGURE 19.8

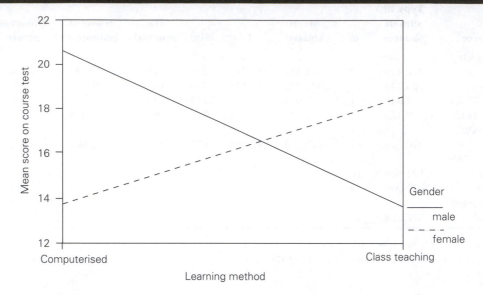

significant differences lie. However, there is a problem associated with multiple pairwise testing, or family-wise testing as it is sometimes called.

Methods for controlling Type I error across multiple tests

You will remember that Type I error is the probability of rejecting the null hypothesis when it is true. When we are only testing one comparison as in a *t* test we designate significance at .05 or less to minimise our chances of committing a Type I error.

However, in ANOVA (and also when testing a group of inter-correlations), when multiple hypotheses are being tested there is a greater chance of a Type I error because we know that even at the 5 per cent level a result of this magnitude will occur in the long run one in twenty times. So with a group (or family) of multiple hypotheses to check after—for example, a significant F on a one-way independent ANOVA with six groups—there is a greater chance of a Type I error, i.e. that one of our between-group comparisons is apparently significant when it may be one of the five in 100 that occur by chance.

To control for this, several statistical methods have been introduced and are conveniently available on SPSS, thus easy to apply. These are:

- *The LSD procedure.* This can only be used when there are three groups.
- *The Bonferroni method.* This reduces the chosen level of significance, say 5 per cent, to a level equal to that significance level divided by the number of paired comparisons.
- *The Holm's Sequential Bonferroni procedure.* This method evaluates each pair at a different level of significance. This method is often preferred over the basic Bonferroni since it is less conservative and has greater power to detect differences. Here all post hoc p values from the paired comparisons are ranked for size. The smallest p value is

evaluated first by dividing it by the number of comparisons. If the result is less than the p you have set, then reject the null hypothesis and evaluate the next smallest p. Continue on until a result is more than the 'p' required. At this point, you cannot reject the null hypothesis and all remaining comparisons are also statistically non-significant.

Both Bonferroni and the Holm's variant can be used with any number of comparisons.

These multiple comparisons are often called family wise comparisons.

Non-parametric alternatives of ANOVA

Kruskal-Wallis one-way non-parametric ANOVA

We have only considered parametric ANOVAs above. There are non-parametric options. The Kruskal-Wallis test determines whether independent samples are from different populations. This test uses ordinal data; therefore all scores must be transformed into ranks by combining all scores from all samples into one series. The smallest score is ranked as 1, the next smallest as 2, etc. Tied scores are given the mean of the ranks for which they are tied. When this is completed the sum of ranks in each condition is found. The test determines whether these sums of ranks are so disparate that they are not likely to have come from samples all drawn from the same population.

The Kruskal-Wallis formula is:

$$H = \frac{12}{N(N + 1)}\left(\frac{\Sigma R^2}{N}\right) - 3(N + 1)$$

where

n = no of cases in each condition
R = sum of ranks in each condition
N = total number of cases

H is distributed as chi square with df = number of conditions – 1. If the observed value of H is equal to, or larger than, the tabled value of chi square for the previously set level of significance and correct df, then the null hypothesis may be rejected. With less than five cases in each group the chi square distribution is not as accurate. There is a correction for tied scores but the effect of this correction is negligible and is usually not applied.

Here is an example based on achievement motivation scores of three groups of educators.

Teaching-oriented teachers		Administration-oriented teachers		Administrators	
Score	Rank	Score	Rank	Score	Rank
96	4	82	2	115	7
128	9	124	8	149	14
83	3	132	10	166	15
61	1	135	12	147	13
101	5	109	6	134	11
	$R_1 = 22$		$R_2 = 38$		$R_3 = 60$

$$H = \frac{12}{15(15 + 1)}\left(\frac{22^2}{5} + \frac{38^2}{5} + \frac{60^2}{5}\right) - 3(15 + 1) = 7.28$$

The tabled value for $df = 2$ at 0.05 level is 5.99. As our calculated H is higher than this, we can reject the null hypothesis and support the alternative hypothesis: that significant differences do exist in terms of achievement motivation between the three different types of educator.

STQ101*

Analyse these data using the Kruskal-Wallis test. Do you reject or retain the null hypothesis at p < 0.05?

Condition 1 Scores	Condition 2 Scores	Condition 3 Scores
10	15	21
16	14	18
8	12	13
19	11	16
7	13	19

*Answer on p. 605.

Using SPSS with the Kruskal-Wallis test

SPSS does not report an effect size index for the Kruskal-Wallis. However, a simple index can be computed. For the Kruskal-Wallis test, the median and the mean rank for each of the groups can be reported. Another possibility for the Kruskal-Wallis test is to compute an index that is normally associated with a one-way ANOVA, such as partial eta^2. Eta^2 can be computed directly from the reported chi-square value for the Kruskal-Wallis test using the following formula.

$$eta^2 = \frac{\text{chi square}}{N - 1} \qquad \text{where N is the total number of cases}$$

How to proceed to compute the Kruskall-Wallis test

1 Click *Data,* then *Select Cases.* Next choose *All Cases* and finally *OK.*
2 Select *Statistics* followed by *Nonparametrics,* and choose *K-independent samples.*
3 Click *Reset* to clear dialogue box.
4 Ensure only the *Kruskall-Wallis* option is selected in the *Test Type* box.
5 Click the treatment variable and move it to the *Test Variable* list box using the arrow button.
6 Select *Group* and move that to the *Grouping Variable* box.
7 Choose *Define Range.*
8 Type 1 as the minimum value; type as maximum value the total number of groups.
9 Select *Continue* then *OK* to produce output.

How to interpret output

- The table will provide a chi square with a significance level to indicate whether there is a significant difference between median ranks.
- If there is significant differences, pairwise comparisons among the groups needs to be conducted using the Mann-Whitney test (p. 189).

How to report results

'A Kruskal-Wallis test was conducted to evaluate differences between the three influenza vaccine dosage conditions (placebo, low dose, and high dose) on change in the number of days of absence (number of days with colds during treatment minus number of days with colds prior to treatment). The test, which was corrected for tied ranks, was significant, chi square (N = 100) = 26.92, p = .001. Post hoc pairwise comparisons using Mann-Whitney demonstrated a significant difference between the placebo group and the low-dose group. The typical decrease in number of days with cold symptoms after treatment was greater for the low-dose treatment group than for the placebo group. There was no significant difference between the two levels of vaccine dosage.'

Friedman two-way non-parametric ANOVA

This test can be applied to matched samples. For example, if one wanted to study the differences in learning attained under four teaching conditions with small matched samples, this would be the appropriate test. The data is cast in a two-way table with rows representing the various subjects and the columns the various conditions. The data in each row is ranked separately. The Friedman test determines whether it is likely that the different columns of ranks (samples) came from the same population.
The formula is:

$$X^2 = \frac{12}{Nk(k+1)} \Sigma R^2 - 3N(k+1)$$

where N = number of rows
k = number of columns
R = sum of ranks in each column
X^2 is approximately the chi square distribution with $df = k - 1$, with accuracy declining as number of rows and/or subjects decreases below 4.
Here is an example:

	Conditions			
	I	**II**	**III**	**IV**
Group A	9	4	1	7
Group B	6	5	2	8
Group C	9	1	2	6

We must first rank the scores in each row. The table then becomes:

	Conditions			
	I	II	III	IV
Group A	4	2	1	3
Group B	3	2	1	4
Group C	4	1	2	3
R	11	5	4	10

If the null hypothesis were true, there would be no significant difference between the sum of ranks for each condition. The distribution of ranks in each column would be on a chance basis. We would expect the ranks 1, 2, 3 and 4 to occur in all columns in about equal frequency, with rank totals about equal. If ranks depend on conditions then totals would vary from column to column.

The calculation for above data is:

$$X^2 = \frac{12}{(3)(4)(4+1)}(11^2 + 5^2 + 4^2 + 10^2) - (3)(3)(4+1) = 7.4$$

The tabled value with $df = 3$ and p set at 0.05 is 7.82. We must therefore retain the null hypothesis.

STQ102*

Analyse the following data (raw scores) using Friedman's test and make a statement about the null hypothesis.

	Conditions			
	I	II	III	IV
Group A	20	13	6	9
Group B	18	15	8	7
Group C	27	17	11	5
Group D	22	19	3	14
Group E	16	10	12	4

*Answers on p. 605.

STQ103*

Match the test on the left with the definitions on the right. (There is one test with no definition.)

a Mann-Whitney U test   1 Used following a significant F ratio.

b Scheffe test   2 Used to determine whether a set of ranks on a single factor differ significantly.

c Wilcoxon   3 Used to determine whether mean scores on two or more factors differ significantly.

d Chi square   4 A non-parametric test used to determine whether two uncorrelated means differ significantly.

Using SPSS for Friedman test

To obtain an effect size using the Friedman test, Kendall's coefficient of concordance (Kendall's W), a strength-of-relationship index, which SPSS calculates, can be used. The coefficient of concordance ranges in value from 0 to 1, with higher values indicating a stronger relationship.

How to proceed to compute a Friedman test

1 Select *Statistics* then *Nonparametric tests* and click on *K Related samples*.
2 Click *Reset* to empty the dialogue box.
3 Transfer the variables to the *Test variables List* box using the arrow button.
4 Choose *Friedman* and *Kendall's W* in the *Test Type* area.
5 Select *OK* to produce the output.

How to interpret the results

- The output will indicate the level of significance reached.
- Kendall's W can be used as an effect size index.
- If significance is reached, a follow-up test must be applied to determine where the differences lie. For this use Wilcoxon (see p. 205).

How to report results for the Friedman test

'A Friedman test was conducted to evaluate differences in medians among social workers on concerns for promotion (median = 6.50), for job satisfaction (median = 4.50) and for job security (median = 3.00). The test was significant, chi square (N = 50) = 27.49, p = .001, and the Kendall coefficient of concordance of .31 indicated fairly strong differences among the three concerns. Follow-up pairwise comparisons were conducted using a Wilcoxon test. The median concern for promotion was significantly greater than median concern for job satisfaction, p = .005, and the median concern for job security p = .009, but the median concern for job satisfaction did not differ significantly from the median concern for job security, p = .356.'

Some general guidelines on writing a results section for ANOVA

As ANOVA procedures are more involved than most of the previous statistical procedures discussed, here are some guidelines for writing a results section for statistical procedures that may require follow-up tests, such as one-way ANOVA or the Friedman test.

Steps

1 Describe the statistical test(s), the variables, and the purpose of the statistical test(s). For example: 'A one-way analysis of variance was conducted to evaluate the relationship between multi-vitamin treatment and the change in the number of days absent over a year.'
   - Describe the factor or factors. If a factor is a within-subjects factor, be sure to label it as such. Otherwise the reader may assume that it is a between-subjects factor. If a multifactorial design has one or more within-subjects factors, describe each factor as a between-subjects or a within-subjects factor.
   - Indicate the number of levels for each factor. It may be also be informative to the reader to have a description of each level if the levels are different treatments. However, it is not necessary to report the number of levels and what the levels are for factors with obvious levels such as gender.
   - Describe what the dependent variable(s) are.
2 Report the results of the overall test(s).
   - Describe any decisions about which test was chosen based on assumptions.
   - Report the F value and significance level (e.g. $F_{(2, 27)} = 4.84$, V = .016). For p-values of .000, quote $p < .001$. For multifactor designs, report the statistics for each of the main and interaction effects. Tell the reader whether the test(s) are significant or not.
   - Report statistics that allow the reader to make a judgment about the magnitude of the effect for each overall test (e.g. $eta^2 = .45$).
3 Report the descriptive statistics usually by reference to a table or figure that presents the means and standard deviations.
4 Describe and summarise the general conclusions of the analysis. An example: 'The results of the one-way ANOVA supported the hypothesis that different types of stress management treatment had a differential effect on the reduction of absences for individual teachers'.
5 Report the results of the follow-up tests:
   - Describe the procedures used to conduct the follow-up tests.
   - Describe the method used to control for Type I error across the multiple tests.
   - Summarise the results by presenting the results of the significance tests among pairwise comparisons with a table of means and standard deviations.
   - Describe and summarise the general conclusions of the follow-up analyses. Make sure to include in your description the directionality of the test.
6 Report the distributions of the dependent variable for levels of the factor(s) in a graph if space is available.

ANOVA is a statistical technique that is used to test for mean differences among two or more treatment conditions or populations. ANOVA can be used in both independent and repeated measures designs.

The test statistic is the ratio of two variances, termed the F ratio. It is structured so that the numerator and denominator measure the same variance when the null hypothesis is true. An 'unbalanced' F ratio indicates a treatment effect.

The F ratio has two values for *df*, one associated with the MS in the numerator, and the other associated with the MS in the denominator. The *df* values are used to locate the critical tabled value of F.

When a decision is made to reject the null hypothesis and the experiment contains more than two treatment conditions, a post hoc test such as Scheffe must be used to determine the significantly different treatments. This is because when an obtained F is significant, there is a significant difference between at least two of the conditions and we don't know which.

A repeated measures ANOVA eliminates the influence of individual differences from the analysis, because the same sample of subjects serves in all treatment conditions.

An investigation with two independent variables is termed a two-factor or two-way experiment and by tradition the two factors are identified as A and B: the two-factor (or way) ANOVA tests are for main effects for A and B, and for interaction effects between A and B. An interaction exists when the effect of one factor depends on levels of the other factor.

The Kruskal-Wallis and the Friedman tests provide non-parametric versions of ANOVA for independent and related designs.

Reference

Cohen, J. (1988), *Statistical Power Analysis for the Behavioural Sciences*, Laurence Erlbaum, New York.

Reliability and validity

20

twenty

When data are obtained from a data gathering instrument or technique, we need to know what faith we can put in the data as truly indicating the person's performance or behaviour. With all data we must ask:

- Was the assessment instrument/technique reliable and valid?
- Were the conditions under which the data were obtained such that, as far as possible, only the subject's ability is reflected in the data and that other extraneous factors had as minimal an effect as possible?

Reliability

Synonyms for reliability are dependability, stability, consistency, predictability, accuracy. A reliable person, for instance, is one whose behaviour is consistent, stable, dependable, and predictable—what he or she will do tomorrow and next week will be consistent with what he or she does today, and what he or she did last week. An unreliable person, on the other hand, is one whose behaviour is much more variable, often unpredictably variable. Sometimes he or she does this, sometimes that.

Psychological and social science measurements are similar to humans; they are more or less variable from occasion to occasion. They are stable and relatively predictable, or they are unstable and relatively unpredictable; they are consistent or not consistent.

If they are reliable, we can depend on them. If they are unreliable, we cannot depend on them.

It is possible to approach the definition of reliability in three ways:

1 One approach asks the question, 'Is the score which I have just obtained for student A the same score I would obtain if I tested him or her tomorrow and the next day and the next day?'.

This concept of reliability considers whether the obtained score is a stable indication of the student's performance on this particular test. This question implies a definition of reliability in terms of stability, dependability and predictability. It is the definition most often given in discussions of reliability.

2 A second approach asks, 'Is this test score which I have just obtained on student A an accurate indication of his or her 'true' ability?'.

This question really asks whether measurements are accurate. Compared to the first definition, it is further removed from common sense and intuition, but it is also more fundamental. These two approaches or definitions can be summarised in the words *stability* and *accuracy*.

3 The third approach, which helps in the understanding of the theory of reliability, also implies the previous two approaches. This approach asks how much error there is in the measuring instrument.

The two sources of error are:

1 experimental variability induced by real differences between individuals in the ability to perform on the test;
2 error variability which is a combination or error from two other sources:
   a random fluctuation. Subtle variations in individual performance from day to day; and
   b systematic or constant error. This is the result of one or more confounding variables which always push scores up or always push scores down, e.g. practice effect.

The amount of error in a score is a measure of the unreliability of the score. The less error, the more reliable the score, since the score then represents more closely the 'true' performance level of the subject.

Errors of measurement are assumed to all be random error. They are the sum or product of a number of causes: the ordinary random or chance elements present in all measures due to unknown causes, temporary fatigue, fortuitous conditions at a particular time that temporarily affect the object measured or the measuring instrument, fluctuations of memory or mood, and other factors that are temporary and shifting. Reliability can be defined as the relative absence of errors of measurement in a measuring instrument. Error and reliability are opposite sides of the same coin. The more error, the less stable, and less accurate the measurement. Our three approaches above recognise that reliability is the accuracy, stability and relative lack of error in a measuring instrument.

A homely example of reliability will further clarify the concept for those still in the fog. Suppose we wished to compare the accuracy of two crossbows.

One is an antique, well used and a bit sloppy in its action. The other is a modern weapon made by an expert. Both pieces are solidly fixed in granite bases and aimed and zeroed in by an expert toxophilite. Equal numbers of darts are fired with each. The target on the left represents the pattern of shots produced by the older weapon. Observe that the shots are considerably scattered. Now observe that the pattern of shots on the target on the right is more closely packed. The shots are closely clustered around the bullseye (see Figure 20.1).

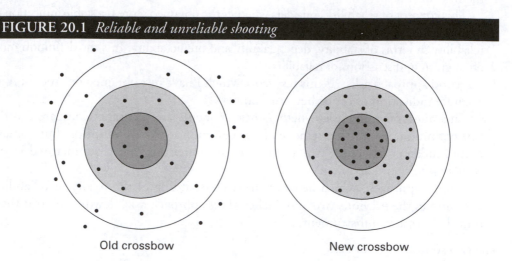

FIGURE 20.1 *Reliable and unreliable shooting*

Old crossbow

New crossbow

It is obvious that if we computed measures of variability—say, a standard deviation, or a variance from the two shot patterns—the antique bow would have a much larger measure of variability than the newer bow. The smaller variability measure of the new one indicates much less error, and thus much greater accuracy, stability and predictability. The new bow is reliable; the old bow is unreliable.

Similarly, psychological and educational measurements have greater and lesser reliabilities. A measuring instrument, say a personality scale, is given to a group of children—usually only once. Our goal, of course, is to hit the 'true' score of each child. To the extent that we miss the 'true' scores, to this extent our measuring instrument, our test, is unreliable and contains error too.

The theory of reliability

The measurement of a subject's 'real' level of performance will be blurred by these influences, such as fluctuations in motivation and fortuitous context conditions which give rise to the error 'score' component in the observed score. For any form of assessment or data gathering technique, there is the *true score*, the *observed score* and the *error score*. A simple equation can be written which links these three scores. Observed score = true score ± error 'score', or more simply:

$$X_{obs} = X_{true} \pm \text{error}$$

The error score may, of course, be positive or negative, depending on whether a person 'overscores' or 'underscores' with reference to his or her true performance level. The smaller the error score, the closer the observed score approximates the true score and the greater the reliability.

part 2 | quantitative methods

Where there is no error component, $X_{obs} = X_{true} + 0$, i.e. perfect reliability.

As the error component increases, the true score component decreases. Similarly, it can be shown that total variance in obtained data is equal to the sum of the 'true' variance and the error variance, that is:

$$\sigma^2_{obs} = \sigma^2_{true} + \sigma^2_{error}$$

We can define the reliability of any set of measurements as the proportion of their variance which is true variance; in other words, the ratio of true variance to observed variance. When the true variance is equal to the observed variance, i.e. when there is no error variance, this ratio has a value of +1.0. This is the 'perfect reliability' value:

$$\frac{\sigma^2_{true}}{\sigma^2_{obs}} = 1 \qquad r_{tt} = +1.0 \ (r_{tt} \text{ symbolises reliability})$$

When there is no true variance present, i.e. when the observed variance is entirely error, the ratio has a value of zero. This is the 'nil reliability' value:

$$r_{tt} = 0$$

That is,

$$\frac{\sigma^2_{true} \ (0)}{\sigma^2_{obs}} = 0$$

or conversely,

$$\frac{X_e}{X_{obs}} = 1 \text{ (i.e. entirely error variance)}$$

Hence, reliability equals 1 minus the error variance divided by the obtained variance.

$$r_{tt} = 1 - \frac{\sigma^2_{error}}{\sigma^2_{obs}} \qquad \text{Definition of reliability}$$

STQ104

Explain the meaning of $X_{obs} = X_{true} \pm X_{error}$. How does this expression help us to understand the concept of reliability?

Methods of determining reliability

There are four approaches to computing reliability coefficients in general use. These are based on the principle that sets of scores can be correlated to determine the reliability of the test, i.e. to determine the amount of variance in the test scores which may be attributed to true differences among individuals. Reliability coefficients are thus correlation coefficients between two sets of scores. The methods used in computing reliability estimates are:

1 test–retest method
2 alternate forms method
3 split-half method
4 internal consistency method

Test–retest method

When reliability is measured by the test–retest method, a coefficient of stability is obtained. This reliability coefficient measures error variance due to temporal variations in characteristics of those being assessed, as well as variation in conditions of test administration. Some of this temporal instability in test scores is due to variations from one testing occasion to another in the subject's general characteristics, such as in their health or emotional tension; part of it is due to variations in their reactions to the specific test or assessment.

The test–retest reliability of a test is simply expressed as the correlations between the scores from two administrations of the same instrument to the same students. There is no standard duration of time which should separate the two administrations. However, a minimum of one day and perhaps a maximum of one year are boundaries generally considered acceptable for test–retest reliability estimates. In general, a two- to three-month period is best.

STQ105

1　Why does a two- to three-month lapse of time between test and retest seem the optimum?
2　What would you see as the problems stemming from:
  a　too short a time lapse?
  b　too long a time lapse?

If the period is too short, the subjects may remember the answers they gave on the first occasion, and so spuriously increase the consistency of scores. On the other hand, boredom, decreased motivation, etc. may influence the second testing, thus reducing the congruence of results between the two occasions of testing. If the period is too long, maturational factors—for example, learning experience, age—will influence changes of score on the second occasion and cause an underestimation of the reliability. It is difficult to state any general rule concerning an appropriate period of intervening time for all tests. If the test is designed to measure a relatively stable trait or characteristic and the individual is not subjected during the intervening time to experiences which may, in some way, affect the particular characteristic involved, then the intervening period can be relatively long. However, when measuring a trait which is influenced by the individual's intervening experiences, the time should be shorter, but not short enough to allow memory or practice effect to inflate artificially the relationship between performance on the two administrations. Thus an appropriate period of intervening time can only be decided on in the next context of the situation.

STQ106

For each of the following, indicate whether they would contribute to true score or error score variance when a test–retest method is employed.
1　Noise in the next room on the first test.

Since the rationale of the test–retest method implies that the same level of cognitive, intellectual, motivational and personality variables are demonstrated on each occasion, so that any changes are due to the instability of the test itself, changes which occur within the subjects during the interval between test and retest are the largest source of error in the test–retest reliability estimate. However, the subject must always be a 'different' person for the sole fact of having taken the test on the first occasion.

STQ107

If the correlation between the scores from two occasions of testing was +1.0, what does this imply for reliability and error?

If you recall your studies of the correlation coefficient, you should realise that $r = +1.0$ would imply perfect reliability with no measurement error evident.

STQ108

If reliability is less than +1.0 what does this imply?

As the test–retest correlation declines from unity, we are measuring the effects of increasing random error.

Alternate (or parallel) forms method

Because both general ability and specific knowledge may change differentially among students from test to retest, the alternate forms method can be used. Some standardised tests have two or more equivalent forms that have been designed to be comparable in content, length, difficulty level and variance. When two equivalent forms (say forms A and B) are administered to students on the same occasion, these are correlated and a coefficient of equivalence is obtained which measures the consistency of examinee performance from one specific sampling of test content to another. This method does not take into account temporal fluctuations in examinee performance.

This procedure has two advantages over the previous method. First, one need not be as concerned about memory and practice effect since the two forms of the test are composed of different items. Second, a more accurate estimate of reliability is likely to be obtained because the estimate is based on a larger sampling of the universe of test items. However, these advantages are gained at the price of further time and effort involved in the construction of the instrument itself. It is obviously more difficult to construct two forms of a test than to construct just one. In addition, there are problems of ensuring that the forms are indeed equivalent. If they are not, the estimate of the reliability of either form is likely to be too low, since non-equivalency will tend to lower the correlation between the two tests.

This estimate is still influenced by temporary factors in the environment, by the test administration, and temporary conditions of the students, such as boredom or fatigue. It cannot be assumed that these factors will be present on the successive administrations of the tests and therefore they contribute to the error variance and reduce the estimated reliability of the tests.

Split-half method

The split-half method is based on the proposition that many of the temporary factors which influence the test–retest and alternate forms methods of estimating reliability could be eliminated if a reliability coefficient could be determined from the scores of a single administration of a test. Two scores can be obtained simply by splitting the test into halves. The scores obtained on one half of the test can be correlated with scores on the other half of the test.

STQ109

Can you think why splitting a test into a first half and a second half would not be a good way of splitting the test for a split-half reliability estimate?

The major problems with that sort of split are that:

1 different types of items with different difficulty levels may occur in each half;
2 some subjects may run out of time and not finish the second half; and
3 boredom may set in on the second half.

Hence, a commonly accepted way of splitting a test into two halves is to divide it into odd-numbered items and even-numbered items. If the test is constructed so that adjacent items tend to be similar in difficulty level, discriminatory power and content, this is not an unreasonable procedure. However, one might ask what difference in the computed coefficient there would have been if the test had been split in some other way. A test of twenty items, for example, may be divided into two equal parts in exactly 184 756 different ways. Unless the twenty items are exactly equivalent there would probably be some variation in the reliability estimates obtained by splitting the test in so many different ways. In spite of this difficulty, the split-half reliability coefficient based on the odd–even split still provides the test constructor with useful information.

A further problem exists. When a test is divided into two parts and the scores are correlated, the result is a correlation between scores on tests that have only one-half as many items as were originally administered. The Spearman-Brown formula is used to estimate the reliability of the test in its original length. The general formula for the reliability of a test n times as long as the given test is:

$$r_{tt} = \frac{n r_{tt}}{1 + (n - 1)\, r_{tt}}$$

In this formula, n is the ratio of the length of the desired test to the length of the present test (length is defined as number of test items), and r_{tt} is the already obtained reliability. If the correlation between the scores on the odd items and the scores on the even items were 0.50, this correlation based on 10 items would be substituted into the Spearman-Brown formula as follows:

$$r_{tt} = \frac{(2)(0.50)}{1 = (2-1)(0.50)} = \frac{1.0}{1.5} = 0.67$$

The value 2 has been substituted for n because it was necessary to determine the reliability of the test twice as long as the two 10-item tests used to obtain the original reliability coefficient. The formula indicates that the split-half reliability of the 20-item test is 0.67.

It is important to remember that any time the split-half method of reliability estimate is utilised, the Spearman-Brown formula must be applied to the correlation coefficient in order to obtain a reliability estimate which is appropriate for the total test length.

STQ110

The split-half reliability of a 50-item test is 0.79. What is the reliability of the whole test?

Internal consistency method

Another form of reliability measure which is commonly used is one developed by Kuder and Richardson (1937)—the internal consistency method. As we have seen, there are a 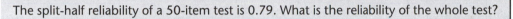 number of ways in which a test may be split in order to compute 'half-test' scores, which then enter into the computation of a correlation coefficient. For each split, a different reliability coefficient might be obtained. Kuder and Richardson formulated measures of reliability that used item statistics, as opposed to part or total scores, as the basic unit of measurement. The result is a reliability estimate which is equivalent to the average of all possible split-half coefficients. Cronbach' coefficient alpha is another form of internal consistency reliability index, and is used by SPSS.

The simplest Kuder-Richardson formula is Formula 21 (often referred to as KR 21). With this reliability, coefficients can be computed fairly easily, just on the basis of M, the number of test items (n) and σ. The KR 21 formula is:

$$KR\ 21 = \frac{n}{n-1}\left(\frac{1 - m(n-m)}{n\sigma^2}\right)$$

For example, on a self-concept scale, where n is 100, the mean is 78, and the SD is approximately 10, the computation is as follows:

$$KR\ 21 = \frac{100}{99}\left(1 - \frac{78 \times 22}{100 \times (10)^2}\right)$$

$$= 1.01\left(1 - \frac{1716}{10\ 000}\right)$$

$$= 1.01(0.83) = 0.84$$

This method, like the equivalent-forms method, takes into account variance due to the specificity of the tests and fails to measure temporal instability in test performance of students. It measures the consistency of performance on each test item. The more the test items inter-correlate, the higher the KR 21, i.e. all the items in the test are measuring the same characteristic of the individual. The greater the diversity of test items, in terms of the skills required to determine the correct answers, the lower the correlations of the performance on the various test items. This decrease in the inter-item correlations reduces the obtained internal-consistency reliability estimate. An assumption is that the test items are scored '1' for correct responses, and '0' for incorrect responses, and the total score is the sum of the number of items correct.

Review of methods

Other things being equal, a researcher will choose the test with the highest quoted reliability. A test with a reliability of +0.90 is surely better than one with a reliability of +0.80!

However, the quoted values need interpretation, in terms of the method chosen to estimate reliability data, in terms of the situation in which the particular data were gained, and in terms of the sources of error they control (or don't control).

An interesting way of differentiating between these kinds of reliabilities is to note some of the causes of error variance in observed scores.

Complete Table 20.1, indicating where the appropriate error variance will be present. The 'Parallel form' column has been completed for you. There is a completed Table 20.1 on p. 348.

Clearly, we cannot always be certain that no error variance will be present. For example, if an immediate test–retest method is used, it is possible that error variance associated with the children will still be present, since they may be a little more tired on the retest. But it is unlikely to be as great as error variance associated with the children if a delayed test–retest method is used, with a long time interval between retests. And the longer the interval, the lower will be the reliability figures obtained. So the important point is not the exact specification of the source of error variance. The point is that a reliability quoted by a test constructor must be interpreted according to the method used to calculate it.

TABLE 20.1				
		Type of reliability coefficient		
Source of error variance	**Test–retest immediate**	**Test–retest delayed**	**Parallel form**	**Split half**
The procedure			Yes	
The child			No	
The conditions			No	
The marking			Yes	

STQ111

1   What sort of reliability method is used when:
    a   different forms of the same test are administered?
    b   one test is administered on two separate occasions?
2   To which sort of variance (time or error) does knowledge of a specific item of information contribute with:
    a   the test–retest method?
    b   the alternate forms method?
3   On how many administrations of a test are internal consistency reliability estimates based?
4   In the split-half technique, why are the various ways of splitting a test in half not all equally acceptable?
5   Why does the split-half technique not indicate the stability of obtained scores?
6   Using the reliability information set out below, which one of the following tests would you select as being most reliable?

Test	Reliability estimate
A	0.96 (split half)
B	0.96 (parallel form delayed)
C	0.96 (parallel form immediate)
D	0.96 (test–retest immediate)

Factors that influence test reliability

A number of factors may influence the reliability of any test. These factors can be grouped in the following three categories:

1   Factors dealing with the nature of the test items and the test itself.
2   The nature of the persons who are being tested.
3   Factors related to the administration of the test.

The three basic methods for computing a reliability coefficient that have been presented often lead to differing estimates of the reliability of the test scores. The various conditions which can influence the outcome of the computation of a reliability coefficient further emphasise the notion that no assessment or technique has a single reliability coefficient.

Length of test

One of the major factors which will affect the reliability of any test is the length of that test. On an intuitive basis, one can see that as the number of items in any particular test is increased, the chance factors which might enter into a score are greatly reduced or balanced out. For example, performance on a three-item multiple-choice test could be greatly influenced by various chance factors which might influence student responses.

However, if the three-item test were lengthened to thirty or forty items, the error sources would have a greater tendency to cancel each other out, and a better estimate of the true scores of the students would be achieved.

In addition, it can also be assumed that, as a test is lengthened, the test maker is providing a more adequate sample of items which will measure the trait in question.

You may already have noted that increasing the length of the test increases its reliability. This assumption is inherent in the use of the Spearman-Brown formula. Although this formula is used most often in the computation of the split-half reliability coefficient, it may also be used to compute the increased reliability due to tripling or adding ten times as many items to a test.

The Spearman-Brown formula may also be used to determine the number of items which must be added to an already existing test in order to increase its reliability to some desired level. However, a law of diminishing returns sets in, so that as reliability increases it requires a tremendous extension in length to improve reliability a little. For example, if a test with a reliability coefficient of only 0.82 is doubled in length, the estimated reliability coefficient of the longer test would be 0.90; if it were tripled in length, the estimated reliability coefficient would be 0.93.

Restrictions in group performance

This refers to the range of ability or spread of scores within the group on which r_{tt} is computed. For example, the reliability coefficients for intelligence tests, computed on all school groups, tend to be higher than those computed on Year 12 groups, which show much less dispersion with respect to IQ.

Methods of estimating reliability

Methods that take into account both stability and equivalence will tend to give lower coefficients than the other methods because all major types of error variance are included. The Kuder-Richardson method and Cronbach alpha will tend to yield lower coefficients than the split-halves method because the former reflects test homogeneity, as reflected in all inter-item relationships, rather than merely the consistency of two scores from the halves of a subdivided test.

With any method involving two testing occasions, the longer the interval of time between two test administrations, the lower the coefficient will tend to be.

Objectivity of assessment

Another major factor affecting reliability of measurement is subjectivity of judgement. We tend to get low reliability coefficients for rating scales, essay examinations, interviewing, projective tests, etc. Objective tests produce high reliabilities because the marker does not have to decide how good an answer is; it is either right or wrong.

Standard error of measurement

The standard error of measurement (SE_{meas}) is a necessary statistic for interpreting the value of a reliability coefficient. A series of scores obtained by an individual on repeated administration of a single test will approximate to a normal distribution. The spread of this distribution is another way of conceptualising the reliability of the test. The smaller the spread, the greater the fidelity with which any one observed score can be taken to represent the individual's 'true' score. We use the SD of this distribution as the index of its spread. This SD of the error distribution is known as the standard error of measurement, or SE_{meas}.

The formula is:

$$SE_{meas} = \sigma\sqrt{1 - r_{tt}}$$

where σ is the standard deviation of the test scores and r_{tt} is the reliability coefficient of the test.

The interpretation of the standard error of measurement is similar to that of the SD of a set of test scores. There is a probability of 0.68 that a student's obtained score does not deviate from his or her true score by more than plus or minus one standard error of measurement. The other probabilities are

$$\text{0.95 for } X_{obs} \pm 2SE_{meas} \text{ and 0.99 for } X_{obs} \pm 3SE_{meas}$$

This interpretation of the SE_{meas} assumes that errors in measurement are equally distributed throughout the range of test scores. If a subject obtains a score of 114 on a standardised intelligence test which has M = 100, σ = 15 and r_{tt} = 0.96, what are the IQ limits within which 95 per cent of the scores from an infinite number of testing would lie? Here we need to know the SE_{meas}, since $2 \times SE_{meas}$ will define the 95 per cent limits.

Substituting, we obtain:

$$SE_{meas} = 15\sqrt{1 - 0.96}$$
$$= 15\sqrt{1.04}$$
$$= 15 \times 0.2$$
$$= 3$$

That is, the IQ scores the student would obtain from an infinite number of testings would have a σ = 3. The 95 per cent limits are therefore 2×3 IQ points above and below the only real score we know he or she has. So the range of error using the 95 per cent confidence limits are 114 ± 6, i.e. 108 – 120. This range is quite revealing for it shows that even with a highly reliable test there is still quite a considerable band of error round an obtained score.

If the reliability is lower this range increases. For example, with an r_{tt} of 0.75 and σ = 15, the 95 per cent limits are ± 15 marks on each side of the obtained score. The limiting cases are when r_{tt} = 0 or r_{tt} = 1. In the former case SE_{meas} is the same as the σ of the scores; in the latter case SE_{meas} is zero, for there is no error.

STQ112

1 Calculate the 95 per cent and 99 per cent score ranges for the following:
   a   raw score 114, σ = 10, r_{tt} = 0.91
   b   raw score 62, σ = 5, r_{tt} = 0.84

2   To have confidence in an obtained score, would you want a small or a large SE_meas?
    Justify your answer.
3   A child achieves a score of 90 on each of five tests of academic ability. Standard
    deviations and reliability coefficients for each test are supplied below. Which of tests
    A, B, C, D or E probably represents the child's 'true' score on the ability the test
    measures with greatest fidelity?

Test	A	B	C	D	E
σ	10	25	10	20	25
r_{tt}	0.84	0.91	0.96	0.96	0.99

4   Describe the usefulness in reporting the standard error of measurement as well as the
    reliability for a test.

COMPLETED TABLE 20.1

	Type of reliability coefficient			
Source of error variance	Test–retest immediate	Test–retest delayed	Parallel form	Split half
The procedure	Yes	Yes	Yes	No
The child	No	Yes	No	No
The conditions	No	Yes	No	No
The marking	Yes	Yes	Yes	Yes

Using SPSS to compute Cronbach's alpha

How to proceed

1   Select *Statistics*, choose *Scale,* then click on *Reliability Analysis* to open the *Reliability Analysis* dialogue box.
2   Transfer all the scale or test items to the *Items* box.
3   Ensure *Alpha* is chosen in the *Model* box.
4   Click on *Statistics* to open the *Reliability Analysis Statistics* dialogue box.
5   In the *Descriptives for* area, select *Item, Scale* and *Scale if item deleted.*
6   In the *Inter-item area* choose *Correlations.*
7   Select *Continue* then *OK* to produce the output similar to that shown in Table 20.2
    At step 2, if you wish to determine the alpha of a subscale (subset of the whole test)
then only transfer those items you require.

How to interpret Table 20.2

- The table shows the iter-item statistics for the sixteen-item scale.
- The two columns to focus on are the last two.
- The *Corrected Item-Total Correlation* reveals those items that have low correlations with the test or scale as a whole.

TABLE 20.2 *Example of Cronbach alpha printout for an attitude scale*

Item-total statistics

	Scale mean if item deleted	Scale variance if item deleted	Corrected item—total correlation	Alpha if item deleted
VAR00001	53.7273	33.1602	.3893	.7472
VAR00002	54.8636	34.8853	.3217	.7529
VAR00003	53.5909	35.0152	.2874	.7560
VAR00004	53.6818	37.2749	.0485	.7768
VAR00005	53.6818	36.1320	.2046	.7619
VAR00006	54.2273	34.5649	.4357	.7449
VAR00007	53.3182	32.8939	.5688	.7325
VAR00008	53.8182	31.3939	.6269	.7236
VAR00009	53.7273	33.1602	.3893	.7472
VAR00010	54.8636	34.8853	.3217	.7529
VAR00011	53.5909	35.0152	.2874	.7560
VAR00012	53.6818	37.2749	.0485	.7768
VAR00013	53.6818	36.1320	.2046	.7619
VAR00014	54.2273	34.5649	.4357	.7449
VAR00015	53.3182	32.8939	.5688	.7325
VAR00016	53.8182	31.3939	.6269	.7236

Reliability coefficients
Number of cases = 22.0
Number of items = 18
Alpha = .7621

- The last column shows the overall scale alpha or internal reliability if that item is removed. The overall alpha is .7621, printed below the table, which is just acceptable. A higher level is preferred.
- Variables 4, 5, 12 and 13 have the lowest item correlations with the scale as a whole. These could be omitted and the reliability assessed again on the remaining twelve-item scale.
- Table 20.3 displays the new data for the twelve-item scale.
- It is apparent that the reliability has been improved by eliminating the four items. Internal reliability is now .8176.

SPSS also produces for this test a table of intercorrelations and a set of descriptive statistics for each item. These have not been shown here. Note that the items eliminated because of their low correlation with the test as a whole may not be poorly worded or ambiguous but may measure another dimension very well, and could be assessed for reliability as a set on their own to determine if they form a separate subscale, which would be indicated by a high alpha. A more acceptable and sophisticated way of determining the structure of a test or scale in terms of its subgroupings of items (factors) is to submit it to factor analysis.

How to report

Internal reliability of a sixteen-item scale was assessed using the Cronbach alpha technique. The scale produced an alpha of .7621. Inspection of the table suggested that four items

TABLE 20.3

Item-total statistics

	Scale mean if item deleted	Scale variance if item deleted	Corrected item—total correlation	Alpha if item deleted
VAR00001	38.6364	27.2900	.4982	.8020
VAR00002	39.7727	29.5173	.3737	.8120
VAR00003	38.5000	29.4048	.3635	.8131
VAR00006	39.1364	29.4567	.4649	.8052
VAR00007	38.2273	28.3745	.5347	.7990
VAR00008	38.7273	27.0649	.5866	.7932
VAR00009	38.6364	27.2900	.4982	.8020
VAR00010	39.7727	29.5173	.3737	.8120
VAR00011	38.5000	29.4048	.3635	.8131
VAR00014	39.1364	.29.4567	.4649	.8052
VAR00015	38.2273	28.3745	.5347	.7990
VAR00016	38.7273	27.0649	.5866	.7932

Reliability coefficients

Number of cases = 22.0

Number of items = 12

Alpha = .8176

should be eliminated because of their low correlation with the test as a whole. A further reliability test then produced an alpha of .8176, which is acceptable for an attitude scale.

Validity

The subject of validity is complex, controversial, and peculiarly important in research. Here perhaps more than anywhere else, the nature of reality is questioned. It is possible to study reliability without inquiring into the meaning of the variables. It is not possible to study validity, however, without sooner or later inquiring into the nature and meaning of one's variables.

A measurement or assessment technique which is perfectly reliable would seem to be quite valuable, but the test user should also raise the questions: 'How valid is it? Does the test measure what I want it to measure?'. A perfectly reliable test may not measure anything of value, and it may not correlate with any other test score. Validity information gives some indication of how well a test measures a given area, under certain circumstances and with a given group. It is for this reason that any one test may have many types of validity, and a unique validity for each circumstance and group tested.

The difference between reliability and validity

Initially many students confuse these two terms. Let us imagine that the quality control department of a factory that manufactured 12-inch wooden school rulers went on strike and some rulers were retailed which were inaccurate. The inaccuracy lay in the fact that each inch division was slightly longer than one inch; each was one and one-twelfth inches long. Hence, when we thought we were drawing a line 12 inches long, we were in fact drawing a line 13 inches long ($1^{1}/_{12} \times 12$).

Surprising as it may seem, the ruler is quite reliable, for it produces consistent results, even though the measurements are not what we think they are. Every time we draw what we assume to be a line 12 inches long, we produce a line 13 inches long consistently. The ruler produces a reliable measurement *but it is not a valid measure of 12 inches*. It is a valid measure of 13 inches, but since we bought it on the presumption that it measured 12 inches it cannot be measuring what it purports to measure. Similarly, test instruments and techniques can be very reliable, producing consistent results from occasion to occasion, but may not be valid as measures of what they set out to measure. On the other hand, if an instrument is unreliable it cannot be valid.

So validity relates to the question, 'What does the test measure?'. The importance of this question would seem obvious; yet research literature contains many examples of tests/techniques being used without proper consideration of their validity for the user's purpose. This lack of attention to validity may seem somewhat surprising, since most tests are clearly labelled with a title intended to indicate quite specifically what is measured. But one of the first steps in evaluating a new test is to disregard the title, which may represent only what the test author had hoped to measure. A test of reading comprehension may, in fact, measure only a general intelligence factor. A test of achievement may be an equally good measure of general test-taking ability, particularly if the items are poorly constructed. The possibility that a scale of neuroticism might measure something else, such as a response set, or the ability to see through the test and give a favourable impression, was seldom considered. It is important, therefore, that the researcher be able to judge whether a test is valid for its purposes.

Types of validity

Five types of validity can be distinguished: predictive, concurrent, content, construct and face. Each of these will be examined briefly, though we put the greatest emphasis on construct validity, since it is probably the most important form of validity from the research point of view.

Content validity

Content validity is most appropriately considered in connection with achievement testing. An achievement test has content validity if it represents faithfully the objectives of a given instructional sequence and reflects the emphasis accorded these objectives as the instruction was carried out. It is assumed, of course, that the teacher did, in fact, follow a plan based on specific objectives during the course of their teaching and that the test was based on that plan. A test in algebra would have no content validity for measuring achievement in history. A test in long division would have low content validity if administered to infant school pupils. When students criticise a test as not fairly representing the actual content of the course, they are in reality remarking about the test's content validity.

Content validity then is the representativeness or sampling adequacy of the content (the substance, the matter, the topics) of a measuring instrument. Content validation is guided by the question: 'Is the substance or content of this measure representative of the content or the universe of content of the property being measured?'.

Content validity is most often determined on the basis of expert judgement.

It should be pointed out that an achievement test may have adequate content validity at a given time for a particular class and teacher, but may not be equally valid for testing another group taught by a different teacher at a different time. A criticism of commercially published standardised tests is that they sometimes do not fairly test the achievement of pupils in 'my' classes; i.e. they do not have satisfactory content validity in some situations. This criticism suggests one of the cautions which must be kept in mind in interpreting the scores on such tests, and one which might well apply to the teacher's own tests if they are not made up especially for the groups to be tested. It should not be inferred that the results of standardised tests are useless; they actually form an important part of the body of necessary information about pupils. Neither should one infer that teacher-made tests should be used only once and then discarded. One should, however, keep in mind that the content validity of a test is not necessarily a fixed and changeless characteristic. It must be examined whenever the test is used with a different group or when the testing situation is altered.

Predictive validity

Predictive validity involves the wish to predict, by means of assessment or technique, performance on some other criterion. An example of such a situation is the use of Year 12 matriculation for tertiary study. The correlation between performance on the Year 12 exams and final degree results is a measure of the predictive validity of the Year 12 exams. Predictive validity is vitally important for vocational selection research techniques, because a person responsible for the selection of those likely to succeed in a given job, college or curriculum is concerned with test scores as aids in doing a better job of selection.

Primary teachers use reading readiness and intelligence tests as predictors when they use them as aids in grouping children. Predictive validity cannot be judged by an examination of a test's content. It can only be assessed by comparing a later performance (perhaps several years later) with the original test scores. This later performance, which is to be predicted, is often termed the *criterion performance* and may be a rather crude one such as successfully completing an apprenticeship, achieving an acceptable shorthand rate, making at least a C average on a course, or developing a particular neurotic or psychiatric symptom. We rarely require the prediction of a precise score.

It is usually possible to express predictive validity in terms of the correlation coefficient between the predicted status and the criterion. Such a coefficient is called a validity coefficient. Suppose, for example, that a college admissions officer predicts the status (either passed or failed) at the end of the first year for each of 100 first-year college students, using information available to her at the beginning of the year. Then their actual status is observed at the end of the year and the admissions officer determines the extent of agreement between the predictions and the observed status. The extent of the agreement may be expressed in the form of the coefficient of predictive validity for the method of prediction used. If a single test was used for this prediction, then this coefficient may be regarded as a measure of the predictive validity of that test.

Many criteria are unfortunately very remote in time and difficult to define. For example, with 'success on the job', should one consider income or self-ratings of ability, or happiness in one's profession, or supervisor's ratings, or perhaps some combination of a number of these individual criteria?

Although there is no simple answer to the problem of how best to choose a criterion measure, a few suggestions might be given.

- One should be sure that performance on the criterion measure is a result of the same individual characteristics and external environmental conditions which affected performance on the test one is attempting to validate.
- The criterion measure should be reliable; i.e. it should be stable or consistent from day to day or time to time. Obviously, it is very difficult to predict something that fluctuates markedly over short periods of time.
- In choosing a criterion measure, one should consider such factors as the time and the expense required to obtain the measure.

STQ114

Which of the following requires a test with predictive validity?
1   A mental patient is given a personality test prior to discharge.
2   A student requires an estimate of success before commencing training.
3   A teacher wishes to assess what her history class has learned.

Concurrent validity

Concurrent and predictive validity are very much alike. They differ only in the time dimension. For example, if we developed a neuroticism scale, we would require an answer to the question, 'Will a high scorer on this test become a neurotic at some time in the future?' for predictive validity, but an answer to the question, 'Is the high scorer a neurotic now?' for concurrent validity. Predictive and concurrent validity are both characterised by prediction to an outside criterion and by checking a measuring instrument, either now or in the future, against some outcome. A test predicts a certain kind of outcome, or it predicts some present or future state of affairs. In a sense then, all tests are predictive. Aptitude tests predict future achievement; achievement tests predict present and future achievement; and intelligence tests predict the present and future ability to learn and to solve problems.

Since concurrent validity coefficients, in which we relate test scores to present performance, can be obtained with less expense and delay than predictive validity coefficients (involving future performance), many aptitude test manuals present concurrent validity data only. But high concurrent validity is no guide to high predictive validity.

The concurrent validity of a test must be considered when one is using the test to distinguish between two or more groups of individuals whose status at the time of testing is different. An example of a test originally developed to have high concurrent validity to a specific purpose is the Minnesota Multiphasic Personality Inventory, better known as the MMPI. The MMPI has been used as a screening device for identifying persons who, at the time of testing, have a personality disorder which requires treatment. A preliminary form of this instrument was administered to a group of hospitalised mental patients and also to their normal visitors. Items of the test were then carefully analysed to identify those who distinguished clearly between the two groups, i.e. patients and visitors. These items were then administered to other groups of patients and visitors, and on the basis of their responses (and without knowledge of their actual status), these individuals were classified as either patients or visitors. A comparison of test-based categorisation and actual status provided a measure of the concurrent validity of the test. Concurrent validity is thus always expressed in terms of the relationship between test performance and an accepted contemporary criterion. The correlation coefficient provides a quantitative measure of this relationship.

Concurrent validity may also be a relevant concern in the evaluation of achievement tests. In everyday classroom experiences there frequently are appropriate contemporary criteria with which achievement test performance should be compared. A pupil who performs well in a spelling test, for example, may be expected to exhibit his or her spelling skill in such tasks as writing compositions, finding spelling errors in their own work, and performing in classroom spelling games. The score on a test of reading comprehension should be related to teacher observations of the pupil's skill in classroom recitation or of their work in small reading groups. Test performance in arithmetic computation should be related to computational skill exhibited in other subject areas such as science or geography. The failure to find such relationships between test performance and contemporary behavioural criteria may indicate: (a) that the criteria themselves are not acceptable; (b) that the same behaviours are not being assessed by the test and the criteria; or (c) that the test itself has low concurrent validity. The latter conclusion should be drawn only after the first two have been carefully examined and discounted.

STQ115

1 What is the purpose of a criterion in concurrent and predictive validity?
2 Criticise the following criteria:
   a   Ratings by pupils as an index of teaching ability.
   b   Success at university as a criterion of the school-leaving certificate.

Construct validity

A 'construct' is a quality which has been suggested to explain aspects of human behaviour. Thus we find it helpful to use hypothetical constructs such as 'intelligence', 'sensitivity', 'self-concept', etc. to explain behaviour, although we cannot observe the constructs themselves. Some tests are intended to measure such constructs. How, for example, can we be sure that a test of 'sensitivity' is measuring this construct? We cannot specify the content to everyone's satisfaction; we may not intend to use the test for prediction; there may well be no other such test which we can use concurrently with our test.

We must validate our test through a variety of kinds of indirect evidence. For example, the items must be internally consistent, i.e. show good agreement, one with another (i.e. a high alpha coefficient) for if not, they are measuring different qualities. We could collect careful ratings of the construct from teachers and determine how well our test correlated with the ratings. We should expect reasonable correlations with tests measuring in related areas. The techniques of factor analysis would help us decide whether our test was assessing an underlying quality common to all measures and ratings in the area.

The process of construct validation is the same as that by which scientific theories are developed. A researcher will note that previous evidence may suggest that construct X accounts for performance in test Y. They then hypothesise that if that is so, construct X should also influence performance in certain other scales or demonstrate itself in certain observable behaviours. An experiment is performed, deductions are tested. The construct may then be accepted as part of a theory, or a theory may have to be modified.

Thus, by using construct validity in correlating the results of several tests which had not been previously validated, a closer approach to the construct of, say, intelligence and the construction of an intelligence test is made. Of course, in specific instances with only two tests, say, a correlation between the results on the tests, it could simply imply that they were both measuring the same thing to a certain degree but not *what* they were measuring. The inclusion of more and more tests of various types helps us to see that over these many tests the only common element remaining is a general mental ability.

So in designing a test to measure a construct (for example, ego strength, intelligence, neuroticism), we are concerned with all types of evidence which make the interpretation of test scores more meaningful; which help us to understand what the scores signify. Construct validity is an analysis of the meaning of test scores in terms of psychological concepts. Let us take an example. We might attempt to study the construct of social withdrawal. Some persons who rank high on this 'construct' may actually appear unsociable; others may engage in some social activities but reveal and experience more emotional stress in doing so; for example, they may talk very little to others, blush on being talked to. Hence, scores in any test of social withdrawal would not be consistently associated with, or highly correlated with, any single criterion.

However, we might be able to make several hypotheses about ways in which individuals who are socially retiring would differ from those who are not—with respect to types of occupations pursued, leadership or follower roles assumed, symptoms of emotional stress when engaged in social activities, behaviour in experimental situations that allow opportunities to measure suggestibility, initiative in a leaderless group discussion, and other factors presumably related to the construct. When correlations between the test and all these other criteria are analysed by factor analytic techniques one hopes that a major common factor will emerge, which theoretically is the underlying social withdrawal factor.

Evidence of a test's construct validity may be provided by: (a) its correlations with other tests, particularly those which are accepted measures of the same construct; (b) its correlations with other characteristics of the individual, for example attitudes, personality, interests; and (c) its correlations with factors in the individual's environment which would be expected to affect test performance. Insofar as these relationships can be demonstrated, particularly by factor analysis, the construct validity of the test is supported. If such relationships cannot be demonstrated, then one must conclude either that the test is not valid for measuring the construct involved, or that the rationale for predicting the relationships was in some sense faulty. A large common factor revealed by factor analysis can be taken as evidence that performance on a set of measures reflects the proposed hypothetical construct. Thus the tests have construct validity.

Scientifically speaking, construct validity is one of the most significant advances of modern measurement theory and practice. It is a significant advance because it unites psychometric notions with scientifically theoretical notions. Construct validity really gets down to the question of what property is actually being measured.

The significant point about construct validity—that which sets it apart from other types of validity—is its preoccupation with theory, theoretical constructs and scientific empirical inquiry involving the testing of hypothesised relations. Construct validation in measurement contrasts sharply with empiric approaches that define the validity of a measure purely by its success in predicting a criterion. For example, a purely empiric researcher might say that a test is valid if it efficiently distinguishes individuals high and low in a trait. Why the test succeeds in separating the subsets of a group is of no great concern. It is enough that it does.

Face validity

In certain circumstances, one may be concerned with the question, 'Does the test appear, from examination of the items, to measure what one wishes to measure?', or with 'Does the test appear to test what the name of the test implies?'.

This is usually the concern of the lay person who knows little or nothing about measurement, validity or reliability. Researchers often require 'high face validity' for tests or techniques which they use in research programs for industry, the military and schools. However, it is difficult, if not impossible, to measure a validity of this type.

The high face validity will, hopefully, motivate the subjects to tackle the test in a businesslike way. If the naive subjects looked at a test and started thinking that the items were ridiculous and seemed (to them) unrelated to the aim of the tests, then motivation would be considerably reduced. Up to a few years ago, we often chuckled when we read abusive letters in national newspapers from parents asking how on earth some particular (quoted) question could ever measure IQ. Obviously face validity had failed in instances like this, yet the items probably had high construct, predictive and concurrent validity.

Face validity can also serve other functions. When one researches mental illness, it would be better to give a test with low face validity—for example, a projective technique—so that the naive remain naive. Tests must be disguised where faking expected answers or faking bad ones could have serious consequences. Face validity is important in the field of attitude measurement. With attitude scales there may be large differences between *what a scale looks as though it is measuring* (face validity) and *what it is in fact measuring* (explored through concurrent validity with respect to other attitude scales or construct validity). It is possible to hide the true aim of a test or scale and at the same time increase its face validity by including a lot of filler items that are not going to be marked. In this way, a false face validity is created; subjects believe it is measuring one thing when in fact it is measuring another.

Internal and external validity

Some research workers distinguish between internal validity and external validity.

Internal validity is concerned with the question, 'Do the experimental treatments, in fact, make a difference in the specific experiments under scrutiny, or can the differences be ascribed to other factors?'.

External validity, on the other hand, asks the question, 'Given these demonstrable effects, to what populations or settings can they be generalised?'.

STQ116

1 In what research situations might you find it desirable to have low face validity in an assessment instrument?

2 Which one of the following properties of a test would be taken as evidence of its reliability and not its validity?

  a The scores obtained by children on two successive administrations of the test were correlated 0.95.

  b The even-numbered questions on the test were found to yield a substantially higher mean score than the odd-numbered questions.

  c Scores on the test correlated highly with scores on another test designed to measure the same ability.

  d Scores on the test at the beginning of the school year predicted scores on the final examination.

Factors affecting internal validity

History

Often in educational research, events other than the experimental treatments occur during the time between pre-test and post-test observations. Such events produce effects that can mistakenly be attributed to differences in treatment.

Maturation

Between any two observations, subjects change in a variety of ways. Such changes can produce differences that are independent of the experimental treatments. The problem of maturation is more acute in protracted educational studies than in brief laboratory experiments.

Statistical regression

Like maturation effects, regression effects increase systematically with the time interval between pre-tests and post-tests. Statistical regression occurs in educational (and other) research due to the unreliability of measuring instruments and to extraneous factors unique to each experimental group. Regression means, simply, that subjects scoring highest on a pre-test are likely to score relatively lower on a post-test; conversely, those scoring lowest on a pre-test are likely to score relatively higher on a post-test. In a word, in pre-test/post-test situations, there is regression to the mean. Regression effects can lead the educational researcher mistakenly to attribute post-test gains and losses to low scoring and high scoring respectively.

Testing

Pretests at the beginning of experiments can produce effects other than those due to the experimental treatments. Such effects can include sensitising subjects to the true purposes of the experiment and practice effects which produce higher scores on post-test measures.

Instrumentation

Unreliable tests or instruments can introduce serious errors into experiments. With human observers or judges, error can result from changes in their skills and levels of concentration over the course of the experiment.

Selection bias

Bias may be introduced as a result of differences in the selection of subjects for the comparison groups or when intact classes are employed as experimental or control groups. Selection bias, moreover, may interact with other factors (history, maturation, etc.) to cloud even further the effects of the comparative treatments.

Dropout

The loss of subjects through dropout often occurs in long-running experiments and may result in confounding the effects of the experimental variables, for whereas initially the groups may have been randomly selected, the residue that stays the course is likely to be different from the unbiased sample that began it.

Factors affecting external validity

Threats to external validity are likely to limit the degree to which generalisations can be made from the particular experimental conditions to other populations or settings.

Failure to describe independent variables explicitly

Unless independent variables are adequately described by the researcher, future replications of the experimental conditions are virtually impossible.

Lack of representativeness of available and target populations

While those participating in the experiment may be representative of an available population, they may not be representative of the population to which the experimenter seeks to generalise his or her findings.

Hawthorne effect

Medical research has long recognised the psychological effects that arise out of mere participation in drug experiments, and placebos and double-blind designs are commonly employed to counteract the biasing effects of participation. Similarly, so-called Hawthorne effects threaten to contaminate experimental treatments in educational research when subjects realise their role as guinea pigs.

Inadequate operationalising of dependent variables

Dependent variables that the experimenter operationalises must have validity in the non-experimental setting to which the researcher wishes to generalise his or her findings. A paper-and-pencil questionnaire on career choice, for example, may have little validity in respect of the actual employment decisions made by undergraduates on leaving university.

Sensitisation to experimental conditions

As with threats to internal validity, pre-tests may cause changes in the subjects' sensitivity to the experimental variables and thus cloud the true effects of the experimental treatment.

Interaction effects of extraneous factors and experimental treatments

All of the above threats to external validity represent interactions of various factors with treatments. As well as these, interaction effects may also arise as a result of any or all of those factors identified under the section on internal validity above.

By way of summary, an experiment can be said to be internally valid to the extent that within its own confines its results are credible, but for those results to be useful they must be generalisable beyond the confines of the particular experiment, i.e. they must be externally valid also. Without internal validity, an experiment cannot possibly be externally valid. But the converse does not necessarily follow; an internally valid experiment may or may not have external validity. Thus, the most carefully designed experiment involving a sample of English-speaking children is not necessarily generalisable to a target population which includes non-English-speaking subjects.

It follows, then, that the way to good experimentation in schools and classrooms lies in maximising both internal and external validity.

summary

Reliability refers to the stability, accuracy and dependability of data. Methods of measuring reliability include the test–retest, parallel forms, internal consistency and split-half methods. The SE_{meas} interprets the value of a reliability coefficient. Reliability is affected by the length of the test and the objectivity of the scoring.

Validity assesses whether the test measures what it claims to measure. The main types of validity are content, construct, concurrent and predictive validity. Some researchers distinguish between internal validity and external validity.

Reference

Kuder, G. and Richardson, M. (1937), 'The theory of the estimation of test reliability', *Psychometrika* 2, pp. 151–6.

21
twenty one

What is meta-analysis?

Each strand of a rope contributes to the strength of that rope. But the rope is stronger than any individual strand. Similarly, when a particular finding is obtained again and again under a variety of conditions, we are strongly confident that there exists a general principle of behaviour. The results of individual studies, no matter how well conducted, are unlikely to be sufficient to provide us with confident answers to questions of general importance. *Meta-analysis* is a quantitative tool for comparing or combining results across a set of similar studies. In the individual study the unit of analysis is the responses of individual *subjects*. In meta-analysis the unit of analysis is the results of individual *studies*.

The term 'meta-analysis' means an 'analysis of analysis'. Many studies are replicated in various degrees using, for example, differently sized samples, different age ranges, and are conducted in different countries under different environmental conditions. Sometimes results appear to be reasonably consistent; others less so. Meta-analysis enables a rigorous comparison to be made rather than a subjective 'eyeballing'.

In chapter 3 you were introduced to the traditional literature review, a strategy in which you read research relevant to the topic you wish to investigate further, then summarise the findings and integrate the existing knowledge. From this you may conclude that a particular variable is of crucial importance, or that the relationships between particular variables are worthy of note. However, the conclusions you are drawing are essentially subjective, based on your critical evaluation of the literature. You often use a 'voting method' as a crude index of where the balance of results lie. The possibility exists that your subjective conclusion may not accurately reflect the actual strength of the relationship. You can reduce this possibility by adding a meta-analysis to your review. This allows you to compare or combine results from different studies, facilitating statistically guided decisions about the strength of observed effects and the reliability of results across a range of studies. Meta-analysis is a more efficient and effective way to summarise the results of large numbers of studies. A good source of reviews using meta-analysis is the journal, *Review of Educational Research*.

Meta-analytic techniques have been used to answer questions such as:

- Are there gender differences in conformity?
- Is there a relationship between self-concept and academic attainment?
- What are the effects of class size on academic achievement?

A few examples

1 In the first classic meta-analysis study, Smith and Glass (1977) synthesised the results of nearly 400 controlled evaluations of psychotherapy and counselling to determine whether psychotherapy 'works'. They coded and systematically analysed each study for the kind of experimental and control treatments used, and the results obtained. They were able to show that, on average, the typical psychotherapy client was better off than 75 per cent of the untreated 'control' individuals.

2 Rosenthal (1994) used meta-analysis to summarise the results of 345 studies on experimenter effects. Experimenter effects occur when the participants in an experiment respond in ways that correspond to the expectancies of the experimenter. Rosenthal investigated this effect in eight areas in which the effect had been studied (e.g. learning material, person perception, athletic performance), and the mean effect size was .70. This suggests a strong effect size, so we can confidently state that interpersonal expectancies can influence behaviour as a general principle.

3 Horton et al. (1993) performed a meta-analysis on nineteen studies related to concept mapping by secondary school students. The analysis revealed that concept mapping had generally positive effects and raised individual student achievement by 0.46 standard deviations.

Although meta-analysts use a number of more advanced techniques, we will concentrate on some basic techniques that incorporate some fundamental statistical procedures such as 'significance', 'p' and '*r*', discussed earlier in the book, to give you the flavour of what meta-analysis is. Students interested in a more comprehensive and advanced treatment should consult specialised accounts in a number of advanced texts (e.g. Rosenthal 1991).

Conducting a meta-analysis

There are three stages to this:

1 Identify the relevant variables.
2 Locate relevant research.
3 Conduct the meta-analysis.

Step 1 Identify the relevant variables

This sounds easy; however, like defining a hypothesis and determining research questions you must be specific and clear about what your real focus is. You cannot simply say, 'I want to do a meta-analysis of attitude change research'. As Rosenthal (1984) indicates, the unit of analysis in meta-analysis is the impact of variable X on variable Y. So you must limit yourself to conducting an evaluation of a much smaller segment, such as attitude change towards self as a result of Rogerian counselling.

Step 2 Locate the relevant research

This topic will not be discussed here as it has already been dealt with in chapter 3. However, one issue that is vital and potentially serious for the meta-analyst is the *file drawer problem.*

The file drawer problem

Because many journal editors are reluctant to accept 'non-significant' results, researchers' file drawers (or in more modern parlance, their 'C' drives and diskettes) may contain unpublished studies that failed to yield significant results. If there are a substantial number of such studies in the file drawers, the meta-analyst's evaluation of the overall significance level may be unduly optimistic. The problem posed by the file drawer phenomenon is potentially serious for meta-analysis because it results in a biased sample—a sample of only those results published because they produced acceptable statistically significant results. This bias inflates the probability of making a Type II error (concluding that a variable has an effect when it does not). Studies that failed to be published because the investigated variables did not show statistically significant effects are not available to include in the meta-analysis. Because meta-analytic techniques ultimately lead to a decision based on available statistical information, an allowance must be made for the file drawer phenomenon.

There are two ways of dealing with the file drawer problem:

1 First, you can attempt to uncover those studies that never reach print. This can be done by identifying as many researchers as possible in the research area you are covering. You then send each researcher a questionnaire, asking if any unpublished research on the issue of interest exists. This may be impracticable as non-response may be high and identification of researchers difficult.
2 A more practical approach suggested by Rosenthal (1991) involves calculating the number of studies and averaging null results (i.e. that did not reach significance) that would be required to push the significance level for all studies, retrieved and unretrieved combined, to the 'wrong' side of $p = .05$. If the overall significance computed on the basis of the retrieved studies can be brought down to the wrong side of p (i.e. $p > .05$) by the addition of just a few more null results, then the original estimate of p is clearly *not robust* (i.e. not resistant to the file drawer threat).

Table 21.1 illustrates such a calculation. It shows a table of 'tolerance' values in which the rows represent the number of retrieved studies and the columns represent three different levels of the average statistical significance of the retrieved studies. The intersection of any row and column shows the sum of old and new studies required to bring the combined 'p' value for all studies, retrieved and unretrieved combined, down to the level of being just barely 'non-significant' at p > .05. Suppose we meta-analysed eight studies and found the average 'p' value to be .05. The 64 that is shown tells us that it will take an additional 56 unretrieved studies averaging null results to bring the original average p = .05 based on eight studies (i.e. 64 – 8 = 56) down to p > .05.

As a general rule of thumb, it has been suggested that we regard as robust any combined results for which the tolerance level reaches 5k + 10, where k is the number of studies retrieved (Rosenthal 1991). In our example of eight studies retrieved, this means that we will be satisfied that the original estimate of p = .05 is robust if we feel that there are fewer than an additional 5(8) + 10 = 50 studies with null results squirreled away in file drawers. Because Table 21.1 shows a tolerance for an additional 56 studies, it appears to us that the original estimate is indeed robust.

TABLE 21.1 *Tolerances for future null results as a function of the original average level of significance per study and the number of studies summarised*

Number of studies summarised	Original average significance level		
	.05	.01	.001
1	1	2	4
2	4	8	15
3	9	18	32
4	16	32	57
5	25	50	89
6	36	72	128
7	49	98	173
8	64	128	226
9	81	162	286
10	100	200	353
15	225	450	795
20	400	800	1412
25	625	1250	2206
30	900	1800	3177
40	1600	3200	5648
50	2500	5000	8824

Note: Entries in this table are the total number of old and new studies required to bring an original average p of .05, .01, or .001 down to p > .05 (i.e. 'non-significance').

If, however, you determine (based on your analysis) that at least several thousand studies must be in the file drawer before biasing of your results takes place, then you can be reasonably sure that the file drawer phenomenon is not a serious source of bias.

Step 3 Doing the meta-analysis

When you have located relevant literature, collected your data, and are reasonably certain that the file drawer phenomenon isn't an issue, you are ready to apply one of the many available meta-analytic statistical techniques. The heart of meta-analysis is the statistical combination of results across studies. Therefore, as well as recording the methodology, sample, design, hypotheses, conclusions, etc., you must record information, particularly from the results section of research papers you are reviewing, such as r's, t's, chi squares, F's, and p-values. Table 21.2 illustrates meta-analytic techniques that can be applied to the situation where you have two studies.

- The first general technique is that of *comparing studies*. This comparison is made when you want to determine whether two studies produce significantly different effects.
- The second general technique involves *combining studies* to determine the average effect size of a variable across studies.

For each approach, you can evaluate studies by comparing or combining either p-values or effect sizes.

TABLE 21.2 *Meta-analytic techniques for comparing and combining two studies*

Technique	Method/purpose
Comparing studies	*Used to determine if two studies produce significantly different results.*
Significance testing	Record p-values from research and convert them to exact p-values (such as a finding reported at $p < 0.05$ that may actually be $p = 0.036$). Used when information is not available to allow for evaluation of effect sizes.
Effect-size estimation	Record values of inferential statistics (F, t, for example), along with associated degrees of freedom. Estimate effect sizes from these statistics. Preferred over significance testing.
Combining studies	*Used when you want to determine the potency of a variable across studies.*
Significance testing	Can be used after comparing studies to arrive at an overall estimate of the probability of obtaining the two p-values under the null hypothesis.
Effect-size estimation	Can be used after comparing studies to evaluate the average impact across studies of an independent variable on the dependent variable.

Source: Based on Rosenthal (1984).

Comparison of effect sizes of two studies generally is more desirable than simply looking at p-values. This is because effect sizes provide a better estimate of the degree of impact of a variable than does the p-value. (Remember, all the p-value tells you is the likelihood of making a Type I error.) The p-values are used when the information needed to analyse effect sizes is not included in the studies reviewed. Consequently, the following discussion focuses on meta-analytic techniques that look at effect sizes. For simplicity, only the case involving two studies is discussed. The techniques discussed here can be easily modified for the situation where you have three or more studies. For more information, see Rosenthal (1979, 1984), and Mullen and Rosenthal (1985).

Replication and meta-analysis

Table 21.3 illustrates why researchers prefer to work with effect sizes rather than p-values. Set A shows two results, with the p-values both rejecting the null (i.e. both p's = .05), and with a difference in effect sizes of .30 in units of r (i.e. $.50 - .20 = .30$). The fact that both studies were able to reject the null and at exactly the same p-level is a function of sample size, whereas the difference in effect sizes implies the degree of failure to replicate. Set B shows two studies with different p-values, one significant at $p < .05$ and the other not significant; the two effect sizes, on the other hand, are in excellent agreement.

The meta-analyst would say, accordingly, that set B shows more successful replication than does set A. Set C shows two studies differing markedly in both level of significance and magnitude (and direction) of effect size. Observe that one of the effects is reported as a 'negative' r, which tells us that this result was not in the same direction as the other result. Set C, then, is a not very subtle example of a clear failure to replicate. That the combined probabilities of all three sets are identical to one another (combined $p = .0028$) tells us that the pooled significance level is uninformative in differentiating successful from unsuccessful sets of replication studies.

TABLE 21.3 *Comparison of three sets of replications*

	Set A		Set B		Set C	
	Study 1	**Study 2**	**Study 1**	**Study 2**	**Study 1**	**Study 2**
N	96	15	98	27	12	32
p level (two-tailed)	.05	.05	01	.18	.000001	.33
r (effect size index)	.20	50	.26	.26	.72	−.18
Pooled p i.e. combining both studies (one-tailed)	.0028		.0028		.0028	

Comparing studies by effect size

What is effect size?

In chapter 12 we indicated that this is the *degree* to which the phenomenon is present in the population. In meta-analysis, the finding of a study is converted into an effect size estimate. The various ways of estimating effect size such as the standardised mean difference (d), the correlation coefficient (r), and eta^2 are used. You should refer to chapter 12 for the various formulae used to calculate these estimates of effect size.

However, before synthesising the effect sizes of separate studies, the meta-analyst usually finds it instructive to compare the results to discover the degree of their actual similarity. One approach is to define effect size r's as dissimilar if they are significantly different from one another, and to define them as similar if they are not significantly different from one another.

In statistical terms, such significance testing involves:

1 converting the quoted statistic from both studies, e.g. *t* or chi square into *r*'s;
2 giving the *r*'s when calculated the same sign if both studies show effects in the same direction, but different signs if the results are in the opposite direction;
3 finding for each *r* the associated 'Fisher z' value. Fisher's z (i.e. lower case z to differentiate this statistic from the upper case Z denoting the standard normal deviate, or Z score described in chapter 4) refers to a set of log transformations of *r* as shown in Tables 21.4 and 21.5;
4 substituting in the following formula to find the standard normal deviate or Z score:

$$Z = \frac{z_1 - z_2}{\sqrt{\dfrac{1}{N_1 - 3}\dfrac{1}{N_2 - 3}}}$$

TABLE 21.4 *Fisher z transformations of r*

z	.00	.01	.02	.03	.04	.05	.06	.07	.08	.09
.0	.000	.010	.020	.030	.040	.050	.060	.070	.080	.090
.1	.100	.110	.119	.129	.139	.149	.159	.168	.178	.187
.2	.197	.207	.216	.226	.236	.245	.254	.264	.273	.282
.3	.291	.300	.310	.319	.327	.336	.345	.354	.363	.371
.4	.380	.389	.397	.405	.414	.422	.430	.438	.446	.454
.5	.462	.470	.478	.485	.493	.500	.508	.515	.523	.530
.6	.537	.544	.551	.558	.565	.572	.578	.585	.592	.598
.7	.604	.611	.617	.623	.629	.635	.641	.647	.653	.658
.8	.664	.670	.675	.680	.686	.691	.696	.701	.706	.711
.9	.716	.721	.726	.731	.735	.740	.744	.749	.753	.757
1.0	.762	.766	.770	.774	.778	.782	.786	.790	.793	.797
1.1	.800	.804	.808	.811	.814	.818	.821	.824	.828	.831
1.2	.834	.837	.840	.843	.846	.848	.851	.854	.856	.859
1.3	.862	.864	.867	.869	.872	.874	.876	.879	.881	.883
1.4	.885	.888	.890	.892	.894	.896	.898	.900	.902	.903
1.5	.905	.907	.909	.910	.912	.914	.915	.917	.919	.920
1.6	.922	.923	.925	.926	.928	.929	.930	.932	.933	.934
1.7	.935	.937	.938	.939	.940	.941	.942	.944	.945	.946
1.8	.947	.948	.949	.950	.951	.952	.953	.954	.954	.955
1.9	.956	.957	.958	.959	.960	.960	.961	.962	.963	.963
2.0	.964	.965	.965	.966	.967	.967	.968	.969	.969	.970
2.1	.970	.971	.972	.972	.973	.973	.974	.974	.975	.975
2.2	.976	.976	.977	.977	.978	.978	.978	.979	.979	.980
2.3	.980	.980	.981	.981	.982	.982	.982	.983	.983	.983
2.4	.984	.984	.984	.985	.985	.985	.986	.986	.986	.986
2.5	.987	.987	.987	.987	.988	.988	.988	.988	.989	.989
2.6	.989	.989	.989	.990	.990	.990	.990	.990	.991	.991
2.7	.991	.991	.991	.992	.992	.992	.992	.992	.992	.992
2.8	.993	.993	.993	.993	.993	.993	.993	.994	.994	.994
2.9	.994	.994	.994	.994	.994	.995	.995	.995	.995	.995

TABLE 21.5 *Transformations of r to Fisher z*

Second digit of r

r	.00	.01	.02	.03	.04	.05	.06	.07	.08	.09
.0	.000	.010	.020	.030	.040	.050	.060	.070	.080	.090
.1	.100	.110	.121	.131	.141	.151	.161	.172	.182	.192
.2	.203	.213	.224	.234	.245	.255	.266	.277	.288	.299
.3	.310	.321	.332	.343	.354	.365	.377	.388	.400	.412
.4	.424	.436	.448	.460	.472	.485	.497	.510	.523	.536
.5	.549	.563	.576	.590	.604	.618	.633	.648	.662	.678
.6	.693	.709	.725	.741	.758	.775	.793	.811	.829	.848
.7	.867	.887	.908	.929	.950	.973	.996	1.020	1.045	1.071
.8	1.099	1.127	1.157	1.188	1.221	1.256	1.293	1.333	1.376	1.422

Third digit of r

r	.000	.001	.002	.003	.004	.005	.006	.007	.008	.009
.90	1.472	1.478	1.483	1.488	1.494	1.499	1.505	1.510	1.516	1.522
.91	1.528	1.533	1.539	1.545	1.551	1.557	1.564	1.570	1.576	1.583
.92	1.589	1.596	1.602	1.609	1.616	1.623	1.630	1.637	1.644	1.651
.93	1.658	1.666	1.673	1.681	1.689	1.697	1.705	1.713	1.721	1.730
.94	1.738	1.747	1.756	1.764	1.774	1.783	1.792	1.802	1.812	1.822
.95	1.832	1.842	1.853	1.863	1.874	1.886	1.897	1.909	1.921	1.933
.96	1.946	1.959	1.972	1.986	2.000	2.014	2.029	2.044	2.060	2.076
.97	2.092	2.109	2.127	2.146	2.165	2.185	2.205	2.227	2.249	2.273
.98	2.298	2.323	2.351	2.380	2.410	2.443	2.477	2.515	2.555	2.599
.99	2.646	2.700	2.759	2.826	2.903	2.994	3.106	3.250	3.453	3.800

EXAMPLE

Here is an example comparing two studies.

Imagine you are interested in comparing two experiments that investigated the impact of the credibility of a communicator on persuasion for similarity of effect size, to determine whether it is worthwhile combining them. In the results sections of the two studies, you found the following information concerning the effect of credibility on persuasion:

Study 1: $t = 2.57$, $p < 0.01$, N = 22;

Study 2: $t = 2.21$, $p < 0.05$, N = 42.

The first thing you must do is to determine the size of the effect of communicator credibility in both studies. Unfortunately, neither study provides that information (you will rarely find such information). Consequently, you must estimate the effect size based on the available statistical information which is t. Using the formula for t (see p. 170) gives the following results when converted into r. The formula is:

$$r = \sqrt{\frac{t^2}{t^2 + df}}$$

Study 1: $r = \sqrt{6.59/(6.59 + 20)} = 0.50$

Study 2: $r = \sqrt{4.89/(4.89 + 40)} = 0.33$

The next step in the analysis is to convert the *r*-values into Fisher z-scores. This is necessary because the distribution of *r* becomes skewed as the population value of *r* deviates from zero. Converting *r* to z corrects for this skew (Rosenthal 1984). Table 21.5 shows that for the *r*-values calculated above, the z-values are 0.55 and 0.34, respectively.

When you have found the respective z-scores, you test for the difference between the two Fisher z scores with the following formula:

$$Z = \frac{z_1 - z_2}{\sqrt{\dfrac{1}{N_1 - 3} \ \dfrac{1}{N_2 - 3}}}$$

In this example, you have:

$$Z = \frac{0.55 - 0.34}{\sqrt{\dfrac{1}{19} - \dfrac{1}{39}}} = \frac{0.21}{0.279} = 0.75$$

This Z score (standard deviate) of 0.75 is then evaluated for statistical significance by using a table of areas under the normal curve (see Table 5.1). As it turns out, 0.75 is not significant beyond $p < .05$. Consequently, you would conclude that the effect sizes produced by the two evaluated studies do not differ significantly. They are therefore good candidates for combining. Had a significant difference been obtained, you would conclude that one study produced a significantly larger effect than the other study.

Here is another example. The effect size estimates using *r* for studies A and B are 0.7 (N = 20) and 0.5 (N = 80). First, convert each *r* into the associated Fisher's z, using Table 21.5, giving $z_1 = 0.867$ and $z_2 = 0.549$.

Next compute:

$$Z = \frac{z_1 - z_2}{\sqrt{\dfrac{1}{N - 3} \ \dfrac{1}{N - 3}}}$$

= 1.19, its p-value is .117 (one-tailed) or .234 (two-tailed).

The effect size estimates do not differ significantly; the two studies show significant relationships between variables X and Y and they also agree in their estimates of the size of the relationship.

If you do find a significant difference between effect sizes, you should investigate why the difference exists. You might look at the methods, materials, sample sizes and procedures used in each study, as any or all of these may differ considerably between the studies and may be likely causes of the different effects.

STQ117*

Suppose you have used 100 subjects to try to replicate an experiment that reported a large effect ($r = .50$) based on only ten subjects. You find a smaller sized effect in your study ($r = -.31$), but it is in the opposite direction of the one previously reported.

a   Do you code your effect as negative or positive?
b   From Table 21.4 what are the Fisher z's corresponding to each *r*?
c   Compute Z and find the associated p-value.
d   What is your conclusion about the merits of combining these two studies.

Answers on p. 605.

STQ118*

Alternatively, suppose your result is in the same direction as the original one and of a similar magnitude, and you have used the same number of subjects. This time, imagine that the original effect size was $r = .45$ (N = 120), and your effect size is $r = .40$ (N = 120). Following the same procedure as above, find:

a   the corresponding Fisher z's;
b   Z; and
c   p.
d   Now comment on your findings.

Answers on p. 606.

Combining studies by effect size

Given two effect sizes that are not significantly different and therefore combinable on statistical and/or logical grounds. You may want to determine the average size of an effect across studies. The formula to be used again employs the Fisher z transformation (Rosenthal 1984):

$$\text{Mean z or } z_m = \frac{z_1 - z_2}{2}$$

in which the denominator is the number of Fisher z scores in the numerator; the resulting value is an average (or z_m).

The first step to take when combining the effect sizes of two studies is to calculate r for each and convert each r-value into corresponding z-scores. Using the data from the example used above to demonstrate comparing studies, we already have z values of 0.55 and 0.34.

$$z_m = \frac{(0.55 + 0.34)}{2} = 0.45$$

This z is reconverted back to an r using Table 21.4. The r-value associated with this average Fisher z is 0.42. Hence, you now know that the average effect size across these two studies is 0.42.

Here is another example. Given effect size estimates of $r = .7$ (N = 20) for study A and $r = .5$ (N = 80) for study B, find a combined estimate of the effect size.

We first convert each r into z scores and then substitute into the formula. This gives

$$z_m = \frac{(0.867 + 0.549)}{2} = .708$$

This average Fisher z converts back to a combined effect of $r = 0.65$. This is larger than the mean of the two r's.

Remember, always compare the studies before combining them. If the effect sizes of the two studies are statistically different, it makes little sense to average their effect sizes.

Obviously, if the results from the studies are in opposite directions (for example, one study shows a positive effect of the independent variable, while the second shows a negative effect), combining should never be considered.

Unfortunately, there is no established criterion to judge whether or not the combined effect size is significant or, for that matter, important.

STQ119*

Given two studies, with effect sizes $r = .45$ and $r = .40$ (both coded as 'positive' to show that both results were in the predicted direction),
a   find Fisher z's for each;
b   compute mean z;
c   find combined effect size.

Answers on p. 606.

Comparing studies by significance levels

While meta-analysts are usually more interested in effect sizes (usually r's as we have seen) than in p-values, they sometimes evaluate the overall level of significance as a way of increasing power. It is again instructive to find out whether the individual values are homogeneous (i.e. telling the same story) and therefore combinable. To make such a comparison, the meta-analyst first obtains an accurate p-level—accurate, say, to two digits (not counting zeros before the first non-zero value)—such as p = .43 or .024 or .0012. Tables of the t distribution, such as the one on p. 178, are needed.

For each p, the meta-analyst then finds Z (i.e. not the Fisher z, but the standard normal deviate Z) using the table of Z (p. 73). Both p's should also be one-tailed, and we give the corresponding Z's the same sign if both studies showed effects in the same direction, but different signs if the results are in the opposite direction. The difference between the two Z's when divided by $\sqrt{2}$ yields a new Z. This new Z corresponds to the p-value of the difference between the Z's if the null hypothesis were true (i.e. if the two Z's did not really differ).

Recapping,

$$Z = \frac{Z_1 - Z_2}{\sqrt{2}}$$

is distributed as Z, so we can enter this newly calculated Z into a table of standard normal deviates (p) to find the p-value associated with a Z of the size obtained or larger.

EXAMPLE

Suppose that studies A and B yield results in opposite directions, and neither is 'significant.' One p is .075 one-tailed, and the other p is .109 one-tailed but in the opposite tail. The Z's corresponding to these p's are found in Table 5.1 (p. 73) to be +1.44 and −1.23 (note the opposite signs which indicate results in opposite directions). Then, from our equation we have:

$$Z = Z_1 - Z_2 = 1.44(-1.23) = \frac{2.67}{1.41} = .189$$

as the Z of the difference between the two p-values or their corresponding Z's. The p-value associated with a Z of 1.89 is .0294 one-tailed (rounded to .03). The two p-values may thus be seen to differ significantly (or nearly so, if we used the two-tailed p of .0294 × 2 = .0588), suggesting that the results in terms of the p-values of the two studies are heterogeneous, even when we allow for normal sampling fluctuations. Thus the p-levels should not be combined without special thought and comment.

Here is another example. Imagine the p-values (one-tailed) for studies A and B are: p = .02 (significant) and p = .07 (not significant). Compute new Z as:

$$Z = \frac{Z_1 - Z_2}{\sqrt{2}} = \frac{2.06 - 1.48}{1.41} = 0.41$$

Its p-value is .341 (one-tailed) or .682 (two-tailed).

Hence, the difference between these two studies (one significant, the other not significant) is not significant.

Combining studies by significance levels

After we compare the results of two separate studies, it is an easy matter to combine the p-levels. In this way, we get an overall estimate of the probability that the two p-levels might have been obtained if the null hypothesis of no relation between X and Y were true. To perform these calculations, we modify the numerator of the formula for comparing p-values that we just described. We obtain accurate p-levels for each of our two studies, and then find the Z corresponding to each of these p-levels. Also as before, both p's must be given in one-tailed form, and the corresponding Z's will have the same sign if both studies show effects in the same direction, and will have different signs if the results are in the opposite direction.

The only change from the previous equation is to add the Z values instead of subtracting them:

$$Z = \frac{Z_1 + Z_2}{\sqrt{2}}$$

That is, the sum of the two Z's divided by the square root of 2 yields a new Z. This new Z corresponds to the p-value of the two studies combined if the null hypothesis of no relation between X and Y were true.

Suppose studies A and B yield homogeneous results in the same direction but neither is significant. One p is .121, and the other is .084; their associated Z's are 1.17 and 1.38, respectively. From the preceding equation we have:

$$Z = \frac{Z_1 + Z_2}{\sqrt{2}} = \frac{1.17 + 1.38}{\sqrt{2}} = \frac{2.55}{1.41} = 1.81$$

as our combined Z. The p associated with this Z is .035 one-tailed (or .07 two-tailed). This is significant one-tailed even though the original p's were not.

As another example, imagine p-values (one-tailed) for studies A and B are p = .02 (significant), p = .07 (not significant).

The two p-values can be combined to obtain an estimate of the probability that the two p-values might have been obtained if the null hypothesis of no relation between X and Y were true.

$$Z = \frac{Z_1 + Z_2}{\sqrt{2}} = \frac{2.06 + 1.48}{1.41} = 2.51$$

Its p-value is .006 (one-tailed) or .012 (two-tailed). This combined p-value is significant; it supports the significant study A.

Summary of general procedures for meta-analysis

Table 21.6 summarises the procedures and problems.

TABLE 21.6

Step	Procedure	Caution
Identify and collect studies.	Define the criteria used to include or exclude studies. Describe how the search is conducted and the studies collected. Search for unpublished studies to test for Type I error publication bias.	Tendency to include studies not very similar; mixing 'apples' and 'oranges'. Time consuming to locate unpublished studies. May have included studies of poor quality. Stronger effects are found in journal articles than in theses; unpublished studies tend to be non-significant—sampling bias.
Quantify criteria.	Convert reported results to common metrics for meta-analysis, e.g. effect size, t, r, p.	Over-emphasis on a single value, i.e. effect size. A wide variety of effect size estimates and corrections. Effect size estimates not directly comparable among some studies due to arbitrary scales used.

TABLE 21.6 *Continued*

Step	Procedure	Caution
Code characteristics of studies—the crucial aspect.	Code substantive characteristics, e.g. nature of sample, types of instruction, classification of outcomes using theory. Code methodology characteristics, e.g. dropout rate, design used, source of studies, date of study. Check validity and reliability of coding.	No systematic or logical procedure to build coding. Consult the literature and others with respect to the coding used.
Analyse data.	Average effect sizes. Estimate variation in effect sizes. Divide studies into subgroups and test for homogeneity.	Calculate parametric and non-parametric estimates, if possible.
Discuss results.	Describe limitations of review. Provide guidelines for future research.	

Comparing and combining more than two effect sizes and significance levels

Although the discussion in this chapter has focused on comparing or combining only two studies, you will probably want to compare more than two studies. Fortunately, meta-analytic techniques are available that follow the logic developed. Multiple studies can either be combined or contrasted with significance testing or effect-size estimation, as is the case with two studies.

The mathematical formulas used to meta-analyse several studies are a bit more complex than those used in the two-study case. However, the general logic applied to the two-study case applies to the multi-study case. The formulas for comparing and combining more than two studies can be found in Rosenthal (1984). Additionally, Mullen and Rosenthal (1985) provide several computer programs that do most of the tedious calculations needed to perform such meta-analyses. Another useful computer program is DSTAT (Blair Johnson, Syracuse University, published by Lawrence Erlbaum, New Jersey, ISBN 1 56321 137 8).

Some issues in meta-analysis

Meta-analysis can be a powerful tool for evaluating results across studies. Even though many researchers have embraced the concept of meta-analysis, others question its usefulness on several grounds. This section explores some of the drawbacks to meta-analysis, and presents some of the solutions suggested to overcome those drawbacks.

Assessing the quality of the research reviewed

Not all journals are created equal. The quality of the research found in a journal depends on its editorial policy. Some journals have more rigorous publication standards than others. This means that the quality of published research may vary considerably from journal to journal.

One problem facing the meta-analyst is how to deal with this uneven research quality. For example, should an article published in a non-refereed journal be given as much consideration as an article published in a well-regarded reputable refereed journal? There is no simple answer.

While Rosenthal has suggested weighting articles according to quality, on what bases should they be weighted? The refereed/non-refereed dimension is one possibility. However, simply because an article was not refereed is not a reliable indicator of the quality of that piece of research. Research in a new area, using new methods, is sometimes rejected from refereed journals even though it is methodologically sound and of high quality. Conversely, publication in a refereed journal is no guarantee that the research is of high quality.

A second dimension along which research could be weighted is according to the soundness of methodology, regardless of journal quality. Several experts could rate each study for its quality (perhaps on a zero to ten scale). The ratings would then be checked for inter-rater reliability and used to weight the degree of contribution of each study to the meta-analysis.

Combining/comparing studies using different methods

A frequent criticism of meta-analysis is that it is difficult to understand how studies with widely varying materials, measures, and methods can be compared. This is commonly referred to as the 'apples versus oranges argument'.

Although common, this criticism of meta-analysis is not valid. Comparing results from different studies is no different than averaging across heterogenous subjects in an ordinary study. If you are willing to accept averaging across subjects, you should also be willing to accept averaging across heterogenous studies.

The core issue is not whether averaging should be done across heterogenous studies, but rather whether or not differing methods are related to different effect sizes. If methodological differences appear to be related to the outcome of research, studies in a meta-analysis could be grouped by methodology to determine its effects.

Practical problems

The task facing a meta-analyst is a formidable one. Not only may studies on the same issue use widely different methods and statistical techniques, some studies may not provide the necessary information to conduct a meta-analysis and have to be eliminated. The problem of insufficient or imprecise information (along with the file drawer problem) may result in a non-representative sample of research being included in a meta-analysis. Admittedly, the bias may be small, but it may nevertheless exist.

Do the results of meta-analysis differ from those of traditional reviews?

A valid question is whether or not traditional literature reviews produce results that differ qualitatively from those of a meta-analysis. To answer this question, Cooper and Rosenthal (1982) directly compared the two methods. Graduate students and professors were randomly assigned to conduct either a meta-analysis or a traditional review of seven articles dealing with the impact of the sex of subject on persistence in a task. Two of the studies showed that females were more persistent than males, whereas the other five either presented no statistical data or showed no significant effect.

The results of this study showed that subjects using the meta-analysis were more likely to conclude that there was an effect of sex on persistence than were subjects using the traditional method. Additionally, subjects doing the traditional review believed that the effect of sex on persistence was smaller than did subjects doing the meta-analysis. Overall, 68 per cent of the meta-analysts were prepared to conclude that sex had an effect on persistence, whereas only 27 per cent of subjects using the traditional method were so inclined. In statistical terms, the meta-analysts were more willing than the traditional reviewers to reject the null hypothesis that sex had no effect. It may be, then, that using meta-analysis to evaluate research will lead to a reduction in Type II decision errors.

summary

Meta-analysis is a quantitative tool for comparing or combining results across a set of similar studies, facilitating statistically guided decisions about the strength of observed effects and the reliability of results across a range of studies. Meta-analysis is a more efficient and effective way to summarise the results of large numbers of studies.

- The first general technique is that of *comparing studies*. This comparison is made when you want to determine whether two studies produce significantly different effects.
- The second general technique involves *combining studies* to determine the average effect size of a variable across studies.

For each approach, you can evaluate studies by comparing or combining either p-values or effect sizes.

The problem posed by the file drawer phenomenon is potentially serious for meta-analysis because it results in a biased sample—a sample of only those results published because they produced acceptable statistically significant results. But even published research may be of uneven quality.

References and further reading

Cooper, H. & Rosenthal, R. (1982), 'Statistical versus traditional methods for summarising research findings', *Psychological Bulletin*, 87, pp. 442–9.

Horton, P., McConney, A., Woods, M. & Hamelin, D. (1993), 'An investigation of the effectiveness of concept mapping as an instructional tool', *Science Education*, 77, pp. 95–111.

part 2 | quantitative methods

Mullen, B. & Rosenthal, R. (1985), *Basic meta-analysis,* Laurence Erlbaum, Hillsdale.

Roberts, J. (1985), 'The attitude memory relationship: A meta analysis of the literature', *Basic and Applied Social Psychology,* 6, pp. 221–42.

Rosenthal, R. (1979), 'The file drawer problem', *Psychological Bulletin,* 86, pp. 638–41.

Rosenthal, R. (1984), 'Meta analytic procedures for social research', *Applied Social Science Research Methods,* vol. 6, Sage, Beverly Hills.

Rosenthal, R. (1991), *Meta-analytic Procedures for Social Research,* Sage, Newbury Park.

Rosenthal, R. (1994), 'Interpersonal expectancy effects. A 30 year perspective', *Current Directions in Psychological Science,* 3, pp. 176–9.

Smith, M. & Glass, G. (1977), 'Meta-analysis of psychotherapy outcome studies', *American Psychologist,* 32, pp. 752–60.

The experimental research report

22

twenty two

There is an art in writing an experimental report, and you will find that it becomes easier with practice. Research work must be written up systematically and with great care, so that the reader is not faced with the prospect of having to sort out ambiguities or misunderstandings. You must be prepared to write up a report a couple of times at least before you are satisfied that there is no room for improvement. Researchers who are experts in writing up their results often have to make several drafts before writing up the final report. Extremely valuable and interesting practical work may be spoiled at the last minute by a student who is not able to communicate the results easily. The report should be written in an impersonal third person style, with a minimum of rhetorical excess. Scientific writing is a stripped-down cool style that avoids ornamentation.

- **You must write in an accepted style.** Most universities and journal editors will provide a style manual which details the organisation, presentation, format and language to be used. It will pay to examine some previous studies printed in the journal in which you wish to publish, or some successful theses/dissertations at your university. Your material will be subject to the same format and style requirements.

- **It is essential to write clearly and precisely in presenting your material.** You should avoid jargon and assume that your readers will have a general understanding of, and familiarity with, basic statistical concepts such as standard deviation and the normal distribution curve. These concepts need not be explained. The entire report should have a coherent structure with an orderly progression in the presentation of ideas, data and arguments.

- **Always acknowledge the work of others.** If you quote from another person's work present the passage within quotation marks with a reference at the end of the quotation. Don't try to pass off the work of others as your own; this is plagiarism. You need to cite other authors in the text by placing the date of publication after their name, e.g., 'In a follow up study, Jones (1993) found . . .'. You can also include the name and date in parentheses at the end of a sentence if the name is not part of the narrative, e.g. 'Students from single parent families had significantly lower self-concepts (Smith 1994)'. The name and date can then be looked up in the references, where full details of the texts referred to are given. Where there are two authors, join their names with 'and'. Where there are three or more use 'and' on the first occasion; on subsequent occasions cite only the first author followed by the abbreviation 'et al.', e.g. Jones, Smith and Wilson become 'Jones et al.'.

- **Avoid sexist language** by rephrasing sentences, e.g. change 'the teacher completed her questionnaire...' to 'the teacher completed the questionnaire...'. 'He' and 'she' can often be replaced by 'they'.

- **Begin writing up data as soon as possible.** Do not wait until all the data have been collected and all analyses have been completed before commencing to draft the first sections of your thesis/paper. If you leave it all to the end you may find difficulty in meeting deadlines. The Introduction and Methodology sections can certainly be drafted while data collection is under way, as these include your review of the literature, theory and previous research, the statement of the problem, the hypotheses, the sample, design and any other matters that must have been dealt with before data collection commenced. Your original research proposal could provide a basis for the introduction as it should contain a detailed statement of the problem and hypotheses. This could be extended with a fuller literature review. From your computer search of the literature you can also start organising your bibliography.

  The time factor is important. Writing up experiments cannot be rushed without doing an injustice to the results and conclusions of these experiments. Unless enough time is devoted to the writing up, serious errors can be made. The purpose of writing up one's findings is to enable others to understand clearly what you have done; to replicate the work if they are interested or to modify aspects of it. Each part of the experiment should be reported carefully and accurately. Most research articles in the behavioural sciences are organised in essentially the same way; so too are theses and dissertations although most aspects of the research is covered in greater detail than in an article. The usual format is based on the *Publication Manual* of the American Psychological Association and is used in most journals in education and psychology.

  The following sequence is recommended as being one which students find easy to use and which sets out the stages of the report in a logical fashion.

Title

Here is an example of a point referred to above about rewriting aspects of the report. The title should be as short as possible but it should retain meaning. You may have to make several attempts at writing down the title until you are satisfied with it. The title should reflect the main idea, topic or theme of the experiment. It should be brief but succinct (12–15 words at the most), providing sufficient specific description so that a potential reader will have a good idea of what the study is concerned with. The study might be a comparison of achievement between a group of students undertaking face to face teaching with a matched group who are studying the same course through distance education. The novice might, at their first attempt, entitle this:

'An investigation of the comparative effects on achievement of normal classroom teaching versus distance education in a matched group of first year university students studying a unit in human biology.'

This is bit of a mouthful and the researcher will realise this. Gradual refinement should lead to a title similar to the following:

'Classroom teaching versus distance education in a first year university biology unit.'

Similarly a draft title,

'The effects of lunchtime involvement in exercise on the stress levels of teachers in secondary schools in inner city areas.'

might be just as clear and yet less of a mouthful if rewritten:

'Exercise and stress levels in inner city secondary school teachers.'

STQ121

Rewrite the following titles so that they are succinct yet informative.

a   A study investigating the relationship between selected socioeconomic factors among 7-year-old and 10-year-old boys and girls and their attitudes towards certain aspects of their schooling.

b   A pilot study of the effectiveness of individual versus group counselling on the self-concepts of forty high school students selected on the basis of suffering physical and emotional child abuse during their primary school years.

c   An investigation to test the hypothesis that 10-year-old girls are significantly better at reading but significantly poorer at mathematics than 10-year-old boys.

Summary

In printed research papers, this may be referred to as the abstract, and it may appear at the beginning or end of the paper. For our purposes, it seems sensible to call it the summary, as this acts as a reminder to us that its purpose is to present an overview of the design, contents and results of the experiment. Another reason for placing the summary early in the write-up is to enable the reader to determine whether or not it is worthwhile ploughing through the whole report.

As with the title, *brevity* is the key word. The summary should be as short as possible and should contain only one paragraph. Essentially, it should refer to the hypothesis, the experimental design, the results and the most significant findings, all concisely reported. Clearly the summary cannot be written until all the other parts of the report have been completed.

Introduction

This is best started with a general statement of the problem which enables the reader to gain an appreciation of the issue, its importance, pertinence, and its place within the ambit of education. A brief review of research findings and theories related to the topic follows. This is to provide an understanding of previous work that has been done and a context into which the current study fits. If you have conducted a computer review of the pertinent literature the printout should provide the basis for a chronological or topic order of the review. Some researchers put a summary of each study reviewed on their word processor as they progress with their reading. This offers a basis for the writing of this section.

However, you should not simply regurgitate the summary of each reviewed study, but attempt to synthesise and analyse the material, distilling the essential themes, issues, methodologies, discrepancies, consistencies and conclusions, as well as the specific results and conclusions of particular studies where appropriate. The aim is a clear, unified and thorough picture of the status of research in the area and not a boring, stereotyped sequential presentation of all the separate summaries of each study taken from the indexes and abstracts consulted like a furniture sale catalogue commencing with 'Professor X (19YY) discovered that . . . and Dr Smith (19ZZ) found that . . . '. There are of course some significant and seminal studies that should be reviewed individually. The process of combining and interpreting the literature is more difficult than simply reviewing. You should also avoid an excessive use of quotations. Any quotation used should be a significant one that bears a relationship to what you propose to investigate in your study.

Out of this review of the literature, and linked to the original problem, there should emerge a statement of the hypothesis to be tested. This could be followed by a definition of terms and concepts to be used in the study. It is imperative to know what is meant, for example, by such terms as 'disadvantaged student', 'holistic education', 'aggressive behaviour' or 'creativity', as these can be deployed with a variety of meanings by different authors. The hypothesis should stem out of the matrix of knowledge and interpretation already presented. It should be succinct, be consistent with known facts and be testable.

After reading the introduction, a reader should understand why you decided to undertake the research, how you decided to set about doing it and what your hypothesis is. This is a general to specific organisation, as indicated below:

- General introduction to topic.
- Literature review.
- Link literature review to your topic.
- State your hypotheses.

Methodology

Subjects

Here you must indicate who took part and how many subjects there were. You may find it necessary to give a little more information about them if you think it could be relevant to the progress of the experiment and the subsequent results. For instance, the age range of your subjects could be important, and in certain types of experiments (e.g. interpersonal attraction), the sex of the subjects could be most influential. The same applies to the experimenter(s)—is their age important, or their sex? Is the experimenter known to the subjects, and could this be relevant?

One final, extremely significant piece of information should be given about the subjects, i.e. how were they obtained? Were they enlisted because they were friends? Were they 'captive' and somewhat unwilling subjects? Were they chosen 'because they were there'? In other words, did your subjects constitute an opportunity sample, or did you have the good fortune to be able to take a random sample ? Do you remember what we said in chapter 6 about sampling and being able to generalise our results to the population from which the sample was taken? This kind of information needs to be included at this point. Providing this information enables another researcher to replicate the study. In fact, the whole of the method section should be written with this purpose in mind.

Test instruments/apparatus/materials

Details of all tests should be given, including name, source, reliability and validity data. If the tests are self-created, evidence of reliability and validity from pilot studies is needed.

If you construct equipment or manufacture material specifically for your experiment, then it is essential that you describe it in some detail. When you have done this, read over what you have written and ask yourself whether another person, unfamiliar with your work, would be able to reconstruct your equipment or material.

A photograph, or photographs, of new equipment will be welcomed by a reader who is unacquainted with your work, and examples of your actual material should be appended to the report where possible. For example, to refer to a list of anagrams without specifying their length, their difficulty or even their number is singularly unhelpful. Moreover, if material is available in the report, you will have little difficulty describing your work and discussing it.

Design

Some researchers would regard this as being the most important section in the report. Since, in theory, the purpose of writing a report is to enable others to replicate your work, great care must be taken in describing your design clearly, concisely and logically. You will need to furnish information as to how each stage of the experiment was conducted. Once again, we must emphasise that this will demand much patience on your part, and you must be prepared to rewrite the section several times before producing an acceptable version.

You will need to state which experimental design you used, and it is a good idea to say briefly why you used it. Remember that your choice of design dictates the statistical procedure you will later apply to your results. Having described your apparatus and equipment in the previous section, you must now explain how it was used, mentioning the number of trials per subject, the rate of presentation of material, the instructions given to the subjects, etc. Since the instructions to subjects are so important, they could be set out *en bloc* and/or underlined, or even printed on a separate sheet and inserted at a suitable place in the report.

Results obtained in experiments can sometimes be affected by unacceptable conditions, and their authenticity is thereby either enhanced or diminished accordingly. Spurious results lead to incorrect conclusions, in spite of the fact that great care may have been taken in choosing subjects, selecting the most appropriate experimental design, and applying the correct statistical procedure. Results obtained under one set of conditions may not be faulty in a particular instance, but may be faulty when produced under different conditions.

Learning lists of words in a memory experiment could quite easily be affected by the time of day and the room in which the experiment was conducted. For example, subjects might be more alert in the morning than in the afternoon, or the room in which they undergo the memory task may be next to a workshop where lathes are turning.

It is therefore essential that you give a detailed description of the conditions which operated at the time of your experiment, but only those conditions which were relevant to the outcome of the experiment need to be stressed. You may need to refer to environmental conditions such as place, time of day, room temperature, etc. if you think these could be important factors. Subject variables, such as fatigue and cooperativeness, may also deserve some mention.

Data analysis

This describes the statistical analyses undertaken. If they are commonly known—e.g. chi square, independent *t* test—then the tests only need to be named. Unusual approaches should be detailed. The significance level to be accepted should be stated.

Results

Clarity! This is the key word in this section. Sound studies which have produced excellent results are often spoiled at this stage simply because students either do not know the best way to present their results, or do not pay sufficient attention to their presentation. The major failing seems to be in trying to present too much information at once; graphs become confusing and tables are difficult to interpret simply because the student has tried to convey too many results in one display. Present your results clearly, simply and neatly. Your results should be presented in tables or other diagrams which have appropriate, meaningful, short headings. Short comments on the results are permissible, such as, 'Introverts scored significantly higher than extroverts on this scale', but do try to avoid detailed and penetrating comments which are better placed in the 'Discussion' section.

The best way to structure the results section is in terms of the hypotheses which the study has set out to test. Hypothesis One would be the first heading, Hypothesis Two, the second, and so on. (Such subdivisions would not be necessary, of course, in a study with only a single hypothesis.) Each heading would then be followed by a brief restatement of the hypothesis, a reference to an appropriate table or graph, and a descriptive statement of the outcome in testing the hypothesis, i.e. F ratios, *t* values, correlations, means, or whatever statistic was used. The description of statistical outcomes would parallel the table in which these data are found. Significance levels should be quoted and a brief statement (one sentence) should be offered to say whether the results were significant, and whether the null and alternative hypotheses were supported or rejected.

Discussion

Instead of moving from the general to the specific, as we did in the introduction, we move from the specific to the general in the discussion.

Restate major hypotheses and findings

Tie results into previous research and theory

Broad implications; methodological implications;
directions for future research

The purpose of this section is to enable you to assess your results and draw sensible conclusions from them. It is quite common to find students who have painstakingly undertaken an interesting experiment, produced a set of results, and applied appropriate statistical procedures, yet are incapable of explaining their significance. What do the results mean in terms of your hypothesis? What implications or inferences can be made from your results? Are you able to summarise your conclusions, perhaps suggesting ideas from your experiment which could be developed by another person?

Do not be afraid to mention any failings in your experimental design, your sampling difficulties, or your procedure. The discussion section has a frame of references—the introductory section. The points raised in the introduction must be responded to in the discussion. But within this frame of reference, the writer is free to use whatever art and imagination they can to show the range and depth of significance of their study. The discussion section ties the results of the study to both theory and application by pulling together the theoretical background, literature reviews, potential significance for application, and results of the study.

Conclude this section by summarising the major conclusions and results of the experiment, and restate the hypothesis in its original wording, pointing out whether or not it was supported.

References

You must record all the references you have mentioned in your experiment, but no others. Accuracy is important, as other people may wish to follow up your work by reading some of the references in the library, and much time can be wasted if a librarian has to search for a non-existent manuscript, or one which is contained in an entirely different journal. References are written in a standard format. They appear in alphabetical order according to the name of the author. When a reference is made to the title of a book, you should underline the title, but when you refer to an article in a journal it is the name of the journal which is underlined. The parts which you underline would appear in italics in a printed experimental report. The following are examples of the format:

Hunter, I.M.L. (1966). *Memory*, Penguin: Harmondsworth.
Bower, G.I. (1970). 'Organisational factors in memory.' *Cognitive Psychology*, 1, 18–41.

Within the text, any reference appears as the author's surname and year of publication. This model for writing an experimental report is, of course, only one particular model.

But whatever model or pattern you use, the basic criterion is that it should provide a logical sequence, concisely expressed, enabling another interested person to understand what has been done, why, and with what results.

Checklist for writing an experimental research report

- **Title** Is it sufficiently brief, yet able to provide a clear indication of the content?

- **Abstract/Summary** Does it convey a brief essential impression of the research in less than 200 words, covering aims, subjects, variables, design, and conclusions?

- **Introduction** The introduction should contain brief overview of issues and concepts to place research in its context. Aim(s) and hypotheses should be stated clearly in a predictive form.

- **Method** Give enough detail to enable readers to repeat the study as you did it.

- **Design** Detail the variables, the design form, the statistics employed, the subjects, materials/tests, procedures/instructions.

- **Results** Verbal description of results plus summary tables clearly titled and labelled (raw data in appendix if necessary) are essential with significance levels stated and statements about rejection or support for null hypotheses.

- **Discussion** Relate results to hypotheses, background theory and previous research. Note and explain, if possible, unexpected results. Suggest modifications and future directions for the research area. Discuss limitations.

- **References** List all studies referred to using standard format.

Further reading

American Psychological Association (1993), *Publication Manual*, 4th edn, APA, Washington DC.
Campbell, W., Ballou, S. & Slade, C. (1986), *Form and Style: Theses, Reports and Term Papers*, 7th edn, Houghton Mifflin, New York.
Light, R.J. & Pilliner, D.B. (1984), *Summing Up: The Science of Reviewing Research*, Harvard University Press, Cambridge.
Mauch, J.E. & Birch, J.W. (1983), *Guide to the Successful Thesis and Dissertation*, Dekker, New York.

PART 3
QUALITATIVE METHODS

The purists assert that qualitative and quantitative methods are based in paradigms that make different assumptions about the social world, about how science should be conducted, and what constitutes legitimate problems, solutions, and criteria of 'proof'.

So far, we have been considering a pervasive, scientific mode of inquiry—a mode characterised by objectivity, reliability and prediction. The assumption that 'truth' and 'knowledge' are fixed and singular entities has predisposed research towards numerical quantification procedures and technical controls, generally statistically oriented.

During the late 1960s and throughout the decade of the 1970s, a new critical form of inquiry began to emerge. A more diffuse recognition of the implicit relationship between knowledge and human interests led to the advocacy of an alternative, more humanistic, investigative paradigm. This paradigm is based on the concept of *verstehen*, a form of subjective understanding.

In current research, movements towards humanness are based on a recognition of the need for critical inquiry and meaning in educational action. The traditional emphasis on 'factual' knowledge and singular truths has become obsolete as the avenues for knowledge generation and cultural interchange increase. The qualitative researcher attempts to gather evidence that will reveal qualities of life, reflecting the 'multiple realities' of specific educational settings from participants' perspectives.

Social reality

Qualitative researchers believe that since humans are conscious of their own behaviour, the thoughts, feelings and perceptions of their informants are vital. How people attach meaning and what meanings they attach are the bases of their behaviour. Only qualitative methods, such as participant observation and unstructured interviewing, permit access to individual meaning in the context of ongoing daily life. The qualitative researcher is not concerned with objective truth, but rather with the truth as the informant perceives it. If a student believes a teacher dislikes him or her, then every act of that teacher towards the student will be interpreted by the latter in terms of that belief. This information is necessary in order to fully understand the behaviour of the student towards the teacher. In an objective sense, only a disruptive student is seen.

Social reality is the product of meaningful social interaction as perceived from the perspectives of those involved, and not from the perspectives of the observer. Thus, the central data-gathering techniques of a qualitative approach are participant observation and unstructured interviewing. Qualitative methods attempt to capture and understand individual definitions, descriptions and meanings of events. Quantitative methods, on the other hand, count and measure occurrences. Abercrombie (1988) argues that social science research can never be objective because of the subjective perceptions of those involved, both informant and researcher; because all propositions are limited in their meaning to particular language context and particular social groups; because all researchers impose unwittingly their own value judgements and because all observations are theory laden.

Analytic induction

Analytic induction and theoretical sampling are essential features of qualitative studies. These two processes enable the investigator to construct, elaborate and test propositions and hypotheses while the study is ongoing. Analytic induction requires that each interview supports the proposition being developed. If the interview does not substantiate the proposition, then a revision of the initial proposition is formulated. This constant development allows the research question to evolve in response to emerging insights, focusing more closely on some specific event or behaviour. As a result, sampling will also alter as the focus of the study subtly changes.

Sampling

Whereas quantitative research uses probability sampling, qualitative research employs non-probability sampling, especially snowball sampling and theoretical sampling. In snowball sampling, a person, who is identified as a valid member of a specified group to be interviewed, is asked to provide the names of others who fit the requirements. This is because in many situations the interviewer would not know the potential members of the sample; for example, in a study of delinquent gangs, one gang member can provide names of other gangs and gang members—information that may only be known to a select few and which would remain confidential. The gang member would be asked to introduce the interviewer to the further potential interviewees. In theoretical sampling, data collection is controlled by the developing theory. As information is gathered from the first few cases the underlying theory becomes extended, modified, etc., and therefore informs the investigator as to which group(s) are relevant to interview. For example, in a study investigating how students respond to sports injuries that leave them unable to take part in that sport again, successive interviews might gradually narrow down the range of sports to be covered, as the investigator determines that some sports have no participants that ever suffer such disabling injury. Eventually, because of the incidences noted, the study begins to limit its focus to rugby and skiing participants. Thus the purpose of theoretical sampling is the discovery and development of categories. It is a recurrent process, as incoming data provides new evidence and suggests new categories. Cases are analysed until new categories and disconfirming cases no longer appear to change the theoretical and conceptual model. At this stage we have reached theoretical saturation. This approach is linked to analytic induction in which a search for falsifying evidence is made which leads to modification of the theory until no further disconfirming evidence is found. There is a resemblance between analytic induction and Popper's emphasis on the importance of setting up null hypotheses.

As Glaser and Strauss (1967) suggest, sampling is often guided by the search for contrasts which are needed to clarify the analysis and achieve maximum identification of emergent categories. So no representative sample is found here but particular samples to identify specific classes of phenomena are emerging. This strategy permits the investigator to develop and study a range of types rather than determine their frequency or distribution. Then, once this identification of events/types has been effected, more in-depth study can be made. For example, having identified four types of teacher response to some classroom event through unstructured interviews, a deeper study of these responses in specific contexts can be made to expand the explanations being offered to account for the differences in response.

Reliability and validity

You remember from chapter 20 that reliability was concerned with giving the same result consistently under the same conditions, while validity was concerned with an assessment or judgement measuring what it is supposed to measure. When we are dealing with human beings, rather than inanimate scientific material, it is easy to realise that while we can measure something reliably, it may well not be valid. A questionnaire to students about why they absent themselves from school may well produce consistent results (reliable) in that they all claim they were ill. However, some in-depth unstructured interviewing would certainly discover that many of these illness responses were not true (invalid), with students staying away for a variety of reasons, such as homework not done, dislike of school, a preference for hanging around the city centre, and so on. Who has the power to decide what is the truth in the informant's social world?

How do we know what is reliable and valid in qualitative research where the responses of individuals to interviews and general conversation noted in participant observation may be distorted by all sorts of idiosyncratic factors? The best way is triangulation, in which we can argue that if different methods of assessment or investigation produce the same results, then the data are likely to be valid.

Literature review

Qualitative researchers do not search for data that will support or disprove their hypothesis. Rather as we read above, they develop theories and propositions from the data they collect as the research develops. The literature review is a stimulus for your thinking and not a way of summarising in your own mind the previous work in the area that can blind you to only considering existing concepts and conceptual schemes, as in quantitative method. New findings cannot always be fitted into existing categories and concepts, and the qualitative method, with its more open-minded approach, encourages other ways of looking at the data. The literature review should be a sounding board for ideas, as well as finding out what is already known and what specific methodologies have been used. Often research reports identify additional questions that would be fruitful to pursue.

The promise of the qualitative mode can be seen in its emphasis on naturalistic investigative strategies. These methods could enable the researcher to focus on complexities and qualities in educational action and interaction that might be unattainable through the use of more standardised measures. An explication of 'meaning', rather than the isolation of 'truth', is identified as the goal.

Within social science research, the typical qualitative approaches involve ethnography survey and action research, with observation and interviewing as the major techniques.

As a result, the qualitative researcher is likely to become quite personally involved in the study, while the quantitative researcher attempts to be dispassionate, neutral and detached so as to avoid bias.

Qualitative research methods are another way of understanding people and their behaviour. Qualitative research methods should not be regarded as 'the other way' of doing research. Quantitative and qualitative methods may appear to be opposites derived from different philosophies, yet both are legitimate tools of research and can supplement each other, providing alternative insights into human behaviour. One method is neither better nor poorer than the other. The choice of which research method is used should be based on an informed understanding of the suitability of that method for that particular research. It is impossible to judge one method using the concepts derived from another totally different approach, thus concepts of reliability, validity, or sampling may not be relevant or require redefinition when used in another method. The research problem should determine the method.

The value of qualitative studies lies in their ability to research issues that:

- explore folk wisdom and practices that do not work;
- investigate real or hidden agendas of organisations as opposed to stated agendas;
- cannot be done experimentally, for ethical or practical reasons;
- unravel informal and unstructured links and processes in organisations;
- delve in depth into processes.

The strength of qualitative studies then lies in research that is descriptive or exploratory and that stresses the importance of context and the subjects' frame of reference.

Comparison of qualitative and quantitative methods

Qualitative	Quantitative
Assumptions	
Reality socially constructed	Facts and data have an objective reality
Variables complex and inter-woven; difficult to measure	Variables can be measured and identified
Events viewed from informant's perspective	Events viewed from outsider's perspective
Dynamic quality to life	Static reality to life
Purpose	
Interpretation	Prediction
Contextualisation	Generalisation
Understanding the perspectives of others	Causal explanation
Method	
Data collection using participant observation, unstructured interviews	Testing and measuring

Qualitative	Quantitative
Method (continued)	
Concludes with hypothesis and grounded theory	Commences with hypothesis and theory
Emergence and portrayal	Manipulation and control
Inductive and naturalistic	Deductive and experimental
Data analysis by themes from informants' descriptions	Statistical analysis
Data reported in language of informant	Statistical reporting
Descriptive write-up	Abstract impersonal write-up
Role of researcher	
Researcher as instrument	Researcher applies formal instruments
Personal involvement	Detachment
Empathic understanding	Objective

As the table suggests, the choice of research method will be influenced by the assumptions that the researcher holds about the social world and the people who inhabit it, and by the sort of study required by the topic under investigation.

References

Abercrombie, N. (1988), *The Penguin Dictionary of Sociology*, Penguin, Harmondsworth.

Glaser, B. and Strauss, A. (1967), *The Discovery of Grounded Theory*, Aldine, Chicago.

Further reading

Berg, B. (1989), *Qualitative Research Methods for the Social Sciences*. Allyn & Bacon, Boston.

Eisner, E. & Peshkin, A. (eds) (1990), *Qualitative Enquiry in Education*, Teachers College Press, New York.

Firestone, W. (1987), 'Meaning in method: the rhetoric of quantitative and qualitative research' *Educational Researcher* 16, pp. 16–21.

Flick, U. (1998), *Introduction to Qualitative Research*, Sage, London.

Glesne, C. & Peshkin, A. (1992), *Becoming Qualitative Researchers*. Longman, New York.

Goodwin, L. & Goodwin, W. (1984), 'Qualitative vs quantitative research or qualitative and quantitative research', *Nursing Research* 33, pp. 378–9.

Jacob, E. (1988), 'Clarifying qualitative research.' *Educational Researcher* 17, pp. 16–24.

Marshall, C. & Rossman, G. (1989), *Designing Qualitative Research*, Sage, Newbury Park.

Mason, J. (1996), *Qualitative Researching*, Sage, London.

Reismann, C.K. (ed.) (1993), *Qualitative Studies in Social Work Research*, Sage, London.

Strauss, A. & Corbin, J. (1999), *Basics of Qualitative Research*, Sage, London.

Richardson, J.T. (ed.) (1996), *Handbook of Qualitative Research Methods for Psychology and Social Science*, BPS Books, Leicester, UK.

23

twenty three

Introduction

The word *ethnography* literally means 'writing about people'. In a broad sense, ethnography encompasses any study of a group of people for the purpose of describing their socio-cultural activities and patterns.

In early anthropological studies, ethnographers (for example, Malinowski 1922), working through in-culture informants, gathered data first-hand about the ways in which members of a group ordered their life by means of social custom, ritual and belief. By compiling and organising this information, ethnographers constructed pictures of that group's cultural and perceptual world. In ethnography, people are not subjects; they are experts on what the ethnographer wants to find out about. Over time, a greater range of theory and method for ethnographic fieldwork has developed, involving concepts and approaches suitable for describing such social subgroups as motorcycle gangs and juvenile delinquents, social situations such as classrooms and courtrooms, and open public scenes such as street corners and hospital wards.

Ethnography essentially involves descriptive data collection as the basis for interpretation. It represents a dynamic 'picture' of the way of life of some interacting social group. As a process, it is the science of cultural description. Ethnography is a relevant method for evaluating school life, hospital life, prison life, etc., since these contexts are essentially cultural entities.

Typical concerns have been the development of pupil identities, teachers' perceptions of pupils and their abilities, the 'management' of classroom knowledge, pupils' definitions of school subjects, prisoner–guard relationships, sick role behaviour, and so on. (Examples of such work are collected in Stubbs and Delamont (1976) and Woods and Hammersley (1977).)

An ethnographic approach, for example, to the everyday tasks of teaching and curriculum planning, whatever the professional area, does not define curriculum simply as 'a relationship between a set of ends and a set of means', as a statement of intended learning goals together with methods for goal achievement. We can view a curriculum as a process in which there is constant interpretation and negotiation going on among and between academic staff and students. In this sense, a curriculum is the everyday activities in the classroom. The conceptual and methodological tools of ethnography get at this aspect of curriculum planning and teaching.

Ethnography accepts that human behaviour occurs within a context. A classroom never stands in isolation from larger cultural and social landscapes, such as local and national, political or economic processes and values. Educational activities take place against a background of premises, interests and values concerning what it means to be a student or teacher, and what constitutes worthwhile knowledge and learning. These features are implicit in the choices made, and in justifications given by participants. In other words, academic tasks are accomplished with prior presuppositions, beliefs, and anticipations. Inevitably, these perspectives are shaped within larger social and political contexts. These relationships need to be examined as part of the classroom. Ethnography takes this larger context into account.

Ethnography can be a useful way of providing descriptions of what actually happens in a school district, health authority, etc. These descriptions may help administrators ensure that policy development is based on, and directed to, the actual situation rather than to an ideal or imaginary situation. For example, administrators developing policy concerning 'rowdiness' in schools should have some idea about the extent and varying interpretations of 'rowdiness' already occurring. To develop a policy dealing with 'rowdy acts', descriptions of various contexts of such acts are needed. Players in the context of a game in the gymnasium give particular meanings to 'rowdiness' recognised by all participants as a part of physical education; on the other hand, similar relations in the school cafeteria would incur the wrath of the administrators. Social–cultural factors of an educational institution, time of day, relationship to holidays and community events, or final examinations, are just a few of the factors which may give meaning and situational legitimacy to the notion of rowdiness. To make sense at all, policy has to take into account the contextualness of this student behaviour. Even more realistic examples of policy development could be given in the areas of report cards and reporting procedures, student attendance, community use of facilities, vandalism, and many other school-related issues which may arise. These kinds of policy formulations benefit from (and even require) explicit descriptions of the situationally defined rules, expectations, intents, perceptions and interpretations held and utilised by participants. Without an understanding of these contextual factors, policy makers misunderstand and distort the issues they purport to redress. Ethnographic methods can be one way to help supply the needed descriptive basis for policy development and its implementation in the changing world of education, social work, health, etc.

The purpose of ethnographic research is to uncover social, cultural, or normative patterns. Generally, this involves an analytic description in terms of a social setting, organisation, behaviour, and activities. The fieldwork incorporates participant observation, triangulation, interviewing and qualitative analysis—essentially, interpretation—in order to arrive at an understanding of the observed patterns of behaviour engaged in by those being studied.

This generalised and, to many researchers, less rigorous approach has gained credibility in social science research because it has become increasingly evident that over-concern with quantitative data may miss significantly important links and relationships within a context or process. Without doubt, some elements of a qualitative approach are impressionistic and subjective, but it would be equally true to argue that an investigation conducted under the most rigorous conditions and employing sophisticated statistical analyses is still often open to question in its sampling procedures, choice of statistical tools and techniques of analysis. Above all, however, such research methodology in its attempts to isolate variables may be reporting an unrealistic scenario with little practical applicability. In contrast, the more questionable and soft approach allows greater speculation and an arena for explanation. There are no formulae, flow charts or standardised procedures for the ethnographer to follow. Much of the ethnographic work is inductive because of its situational character. This makes the fieldworker's attitude to the situation, flexibility in planning, sensitivity to contextual clues, and ability to be comfortable with change and emergence, all-important aspects of 'methodology'.

The varied situations within schools, hospitals and workplaces are too complex to be viewed from any single perspective. In the past, most research activities relied heavily on quantification, measurement, and 'objective' category systems. There was seldom interest in how participants expressed their own intentions and interactions within the context. Individuals bring priorities, concerns, and other personal constructs which influence their participation in programs and interaction with one another. In a school there are as many programs as there are teachers and students who experience curricula. Adequate understanding of school programs requires thorough descriptions of what happens in the classroom from the perspective of the participants. In other words, we see a need for deeper exploration into the experience of classroom situations. Ethnography is one way to understand this experience, for ethnographic procedures allow us to grasp subjective aspects of life that other procedures neglect.

STQ122

List a number of areas/topics/situations/relationships which would be amenable to ethnographic investigation.

Ethnographic approach to research

Whereas the emphasis in quantitative research is on the testing of theory, the ethnographic researcher has a much more central concern with generating and developing theory. Ethnographers are attempting to capture the social reality of a group, so that formulating the appropriate research problems and asking the appropriate questions become the most important features of the research; yet these also are difficult items to pose correctly. Ethnographic projects can often be divided into three phases:

1 **The initial phase.** Guided by broad research interests, the investigator collects data with a view to exploring a range of possible ideas.
2 **The second phase.** Significant classes of events and persons begin to emerge leading to reformulation of initial guiding propositions.
3 **The third phase.** The collection of data relevant to the reformulation occurs.

There is an interplay between personal observations and theory which leads to decisions about what might be useful to observe and what questions it might be relevant to ask. Often the primary research goal is to discover those questions which will emerge along with the concepts and theoretical framework as the study proceeds. The qualitative approach demands great flexibility and an openness to change rather than a narrow focused approach from the outset. This indeterminacy can be threatening to the novice, but they should be reassured that even experienced qualitative researchers are often grasping for direction at times when commencing a new study. It is important to remember that the general research question, related literature, theory and research design are all interrelated, each building on the others in a process of unfolding, incubation, creativity, intuition, or just plain commonsense. The initial operation of a study is like a strategy of attack which takes shape as a function of previous activity, rather than a fixed roadmap taking one from A to B without deviation.

Guiding hypotheses are crucial in this process of gradual refinement. The guiding hypothesis is merely a tool to generate questions and search for patterns. It can be discarded or refined, as this research process itself leads to a clearer focus and more precise formulation of the problem.

Of course, as the study proceeds, this sequence may be traversed several times. This process is sometimes termed *progressive focusing*, i.e. adopting a stance as a naive observer and avoiding placing self-obvious categories on what is observed until considerable exploratory fieldwork has occurred, and then permitting this learning and assimilation to provide guides on what propositions to offer and how to categorise and interpret the data.

In ethnography, research design refers to a multitude of decisions that have to be taken over the whole course of the fieldwork. In each case, the strategy that is adopted depends to a great extent on the nature of the social situation chosen for study. There can, therefore, be no single ideal to which all such research can be expected to conform. However, ethnography does provide a set of general commitments or orientations to research which is rather different from those of the experimental and survey styles. These can be identified as:

1 The problem of understanding social action (understanding and interpretation).
2 The emphasis on process (process).
3 The investigation of 'natural' settings (naturalism).
4 The study of social phenomena in their context (holism).
5 The assumption that there are always multiple perspectives (multiple perspectives).
6 The use of multiple techniques, with emphasis on participant observation and interviewing.

Understanding and interpretation

The social world differs from the natural world because it is essentially a world of interpretations and meanings. People differ from natural objects in their ability to interpret their own actions and those of others; to act on their understandings and to endow their lives and actions with meaning. The social world of a particular culture is, therefore, socially constructed; it is the active accomplishment of the members of that culture. For this reason, the language of ethnography refers to actors and actions, rather than, say, 'subjects' and 'behaviour', and the question is always 'How is it done?'; 'What cultural resources, stocks of knowledge, routines and strategies do the actors bring to bear?'; 'How do the actors collectively negotiate and achieve social order, understanding and working relationships?'.

Process

Ethnographers argue that meanings and interpretations are not fixed entities. They are generated through social interaction and may change over the course of interaction. Actors' identities are also subject to processes of 'becoming', rather than being fixed and static. No single meaning or identity is assumed; there are multiple and competing definitions current in almost every social situation. The metaphor of negotiation is often used to capture the processes of interaction whereby social meanings are generated, and a precarious social order is produced.

Naturalism

Ethnographers recognise that the things people say and do depend on the social context in which they find themselves. They urge, therefore, that social life be studied as it occurs, in natural settings rather than 'artificial' ones created only for the purposes of the research. Furthermore, they do not seek to manipulate and control what goes on in these settings, but rather to minimise their own impact on events so as to be able, as far as possible, to observe social processes as they occur naturally without the intervention of researchers. Their aim is thereby to maximise the ecological validity of their findings. Just as Lorenz swims with his goslings, or Schaller lives with mountain gorillas, so ethnologists live the lives of the people they study. To expect more from the ethnological study of teachers and children for a lesser effort seems naive indeed.

Holism

Those working in the ethnographic tradition also stress the need to see social life within the general context of a culture, subculture or organisation as a whole. The actions of individuals are motivated by events within the larger whole and thus cannot be understood apart from it.

The ethnographer must be aware of the classroom setting within a wider context: the surrounding vicinity, the milieu of the values and beliefs, the larger social environment. A school is a reflection in some way of the neighbourhood in which student and teacher live, with its various kinds of groups, events of community life, economic activities, industry and transportation, ethnic and cultural patterns, or street life. These factors influence the interpretations students and teachers collectively and individually ascribe to school.

Multiple perspectives

Early anthropological ethnographers argued that 'savages' were not 'superstitious' or 'mentally inferior' to western observers, but rather employed different, equally rational 'world-views'. Contemporary ethnographic approaches take a similar view and, rather than imposing their own modes of rationality on those they study, attempt to comprehend social action in terms of the actors' own terms of reference. As a result, they are well suited to the detection of 'unofficial' versions of social reality. What people do and what they ought to do are very often different. Because of this, there is frequently a discrepancy between what people do and what they say they do. Therefore, one must look beyond the 'public' and 'official' versions of reality in order to examine the unacknowledged or tacit understandings as well.

Thus, studies in education have highlighted 'unofficial' perspectives in a number of contexts; for example, by drawing attention to the 'hidden curriculum'. This is the set of implicit messages and learning that go on in addition to, and sometimes in opposition to, the 'official' curriculum. A classic example of such an approach was undertaken by the authors of *Boys in White: Student Culture in Medical School* (Becker, Geer, Hughes & Strauss, 1961), in which the authors documented in considerable detail the hidden curriculum of medical education at Kansas University.

Individuals have interpretations based on their experience from the unique vantage point of their life and biography. These personal interpretations include the perceptions, intentions, expectations and relevances through which each one of us makes sense of things. Participants understand classrooms and programs in accord with their own subjective interpretations. A teacher may interpret a classroom and program in terms of formal training (for example, theories of learning, psychological constructs, instructional methodologies), instructional goals, and beliefs about students and the subject matter. On the other hand, each student may interpret the same class in terms of past school experiences, immediate goals, beliefs about teachers and the subject matter, expectations of education, purposes for attending school, and views of their own potential. Factors such as these influence each participant's experiences in that classroom.

The purposes for using ethnography are to uncover and describe group social relations such as:

- the understandings (e.g. beliefs, perceptions, knowledge) which participants share about their situation;
- the routine methods (e.g. social rules, expectations, patterns, roles) by which their situation is structured;
- the legitimisations by which participants justify the normality and unquestioned character of their situation; and
- the motives and interests (for example, purposes, goals, plans) through which participants interpret their situation.

In other words, ethnographers focus on how different people define an event through their actions, perceptions, interpretations and beliefs. Investigators, therefore, must become immersed in a particular situation in order to describe and interpret people's actions.

Multiple techniques

Ethnographic 'fieldwork' is not a homogeneous method, but involves a variety of techniques of data collection. The most commonly employed approach is that of participant observation, whereby the fieldworker directly observes, and to some extent takes part in, everyday life in a chosen setting (a school, prison, bureaucracy, rural community, adolescent gang, etc.).

Observations are recorded in the form of detailed fieldnotes, which may be made on the spot and amplified subsequently, or written up as soon as possible after leaving the field. In recent years, audio and videotape recordings have been increasingly used to obtain permanent records of social interaction. In addition, the ethnographer may engage in interviewing, collecting and analysing documentary material, and may also use the techniques of survey research to supplement the field notes. All the material gathered is reported, described and interpreted to form the ethnographic study.

STQ123

What do you regard as the major characteristics of the ethnographic method?

Ethnographic fieldwork

Ethnography does not fit a linear model of research. Instead, the major tasks follow a kind of cyclical pattern, repeated over and over again, as outlined in Figure 23.1. Compare this figure with the quantitative linear sequence in Figure 4.1, p. 42.

Selecting an ethnographic project

The cycle begins with the selection of a research project.

Collecting ethnographic data

The second major task in the ethnographic research cycle (see Figure 23.1) is collecting ethnographic data. By means of participant observation, the activities of people, the physical characteristics of the social situation, and what it feels like to be part of the scene are observed. During the course of fieldwork, whether one studies a classroom for a year or college administrators for a few months, the types of observation will change. One starts by making broad descriptive observations, trying to get an overview of the social situation and what goes on there. Then, after recording and analysing the initial data, research narrows and the researcher begins to make more focused observations. Finally, after more analysis and repeated observations in the field, investigations narrow still further to make selective observations.

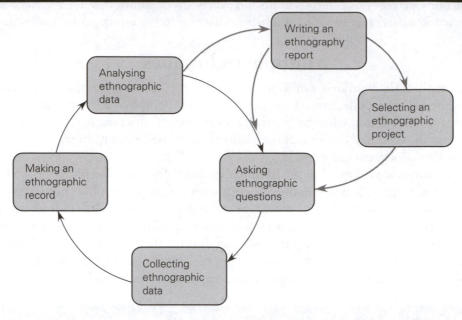

FIGURE 23.1 *The research cycle in ethnography*

Writing an ethnography report

Analysing ethnographic data

Selecting an ethnographic project

Making an ethnographic record

Asking ethnographic questions

Collecting ethnographic data

Making an ethnographic record

The next step in the research cycle, following fast on the heels of each observation period, is making an ethnographic record. This includes taking fieldnotes, taking photographs, making maps, and using any other means to record observations. This ethnographic record builds a bridge between observation and analysis. Indeed, most of the analysis will rely heavily on what has been recorded.

Analysing ethnographic data

The next step in the cycle cannot wait until a large amount of data is collected. In ethnographic inquiry, analysis is a process of question–discovery. Instead of coming into the field with specific questions, the ethnographer analyses the field data compiled from participant observation to discover questions. There is a need to analyse fieldnotes after each period of fieldwork in order to know what to look for during the next period of participant observation.

Writing an ethnography

This last major task in the research cycle occurs toward the end of a research project. However, it can also lead to new questions and more observations. Writing an ethnography forces the investigator into a new and more intensive kind of analysis. Those who begin their writing early, and when they still can make observations, will find that writing becomes part of the research cycle.

Ethnographic research involves an open-ended inquiry; it requires constant feedback to give the study direction. Ethnographers can only plan ahead of time the course of their investigation in the most general sense.

Methodology used for collecting and analysing data from the everyday school world may be classified broadly into:

1 pre-entry;
2 into the field;
3 analysis.

STQ124

Why is ethnographic research cyclic rather than linear?

Pre-entry

Ethnography is conducted in the context of the situation under study. Ethnographers recognise the fundamental need to go where participants spend their time. Therefore, preparation for entry must be carefully planned, as the entire study depends in large part on the group's acceptance of the researchers.

In organisations, official agencies and so on, there are individuals who, by virtue of their office, have the authority to act as gatekeepers. They can grant or withhold formal permission to enter and participate in the life of the organisation. Dealings with such gatekeepers can therefore be an extremely important part of the design and conduct of ethnography.

Gaining entry is best accomplished through a mutual contact who can recommend the researcher to the gatekeeper. Gatekeepers are often wary of the proposed length and intimate participation of the fieldworker; they normally seek reassurances that the research will not prove unduly disruptive, i.e. that the fieldworker will not prevent people from getting on with their normal work, force an entry into private meetings or conversations, and so on. Gatekeepers need to be reassured that relations of trust and confidentiality will not be abused; as in any variety of research, ethnographers have to ensure the anonymity of the members concerned and that nothing will be made public that is detrimental to individuals. These issues are particularly critical in the context of ethnography, since the actions and beliefs of the actors will be documented in some detail, and ethnographers are more likely than most other researchers to see 'behind the scenes'.

Gatekeepers often engage in impression management. Quite naturally, they do not want to find the ethnographer producing an unflattering portrait of them and their work or their organisation. Consciously or unconsciously, they will 'put on a show', attempting to influence the initial impressions the fieldworker receives. The fieldworker must remain alert to such possibilities and record them systematically, since they constitute valuable data in their own right—throwing light on the gatekeepers' perceptions and preoccupations.

STQ125

You might like to reflect on some social group, association or organisation that you know. If you were acting as gatekeeper, would there be any aspects that you would try to 'play down' or 'play up' in your dealings with a potential researcher?

Most gatekeepers are not familiar with the ethnographic style of research. If they have any expectation of social research, the survey will probably be their model. Fieldworkers are often asked, therefore, to spell out their 'hypotheses' and to show their draft questionnaires or interview schedules. Given a commitment to progressive focusing and a flexible research strategy, it may be rather difficult to establish one's legitimacy as a social researcher.

It may be a good tactic for researchers and initial contact person(s) to form a community steering committee of five or six. This provides ethnographers with several research advantages. Members of this committee give the support and legitimacy needed to help overcome possible suspicion when conducting a local study. In the eyes of community members, the study may have greater relevance and acceptance if they perceive the steering committee as having some control over what is done by the outsiders, thereby making easier entry for negotiations with members of the group. By working through a steering committee, researchers find it easier and faster to acquire documents such as old newspapers, minutes of meetings, pupil absence figures, former curricula, or even letters. If this committee is representative of wide school interests—for example, parents, labour, administration—it becomes invaluable for validating data collected by ethnographers; the members determine whether the ethnographer's descriptions actually reflect the situation. In this manner, a self-correcting procedure (triangulation, p. 419) is built into data collection and interpretation.

Costing the study is also an important pre-entry task. Ethnographic methods require considerable time to use, as does the analysis of data and writing of descriptions.

STQ126

A school classroom is a familiar setting for research and potentially requires negotiation with many gatekeepers. List the various persons with whom a researcher might have to negotiate in order to gain access.

During the first few days of entry, observers should be somewhat unobtrusive and learn how to act and behave in the setting. Collecting data is secondary to becoming familiar with the setting and putting 'locals' at their ease. Rapport can be helped by fitting in with established routines, showing interest in all that goes on, and being honest about what you are doing.

No less important is the time of entry. Just about every group, organisation, social movement (or whatever) has its own rhythms, timetables and calendars. It may therefore be important to plan the timing of the research to take account of such timetables (for example, the cycle of the school year). Particular periods of the school calendar can have great significance. 'First days' are important; the 'reality shock' experienced by new pupils can be crucial in the formation of their perspectives and identities, and illuminating for the observer. At such times, new members have to work out how things operate in their novel situation. At the same time, 'old hands' may help them by making explicit what usually passes unnoticed.

All of these activities are a part of negotiating entry. Ethnography cannot simply be done anonymously by mailing out questionnaires, but depends on the ethnographer's personal presence for establishing relationships with the inhabitants of situations. The ethnographer needs to be granted open entry.

Ethnographers normally study only a single setting, or a small number of settings at one time. There is a trade-off between depth and breadth of coverage; the limitations of time and labour often preclude the exhaustive investigation of many different settings or locales within the same research project. The nature of the chosen research setting(s) is therefore crucial. A recurrent question for ethnographic research is, 'Was the setting of the research typical of its sort?'. If it was not, the study lacks external validity in that the findings cannot be generalised to another setting.

However, research settings may prove fruitful precisely because they are not typical, or do not fit an expected pattern. The exploration of unusual or extreme examples may help to illuminate more general features—throwing them into sharp relief, casting doubt on cherished, taken-for-granted ideas, and pushing existing theories and concepts to the limits of their application. The close examination of the unusual case can highlight aspects of the 'typical' and the 'routine' which might otherwise pass unnoticed as 'obvious' or 'normal' and hence unremarkable. 'Deviant' or critical case analysis thus plays an important part in the generation of hypotheses and testing them in different contexts.

The choice of a particular setting may be prompted by a period of change and innovation in that setting. The process of innovation may be studied for its own sake, or may be used to highlight other concerns. During periods of change and upheaval, actors may need to question their beliefs and their taken-for-granted views of themselves and the social world. It may therefore prove a fruitful strategy deliberately to select fields for research in which innovatory processes are taking place. Thus, for instance, there have been ethnographic studies of the institution of new curricula in schools. Here the emphasis on the 'unofficial' plays an important part. Although such changes are directed towards specific aims and objectives, there are always unintended consequences; no new curriculum can be guaranteed to be 'child-proof' or 'teacher-proof'. Thus it becomes extremely important that investigators should trace the day-to-day processes of change and its unforeseen consequences (cf. Hamilton 1976; MacDonald & Walker 1976).

The ideal site is one where entry is possible and welcome; where there is a high probability of the mix of processes/people/interactions/structures that are central to the research question; where the researcher can devise an appropriate role to maintain an unobtrusive presence. In some studies the site is critical and little choice is available. Part of the validity of the study rests on the suitability of the site. In some research the site is actually the study. For example, where and under what circumstances do students meet at night to smoke marijuana?

STQ127

What are the advantages and disadvantages of selecting a 'typical setting' for study?

Into the field

Progressive focusing: Formulating problems and testing hypotheses

We can identify three broad phases in the development of fieldwork projects.

The initial phase

Guided by broadly defined research interests, the fieldworker collects data with a view to trying out a wide range of possible ideas and lines of inquiry.

The second phase

Significant classes of persons and events begin to emerge. Initial research problems may have undergone reformulation, and ideas start to come into focus. Working hypotheses and propositions are formulated with reference to specific aspects of the field of study.

The third phase

The testing of a restricted number of hypotheses is undertaken. The guiding principle of ethnographic fieldwork, at least in the early stages, is *learning*. The researcher tries to adopt the role of 'acceptable incompetent'. The stance adopted is one of a radically naive observer who does not take it on trust that 'everyone knows' what goes on in any given context. By watching, listening and asking questions, the ethnographer comes to assimilate the knowledge and perspectives of the actors concerned.

Ethnographers try to avoid sharpening their problems into specific research hypotheses until considerable exploratory investigation has occurred (a process termed *progressive focusing*). This is another facet of the attempt to avoid commitment to existing theoretical and/or commonsense categories or sources of data.

In the light of emergent hypotheses, the fieldworker seeks out new cases (settings, groups or individuals) in order to develop, test, modify and extend the hypotheses and the concepts in terms of which they are expressed.

Strategies in the field

Observation

The basic ethnographic approach involves the observation, organisation and interpretation of data. Data collection is done principally through participant observation, whereby the observer is part of the context being observed; being both modified and influenced by this context. The end result is an analytical description and interpretation of a highly complex system.

The kinds of data researchers gather will depend in part on how they participate in the setting. There are four possible research stances for the participant observer: the complete participant; the participant-as-observer; the observer-as-participant; and the complete observer.

1 The complete participant operates under conditions of secret observation and full participation; for example, Hargreaves (1967).
2 The complete observer is entirely removed from interaction with those under observation; for example, using a two-way mirror to observe children at play.
3 The observer-as-participant is a role intermediate between the first two, where the researcher's identity is known to the hosts, but he or she remains a relative 'stranger', as in interviewing.
4 The participant-as-observer is a similar role, but characterises situations in which the fieldworker becomes more closely involved and identified with the actors; for example, Whyte (1955).

Participant observation

Participant observation is the primary technique used by ethnographers to gain access to data. In this mode the investigator lives as much as possible with, and in the same manner as, the individuals being investigated. Researchers take part in the daily activities of people, reconstructing their interactions and activities in fieldnotes taken on the spot, or as soon as possible after their occurrence.

Participant observation has been described as a process of waiting to be impressed by recurrent themes that reappear in various contexts. Wolcott's (1973) account of the career of a primary school principal illustrates this waiting role. Wolcott shadowed the principal for two years, spending several days each week with him at school and on school business away from the school building. A constant written record of behaviour seen and conversations held between principal, staff, pupils, family and friends was maintained. The principal also kept a written account of recurring school problems for a period of several weeks and over a period of several weeks Wolcott recorded the patterns of interaction of the school principal every minute for two-hour periods. As a result, a detailed picture was built up of the multifarious demands made on a school principal in his day-to-day life.

Another example of participant observation involving painstaking involvement in the life of a school, without being fettered by pre-planned questionnaires and interview schedules, is that of King (1978) on kindergartens. Of his start he says: 'I asked the headmistress of a large kindergarten if she would allow me to make observations in one of the classrooms. I was not able to give her any clear idea of what I was trying to do because I did not know exactly myself'.

King began to make sense of the myriad of things that were happening in a busy classroom by using quota sampling, snowball sampling and the search for exceptions. Quota sampling involves the interviewing of individuals from specific categories, and in his case it was the kindergarten teacher. His observations of kindergarten teachers in action led him to the conclusion that what happened in the classroom was not haphazard, but was arranged to happen or allowed to happen by the teacher. This subtle structuring was guided by the teacher's ideology, and King concluded in his analysis that kindergarten education can be viewed as a middle-class institution.

Snowball sampling involves recording a particular incident and then looking for another example of it. By this technique King was able to categorise five types of teacher voices.

The search for exceptions is a way of falsifying working hypotheses or reformulating them. Occasionally a child might be allowed to get away with behaviour—'permitted eccentric children from professional homes', e.g. 'strange child—her father is a psychologist'. Essentially what King was able to do was show the consequences in their teaching of teachers' adherence to concepts of 'play is learning' and 'family-home background' theories of performance/behaviour.

Participant observation serves to elicit from people their definitions of reality and the organising constructs of their world. Because these are expressed in particular linguistic patterns, it is crucial that the ethnographer studying children and teenagers in schools should be familiar with, and imperturbable toward, current juvenile word usage. They also should recognise the tendency for teacher-talk to centre around descriptions of what is socially acceptable, rather than what teachers actually do. Most important is the collection of stories, anecdotes and myths—such as are found in the daily round of gossip in the staff room or among student groups—with which a sense of the dominant themes of concern to teachers, parents and children can be developed.

These data indicate what is important and unimportant, how people view each other, and how they evaluate their participation in groups and programs. They provide the basis for determining the extent to which formal and informal goals and objectives of a group are being met.

The attempt to be both a member and a researcher can often lead to problems of role conflict. This is well illustrated by Hargreaves (1967). In the course of his study of a boys' secondary school, Hargreaves worked as a teacher. In doing so, he believed that he would demonstrate to the teachers that he was willing and able to see things from their point of view, and that he was not a 'spy' from the education authority. But as soon as he turned from teaching to data collection in other teachers' classrooms, this conflicted with the normal behaviour expected of colleagues. They saw him as a sort of school inspector and his relations with them were compromised. His participation with the pupils was also hampered by activities as a teacher and he was forced to abandon the teacher role. Hargreaves' difficulties also show how short-term strategies for gaining access or establishing a role in the field may, in fact, lead to long-term difficulties and place constraints on the collection of data.

Main elements to focus on

The first days in the field can produce anxiety about acceptance and whether your approach is right. Don't try to get in with everyone; look for the easy openings with welcoming people. They can reassure others. If visiting classrooms, arrive at the beginning of a lesson and leave at the end; do not draw attention to yourself. Ask to be introduced on the first occasion to reassure the class that you are there to observe, not to judge. Get to know teachers in their safe places where they can be comfortable and open with you, e.g. the staff room or the cafeteria. Guard against bringing preconceived notions with you. This is particularly easy if you are a teacher who is going into schools.

You cannot safely assume that what is going on is what you think from your own experience.

Try to observe and note everything. Take notes of the participants in the setting: who they are in terms of gender, age, ethnicity, etc; what they do and say; who interacts with whom. Take notes of events and the acts within the event: at a teachers' staff meeting note who greets whom, what the informal chat is about, what questions are asked of the principal, who sits where or with whom, what gestures are used, etc. The following five areas must be covered:

1 **Who** is in the group or scene? How many people are there, and what are their kinds, identities and relevant characteristics? How is membership in the group or scene acquired?

2 **The setting**. A social situation may occur in different settings; for example, a youth club, a busy street intersection, a staffroom, a nursery school, a slum dwelling. About the setting one wants to know, in addition to its appearance, what kinds of behaviour it encourages, permits, discourages or prevents. Or the social characteristics of the setting may be described in terms of what kinds of behaviour are likely to be perceived as expected or unexpected, approved or disapproved, conforming or deviant.

3 **The purpose.** Is there some official purpose that has brought the participants together, or have they been brought together by chance? If there is an official purpose, what is it? For example, to attend a lesson, to compete in a football match, to participate in a religious ceremony, to meet as a committee, to have fun at a teenage party? How do the participants react to the official purpose of the situation? For example, with acceptance or rejection? What goals other than the official purpose do the participants seem to be pursuing? Are the goals of the various participants compatible or antagonistic? What meanings do participants attribute to what they do?

4 **The social behaviour.** Here one wants to know what actually occurs. What do the participants do, how do they do it and with whom, and with what do they do it? With respect to behaviour, one usually wants to know the following:
   a What was the stimulus or event that initiated it?
   b What appears to be its objective?
   c Toward whom or what is the behaviour directed?
   d What is the form of activity entailed in the behaviour (for example, talking, running, questioning, gesturing, sitting)?
   e What are the qualities of behaviour (for example, its intensity, persistence, unusualness, appropriateness, duration, affectivity, mannerisms)?
   f What are its effects (for example, what behaviour does it evoke from others)? How is stability maintained? How does change originate and how is it managed? How are the identified elements organised? What rules, norms or mores govern this social organisation? How is this group related to other groups, organisations or institutions?

5 **Frequency and duration.** Here one wants to know the answer to such questions as the following: When did the situation occur? How long did it last? Is it a recurring type of situation, or unique? If it recurs, how frequently does it recur? What are the occasions that give rise to it? How typical of such situations is the one being observed?

It should be emphasised that this list is not meant to apply in its entirety to every situation observed.

Sampling

Even when settings have been specified, it is usually necessary to be more selective still. Even in fairly circumscribed social settings, there will be too much going on for it all to be observed equally. As with other styles of research, therefore, samples must be drawn for detailed investigation and recording.

The highly rational prescriptive procedures of experimental statisticians are seldom truly applicable in sampling informants or events for participant observation studies. Rather, the 'most common' data referents are the units themselves—the 'persons, acts (or events) and time' that serve as representative dimensions of the study.

STQ128

Make a list of some specific educational situations in which one could engage in participant observation.

Observation

Most well-documented observation studies have involved the researcher spending many months, or even a year or so, immersed in a community or group, and becoming generally accepted as one of the group. Most of these studies start off largely unstructured, as the researcher has little idea about what it is they precisely want to observe, or what might go on. There are no initial checklists, simply observation of events, situations and behaviours, which are then written up and gradually, as more data accumulates, tentative guiding hypotheses, categorisation, conceptual frameworks and some theoretical underpinning coalesce to give some body, focus and direction to later stages.

Observing groups

A great number of observation schedules have been produced for observing groups. Many have been developed out of the interaction process analysis approach of Bales (1950). This is a way of coding the individual's behaviour within a group context under twelve headings, sufficiently comprehensive to cover most behaviour exhibited in groups. One of the most frequently used systems in education has been that of Flanders (1970) which was derived from the original Bales' method. Flanders established ten categories of teacher/pupil behaviour which the observer could use to categorise and record classroom behaviour. Observers are required to record the behaviour every three seconds by entering an appropriate number on a prepared chart. This proved to be very demanding, as many of the categories had subsections. Moreover, making a judgement every three seconds proves too exacting for most observers, even after memorising the categories. Hardly have you put in a tally mark for a particular category, than another value judgement is immediately required for a sample of behaviour you have just glanced at, and so on—a veritable treadmill.

A more manageable system useful for observing groups holding a meeting is formed of the following six categories:

1 **Proposing**   Putting forward suggestions, new course of action
2 **Supporting**   Giving support/agreement to a proposal
3 **Disagreeing**   Criticising/declaring difference of opinion
4 **Giving information**   Offering facts/opinion/clarification
5 **Seeking information**   Asking for facts/opinions/clarification
6 **Building**   Extending/developing proposal made by other

These categories only describe the behaviour and not the content. A statement may also contain more than one category, as when a person disagrees and puts forward an alternative proposal. How these are dealt with is a matter of personal preference. Many observers code a dual statement both ways. It is also useful to note who made the various statements by designing a grid with participants along one dimension and the six categories forming the other dimension (see Figure 23.2). Other observations might include a seating plan or multiple seating plans (see Figure 23.3), on which arrows can designate the sequence of the conversation of who replied to whom, etc. This sort of observation guide is malleable, to be altered to suit the purposes and resources of the researcher.

FIGURE 23.2 *Records of participant X category for whole of meeting on funding proposal held 6.10.95*

Group members	Categories						Totals
	1	2	3	4	5	6	
Chairperson	✓✓✓✓			✓✓	✓	✓✓✓	10
Secretary				✓✓✓✓		✓✓	6
José		✓			✓	✓	3
Sasha	✓					✓	2
Kim		✓		✓	✓	✓	4
Mary			✓✓	✓			3
Pat			✓		✓		2
Leon	✓✓	✓✓			✓		5
Totals	7	4	3	8	5	8	

Far more complex systems can be devised by a determined researcher if audio- or video-taping is used. Content, time of speaking and emotion/gesture/nonverbal signals can all be recorded and with ingenuity displayed in tables, graphs and diagrams, etc.

You may need to try out several methods for any particular group study or particular focus. There will never be a made-to-measure observation technique for you. You will have to adapt and refine an existing one, even inventing your own shorthand symbols. Preparation is all important, so that all your charts are ready and you know exactly what items you are going to focus on: is it content, interaction or process, or all of these? Remember that meetings are only the final stage of other activities that may have been going on in private over preceding weeks, such as quiet conversations in corners, manoeuvring, delaying tactics and lobbying. There are hidden agendas, anxieties and emotions which need to be considered. The micropolitics may well be more important that what transpires at a well organised staff meeting or governing body meeting where the chairperson has already done his or her 'homework'.

FIGURE 23.3 *Seating plan recording individual verbal behaviour over first five minutes of discussion. The category numbers refer to the behaviour categories listed on p. 409.*

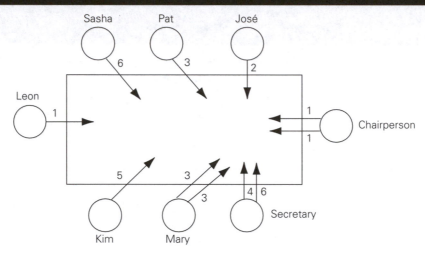

Interviews

Many fieldworkers complement data from participant observation with information taken from interviews. In the course of an interview the researcher can, among other things, investigate in more detail an informant's typifications of persons and events ('Is he usually like that . . .?', 'Would you say that was typical . . .?', 'Could you give me an outline of a typical . . .?'). Informants may be asked to reflect and comment on events that have already been observed directly by the ethnographer. In addition though, they may be used to gain information about events which occurred in this setting before the ethnographer arrived, and events within the setting to which the ethnographer does not have access. 'Informal' interviewing is often a part of ethnographic fieldwork. Such interviews, which are conversational in style rather than based on a fixed schedule of questions, are natural extensions of the social relationships established in the course of participant observation. More formal interviews are also sometimes used by ethnographers. (Interviewing is dealt with in detail in chapters 24 and 30.)

Survey techniques

Some fieldworkers employ survey techniques in the course of ethnographic projects, to gather background data on populations or samples under investigation, or to try to assess the generality of observations made in a limited range of situations. Such an approach assumes that a survey can be used to 'check' the representativeness of the ethnographic data, and hence the generality of the interpretations. (Chapters 29 and 30 consider survey methods in more detail.)

In ethnographic investigations, surveys are based on information first gathered through the preceding less formal and more unstructured methods. Once this background work has been done, construction of survey instruments can begin. These generally take the form of confirmation instruments.

Advantages of observation

The implicit assumption behind observation is that behaviour is purposive and expressive of deeper values and beliefs. Perhaps the greatest asset of observational techniques is that they make it possible to record behaviour as it occurs. All too many research techniques depend entirely on people's retrospective or anticipatory reports of their own behaviour. Such reports are, as a rule, made in a detached mood, in which the respondent is somewhat remote from the stresses and strains peculiar to the research situation. The degree to which one can predict behaviour from statistical data is at best limited, and the gap between the two can be quite large. In contrast, observational techniques yield data that pertain directly to typical behavioural situations—assuming, of course, that they are applied to such situations. Where the researcher has reason to believe that such factors as detachment or distortions in recall may significantly affect the data, they will always prefer observational methods. Sometimes a study demands that what people actually do and say be compared with their account of what they did and said. Obviously, two methods of collecting data must be employed in such inquiries—observation and interviewing.

Moreover, some investigations deal with subjects (for example, infants) who are not able to give verbal reports of either their behaviour or their feelings, for the simple reason that they cannot speak. Such investigations necessarily use observation as their method of data collection. Spitz and Wolf (1946), through the observation of behaviour of babies in a nursery, were led to the conclusion that prolonged separation of a child from a previously attentive mother may lead to a severe depression.

In addition to its independence of a subject's ability to report, observation is also independent of the subject's willingness to report. There are occasions when research meets with resistance from the person or group being studied. Teachers may not have the time, or they may not be inclined, to be interviewed; pupils may resent being singled out or being asked questions whose purpose is obscure to them; they may object to being tested, out of fear that they may not come up to the standards of their group; and so on. Although observation cannot always overcome such resistance to research, it is less demanding of active cooperation on the part of the subjects.

Limitations of observation

On the other hand, observation has its limitations. We have listed as an asset the possibility of recording events simultaneously with their spontaneous occurrence. The other side of the coin is that it is often impossible to predict the spontaneous occurrence of an event precisely enough to enable us to be present to observe it; for example, incidents of aggressive behaviour in the classroom.

One prevalent notion about a limitation of observational techniques, however—the idea that observational data cannot be quantified—is a misconception. Historically, observational data have, it is true, most frequently been presented without any attempt at quantification. This is not to imply that all observational data must be quantified, but it is important to note that they can be, for example into categories for chi-square analysis.

Whatever the purpose of the study, four broad questions confront the observer:

1 What should be observed?
2 How should observations be recorded?
3 What procedures should be used to try to assure the accuracy of observation?
4 What relationship should exist between the observer and the observed, and how can such a relationship be established?

STQ129

1 Observe a young child and in long hand record everything you observe in his/her behaviour during a 5–10 minute period. Choose a time when the youngster is playing to simplify the observations. When you have done this, answer the following questions:
   a To what extent do you feel you were able to record all of the behaviour? What might you have missed?
   b Do you feel you were biased towards observing only certain features?
   c Did you concentrate on motor activity or verbal activity?
   d What did you learn about the child's behaviour that you did not know before?
   e Do you feel that observing the child altered his/her behaviour in any way? How? Could you have avoided it?
   f Did you interpret his/her behaviour from your point of view?
2 Repeat the above exercise with a different child. Use two observers simultaneously. Compare the two records at the end.
   a To what extent were the two observers looking at the same type of behaviour? Was one observer recording more general behaviour than the other?
   b How might we increase inter-observer agreement?
   c Was there any behaviour which was interpreted differently by each observer?

Non-participant observation

Non-participant observation involves merely watching what is happening and recording events on the spot. As a discrete category, non-participant observation exists only where interaction is viewed from hidden cameras and recorders or through one-way mirrors. With these exceptions, interaction is impossible to avoid in social situations. Thus, the functional distinction between participant and non-participant observation is ambiguous. Observers typically label themselves as non-participants when they minimise their interactions with participants to focus attention unobtrusively on the stream of events. Non-participant observation emphasises the researcher's role as a dispassionate recorder. By contrast, participant observation is reflexive; it involves researchers studying themselves as well as other participants in a social setting. However, regardless of their reticence or immersion in a research site, whenever researchers are observing on the scene they acquire some role and status. In conducting studies in school settings, for example, investigators necessarily interact with the teachers and pupils under consideration, even if only non-verbally, and become, to some extent, participants. This need not be a liability; it simply means that estimated consequences of being a participant must be noted in the research report.

Participant and non-participant observers and interviewers need to learn how to manage their role. The role is one of eliciting cooperation, trust, openness and acceptance. At times this may mean play-acting, dressing appropriately, and even allowing oneself to be manipulated. Multiple roles must be nurtured for interaction with different individuals. All this requires careful planning so that subjects have no reason to reject an insincere and manipulating researcher. Often the researcher has to teach the subjects what the role of the researcher is; with the activities that role involves, and with the uses of the information and the manner in which the subjects can aid the research. The researcher cannot be a spongelike observer soaking up the data, but one who is proactive in ensuring that subjects behaviour is valid, understood and willingly displayed.

The process of analysis: segmenting and filing the data

Very soon after the beginning of the data collection process, the researcher is faced with the problem of a gradually mounting body of documents, fieldnotes from participant observation and interviews, and perhaps also transcripts. This material has to be filed.

The most obvious kind of filing system is a running record by time of collection. This is the basic file used by the ethnographer. In itself, though, it is not sufficient; it is also necessary to begin to file data according to its relevance to the categories that are emerging from the analysis. The running record still remains a crucial resource, however, since it allows any piece of data to be examined in the context in which it emerged.

Ethnographers use a form of analytic induction. This strategy involves scanning the data for categories of phenomena and for relationships among such categories, developing working typologies and hypotheses on an examination of initial cases, then modifying and refining them on the basis of subsequent cases.

The first step in analysis is to segment the data. Often there are 'natural' breaks in the material which can be used to break it up into chunks that can then be allocated to particular categories. This is usually the case with participant observation fieldnotes which often consist of notes on a sequence of incidents, each of which can be treated as a separate segment. However, sometimes the 'natural' breaks are so few and far between that, simply for practical purposes, the data must be broken up in a more artificial way.

Each data segment is then allocated to one or more categories, either by being physically placed in a pile of data relevant to that particular category or by the use of punched cards or some other system.

Some of the categories used will be substantive—for example, relating to particular persons or sites—others will be theoretical, concerned with particular types of aspects of social process. The filing of data records will, in line with the discovery-based strategy, undergo development and change as the fieldwork progresses; some categories and category systems may be dropped, others may emerge as the research takes shape and sharpens its focus.

Emerging patterns

Once a researcher has established the categories within which the data are organised and has sorted all bits of data into relevant categories, the ethnography, as a portrayal of a complex whole phenomenon, begins to emerge. The process is analogous to assembling a jigsaw puzzle. The edge pieces are located first and assembled to provide a frame of reference. Then attention is devoted to those more striking aspects of the puzzle picture that can be identified readily from the mass of puzzle pieces and assembled separately. Next, the puzzle worker places the assembled parts in their general position within the frame and, finally, locates and adds the connecting pieces until no holes remain. Thus, analysis can be viewed as a staged process by which a whole phenomenon is divided into its components and then reassembled under various new rubrics. The creativity of ethnographic analysis, however, lies in the uniqueness of the data (or parts), and in the singularity of reconstructed cultures (or pictures).

Problems of interpretation

Qualitative researchers, whether in the tradition of sociology or anthropology, have wrestled over the years with charges that it is too easy for the prejudices and attitudes of the researcher to bias the data. Particularly when the data must go through the researcher's mind before it is put on paper, the worry about subjectivity arises. Does perhaps the observer record only what they want to see rather than what is actually there? Qualitative researchers are concerned with the effect their own subjectivity may have on the data they produce. Is a pupil climbing a tree in the playground adventurous/foolhardy/naughty, etc.?

How do you make interpretations about the emotional states of the persons you observe? If you say the child was angry/pleased/contented/anxious, then you are making inferences which are of a different order than those based on sex and age, or on role relationships. We say they are of a different level because they are much less closely tied to what you actually observe, and there is more room for alternative explanations. Suppose, for instance, you said that the child was happy because he or she was smiling.

There are many kinds of smiles—a smile of surprise, a nervous or stage-fright smile, a patronising smile, a leering smile, a smile of determination, etc. In order to determine a person's emotional state, we have to look not only at their facial expressions, but also at voice tone and the total use of the body and limbs, including gestures and rhythm, and we must also take into account the situational context in which the behaviours occur. We might also have to take into account the person's cultural and social class background, for the same facial expression may have different meanings in different cultures or subcultures. For example, according to Argyle (1969), sticking out the tongue means an apology in some parts of China, a sign of deference in Tibet, a defence against the evil eye in some parts of India, 'no' in the Marquesan Islands. What does it mean in Australia? On the other hand, there are certain universalities in emotional expression across culture, which is why it is possible at all for a person from one culture to observe and learn from a person from a different culture. It may be that it is the most basic emotions—for example fear, anger, happiness, sadness—which are most universal in their expression; and the most subtle ones, which are culture and subculture specific (Ekman 1982).

In attempting to discover people's attitudes, feelings and need states, it is essential that you justify your interpretations by stating quite clearly what aspects of the individual's overt, manifest behaviour made you believe that to be true.

While the idea that researchers can transcend some of their own biases may be difficult to accept at the beginning, the methods that researchers use aid this process. For one thing, qualitative studies are not impressionistic essays made after a quick visit to a setting, or after some conversations with a few subjects. The researcher spends a considerable time in the empirical world laboriously collecting and reviewing piles of data. The data must bear the weight of any interpretation, so the researcher must constantly confront his or her own opinions and prejudices with the data. Besides, most opinions and prejudices are rather superficial. The data that are collected provide a much more detailed rendering of events than even the most creatively prejudiced mind might have imagined prior to the study.

Additionally, the researcher's primary goal is to add to knowledge, not to pass judgement on a setting. Qualitative researchers guard against their own biases by recording detailed fieldnotes which include reflections on their own subjectivity. Some qualitative researchers work in teams and have their fieldnotes critiqued by a colleague as an additional check on bias. It should be noted that we are talking about limiting observers' biases, not eliminating them. Qualitative researchers attempt to seek out their own subjective states and their effects on data, but they never think they are completely successful. All researchers are affected by observers' bias. Questions or questionnaires, for example, reflect the interests of those who construct them, as do experimental studies. Qualitative researchers try to acknowledge and take into account their own biases as a method of dealing with them.

A danger in participant observation is that the investigator will 'go native'. The investigator must always remain conscious of the roles they are playing, and be able to detach themself from the situation. It is a tightrope between being accepted, yet not allowing this new perspective to interfere with their own analytic perspective.

Observer-observed interaction

The presence of the researcher changes the behaviour of the people being studied. Almost all research is confounded by this problem. Take surveys that try to tap opinions. Asking people to sit down and fill out a questionnaire changes their behaviour. Might not asking a person for their opinion create an opinion?

Qualitative researchers try to interact with their subjects in a natural, unobtrusive and non-threatening manner. The more controlled and obtrusive one's research, the greater is the likelihood that one will end up studying the effects of one's methods. If you treat people as 'research subjects', they will act as research subjects, which is different to how they usually act. Since qualitative researchers are interested in how people act and think in their own settings, they attempt to 'blend into the woodwork', or to act so that the activities that occur in their presence do not differ significantly from those that occur in their absence. Similarly, since interviewers in this type of research are interested in how people think about their lives, their experiences and particular situations, they model their interviews after a conversation between two trusting parties rather than on a formal question-and-answer session between a researcher and a respondent. It is only in this manner that they can capture what is important in the minds of the subjects themselves.

One can never eliminate all of one's own effects on subjects or obtain a perfect correspondence between what one wishes to study—the 'natural setting'—and what one actually studies—'a setting with a researcher present'. One can, however, understand one's effect on the subjects through an intimate knowledge of the setting, and use this understanding to generate additional insights into the nature of social life. Researchers learn to 'discount' some of their data, i.e. to interpret them in context. One often finds subjects' attempts to manage impressions of researchers and their activities especially during the early stages of the project. Teachers, for example, might not yell at their students in front of you, or in other ways act more reserved. Knowing that you are seeing teachers' behaviour before strangers is important to take into account. Principals may engage in behaviour they consider principal-like, and, in order to do this, upset their normal behaviour.

The ethnographer must distinguish in their analysis between statements which are direct responses to questions asked and those which are volunteered. This is certainly an important distinction to bear in mind, but we must remember that even 'spontaneous' utterances may be shaped to certain conceptions of the interviewer. However, the interviewer may not be the only perceived audience. The informant may suspect that the interviewer will pass on or mention what they have said to others, or may feel that they are speaking 'for posterity'.

STQ130

What do you regard as the relative merits of participant and non-participant observation?

STQ131

If I ask a teacher what he or she finds to be the major problem in his or her work:

a   in what way might the 'surrounding context' affect his or her answer?

b   in what way might the 'perceived audience' influence his or her answer?

Reliability and validity

As chapter 20 revealed, among quantitative research approaches the expectation exists that there will be consistency in results of observations made by different researchers or the same researcher over time. Qualitative researchers do not share exactly this expectation.

Qualitative research does not pretend to be replicable. The researcher purposely avoids controlling the research conditions and concentrates on recording the complexity of changing situational contexts.

Qualitative researchers tend to view reliability as a fit between what they record as data and what actually occurs in the setting under study, rather than the literal consistency across different observations.

Reliability

Reliability is based on two assumptions. The first is that the study can be repeated. Other researchers must be able to replicate the steps of the original research, employing the same categories of the study, the same procedures, the same criteria of correctness and the same perspectives. But because ethnographic research occurs in natural settings and often is undertaken to record processes of change, it is especially vulnerable to replication difficulties. A study of a racial incident at an urban secondary school, for example, cannot be replicated exactly because the event cannot be reproduced. Problems of uniqueness and idiosyncracy can lead to the claim that no ethnographic study can be assessed for reliability.

The second assumption is that two or more people can have similar interpretations by using these categories and procedures. However, in ethnographic research, it is difficult for an ethnographer to replicate the findings of another, because the flow of information is dependent on the social role held within the group studied and the knowledge deemed appropriate for incumbents of that role to possess. Thus, conclusions reached by ethnographers are qualified by the social roles which investigators hold within the research site. Other researchers will fail to obtain comparable findings unless they develop corresponding social positions or have research partners who can do so.

Crucial also to reliability is inter-rater or inter-observer reliability, or the extent to which the sets of meanings held by multiple observers are sufficiently congruent that they describe and arrive at inferences about phenomena in the same way.

This is a key concern to most ethnographers. Of necessity, a given research site may admit only one or a few observers. Without the corroboration of other observers, such investigations may be seen as idiosyncratic, lacking a careful and systematic recording of phenomena.

The optimum guard is the presence of multiple researchers, who undergo extensive prior training and who discuss the meaning of what has been observed during fieldwork until agreement is achieved.

Reliability is also restricted by the informants who provide data. Each individual informant has access to unique and idiosyncratic information. No single informant can provide universal information. The researcher who hopes to replicate a study must contact individuals similar to those who served as informants in previous studies. This threat to reliability is handled most commonly by careful description of those who provided the data.

Delineation of the physical, social and interpersonal contexts within which data are gathered enhances the replicability of ethnographic studies.

Reliability can be enhanced in these ways:

- Investigators outline the reason for the research and the major question they want to address.
- They explicate their perspectives on the question, stating their research assumptions and biases.
- They explain their data-gathering procedures, including timing and timelines of observations, spatial arrangements of interviews, relationships with subjects and categories developed for analysis.

STQ132

What are the major problems in ensuring reliability in an ethnographic study?

Validity

Establishing validity necessitates demonstration that the propositions generated, refined or tested, match the causal conditions that exist in human life. The issues involved in matching scientific explanations of the world with its actual conditions resolve into two questions.

First, do scientific researchers actually observe or measure what they think they are observing and measuring? This is the problem of internal validity. Solving it credibly is considered to be a fundamental requirement for any research design.

Second, to what extent are the abstract constructs and postulates generated, refined or tested by scientific researchers applicable across groups? This addresses the issue of external validity.

The claim of ethnography to high internal validity derives from the data collection and analysis techniques used by ethnographers. First, the ethnographer's common practice of living among participants and collecting data for long periods provides opportunities for continual data analysis and comparison to refine constructs and to ensure the match between scientific categories and participant reality. Second, informant interviews, a major ethnographic data source, necessarily must be phased close to the empirical categories or participants, and are less abstract than many instruments used in other research designs. Third, participant observation—the ethnographer's second key source of data—is conducted in natural settings that reflect the reality of the life experiences of participants more accurately than do more contrived or laboratory settings. Finally, ethnographic analysis incorporates a process of researcher self-monitoring, termed disciplined subjectivity, that exposes all phases of the research activity to continual questioning and re-evaluation.

Internal validity can be reduced by the reactivity generated by participant observation. In the initial stages of research, informants may dissemble, present an ideal self or tell the researcher what they think the researcher should or wants to hear.

Parallel to this problem in observation is the credibility of informant reports in interviewing. Informants may lie, omit relevant data or misrepresent their claims. Independent corroboration from multiple informants or other fortuitous observers of the social scene, and sufficient residence in the field to reduce artificial responses from informants, improve validity.

Finally, ethnographers must demonstrate—in cases where presentation of the perspective of participants is important—that the categories are meaningful to the participants, reflect the way participants experience reality and are actually supported by the data.

STQ133

How would you improve the internal validity of an ethnographic study?

Triangulation

A commonly used technique to improve the internal validity is **triangulation**. Triangulation may be defined as *the use of two or more methods of data collection in the study of some aspect of human behaviour*. In its original and literal sense, triangulation is a technique of physical measurement—maritime navigators, military strategies and surveyors, for example, use (or used to use) several locational markers in their endeavours to pinpoint a single spot. By analogy, triangular techniques in the social sciences attempt to map out, or explain more fully, the richness and complexity of human behaviour by studying it from more than one standpoint and/or using a variety of methods, even combining qualitative and quantitative methods in some cases.

Exclusive reliance on one method may bias or distort the researcher's picture of the particular slice of reality being investigated. The researcher needs to be confident that the data generated are not simply artefacts of one specific method of collection. Where triangulation is used in interpretive research to investigate different actors' viewpoints, the same method—for example, observation—will naturally produce different sets of data. Further, the more the methods contrast with each other, the greater the researcher's confidence. If, for example, the outcomes of a questionnaire survey correspond to those of an observational study of the same phenomena, the researcher will be more confident about the findings.

A more complex triangulation in a classroom ethnography study may involve teachers' ratings of pupils, school records, psychometric data, sociometric data, case studies, questionnaires and observation. Triangulation prevents the investigator from accepting too readily the validity of initial impressions.

Triangulation contributes to verification and validation of qualitative analysis by:

- checking out the consistency of findings generated by different data-collection methods; and
- checking out the consistency of different data sources within the same method.

In educational research there is also justification for the use of at least three different viewpoints in analysis. Each point of the triangle stands in a unique position with respect to access to relevant data about a teaching situation. The teacher is in the best position to gain access via introspection to their own intentions and aims in the situation. The students are in the best position to explain how the teacher's actions influence the way they respond to the situation. The participant-observer is in the best position to collect data about the observable features of the interaction between teachers and pupils (MacDonald & Walker 1976).

By collecting and analysing these viewpoints, the evaluator ensures that the final evaluation report reflects the multiple realities of specific social relationships.

External validity

External validity depends on the identification and description of those characteristics of phenomena salient for comparison with other similar types. Once the typicality or atypicality of a phenomenon is established, bases for comparison then may be assumed, and results may be translated for applicability across sites and disciplines.

A study is of little use to other researchers if its theoretical basis, or the constructs around which it is organised, are so idiosyncratic that they are understood only by the person who executed the study. The lack of comparability and translatability reduces the usefulness of a study to interesting but unscientific reading. Ethnographic studies are generally case studies from a single setting and it is difficult to translate them to other similar settings.

Writing up and publishing the ethnographic research report

Research reports are generally written to a fairly standard pattern: the hypotheses to be tested are stated first, the research procedures outlined, the findings analysed and, finally, an interpretation of the findings is given (chapter 22). The diverse and discovery-based character of ethnographic research makes any such standard pattern of reporting impossible. In any case, ethnographers often feel that this standard pattern of reporting employed by the other styles disguises as much as it reveals. The form of ethnographic reports is thus largely a product of the particular course of the research; the report usually being structured around certain major themes which emerged as the fieldwork and analysis progressed. However, there are certain general principles which underlie the construction of ethnographic research reports.

Perhaps the most distinctive feature of ethnographic analysis is the emphasis on reflexivity: description and analysis of the research process itself. One important element of reflexivity in connection with research reporting is the provision of extracts from the data. This provides a basis for the reader's assessment of the study: it gives the reader some idea of how the ethnographer interpreted the data, as well as some materials with which one can attempt various kinds of re-analysis. Some selection is inevitable in the presentation of data to the reader; the whole running record cannot be published. Often quotations from the data records seem to be chosen simply to illustrate the argument.

That is certainly an important function but it should not be the only one. Illustration ought to be given from each stage of the analysis, and the set of illustrations provided for each stage needs to be representative of the body of data used. Of particular interest and importance are deviant cases; these should be presented to the reader even if the analyst has found no way of incorporating them into the analysis. The fact that there are such cases does not necessarily undermine the theory, nor does it mean they cannot be incorporated into it; the reader may find ways of doing this.

Another difference is that for qualitative reporting the traditional 'third person' literary format that neutralises any sense of the personality of the investigator is inappropriate. A recognition of this element has advanced the use of 'first person' reporting.

A thorough report of an ethnographic or quasi-ethnographic study includes the description and discussion of each stage. These are:

1 the focus and purpose of the study and the question it addressed;
2 the research model or design used and justification for its choice;
3 the participants or subjects of the study and the setting(s) and context(s) investigated;
4 researcher experience and roles assumed in the study;
5 data collection strategies used in the study;
6 techniques used to analyse the data collected during the study;
7 findings of the study and their interpretations and applications.

summary

Ethnography is the study of people in their context. It is aimed at understanding behaviour from the perspective of the participants, and to capture social reality through fieldwork in natural settings. Ethnographic research is cyclic, as incoming data raises more questions and emerging hypotheses.

Observation and interviewing are the main data gathering techniques. Ethnographic research cannot employ the conventional judgements of reliability and validity. Replication is impossible given the subjective and once-only nature of the data. Generalisation is not feasible as statistical sampling is not involved. Triangulation is the major way in which validity can be assessed in ethnographic studies.

References

Argyle, M. (1969), *Social Interaction*, Methuen, London.
Bales, R.F. (1950), *Interaction Process Analysis*, Addison-Wesley, Reading, Massachusetts.
Becker, H.S., Geer B., Hughes, E.C. & Strauss, A.L. (1961), *Boys in White: Student Culture in Medical School*, University of Chicago Press, Chicago.
Ekman, P. (1982), *Emotion in the Human Face*, Cambridge University Press, New York.
Flanders, N. (1970), *Analysing Teaching Behaviour*, Addison-Wesley, Reading, Massachusetts.
Glaser, B.G. & Strauss, A. (1967), *The Discovery of Grounded Theory*, Aldine, Chicago.
Hamilton, D. (1976), *Curriculum Evaluation*, Open Books, London.
Hargreaves, D. (1967), *Social Relations in a Secondary School*, Routledge and Kegan Paul, London.

King, R. (1978), *All Things Bright and Beautiful*, Wiley, Chichester.

MacDonald, B. & Walker, R. (1976), *Changing the Curriculum*, Open Books, London.

Malinowski, B. (1922), *Argonauts of the Western Pacific*, Routledge, London.

Spitz, R.A. & Wolf, K.M. (1946), 'Anaolitic depression: An enquiry into the genesis of psychiatric conditions in early childhood, II', *The Psychoanalytic Study of the Child*, vol. II.

Stubbs, M. & Delamont, S. (eds) (1976), *Explorations in Classroom Observation*, John Wiley & Sons, London.

Whyte, W.F. (1955), *Street Corner Society*, University of Chicago Press, Chicago.

Wolcott, H. (1973), *The Man in the Principal's Office*, Holt Rinehart & Winston, New York.

Woods, P. & Hammersley, M. (eds) (1977), *School Experience*, Croom Helm, London.

Further reading

Adelman, C. (1981), *Uttering, Muttering: Collecting, Using and Reporting Talk for Social and Educational Research*, London, Grant McIntyre.

Bailey, K. (1989), *Methods of Social Research*, Free Press, New York.

Blaikie, N. (1988), Triangulation in Social Research: Origins, Use and Problem, Paper presented at the Conference of the Sociological Association of Australia and New Zealand, Canberra.

Bliss, J., Monk, M. & Ogbom, J. (1983), *Qualitative Data Analysis for Educational Research*, Routledge, London.

Burgess, R. (ed.) (1985), *Field Methods in the Study of Education*, Falmer Press, London.

Cobb, A. & Hagemaster, J. (1987), 'Ten criteria for evaluating qualitative research proposals,' *Journal of Nursing Education*, 26, pp. 138–43.

Dillon, D.R. (1989), 'Showing them that I want to learn and that I care about who they are. A micro ethnography of an English-reading classroom,' *American Education Research Journal* 26, pp. 227–59.

Fetterman, D. (1998), *Ethnography: Step by Step*, Sage, London.

Glesne, C. & Peshkin, A. (1992), *Becoming Qualitative Researchers*, Longman, NY.

Goetz, J.P. & Le Compte, M.D. (1984), *Ethnography and Qualitative Design in Educational Research*, Academic Press, Orlando.

Grills, S. (ed.) (1998), *Doing Ethnographic Research*, Sage, London.

Hammersley, M. (1991), *What's Wrong with Ethnography*, Routledge, London.

Henwood, K. & Pidgeon, N. (1995), 'Grounded theory and psychological research', *The Psychologist*, March, pp. 115–18.

Jorgensen, D. (1989), *Participant Observation: A Methodology for Human Studies*, Sage, Newbury Park.

Kirk, J. & Miller, M. (1986), *Reliability and Validity in Qualitative Research*, Sage, Beverly Hills.

LeCompte, M.D. & Pressle, S. (1993), *Ethnography and Qualitative Design in Educational Research*, Academic Press, New York.

Lincoln, Y.S. & Guba, E.G. (1985), *Naturalistic Inquiry*, Sage, Beverly Hills.

Miles, M.B. & Huberman, A. (1984), *Qualitative Data Analysis: A Sourcebook of New Methods*, Sage, Beverly Hills.

Potter, J. & Wetherell, M. (1987), *Discourse and Social Psychology*, Sage, London.

Rossman, G.B. & Wilson, B.L. (1985), 'Numbers and words: Combining quantitative and qualitative methods in a single large-scale evaluation study', *Evaluation Review*, 9(5), pp. 627–43.

Schonsul, J. & Le Compte, D. (eds) (1999), *The Ethnographer's Toolkit*, 7 vols, Sage, London.

Stringer, E., Agnello, M.F. & Conant-Baldwin, S. (eds) (1997), *Community Based Ethnography*, Laurence Erlbaum, New York.

Wolcott, H. (1986), *Inside Schools: Ethnography in Educational Research*, Routledge & Kegan Paul, New York.

Wolcott, H. (1990), *Writing up Qualitative Research*, Sage, Newbury Park.

Unstructured interviewing

24
twenty four

As well as participant observation, unstructured and semi-structured interviews are other major tools in the qualitative researcher's pack. Accounts derived from interviews are studied for themes. This data is reported as narrative containing direct quotations from interview statements, fieldnotes, etc. This illustrative data provides a sense of reality, describing exactly what the informant feels, perceives, and how they behave.

Participant observation, as presented in chapter 23, depends on participation in, and observation of, behaviour in its context, and this approach puts one in a better position to understand the everyday life of the group, as the participant observer actually experiences life as the group does. Open-ended interviewing, on the other hand, is advantageous for obtaining secondhand accounts.

An interview is a verbal interchange, often face to face, though the telephone may be used, in which an interviewer tries to elicit information, beliefs or opinions from another person. A crude categorisation of the forms interviews can take is listed below.

Unstructured (open-ended)	Semi-structured	Structured
Oral or life history interviews	Survey interviews	Standardised interviews
	Group interviews	
In-depth interviews	In-depth interviews	Survey interviews
Clinical interviews		Clinical history taking
Group interviews		

Structured or standardised interviews are used predominantly in surveys and opinion polls with consequent quantitative analysis, and are considered in this text in more depth in chapter 30. In such standardised interview procedures:

- every interviewee receives the same questions in the same specified order so that comparisons between defined groups can be made with statistical comparability being the main objective;
- specific questions receive specific answers, so that a conversational approach cannot be maintained;
- all or nearly all the questions will be close-ended, in that the respondent is forced to select their answer from a limited set of responses previously established by the designer of the questionnaire;
- there is no flexibility or latitude allowed to either interviewer or respondent. The data coding of responses is done relatively easily.

The disadvantages of closed-ended structured surveys are obvious:

- Firstly, the researcher has no scope to find out the beliefs, feelings or perceptions of the respondent that do not fit into the pre-ordained response categories.
- Secondly, there is the assumption that the trained interviewer can be so standardised themselves, becoming a neutral medium in their manner of presentation of the questions, that no bias or subjectivity is introduced.
- Thirdly, this detachment and impersonal approach can prevent trust and rapport building up between interviewer and respondent.

As a result, qualitative researchers use unstructured or semi-structured interviewing techniques.

Semi-structured interviewing

This has been used either as part of a structured interview or an unstructured interview, as investigators from both persuasions feel that this may help their study. Rather than having a specific interview schedule or none at all, an interview guide may be developed for some parts of the study in which, without fixed wording or fixed ordering of questions, a direction is given to the interview so that the content focuses on the crucial issues of the study. This permits greater flexibility than the close-ended type and permits a more valid response from the informant's perception of reality. However, the comparability of the information between informants is difficult to assess and response coding difficulties will arise.

It is the making public of private interpretations of reality.

According to Taylor and Bogdan, open-ended or in-depth interviews are:

. . . repeated face-to-face encounters between the researcher and informants directed towards understanding informants' perspectives on their lives, experiences or situations as expressed in their own words (1984, p. 77).

The advantages are that:

- with the contacts being repeated, there is a greater length of time spent with the informant, which increases rapport;
- the informant's perspective is provided rather than the perspective of the researcher being imposed;
- the informant uses language natural to them rather than trying to understand and fit into the concepts of the study;
- the informant has equal status to the researcher in the dialogue rather than being a guinea pig.

The rationale behind open-ended interviewing is that the only person who understands the social reality in which they live is the person themself. No structure imposed by the interviewer will encapsulate all the subtleties and personal interpretations. At the end of the academic year a student reports sick to the university's health service complaining of headaches, fatigue, stomach upset. The doctor imposes an often-used structure on this and informs the student that they have a virus infection which will clear up in a few days' time. If the doctor had used a more open-ended approach and encouraged the student to talk, the dialogue would provide revelation of worry over exam failure, loss of esteem feelings, difficulties of facing parents and friends with the results, deciding whether or not to drop out, etc. The apparent lack of structure to the dialogue will provide a window into the routinely constructed interpretations and habitual responses of each individual. Open-ended interviewing depends on verbal accounts.

Open-ended interviewing (or in-depth interviewing)

This form of interviewing takes the form of a conversation between informant and researcher. It focuses, in an unstructured way, on the informant's perception of themself, of their environment and of their experiences. There is no standardised list of questions. It is a free-flowing conversation, relying heavily on the quality of the social interaction between the investigator and informant, that can be subtly redirected by the interviewer if it should stray too far off the track of the research study. Thus, while it is made to be as natural as possible, the direction of the conversation is always controlled somewhat minimally to ensure the focus stays relevant to the problem.

When should open-ended interviewing be employed?

- It should be used to obtain an individual's subjective experiences when a life or oral history is being elicited. The individual's subjective life experiences are reported in the individual's own language in a case study approach. This evidence is often combined with the study of documents, photographs, letters and other personal effects.
- It facilitates access to events and activities that cannot be directly observed by the researcher because perhaps they occurred in the past; for example, a school leaver's reactions and feelings to not gaining entry to the university and/or course of their choice.

- In a variant of the first point, it can be used in a clinical interview to obtain a case history for counselling or medical purposes.
- It enables more subjects to be studied in detail than does participant observation; for example, in studying the integration of migrant children into state schools it is more economical to give open-ended interviews than to attend and immerse oneself in a number of school classes across a variety of schools as a participant observer.
- It can also be used in a group interview context where the form would be an open-ended group discussion. Group dynamics can be studied in this way too. There is the danger that members will not fully reveal their beliefs and feelings when other persons are present.

Advantages and disadvantages of open-ended interviewing

A major disadvantage is that the researcher is open to the vagaries of the informant's interpretation and presentation of reality. This is a problem of validity, but, of course, if the informant genuinely perceives events in the way stated, then their behaviour follows as a corollary. The researcher is deprived of an ethnographic context in which the informant's reported perceptions occur, as they are never able to directly observe the informant in their everyday context.

Prior to conducting the interviews, the researcher does not know how many sessions are going to be needed or what their length will be. These matters will depend on the verbosity of the informant, their willingness to talk, and the value of what they are saying.

STQ134

Explain when you would use open-ended interviewing rather than structured interviewing.

Questioning techniques

The techniques which counsellors—particularly non-directive counsellors—use in their counselling sessions are equally valuable to open-ended non-directive interviewers.

In non-directive counselling the counsellor makes considerable use of parroting (mirroring) and minimal encouragers to keep the informant conversing. These must be used effectively too by the open-ended interviewer. 'Parroting' or 'mirroring' is repeating back to the informant the last few words they said, or the gist of what they said, e.g. 'You were late'. When the mirroring involves feeling, it is often termed 'reflecting', e.g. 'You feel unhappy with the support you get from your principal'. Accurate mirroring shows the informant that you are listening and understanding, encouraging them to continue.

Minimal encouragers are single words or short phrases that encourage or reinforce the informant, e.g. 'I see', 'Go on', 'Can you tell me more?', 'Yes', 'Hmm', 'What happened next?'. Parroting and minimal encouragers combined with such non-verbal communication techniques as eye contact and head nods will ensure that the informant continues to speak in what they perceive as a warm, accepting interpersonal context.

When questions are asked they are usually descriptive, requesting informants to describe experiences, places, people and events. These are useful at the start of an interview as general non-threatening questions. They allow the respondent to control the flow of information. Other types of questions are contrast questions and structural questions. The former ask for comparisons of experiences/events, e.g. 'How did your first day as a teacher compare to today?'. Then, of course, using the funnelling technique, the comparisons can become more specific about feelings of competency, pupil behaviour, etc. The structural question is used to discover how a person organises their information/experiences, e.g. 'What sort of activities does a classroom teacher involve themselves in during a typical day?'. The above type of questions are focused on knowledge. Feeling questions are focused on emotional responses, e.g. 'How do you feel about the way the parents of your pupils respond to you?'.

STQ135

Devise some minimal encouragers you could use as part of your interviewing technique.

Listening skills

These are better thought of as attending skills and involve the same qualities and skills as those required by good counsellors. Only by displaying empathy and acceptance, conveying respect and creating an ethos of trust will the interviewee be able to enter into a valid relationship with you, in which they are willing to convey their real feelings, thoughts and emotions. In attending to an interviewee you must be an active listener, look interested, be sensitive to verbal and non-verbal cues, using as it were a third ear. Remember, the interviewee is noting your verbal and non-verbal signals and building up a picture of how open, genuine, interested and encouraging you are.

Words are not the whole message. Listening is not simply hearing, for we can hear without listening. You must attend to the content of the words and the feeling behind them. You can ask for clarification, you can summarise and check out inconsistencies so you are sure you are picking up the message accurately. Never jump to conclusions, and avoid personal prejudices and blocks that hinder understanding of what the other person is really saying. Take time to listen and give time for the other person to finish.

Non-verbal communication

We communicate with our whole bodies, not just with our tongues. Actions, gestures, facial expressions, body movements and body positions—all speak louder than words. Interviewees often don't realise they are communicating non-verbally, confirming, emphasising, or even contradicting the verbal message. Learn about some of the more significant non-verbal cues and how these vary from culture to culture. Non-verbal signals are an important part of the interview data.

A pilot study

A pilot study can test many aspects of your proposed study. It does so under circumstances that do not count, so that when they do count you have more faith in what you are doing.

Pilot observations and interviews need to be as close in context to the realities of the actual study as possible. The idea is not to gain data but to learn. Clarify these piloting intentions with your respondents so that after the interview you can talk about the questions themselves. Are they clear? Appropriate? What else should I be asking? Were there too many questions? Was my introduction appropriate? Did I establish rapport?

A cover story

A cover story is the initial verbal or written presentation of yourself to the gatekeeper and others who will be involved in your research. It does more than simply say who you are and what your study is about; it also prepares others to take part more effectively. It must cover what you will do with the results, their confidentiality, how you will record the data, how long a session will last, how many sessions, reassurance that there are no right answers, and that your role is not judgemental or evaluative, but understanding.

Initial interviewing activities

Before the interview starts, whether it is structured or unstructured, there are a few pragmatic issues to cover. For example, it may be prudent to discuss whether any payment will be made, where the interview will take place, at what time, the method used to record the information, the general nature of the research, and issues of confidentiality and anonymity. In addition, these initial discussions should help to develop rapport.

The form of questioning best suited to open-ended interviewing is the recursive model. This is the conversational approach, in that a natural flow between two persons occurs with a connection between the previous, current and next remark. The criticism of this recursive approach is that as it is directed by the conversation it is quite possible for the interchange to go completely off the topic. If this occurs, the interviewer must guide the attention of the informant back to the topic, e.g. by recalling something they said.

While the open-ended interview or non-directed interview does not have a structured set of questions, the interviewer will create a guide of the general issues they wish to cover. It is an *aide-mémoire* which can be revised as respondents provide new insights and further topics for exploration. This guide does not determine the order of topics discussed. Burgess (1984) found in interviewing primary school pupils that the latter would talk first about what each in their own way saw as being at the top of their agenda.

How do you start to get the informant to talk about at least one of the topics or themes that interest you? One technique is the storytelling technique, whereby the respondent can tell a story about themselves or an event, e.g. in response to a question like, 'I hear that students at this school often play jokes on teachers. Have you ever done this?', there is likely to be an extended response in the form of a story. Another example would be asking students to talk about their first day at secondary school. The story approach is encouraged if the interviewer shows considerable interest in the events and appears to enjoy the account.

Funnelling

In this approach the interviewer gradually guides the direction of the interview by commencing with broad general questions and focusing progressively onto the topic with more specific questions. For example, the interviewer interested in the drinking behaviour of adolescents might start by questioning their views on advertising alcohol at sports grounds, and sponsorship of sport by brewing companies. Gradually the focus narrows to alcohol and health, then to their drinking habits and effects on their health, finally targeting the issues to do with personal reasons for drinking. Only as rapport develops are respondents posed questions which could be personally threatening.

Solicited narrative

Here the researcher obtains a written account of the story and uses this as a source of discussion points in follow-up sessions. This technique is often used in life history and diary interview methods.

Recording the interview

Tape-recording is the best method, as the raw data remain for later study. Not having to take notes enables the researcher to take part in the conversation in a natural way. However, interview notes are a useful supplement to record non-verbal activity, and transcribing the data from a tape recording is a laborious and time-consuming task.

Closing an open-ended interview

Try not to give any verbal or non-verbal cues that you are glad the interview is coming to an end. That would destroy your relationship with the informant. Several strategies exist which facilitate the closing of the session, yet leave the door open for further sessions. Summarising the interview is one way. You could say, 'I think we have covered all the topic(s) we planned for today. Have you anything else you can add? Now that we have covered w, x and y, could we talk about z next time?'. Another ploy is to signal that the planned time is up: 'Hasn't our hour together gone quickly today? I am looking forward to our next hour together tomorrow.' However you close, always thank the informant, e.g. 'Thank you for your involvement; your contribution is really helping this project'.

Disengaging from the research field

Rather than this being a single event it is more of a process. The informant's involvements in the research will have had a lasting effect on them, as often it can involve them in revealing incidents and experiences known only to themselves, and there are obvious ethical, psychological, social and political issues at stake too for both parties. For example, both interviewer and respondent may have become very close; through the passage of time and changes in the direction of the research the original bargains and moral obligations struck with the gatekeeper and informants may be difficult to keep. Unfortunately there is no one routine way of disengaging.

Withdrawing gradually has its merits, as this enables the interviewer to return to informants during the writing up and analyse stages to recheck and clarify points. A quick, clean break can create a minimum of possible future complications.

Fieldnotes

Many ethnographic and open-ended interview research projects can generate over 1000 pages of fieldnotes which need to be analysed. Fieldnotes usually cannot be coded into numerical data and usually are transcribed, category-coded and filed. The purpose of the coding and filing is to enable the investigator to sort and organise the obtained information into patterns and themes.

Fieldnote data will not only include records of conversations, but also details of setting and investigator's impressions/observations. The fieldnotes will additionally include the investigator's reflections on the conversation and setting. Many interviewers like to keep the descriptive content and reflexive parts separate, as they derive from different persons.

Fieldnotes should be written up as soon as possible, and note-taking must be considered compulsory. Like all other types of research, it involves hard work, time and discipline.

During the first days of a research project the investigator will take down everything; as the project becomes refined and focused, the notes will be more selective. Notes should concentrate on answering *who/what/where/when/how/why* questions.

The fieldnotes really separate into three files. The *transcript file* contains the records of the interviews (see Figure 24.1). The transcript file should have a large margin on the right in which comments can be placed, and on the left, numbers alongside, to locate the conversation on the tape.

The *personal file* holds the reflections of the interviewer and a description of the setting. All your thoughts and impressions should be included in a frank way. It should read as you think—forget the grammar. The personal file should also contain full details of how you gained permission, how you maintained relations, and how you left the field and the success of these strategies. Comments on methodological problems are relevant in the personal file.

The third file is the *analytic file* which identifies and discusses the conceptual issues and emergent themes. It is usually organised around topic areas and is the basis for the analysis of the data.

Analysing the data

The purpose of analysing the data is to find meaning in the data, and this is done by systematically arranging and presenting the information. It has to be organised so that comparisons, contrasts and insights can be made and demonstrated. But the data are categorised not just to count occurrences. Instead, they are categorised to permit analysis and comparison of meanings within a category. For example, from interviews with adolescent drug users on their experiences in trying to break the habit, various perceptions and fears of the 'straight' world may emerge that are unique, and paint a picture of personal experience of considerable use to drug

FIGURE 24.1 *Example of transcript file*

Informant:	John Smith	2nd interview
Interviewer:	RBB	
Date:	1. 9. 99	
Subject:	How school principals perceive their role	
Place and time:	Principal's Office, Western H.S. 2 p.m.	
Other Relevant Information	Principal for ten years. Committee member State Teachers' Association. Tape recorder used with permission.	

0000   RBB Last session we talked about your experiences as a principal. I really enjoyed the stories you told me. I would like you now to tell me how you see your role.
JS What do you mean by role? Do you mean my day-to-day activities and responsibilities or the things, er, I should ideally do? *Possible way of categorising*
RBB I am interested in both, but let's start by you telling me about a typical day.
JS I find I do a lot of simple yet important things at the beginning of each day. For example, er, well, I try to be first at school and check with the caretaker that everything is alright—no break-ins, rooms all cleaned and so on.
RBB How would you describe this role?
JS I believe the principal is responsible for ensuring the school is in working order every day before students and staff arrive. I suppose it is part of the overall role of the *Pause* principal to see that the school functions but what to call *confusion?* this sub-role . . .

0010   RBB We can come back to naming roles later. What else do you do? (Interview continues for another 40 minutes)

Example of personal file for above

1.9.99   JS appeared agitated when I arrived as he had just faced some critical parents who had demanded explanation for their child's poor school report. As in the first interview he seemed a person under pressure; he looked tired and spoke hesitantly. Although he had volunteered to take part in the project, I felt that he viewed the situation as an examination of his performance as a principal: was he doing the 'right' things? He was again dressed in a suit—was this for me?—impression: management. He sat behind his desk. Does a hierarchical, authoritarian structure and role set dominate his thinking? Only time will tell. JS asked the secretary to bring us a cup of tea each so we relaxed a little before the interview began. I chatted about the weekend rugby league match, knowing he was an ardent supporter, hoping this would put him more at ease than in the first interview. However, he still seemed on edge and throughout the interview he focused on the minutiae of his job, itemising activities almost on a diary basis and seemed unable to perceive patterns to his work or categorise the activities into roles from his point of view . . . In later interviews I shall try to get JS to look for major role categories.

rehabilitation therapists trying to assist the user. The richness of unique qualities is preserved in qualitative analysis.

The qualitative researcher will begin by categorising. As notes are read and re-read it is possible to start grouping items together. For example, if you asked students to discuss in unstructured interviews their reactions to their college courses, statements might fall into the following groupings: relevancy, quality of teaching, timetable, textbooks, link to career, amount of work, assessment, etc.

Other categories might come from the participants themselves. They might divide themselves in perception and actual friendship groups into 'the workers', 'the smokers' and 'the thick-heads'. These categories might prove vital in looking at different perceptions of school, levels of academic commitment and future career plans.

Some researchers may cross categories to produce types. For example, a teacher who is a disciplinarian might also be distant and cold in their relationship with the students. This combination of qualities might be given the type name 'autocrat'. Types are useful in that if a subject does not fit any type this may lead to fresh insights and another way of classifying. An example of a category system or taxonomy is seen in Table 24.1 (p. 433).

Coding

So the first stage in analysing the interview data is coding, i.e. classifying material into themes, issues, topics, concepts, propositions. Coding cannot be done overnight. Many interviewers re-read their notes many times before they can begin to grasp the major themes. Some of this coding may begin while the data is still being collected, as particular issues are raised consistently across interviews. This early coding assists the interviewer to focus on essential features of the project as they develop.

This is part and parcel of the analytic induction method where the general statement about the topic is constantly refined, expanded and modified as further data are obtained. For example, you may be studying why some tertiary students apply to live in university halls/colleges. After interviewing the first six students you develop some tentative propositions about why they make this choice. In subsequent interviews you will tend to refine your questions along the line of these propositions. Further propositions will emerge as more interviews are conducted. Later interviews will test the validity of the propositions.

Woods (1976) used open-ended interviews to explore pupils' experiences of school and found that 'having a laugh' was a recurrent theme. Woods then set about classifying types of laughter in the classroom and their functions.

Content analysis

Content analysis is used to identify themes, concepts and meaning. It is a form of classifying content. These elements can be counted in numerical terms as well as examined for meaning. But when looking at the latter there is the problem of hidden meaning, of reading between the lines, and we will never know whether our reading between the lines is what the informant was meaning. Each interview is analysed for themes/topics. As the research focus becomes narrower, the file should include discussion about why certain focuses were chosen rather than others, and should reveal emerging ideas which are strengthened or weakened by successive interviews. This discussion will involve from time to time the relating of present findings to previous research and theory. Is there support for, extension or rejection of previous findings/theory? Include speculative ideas that come to you as you write the analytic file which you can test in later interviews. Theory emerges from the data in qualitative research. This has been termed *grounded theory* by Glaser and Strauss (1967). Thus observers enter the research situation with no prior theoretical preconceptions and create, revise and refine theory in the light of the data collected.

TABLE 24.1 *Example derived from open-ended interviews*

Taxonomy of things students do in school

Pick on other students	fight
	push
	threaten
	call names
	tease about looks
	trip up
	steal books, pens, etc.
	make fun of them
Behave in class	take tests
	sit in classes
	don't talk in class
	don't shout out
	stay in seat
	do work requested
	try to become teacher's pet
	extra work
	volunteer
	carry equipment
	clean boards
Fool around	fight in class
	drop things on floor
	shout out
	don't do work
	smoke in toilets
	set off fire alarm
	skip class
	sit in another's seat
	give silly answers
	throw things across room
	ignore teacher
	eat in class
	walk around in class
	read comics in class
	push another off chair
	whistle in class
	tell jokes
	get others into trouble

Grounded hypotheses should be truer to life than those generated through deduction within, say, behaviourism or Piagetian theory. The final qualitative research paper can then give an account of early hypotheses and the extent to which these are modified or discarded by further inquiry and data analysis. The report becomes a diary of insights and project development.

Content analysis needs a coding system that relates to the theoretical framework or research question. If our research question is who influences a student's decision to apply for university campus accommodation, then our coding categories would involve significant others such as parents, friends, counsellor, etc. The coding of a qualitative research is important, as it operates as a labelling, retrieval and organising device. If a coding system appears not to be working, in that it is difficult to code some elements, then a new coding system may emerge that brings material together in completely new way and adds insight into the topic. The coding scheme is, in fact, the conceptual model. The coding categories should start developing as soon as the first interview is being conducted, as coding facilitates the understanding of the information which may direct the focus of the next interview. As Miles and Huberman (1984, p. 63) state, 'Coding is not something one does to get data ready for analysis, but something that drives ongoing data collection. It is, in short, a form of continuing analysis'.

Content analysis is more an art than a science. The process of category generation involves noting regularities and recurring ideas/themes in the setting, or people, chosen for study. The categories may be those that are generated by the people in the setting as they perceive their environment, or may be constructed by the observer/interviewer. The greatest strength of content analysis is that it can be conducted later, so that the setting is not disturbed in any way, and that the researcher determines the coding after the event, not setting out to prove or disprove a hypothesis by gathering facts to support their position, though guiding hypotheses may serve as flexible boundaries to provide a focus for the coding and selection of relevant elements of content. This must not lead to premature coding, forcing data into some theoretical framework, closing off alternative conceptualisations, or precluding the discovery of formerly hidden unrecognised data, connections and processes.

As categories and patterns become evident in the data, the researcher can then commence to evaluate the plausibility of emerging hypotheses and test them against further data. This entails attempts to challenge the hypotheses by seeking further positive instances and disconfirming instances. An apparent pattern must be challenged. Other plausible explanations always exist, and the researcher must demonstrate how and why their explanation is the most plausible of all.

In order to control for bias in the analysis and interpretation, the researcher should engage another researcher who can play devil's advocate and critically question the researcher's coding and analysis. Additionally, there should always be a search for negative instances.

Some of the sort of code categories that generally are useful include:

event codes, i.e. specific activities
definitions of the situation codes, i.e. how informants define setting
process codes, i.e. stages, steps, phases
social structure codes, i.e. patterns of behaviours and relationships

strategies codes, i.e. how people do things

subject perspective codes, i.e. how informants think about their situation

Stages in coding

1 The first stage in coding is to develop a list of coding categories. Then a short name is assigned to each and a number to each subcategory. For example, classroom activities (CA in short) may be a category, while teaching (CAl), marking (CA2) and administration (CA3) are sub-categories.
2 In the margin of the transcript file, the data can now be coded by the appropriate code, e.g. CA2, as the file is read. The code may refer to a phrase, a sentence or a paragraph. On occasions, there may be a double reference in the verbal unit and in this case it is double-coded.
3 After codes have been allocated to the text in the transcript file, data coded to each category needs to be collected together. Here you can use either index cards on which you paste cut-up sections of the text, or place the cuttings into manila folders. The former method is the best. You must photocopy your transcript file or ensure it is held on a PC so you do not lose your only copy when you cut and paste.

Computer-aided methods in qualitative research

It was not until the early 1980s that qualitative researchers discovered that the computer could assist them in working with their data. Even then there was a reluctance to employ information technology—a reluctance exemplifying the antipathy held by qualitative researchers towards those who pursued experimental research for whom the computer was becoming an indispensable aid. Qualitative researchers did and still do believe that ambiguity and context relatedness have to be regarded as central characteristics of everyday language and behaviour.

Therefore, they argue it is impossible to make sense out of written or spoken messages in everyday contexts without some tacit knowledge that cannot easily be formalised. The attempt to apply the logical, unambiguous precise rules and context-free conditions that computer analysis requires to human understanding was perceived as a futile and erroneous approach. An additional argument claimed that quantitative content analysis is too atomistic and over-simplistic to capture the richness of human communicative and social interaction.

It is therefore only recently that the idea of electronic data processing being an indispensable tool for the storage, retrieval and manipulation of text has become acceptable. The event that really changed the situation was the advent of small personal user-friendly desk computers, instead of impersonal mainframes. This led to a change in the dominant paradigm of computer use from 'computers as number crunchers' to computers as devices for the intelligent management of data, incorporating storage and retrieval facilities. This led to the PC becoming regarded as being of assistance to qualitative research.

The central task in qualitative research—understanding the meaning of communication and behaviour—cannot be computerised as a mechanical task, but there are many mechanical tasks involved in interpretive analysis. Huge amounts of unstructured data such as interview transcripts, fieldnotes, personal documents, etc., need to be managed and organised, in addition to the numerous codings, notes, memos, and marginal comments made as the researcher wades through the material. Another important aspect of qualitative research is pulling together interview data, textual material, etc., that have 'something' in common. Qualitative researchers used to cut up file notes and transcripts, and code them into separate manila folders. Unfortunately this mechanical method dislocated the removed section of text from its original context.

The advantage of the computer is that it does not decontextualise the text which can be copied into files as a form of an electronic concordance, making it possible to electronically restore the original context of the segment, allowing for the coding system to be changed if necessary, and permitting networks and hierarchies of codes, as well as quantitative attributes such as frequency counts within codes. All this makes qualitative theory building an easier task, with a network of codes acting as the representation of an emerging theory or hypothesis. Most recent computer programs in this area allow such networks to be graphically displayed.

Some useful software for qualitative analysis

The following are just a few of the existing softwares available. Researchers should keep their eyes open for updates and new ones coming on the market.

ATLAS/ti Version 1.1E

Thomas Muhr, Trautenaustr. 12, 10717 Berlin, Germany

ATLAS/ti is extremely useful for text interpretation, text management and theory building. It could be the preferred program if a researcher wishes to construct linkages between any elements of the qualitative database—for example, text segments and memos. This is a very flexible tool for constructing any kind of network.

The design of the user interface is such that most of the analysis is conducted on-screen. Consequently, a wide variety of functions to support this style of working is offered. The program is especially useful for research groups whose members want to do coding, memoing and theory building independently, but want to share their results.

HyperRESEARCH Version 1.5x

Sharlene Hesse-Biber, T Scott Kinder, Paul R. Dupuis ResearchWare, Inc., PO Box 1258, Randolph, MA 02368-1258, USA

As well as permitting ordinary coding and retrieval, this program is particularly designed for the approach towards qualitative hypothesis testing. The researcher formulates hypothesis in terms of 'if-then' statements about the co-occurrence of certain codes within a document.

TextSmart by SPSS Inc.

This software uses cluster analysis and multi-dimensional scaling to analyse key words and group texts, such as open-ended survey responses, into categories.

TEXTPAC PC

This package is useful for content analysis of open-ended questions from surveys. It can also deal with many aspects of text analysis and content analysis. There are options for validity and reliability studies.

MAx Version 3.5

Udo Kuckartz, Andreas Maurer, Bilro far Softwareentwicklung und Sozialforschung, Schiltzallee 52, 14169 Berlin, Germany

This program was originally developed to support the analysis of open-ended questions in survey questionnaires, where the method of case-oriented quantification is employed. Since then, additional features have been added, for example, for the retrieval of co-occurring text segments. All files used and created by the program that contain code or case information are stored in standard dBase format. This offers the competent user extensive possibilities for using other software tools in order to modify these files, or to subject them to a different type of analysis from that offered by the program.

All files (texts, codes, numerical and other case-oriented data) are saved in dBase format and can therefore easily be exported to statistical programs such as SPSS and SAS and re-imported to MAx after modification. SPSS files can also be directly created for exporting numerical data. Documents can be divided into *paragraphs,* permitting a structuring of texts such as open-ended questions. Code and word frequencies can be calculated.

Code-a-Text

Dr A. Cartwright, Centre for the Study of Psychotherapy, University of Kent, Canterbury, UK

Originally designed to aid analysis of therapeutic conversations, it has now been applied to other texts such as fieldnotes, and responses to open-ended questions.

QSR NUD*IST

Lyn Richards and Tom Richards. Qualitative Solutions & Research Pty. Ltd., Box 171, La Trobe University Post Office, Victoria 3083, Australia
Distributed by Sage Publications Ltd., 6 Bonhill Street, London EC2A 4PU, UK

NUD*IST is a program for facilitating theory building by searching for words and phrases and coding data. From the coding it will search for links among the codes and build a hierarchical network of code patterns, categories and relationships in the original data. It will code data in more than one way to provide multiple perspectives and enable changes in codes to be effected as a deeper understanding of the data emerges. This makes it a very useful tool in strategies of hypothesis development and grounded theory.

The user is invited (but not forced) to develop a hierarchical code structure that can be represented graphically and can be used for multiple types of retrievals. Among the most powerful retrieval functions are COLLECT, which allows for retrieving all segments or memos attached to a code and all of its subcodes, and INHERIT, which permits the retrieval of all memos or segments attached to a code and its 'ancestors' (that is, the codes in a direct line above the code in question). Memos can be linked to codes, case-variables, and whole documents.

A great variety of retrievals can be conducted to identify the co-occurrence of codes, which is defined as the overlapping, nesting, proximity and sequential order of text segment to which the codes under investigation are attached. All Boolean operators can be employed. The program attaches a new code to the retrieved text segments, which may then be incorporated into an existing hierarchical code structure.

Code and word frequencies can be calculated. Additional functions are available for the building of matrices, and for automatic coding according to user-defined keywords. NUD*IST files can be imported into SPSS.

QUALPRO Version 4.0

Bernard Blackman. Impulse Development Company, 349, Thomasville Road, Suite 202, Tallahassee, FL 32308, USA

QUALPRO was originally a collection of routines for ordinary coding and retrieval that could be executed via DOS and by using a simple command shell. This collection has now been extended by the addition of functions for co-occurring code searches and matrix displays. Algorithms for the calculation of interceder reliability and for computing matrices displaying agreement and disagreement between coders, are unique features of this program. This information can be used to improve the code definitions and procedures, and hence the precision of coding. The program is particularly useful for research groups concerned with the robustness of the coding scheme.

Text can be entered into the program directly or imported as an ASCII file. The smallest coding unit is the text line. Up to 1000 codes can be attached to one document. Selective retrievals of text segments are supported and memos can be recorded. Memos can be linked to whole documents and text segments.

In every ordinary retrieval, the program can retrieve, together with the text, the line numbers of overlapping presented segments coded with another code. All Boolean operators can be applied in a search for text segments so that nested and overlapping text segments can be retrieved, and also text segments to which a certain combination of codes does or does not apply. Code frequencies can be calculated. The interceder reliability can be determined too.

The ETHNOGRAPH v.4.0

John Seidel, Susanne Friese, D. Christopher Leonard
Qualis Research Associates, PO Box 2070, Amherst, MA 01004, USA

This was one of the earliest and most widely distributed programs in the field. The strength of the program is its functions to assist researchers working in the tradition of ethnography and interpretive sociology who are more concerned with the interpretive analysis of texts than with theory building and hypothesis examination.

The software facilitates the management and analysis of text-based data, such as transcripts of interviews, focus groups, fieldnotes, diaries, meetings and other documents.

Searches for co-occurring codes are also available. Linkages can be established between one text segment and up to twenty-six memos. Several codes can be subsumed under one 'parent code' for structuring the coding scheme.

The 'Multiple Code Search' function helps to find co-occurring codes, whereby co-occurrence can be defined as the overlapping, nesting, sequential ordering or proximity of text segments. Code frequencies can be calculated and additional functions are available for identifying different speakers in transcripts and for entering contextual comments within the texts.

The above descriptions are sparse and cannot be exhaustive. Although we have tried to ensure that all the information is accurate, we cannot guarantee this, as newer versions are always being prepared. By accessing the following site you can download demonstration versions of many pieces of software that undertake qualitative analysis: www.gwdg.de/~mromppe/contsoft.htm/

Case summaries

Many researchers use case summaries as a means of analysing their data. For example, it is useful to employ case studies of students to illustrate and support arguments in investigating student behaviour or school processes. However, the basis on which case studies are chosen is often obscure and may simply reflect a bias towards, or desire to support, a particular theoretical rationale. Again, the use of index cards is advised. Each card can contain information on the informant, including their categorisation on a number of concept codes, a summary of the interview and analytic comments taken from the analytic file. These case summaries not only clarify and sort information from within a case but permit comparison across cases too.

The diary as a preliminary to interviewing

Most of us keep diaries for the very practical purpose of knowing when we have a meeting to attend, or when it is our turn to pick up the children from school. Since most people keep diaries, they provide a simple and cheap way of finding out information, particularly about how people spend their time. The diaries used for research purposes include not usually those containing personal thoughts or shopping lists, but logs of professional activities which give clear information about work patterns.

Diaries are often used as a preliminary to interviewing. The record provides a basis for further questions that explore job-related activities in more depth. In some research it may not be clear initially exactly what questions to ask. Therefore the diary content will generate ideas. The diary, in conjunction with a diary interview, has been used as an approximation to participant observation. You are now aware of the difficulties of participant observation, such as the time involved and the possible change in behaviour. A combination of diary and interview is valuable for those situations where observation might be too intrusive, such as being present at a parent–principal interview, or when extended observation would be too resource intensive. In this approach the diarist is requested to write on the what/when/where/who and how matters. For example in-service teacher education students might be asked to maintain a diary of the events that caused them problems each day, how they sought to solve the problems, who they sought support from and how successfully they resolved the issue. Participant observation may well have prevented some of the problems—particularly pupil misbehaviour—from occurring, or may have led to advice being sought from the observer.

As in all research, the diary method requires subjects who are willing to undertake the tasks conscientiously. If subjects are persuaded against their better judgement, or have little sympathy with the research, then the diary they eventually hand over may well be incomplete or contain matters not requested. Subjects must be given clear instructions about what they are being asked to do, what type of words are needed and why. While completing a diary at regular intervals during a day can be time-consuming for those who already maintain a diary, the task is of little consequence or additional effort.

A major problem, as with observation or interviews, is that the subject may modify their behaviour so that the diary record reveals a different range of activities than normal to create a favourable impression. A diary showing hours spent and activities related to preparing schoolwork at home each evening may well be inflated to give the impression of a dedicated teacher.

A major way of investigating the work people do, without inconveniencing them with the constant presence of an observer, is to ask them to describe the critical incidents that have occurred over a specified time period. Heads of departments, principals or education administrators could be asked how they distinguish between trivial aspects of their job and key ones; how they prioritise their time; what events/issues they regard as critical and why. A critical task might be defined as one which makes a difference between success and failure in carrying out the duties associated with a job. The idea is to collect reports as to what issues occur, how they are defined, how they can be dealt with effectively, and how they contributed to good performance. The diary becomes a log focusing on specific happenings, almost like an accident or incidents file maintained at a police station. If they had time (which is unlikely) you could ask postgraduate students undertaking thesis research to keep a log of the issues or problems that they faced in conducting the various aspects of their research. They would describe each problem as it arose, why it arose, and how they tackled it.

Diaries generally cover an agreed timespan. It may be a week, a month or even longer. Content usually deals with facts and activities rather than emotions, although some researchers may be interested in some additional commentary to accompany the record. Diary requests often take the form of:

Every day at 11.00 a.m., 2.00 p.m. and 5.00 p.m. write down all the things you did in the previous hour;

or

Keep a record of all interviews with parents, their length, reason, content, conclusion/result, etc.

In research we are usually only interested in job-related activities; therefore instructions must be explicit and indicate that you do not require details such as that you washed your hands or made a coffee. It is also useful to have the diarist indicate how usual the week or the day was and whether there were any unusual events, crises, etc.

Completed diaries can provide a wealth of information if they have been completed conscientiously and thought has been given in advance to what information is to be sought.

summary

Unstructured and semi-structured interviewing are the major tools of qualitative research. Their advantage is that the informant's perspectives are provided using language natural to them. This limits the effect of the researcher's preconceptions and biases and beliefs in directing the line of interviewing. The interviewer requires listening skills and non-directive questioning techniques. Interview data requires coding so that a content analysis can be used to identify themes, concepts and categories.

References

Burgess, R. (1984), *In the Field*, Unwin, London.
Glaser, B.G. & Strauss, A.L. (1967), *The Discovery of Grounded Theory*, Aldine, Chicago.
Miles, M. & Huberman, M. (1984), *Qualitative Data Analysis*, Sage, Beverly Hills.
Taylor, S. & Bogdan, R. (1984), *Introduction to Qualitative Research Methods*, Wiley, New York.
Woods, P. (1976), 'Having a Laugh', in *The Process of Schooling*, eds M. Hammersley & P. Woods, Routledge and Kegan Paul, London.

Further reading

Berg, B. (1989), *Qualitative Research Methods for the Social Sciences*, Allyn and Bacon, Boston.
Boyatis, R. (1998), *Thematic Analysis and Code Development. Transforming Qualitative Information*, Sage, London.
Brooks, M. (1989), *Instant Rapport*, Warner Books, New York.
Cohen, A.K. (1955), *Delinquent Boys*, Free Press, New York.
Foddy, W.H. (1988), Open Versus Closed Questions: Really a Problem of Communication. Paper presented to the Australian Bicentennial Meeting of Social Psychologists. Leura, New South Wales, August.
Gerson, E. (1985), 'Computing in qualitative sociology', *Qualitative Sociology*, 7, pp. 194–8.
Gahan, C. & Hannibal, M. (1998), *Doing Qualitative Research Using QSR NUD*IST*, Sage; London.
Green, A. (1995), 'Verbal protocol analysis', *The Psychologist*, March, pp. 126–9.
Hargreaves, D.H., Hestor, S.K. & Mellor, F.J. (1975), *Deviance in Classrooms*, Routledge and Kegan Paul, London.
Kelle, U. (ed.) (1995), *Computer Aided Qualitative Data Analysis*, Sage, London.
Lacey, C. (1970), *Hightown Grammar*, Manchester University Press, Manchester.
Minichiello, V. et al. (1990), *In Depth Interviewing*, Longman Cheshire, Melbourne.
Richards, L. & Richards, T. (1987), 'Qualitative data analysis: Can computers do it?' *Australian and New Zealand Journal of Sociology*, 23, pp. 23–35.

Richards, T. & Richards, L. (1988), NU*DIST: a System for Qualitative Data Analysis. Paper presented at Australian Computer Society. Victorian Branch.

Tesch, R. (1990), *Qualitative Research. Analysis Types and Software Tools*, Falmer, New York.

Van Galen, J., Noblit, G. & Hare, D. (1988–89), 'The art and science of interviewing kids: The group interview in evaluation research', *National Forum of Applied Educational Research Journal*, 1(2), pp. 74–81.

Action-research

25
twenty five

What is action-research?

Action-research is the application of fact-finding to practical problem-solving in a social situation with a view to improving the quality of action within it, involving the collaboration and cooperation of researchers, practitioners and laymen.

Kemmis and Grundy (1981) define action-research in education as:

> A family of activities in curriculum development, professional development, school improvement programmes, and systems planning and policy development. These activities have in common the identification of strategies of planned action which are implemented, and then systematically submitted to observation, reflection and change. Participants in the action being considered are integrally involved in all of these activities.

It aims to improve practical judgement in concrete situations, and the validity of the 'theories' it generates depends not so much on 'scientific' tests of truth, as on their usefulness in helping people to function more intelligently and skilfully. In action-research, 'theories' are not validated independently and then applied to practice. They are validated through practice. Action-research is a total process in which a *'problem situation' is diagnosed, remedial action planned and implemented, and its effects monitored*, if improvements are to get underway. It is both an approach to problem-solving and a problem-solving process. The development of action-research philosophy and method has had a strong Australian input through the work of Kemmis and his colleagues at Deakin University.

The focus in action-research is on a specific problem in a defined context, and not on obtaining scientific knowledge that can be generalised. An on-the-spot procedure designed to deal with a concrete problem, it is a logical extension of the child-centred progressive approach. If children can benefit intellectually, socially and emotionally from working together to solve problems in group activities, so too, it is argued, can their teachers.

There are four basic characteristics of action-research:

1. Action-research is *situational*—diagnosing a problem in a specific context and attempting to solve it in that context.
2. It is *collaborative*, with teams of researchers and practitioners working together.
3. It is *participatory*, as team members take part directly in implementing the research.
4. It is *self-evaluative*—modifications are continuously evaluated within the ongoing situation to improve practice.

Lewin's model of action-research

The term *action-research* was first coined by the social psychologist Kurt Lewin. Lewin's model involves a cyclic sequence (see Figure 25.1).

STQ136

What do you perceive as the main characteristics of action-research?

Lewin challenged an orthodoxy about the role of the social scientist as the disinterested, 'objective' observer of human affairs.

Lewin's model is an excellent basis for starting to think about what action-research involves. Two major stages can be identified:

1. diagnostic, in which problems are analysed and hypotheses developed; and
2. therapeutic, in which hypotheses are tested by a consciously directed change experiment in a real social life situation.

Action-research usually commences with observations in the real world that raise such questions as 'Why don't my everyday experiences in the classroom fit with theory?', 'Why hasn't practice led to predicted results?'. To cope with these and other similar situations, we tend to formulate our own intuitive implicit theories. These are really the start of the qualitative research process. Personal theory helps to bring a problem into view and leads into a more systematic approach to investigating the issue. For example, the real-world intriguing observation that boys in my class try to avoid obtaining verbal reinforcement from me by not answering questions leads to a personal theory that boys don't want to counter peer group norms. This leads into a tentative guiding hypothesis for research purposes that suggests that the expectations of the boys' subculture is stronger than teacher expectations in relation to aspects of classroom behaviour.

FIGURE 25.1 *Lewin's cyclic model*

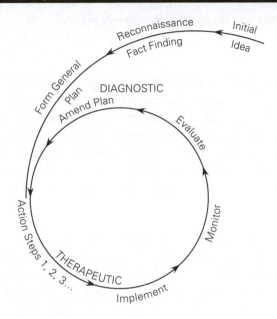

This cyclic model of problem identification, therapeutic action and evaluation can be divided into seven substages.

Stage 1

This involves the identification, evaluation and formulation of the problem or general idea perceived as critical in an everyday teaching situation. 'Problem' should be interpreted in as wide a way as possible to prevent constraints too early about issues/ideas creating too narrow a focus. Some examples of problems or general ideas are listed here.

- Students are dissatisfied with the methods by which they are assessed. How can we collaborate to improve student assessment?
- Students seem to waste a lot of time in class. How can I increase the time students spend 'on-task'?
- Parents are fairly keen to help the school with the supervision of students' homework. How can we make their help more productive?

In other words, the 'general idea' refers to a state of affairs or situation a participant wishes to change or improve on. The original problem may, in fact, change and be revised in the cyclic process. For example, pupils' dissatisfaction with the way they are assessed may merely be a symptom of a more fundamental problem, which may 'come to light' during the course of action-research; for example, the real purposes of assessment. In which case, a teacher would want to undertake subsequent actions which tackle that deeper problem, rather than merely treating the symptom. Goals are variables, not constants. They change over time as a result of the development project itself.

Stage 2

This is the time for fact finding, so that a full description can be given of the situation. For example, if the problem is 'pupils wasting time in class', one will want to know things such as: Which pupils are wasting time? What are they doing when they are wasting time? Are they wasting time doing similar or different things? What should they be doing when they are wasting time? What are they doing when they are not wasting time? Is there a particular point in the lesson, or time of day, or set of topics, where pupils waste time the most? What are the different forms in which 'wasting time' manifests itself?

All these facts help to clarify the nature of the problem. The collection of this information can provide a basis for classifying the relevant facts; for example, generating categories for classifying the different kinds of 'time-wasting' which go on.

It can also lead to some fairly radical changes in one's understanding of the original idea. For example, one may decide, in the light of this exercise, that many of the things thought to be 'time-wasting' are not, and that many of the things thought not to be 'time-wasting' in fact are.

Stage 3

This may involve a review of the research literature to find out what can be learned from comparable studies, their objectives, procedures and problems encountered. All this is related and synthesised with the critical review of the problem in Stage 2. Hypotheses can now be formulated; for example, utterances such as 'fine', 'interesting', 'correct', by teachers in response to ideas expressed by pupils can prevent the discussion of alternative ideas, since pupils tend to interpret such feedback as attempts to legitimate the development of some ideas rather than others. These hypotheses are general statements which attempt to explain some of the facts of the problem.

Stage 4

Having, through 'brainstorming' around a problem, generated some hypotheses, one can then proceed to gather information which is relevant to testing them. For example, evidence can be gathered about the extent to which one uses terms such as *good, interesting, right*; their effects on pupils' classroom responses; and the ways pupils interpret their use. The gathering of this evidence may also suggest further explanations of the problem situation, which in turn leads to more gathering of information, etc. This 'testing' of the hypothesis is not a statistical testing. It is seeing whether the evidence is congruent with the hypothesis. Even when one has tested hypotheses and found them to apply, they should retain the status of 'hypotheses' rather than 'conclusions', since one can always encounter instances where they do not apply, and which will prompt a search for more comprehensive explanations. The process of analysis is an endless one, but in action-research it must be interrupted for the sake of action. And the point of interruption should be when one has sufficient confidence in the hypotheses to allow them to guide action. At this point, the revised statement of the general idea or problem is feasible.

STQ138

How do hypotheses in action-research differ from those in quantitative research?

Stage 5

Before going into action, there is the need to decide on the selection of research procedures such as choice of materials, resources, teaching method, allocation of tasks. Equally important are discussion and negotiations among the interested parties—teachers, researchers, advisers, sponsors. A teacher may need to negotiate some of the proposed actions with colleagues, or a 'superior'. Their capacity to do their job properly could be influenced by the effects of the proposed changes, or perhaps they will 'carry the can for them', or even intervene unconstructively if not consulted. For example, a proposed change of syllabus might need to be negotiated with the relevant head of department, departmental colleagues, the head teacher, or even pupils and their parents.

As a general principle, the initial action-steps proposed should lie within areas where the action-researchers have the maximum freedom of decision.

Stage 6

This stage involves the implementation of the action plan. Decisions about the conditions and methods of data collection (for example, bi-weekly meetings, the keeping of records, interim reports, final reports, the submission of self-evaluation and group-evaluation reports, etc.); the monitoring of tasks and the transmission of feedback to the research team; and the classification and analysis of data.

Even if the action step is implemented with relative ease, it may create troublesome side-effects which require a shift into fact finding in order to understand how these arise. And this in turn may require some modifications and changes to the 'general plan' and a revamped action-step.

The choice of evaluative procedures is considered here too, in order to monitor the implementation:

- One needs to use monitoring techniques which provide evidence of how well the course of action is being implemented.
- One needs to use techniques which provide evidence of *unintended* as well as intended effects.
- One needs to use a range of techniques which will enable one to look at what is going on from a variety of angles or points of view (triangulation).

A huge range of techniques is available to record and report on the implementation. Some of these are plainly qualitative but others are taken from the quantitative stable. Among the usual techniques are diaries, analytic memos, document analysis, audio tape/video, outside observer, interviewing, and questionnaires.

Stage 7

This final stage involves the interpretation of the data and the overall evaluation of the project, often by writing a case study. Ideally, case study reports should be written at the end of each cycle, each building on and developing previous reports. At least one full report should be written at the point where one decides to end a particular spiral of action and research, and switch to a quite different issue or problem.

A case study report should adopt a historical format; telling the story as it has unfolded over time, showing how events hang together. It should include (but not necessarily in separate sections) accounts of the following:

- How one's 'general idea' evolved over time.
- How one's understanding of the problem situation evolved over time.
- What action-steps were undertaken in the light of one's changing understanding of the situation.
- The extent to which proposed actions were implemented, and how one coped with the implementation problems.
- The intended and unintended effects of one's actions, and explanations for why they occurred.
- The techniques one selected to gather information about:
  - the problem situation and its causes; and
  - the actions one undertook and their effects.
- The problems one encountered in using certain techniques and how one 'resolved' them.
- Any ethical problems which arose in negotiating access to, and release of, information, and how one tried to resolve them.
- Any problems which arose in negotiating action-steps with others, or in negotiating the time, resources and cooperation one wanted during the course of the action-research.

The mode of explanation in case study is naturalistic rather than formalistic. Relationships are 'illuminated' by concrete description rather than by formal statements of causal laws and statistical correlations. As action-research necessarily involves participants in self-reflection about their situation—as active partners in the research—accounts of dialogue with participants about the interpretations and explanations emerging from the research should be an integral part of any action-research report.

Discussions of the findings will take place in the light of previously agreed evaluative criteria. Errors, mistakes and problems will be considered. At this stage, the cycle is likely to begin again, with the problem and action modified to meet the evaluation comments. At the end of several cycles, outcomes of the project are reviewed, recommendations made and arrangements for dissemination of results to interested parties decided.

This is a basic framework; much activity of an incidental and possibly ad hoc nature will take place in and around it. This may comprise discussions among teachers, researchers and pupils, and regular meetings among teachers or schools to discuss progress and problems, and to exchange information.

In summary, we have a step-by-step process constantly monitored over varying periods of time by a variety of mechanisms (for example, diaries, questionnaires, interviews, tape recordings), so that feedback may be translated into modifications, directional changes and redefinitions, so as to bring about lasting benefit to the ongoing process. No attempt is made to identify one factor and study its effect in isolation, divorced from the context that gives it meaning. The findings tend to be applied immediately. Action-research should not only contribute to practice but aim at creating a theory of education and teaching which is available, meaningful and significant to other teachers.

Timing

With respect to classroom action-research, a teacher should decide exactly how much time can be set aside for monitoring the next action-step, when, and its effects. It is no good collecting more evidence than one can afford to 'process' and reflect about. And it is no good 'deciding' to transcribe all recordings when one knows one hasn't the time to do it. So the number of lessons monitored and the techniques selected should all be matched to a realistic estimate of available time. The 'matching' process is helped by working out a timetable.

In schools, the fact that 'terms' are usually interspersed by vacations suggests that this is a natural organisational unit of time in which to complete a 'cycle' of classroom action-research activity. I would normally feel it necessary to complete at least three, and perhaps four, cycles before one ought to be sufficiently satisfied with the improvements effected. In the context of classroom action-research, this could well mean a commitment of at least a year.

What can action-research be used for?

The purposes of action-research in school and classroom fall broadly into categories.

1 It is a means of remedying problems diagnosed in specific situations, or of improving in some way a given set of circumstances.
2 It is a means of in-service training, thereby equipping the teacher with new skills and methods, sharpening analytical powers and heightening self-awareness.
3 It is a means of injecting additional or innovatory approaches to teaching and learning into an ongoing system which normally inhibits innovation and change.
4 It is a means of improving the normally poor communications between the practising teacher and the academic researcher, and of remedying the failure of traditional research to give clear prescriptions.
5 Although lacking the rigour of true scientific research, it is a means of providing a preferable alternative to the more subjective, impressionistic approach to problem-solving in the classroom.

6 It is a way of studying human relations, morale and personnel functioning in the organisation.
7 It can facilitate job analysis.

Comparison between action-research and quantitative research

Purpose of research

Quantitative researchers believe the primary purpose of educational research is to establish new generalisations stated as observed uniformities, explanatory principles, or scientific laws. They test hypotheses in order to justify conclusions extending beyond the populations and situations studied. They use sampling theory and describe, within stated limits, population or situation universes. They are interested in discovering 'the truth'.

Action-researchers have a different primary purpose. They are not immediately concerned with adding more 'truth' to that body of educational knowledge which appears in articles and books. The action-researchers are interested in the improvement of the educational practices in which they are engaging—how to do their jobs better. Their investigations are conducted into those activities which they wish to handle more capably.

Those who conduct quantitative educational research believe that practice will improve because of the findings of their studies. They assume that the discovery and publication of truth will, in due course, and almost by the very nature of things, bring about change for the better. The action-researcher argues that it is the responsibility of practitioners, in contrast to investigators, to take new findings into account.

Reliability and validity

Quantitative research has a great investment in reliability and validity. If the data is not reliable and valid, if the assessment techniques are not reliable and valid, if the design features are not able to create satisfactory internal and external validity, then the research is worthless in scientific eyes. However, action-research can really only possess internal validity, as it is a one-off intervention in a specific context. The results, findings and recommendations can only have relevance for that unique setting. Replicability is doubtful, as change is an integral part of the process. The use of triangulation facilitates the validity of each participant's perspective and understanding.

An account can be judged to be internally valid if the author demonstrates that the changes indicated by the analysis of a problem situation constitute an improvement to it. Such an account would, therefore, need to contain not only an analysis of the problem situation, but an evaluation of the action steps undertaken. An account can be judged to be externally valid if the insights it contains can be generalised beyond the situation(s) studied.

Readers of an action-research case study may identify themselves with the predicament of the teacher and thereby gain fresh insights into their own classroom problems.

Intuitive validation of this kind needs to be tested through action. In other words, it is only when the insights gained from a case study are translated into an improved quality of action that its external validity, and therefore generality, can be demonstrated.

The value of general hypotheses lies in the extent to which, in reflecting on the question of whether a general hypothesis applies to and explains his or her own situation, a teacher may begin to generate and test an alternative explanation, which in turn could contribute to the evolution of a common stock of professional knowledge.

Research and the consumer

People who engage in action-research do not make any such neat separation between the research function and the practice function. When this separation occurs, the assumption is that, if the researcher reports their findings to the teacher, the latter will modify their practices to make them correspond with the newly discovered data. The advocates of action-research deny the efficiency of this method of getting research data into action. There is available, in hundreds of libraries and thousands of books and articles, a tremendous amount of information about education derived from research. Yet this scientific truth frequently has little, if any, effect on practice. Even the teachers who hear about or read these reports are, in most instances, slightly, if at all, influenced by them.

Many traditional or fundamental investigators believe that the problem is largely one of communication. If the research reports were more lucid, or if the implications for practice were stated more clearly, teachers would be able to incorporate the findings into their practices. Action-researchers contend that the difficulty extends beyond communication and involves important principles of learning. They claim that teachers are most likely to change their ways of working with pupils because of information they accumulate about these same pupils in order to work more effectively with them. Reading fundamental research studies conducted by someone else and describing boys and girls in general may have some influence on the practices of teachers. A greater influence will be exercised, however, by the data teachers bring together and interpret in connection with attempts to solve an instructional problem about which they are intimately concerned.

A cornerstone of the action-research movement is its criticism of traditional research for trying to initiate change through dissemination of research results, rather than through the involvement of more people in the process of research.

Research has too often failed because of lack of cooperation between the researcher and the consumer. A common reason given for non-acceptance of research results is that 'it is not applicable to my situation'. The 'solution' to the problem is in terms of the producers' rather than the consumers' orientation. The cooperative search for plans of action assures that the research results will be realistically oriented and applicable to the lives and situations of the participants.

Design issues

Scientific research involves a fixed purpose and design. Action-research is adaptive, tentative and evolutionary. Scientific research cannot interpret the present until it knows the answers to its investigation. Action-research does not know what questions to ask until it has interpreted the present.

Qualifications for research

There are some differences, too, in the qualifications that seem most appropriate for those who do traditional or action-research. In the former case, great competence is required in the type of logical analysis represented by mathematical statistics, particularly those concepts that have to do with sampling theory. Knowledge about such matters is of less significance for action-researchers because they are not so interested in extending their generalisations to populations beyond those they are studying. The action-researcher needs to have a great deal of experience in the cooperative study of educational problems. They must be able to work effectively with others who are also involved in the situation they are trying to improve. This is not to deny that fundamental research frequently involves team activity, but action-research almost invariably requires the joint effort of a group of people who want to get whatever data they need to improve their practices.

Evaluation criteria

The quality of fundamental research and the quality of action-research are judged by somewhat different criteria. The former is considered to be superior in the degree to which the methods and the findings warrant generalising to persons and situations beyond those studied. An investigation is a good one if it adds knowledge to that already recorded and is available to anyone who wants to read it. The value of action-research, on the other hand, is determined by the extent to which the methods and findings make possible improvements in practice.

Society and research

Ordinarily, the scientist's job comes to an end, as far as society is concerned, when they have made some technological advance or some socially applicable scientific discovery. It is up to society to make use of this development. If it fails to do so, the scientist may perhaps react with a sense of personal futility, but they still consider that they have done their job.

Suppose, however, that the scientist redefines their job to include not merely teasing out the secrets of nature but also directing the application of their discoveries. The scientist would suddenly be confronted with a host of problems that have little to do with traditional physics or chemistry, but which have a great deal to do with human, personal and social resistance. Weapons scientists have a slight taste of this sort of problem and find themselves unequipped.

This is precisely the way in which the action-researcher defines their job. Not only must they make discoveries, but they must see to it that their discoveries are properly applied. It is largely in terms of this job definition that the action-researcher differs from the ordinary academic scientist.

STQ139

1   What do you regard as the main advantages of action-research over conventional qualitative research?
2   What are the advantages and disadvantages of teachers acting as a researchers in their own classroom?

Action-research as professional development

Action-research tries to enhance the capacity of teachers as generators of professional knowledge in contrast to enhancing their capacity to apply someone else's knowledge, for example, the findings of specialist researchers.

Action-research implies a 'bottom-up' rather than a 'top-down' view of teacher development. The knowledge-generating model assumes that improvements in educational practice ought to be grounded in insights generated by teachers. This gives teachers greater influence over what is to count as valid educational knowledge. And this implies making professional educational researchers, and the government or quasi-government agencies which sponsor work, more accountable to teachers in schools. In other words, it is a model which seeks to shift the locus of control over what is to count as valid educational knowledge and research from external agencies to schools themselves; the teacher–researcher model.

One aspect of the professional development of teachers is their capacity to adopt a research stance towards their teaching, producing accounts of their reflections, encouraged to research collaboratively on a common theme or issue. Development is limited if individuals only have their own experience to draw on when reflecting on practical problems. Individual reflection needs to be informed by a sharing of insights about common problems. Hence the need for collaborative investigations which can evolve common stocks of professional knowledge; a 'collective culture' which enhances the reflective capacities of individual teachers, and which in turn is enhanced by the contributions they feed back into it.

By becoming more collectively aware, through action-research, of the relationship between problems in the teaching situation and contextual factors, teachers place themselves in a stronger position to influence the policies which shape their practice in classrooms.

Action-research as a political process

The implication of the professional development of teachers through action-research is that, at a classroom level, teacher awareness of policy implications is increased. This enhances their collective capacity to influence structural changes within schools and the wider educational system. Any classroom action-research capable of fostering a 'bottom-up' approach to professional development must generate ideas which link problems of teaching and learning with broader questions of institutional and social policy. It then becomes a means not simply of fostering teacher development, but of developing schools as institutions and the educational system more generally. Both must be part of one and the same process, and not conceived of as two quite independent processes.

Different modes of educational research are related to differing views on educational change, on its method and direction, and to differing opinions on the role and aim of education, and action-research is seen as belonging to critical social science in an emancipatory process, and has the aim of *transforming* education.

Action-research is about involving teachers, students, parents and school administrators (among others) in the tasks of critical analysis of their own situations with a view to transforming them in ways which will improve the situations as educational contexts for students, teachers and society. It is a form of 'conscientisation', a commitment to the *improvement* of education. If research is to achieve concrete transformation of educational situations, then this requires a theory of change which links researchers and practitioners in a common task in which the duality of the research and practice roles is transcended. It requires joint participation and collaboration in the process of social transformation, expressed in joint participation in the decision-making processes of transformation. It is therefore democratic in operation.

This 'political' stance is not a prerogative of only the action-research mode. Even the scientific objective quantitative mode has a 'political' underpinning. Many radical educationalists would see conventional research as the maintenance of a hierarchical superordinate–subordinate relationship between the elite researcher with skills, knowledge and jargon to mystify the naive classroom teacher, who imposes 'truth' without question, and manipulates subjects with little regard for their feelings or ability to make meaning out of events.

This sets up a power situation; researchers tell teachers what to do, teachers resent and reject the research and theories.

STQ140
What do you believe the purpose of research is?

Action-research promotes teacher self-improvement

Action-research encourages group cooperation and group cohesiveness, releases creativity and critical thinking, and promotes change. An action-research movement is potentially a grass-roots approach to the solution of school problems.

Working together on a common problem is a source of security, status and recognition. The participant learns that they are not an ugly duckling who has 'problems'. They find that to a great extent these problems are common and shared by others. The individual accepts having a problem, not as a stigma, but as a normal aspect of a teacher in their professional life.

Studies in group dynamics point out that it is easier for individuals to change as members of a group than it is for them to change as individual members, isolated from others. Lewin found that the dependence of the individual on a valued standard and norm interferes with the attempt of change from that standard. On the other hand, when group norms change, the same dependence on group values will facilitate change in the individual and will strengthen their decision to continue with the new group norms of behaviour.

Action-research does not see teachers as naive, that is, incompetent, but as possessing skills that can contribute to the research task. In the team, each teacher can offer their specific strengths.

The role of the researcher in participatory research

In classical research, the researcher's role is, in principle, clearly defined. They are responsible for the design of the study, planning, preparation, execution, data treatment and interpretation, and result dissemination.

The role of the researcher is fundamentally changed in action-research as compared to the classical role; in all participatory research, the researcher may adopt a completely new one. In this, they assume several responsibilities:

- possibly being the initiator of the research;
- being a resource person to whom the participants can turn for advice and information;
- being a teacher, training other participants to play their parts.

Participatory research is usually initiated by a decision-maker who experiences a need or a problem. The researcher cooperates with the group members on equal terms. Their research training and general experience make it possible for them to provide the group with information; for example, data on previous studies in the field, suggestions for suitable research methods and adequate instruments, interpretations of the data as seen by a critical eye, and so on. The provision of factual information makes it possible for the researcher to guide the research so as to provide the best solution to the problem at hand; for example, by pointing to pitfalls, by showing that several possible roads are open, by convincing the participants about their capacities, and by showing what can be accomplished. In most cases, particularly with inexperienced participants, this guidance will at first be rather important, but will diminish as the participants gain knowledge and experience.

The very philosophy behind participatory research demands that the participants are called on to use their own capacities. A fundamental aim of the research supervisor must be that they prepare the participants in such a way that the participants can take over the work themselves when the researcher leaves the group. The researcher is nurturing the embryo teacher-researcher.

There are three possibilities for initiating and conducting action-research in schools. First, there is the sole teacher who feels the need for some kind of change or improvement in such areas as teaching, learning or organisation, and will be in a position to translate their ideas into action in their own classroom. They are both practitioner and researcher and will integrate the practical and theoretical orientations. Second, action-research may be pursued by a group of teachers working cooperatively within one school. They may or may not be advised by an outside researcher.

And third, there is the situation where a team of teachers work alongside researchers in a sustained relationship, possibly with other interested parties, like advisers, university departments and sponsors, on the periphery. This third possibility, though potentially the most promising, may also be the most problematic because of the possibility of incongruent aims and expectations by the teachers and researchers respectively.

Advocates of action-research believe that little can be achieved if only one person is involved in changing their ideas and practices. For this reason, cooperative research tends to be emphasised and encouraged. It is important, therefore, that the teachers taking part are involved, know what the objectives are, and are adequately motivated. Another important factor concerns the organisational aspect of the school so that there is a reasonable amount of congruence between the setting and the program to be initiated. This can be achieved without too much discord when a program is internally organised by the school itself.

The combination of a teacher with a researcher seems a useful way to get action-research on the road, since the successful teacher is continually seeking to understand what is taking place in the classroom and why, in order to make the best provision for students and to intervene in their work in the most suitable manner, as well as in order to evaluate the teacher's own performance.

There is a danger in the 'outsider' or 'consultant' or 'facilitator' role, even by a researcher committed to the action-research philosophy. The 'self-reflective spiral' of cycles of planning, acting, observing and reflecting in action-research are tasks primarily for the participants in educational situations who, by their practices, construct and constitute these situations as educational, transform them by transforming their own practices, and live with the consequences of the transformations they make. The 'outsider' researcher who may interpret or inform these practices, but does not constitute them, has limited power to transform them, and rarely lives with the consequences of any actual transformations that occur.

STQ141

Who should 'control' classroom research? Why?

Because teachers do tend to find one way of doing things as they advance in years, action-research has been much more successful in the primary school than in the senior high school. There are many other factors which may be responsible for this. The departmental feeling is probably stronger in high school than in the primary school and there is a strong possibility that if a high-school teacher attempts some action-research in their subject area, other members of the subject team may feel threatened, or believe that the syllabus is being neglected. Also, the high school teacher probably handles more pupils per day and has them for shorter periods of time than does the primary teacher. This means less interaction with each pupil. As a result, the primary school teacher is perhaps in a more favourable position to involve themselves in action-research. They are not bound in tight subject matter compartments, remember more of their own academic training, and are still selecting teaching methods and materials from a fairly wide repertoire.

Favourable conditions for action-research would include:

- a willingness on the part of a teacher to invest time in efforts associated with research and change;
- a mutual trust between researcher(s) and participants; and
- a recognition of the importance of professional development. Advocates of action-research also suggest that 'the principal justification for the use of action-research in the context of the school is improvement of practice'.

These considerations suggest that the most appropriate type of classroom in which to operate the teacher-researcher strategy would be an 'informal' classroom. By 'informal' is meant, in very general terms, a classroom in which there is a relatively high degree of autonomy on the part of the students, a flexible approach towards the allotment of time to the different areas of the curriculum and a relatively high priority given to work in which the students are able to interpret meaning and context in their own individual ways.

The use of triangulation in action-research

Triangulation involves gathering accounts of a teaching situation from three quite different points of view; namely, those of the teacher, the students, and a participant-observer. Who in the 'triangle' gathers the accounts, how they are elicited, and who compares them, depends largely on the context.

The teacher is in the best position, via introspection, to gain access to their own intentions and aims in the situation. The students are in the best position to explain how the teacher's actions influence the way they respond to the situation. The participant-observer is in the best position to collect data about the observable features of the interaction between teachers and students.

Triangulation can not only foster dialogue between outside-researcher and a teacher-researcher; it can also foster three-way discussion and develop research potential in students.

The teacher should be interviewed before the pupils, as it is less threatening to the teacher. The teacher tends to feel freer to say what they want because they are not worrying about how the interviewer's questions are influenced by what the students have said to the interviewer, and whether the teacher's own account is wildly different from the students' accounts. The problem with interviewing the teacher first is that it can create an over-structured interview with the students and limits a focus on the student concerns.

The participant-observer can also exercise the initiative in negotiating the teacher's access to student accounts, only interview students with the teacher's permission, and make it clear that teacher access would have to be negotiated with students. Prior to an interview with students, they should be told that honest accounts are sought and that in order to ensure this, they have control over the teacher's access. Many student groups demand some reassurance from teachers that they would discuss their accounts with them and not react overdefensively to what was said.

STQ142
What is the role of the 'outside researcher' in action-research?

summary

Action-research is the application of fact-finding to solving practical problems. It is situational, collaborative and participatory. Action-research involves teachers as generators of knowledge in a bottom-up approach to professional development with the professional researcher as the resource person for the teacher.

References

Kemmis, S., & Grundy, S. (1981), 'Educational Action Research in Australia'. Paper presented at annual conference of AARE, November, Adelaide.

Lewin, K. (1952), 'Group decision and social change' in eds T. Newcomb & F. Hartley, *Readings in Social Psychology*, Holt, New York.

Further reading

Atweh, B., Kemmis, S. & Wecks, P. (1998), *Action Research in Practice*, Routledge, London.

Ball, S. (1985), 'Participant observation with pupils,' in *Strategies of Educational Research*, ed. R. Burgess, Falmer Press, Philadelphia.

Burgess, R. (ed.) (1984), *The Research Process in Educational Settings: Ten Case Studies*, Falmer Press, London.

Carr, W. & Kemmis, S. (eds) (1986), *Becoming Critical: Education, Knowledge and Action-research*, Falmer Press, London.

Clandinin, D.J. (1986), *Classroom Practice: Teachers' Images in Action*, Falmer Press, London.

Connell, R.W. (1985), *Teachers' Work*, George Allen & Unwin, Sydney.

Croll, P. (1986), *Systematic Classroom Observation*, Falmer Press, London.

Deakin University, (1988), *The Action-research Reader*, Revised edn, Geelong, Deakin University Press.

Erickson, F. (1986), 'Qualitative methods in research on teaching.' in *Handbook of Research on Teaching*, ed. M.C. Wittrock, Macmillan, New York.

Goswami, D. & Stillman, P. (eds) (1987), *Reclaiming the Classroom: Teacher Research as an Agency for Change*, Boynton Cook, Upper Montclair, New Jersey.

Gregory, J.P. (1989), *Action-Research in the Secondary School*, Routledge, London.

Hart, E. & Bond, M. (1995), *Action-Research for Health and Social Care*, Open University, Milton Keynes.

Hustler, D., Cassidy, T. & Cuff, T. (eds) (1986), *Action-Research in Classrooms and Schools*, Allen & Unwin, Boston.

Kilpatrick, J. (1988), 'Educational research: Scientific or political,' *Australian Educational Researcher*, 15(2), pp. 13–30.

Mohr, M. & Maclean, M. (1987), *Working Together: A Guide for Teacher Researchers*, National Center of Teachers of English, Urbana, IL.

Nias, J. & Groundwater-Smith, S. (1988), *The Enquiring Teacher: Supporting and Sustaining Teacher Research*, Falmer Press, London.

Walker, R. (1989), *Doing Research: A Handbook for Teachers*, Routledge, Cambridge.

Whyte, W. (ed.) (1991), *Participatory Action-research*, Sage Publications, Newbury Park.

Case studies

26
twenty six

Case study research is not new. Significant cases are central to the world of medicine and law, and have long been included in the disciplines of anthropology, psychology, political science, social work and management.

The case study has had a long history in educational research and has been used extensively in such areas as clinical psychology and developmental psychology. For example, both Freud and Piaget typically used case studies to develop their theories. Criticism of their techniques damaged the case study approach, but the increased acceptance of qualitative research and, in particular, participant observation has, as a corollary, revived the acceptability of the case study.

The case study has unfortunately been used as a 'catch-all' category for anything that does not fit into experimental, survey or historical methods. The term has also been used loosely as a synonym for ethnography, participant observation, naturalistic inquiry and fieldwork. This has occurred because case study is a method that can be usefully employed in most areas of education from a historical case study of a particular school to a case study of a particular child in psychology, counselling, special education, social work, or a psychological process, such as Ebbinghaus' work on himself in the field of memory, to sociological case studies involving the role of a particular pressure group or religious order on education provision or the hidden curriculum in a specific private school.

The case study is rather a *portmanteau* term, but typically involves the observation of an individual unit, e.g. a student, a delinquent clique, a family group, a class, a school, a community, an event, or even an entire culture. It is useful to conceptualise a continuum of unit size from the individual subject to the ethnographic study. It can be simple and specific, such as 'Mr Brown, the Principal', or complex and abstract, such as 'Decision-making within a teacher union'. But whatever the subject, to qualify as a case study *it must be a bounded system*—an entity in itself. A case study should focus on a bounded subject/unit that is either very representative or extremely atypical.

The key issue in deciding what the unit of analysis shall be is to decide what it is you want to be able to say something about in the report. As a sociologist you may wish to focus on roles, subsystems, etc; as a psychologist you would tend to focus on individuals; with an interest in educational management you could focus on change in a particular establishment, the implementation of a particular program, or decision-making processes of a board of school governors, etc.

A case study is not necessarily identical to naturalistic inquiry. Many are studies of persons or events in their own environment with rigorous research design, but others are not. A researcher's report of observations of a school board is usually naturalistic, but the school psychologist's report of special tests on a child is a formal, not naturalistic, study.

While a case study can be either quantitative or qualitative—or even a combination of both due to the constraints of a sample of one or a single unit being studied, with the restrictions that brings for statistical inference—most case studies lie within the realm of qualitative methodology. Case study is used to gain in-depth understanding replete with meaning for the subject, focusing on process rather than outcome, on discovery rather than confirmation.

A case study must involve the collection of very extensive data to produce understanding of the entity being studied. Shallow studies will not make any contribution to educational knowledge. One study the writer is aware of involved interviewing a teacher for several hours and observing the teacher teach for two periods.

The case study is the preferred strategy when 'how', 'who', 'why' or 'what' questions are being asked, or when the investigator has little control over events, or when the focus is on a contemporary phenomenon within a real life context. In brief, the case study allows an investigation to retain the holistic and meaningful characteristics of real life events. The main techniques used are observation (both participant and non-participant depending on the case), interviewing (unstructured and structured), and document analysis. In a case study the focus of attention is on the case in its idiosyncratic complexity, not on the whole population of cases. It is not something to be represented by an array of scores. We want to find out what goes on within that complex bounded system.

Purposes of the case study

1 Firstly, they are very valuable as preliminaries to major investigations. Because they are so intensive and generate rich subjective data they may bring to light variables, phenomena, processes and relationships that deserve more intensive investigation. In this way a case study may be a source of hypotheses for future research by showing that things are so, or that such an interpretation is plausible in a particular case and therefore might be so in other cases. As a pilot study, methods, approaches or policies are tried out to see what the difficulties are that need to be dealt with before the main

study is attempted. Clearly such use must assume that the case is representative in at least some ways to others, or the exercise would be pointless. Conclusions reached are instrumental rather than terminal.

2 Secondly, observation case studies may have the aim of probing deeply and analysing intensively the multifarious phenomena that constitute the life cycle of the unit, with a view to establishing generalisations about the wider population to which the unit belongs. Case studies fit many purposes, but most case studies are based on the premise that a case can be located that is typical of many other cases. Once such a case is studied it can provide insights into the class of events from which the case has been drawn. Of course, there is no way of knowing how typical the selected case really is, and it is therefore rather hazardous to draw any general conclusions.

3 Thirdly, a case study may provide anecdotal evidence that illustrates more general findings.

4 Fourthly, a case study may refute a universal generalisation. We are considering here the critical case which is used to confirm, challenge or extend a theory. A single case can represent a significant contribution to theory building and assist in refocusing the direction of future investigations in the area.

5 Fifthly, a case study is preferred when the relevant behaviours cannot be manipulated.

6 Finally, a case study may be valuable in its own right as a unique case. This is often the position in clinical psychology or in special education, where a specific disorder, behaviour manifestation or physical disability is worth documenting and analysing; or in a school setting where an occasional event such as a teacher being charged for assault by a pupil, or the planning of shared resources by a primary and secondary school on the same site would be of interest. The case study may be the best possible source of description of unique historical material about a particular case seen as inherently interesting in its own right. Gruber's (1974) study of Darwin and the processes by which he arrived at the theory of evolution is an example of this.

Types of case study

Historical case studies

These studies trace the development of an organisation/system over time. A study of the development of an experimental school such as Summerhill or of a denominational church school, or of the development of a curriculum, would be examples. This type of case study depends heavily on records, documents and interviews. One must be sure that the necessary documents and records are available, and that you can have access to them to do some preliminary checking as to who is available to interview and what documents have been preserved.

Observational case studies

These studies often focus on a classroom, group, teacher or pupil, often using a variety of observation and interview methods as their major tools. Case study researchers are rarely total participants or total observers. Although it has been a tenet of faith of the qualitative school that the aim is to get inside the perspective of the participants, it is not always possible. In any case, there are many times when the spectator or television viewer gets a better perspective on what is going on than an individual player.

The parts of an organisation that can become a focus for an observational case study include:

- a classroom, a cafeteria, or other specific place;
- a specific group of people, such as members of the school choir, the science department teachers;
- some activity of the school such as annual prizegiving night or sports day.

Some case studies may use a combination of these focuses. In a case study of a high school one could focus on leadership assignment (an activity) among Year 12 (a group). Picking a focus, be it a place in school, a particular group, or some other aspect, is always an artificial act, for you break off a bit that is normally integrated into the whole. The qualitative researcher tries to take into account this relationship of the part to the whole, but out of necessity narrows down the subject matter to make the research manageable. The distortion is reduced by choosing a naturally existing unit that the participants may see as distinct, and which the observer recognises has a distinct identity of its own. A good physical setting to study is one that the same people use in a regular and consistent way, e.g. staff room, governing body meeting, morning assembly, basketball training sessions, etc.

Crucial to any successful case study of a group is the definition of the group as a unit which separates it in some way from the general population. You must make sure that they are not just people of the same age, sex, or other attribute, but actually identify with each other, share expectations and interact in a close way.

All science teachers in a school may not form a group in that they have different friendship groups in the staff room, and rarely interact except on a formal level to ensure that the science curriculum is taught. Of course, it may be that you are interested in why the staff with similar academic interests do not form a group. But it does depend on your particular focus as to what will serve you best as a group. Examples of case studies involving a group as the unit include Helson's (1980) study of creative women mathematicians, and Bernard's (1966) study of women university staff.

A community may be a distinct social unit that functions within a culture, such as Srole's (1977) study of mental health in Manhattan. In studying an entire culture as a group we enter into the world of ethnography again. A useful example here is Gorer's (1955) investigation of the British character.

Participant observation is the usual technique in the group case study, but make sure your group has sufficient members in it so that you don't stick out like a sore thumb. With a small group there is more danger of your changing their behaviour by your presence.

This has been a major concern. The ideal has been to ensure that the observer has a neutral effect. As this ideal is unlikely to be met, the question in reality becomes how able we are to monitor the effects of the observer and take them into account. The major alterations of subjects' behaviour are well known in psychology and involve participants, *inter alia*, producing socially acceptable behaviour; behaviour they believe the observer wishes to record or behaviour based on subjective interpretation of feedback from the observer; or deliberately trying to mislead the observer, which is all too common with adolescent or deviant groups. However, many deeply entrenched customs, practices and routines built up over many years will not alter very much in the presence of an observer.

Oral history

These are usually first person narratives that the researcher collects using extensive interviewing of a single individual, for example, the development of a program for deaf children as seen by a teacher closely associated with the scheme, or a retired person recounting how they were taught in the early part of this century. The feasibility of this approach is mostly determined by the nature of the respondent. Do they have a good memory? Are they articulate? Do they have the time to spend with you? Often the researcher does not have a person in mind but meets a person as they are exploring the topic who strikes them as a good subject on the basis of initial conversations.

Situational analysis

Particular events are studied in this form of case study. Often the views of all participants are sought as the event is the case. For example, an act of student vandalism could be studied by interviewing the student concerned, the parents, the teacher, the local magistrate, witnesses, etc. When all these views are pulled together they provide a depth that can contribute significantly to the understanding of the event. Interviews, documents and other records are the main sources of data.

Clinical case study

This approach aims to understand in depth a particular individual, such as a child having problems with reading, a newly immigrant child in their first term at school, or a teacher with disciplinary difficulties. Such case studies usually employ detailed interviews, non-participant observation, documents, records and even testing, with a view to understanding the problem and identifying possible treatments. Often the individual case study or a collection of individual case studies is used to define the typical case. Well-known examples include Jones' (1924) classic study of deconditioning Albert, Bacharach's (1965) study of an anorexic, and Piaget's (1929) studies of cognitive growth.

Multi-case studies

A collection of case studies, i.e. the multi-case study, is not based on the sampling logic of multiple subjects in one experiment. If the cases are not aggregated it is convenient to apply the term 'case study' to such an investigation. It is a form of replication, i.e. multiple experiments. If you had, for example, access to three cases of a very rare psychological syndrome, the appropriate research design is to predict the same results for each case—the replication logic. This logic argues that each case must be selected so that it either produces contrary results for predictable reasons or produces similar results. The outcome will demonstrate either compelling support for the initial propositions or a need to revise and retest with another set of cases, in exactly the same way as scientists deal with disconfirming experimental findings.

A useful example of the multi-case method is Szanton's *Not Well Advised* (1981), which studied the experiences of university researchers attempting to provide advice to city officials. Eight cases are used to show how different university groups failed to help cities. A further five cases of non-university groups which failed are also analysed. The conclusions were that failure was not inherent in university endeavours only, and a third group of successful university cases revealed that success was associated with implementation and not advice alone.

Multi-case designs can be considered advantageous in that the evidence can be more compelling. However, the conduct of a multi-case study requires more time and effort than most investigators can spend.

Planning the case study

The general design of a case study is best represented by a funnel. The start of the study is the wide end—trawling around, scouting for possible places and people who might be the subject or source of data, looking for clues on how to start, and the feasibility of it all. A choice having been made, a more detailed exploration begins with the chosen case. A focus develops and data collection narrows down.

In case studies there are four main components to the research design:

1 **Initial case study questions**—these are who, what, where, when and how, and must be clarified and stated succinctly before moving on, e.g. how and why do educational organisations cooperate with one another to provide joint services? This is the question the case study is seeking to answer and provides the focus for the study. Without at least one initial question to which you wish to find the answer, no start can be made.

2 **Study proposition**—each proposition directs attention at something that should be examined within the scope of the study. For instance, the how and why examples in component 1, above, are too vague. You still need to specify some succinct propositions that will enable the questions to be answered, e.g. educational organisations collaborate because it is cheaper to run joint courses. This proposition directs you to look for specific evidence.

3 **Unit of analysis**—this component is concerned with defining what the 'case' really is. While the proposition has narrowed down the focus and provided something to tackle, the actual context, person, or event needs stating. For example, we may restrict our case in 1 and 2 above to one particular joint venture between two specific institutions. As another example, a proposition that claims there is a relationship between parenting behaviour and adolescent peer relationships needs to be vastly narrowed to a specific case. Without this, the investigator will have no bounded system and will be tempted to collect everything that randomly may have a bearing on the issue. Many investigators have confused a case study of a neighbourhood with

a case study of a small group. *Street Corner Society* (Whyte 1943) is a study of a group, not a neighbourhood. Once the case has been established, then other units of analysis become apparent. If the unit is a group, then the persons to be included in the group must be established.

4 **Linking data to propositions and criteria for interpreting findings**—the fourth component is least well developed and relates to the data analysis step.

Sampling

You have already been introduced to probability sampling in chapter 6. However, non-probability sampling is more often applied in a case study. The difference is that in probability sampling one can specify the probability of including an element of the population in the sample, make estimates of the representatives of the sample, and generalise the result back to the population. In non-probability sampling, there is no way of estimating the probability of being included; there is no guarantee that every element has had an equal chance of being included, or that the case is representative of some population; and therefore there is no validity in generalising the account.

The usual form of non-probability sampling is termed *purposive, purposeful* or *criterion-based sampling*; that is, a case is selected because it serves the real purpose and objectives of the researcher of discovering, gaining insight and understanding into a particularly chosen phenomenon. This sort of sampling is based on defining the criteria or standards necessary for a unit to be chosen as the case. A blueprint of attributes is constructed and the researcher locates a unit that matches the blueprint recipe. Table 26.1 lists some types of cases often sought in purposive or criterion-based sampling.

TABLE 26.1 *Some ways of choosing the purposive case unit*

Initial case

Typical	Profile of average case made and instance sought, e.g. pupil who passed end-of-year examinations with average marks.
Extreme/deviant	After norm is established, extreme case sought to enable comparison to be made, e.g. pupil who failed all end-of-year examinations.
Convenient	Available.
Comprehensive	Review of all available instances before choice made.
Quota	Arbitrary number of individuals/events/contexts to form case, e.g. the last five physically handicapped pupils mainstreamed in the school.
Network	Case collected by participant referral, e.g. single parent names another single parent known to them and so on.
Unique	Rare, such as hardened criminal with PhD.
Reputational	Chosen on recommendation of expert/news report, etc.
Ideal	Profile developed of most effective, desirable, best instance then search for real world case.

Subsequent case

Discrepant/negative	Often chosen subsequently to show contrast.

Internal sampling

By internal sampling, we mean the decisions you make once you have a general idea of what you are studying, with whom you wish to talk, what settings are involved, what documents are required, etc. Decisions and choices you will make determine the sort of data you eventually end up with. Even the time of day you visit or interview will affect the outcome. For example, schools are very different places at 9.00 a.m. compared to 3.00 p.m., as school routines, timetables and tiredness levels will reveal. Even different times of the year will show variation, as examinations, sports day and vacations, etc. play their roles.

But whatever choices you make at the outset and during your case study they must be made in the context of the study and relate to the purpose of the study. The choices logically flow from both the premises of qualitative approaches and the contingencies of the study, as these become apparent in the course of the work. You must often step back and ask, 'If I do it this way what am I missing, what am I gaining?'. The more you are aware of the ramifications of the choices, the more likely you will choose wisely.

The length of a case study

The amount of time you have available can often determine the range and limits of your case study. The case study can be quite time-consuming. After collecting data for a while you get a feel for whether you have under- or overestimated your time allowance. You can adjust it by extending the scope and depth, or narrowing the focus. Many case study researchers gauge when they have finished by what they term 'data saturation', or the point at which the data coming in become redundant. Remember too that the study has to be written up, and by staying on the study too long you will have far more material than you can analyse.

Case study protocol

The case study protocol contains the procedures and rules that should be followed in the study. It increases the reliability of the study by ensuring the standard procedure is followed, an essential if several persons are to do the interviewing or observing. The protocol should contain the purpose of the study, the issues, the setting, the propositions being investigated, the letter of introduction, review of theoretical basis, operational procedures for getting data, sources of information, questions and lines of questioning, guidelines for report, relevant readings and bibliography.

STQ143

Name a topic you think is a valuable one for a case study. Identify three major questions your study would try to answer. Try to rewrite these as propositions that are amenable to being supported or refuted by evidence.

Sources of evidence

Documents

A variety of documents are likely to be used by a case study investigator. They would include letters, agendas, minutes, administrative reports, files, books, diaries, budgets, news clippings, photographs, lists of employees/pupils, etc. It is essential to remember that these documents may not be accurate or lack bias, and that they have been written with a specific audience in mind, for a specific purpose. In fact, many are deliberately edited before issue. But they are important as another way to corroborate evidence derived from other sources. They may specify events and issues in greater detail than interviewees can.

Interviews

These are one of the most important sources of information. Chapter 24 *Unstructured Interviewing* and chapter 30 *Structured Interview and Questionnaire Surveys* cover interviewing in considerable detail. Interviews are essential, as most case studies are about people and their activities. These need to be reported and interpreted through the eyes of interviewees who provide important insights and identify other sources of evidence. Most commonly, case study interviewers use the unstructured or open-ended form of interview, so that the respondent is more of an informant than a respondent. The case study investigator needs to be cautious about becoming too dependent on one respondent and must use other sources of evidence for confirmatory and contrary evidence.

Case study workers will also use the focused interview in which a respondent is interviewed for about one hour on a specific topic, often to corroborate facts already gleaned from other sources. The questions are usually open-ended with a conversational tone.

However, at times a more structured interview may be held as part of a case study. For example, as part of a case study of a neighbourhood creche some formal survey might be taken of its use by different ethnic groups or family types. This could involve sampling procedures and survey instruments. But it would form only one source of evidence, rather than the only source of evidence as in a survey.

Participant and non-participant observation

Both participant and non-participant observation can be used in case studies. Participant observation has been well developed in ethnographic studies, as chapter 23 details. As observers take a role and involve themselves in the group or activity being studied, often without the other members being aware, unusual opportunities for collecting data that might otherwise not be collected are available. For some topics there may be no other way than to observe through being involved as a participant. This also gives the opportunity to perceive reality from the viewpoint of an insider.

The major problems associated with participant observation are concerned with potential for bias. The investigator may become too closely involved and lose detachment, or assume advocacy roles detrimental to unprejudiced reporting.

One researcher became one of a Glasgow gang he was studying. Born and bred in Glasgow, his role remained hidden from other members of the group in whose activities he participated for four months. Such complete anonymity is not always possible and cover is not always a prerequisite of participant observation. Another investigator, studying a downtown Liverpool adolescent gang, made it generally known that he was waiting to take up a post at the university. In the meantime he was 'knocking around' as an unemployed person during the day with the lads and frequenting their pub at night, rapidly establishing himself as an OK person. 'I was a drinker, a hanger around and had been tested in illegal business matters, and could be relied on to say nothing since I knew the score.' Willis (1977) in a study of the first months of employment worked alongside each boy in industry for a short period.

On the other hand, a non-participant observer stands aloof from the case being investigated and eschews group membership. This is obviously necessary where it is impossible to be a member of the case study group, e.g. a pre-school group. King (1978) acted as an adult observer in his case study of an infant classroom. He describes how he deliberately established his non-participant status:

> I rapidly learnt that children in infant classes define any adult as another teacher or teacher surrogate. To avoid being engaged in conversation, being asked to spell words or admire pictures, I evolved the following technique. To begin with I kept standing so that physical height created social distance . . . Next I did not show immediate interest in what the children were doing or talk to them. When I was talked to I smiled politely and referred the child to the teacher . . . Most importantly I avoided eye contact; if you do not look you will not be seen (1978, p. 24).

Participant and non-participant observations can range from the casual to the formal. In the formal mode the observer will measure the incidence of various types of behaviour during certain time periods. This might involve observations in classrooms, play areas, staff meetings or games arcades. This form of observing will give rise to some quantitative data. The casual mode may be ad hoc observations made during a visit when other evidence is being obtained. It is fairly easy to notice such items as how staff greet each other, how staff divide into subgroups in a staff room while having a tea break, the condition of equipment, pupil behaviour in corridors, etc. These impressions and perceptions add to the flavour of the context and to the possible events that may need further study by interview or more formal observation. Photographs are a useful extra that can help convey site or behavioural characteristics to a report. The use of more than one observer is recommended in order to increase reliability of the observations.

Artefacts

Artefacts may be a technological device, a tool, a work of art, etc. Computer printouts can be used to assess the use of computers by students and the applications of computers in the classroom.

Principles of case study data collection

1 **Use multiple sources**. It is a poor study that uses only one source of evidence. Most studies are capable of producing several sources. The use of multiple sources is the major strength of the case study approach. Much lauded experiments are often concerned solely with measurement of the IV and DV.

   Multiple sources allow for triangulation (p. 419) through converging lines of inquiry, improving the reliability and validity of the data and findings. Corroboration makes a case study report more convincing.

   However, using multiple sources places considerable pressure on case study investigators. They have to be competent in carrying out a range of data collection methods—interviewing, observation, analysing records, survey questionnaires.

2 **Maintain a chain of evidence.** The reader of a research report should be able to trace the chain of evidence, either from initial research questions to conclusions, or from conclusions back to initial research questions. In a case study, evidence should be built up from multiple sources if possible and shown to be congruent with the conclusions; almost like a criminological investigation. The evidence should also be stated and specific observations, documents and interviews cited.

3 **Record data**. On-site recording can range from sketchy notes to the minute detail encoded on video or tape. If a few notes are taken at the time, it is imperative that full notes be written up as soon as possible after the observation in view of the fallibility of human memory. A useful way to aid later recall is to focus observation on a specific person, interaction or activity, note key words and actions, and concentrate on the first and last remarks in each conversation.

   It is also useful to draw a diagram of the setting, tracing movements through it, or seating positions or suchlike, if appropriate. Be more concerned with remembering the substance of conversations rather than a perfect reproduction. The actual content of any observation should include verbal descriptions of the setting, the people and the activities; the substance of what was said and who said it; the observer's comments, feeling, reactions and interpretations.

Skills needed by the case study investigator

1 The person needs to be able to formulate relevant and precise questions that enable the data to be extracted from the subject. Some of these questions cannot be prepared in advance, so clear insight must be used to know what line of questioning to follow, and how to dig deeper after a tentative or unexpected response.

2 The investigator needs to be a good listener, observing and sensing, as well as using their ear. In other words, they are attentive to all the cues and information being given. Mood and affective elements are as important as the actual words. Reading between the words and valid interpretation is necessary, without being trapped by preconception and ideology.

3 Adaptiveness and flexibility is a vital trait, as few case studies ever proceed exactly as planned. Inevitably, changes are made as new evidence comes to light and the focus can even change. Unexpected situations are new opportunities, not threats.

4 The investigator must have a grasp of the issues they are studying. Without this, important points and issues can be missed. Recording data is not a mechanical act. The investigator must be aware immediately if several sources of information are at variance with one another and lead to the need for more evidence.

5 Lack of bias is essential to prevent an investigator interpreting evidence to support a preconceived position. Openness to contradictory evidence is a must.

There are two seemingly incompatible qualities that the case study exponent must employ. They must know how to observe, allowing the subject to talk freely, and at the same time be alert for something definitive that may relate to a hazy hypothesis which they are seeking to check. The following suggestions reduce the chance of having the individual tell you what you want to hear, or come to perceive the situation from your own perspective because of the way you state the question:

- Minimise direct questions and use non-directive probes, e.g. 'What happened next?', 'What do you think?'.
- Use words, terms and structures used by the respondent.
- Join in the conversation as a relatively disinterested participant while other members of the group talk, influence, argue and decide.

STQ144

Identify some incident that has occurred to you recently. How would you establish the facts of the incident? Who would you interview? Are there any documents to rely on?

STQ145

To what extent do you think a case study is distinguished from other methods of educational research by the techniques it employs?

Analysing case study data

Case study notes

For most studies, notes are the most common form of data and may have been derived from interviews, observations and documents. They may be in the form of written or typed notes in a pad, diary or index card, audio tapes, computer disks, video/film. These notes should be organised as an ongoing process so that as the study progresses the investigator has some sense of the direction in which it is going, and the confirmations and contradictions that are arising. The building up of the case record facilitates the later writing of the report. An annotated bibliography of documents should be built up as they are collected. Narratives taken verbatim from interviews should be content analysed as soon as possible. Chapter 24 shows how this can be done.

Once all the observations and data are in and organised chronologically or by topic, they should be closely perused and the main aspects of the data isolated. This is the beginning of the process of organising, abstracting, synthesising and integrating. Initially a primitive classification system will be created which will be continually revised as more data are sorted. Many researchers look initially for patterns that recur, and regularities which can form the basis of initial categories into which can be placed units of data. Each unit should be placed on a separate index card and coded according to the category or categories into which it could go. An example of this task is that of trying to classify all the data about new cars. Each item could be classified in terms of make, colour, price, engine size, number of doors, seating capacity, safety features, etc. Many ways of sorting the data will come to mind as they are initially scrutinised. The researcher's dilemma is which one will best suit their purpose and reflect the findings in the most sensible and valid way.

As well as coding units of data by obvious factors such as who, what, where, how, and when, the analysis involves the development of conceptual categories at a higher level in order to integrate the material and develop theories and themes. This is a somewhat intuitive process but it is not haphazard. It is informed by the purpose of the study, the researcher's knowledge and the constructs made explicit in the behaviours and verbalisation of the participants. It involves looking for regularities and contrasts. In developing these categories at both the initial sorting and later levels, it is useful to use small index cards on which initial content has been written. These cards are then sorted into 'yet to be named' categories. Once this is done, it is possible to consider giving the categories a name and writing a covering rule. Categorisation is complete when there is a minimum of unassignable data items. All the categories should be congruent with the research purpose and mutually exclusive.

In some research projects the categories might be suggested by the participants. For example, teachers might, in their discussions with the researcher, unwittingly provide a classification system for classroom behaviour problems; students may provide the basis of a classification of teacher effectiveness criteria.

FIGURE 26.1 *Example of an index card*

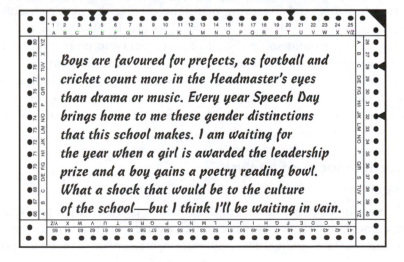

Boys are favoured for prefects, as football and cricket count more in the Headmaster's eyes than drama or music. Every year Speech Day brings home to me these gender distinctions that this school makes. I am waiting for the year when a girl is awarded the leadership prize and a boy gains a poetry reading bowl. What a shock that would be to the culture of the school—but I think I'll be waiting in vain.

The most useful cards are information retrieval cards which have holes punched along their edges. By numbering or labelling the holes on a master card and then punching out the edge of the hole where particular data exists on a card it is possible, using a knitting needle, to draw out cards not containing data on a particular topic, as the edge of the hole for that topic will not be punched out. Using this technique, cards reflecting single and combinations of categories can be left after the other cards have been lifted out. For example, statements made by 'males who are between 30 and 45 years old' on 'job satisfaction' could be selected. Figure 26.1 shows a card coded in a number of different ways for a verbal unit in a study on school culture. Hole 2 represents female participants; hole 4 is for age group under 30; hole 5 represents a reference to the headmaster; hole 20 represents a reference to the prefect system; hole 28 represents a reference to speech day; hole 32 represents a reference to gender discrimination, etc. There are computer programs that will undertake this task too, such as The ETHNOGRAPH (p. 439) which allows each unit of information to be classified in twelve different ways and which will then retrieve and print by category.

Other approaches involve creating flow charts and diagrams, tabulating frequencies, and sorting information into chronological order. But these strategies are only preliminary data manipulations. The ultimate goal is to analyse the evidence in relation to the original propositions and to any feasible alternative interpretations.

Thus a preferred strategy is to focus on the theoretical propositions that led to the case study, since presumably these influenced the design, the review of literature, the research questions asked, the sort of evidence investigated and data assembled. Thus in analysing the data, a good test is to decide what data you would cite if you only had five minutes to defend the proposition in your case study. Answers to 'how' and 'why' questions are also useful in guiding the investigator in what to analyse.

Where theoretical propositions are not available, as in a descriptive case study, another strategy is to develop a descriptive framework as a basis within which the data can be analysed. For example, the descriptive case study of the introduction of a new curriculum can be described as a sequence of decisions along a timeline involving such elements as project approval, negotiation with principal, negotiation with class teacher, production of new curriculum materials, training of teacher, using the new curriculum, and evaluation. Within each element the relevant data can be assembled and analysed. Whatever the study, without some logical plan the data can be so overwhelming in volume that it would be difficult to know where to start with the analysis.

Unlike quantitative analysis there are no cookbook formulae. Much depends on the investigator's ability to plan beforehand what they intend to do with the copious amount of information. The analysis of case study evidence is the most difficult and least developed aspect of the case study methodology.

Other specific modes of analysis

Pattern matching

The pattern matching strategy compares the obtained pattern with a predicted one. If the patterns coincide and there is no pattern to fit rival alternative theories, then the case study can claim internal validity. The important characteristic is that each potentially rival theory or explanation would involve a different pattern of variables or evidence. Hence, if one pattern is valid, the others cannot be. The variables producing these patterns may involve several types of events or characteristics, each assessed by different methods or measures (triangulation). The concern of the case study is the overall pattern of events and the degree to which the pattern matches the predicted one.

Explanation building

This procedure is similar to pattern matching, in which the case study data are analysed by building an explanation about the case. To explain a phenomenon implies stipulating a set of causal links about it. In most case studies, explanation building has been employed in those producing narrative data in which explanations reflect some theoretical propositions. The explanation building process is often iterative; that is, as the initial proposition is compared with some initial findings it is revised and compared with further data. This process repeats itself as many times as is needed until the explanation and theoretical proposition fit. Thus it will be the case that the original proposition will have changed in some degree as evidence is examined and new perspectives obtained. This gradual reciprocal building up of theory and proposition allows for the testing of rival explanations and propositions. It may seem as though the case study investigator is trying to make the proposition fit the evidence, but the congruence between evidence and theory is the vital issue and in the process alternative theories are being tested and discarded.

Time series analysis

One of the major strengths of a case study is to trace changes over time and relate these changes to previously enunciated theoretical propositions. For example, to study the course of events that lead to cigarette smoking in a teenager, one might hypothesise a sequence of events such as being friendly with others who smoke, going to evening activities with them, being 'encouraged' to join in, enjoying the experience, and repeating the experience immediately. Obviously a pattern of events can be more complicated than this naive example, with many interacting variables. The essential logic involves a specified event or trend specified before the onset of the investigation, versus some rival specified trend, traced with precision over time.

Another variant of the time series does not involve the preselection of events, but an analysis of chronological events in retrospect. This sort of study will use many sources of evidence and cover many variables. But again the chronology must be related to some explanatory theory which might specify *inter alia* some sequence to the events.

Some issues in the case study approach

Subjective bias

Many research investigators regard the case study method with disdain, viewing it as a less desirable form of inquiry. The greatest concern has been the role of human subjectivity when selecting evidence to support or refute, or when choosing a particular explanation for the evidence found. It is easy for the case study investigator to allow equivocal evidence or personal views to influence the direction of the findings and the conclusion. But what is forgotten is that bias can also enter into the conduct of experiments, and in the designing of questionnaires to an unknown degree too.

In all research the interpretation of collected observations is problematic, but especially so with case study. Content analysis will often be invoked to convert qualitative data into quantitative, but in so doing the richness, uniqueness and contextuality of case study data are lost. The opportunity to advance personal causes and views is strong, while external checks are weak.

Generalisation

A second concern is that case studies provide very little evidence for scientific generalisation. This objection is where a case is studied to provide a basis for inference to points not directly demonstrated and with relevance to cases not studied. It has been a common feature of literature critical of the case study method to assume that generalising theory is the only worthwhile goal. A frequently heard complaint is, 'How can you generalise from a single case?'. Of course, the same question could be raised about experiments. 'How can you generalise from a single experiment?' In fact, scientific facts are rarely based on one experiment, but on replications that produce consistent results. The short answer is that case studies, like experiments, are generalisable to theoretical propositions, not to statistical populations, and the investigator's goal is to expand theories and not to undertake statistical generalisation.

While the case study has been criticised as a weak vehicle for generalisation, its purpose has generally not been that. Case studies are focused on circumstantial uniqueness and not on the obscurities of mass representation. Complicating interaction effects are not thought of as hindering understanding. The case study worker appreciates the complexity of the environment and expects that behaviour is a response to the Gestalt, a response to the wholeness as perceived by the client, a response to interactions between the subjective and objective of the situation. Every case is embedded in historical, social, political, personal and other contexts and interpretations. Clean data sanitised by control in experimental techniques are not true to life.

The generalisation issue is the one that raises most intellectual problems because what is inferred is a general proposition from a sample of one. If the uniformity of nature is assumed, then the objection disappears as any case will do to demonstrate what is true of all other cases of the same class. This is a standard assumption in the natural sciences but perhaps non-existent in the social sciences. Yet in psychology, for example, there are two notable examples. Both Piaget and Freud erected general theories on the basis of unsystematically selected cases. Piaget in many instances used his own children. He is so naive about it that in *The Origins of Intelligence in the Child* he has no discussion of method or even description of the cases when they are first introduced; names are simply attached to the reported observations from which general conclusions are reached. An example of Freud's use of the case study was the celebrated study of Little Hans, which he used to prove his theory that neuroses are caused by repressed impulses that surface in a disguised form.

Piaget termed his method the 'clinical method'. He is aware of his problems:

[I]t is so hard to find a middle course between systematisation due to preconceived ideas and incoherence due to the absence of any directing hypothesis (1929, p. 69).

However, with the problems of inference from a sample of one we are left uncertain about what to expect from a teacher given a different class, or from one delinquent gang to another. Quite a different strategy for claiming representativeness is adopted by Lacey in *Hightown Grammar* (1970). This is a case study of one school. In one chapter Lacey presents eight cases of pupils selected to illustrate the nature of the relationship between a number of the major social factors relevant to the study. The cases are taken one from each cell of a typology defined by three variables: parental interest, encouragement, and achievement. Each is presented separately and then they are compared and general conclusions drawn in terms of the resources which each family brought to the school context. The case studies do more than illustrate points: they represent categories. However, the author's detailed familiarity with the institution using participant observation and other data does give a measure of confidence to his judgements.

Many case study proponents would argue that any generalisations should be reader-made ones. Thus, the reader decides the extent to which the researcher's case is similar to and likely to be instructive to theirs. Quantitative research has a tendency to increase the authority of, and dependence on, the specialist. Conversely, case study aims at enabling the use of the reported material to increase understanding through the naturalistic generalisation that the readers do themselves, thus emphasising autonomy and responsibility on the part of the practitioner. The case study investigator is trying to facilitate the reader's own analysis more than deliver statements of generalisation.

Time and information overload

A third complaint about case studies is that they are time-consuming and produce for the investigator a massive deluge of information which is impossible to adequately analyse. This increases the tendency to selectivity and bias. However, a case study need not be long if it focuses on a specific person or event, and need not involve lengthy participant observation with tomes of ethnographic fieldnotes. The solution lies in choosing a manageable focus/theme/topic, specifying succinctly the initial proposition, identifying the essential observational settings and/or interviewees, and analysing data as it comes in rather than leaving it to the end.

Reliability

It is impossible to establish reliability in the traditional sense. However, the notion of reliability as applied to testing instruments can be applied to human observers. With training and practice, the human becomes a more reliable observer. Rather than replicability, reliability in case studies is more focused on dependability that the results make sense and are agreed on by all concerned. Ways of establishing reliability involve triangulation, reporting of any possible personal bias by the investigator, the existence of an audit trail to authenticate how the data were obtained and decisions made about data and categories.

To improve reliability and enable others to replicate your work, the steps and procedures must be clearly explicit and well documented in the final report.

Validity

The checks and balances of random sampling, of standardised and reliable instruments are missing. Mainly available are the techniques of triangulation plus the commitment to seek deliberately to disconfirm one's own interpretations. The able case study researcher indicates the validity of the report by giving a detailed account of how they carried out the study. The researcher assumes the primary burden of selecting the case, appropriate observational techniques, interview procedure, documents, and making the appropriate interpretations.

As with tests, the validity of the case depends on the purposes to which it is put. A major validation may be that the case contributes to the reader's vicarious experience, each reader relating it to their own context and method and inferring the quality of contribution it can make for their particular context.

Construct validity

Many case study investigators fail to develop a sufficiently operational set of measures, and subjective judgement is used to collect the data. There are two ways of improving construct validity. Firstly, use multiple sources of evidence to demonstrate convergence of data from all sources. Secondly, establish a chain of evidence that links parts together.

Internal validity

This deals with the question of how well the findings match reality. However, if the major assumption underlying qualitative research is that reality is ever-changing, subjective in interpretation and wholistic, and not a single fixed entity, then it is not feasible to try and measure congruence between the data collected and some notion of reality. In a case study what is being observed is a participant's notion or construction of reality, their understanding of the world. What *seems* true may be more important than what *is* true.

Internal validity has been assessed by a number of strategies, such as triangulation, re-checking with participants as to observer interpretations made, peer judgement, and long-term observation.

External validity

We need to know whether the study's findings are generalisable beyond the immediate case. The analogy being made is the sample-population one of quantitative methodology. This analogy is incorrect because case studies attempt analytic generalisation in which the investigator tries to generalise a particular set of data to some broader theory. Of course, the theory can then be tested by replication. It is important not to confuse the choice of a case study in which the characteristics of the person or community are the issue with the selection of the arena. Every study has to be conducted in some setting. The emphasis of the case study is on the characteristics of the particular case; therefore external validity is not of great importance. A case study need not even be qualitative in toto, as there may well be some data available on a person, although no inferential statistics will be applied. There is, however, an implicit assumption that a case study is a bounded system. It is a presentation, interpretation and investigation of detailed information on a single unit developing idiographic interpretations. Other difficulties associated with case study validity involve incorrect identification of the case as typical or atypical. Is this case a valid example of what we are supposed to be studying? This question only makes sense if a population or reference group is agreed upon. Many case study proponents argue that the understanding of the general is enhanced by the study of the atypical. The atypical can alert us to variables and events that are often overlooked, and the atypical case long studied may be more revealing than the brief experimental intervention manipulating one variable. Of course, it is the researcher who has to determine what it is they are studying—of what is this a case? Most qualitative investigators are sceptical of conventionally defined categories anyway, and do not assume that things called by the same name are necessarily similar.

The case study can oversimplify or exaggerate, leading to erroneous conclusions. There is an easy seduction into thinking that case studies are accounts of the whole, when they are no more than a slice of life. They are limited too by the sensitivity and integrity of the researcher.

The aim has been to understand in depth one case and not what is generally true for most. Generalisability is often left up to the reader, who may ask, 'To what extent can I relate what is in this study to my own situation?'. This is helped by the study providing a rich description, so that readers can see whether the study is applicable to their situation. As a qualitative report is often written with a particular audience in mind, this can assist in framing the depth and focus of description. Policymakers, practitioners, funding agencies, the scientific community, or the members of the project under study will all require a different approach in a report in terms of what could be generalised. The audience also affects the type of report. The scientific community likes data wrapped around a thesis. General audiences might prefer a theme. Practitioners may relish a topic.

Another threat to validity is the reactive problem. The investigator by their presence or actions may affect the behaviour of the observed unit but not allow for this in the report nor interpret the observations while recording them.

Rigour

Another objection is that since methodological rigour appears slight then results are suspect and writings of case studies reveal more literary artistry than reliable and valid explanation. Perhaps it takes longer for exponents of qualitative work to develop the skills needed for a rigorous study. The routines and research activities are not as neat, orderly and cookbook-like in fashion as quantitative methods.

STQ146

Is generalisation necessary if a case study is to have value?

So in summary there are critical issues and questions to answer. Case study accounts can be decried as subjective, biased, impressionistic, and lacking in precision. There are dangers in 'going native' and thereby losing perspective and becoming blind to the very idiosyncrasies that are meant to be the subject of the investigation. The external validity question is hard to answer too. How do we ever know that the results from one case are applicable to other, on the face of it, similar cases? How was the material selected? Fears that the observer's judgement will be affected by their close involvement with the case relate to the internal validity of the method. How do we know that the results do represent the real thing? Of course, there are ways to check, and we offer the methods of triangulation, snowball sampling, and the search for exceptions, as ways of checking the representativeness of the events and behaviours observed.

Case studies can do a variety of things. But some case studies do not do them very well, because no particular rationale has dictated their choice. It is too easy to study a case simply because it is conveniently handy, and hope that something of more interest will come out of it. Case studies that start off with a case in its own right, rather than as an instance, are more likely to uncover unanticipated findings. This openness to surprise and availability for multiple purposes is a real strength. Except for methodological dogmatists, there is no intrinsic reason why case studies should be regarded as more or less powerful than other types of research, for all are subject to the competence and diligence with which the subject(s) are chosen, the research is executed and the results written up.

Case study material gives appeal by providing human interest, good stories and a more humanistic mode of presentation than that of the traditional quantitative style. Since the material must particularise, it is harder to write about it in a theoretical abstract way.

The case study type of research has a highly reputable history, so you should have few qualms about exploiting such a design. However, as some supervisors and external examiners are strongly biased against the case study approach, often because of low external validity and the absence of inferential statistics, you should check carefully to ensure that those likely to be involved in your study are sympathetic to the approach.

The report

The major components of the report are usually these:

- purpose of the study; the problem that gave rise to it, philosophical orientation;
- methodology including the sampling decisions, rich description of site/subject, transaction and processes, and data collection techniques;
- presentation of the data including the patterns, themes and interpretation;
- validation of findings/outcomes;
- conclusions.

Figures and other displays should only be used when really integral to the discussion. While verbatim quotations are often necessary as illustrative examples, long unedited extracts are rarely needed. At the other extreme long, conceptual and philosophical discussion should not be divorced from some real flavouring of direct quotations and succinct descriptions. A 60/40 or 70/30 split between (1) description, data and quotations, and (2) conceptual material is a recommended balance. A sequence of moving from raw data through to patterns, then on to higher levels of abstraction and interpretation is also recommended, so that connection is logically made between single events and more abstract argument and interpretation. The well-chosen instance becomes the concrete road sign that prevents a reader from being lost in a jungle of detail or unable to envision the route back from a stunning conceptual analysis to gain an illuminating retrospective view of a salient detail.

summary

The case study design is chosen when a rich descriptive real-life holistic account is required that offers insights and illuminates meanings which may in turn become tentative hypotheses for further research, possibly in a more quantitative mode. The unit of study must be a bounded system, but can range in size from an individual to a whole program/system.

Many case studies are qualitative and involve ethnographic techniques, particularly participant observation. Sampling is usually non-probability, with the case chosen on the basis of some relevant criterion. Data analysis involves the devising of a coding system that permits higher order categories and conceptual analysis to develop.

Reliability cannot be established in the traditional sense, and external validity with a single case is also unavailable. Internal validity is assessed through triangulation, peer judgement and re-checking with participants.

References

Bacharach, A. (1965), 'The control of eating behaviour in an anorexic', in *Case Studies in Behaviour Modification*, eds P. Ullman & L. Krasner, Holt, New York.

Bernard, J. (1966), *Academic Women*, World Publishing Co, Cleveland.

Gorer, G. (1955), *Exploring British Character*, Criterion Press, New York.

Gruber, H. (1974), 'A psychological study of scientific creativity', in *Darwin on Man*, eds H. Gruber & P. Barrett, Dutton, New York.

Helson, R. (1980), 'The creative woman mathematician', in *Women and the Mathematical Mystique*, eds L. Fox, et al. Johns Hopkins University Press, Baltimore.

Jones, M.C. (1924), 'A laboratory study of fear', *Journal of Genetic Psychology*, 31, pp. 308–15.

King, R. (1978), *All Things Bright and Beautiful*, Wiley, Chichester.

Lacey, C. (1970), *Hightown Grammar*, University of Manchester Press, Manchester.

Piaget, J. (1929), *The Child's Conception of the World*, Adams and Co., New Jersey.

Srole, L. (1977), *Mental Health in the Metropolis*, Harper Row, New York.

Szanton, P. (1981), *Not Well Advised*, Ford Foundation, New York.

Whyte, W. (1943), *Street Corner Society*, University of Chicago Press, Chicago.

Willis, P. (1977), *Learning to Labour*, Columbia University Press, New York.

Further reading

Bartlett, L. et al. (eds) (1983), *Case Study Methods* (vols 1–8), 2nd edn, Deakin University Press, Geelong.

Merrian, S. (1988), *Case Study Research in Education*, Jossey Bass, San Fransisco.

Nisbet, J. & Watt, J. (1978), *Case Study Rediguide No. 26*, Nottingham University, School of Education, Nottingham.

Yin, R.K. (1984), *Case Study Research*, Sage, London.

27

twenty seven

Historical research differs greatly from much of the rest of the research methods discussed in this text. While it shares a great deal in common with qualitative methods in its use of documents, interviews, biographies and events and their interpretation, it may also make use of and analyse quantitative data, such as the changing demographic origins of the teaching profession over the last century. There is also a quest for objectivity in historical research, and it subscribes to the same principles of validity and reliability that characterise all scientific endeavours.

History is a meaningful record, evaluation, systematic analysis and synthesis of evidence concerning human achievement. It is not a list of chronological events like we remember it at school. It is an integrated account of the relationships between persons, events, times and places. For example, it is impossible to discuss the development of programmed learning without also discussing the research of B.F. Skinner and the dominance of the philosophy of behaviourism at the time. There may be different emphases, but it is impossible to separate people, events, time and location. History enables us to understand the past and the present in the light of the past. It is an act of reconstruction, undertaken in a spirit of critical inquiry, and prevents us from re-inventing the wheel.

Historical education research is past-oriented research which seeks to illuminate a question of current interest in education by an intensive study of the material that already exists. Since history deals with the past, the purpose of historical research cannot be to control phenomenon. The research is intended to help understand, explain or predict, through the systematic collection and objective evaluation of data relating to past occurrences in order to explore research questions, or test hypotheses concerning causes, effects or trends that may help to explain present or anticipate future events. The values of historical research are:

- it enables solutions to contemporary educational problems to be found in the past;
- it allows re-evaluation of theories, hypotheses and generalisations held about the past, and how and why educational theories and practices developed;
- it stresses the importance of complex interactions in the actions and situations that determine the past and present; particularly how our present educational system came about;
- it throws light on present and future trends, particularly the guises in which progressive ideas in education re-emerge; and
- it contributes to the understanding of the relationships between politics and education, between school and society, and between pupil and teacher.

Like other forms of qualitative research, historical research is concerned with natural behaviour in a real situation, and the focus is on interpretation of what it means in the context. Unlike other forms of educational research the historical researcher does not create data, but attempts to discover data that already exist.

History and the scientific method

It can be argued that historical education research cannot be scientific:

- The purpose of science is prediction; however, the historian cannot generalise on the basis of past events. Because most past events were unplanned, and even if planned did not develop as planned, many uncontrolled variables were present and the influence of one or two individuals was crucial, so no replication is possible.
- The historian must depend on the reported observations of other witnesses of doubtful competence and of doubtful validity, most of whom are no longer alive.
- The historian is trying to complete a jigsaw puzzle with parts missing, not knowing what the final picture is, and in fact creating that final picture by filling in the gaps with inferences.
- The historian cannot control the conditions of observation or manipulate variables when the events have already happened.

However, in defence it is argued that:

- the historian does delimit a problem, formulate hypotheses, and raise questions to be answered, gathers and analyses primary data, tests hypotheses as consistent or inconsistent with that analysis and evidence, and finally formulates conclusions or generalisations.
- the historian may gather information from a variety of sources and vantage points which can provide a form of triangulation.
- although the historian cannot control variables, it is arguable whether other forms of educational and social science research do so effectively, particularly in non-laboratory studies in the classroom, playground or youth club.

Historical generalisation

There is dispute among historians as to whether historical research can produce generalisations. However, many analytic scholars in other fields have proceeded to generalise from small unrepresentative samples to the universe, including Darwin on the origin of species, Freud on human motivation and personality development, and Weber on the Protestant ethic. This does not make the process of generalisation any more valid, but it shows that historians are not alone in this problematic issue. Finality of knowledge is impossible in all areas of study, and all contain uncertainties and inaccuracies. If the process does no more than furnish general propositions which create focuses for future investigations to support, refine or demolish, then a valuable service has been provided.

The historical hypothesis

Hypotheses may be formulated in historical investigations in education. We might state that demands for university students to pay for their education come at times when economic cycles are on the downturn, or that the British education system ceased to have influence on Australian education after the Second World War. Evidence is gathered; its trustworthiness is evaluated and, if the evidence is compatible with the hypothesis, the hypothesis is confirmed.

Types of historical research

There are a number of types of historical research in the field of education, discussed below:

Biographies of educationalists, institutional histories and histories of particular educational movements

These are very prevalent. They will not have hypotheses or raise startling new issues. The objective is solely to describe something that has not been fully studied before. There are countless local opportunities for such research. Such research helps us understand how and why educational movements arose, evaluate their contribution, and detail the fads and bandwagons that have been discarded. A study of current practices is illuminating in that the practice might have arisen in response to conditions no longer relevant, or the practice may be found to be one that has been recycled from an earlier practice. An examination of many education movements and initiatives in the past confirms that there is little new in education. The ancient Greeks often tried it first. It is useful to discover why existing practices were discarded. The fact is that contemporary education movements and issues usually have a history. Examples readily spring to mind in this area, such as the privatisation of education, attitudes towards technical or vocational education, ethnic, religious and gender issues, access to higher education, assessment of performance, 'back to basics', individualised instruction etc.

Synthesising or comparing old data with new data to illuminate trends

This might involve, for example, data concerning staying on at school after the compulsory period, changes in subject choice between the genders, changes in the curriculum itself, or demand for private education.

Revisionist history

This is an attempt to reinterpret events that others have already studied.

As in all research, it is necessary to determine whether there is a sufficient and accessible data base for your desired topic to permit a successful study. If there is a surfeit of data you will need to narrow the topic down to a shorter time period or a particular aspect. As with all types of quantitative research, the definition process should continue as you collect and analyse the data. In doing so you may uncover new issues and insights, or redirect the focus.

Procedure

Historical research tends to be idiosyncratic, depending both on the individual doing the research and the nature of the topic. In general however, there are six steps:

1 Identification of the topic and specification of the universe of data required to address the problem adequately;
2 Initial determination that such data exists and is available;
3 Data collection through consideration of known data, the seeking of known data from primary and secondary sources and the unearthing of new data and previously unknown data;
4 Initial writing of report;
5 Interaction of writing and additional data search as gaps become apparent;
6 Completion of interpretative phase.

Selecting the topic

This is the most difficult part, as the topic must not be too broad or else only a superficial account can be compiled. A limited focus on a small aspect may, on the other hand, provide difficulties in obtaining the detailed information. One suggested way to define a topic is to ask four questions:

1 Where do the events take place?
2 Who are the persons involved?
3 When do the events take place?
4 What kinds of human activity are involved?

By focusing on these questions a topic will emerge that is capable of being investigated in the timeframe available and with the resources identified. A hypothesis is needed which ties together some of the answers to the four questions above, or else the research will become little more than an aimless collection of facts.

Sources of data

Four types of historical data sources are used: documents, oral records, artefacts and quantitative records. Primary sources are documents written by a witness to the events, whereas secondary sources are secondhand versions and therefore less accurate. Secondary sources are used as back-up data and when primary data is not available.

Primary sources

Documents

These are records kept and written by actual participants in, or witnesses of, an event. Examples are minutes and records of formal and informal organisations, autobiographies and biographies, letters, diaries, census information, contracts, certificates, medical records, community organisation/school newsletters, programs of sports/religious/ educational/social events, curriculum materials, books, films, recordings, reports, newspapers, etc.

Artefacts/relics

These are remains of a person or group and for education research could be sites or remains of old school buildings, hospitals, industrial sites; copies of textbooks, reading books or industrial equipment no longer used; copies of disused procedures, say for school principals, employee rules in industry, social workers' guidelines; old examination papers and student projects found in cupboards; old school furniture, old medical records or disease incidence and outdated treatment procedures, etc. These relics often give valuable clues as to how schooling, working and daily life were conducted in the past.

Oral testimony

This is the spoken account of a witness such as a teacher, pupil, parent, governing body member, etc. This category also includes tales, myths, ballads, songs and rhyming games that can be obtained in personal interviews as witnesses relate their experiences and knowledge.

Secondary sources

The writer of the secondary source merely reports what the person who was actually present said or wrote. It is secondhand material and does not have as much worth or validity as a primary source. Errors often result when information is transmitted from one person to another. A history textbook is obviously a secondary source. A school textbook may be either type of source. It is a secondary source when used as a textbook, but a primary source when a researcher is studying the changes in emphasis given to a topic, such as the dicussion of sexually transmitted diseases in health education textbooks over the last fifty years. Similarly, the records of a school governing body meeting are a primary source if the meeting was held during the period under research, but secondary when used as evidence in developing a history of the school, because the minutes are being used to interpret events of that period.

Documents are the most common, and range from newspapers and committee reports to songs, tales and ballads, and to more personal diaries, letters and memoirs. Some documents are intentional, produced for public consumption, while others are unpremeditated, written for personal use. The intended different purposes of the various types of document affect the validity of the information they contain. Oral records are subject to idiosyncratic change as stories and songs are passed down from one generation to another. Quantitative records such as class lists, birth records and school reports are more valid, yet may not be fully accurate. Old school texts, school rules and photographs are other very valid historical evidence that illuminate education practices in the past.

Data collection

Those involved in historical education research cannot create new data and must work with what already exists although some of it may be unknown at the start of the research and only comes to light through the investigation. Much historical research is conducted in detective-like fashion, whereby information is traced to a source, those knowledgeable about the event or situation contacted and used as informants, and documents located. In general, quality historical research depends on sufficient primary data rather than secondhand data.

The particular research topic will suggest the types of data that must be sought. A study of a local educationalist will require the location of biographical material, letters, interviews with those who knew/were taught by/were colleagues of the person, photographs, diaries, newspaper cuttings, etc. A study of attendance patterns in a region would need access to school records. Most primary sources can be located in libraries, museums, education department and university archives, and personal collections.

Information must be recorded as many records cannot be loaned. This means making photocopies where possible or resorting to manual recording. Photographs of artefacts are necessary.

Data analysis

Most of the data used in historical research have lives of their own, in that they were not created in the first place for research purposes. The data were created for someone else's purpose or administrative function. Therefore the data may be biased, distorted and somewhat invalid when used for other purposes. Thus the researcher must evaluate the data in a critical way, establishing the authenticity of the source, including the date and author, and evaluating the accuracy and worth of the statements. The central role of the historian is the interpretation of data in the light of historical criticism. Each fact and supposition must be carefully weighted and added to the case, leading to the research conclusion. Most researchers organise either by date or by concept/issue.

Historical evidence is obtained from historical data by means of historical criticism. This can be external, or internal, criticism.

External criticism

This establishes the genuineness or authenticity of the data. Is the document a forgery? We may need to establish its age by examining language usage, spelling, handwriting style. This may involve chemical tests on the ink and the paper, or on parchment, cloth, wood and paint, depending on the sort of relic. We also need to check whether the document or relic is consistent with the technology of the period.

Internal criticism

After authenticity has been established, we still need to evaluate the accuracy and validity of the data. So although genuine, we need to ensure that they reveal a true picture. Were the writers honest? Biased? Too antagonistic or too sympathetic? Were they sufficiently acquainted with the topic? What motives did they have to write about or record the event or person? How long after the event was the record made? Does the account agree with other accounts? What was the purpose and in what circumstances was it produced? Is it complete, edited, altered? Was the author an expert or lay person? How long after the event was the document produced? Is it liable to memory distortion? Was the author partisan—a supporter of a particular course of action?

The historian must carefully weigh the extent to which causality can be inferred and generalisation justified. Historical evidence, like a one-shot case study, can never be repeated. There is no control group, so one can never be sure that one event caused another. The best that can be done is to establish a plausible connection between the presumed cause and the effect. Similarly, the historian must assess the extent to which one educator or school was reflective of the general pattern at that point in time. Even if bias is detected, it does not mean that the document is useless. A prejudiced account can reveal the pressures and political processes that were being brought to bear at the time. The principle in document analysis is that everything should be questioned.

Writing the report

As data collection and analysis progresses, the historical researcher synthesises the data and writes it up. This is analogous to the creation of a review of the literature, as there are no set formulas nor prescriptions that lay down how to do it. It is a case of constantly revising, reflecting, obtaining criticism and advice from others, in order to develop the most logical organisation and valid conclusions from the evidence analysed. It is a difficult task to take seemingly disparate pieces of information and meld them into a meaningful whole.

In historical research the review of the literature is not a separate section or done independently of the research itself. Rather it is a integrated part of the data collection, analysis and reporting. Thus reports in historical investigations can take a variety of forms.

Criteria for evaluating historical research

The following criteria are useful to evaluate one's own production before submitting for publication:

- Has the problem been clearly defined?
- Are the data of a primary nature available in sufficient completeness to provide a solution, or has there been an over-dependence on secondary data?
- Has the dependability of the data been established?
- Does the author display insight into the significance of the data? Does he/she maintain objectivity? Are the hypotheses plausible? Are they adequately tested?
- Does the style of writing inform, reflect scholarliness and make a contribution with new data or new interpretations?

Limitations and difficulties

A major limitation is that the problem has to be delimited to make it amenable to research. Historical research must involve a penetrating analysis of a limited problem, rather than a superficial examination of a broad area. The weapon of the research historian is like a target pistol, not a shotgun.

The major limitation of historical research is the opportunity to test the conclusions in a new situation. You will recall that replication is a measure of the reliability of the results in an experimental study. Much is so specific to the actual study situation or event that it may well be unique.

A second limitation is that the data are always incomplete. Conclusions have to be drawn from fragmentary evidence. This can lead to oversimplification in failing to recognise that causes are often complex, and overgeneralisation occurs due to false reasoning, analogy and superficial similarity of situations.

A third limitation revolves around the validity of the data used. Since the data were not created in a controlled way as part of the research process, but were created in the past for a variety of purposes, then much data such as diaries, letters and newspaper reports will be biased—subjective from the point of view of the then recorder. Interviews will be clouded by the lapse of time since the topic of the research (event/situation/person) occurred or was around. Only where there are divergent sources of data and these converge on a similar conclusion (triangulation) is validity demonstrated. Even here the researcher must be wary in case agreement has occurred because all sources were influenced from one original inaccurate source. In using documents of considerable age there is the danger of failing to interpret words and expressions in their accepted meaning at the time of writing.

Many historians are studying events and persons from a previous age. They have to depend on inference and logical analysis, as well as other people's recorded observations at the time. It is necessary to keep the biases and beliefs of those who recorded the events in mind, as well as the social and political context in which they lived and wrote and in which the events took place.

Moreover, all researchers bring their own perspective and personal baggage to the problem. The historian, like the ethnographer, can create a storyline and text which, while shaped by the data, could be massaged into a different history by another historian.

Conclusion

Educational historical research is difficult and demanding, lacking the standard methodology of experimental approaches. It involves considerable time searching for and reading documents, locating individuals and travelling distances on occasion to undertake these tasks. For these reasons, historical research is not frequent in education faculties, as students seldom have sufficient time or financial support to do these tasks.

However, despite these drawbacks, historical research has its own special rewards. It is fun to discover things about the past that give shape to present ideas and patterns of thought in education, and to show the contribution of others, often long since dead, to the process and achievements of education. It is the sort of research that can be pursued alone with no rigid timetables or artificial constraints like experimental approaches. It is a labour of love, limited only by energy and enthusiasm.

Some possible topics in educational historical research

- Education between 1850 and 1900 in some small town.
- X College in the nineteenth century.
- The ideas, work and influence of B, the first principal of C.
- Changes in the state science curriculum 1950–75.
- State–Commonwealth relations in education between 1960 and 1975.
- The development of distance education.
- Changing attitudes to corporal punishment in the second half of the twentieth century in Australia.
- The evolution of the open plan classroom in Y state.
- The influence of Rousseau's book *Emile* on nineteenth century educationalists.
- The development of the school counselling service in Z state.
- Changes in the socioeconomic composition of student applicants to P university 1950–90.
- The history of phonetic approaches to reading.
- Changing methods of financing universities in the period 1945–95.
- The development of legislation to regulate international student recruitment to Australia between 1987 and 1995.
- An analysis of the treatment of Aboriginal peoples in Australian social science textbooks 1945–95.

STQ147

1   Write a proposal for a historical study in a local setting of a school or of an individual involved in education. State an appropriate title, present a hypothesis, indicate the primary sources of data and indicate how you would evaluate the authenticity and validity of the data.

(continued)

2 Select a thesis of the historical type from the university library and analyse it in terms of:
  a hypothesis proposed
  b questions raised
  c primary and secondary sources of data
  d external and internal criticism used
  e soundness of conclusions.

summary

Historical research is an integrated account of people, places, events and times, invoking both qualitative and quantitative methods and data. Historical research involves a wide range of studies from individual biographies and educational movements through to trend analysis, all undertaken in idiosyncratic ways.

The researcher uses both primary and secondary sources of data. It is often difficult to assess reliability and validity as the past event/person cannot be replicated, data are often fragmentary, and authenticity may be difficult to assess. Internal and external criticism are used in an attempt to overcome this.

Further reading

Best, J. (1984), *Historical Enquiry in Education: A Research Agenda,* American Educational Research Association, Washington DC.

The presentation of findings is the culmination of the qualitative research process. After all, the purpose of research is not only to increase your own understanding, but also to share that knowledge with others. Your efforts are wasted if you cannot disseminate the results. Writing a report also helps you to clarify your thoughts and arguments.

But when it comes time to write up your qualitative study you can feel completely out of control, facing too many choices: what is the order of presentation? which evidence? active or passive voice? how long or short? etc. The reporting phase is more difficult to do in qualitative research than in quantitative research, where there is a conventional linear sequence to a research report which deals in a quite short and precise way with the study for publication in a journal. Unfortunately, qualitative reports do not have a uniformly acceptable outline. Nor do ethnographic, action-research or case study reports usually end up as journal articles.

Because of the uncertain nature of qualitative reporting, investigators find that this compositional phase puts the greatest demand on them. Inexperience in composing should not deter an investigator from utilising quantitative methodology. However, much more practice is needed than for a journal article in the quantitative mode. One indicator of whether a person will do well at writing a qualitative report is whether they are good at and enjoy writing essays and detailed letters. Another pointer is whether the report is seen as a chore or an opportunity to make a significant contribution to knowledge.

A report or article based on qualitative research is not an opportunity to 'fly a kite'; to provide an 'off the cuff' view of an event. Rather, it should be a logical, descriptive and analytic presentation of evidence that has been systematically collected and interpreted. It seems formidable if viewed as a single task. It is therefore more encouraging to break down the task into smaller sections, some of which are drafted while the research goes on, and then place all the subtasks in sequence. No one can sit down at the end of a qualitative investigation with blank paper and all the fieldnotes, and start writing. The first step is to decide who the audience will be.

Who is the audience?

Qualitative reports have a more diverse audience than do formal journal articles, which are read often only by particular subject specialists. Possible audiences for qualitative reports include colleagues, policy makers, community leaders, specialists from other fields who do not have a thorough background in your specialism, teachers, parents, funding bodies, politicians, etc. (possibly a thesis examiner as well!). Each audience has different needs, and no single report is likely to suffice.

For colleagues, the findings and how they fit into previous research may be the most important aspect. For non-specialists, the descriptive elements portraying real life situations, issues and feelings with implications for action are the relevant elements. For a thesis, understanding of the theoretical issues, mastery of the methodology, and the presentation of conclusions derived from the evidence is sought. Research funders naturally look for the significance of the findings in practical terms. Thus, successful communication of the report may require more than one version. The usefulness of qualitative research studies may go well beyond the role of the normal research report.

Getting started

Novice investigators are big procrastinators. The key to decreasing the composition problem at the end of the research phase is to commence writing and preparing the report as the study is progressing. Don't leave it all to the end. Re-formatting observational notes/interview details, analysing and coding recent observations and interviews, reviews of literature, building up a bibliography/reference file are ongoing activities while the research continues, but are part of the report writing process. This is the splitting up of the task into subtasks referred to above.

Report writing should start early in the conduct of the study. Certain sections of the report will always be draftable before data collection and analysis have begun. For example, after literature has been reviewed, a first draft of the bibliography and methodology section can be made. Additional citations can always be added to the bibliography, and if some are incomplete these can be tracked down as the study proceeds rather than become a chore holding up the final report at the end.

The methodology section can be drafted early as the major procedures for data collection and analysis should already be part of the design. The methodology section should contain arguments and issues concerning the selection of the cases/informants/techniques. The next section on qualitative and quantitative information gleaned about the cases/issues can be started before analysis begins. While the evidence should demonstrate the case convincingly, all the evidence and documentation should not be placed in the text. Footnotes, appendices and a reference list of sources and contributors are often appropriate instead. In fact, the location of the database is simply required so it can be accessed by anyone considering a replication. Only specimen responses or examples of the evidence need be included in the report, but these must be critical ones or illustrate critical points.

It is worthwhile remembering too that the report is not meant to be a vehicle to convey all the detail you have gleaned. The evidentiary base, as with the raw scores of the quantitative report, should be stored elsewhere as a database, to be accessed by yourself and future researchers as required.

You will eventually write several drafts before you have a report with which you are satisfied. Paragraphs should be kept short so that they cover one point and appear inviting to read. Quotations should be included as they 'tell it like it is'; they encapsulate people's positions on issues or illuminate perspectives.

There is no standard way to write a qualitative report. The type of investigation and the sort of data produced will guide the structure, but a sound report always has a focus, states a purpose and then fulfils the promise. There are many types of focus including a thesis or proposition, a theme or a topic, and there may be several of these within one study. Most crucial in deciding your specific thesis, theme or topic will be the data that has been collected, analysed and coded. You cannot write about a focus on which you have little evidence. One simple way of finding a focus is to look over your coding categories and see which have yielded the greatest amount of data. If you have used the folder method for sorting your data, pick the fattest ones.

A good report also has a beginning or introduction, a middle or a core, and an end or conclusion. Too many reports have indeterminant, or too many, beginnings. They resemble a train wreck rather than a line of carriages headed by an engine proceeding down the single line track passing through one station after another to reach the destination.

Another goal is to present enough evidence to convince the reader that the investigator has been in the field, acted thoughtfully and become steeped in the issues found there. In multi-case studies the author must present enough evidence on each so that the reader can accept that each has received fair treatment. So how much evidence is presented is a decision made by the author, giving due consideration to the particulars of the research; enough to convince, not too much that it overwhelms. A common complaint about qualitative research is that it is lengthy, cumbersome to read and boring. The report must be written in a succinct and clear style and engage the reader.

Structures for qualitative reports

There are nine main structures that can be used.

Linear–analytic structure

This could be considered the standard approach. The sequence follows the standard journal report from statement of the problem, through review of literature/theory, methodology, results and discussion. This structure is comfortable for those studies that involve a single issue/problem/case in an explanatory, descriptive or exploratory study;

for example, the classic single case study, action-research narrative augmented where appropriate with tables, charts, etc.

Comparative structure

A study that compares alternative descriptions or explanations of several cases/problems/issues, or is iterative of the same case/issue from different points of view, or involves more complex comparisons between various subprograms of one action-research study, would employ this approach. Each case/problem/subprogram or section will probably be presented initially as a separate chapter with later cross-case analysis and results. For example, this approach could be used to compare different conceptions of how the appointment of a school principal was made from the perspectives of the candidates, the appointment committee, the staff, etc.

In a variant of this structure, the whole of the report may consist of cross-case analysis only with no separate sections devoted to separate cases, issues, programs, etc. Information on different cases would, therefore, be scattered through each chapter; each chapter dealing with a theme or proposition across cases.

Chronological structure

For the study of an event over time—for example, the introduction of a new examination system or the integration of an immigrant pupil—a sequence of chapters covering the early, middle and late phases of the event would be most appropriate. There is a major problem to avoid in this approach: it is that most investigators spend too much of the report on the introductory stages detailing early history and background and insufficient on the later stages.

Theory-building structure

The sequence of chapters or sections in this approach will follow some theory building logic. Each chapter or section will unravel a further part of the argument with compelling evidence. The entire sequence should be a linked argument following through to a well-supported conclusion.

Suspense structure

This study is presented in reverse to the usual. The outcome or conclusions are presented first, while the remainder of the report is employed to support the outcome presenting alternative explanations as required.

Unsequenced structure

This structure is often used in descriptive case studies where the sequence of chapters is of no great importance. A descriptive study of a school might have sections on staffing policy, student discipline and rules, role of parents and friends, groups, etc., but the order in which each is presented is not crucial.

Case analysis structure

Another type of report may involve either single or multiple cases/programs/topics, etc., but be written up based on a series of questions and answers, the former originally set up as specific directions leading out of the theoretical propositions underlying the research. If there are multiple cases, the advantages are enormous, as examination of the same question across cases is possible. This allows the writer to tailor the cross-case analysis to different audiences who may well be interested in different questions.

Micro-ethnological structure

If you choose to do a micro-ethnography, your report must focus on intimate behaviours in a single setting, narrowing in on more specific aspects of interactions in order to break down the setting more and more. This continual breaking down and dissection of events will form the organising sections of your report.

Macro-ethnological structure

In a macro-ethnography, you lay out the whole realm of a complex situation, covering all aspects that are relevant to your theme. Each section may cover a different aspect but demonstrate its relationship to the whole.

Using the linear–analytic structure

The following detailed structure along the linear–analytic model is suggested as one that will help most novices produce a readable and relevant report. With experience they can branch out into more complex structures.

The introduction

This provides the general background and general statement of the problem needed to understand the importance of the focus; in other words, what the research is attempting to do. Placing the study in the context of current literature, theory or debate is a major strategy here. Many investigators apply an existing theory to a study and try to extend or refine it. For example, Hargreaves, Hestor and Mellor (1975) used labelling theory which had been developed in the area of social deviance as a way of explaining deviance in the classroom.

The introduction will include, where necessary, a review of pertinent literature/theory. The literature review is a stimulus for your thinking and not a way of summarising in your own mind the previous work in the area that can blind you to only considering existing concepts and conceptual schemes as in quantitative method. New findings cannot always be fitted into existing categories and concepts, and the qualitative method with its more open-minded approach encourages other ways of looking at the data. The literature review should be a sounding board for ideas, as well as finding out what is already known and what specific methodologies have been used. Often, research reports identify additional questions that would be fruitful to pursue.

This review should not attempt to cover everything you have read, but summarise with specific reference to major studies only. Do not write an article-by-article review. From this review, establish some initial tentative propositions/theses to be the basis of the commencing data collection. These, of course, may and probably will change as evidence accumulates.

The selection and statement of a thesis/proposition/topic in the introduction is essential. You need it in order to make an initial decision on the methodology, the sources of evidence and the particular evidence you will bring to bear to evaluate the thesis, always bearing in mind that you will show in the core of the report why and how such initial decisions were changed as a result of the ongoing investigations and new evidence. Without a thesis/proposition to hang everything round, you will write a meandering conversation piece that has no aim.

The core

This makes up the bulk of the manuscript, getting its direction from the introduction, and must explain the processes by which you obtained your data and how you interpreted them. It usually commences with a justification and account of the research methods used to gain the evidence. The detail of the method enables readers to evaluate the reliability and validity of your approach. The rest of the core is concerned with the presentation of your evidence related to the focus/theme/topic, arguing and illuminating as you go, and, if necessary, revising your initial proposition, enlarging or changing your focus. At all times you must ask yourself: Does this relate directly to my focus/argument/proposition? If it does not, leave it out; it may be the theme of another later paper, but not this one. This will keep you on track and prevent the report becoming a receptacle for every observation, statement, document you obtained.

Other parts of the core depend on the sort of study you did, whether single case, multi-thematic, action-research or ethnography. You may have to write comparative sections and discuss patterns across cases. A variety of different forms of report is briefly itemised below. But whatever the specific content of each section in the core, each should also have an introduction, a middle and an end. The introduction will inform the reader what that section contains and how it relates to other sections. The middle will provide the evidence and argument, while the end will summarise and provide a link to the next section.

What the qualitative researcher is doing is telling a story—'Here is what I found, and here are the details to support that view'. Use subheadings frequently, as these help to structure the report and may often reflect the way respondents have structured their world. Look for places where your general statements are too dense or lengthy, and see if you can insert a brief but telling example to break up the prose. Readers are advised to consult chapters 23 and 24, where detailed methods of analysing observations, interviews and survey data can be found.

Deciding what evidence to use is like a balancing act between the particular and the general. Your writing must clearly demonstrate that your abstract ideas (summaries of what you saw) are firmly grounded in what you saw. A good qualitative report is well documented, with descriptions taken from the data to illustrate and substantiate the assertions made. Successive concepts, themes and issues are presented and illustrated with informants' verbatim material. There is no formal convention used to establish 'truth' in a qualitative paper. Your task is to convince by summarising and quoting to help your reader get closer to the people or events you have studied.

Only rarely will you use graphs, tables or statistical presentation. The qualitative report is a human story rather than a cold detached set of figures. In the following example the author, in a study of immigrants' experiences of schooling, mixes quotations with his own analysis:

> For children who have learned to respect school and take academic study seriously, the experience of total immersion in a foreign language environment is nothing short of devastating. 'I felt like a piece of wood' says a 15-year-old boy . . . Even the simplest question was torture. 'The teacher would ask me my name and I was afraid to say my name because they said it so much different from how I would say my name.' This was from a 12-year-old girl.

The quotations and the author's interpretations intertwine to form a flowing paragraph that integrates the particular with the general.

Another way is to present a general statement then illustrate it. For example, in a study on how pupils evaluate teachers we get:

> Another bit of evidence used to evaluate their teachers was whether the teachers' concern and interests in their job was visible to their students. Teachers were judged as poor if students felt that they did not like their students or teaching. 'The teacher I had the following year was a Mrs X. And she just didn't enjoy kids at all. She was really a mistake for the teaching profession.'

After presenting a number of examples like this, the author should round it out with a concluding interpretation. Another way to present data is to incorporate them into the narrative so they become part of the story.

> Some of the children used to laugh at her in the third, fourth and fifth grade. But by the time she was twelve she was strong and big so no-one ever teased her for they feared she would pound them with her fists.

In the above example, the quotations and descriptions gained from interviews are not isolated but integrated into a story.

To sum up, most or all the following should be covered in the core:

* Method. Detail the methodology and techniques used.
* Time and length of study.
* Nature and number of settings and subjects.
* Selection of subject(s).
* Change in propositions/hypotheses/direction of study.
* Checks on data; evidence trail.
* How you attempted to gain reliability and validity.
* Description, analysis and evidence related by argument to the propositions/thesis.
* Comparison between cases, where relevant.

The conclusion

In a conclusion the thesis/focus can be restated, the argument reviewed and the conclusions highlighted. This is followed by the implications of what you have discovered for policy and practice. Attention is often drawn to deficiencies in methodology in the study.

The end of the report should contain an annotated bibliography of all the documents/records that were used, since most of these will not be presented in the report but filed away and rarely retrieved. Such documents may form a valuable database for a later researcher.

Review of draft report

It is useful to have the draft report read by participants and informants before it is finally issued. Comments and queries can help to further clarify issues and points being made. It is essential that there is agreement over the facts of the investigation, even if there is disagreement with the investigator's conclusions. When Whyte was completing his draft of *Street Corner Society* he had 'Doc', the major contributor, review his work. 'As I wrote, I showed the various parts to Doc and went over them with him in detail. His criticisms were invaluable in my revision' (Whyte 1955, p. 341).

Such corrections will enhance the construct validity of the report, remove the likelihood of falsely reporting an event and where different informants do have different perspectives, these can be represented in the report. This review cycle can be regarded as part of the research, as well as part of the report stage.

Confidentiality

Should informants, events, locations, etc. be accurately identified or remain anonymous? The most desirable option would be to identify everyone and everything, as this disclosure enables readers to recognise the reality of the study and locate it in their own experiences. However, privacy laws and the confidentiality that has been promised before informants would talk, or would allow observation of events, definitely precludes this. If you have promised confidentiality, you must follow that through. It is possible to maintain anonymity of respondents although the context, event, location are identifiable as individual behaviours; open-ended interview responses, etc. can be reported but not attributed to a named individual.

The variety of reports

Qualitative reports need not restrict themselves to the structures outlined above, nor need they restrict themselves to verbal exposition. The nature of the investigation, the sort of evidence derived, may well dictate that a variety of other presentations will be included, such as pictures, video tapes, audio tapes, artefacts and documents. However, written reports do offer advantages, in that more precise information can be conveyed about abstract concepts such as organisational structure, group interaction and implementation, though even here, pictures can help to bring a sense of reality and credibility. But while we are aware of the dangers of bias and selective interpretation when we write, we are all less aware of the selective bias introduced through the editing process in videos, tapes and static pictures. What has been omitted?

Helpful tips

- Break the report down into manageable parts.
- Prepare parts of the report as your research proceeds, e.g. bibliography, literature review.
- Establish the objective(s) or question(s) you wish to answer and write a summary introduction linking general question/focus with the proposition and previous theory/literature.
- Go through the draft looking for words and sentences that can be left out without changing the meaning or through elimination make the meaning clearer.
- Write in the active rather than in the passive voice.
- Use short sentences and avoid jargon.
- Ground your writing in specific examples.
- Have friends/colleagues read the draft and comment.

Remember in writing a qualitative report that there is no single conventional model—diversity reigns. Your style of presentation should suit the topic, be comfortable to you and, above all, present your study in a well-documented argument, providing the reader with a rich flavour of what you investigated.

The following three research reports illustrate the way in which four particular researchers have investigated and written up their topics. As you are aware by now, qualitative research reports can be structured and reported on in a plethora of ways. Even these three topics could have been written up in different ways by other investigators. So do not feel constrained by these examples in the way in which you wish to present your material. Remember, clarity, precision and a logical structure are important to its readers.

The first report, 'I feel sorry for supply teachers' by Wood and Knight, is an example of a mini-ethnographic study in the classroom. A lengthy literature review is avoided and the paper simply lays down the theoretical context—pupil expectations—and the specific issue: why pupils respond to supply teachers as they do. The methodology is outlined, followed by selected evidence in the form of interview responses. The bulk of the paper then relates the findings to theories and previous studies in expectation, labelling and self-fulfilling prophecy areas. Finally, the paper makes suggestions for improving how relief teachers are seen by pupils. It is a short and very readable piece, aimed at an audience of teachers and education administrators.

The second report, 'Nasr's development as a writer in his second language: The first six months' by Elliott, illustrates the case study approach. The paper reports an investigation of the development of writing behaviour in a second language of one child over a six-month period.

The developmental changes are recorded, described and analysed chronologically within categories of genre, language skills and strategies. The argument and discussion are fully supported with examples of the child's written productions. The audience would be ESL teachers and other language educators.

The third report, 'Dimensions of effective school leadership: The teacher's perspective' by Blase, is a case study that looks at effective school leadership from the subjective perceptions of teachers, by using both structured and unstructured interviews. The study attempts to understand the meanings that teachers have attributed to effective school leadership. The data were drawn from the working lives of teachers as they experienced them. This qualitative study commenced with open-ended questions and through an inductive process produced description and theoretical ideas; in other words, grounded theory. Thus, this research does not start off with categories into which the data is manipulated or hypotheses are to be tested, but develops categories and hypotheses from the data as they are analysed.

References

Hargreaves, D.H., Hestor, S. & Mellor, F. (1975), *Deviance in Classrooms*, Routledge, London.
Whyte, W. (1955), *Street Corner Society*, University of Chicago, Chicago.

Further reading

Clark-Carter, D. (1997), *Doing Qualitative Psychological Research. From Design to Report,* Psychology Press, New York.

Report 1

'I FEEL SORRY FOR SUPPLY TEACHERS...'

An ethnographic study

Elizabeth Wood and John Knight

This paper examines pupils' views and expectations of 'supply' teachers in case-study fashion. Given the limited time in which supply teachers are in contact with any one class, teacher reputation and initial encounters are seen to be critical in determining the success or failure of supply teachers in the classroom. Suggestions are offered for improving the situation and effectiveness of supply teachers.

Pupil expectations: Extending the literature

There is an extensive body of research on pupils' views and expectations of teachers. 'This literature suggests a general consensus on pupil expectations of teachers.[1] Woods (1983, p. 54) for instance, notes the most important of these as being that 'teachers should be "human", should be able to "teach" and make you "work", and keep control. Some teachers are felt to be inhuman'.

An Australian ethnographic study (Catsoulis 1981) of 'delinquent' students in a non-state secondary school is typical in its depiction of the details of student perceptions of teachers. 'Good teachers' 'can put across', 'explain things well', 'want you to do well' and have control of their class. They have a sense of humour, 'can hold their tempers', 'don't bore you' and 'get along with students'. 'Bad teachers' are unfair, 'far too strict', 'won't help you' and 'can't put it across'. They may be lazy, bad tempered or moody. They 'play favourites', have 'pets' and 'make it hard for you'.

It is not our intention here to review this literature, but to address a specific issue: why some pupils respond as they do to supply or relief teachers. This is an issue which as yet has received little research attention.[2]

Through pupils' eyes: A preliminary study

As a preliminary investigation of pupil perspectives on such teachers, this paper reports a practitioner's 'mini-ethnographic' study.[3] We are concerned to show how some pupils respond, why they do so, and how the issue might possibly be resolved. Our interest springs from the senior author's experience as a supply teacher, which showed firsthand the differences between being a supply and a classroom teacher. The fieldwork was undertaken in a Queensland state school where (as a supply teacher) she had experienced a large degree of cooperation and had come to know many pupils and teachers. The school has an enrolment of some 600 pupils in a predominantly middle class suburb. Specialist teachers of music, physical education and remedial teaching are attached to or visit this school.

Six children, three girls ('Michelle', 'Karen' and 'Jenny') and three boys ('Chris', 'Scott' and 'Troy'), from Year 7 (the final year of their primary schooling) were selected. They had attended this school for most (or all) or their primary schooling, and at the time of being interviewed were aged eleven or twelve years. They were in an 'open' classroom shared by two teachers who taught as a team. All six classified themselves as 'normal' in their schoolwork. With respect to their responses to supply or relief teachers, Karen claimed to be one of three pupils in the class who start the 'fun'.[4] The claim by Karen was backed up by the others who also labelled her as a 'loud-mouth'. Jenny said she was a 'loud-mouth' also. However, Michelle, Chris, Scott and Troy are all labelled as 'quiets'. All agreed they were to varying degrees 'pests' for their classroom teachers, but were much worse for supply or relief teachers.

Two group and three individual interviews were held in a small withdrawal room next door to the classroom. During the first interview five of the children (Jenny was absent) discussed questions passed by the interviewer, who then jotted down notes in answer to each question. The next session involved individual interviews with Karen, Chris and Scott. This was a question and answer section, during which the interviewer was able to jot down answers verbatim. (Karen was sent in first 'to get her out of the way' according to her classroom teacher.) Jenny's only interview was on the last visit. This final session was another group interview during which the children helped to construct taxonomies on teachers and students.

The direction of questioning was shaped by the interviewer's own recent experiences as a supply teacher, her conversations with other supply, relief and classroom teachers and confessions from her thirteen year old son on the subject of supply teaching.

Initially, the study was to have been limited to the study of responses of pupils to supply teachers. However, due to their inability to differentiate between supply and relief teachers, relief teachers were also included.

Why muck up? Pupils' responses to supply teachers

The interviews indicated that differing responses towards supply/relief teachers had nothing to do with their academic qualifications (which were seen as 'about the same as our teachers') nor was the use of, or need for, supply/relief teachers questioned by the informants ('supply teachers are needed to control us, when our teachers are away'). Critical factors determining whether the supply/relief teacher had pupils' cooperation (and so was able to teach) were the initial encounters, perceived personality, and management skills of the *unknown* supply/relief teacher or the reputation of the *known* supply/relief teacher. Doing more or less work related directly to behaving or having 'fun'. This is explained in Scott's reply to the question, 'Why muck up?' 'Fun. We don't get as much work done!' The amount of work done also related to whom the supply/relief teacher is.

Supply and relief teachers were not only classified as good or bad but also as known or unknown. The children also grouped together those teachers who got more work and cooperation and less 'fun' from the kids. Those teachers who could not control the class got less work and less cooperation from the kids who had 'fun' and more 'fun'. In reply to 'What are supply teachers supposed to do?' and 'Why are supply teachers needed?', Karen, Chris and Michelle emphasised the need for control of the class by the supply teacher so that work could be done as well as to prevent 'accidents' and 'riots'. Supply teachers unable to do this 'got bad reputations', said Chris and Jenny.

Children's reasons for choosing whether to work or have 'fun' related to their perceptions of supply teachers (including their reputations), their interest or lack of interest in what was being taught and the opportunities, costs and payoffs involved:

Karen: 'He's old and boring. Always talking about history. Always! So we have fun! We throw chalk. He can't see properly so we aim at his bald spot—but I do work for our teachers because our teachers would send us to the office or give us an essay.'

Jenny: 'If rubber bands are handy, depending on who the supply teachers are, and if they don't know what's happening, we fling rubber bands about.'

Chris: 'Something to do. Get a lot of fun having rubber band fights. You need a group if you want to make it any fun'.

Scott: 'Don't get as much work done. Do it (have "fun") all over again, till it's not fun anymore. It's more fun if you've got a group.'

Further information on the criteria by which pupils judge whether to cooperate or not came from Michelle, Karen, Chris, Scott and Troy who agreed that supply teachers don't have as much control because 'they don't know us' or 'they don't know us that well' so 'we have fun'. Teacher behaviours that elicit more work also elicit cooperation and so the pupils do not usually have 'fun'. The reverse was also true.

Karen: 'If they aren't strict the kids tend to play up. Also they don't do their work—like, if they get away with one thing they will try something worse and more daring, like starting a rubber band fight.'

While pupil behaviour for the supply/relief teachers varies from that for classroom teachers, as Chris said: 'Children who muck up for the supply teachers, usually muck up for our own teachers, but not as bad. Goody goodies and stiffs don't muck up.' A sense of fair play, of right and wrong and of how far to go with supply/relief teachers entered into their interactions with each other and the supply/relief teachers. They weighed up the risks involved. For example:

Chris: 'I feel sorry for supply teachers to have to put up with us. We shouldn't really muck around. If we had a supply teacher I'd probably do my work because the teacher would report back, but if the supply teacher has no control over the class and gives us no work, I would misbehave and so would everyone else'.

Troy: 'I wouldn't act up if the supply teacher was a neighbour or a family friend 'cause they might tell Mum.'

or Karen: 'Sometimes you get a supply teacher in the face (with a rubber band). That's not fair.'

If the supply teacher has a reputation with other classes, pupils listen to the rumours and 'We believe what they say' (Jenny). They did more work or less work depending on the reputation held by the supply/relief teachers. For known teachers (usually relief teachers) previously built up the reputations led the pupils to act as they previously had acted with this same teacher [sic].

Karen: 'Fun. It's not something that happens every day. Natural instinct for when Mr Smith walks in! Hey fun!'

The 'fun' in this particular classroom is orchestrated by the three 'starters' and spreads rapidly in wavelike motion as each group joins in, if the supply/relief teacher has no control. If there is no control, immediately after the 'starters' have begun some form of 'fun' (be it paper plane or rubber band throwing), the 'loudmouths' and 'fools' join in followed by the others with the exception of the 'stiffs'. If the teacher has some measure of control, the 'quiets', 'goody goodies' and 'squares' are not as likely to join in. In talking about who joins in, informants said:

Karen: 'Stiffs don't. They say they might dob on you. A group at the front might muck up. Stiffs and squares at the back don't.'

Scott: 'Karen, Michael and Adam (the 'starters') start it off . . . spreads very fast. The stiff tells everyone to be quiet. She's trying to work. She won't join in. We don't plan it. Someone just talks to someone else and it spreads.'

Chris: 'I have dares with friends to have rubber band fights. If they're the same standard as me they probably would—not with goody goodies.'

Despite all this, the children genuinely wanted to be controlled by their teacher; no matter whether it was a supply, relief or classroom teacher in charge. Boredom from too easy work resulted in 'fun' sessions, but too much 'fun' in turn led to boredom. Pupil behaviour was shaped (as noted previously) by available opportunities, teacher reputation and behaviour, and concerns for fair play. Who is involved in classroom 'fun' and how and why this involvement spreads quickly is critical. These responses are shaped by teacher control which in turn relates back to teacher reputation, behaviour, personal characteristics and management skills.

Initial encounters and supply teachers' reputations

The literature on classroom interaction stresses the importance of 'initial encounters' for classroom control:

> Initial encounters . . . constitute pessimistic social environments that necessitate, or art conducive to, the continual reflective calibralion of thc congruence between the self and others. (Ball 1980, 158)

Using strategies which are known or come to hand, both teacher and pupil who are 'thrust together in enforced intimacy' negotiate to develop working relationships (Beynon and Atkinson 1984, pp. 256–7). This negotiation, which takes place in two phases, is referred to by Ball (1980) as a 'process of establishment'. He defines this as:

> an exploratory interaction process involving teacher and pupils during their initial encounters in the classroom through which a more or less permanent, repeated and highly predictable pattern of relationships and interactions emerges. (Ball 1980, p. 144)

According to Delamont (1983, pp. 112–13), during phase one the pupils observe their new teacher 'to develop a series of hypotheses about the kind of teacher' they now have. The second phase is an active one during which the pupils are 'real horrible', as they 'muck up' to discover what parameters of control the teacher is seeking to establish over their behaviour and to find out if 'the teacher has the tactical and managerial supply skills' to defend these parameters.

In this interactionist perspective, the focus is on emergence and negotiation. The idea of 'process of establishment' gives an explanation for what goes on in the informants' room when a supply/relief teacher arrives. As noted above, the results of such pupil testing periods are not 'foregone conclusions' (Ball 1980, p. 150). Only known teachers who had in some way already proved themselves were safe from further testing. For them the pupils were willing to work. All unknown supply/relief teachers (except some 'known' by reputation) were tested. Here the conventional wisdom ('most experienced teachers insist that the teacher must, if he (sic) is to survive, define the situation in his own terms at once') seems justified (Hargreave's pupils 1972, p. 232).

This strategy has particular relevance to supply teaching as most encounters are initial encounters and 'long term establishment' of classroom rules and routine which 'takes weeks to establish' is not possible.

What the supply/relief teacher must bear in mind is that teacher reputations are being formed and will be passed on to other classes, who will react positively or negatively depending on the reputation. The Year 7 pupils used their 'fun' to see how far a teacher would let them go. They expected to be controlled. Supply/relief teachers who did not control them were immediately given 'bad' reputations. Beynon and Atkinson (1984, p. 261) showed that such 'mucking up' could:

simultaneously accomplish several things: it could reveal how teachers would react under pressure; it could enhance the reputation of its instigator; it could flush out accomplices in the classroom and provide occasion for joint subversive action.

The supply/relief teachers associated with the Year 7 class have indeed been tested. Not only have they developed reputations but so have the three 'starters' (Karen, Michael and Adam). Groups willing to join in the 'fun' (depending on the risk of punishment involved) were identified as 'fools', 'loudmouths' and even the 'quiets' and 'squares'.

Informants calculate the risks involved from reputations of teachers, previous associations, or 'cues and information' given out by the teacher 'to the pupils the moment he or she walks into the classroom' (Ball 1980, p. 146). While having 'fun', informants and their cohorts were able to find out how much noise or lack of manners (e.g., calling out) individual supply/relief teachers would tolerate and how much or how little work they would have to do. All these points were identified by Ball as information gathered by pupils in his study. Where one teacher may accept certain behaviour as normal, another may feel this type of room behaviour is bad indeed. Hence pupils are faced with differing teacher expectations. In the same way some pupils may see certain teacher behaviour as unreasonable while others perceive the same behaviour as and 'quite within the limits of a teacher's role' (Education Department of Western Australia 1981, p. 151). This study showed the types of teacher for whom these informants do more work or less work. This correlates highly with behaving or having 'fun'. It also coincides with research showing teachers who are liked or disliked by pupils.

The issue and expectation of teacher control remains central. The observation of Marsh, Rosser and Harre (1978, p. 38) on 'softness' was validated by this study's informants:

> Being a soft teacher was seen to be one of the worst categories of offence. The pupils are insulted by weakness on the part of those in authority who they expect to be strong.

For a supply teacher who has lost control of his or her class it is obvious that the subsequent relationship is one dictated by the pupils, not the teacher. This situation results in little or no appropriate learning taking place.

Labelling

Reputations were built up by pupil labelling of supply/relief teachers by pupils as well as by the labelling of pupils by pupils and teachers (classroom, supply or relief). Here it is important to note that for the imputation of 'deviance', the interaction of two parties, labeller and labelled, is necessary (Hargreaves 1976, p. 201). That is to say, deviance arises:

> not when persons commit certain kinds of acts: it arises when a person commits an act which becomes known to some other person(s) who then defines (or labels) the act as deviant. (Hargreaves, Hester and Mellor 1975, p. 3–4)

This process of labelling appears to be taking place in the informants' classroom between at least three different groups of labellers and labelled. These are:

Labelled	Labellers
'starters', 'fools'	supply/relief teacher
supply/relief teacher	pupils
'starters', 'fools'	pupils

However, not all who are labelled take notice of the label or respond to the labelling in any way. To some the labelling does not appear valid and may be discounted (Hargreaves 1976). Factors influencing the acceptance (or otherwise) of the label include how often the labeller labels the labelled, the extent to which the labelled values the labeller's opinion, the extent to which others use the label on the labelled, as well as the 'public nature of the labelling'. Being labelled in front of a class of pupils is more degrading and severe a punishment than being labelled in private. Being repeatedly publicly labelled by respected persons can be seen as possibly leading to some change in the person labelled.

Consequences of labelling can be seen as social control or as leading to deviance. Under conditions of what Edwin Lemert (in Hargreaves 1976, p. 203) sees as primary deviation, where the person who is labelled is deterred from repeating or committing acts seen as deviant, or is able to justify or deny the actions (and hence is able to neutralise or normalise the labelling), the labelling does not appear to cause a loss of self-regard or result in changing social roles. Under these conditions labelling appears as a form of social control and hence can be viewed as having 'positive' results. However, where the person who has been labelled discounts the label (such as when the labeller's opinion is not valued), no social control results but neither does further deviance result from the labelling.

Further deviance resulting from the application of labelling is viewed by Lemert (in Hargreaves 1976, p. 203) a secondary deviation. He defines secondary deviation as:

deviant behaviour, or social roles based upon it, which becomes a means of defence, attack or adaptation to the overt and covert problems created by the societal reaction to primary deviation.

When labelling fails as a form of social control but instead angers the labelled person, this person may react by committing further deviance. His/her coping strategies for dealing with the labelling, which cannot be normalised, may create a cycle of deviant acts from which the labelled person (now deviant) cannot escape. The deviant may become stigmatised and feel victimised. An example of this cycle of behaviour may be interpreted from information of incidents between a supply/relief teacher and the informants' five years prior to the interviews. The teacher concerned, according to informants, was a bad teacher who could not control the class, who threw chalk and blackboard dusters and locked children in a cupboard.

Perhaps these teacher actions were forms of survival strategies that the teacher felt he needed to protect his job, but the children in the class labelled this teacher as bad and did not cooperate. Hence the labelling was communicated to the teacher through pupil behaviour including lack of cooperation. In striving to control the class the teacher was forced into more deviant behaviour and no doubt felt victimised by the actions of the pupils. He was stigmatised by the pupils, who treated the teacher badly and were in turn badly treated by the teacher. This is an extreme example of teacher deviance.

Labelling and self-fulfilling prophecies

Rosenthal and Jacobsen (1968) linked teacher expectations and 'self-fulfilling prophecies' and Hargreaves et al. (1975, pp. 140–1) showed the close relationship between labelling theory and the self-fulfilling prophecy. Although Rosenthal and Jacobsen's work was concerned with positive self-fulfilling prophecies, the notion of negative self-fulfilling prophecies can be compared with labelling theory. In the informants' classroom, supply/relief teacher expectations of 'bad' behaviour by the 'starters', Karen, Michael and Adam, is communicated to these pupils by the teachers. According to Hargreaves (1976, p. 202):

teachers who have little knowledge of pupils...are forced to rely on 'reputations' of classes and pupils as conveyed to them by the less transitory members of staff. Deviant labels would thus tend to be accepted and used by such teachers—'I've heard all about you, Smith'—who might not remain long enough in the school to test the validity of these labels and thus be in a position to revise them.

Petrie (1981, p. 138) holds a similar view. The 'starters' live up to the negative expectations of the supply/relief teacher as well as the rest of the class. Unfortunately since the teacher and pupil expectations are negative, deviant behaviour (negative self-fulfilling prophecies) results from the labelling.

Changes in expectations of supply/relief teachers and pupils may change the amount of 'fun' had while these teachers are present. Ramsay, Sneddon, Grenfell and Ford (1983, p. 279) found in their study that in successful schools 'The children were rarely held to blame . . . Thus the risk of low expectations and subsequent lowered pupil performance was minimised'. Hence they concluded that 'the level of the teachers' expectations, both academically and socially, marked off the 'successful' schools from the less successful'. This points to a need for high positive expectations in the informants' classroom. High expectations of the 'starters' by the supply/relief teacher, high expectations of the supply/relief teacher by the pupils as well as high expectations of the 'starters' by the rest of the class are needed.

Perceptions of supply role

To clarify the type of high expectations needed by the pupils themselves, the role of the supply/relief teacher must be clarified. The children saw a supply/relief teacher as being needed for controlling the class and revising work, but not for teaching new work. Teachers who cannot control them are viewed as wasting the pupils' time as no work can be done. Pupils then waste time themselves. 'Mucking around takes up much school time and is a common focus of students' interests' (Macpherson 1981, p.143). Unless the supply/relief teacher has his or her job viewed by pupils, their parents and teachers as a valuable part of teaching, not just for babysitting (control) purposes, then pupil expectations will remain low, as status of teachers is communicated to pupils by others.

Supply/relief teachers also need high expectations. Hargreaves et al. (1975, p. 261) referring to deviant pupils state that:

The deviance-insulative teacher believes that these pupils, like all pupils, really want to work . . . the deviance-insulative teacher claims to like all children and considers it a privilege to work with any pupil. He (sic) respects and cares about the deviant pupils and tells them so.

Clearly this type of teacher is unlike those supply teachers in this study who 'do not care'. Hence, rather than concentrating on surviving in the classroom, the supply/relief teacher must be aware of not communicating negative feelings or low expectations to his/her pupils.

From the descriptions given by informants some supply/relief teachers are preoccupied with survival. As Dale (1977, p. 49) notes, 'discipline is not necessary only to facilitate teaching, but also for teachers to survive the classroom'. Woods (1979, p. 258) suggests that by 'increasing resources and/or lessening demands', the concern over survival would be lessened. Some teachers possibly are so preoccupied with survival that concern for the pupils is minimised and the importance of high expectations not considered. For successful teaching high expectations must be held.

Effectiveness of supply teachers

As the use of supply/relief teachers is seen as necessary to prevent interruption to other classes, these teachers contribute towards successful or unsuccessful schooling. For successful teaching, Woods' suggestions (given above) could be implemented by the schools. Rumours generated by pupils and supply/relief teachers must have some basis. More weight could be given to such rumours to help weed out the 'rotten eggs', such as the supply or relief teacher who would not only throw chalk and dusters at the pupils but locked some in the cupboard. Others to be weeded out are those who have no control over the class. This lack of control can lead to labelling and perhaps secondary deviation. Schooling which is seen as possibly creating deviants cannot be viewed as successful.

Although bureaucracies are usually resistant to change, they can produce radical change. Hence it is feasible to envisage a Department of Education empowered to radically alter the status, working conditions and job opportunities to those teachers currently employed as supply and relief teachers. Specifically the current system within the Queensland Education Department, whereby a Local Relieving Teacher (LRT) is attached to a school and is on secondment to other schools means that unknown LRTs can be brought in from other schools while the LRT at his/her home school can gain a reputation as a bad or good teacher. With each new initial encounter and consequent 'sussing out' this reputation can be confirmed. A bad LRT then is possibly stigmatised and victimised by the pupils and in return labels pupils and possibly sets in motion the process of deviation. Until each school is free to choose its own supply teachers this situation is likely to recur. For successful schooling the bureaucracies need to empower each school to choose its own supply teachers.

Final comment

Teacher reputations and survival are important in all the initial encounters that supply/relief teachers are involved in. Prevention or lessening of problems caused by this lessens labelling of pupils and prevents the construction of 'deviant' pupils. Aids for supply teachers in the form of resources and/or fewer demands on them could encourage the formation of high expectations being held by the teacher for the pupils and vice versa. Clarification of the teacher's role and acknowledgement by the school, parents and Department of Education of the difficulty and importance (not just baby-sitting) of supply teaching might lead to higher pupil cooperation and less wasted time. Enabling each school to select their own supply teachers should result in pupils facing known, competent teachers, who hold high and yet valid expectations (in the pupil's eyes too) and who thus help with successful schooling through appropriate teaching.

Notes

1 For example, Catsoulis, 1981; Connell, Ashenden, Kessler and Dowsett, 1982; Corrigan, 1979; Delamont, 1983; Denscombe, 1985; Hargreaves, 1972; Jackson, 1968; Macpherson, 1983; Walker, 1987; Werthman, 1977; Willis, 1977; Woods, 1979, 1980a, 1980b, 1983.

2 The literature on the problems of 'substitute' teachers is extensive; there is, however, a dearth of studies on pupils' views of such teachers.

3 The ethnographic approach seeks to 'describe a culture in its own terms'. A 'mini-ethnography' presents the information shared by two or more people that defines some aspect of their experience' (Spradley and McCurdy, 1972) here, pupils' definitions of a grade seven classroom.

4 'Fun' is this group's word for 'stirring'. Occasionally some informants used 'muck up', but Scott's answer when asked to label what he and the others were doing, 'Fun! We don't really call it anything, but that's what it is!'

5 Being a 'quiet' does not mean that the informants are silent, but that they are usually reasonably quiet in the classroom until an opportunity for having 'fun' presents itself.

6 In this context, supply teachers are teachers who are 'on call' to take over a class when a classroom teacher is absent, who usually have no regular teaching and who are not attached to a particular school. Relief teachers are full-time teachers who are based at one school. Depending on teacher absenteeism, relief teachers can be called to relieve at other schools. As with supply teachers, relief teachers take over a class when another teacher is absent and they have no permanent class of their own.

7 When talking about the 'kids' in their class, informants labelled them as: stiffs, squares, goody goodies, fools, loudmouths, love themselves, quiets, special kids, normals, smart and dumb kids. In answer to the question, ' How do you decide who is a stiff, a square, etcetera?', the informants decided after much discussion that this was summed up by: The way they act, who they hang around with, the way they eat, who they are going with, and if they play football they are not a stiff.

References

BALL, S.J. (1980) 'Initial encounters in the classroom and the process of establishment', In Woods, P. (ed.) *Pupil Strategies*. Croom Helm, London, pp. 143–61.

BEYNON, J. and ATKINSON, P. (1984) 'Pupils as data-gatherers: mucking and sussing', in Delamont, S. (ed.) *Readings on Interaction in the Classroom*. Methuen, London, pp. 255–72.

CATSOULIS, C. (1981) 'Teachers and students at Johnholme College', in D'Urso, S. and Smith, R. (eds) *Changes, Issues and Prospects in Australian Education*, 2nd ed. University of Queensland Press, pp. 130–6.

CONNELL, R., ASHENDEN, D., KESSLER, S. and DOWSETT, G. (1982) *Making the Difference: Schools, Families and Social Division*. Allen and Unwin, Sydney.

CORRIGAN, P. (1979) *Schooling the Smash Street Kids*. Macmillan, London.

DALE, R. (1977) 'The hidden curriculum for the sociology of teaching', in Gleeson, D. (ed.) *Identity and Structure. Issues in the Sociology of Education*. Nafferton Books, Driffield, pp. 44–54.

DELAMONT, S. (1983) *Interaction in the Classroom*. 2nd ed. Methuen, London.

DENSCOMBE, M. (1985) *Classroom Control: A Sociological Perspective*. Allen and Unwin, London.

EDUCATION DEPARTMENT OF WESTERN AUSTRALIA (1981) 'Nature and extent of the discipline problem', in D'Urso, S. and Smith, R. (eds) *Changes, Issues and Prospects in Australian Education*, 2nd ed. University of Queensland Press, pp. 151–70.

FOSTER, L.E. (1987) *Australian Education. A Sociological Perspective*. 2nd ed. Prentice Hall, Sydney.

HARGREAVES, D.H. (1972) *Interpersonal Relations and Education*. Routledge and Kegan Paul, London.

HARGREAVES, D.H. (1976) 'Reactions to labelling', in Hammersley, M. and Woods, P. (eds) *The Process of Schooling: Sociological Reader*. Open University Press, London, pp. 201–7.

HARGREAVES, D.H., HESTER, S. and MELLOR, F. (1975) *Deviance in Classrooms*. Routledge and Kegan Paul, London.

JACKSON, P. (1968) *Life In Classrooms*. Holt, Rinehart and Winston, New York.

MACPHERSON, J. (1981) 'Classroom "mucking around" and the Parsonian model of schooling', in D'Urso, S. and Smith, R. (eds) *Changes, Issues and Prospects in Australian Education*. 2nd ed. University of Queensland Press, 143–50.

MARSH, P., ROSSER, E. and HARRE, R. (1978) *The Rules of Disorder*, Routledge and Kegan Paul, London.

PETRIE, S. (1981) 'School structures and delinquency', in D'Urso, S. and Smith, R. (eds) *Changes, Issues and Prospects in Australian Education*. 2nd ed. University of Queensland Press, pp. 137–42.

RAMSAY, P., SNEDDON, D., GRENFELL, J. and FORD, I. (1983) 'Successful and unsuccessful schools: A study in Southern Auckland', *Australian and New Zealand Journal of Sociology*. 19(2), pp. 279–304.

SPRADLEY, J.P. and MCCURDY, D.W. (1972) *The Cultural Experience: Ethnography in complex society*, S.R.A., Chicago.

WALKER, J. (1987) *Louts and Legends. Male Youth Culture in an Inner-city School*, Allen and Unwin, Sydney.

WERTHMAN, C. (1977) 'Delinquents in schools: A test for the legitimacy of authority', in Cosin, B. et al. (eds) *School and Society*, 2nd ed. Routledge and Kegan Paul, London, pp. 34–43.

WILLIS, P. (1977) *Learning to Labour*, Saxon House, London.

WOODS, P. (1979) *The Divided School*, Routledge and Kegan Paul, London.

WOODS, P. (1980a) *Pupil Strategies*, Croom Helm, London.

WOODS, P. (1980b) *Teacher Strategies*, Croom Helm, London.

WOODS, P. (1983) *Sociology and the School*, Routledge and Kegan Paul, London.

Author

Elizabeth Wood is a supply teacher for the Queensland Department of Education. John Knight lectures in the sociology of education at the University of Queensland.

Source: Knight, E. & Knight, J., *Unicorn Journal of the Australian College of Education*, Canberra, vol. 15, no. 1, Feb. 1989, pp. 36–43.

Report 2

NASR'S DEVELOPMENT AS A WRITER IN HIS SECOND LANGUAGE: THE FIRST SIX MONTHS

Marietta Elliott

La Trobe University

During the first 6 months of the school year of 1985, at Brunswick Language Centre, I observed Nasr as he was learning to write in his second language.

The most significant change which occurred is that Nasr gained an appreciation of the way in which English written language is different from spoken language. That is, rather than merely recording his spoken language, Nasr became a writer in English.

The changes manifested themselves not only in the product, namely the texts themselves, but also in the processes by which they were produced. These processes can be both directly observed, as recorded on videotape or in the observational diary, which was kept once weekly, or inferred from the product.

The major ways in which the last piece is more 'developed' is that Nasr has chosen a more 'advanced' genre, and the piece conforms more strictly to one genre, rather than also containing elements of other genres.

Nevertheless, the earlier pieces mark important, transitional stages and I have therefore chosen to call these intermediate forms 'intertext'.

Nasr gains mastery over linking mechanisms more characteristic of written than of spoken language; he moves from co-ordination to subordination, and through the use of reference and ellipsis, he gradually eliminates the various forms of redundancy. Acquisition of form and function of the past tense is regarded as essential for the production of sustained narrative and, as such, can also be viewed as a form of cohesion.

In Nasr's case the changes in the writing behaviour include an increase in pause length and a reduction in the number of pauses, changes in the number and type of revisions made, and differences in the way in which input from the teacher is generated.

Introduction

I last saw Nasr in July, 1986, one year after he had left the Language Centre. He had changed from the playful boy I remembered to a serious young man. His voice had deepened, and he had grown several inches.

He was happy at Brunswick High School, and had just graduated from E.S.L. to mainstream classes, where he had no difficulty participating. He was also studying Arabic, but he found the work too easy.

He showed me two pieces of his current work: a fictitious interview and a fictitious newspaper report. Not only was his expression virtually error-free, but he was using colloquial expressions like 'take care of yourself, kids', and complex sentences such as 'He was wearing an overcoat even though it was a mild day'.

How had Nasr achieved all this in 18 months?

The study

I wished to observe students' writing development in a situation where they would have considerable choice both in topic and language, so that their writing could be as independently conceived as possible, both with regard to content and with regard to the language selected.

The teachers at Brunswick Language Centre were enthusiastic about putting a writing program in place, therefore all the students I have observed have come from this Centre. As these students stay for a period of six months before moving on to school, and have intensive English tuition for this time, six months is the time frame of the study.

Brunswick Language Centre is in inner-suburban Melbourne. It caters for about 60 students, both 'New Arrival' and 'Intensive' (students who have been in Australia for some time but are experiencing problems).

Four cases are currently being analyzed, of whom one will be discussed in this report. The recordings were made during writing classes, so that the individual observed remained within the normal classroom setting. Each student was observed on a weekly basis. A videocamera was trained on his or her script and moving hand. A microphone recorded any speech. Other observations were recorded in a diary which I kept. All scripts from the writing classes were collected. In addition, the case study students and their families were interviewed with an interpreter present.

Using all these different techniques of data collection, I hoped to get an accurate and sensitive description of students' writing development in their second language.

Nasr

Nasr was 14 when he came to Brunswick Language Centre. He had completed 10 years of schooling in Lebanon, and had already been introduced to Roman script through French. He was very proud of his knowledge. Muhammad Alman's (the Arabic-speaking aide at Brunswick Language Centre) opinion of his first language writing was that he had good ideas, but made grammatical and spelling errors.

Nasr was living in Brunswick with his mother, sister, brother-in-law and their baby, and his brother, who was then about 18. His brother had already been in Australia about a year and spoke reasonably fluent English. His father arrived in Australia from Lebanon a few months after the study began.

Nasr is a Lebanese Christian; religion and patriotism are closely linked and of supreme importance to him. Margaret, one of his teachers, reminisced about that mixture of seriousness and playfulness which is so characteristic of him:

> He was so enthusiastic and lively, and he really enjoyed the writing. In fact all that class did. He did take the writing seriously, although he wasn't academic. (Pers. comm. 15.12.86).

General description of Nasr's writing development

What is evidence of writing development?

When we are looking for evidence of change, we must examine not only the actual text, but also the composing behaviour, as well as assessing what was attempted. Though it is impossible to prove intention, it is, I believe, possible to infer it through examining both product and behaviour. These aspects are intricately related, and should not be discussed in rigid separation; however, some aspects of behaviour as captured on videotape will be alluded to as distinct from the writing itself.

Separating the different kinds of data is done merely in the service of every turn to indicate where evidence came from. With the aid of the two kinds of data, text and (sic) should be possible both to document changes which have taken place and strategies used by the writer.

What has Nasr learnt?

Green and Morgan (1981:177) have stated that an

> awareness of the differences between oral and written communication affects the ability to write well . . .

It is the growth of this awareness with reference to his second language that is seen as the most crucial factor in Nasr's development as a writer. Whereas at the beginning his writing seems to be little more than recorded speech, by the end of the six months during which I observed him, Nasr showed both by the texts he was producing, and by his behaviour while composing, that he was aware of the demands of producing written rather than oral English.

Though Nasr produced only a few pieces of writing in his first language, it is clear that from the beginning he had a reasonably sophisticated idea about written language in general. Firstly, as he had learnt some French, he already knew the Roman alphabet. He learnt very early to use the English alphabet orally when enquiring about spelling. Even in the early pieces he was using rhetorical devices in English (*My Contry*).

However, in spite of previous knowledge and aptitude, many language-specific aspects have to be relearnt and the writer must to some extent forge a new identity which incorporates the experiences s/he has undergone. By the end of the first six months Nasr could not be expected to have completed his development. Idea units in the last piece are in fact shorter than in some earlier pieces, owing to the fact that he had not yet gained a clear concept of idea unit boundaries at the earlier time. He has not learnt to revise at the organizational level. He has not written any complete expository text (Martin and Rothery, 1981). However, he has written observation/comment, report, recount and narrative. By the end of 6 months, he has a good appreciation of what is required of narrative. He has gained mastery over various kinds of cohesive links, in particular subordination, ellipsis and reference and the form and function of the past tense, essential to the production of sustained narrative. From the change in his revision strategies we can conclude that he has gained an appreciation of the way writing, as distinct from speech, can be polished.

Differences between spoken and written language

The differences between spoken language and written language have their origin in two factors: the social situation in which each occurs, and the nature of the activities themselves.

Whereas speaking takes place in a context of social interaction and is basically a co-operative enterprise between two or more people, writing is essentially a solitary activity, where text must be created and sustained independent of an interlocutor. This means that the writer must learn to anticipate the needs of an invisible audience, and consequently to be clear and explicit, to concentrate on the message rather than on social relations. Chafe (1985:105) has called this feature 'integration' in the case of written language and 'involvement' in the case of spoken language and Halliday (1985:61) refers to 'high lexical density' and 'low lexical density', describing the relationship of content words to function words in each ease. Cohesive devices need to become internal to the text itself, or 'ties across message chunks' (Gumperz et al, 1982:8) are needed to compensate for the absence of an interlocutor, or of tonal contours to aid the interpretation of the message.

Though writing is ten times slower than speech, reading is faster than writing. As writers have planning time, and reading is a faster form of processing than listening, idea units tend to be longer in writing than in speech (Chafe, 1985:106). Whereas in speech they are independent of each other, in written language they are more often 'integrated' (Chafe, 1985:111). This leads to features such as the following being more characteristic of written, rather than spoken English (see Chafe, 1985:110 for a more complete listing):

use of passives;
use of nominalization;
subordination rather than co-ordination.

Writing is regarded as permanent, as an artifact, whereas speech is considered dynamic and evanescent. Thus with writing, greater accountability, concern with 'evidentiality' (Chafe, 1985:118) is required. At the same time, writing can be altered, restructured, polished.

Successful writers have also learnt which 'register' or 'genre', defined by Martin and Rothery (1981:2) as

> a conventional configuration of meanings that a culture habitually makes use of in social interaction

is appropriate to their particular communication task. Whilst there can be similarities between some spoken and some written genres, they generally call for different structures and language.

It is true that modern technology, in particular the tape-recorder and the computer, are now closing the distance between speech and writing, and that, as Beaman (1982:51), and Tannen (1982:14) have pointed out, many of the differences outlined are a function of genre rather than of medium. Nevertheless, Nasr's English writing does gradually acquire many of the features which have been presented here as characteristic of written language, and by his behaviour, for example his revision strategies, he shows that he has gained an appreciation of the differences between the spoken and the written medium. Therefore these features are considered significant when we examine Nasr's development as a writer in his second language.

Development of genre

In the discussion of Nasr's development of genre, I will use the taxonomy provided by Martin and Rothery (1981). Though it was devised for young English as a mother tongue writers, it may be useful to see whether the system could be applied to second language learner writers. There are, however, several problems inherent in Martin and Rothery's approach, which I will present here as unanswered questions. After examining Nasr's development I will suggest that certain modifications, or perhaps further amplifications need to be made to their concepts.

Martin and Rothery (1981) have given a sequential account of genres required at various stages of schooling, starting with 'observation/comment', which then splits into two strands: a 'narrative' strand, consisting of 'recount', 'narrative' and 'thematic narrative' (for definitions, see Martin and Rothery, 1981:11–12) and an 'expository' strand, which consists of 'report', 'exposition' and 'literacy criticism'. They accuse the system of valuing the 'narrative' above the 'expository' and claim that many never master this latter genre, because it is explicitly taught.

The following questions remain unanswered:

1) Given that report and 'embryonic' exposition appear as early as year 2, what is the significance of the order as presented?
2) What is the place of input in the developmental sequence, or is the sequence an order of difficulty?
3) How do students move from one genre to another, given that, as Martin and Rothery state, any topic or field might call for a number of different responses?
4) Why are mixtures, or 'melanges' regarded as so inferior given that the genre outlines are 'guidelines' rather than 'straight jackets' (Martin and Rothery, 1981:47)?
5) What importance would they assign development *within* the genre?

One way of testing the usefulness of Martin and Rothery's scheme as a developmental tool is to use it to examine a student's development longitudinally, as I am doing here with Nasr. It will be seen that in sequence, 'melanges' or 'mixtures' play a vital role as transitional pieces, facilitating the move from one genre to another, and that Nasr develops considerably within one genre before he attempts another one.

Though, as will be pointed out in relation to the individual pieces, some topics and 'formulae' were suggested by the teachers, Nasr was never forced to use them. Other ideas came through reading student publications and books, and from classmates. Thus Nasr had control over what he wrote and how he wrote it, even whether he wrote or not.

It is not known what genres Nasr had mastered in his L1. It is likely, as he had already completed 10 years of schooling and showed knowledge about written language in general, that some of these were familiar to him. It is remarkable that nevertheless he has followed an order the same as that which Martin and Rothery (1981:5) have indicated for English as a mother tongue learner writers. For this reason, it is suggested that Nasr is following basically a 'begin again' strategy, that is, using his oral L2 as a basis for L2 writing, rather than translating from his L1 writing. One exception could be the piece *My Contry*.

Table 1 Nasr's English pieces in sequence, classified according to genre

(1)	21/2/85	*I like Australia*	observation/comment
(2)	22/2/85	*I like T.V.*	observation/comment
(3)	22/2/85 and 25/2/85	*I like boats*	observation/comment
(4)	4/3/85	*My School B.L is on the Moon*	(a Lie) report
(5)	22/3/85	*I like . . . I don't like*	observation/comment
(6)	15/4/85	*My Contry*	report/observation/comment
(7)	20/4/85	*My Teachers*	observation/comment
(8)	22/4/85	*The first day I came to School*	recount/narrative

(Term II)			
(9)	11/6/85	*The fellow and the red*	observation/comment
(10)	11/6/85	*My house*	observation/comment
(11)	2/7/85	*New Name for teachers*	observation/comment
(12)	2/7/85	*My Memories*	observation/comment
(13)	9/7/85	*I like dogs*	poem
(14)	9/7/85	*I like stars*	poem
(15)	14/7/85	draft 3 of *My Contry (My Country)*	
(16)	18/7/85	*Boy in the Sea*	narrative/observation/comment
(17)	18/7/85	*The names*	observation/comment
(18)	6/8/85	*War in my Village*	narrative

Note: The spelling in the titles has been slightly amended to facilitate comprehension.

I will now briefly discuss the *schematic structure* of the more important L2 pieces, four of which are reproduced in the appendix.

The first recorded English piece, *I like Australia* (21/2/85), consists of a series of autobiographical statements according to two basic sentence models, which could be regarded as the written equivalent of what has often been described as a 'formulaic' stage of oral language development (Nicholas, 1985), where Nasr is making use of 'prefabricated structures' (Hakuta, 1974:287) some of which have been provided by the teacher, and some found in a children's book (e.g. 'I like boats').

In the second piece of significance, a 'Lie': *My School B.L is on the Moon* (3/4/85) Nasr does what Martin and Rothery (1981:52) have considered impossible: he plays creatively with a text before he has mastered its genre. The idea was presented to him by the teacher. He combined his knowledge of school vocabulary with his knowledge of food, names; making teacher, students and classroom into a kind of food or drink. Although the fictitious description he has created is not coherent, Nasr has fun manipulating the few structures (basically the copula and 'have' constructions) and the little vocabulary he has mastered so far.

After this time he became dissatisfied with playing and with writing simple pieces and did not write for almost two weeks.

My Contry (15/4/85) is extremely difficult to categorize. It contains elements of three different genres: of report, the information that Lebanon is being attacked by surrounding nations, observation/comment, as the author's feelings are included, and exposition, as Nasr has attempted to provide a reason for Lebanon's tragedy. The reason is more symbolic than logical. Lebanon is seen as both small and excellent, therefore a threat to surrounding nations, just as Jesus Christ was gentle and good, and so was crucified. It has been suggested (Robert Paths, pers. comm.) that this piece could be a form of written prayer, which fits in with the fact that Nasr attended a Church service just prior to writing it. Though it would still be based on spoken language, it is a more formal spoken genre, and the model would have been in L1.

My Contry is regarded as a transitional piece, where elements of several genres appear in preliminary form. This becomes clear when we look at the next piece, which is predominantly a recount, with elements of narrative beginning to emerge: *The first day I came to School* (22/4/85). Whilst Nasr and his fellow students are the main protagonists, there is also a small crisis: the fear which the Teacher in Charge has inspired and the strangeness of the new situation: Nasr thought 'him came to hit me'. His fear is resolved, we are not told how, except that Nasr refers incidentally to the passing of time in the coda ('and now . . . '). Now students and teachers alike are remembered in his prayers.

When we look at Nasr's activities and output early in Term 2, we are reminded that development does not occur in a nice linear progression, but in fits and starts, with long fallow periods. Nasr retreats back into observation/comment, with short pieces about his house, his favourite colours, using more 'formulaic' sentences about his teachers, his classmates and 'memories'. Some of these constructions are suggested by the teacher, some by classmates or by student publications. One genre which lends itself well to 'prefabricated structures' is poetry, and Nasr takes to this with enthusiasm. He had previously written down some songs and poems that he knew in Arabic and French, and now adapts children's rhymes and follows his teacher Margaret's suggestions to write little poems.

Boy in the Sea (18/7/85) marks a tremendous leap forward. It is predominantly a narrative, as it has a crisis (a boy is drowning in the sea) and resolution (Nasr saves him). At the beginning it sounds more like a recount: Nasr and his family go to the beach. The actual story is fictional, but the excursion to the beach is probably true. This is perhaps why Nasr has trouble integrating the two parts of the story. He realizes the need for some conclusion but is not sure what is appropriate, reverts to observation/comment:

'I was happy and I like to go their (there) and onther (another) time'. (D.1).

War in my Village (6/8/85), written only three weeks later, does not suffer from these problems. It is a pure and unadulterated narrative. There is an introduction which sets the scene. Nasr is contrasting the external conditions, the rain and the cold, with his cheerful mood ('It was a good morning but it was raining and very cold'). He establishes an atmosphere of cosiness ('when we siting near the fire') but we already have warning of an impending event which is to disturb the equilibrium ('Suddenly'). The suspense is increased by the fact that the main message is delayed: ('something was happened'). The time-honoured tragic convention of having a messenger introducing the action is used ('one of my village dead my uncle talled us'). The resolution comes immediately: the young men go out 'to protect the village' but in fact to avenge the death of one of their number. Simultaneously the children are taken to a safe place. Quickly the young men find their mark.

While there are a few confusions: we don't know where the father is, or where the 'cosins' suddenly sprang from—the story is consistently told from Nasr's own perspective. 'Suddnely we hear shooting, so that was the yongs . . . '. In fact he knows that is what happened.

Though Nasr clearly claims the story as his own in the coda, this time he does not state his feelings, rather allowing the effect to arise out of the story itself.

Nasr learnt in six months to control three genres: observation/comment, recount and narrative. He was not specifically instructed in these written forms, nor was the structure of his pieces discussed by the teacher. It is my contention that pieces containing elements of several genres have served as a pilot, helping Nasr in his gradual understanding of the conventions.

The mixed pieces could be understood as a form of 'interlanguage' (Selinker, 1972), not merely as deviations from the target, but as transitional approximations of text, evidence of exploration, and of hypotheses being constructed at the discourse level. I have called these forms 'intertext'. They must not be judged simply on their own, but in sequence, as part of Nasr's acquisition of written genres.

Language

The development of cohesion

The ability to create sustained written text independently is regarded here as the most vital skill for any writer to acquire. One way of observing the acquisition of this skill is to trace the appearance of various types of cohesion. Halliday and Hasan (1976) have provided a useful framework. Though a later version of cohesion analysis has been published (Halliday, 1985a), the 1976 framework has proved productive for the current description. Halliday and Hasan (1976:13) define cohesion as follows:

> The concept of cohesion accounts for the essential semantic relations whereby any passage of speech or writing is enabled to function as text. We can systematize this concept by classifying it into a small number of distinct categories—reference substitution, ellipsis, conjunction, and lexical cohesion . . . Each of these categories is represented in the text by particular features—repetitions, omissions, occurrences of certain words and constructions—which have in common the property of signalling that the interpretation of the passage depends on something else. If that 'something else' is verbally explicit, then there is cohesion.

Of the various forms of cohesion, only reference and conjunction will be considered here. *Reference* is a way of directing the listener or reader to an item which has either gone before (*anaphoric reference*) or which is to come (*cataphoric reference*). The principal linguistic expressions of reference are personal pronouns, possessive adjectives, deictics and the definite article: e.g. Do you know John? *He's* a friend of mine. Reference may be to something else in the text (*endophoric reference*) or in the situation (*exophoric reference*) (Halliday and Hasan, 1976:145).

Conjunction is a way of 'relating to each other linguistic elements that occur in succession but are not related by other structural means' (Halliday and Hasan, 1976:227). They can be *paratactic* or *hypotactic* (Halliday and Hasan, 1976:322), or we could call them *co-ordinating* (e.g. 'but') or *subordinating* (e.g. 'although').

The most marked changes in the development of cohesion in Nasr's writing have occurred in the areas of *Reference* and *Conjunction*. Though Halliday and Hasan are mainly concerned with relations between sentences, at Nasr's stage, the development of cohesive links takes place predominantly, though not exclusively, within sentences.

Nasr has two tasks ahead of him, firstly to find the appropriate linguistic way to create links in English, for example to acquire the standard form of the personal pronoun, which is clearly an ESL function. Secondly he must discover the form of linking which is characteristic of written rather than spoken English (see discussion, page 124). The second task is similar to that facing young English writers (Beaman, 1984:50).

Table 2 Exhaustive list of Nasr's use of endophoric reference

Reference	
21/2/85	(school) *chis* name Bronsvik languiche cintre
25/2/85	I like boats because the boats *its* verry beautufoul
4/3/85	*they* body is lemons the chair is 25 kls and *she* salad the room have six window and *she* (changed to be) is beans
22/3/85	I like red because red . . . I like yellow because the coulour . . . I like cat and bird because the animals . . . I like soccer because *it* I like teacher because—— teacher me
12/4/85	(translation) I love Jesus and evryone love *Him His* protect evryone
15/4/85	My contry was lovely contry <u>it</u> was . . . My contry is . . . but *his* is . . .
22/4/85	Miss R. I like she because *she* . . . Mr Bill I like *him* . . . I like my school because *she* is a moon
11/6/85	I like *this* coulour because the red one it's My books coulor its a happy coulor evry day and I like evryone and happy and the yellow colur I like *it* ('s crossed out) because *it's* my best clothes and *it's* happy too. ' (*my house*) . *it's* a good cat . . . the dog is an Alsatian I like *him* very much I like my house because I was born in *it*.
2/7/85	Mr bill he love all the studints Miss Phon *she* like the camera and she love all the studints too
2/7/85	I remember . . . and when I remember *this* things i cry and i wand from god to protect all Mi memories.
18/7/85	. . . because *it* was a very hot day . . . my father and my mother *they* make the food . . . saw a boy shouting help help . . . I arrived to *him* and talled *him* give *me your* hand *he* gave *me his* hand and I pull *him* to *me* . . . I got him and I went to the beach and I talled my parent *what* happened.
6/8/85	*War in my Village* *Something* was happened one of my village dead . . . my village yong they got the shooting gun and *they* went to protect the village and we went to my grandfather's house to stay *their*. My cosins talled us that someone killed *that* mam (man). Suddnely we hear *someone* is shooting so that was the yongs *how* had the shooting gun *they* found the killer and *that's* all my story and *it's* true.

Note: Only endophoric references have been underlined because they are considered most important for writing development. It is this form of reference which allows the reader to rely only on the text, rather than on outside information, as is the case with exophoric reference.

Nasr attempts to use some form of linking from the very beginning. Initially it is a form of lexical cohesion very similar to that noted by Martin and Rothery (1981:21), links provided by the teller of the story, e.g. 'I'm Nasr Nabbout .'. However, even in early pieces he is attempting reference, e.g. 'My school *chis* Name . . . ' (21/2/85) and 'the boats its verry beautufoul. In '*My school B.L is on the Moon* (4/3/85) there is lexical cohesion provided by the twin themes of food and schools but there are also some non-standard forms of reference. Perhaps Nasr is over-generalizing from his L1 or from French when he uses the personal pronoun for inanimate objects, e.g. 'The chair is 25 kls and she salad'. He also attempts a form of the possessive: 'They body'.

By 22/3/85 he is using the formula 'I like . . . because . . . ' to carry different forms of cohesion. He starts off with repetition: e.g. 'I like red because red . . . ' goes to another form of lexical cohesion: e.g. 'I like yellow/because the colour . . . ' and finally to reference: e.g. 'I like soccer because it . . . '. He then gradually begins to use more pronouns: for example in the pieces dated 11/6/85, he uses 'it' seven times, on 18/7/85 he is using the plural pronoun 'they' and the accusative 'him' referentially.

2/7/85 shows the first evidence of the deictic adjective though not in the standard form: ' . . . and when I remember this things I cry'. By 6/8/85 most of his uses of reference are close to standard (except for 'their') and the doubling up of noun and pronoun as in: 'the village yong, they got the shooting gun'. This construction remains a consistent feature.

Nasr was not corrected and was allowed to explore various structures. He used 'formulaic' expressions and experimented with altering small subsections of theses focussing on one particular element (see 22/3/85). Here as with the development of genres it seemed essential, at least for that he was able to experiment and that he was not prematurely corrected because he did not immediately achieve the standard form. His text gradually became closer to the conventions, though in the first six months some non-standard features remained.

Table 3 Exhaustive list of Nasr's use of conjunction

Conjunction

22/2/85 (a)	beacuse (because) I wath (watch) Saturday and Sunday 'and' as co-ordinator
22/2/85 (b)	I like boats beacuse its verry beautufoul
4/3/85	. . . and the hair is jelly . . . and the cloose (class) is water . . . and one with eye . . . and she salad . . . and verry smale . . . and she is beans
22/3/85	I like red because red is very hot. (Model provided by teacher)
12/4/85	I write story of Jesus because . . . I love Jesus and evryone love Him because His protect evryone and when we go and when we mouve the Jesus protect we (us).
15/4/85	. . . but now . . . . . . because Lebenon . . . . why? because . . . . . . but his is the good and is the lovely . . . . . . an the end . . .
22/4/85	but his the boss . . . and when his open the door and his look

	and said
	after I ask him what your name
	and after 10 minits
	and evryone came
	and the first teacher
	and her name is . . .
	and she start the first lesson
	and she asked . . .
	and now I pray . . .
22/4/85 (b)	because she is very happy . . .
	when she teach . . .
	but I like him . . .
	because she is a moon (written in Arabic first)
11/6/85 (a)	I like this coulour because . . .
	and it's a happy coulor . . .
	and I like
	I like it because
	and it's happy . . .
11/6/85 (b)	. . . cat and a dog . . .
	but the dog is Alsatian . . .
	I like my house because I was born in it
2/7/85	and when I remember this things I cry.
	I wand (want) (from) god to protect all mi memories.
9/7/85	A star that is shooting across the dark sky.
	A dog that is dreaming very still.
4/7/85	Lebanon which I means my country. (*My country* D.2)
18/7/85	. . . because it was a very hot day.
	and my father and my mother they make the food.
	suddnely . . .
	. . . and I arrived to him
	I talled him give me your hand
	and I pull him to me
	and I went to the beach . . .
	and I talled my parents what happened.
	and I like to go to their onther (another) time.
	(the beach) which were my parents ther . . . (D.2)
6/8/85	when I waked up.
	but it was raining and very cold.
	Suddnely when we siting near the fire . . .
	and they went to protect the village.
	and we went to my grandfather's house,
	because my father was not home.
	and my cosine talled us
	that someone killed that mam (man)
	. . . so that was the yongs,
	how (who) had the shooting gun.
	and that's all my story,
	and it's true.

In talking about Nasr's development of conjunction, I shall be mainly concerned with actual *conjunctions* and these mainly within the sentence, though sentence boundaries are not initially clear. Nasr, in fact, is initially under the impression that conjunctions can start a sentence.

I have included in the discussion of 'conjunction' the use of relative pronouns, though strictly speaking these are in a different category, as the links between clauses are structural. However, the aim is to demonstrate Nasr's growing ability to combine idea units. He progresses from using conjunctions to using constructions with relative pronouns, which are more 'integrated'.

In the first piece (21/2/85) no conjunctions are used at all. 'And' is used as a co-ordinator:

' . . . and my father and cisty-in-laws (sister-in-law) and mother'.

The first conjunction used is 'because' spelt beacuse (21/2/85):

'I like T.V. Beacuse I wath (watch) Saturday and Sunday'.

Here it has an additive rather than a causative function. However, the next day (22/2/85) Nasr was using it in the correct way, having found a model in a child's book which he has slightly adapted:

'I like boats because it's verry beautufoul'.

4/3/85—Many units are not joined by any conjunctions at all but 'and' is used six times.
22/3/85—The following pattern was provided:

'I like . . . because . . . '

12/4/85—Nasr translated an L1 report of a church service. In this translation we find not only 'because' but 'and' as an additive conjunction together with 'when' (temporal). Firstly, in this translated section, Nasr has used two new conjunctions. Secondly, he has integrated more clauses. The second 'because' clause is dependent on the first one and there are two 'when' clauses dependent on the main clause. Through translation, Nasr has been able to use several new elements. These have featured in his subsequent writing.

By 14/5/85 Nasr is learning to combine clauses. Four is the highest number there:

It was the good contry of all contries. but now my contry is not good because Lebanon I means my contry the israil soldier shooting the libanes soldier and the people in my contry no just israil and syria, evryone shoot my contry.

He does not have control over the linking process and the effect here is somewhat meandering. Nevertheless this is developmentally a very significant step, because he is already attempting to create longer idea units.

22/4/85—While the predominant conjunction is still 'and' (7×), 'after' (temporal) appears for the first time. At this stage, Nasr is using 'and' together with other conjunctions such as 'when' or 'after'. It is not clear why he does this—though it is a very common characteristic of spoken language (e.g. 'and I said, and then he said and . . . ').

The next 'integration' feature occurs on 9/7/85 in the little poems, the model for which was a children's hook:

'A star that is shooting . . .

'A dog that is running . . . '

Once again, Nasr has used 'prefabricated structures' to' experiment with new forms.
On 14/7/85 and 18/7/85 Nasr tries to link clauses using the relative pronoun:

14/7/85 'which I means my country' (Draft 2)

18/7/85 'which were my parents that' (Draft 2)

In the second instance he has coalesced two ideas:

18/7/85 (the beach) on which/where my parents were.

'Where' is in fact a combination (even in form) of which and there. On 18/7/85 the first link beyond the sentence 'suddnely' also appears. By 6/8/85 (the final piece) his use of the relative pronoun is closer to target (except for spelling):

' . . . How (who) had the shooting gun'.

This piece is remarkable for the number of units which have been 'integrated'.

My village yong they got the shooting gun and they went to protect the village and we went to my grandfather s house to stay their because my father was not home

Nasr retains control of this very long sentence. Everything is happening at once, people are scattering in all directions. In addition, in other parts of the piece, linking has occurred beyond the sentence level as in 'Suddnely, when . . . ' and 'so that was . . . '.

Development of conjunction can be very broadly characterized as going from co-ordination to subordination. However, within this continuum there are further refinements, in the degree of 'integration' or connectedness between the units being joined together. The 'additive' is the simplest one. Though 'because' is used, the relation expressed is an additive one (21/2/85).

Next is 'because', the 'causative' relation which seems out of place but may be explained by the fact that teachers are very fond of asking 'why'. The next is the 'adversative', 'but', then comes the 'temporal', both 'co-ordinating' and 'subordinating' as in 'after' and 'when'. Finally we see some linking at a more profound structural level than conjunction, such as 'which' and 'that' and links beyond the sentence such as 'So that . . . ' and 'Suddnely . . . '

Form and function of the past tense

15/4/85   was (2×)

Verbs that should have been in the past tense

Table 4 Exhaustive list of Nasr's use of past time referring verbs

22/4/85	Draft One	Draft Two
	come	came
	comed	comed
	was think	was think
	I think	I think
	came	came
	open	open
	said	said
	say	said
	is came	is come
	come	come
	take	take
	start	start
	asked	asked
18/7/85	went	went
	was	was
	arrived	arrived

was	was
weared	wore
started	start
make	was making
saw	saw
swam	swam
arrived	araved
talled (told)	talled
gave	gave
full	full
got	got
went	went
	which were
	we ate
	we went home
talled	
happened	
was	was
was	was
waked up	waked up
we siting	we wan siting
was happened	was happened
dead	dead
talled	talled
got	got
went	went
went	went
was	was
tailed	tailed
killed	killed
heap	hear
is shooting	is shooting
was	was
had	had
found	found

As is the case with other features, Nasr faces two separate tasks simultaneously. It is this simultaneity which distinguishes second language writing development from first writing development. One task is to maintain consistency in the use of the past tense. The other task is to learn how the past tense is formed. Though Nasr has progressed in both these areas by the end of six months, mastery is by no means complete.

In the whole of Nasr's output, there are only 4 pieces featuring the past tense at all. By the time he tried a recount he understood what the past tense was for and he had some idea of how to form it. On 15/4/85, though he used only one past verb form, the copula, and he did not attempt to sequence past events, he did contrast a past and a present state.

One week later, on 22/4/85, Nasr's knowledge was clearly at a transitional stage. He knew there are two different ways of forming the past tense, and he was sure of 'asked', which is used correctly throughout. Other verbs he was unsure of, and he tried out different forms, which I would like to claim is not a random phenomenon but is a sign that he had narrowed down his hypotheses about the form and was awaiting confirmation. These include: 'said' where he has:

(Draft 1) 'said', 'said', 'say' and 'is say'

(Draft 2) 'said', 'said', 'said' and 'is said'

'came' where he has

(Draft 1) 'come', 'comed', 'came' and 'is come'

(Draft 2) 'came', 'comed', 'came' and 'is come'

'thought' where he has

(Draft 1 and Draft 2) 'I was think' and 'I think'

There are several verbs that remain in the incorrect form. No variation found in their forms:

(Draft 1 and Draft 2) 'his open', 'his look',

'taken and 'start'.

It is reasonable to assume that Nasr has no basis on which to determine whether these forms are correct or not. For example, both weak and strong verbs are represented.

By 18/7/85 Nasr has added several new forms to his repertoire. There are many more forms that are secure, there is far less of what I have called experimentation. Common strong forms such as 'went', 'saw', 'swam', 'got', and 'ate' (Draft 2) and the weak form 'happened' all remain correct. 'Started' gets the 'ed' added on at a later stage.

By 6/8/85, while he is not completely confident, and not all the verbs used are in their conventional form (e.g. 'was happened', 'tailed', 'waked') he has control over a variety of verbs in the past tense ('got', 'killed', 'went', 'had' and 'found'). He does revert to the present tense at one point

Suddnely I hear someone is shooting, so that was the yongs . . .

However, a single example provides insufficient evidence for any conclusion as to intention.

Strategies

Thus far attention has been focussed mainly on the text. Even so, the aim of the analysis has been to gain some understanding of the processes underlying Nasr's writing development in his second language. One strategy Nasr seems to be using is what I have called 'the exploration of variation', where Nasr has experimented with different possible forms, whether it be the personal pronoun, or the past tense.

Several other strategies may be inferred from the texts. One very important strategy which has received great attention in relation to oral second language development (e.g. Kellerman, 1978:59; Pit Corder, 1978:90) is the use of L1. Another strategy which may be observed by comparing different drafts of Nasr's pieces, is revision. They must be looked at in conjunction with videodata, as Nasr carries out many of his revisions on the run, much like repairs in conversation.

Use of L1

A major hypothesis underlying this research is that a translation strategy is one means by which students who have sound literacy skills in L1 can move themselves a little faster along the developmental track and introduce more complexity and interest in their writing than if they simply began again.

In spite of differences between education systems throughout the world, there are likely to be enough similarities relating to school-based writing to make L1 writing a possible alternative model for L2 writing instead of L2 oral language.

Nasr basically adopted a 'begin again' approach. That is, he preferred mostly to use his L2 oral language as the basis for his L2 writing, instead of using his L1 and translating. There could be personality factors involved in his choice. He found little difficulty in regressing to a more childlike form of behaviour. He is an outgoing, happy student with a sense of fun and play and, as well as enjoying simple children's books he was not seriously frustrated, as some other students have been, by the very basic nature of the texts he initially produced. *My Contry* seems to have been the exception to this, perhaps because his emotions were seriously engaged, and *there* he turned to translation.

Therefore, in Nasr's case, while use of the first language is not his major strategy for generating written text in English, it nevertheless plays an important part. Initially the option of writing in L1 provided a reprieve; a time when he was free to assimilate the new language without the pressure to produce it. Nasr is proud of his writing, not only in Arabic, but also in French, and used material from an L1 autobiography in his English one.

Though Nasr initially wrote several pieces in his L1, he did not make very much use of it as a conscious translation strategy, though he was aware of it as an option. In an interview with me (6/5/85) when asked

When do you write in Arabic?

he replied:

Because I didn't know the English.

When asked, 'If you don't know how to write something, how do you find out?' he said the dictionary was the best way.

He also uses translation, though not very often, to access language which is developmentally in advance of the stage he has otherwise reached. The construction he found remains in his interlanguage, to be used at first in a formulaic way, then gradually assimilated. There are two instances where a translation strategy was used, both from *My Contry* (15/4/85). In the first instance, it is inferred. In the second, there is direct evidence from videotape and from translation of an L1 text.

. . . and now Lebenon crucified on the cross.

Though this item, the only instance of the use of the passive voice, was produced through interaction with the teacher (see page 148) it must have been conceived in L1, firstly because it was a metaphorical rather than a literal use of the concept, secondly because he had written an L1 version of the Easter service so that he had been working on the whole concept in L1 (12/4/85).

I pray to Jesus to protect my contry.

This item is more significant, though less specialized, because it is gradually integrated into Nasr's interlanguage. Initially it is used as a formula, subsequently he is able to manipulate smaller units and recycle them.

We can find the origin of this construction in the L1 piece previously mentioned: a report of the Easter service (12/4/85). Nasr translated part of this piece himself. I was not present so do not know if he used the dictionary.

The self-translated text reads as follows:

I write now story of Jesus because I love Jesus and evryone love Him because His protect evryone. and when go and when we mouve the Jesus protect we.

He could not translate the rest, nor could several puzzled Moslem translators. Some months later we finally discovered by accident that the text consisted of the Lord's Prayer and the Catechism, and Nasr was delighted. He spent some lessons typing out the English version (29/7/85).

The section Nasr left in Arabic (subsequently translated by Muhammad Alman) reads in part:

I ask Jesus Christ to protect Lebanon for us from all those troubles.

As well as evidence from similarities in L1 text and self-translation, we have evidence recorded on videotape (15/4/85) that Nasr actually looked back to the L1 piece during the composition of *My Contry* not once, but several times.

Table 5 Nasr's subsequent use of the construction: 'I pray to Jesus to protect my contry'.

22/4/85	. . . and now I pray to Jesus to protect my school and my teachers and my freinds (sic.: Draft 1)
22/7/85	I wand (from) god to protect all mi memories (Note the time lag—3 months)
29/7/85	And at the end I pray for Jesus to protect my contry and my family and all the world too. ('Jesus story'—English version of Catechism)
6/8/85	they went to protect the village.

We can see from these examples that both the vocabulary item and the structure have remained. Though Nasr has not made extensive use of translation, these two instances are most productive for his development.

Revision

Revision is seen by Graves (e.g. 1983:151) as being at the heart of the writing process and essential to success as a writer. However, the ability to revise involves an understanding of the differences between formal written prose and speech. As speech, at least in terms of the students' experience, is generally more ephemeral than writing, revision of the complete spoken text is not possible (though repairs of course are). Initially, when Nasr is doing little more than recording his oral language, he is not concerned with revision, nor can we expect him to be. Only gradually does Nasr's whole concept of revision change, as he becomes more confident at manipulating English written forms.

There are two places where Nasr's revision strategies may be observed: (1) the videodata, where he shows evidence of making running repairs, and (2) where multiple drafts of the same piece exist.

It would be interesting to compare the phenomenon of running repairs in writing with that of 'repair' in speech, although this is beyond the scope of this paper. One important difference in speech is that repairs are often the result of interaction with another person, whereas in writing, it is the author himself who provides the impetus. The increase in scope of his revisions, and the gradual incorporation of many changes within the first draft itself, is further evidence of Nasr's growth as a writer.

Table 6 Exhaustive list of Nasr's revisions

(1) 14/3/85 *My school B.L is on the Moon* 2 drafts, D.2 12/3/85 1
Arabic version 12/3/55, no differences in the two English versions.

(2) 15/4/85 *My Contry* 3 drafts, D.3 14/7/85
Revisions within D.1:
conty—contry (My contry was lovely contry) 2x
and after said—erased) after "crucified on the cross . . . ")
D.1 to D.2:
palistin—palestan
My Contry D.3
(Note: This draft was typed. Some spelling errors could be typing errors).

Draft Two	Draft Three
contry	coutry
Lebenon	Lebanon
shooting	chooting
Palestan	Palastin
crucified	crusifid
————	like Jeses (after -'on the cross')
contry	country
smaller	smalest
and it is the	but it is the
the lovely	lovely
and the end	———— (omitted)
Jesus	Juses

(3) 22/4/85 *The First day I came to school* 2 drafts (no videodata)
D.1 to D.2: (see page 137)

18/7/85 *Boy in the Sea* 2 drafts
Revisions within D.1
we went—we arrived (see Input)
quickly (orally)—suddnely
I swim (orally)—I swam
I sa (crossed out)—I talled him
I—he gave me his hand
after (crossed out)—and I pull him to me
and (crossed out)—onther (another) time

Draft One	Draft Two
One summer	One summer day
We arrived to the beach	We with the car
I was very happy	I was rearly happy
I weared the sea clothes	I wore the bathers
father and my mother	But my father and my mother
they make the food	they was making the food
I swam very hard	I swam to him very hard
I arrived	I araved

And I talled my parents	Which were my parents
ther	
what happened	We ate and we went home
To their	To ther
Onther time	Onothe time

6/8/85) *War in my Village*
Revisions within D.1:
is happened—was happened
Die—Dead
After they (erased)—Because my father was not their (inserted before 'after my cosins . . .')

(Note: D.2 is the same date as D.1 unless otherwise stated)

The teacher, Rosemary, provided instructions about revision and drafting on 21/2/85. However, Nasr did not start revising independently till 15/4/85. He may have remembered and stored the instructions, but at this stage he was rewriting rather than revising, as he did not look at his first draft and the only change 'palastin ' palestan' corresponds to a change in his pronunciation.

22/4/85 The First Day I Came to School
While there are marginally more verbs in the past tense in D.2 (2 more, though D.1 has 'is came') Nasr mainly seems to be experimenting with different forms instead of consistently revising.

14/7/85 The availability of typewriters in term two was strong motivation for revision. Nasr returned to a much earlier piece (*My Contry*) and revised it, adding elements which improved cohesion ('and'—'but'), correcting spelling or syntax (e.g. *'contry'—'country', 'smaller' 'smalest'*) adding detail (e.g. crusifid *like Juses*).

18/7/85 Boy in the Sea has the most intensive set of revisions both within D.1 and in D.2. Here Nasr is concerned with word choice such as asking for 'arrived' rather than 'went' and 'suddenly' rather than 'quickly'. At the same time we see the growth of 'within draft' revisions, as Nasr develops the ability to stand back from his writing during the composing process itself and anticipate the reader's need.

For example on 6/8/85 (*War in my Village*) he changes 'they' to 'my cosins' and adds 'because my father was not home' as an explanation of why the children did not go to their own home during the shooting.

The past tense continues to feature prominently in revisions, an indication that whilst Nasr is aware of the need to be consistent, he still has not mastered the form completely.

Nasr has developed in the following ways:

— Some of the processes of revision have become more automatic.
— Many of the revisions are now concerned with the needs of the reader and with adding elements more characteristic of written English.
— He is now able to select from alternative wordings in his repertoire (or his teacher's repertoire, see Input page 148).

Pauses

Through observation of Nasr's behaviour while composing, we can come just a little closer to an understanding of his actual processing strategies. By comparing the number, length and reason for the breaks he takes during the composing of an early and a late piece, we can also observe the development which has taken place in his language processing capacities.

Table 7 Pauses in an early and a late text

My Contry

was hove (3) —
ly contry (3)
before
100 years ago
It was the good contry of all contri (20) ies
(asks the teacher for plural of 'country)
but now (15)
my contry is (3)
not good (26)
because (8) (writes 'n' and then erases it)
Lebenon (13)
I means my contry (14)
the Israil soldier shooting the libenes soldier and the people in my contry no just (14)
Israil (5)
and palistin (3)
and syria (22)
evryone (19)
shoot my contry (9)
(corrects spelling—adds 'r')
and now (4)
Lebenon (53)
(See *Input*, page 148—Teacher helps with 'crucified')
Why? because my contry is the smaller (4)
of all contries but his is the good and is the lovely of all the contries (3)
and the end (4)
I pr (5) ay for Je (3) sus (4) to protect my contry.

War in my Village

it was a good morning when I waked up (32)
but it was raining (21)
and very cold (32)
suddnely when we (5)
siting near the (3)
fire (69)
something was happened one of my village die (11)
dead (7)
my uncle tailed us (38) (interruption)
my village
yong they got the shooting gun and they went to protect the village and we went (12)
to my grandfather's house to stay their (17)
(writes 'after they', erases it (5)
because my father was not home after (12)
my cosins talled us that someone killed that mam (man)
suddnely we hear (38)
someone is shooting so that was the yongs (11)

(adds 's')

how had the shooting gun they found the killer (13)

(see *Input*—asks teacher about 'killer')

and that's all my story and it's true.

Note: Numbers refer to time in seconds

Although there are no videotapes in existence for pieces before 15/4/85, it seems reasonable to infer from Nasr's early invented spelling and from the fact that he consistently subvocalizes while writing, that he initially concentrated on merely recording his oral language. On 21/2/85 he wrote 'Bronsvik languiche cintre' for 'Brunswick Language Centre', although he had already learnt some words as 'gestalts': e.g. 'father', 'mother'.

By 15/4/85 he was already beginning to censor himself as he wrote. The most common reason for a break is that he is unsure of spelling: e.g. 'lovely'—he said the word three times, and he initially left out 'r' in 'contry' and went back to put it in.

During the composition of *My Contry* (15/4/85) Nasr stopped more frequently, less time than during *War in my Village* (6/8/85):

Table 8 Pauses in two texts

My Contry (D.1)	War in my Village
Total length: 97 words	Total length: 105 words
Number of pauses: 25	Number of pauses: 18
Average length of pauses: 11.4 seconds	Average length of pauses: 19.3 seconds

The length of pauses is more inconsistent in the earlier pieces because Nasr stopped when he had some difficulty. Otherwise he wrote steadily, keeping pace, word for word, with his subvocalization.

In the later pieces there is more evidence of forward planning as Nasr will say a whole phrase or clause before writing, and also reads aloud what he has written when he reads. He uses a rising intonation rather like taking a running jump, to create a link between what he has written and what is still to come.

Further evidence of more extensive planning at the later stage can be seen in the positioning of pauses, which now coincide more frequently with idea unit boundaries. The first sentence of each piece provides a clear illustration of this point (slashes mark pauses):

(*My Contry*)

My Contry/was love/ly/contry before/100 years ago/it was/the good contry of all contr/ies

(*War in my Village*)

It was a good morning when I waked up/but It was raining/and very cold.

Nasr initially used production strategies more characteristic of speakers than writers in that he worked in very short 'message chunks' (Gumperz et al, 1984:8) and showed little evidence of forward planning.

The video data have provided evidence of the development in Nasr's language processing capacities in English in that he became able to plan and revise increasingly large chunks. This would seem to be an essential pre-condition for the production of written text.

Input from teachers

Both Nasr's teachers were relatively non-interventionist. They left him reasonably free to write or not write, and to choose his own topics. They did not correct him unless he asked, and did not force him to revise.

Most of the interactions on record are initiated by Nasr. Looking at his interaction with the teacher, it becomes clear how much the student has to know before he is able to ask the right question. Even in *My Contry* he had to know that there was something peculiar about the plural ending of 'countries' to stop and get help. He did not ask for help with the first part of the word because he had no doubts about it (c-o-n-t corresponded closely with his pronunciation).

In *My Contry* Nasr used gesture to obtain 'crucified':

NASR: Lebanon—on the Cross—you know Jesus, this one, when he died (throwing his arms wide)
T: You want the special word?
N: Yes
T: 'crucified'. You want me to write it for you?
N: Yes
T: (writes word)
N: (as he writes): And now Lebanon crucified on the Cross.

By 18/7/85 he is using circumlocution in order to obtain the words 'arrived' and 'suddenly'.

NASR: We went . . . we came, not we came, we drove in the car, and after we . . .
T: Arrived?
N: Yes, arrived.
N: Miss, what's this called . . . quickly! quickly!
T: Suddenly?
N: (as he writes) Suddnely . . .

In D.1, Nasr wrote 'sea-clothes' but he knew this was not the conventional word, so that when he was writing D.2 he asked:

Miss, how do you say 'sea-clothes' . . . ?

He also knew that 'weared' is not the right form of the past tense of 'wear', but he was quite content to write it in D.1. Later he asked:

What is the past tense of 'wear'?

By 6/8/86 he is able to describe quite precisely the context in which the item is required. He is using the teacher to confirm a hypothesis:

NASR: Miss who killed the man . . . if I said one killed, and the people found . . . the killer?

Here Nasr is actually demonstrating the process of turning oral language into language more appropriate to formal written text: the transformation of verbs into nouns, or nominalization.

There are possibly personality factors involved in the extent to which students are able to make use of a relatively unstructured situation. Nasr seemed to benefit; he is an outgoing person, who used 'message expansion strategies' (Pit Corder, 1983:17) from the beginning. Initially, while his knowledge of English was limited, he used gesture, which is still a very effective method in some cases. Then he went to circumlocution and to neologism, and finally he was able to specify quite exactly what he needed, either by providing the exact context or by using grammatical terminology for the required item.

Some input from teachers took a long time to percolate, for example the notion of revision. This does not imply that the input should not be provided, but that immediate reaction should not be the only criterion for something having been learnt. It might also suggest that, whilst the relationship between developmental sequence and input is still not clear, it should be taken into account when providing input. For examples, students must learn to co-ordinate before they can subordinate, and they cannot revise their writing if they are still struggling to record their speech. Premature demands may well be detrimental, as they could engender a feeling of failure.

It is encouraging that Nasr seemed to be able to generate the input he needed at the appropriate time, and that he was able to apply knowledge gained elsewhere without being specifically instructed in the writing class.

Conclusion

At the beginning, I posed the question: How had Nasr achieved all this? Nasr's achievements may be summarized so follows:

1) In respect of genre, he followed Martin and Rothery's (1981) sequence part of the way. He learnt gradually to differentiate the school-based genres of observation/comment, recount and narrative.

2) He gradually built up a repertoire of cohesive links in English which enabled him to move from writing a series of statements to creating written text. The ability to create more 'integrated' text was associated with an increase in his English language processing capacity, which enabled him to combine larger chunks of written text.

3) He learnt to revise. Initially he did not revise, as he was occupied with recording his oral language. Next he became concerned with matters of spelling and syntax, and finally came to a limited understanding of style options. He also learnt to revise on the run, to stand back during the composing process itself.

I suggest that these are necessary skills to master, especially for school-based writing.

Nasr also had something to say. Acquiring standard forms of expression may make the writing more accessible, but not necessarily more interesting. I confess to a passing nostalgia for the non-standard eloquence of Nasr's early work (e.g. *My Contry*), with its repetitions, grammatical parallelism of 'no just israil and palistin and syria evryone shoot my contry' and the religious fervour of 'I pray to Jesus to protect my contry'. Nasr learns to cut all that sort of thing out, he learns to play the English game.

When we come to how Nasr did all this, we are left with two problems which, for the moment, must remain unsolved:

1) It is not clear at this stage what the effect of the differences between the Arabic system and the English system—both the school system and the text system—might be.

2) Though it is known that Nasr had basic literacy in his L1, it is not known precisely how sophisticated his understanding of written language was in his L1, so that it is not entirely clear which concepts involved transfer of L1 knowledge and skills, and which involved cognitive advances. I did not specifically ask him to compose in L1 because I wanted to investigate under what circumstances he would do so. There will be data available from other cases in respect of this particular question.

The study has generated the following hypotheses:

1) Nasr learnt because he was not interfered with and was allowed to experiment. He was not corrected unless he asked to be. The question of whether he would have been successful in a more structured classroom is beyond the scope of this study and must remain unanswered.

2) Factors which influence the choice of learning strategy include:
   – personality;
   – linguistic distance between L2 and L1;
   – previous literacy skills.

Nasr chose to use his L2 oral language as a basis for his L2 written language, though he used his L1 at times. Other students may choose a translation strategy. This may involve a different developmental path. After observing Nasr and other students learning to write in their second language for the past two years, I am convinced that the choices are best left in the hands of the learners themselves.

References

Beaman, K. (1984) 'Coordination and subordination revisited: syntactic complexity in spoken and written narrative discourse', in D. Tannen (ed.) *Coherence in Spoken and Written Discourse,* Ablex Publishing Corporation, New Jersey, pp. 45–80.

Chafe, W.L. (1982) 'Integration and involvement in speaking, writing and oral literature', in D. Tannen (ed.) *Spoken and Written Language: Exploring Orality and Literacy,* Ablex Publishing Corporation, New Jersey, pp. 35–54.

Chafe, W.L. (1985) 'Linguistic differences produced by differences between speaking and writing', in D.R. Olsen, N. Torrance, A. Hildyard (eds.) *Literacy, Language and Learning: The Nature and Consequences of Reading and Writing,* Cambridge University Press, Cambridge, pp. 105–23.

Graves, D.H. (1983) *Writing: Teachers and Children at Work,* Heinemann Educational Books, New Hampshire.

Green, G.H. and J.L. Morgan (1981) 'Writing ability as a function of the appreciation of differences between oral and written communication', in C.H. Frederiksen and J.F. Dominic (eds.) *Writing: The Nature, Development, and Teaching of Written Communication—Volume 2; Writing Process, Development and Communication,* Laurence Erlbaum Associates, New Jersey, pp. 177–88.

Gumperz, J.J., H. Kaltman, and H. O'Connor (1984) 'Cohesion in spoken and written discourse: ethnic style and the transition to literacy', in D. Tannen (ed.) *Coherence in spoken and written discourse,* Ablex Publishing Corporation, New Jersey: pp. 3–20.

Hakuta, H. (1974) 'Prefabricated patterns and the emergence of structure in second language acquisition', in *Language Learning,* 24, 2, pp. 298–297.

Halliday, M.A.K. and R. Hasan (1976) *Cohesion in English,* Longman, London.

Halliday, M.A.K. (1985a) *An Introduction to Functional Grammar,* Edward Arnold, London.

Halliday, M.A.K. (1985b) *Spoken and written language,* Deakin University, Victoria.

Kellerman, E. (1978) 'Giving learners a break: native language intuitions as a source of predictions about transferability', *Working Papers on Bilingualism,* March 1978, pp. 59–92.

Kress, G. (1982) *Learning to Write,* Routledge and Kegan Paul, London.

Martin, J.R. and J. Rothery (1981) *Writing Project No. 2: Working Papers in Linguistics,* Linguistics Department, University of Sydney.

Nicholas, H. (1984) 'Is correct usage a relevant target for all second language learners? An overview of some aspects of second language acquisition research', in R.J. Mason (ed.) *Self-directed Learning and Self Access in Australia; From Practice to Theory,* Council of Adult Education, Melbourne, pp. 36–65.

Nicholas, H. (16/4/85) Lecture presented at La Trobe University.

Nicholas, H. (1986) 'The acquisition of language as the acquisition of variation', *Australian Working Papers in Language Development,* 1/2.

Pit Corder, S. (1983) 'Strategies of communication', in C. Faerch and G. Kasper (eds.) *Strategies in interlanguage communication,* Longman, London pp. 15–19.

Tannen, D. (1982) 'The oral literate continuum in discourse', in D. Tannen (ed.) *Coherence in Spoken and Written Discourse,* New Jersey, Ablex Publishing Corporation, pp. 1–16.

Appendix

Typed version of four of Nasr's texts

I LIKE AUSTRAIIa

I'ime NASR NAbbaut I'me gaw scoule chis NAme Bronsvik languiche cintre I live 12 osborne st Me House Not fraway of the scoule

I'Ime libanise. I'ime live and my brother together and My father cisty in-laws and Mother

My schoul B.L is on the moon

My schaul bieng one from big schouls is on the moon. My school is building from chocolate, the teacher is tomato the table is water melon, and the hair is jelly, the books is pineapple the pens is cucumbers the bag is lions the rubber is soup and the cloose is water.

.the students have two very big head and one with the eye, the jeans is Nember 200 and 250 kls there are three hand, 50 fingers and 5 leg. they body is lemons, the chair is 25 kls and she salad. the window is oranges and very smale. The Room have six window and he is beans. two blak.board from the plum.

My COnTry

My conTry was lovely conTry before 100 years ago iT was The good contry of all contries. but Now my contry in Not good because lebanon I means My contry The israil soldier shooting The libanes. soldier and The people in My contry No Just israil and palistin and syria evryone shoot My contry.

and Now Lebanon crucified on the cross. why? because My contry is the smaller of all The contries but His is The good and is The lovely of all The contries. anThe end I pray to Jesus to protect My contry.

war in My village

it was a good Morning when I waked up. buT itwas Raining and verycold. suddnely when we siting near the Fire somthing was happend one of My village dead My uncle talled us.

My village young they got The shooTing gun and they wenT to proTect the village and we wenT to My grandfaTher's house To sTay Their.

Because My Father was NoT home. after My cosins talled us thaT someone killed that Mam.

suddnely we hear someone is shooting so That was The yongs how had the shooting gun They found The Killer. and that's all My story and its' True.

Source: Reprinted from *Australian Review of Applied Linguistics* 9(2), pp. 120–53, 1986.

Report 3

DIMENSIONS OF EFFECTIVE SCHOOL LEADERSHIP: THE TEACHER'S PERSPECTIVE

Joseph J. Blase

University of Georgia

The study reported in this paper examines teachers' perspectives on effective school leadership. Formal interviews, both unstructured and structured, and informal interviews were used to collect data from teachers in one urban high school in the southeastern United States. Data were collected and analyzed according to guidelines for grounded theory research. This article describes factors teachers identified with effective school principals and the impact of these factors on the teachers and their relationships with other faculty, students, and parents. The research data are discussed briefly in terms of their implications for leadership training and research.

Research on principals has increased dramatically in recent years. Much of this research has generated descriptions of what principals do (Dwyer, 1985; Martin & Willower, 1981; Metz, 1978; Peterson, 1977–1978). Other research has specifically investigated the instructional leadership role of the principalship. Whereas researchers have argued the efficacy of the principal in this role, some suggest that the primary effects of a principal's leadership may in fact be indirect (Blumberg & Greenfield, 1980; Hannay & Stevens, 1985; Lipham, 1981; Silver & Moyle, 1984). In addition, the literature on school effectiveness has offered images of principals as 'strong leaders' and has linked leadership to, for example, school climate, teacher morale, and organizational performance.

Despite a developing knowledge base regarding the effective school principalship, definitions of effectiveness and ineffectiveness have relied primarily on test scores or peer nominations. Little attention has been given to the relationship between leadership and school context variables. Even here, for the most part, inquiry has focused on manifest outcomes and has provided scant data regarding the process of leadership associated with such outcomes (Greenfield, 1984). And although some studies provide detailed qualitative descriptions of school context (Becker, 1980; Cusick, 1983; Waller, 1932) and the principalship (Dwyer, 1985; Wolcott, 1973), negligible data exist that describe meanings associated with principals' actions specifically from the teachers' perspective (March, 1984; Sergiovanni & Corbally, 1984). Consequently, the 'thick descriptions' necessary for understanding the complex nature of leadership in terms of its effect on teachers and the sociocultural context of the school are noticeably lacking. These types of qualitative data are essential to building descriptions and substantive theories of school-based leadership grounded in the meanings, values, norms, beliefs, and symbolic structures characteristic of school cultures.

Although this article focuses specifically on dimensions of *effective school leadership*, the data were drawn from a comprehensive case study of the working lives of teachers. By focusing on the teachers' perspective on effective and ineffective principals, this study was able to determine the impact of high school principals on teachers and their relationships with others. Generally, it was found that the leadership orientation of principals appears to have strong effects on the sociocultural contexts of schools. For instance, the data demonstrate that effective principals positively affected the specific meanings teachers attributed to core issues—for example, participation, equitability, and autonomy—from which social and cultural patterns seemed to evolve. This article describes findings associated with teacher perceptions of effective (and to some extent ineffective) principals and briefly discusses these findings in terms of their implications for leadership training and research.

In general, the data base used for this article was detailed and consistent, thereby making possible the exploration of categories as well as emergent relationships. As a result, a high level of theoretical integration (i.e., the strength of interrelationships between and among categories and themes) was achieved. This was evident for relationships between major themes (e.g., principal's effectiveness) and constituent categories (e.g., accessibility), between and among categories associated with the effectiveness theme (e.g., accessibility and problem solving), and for relationships between categories describing the leadership orientation of effective school principals and their impact on teachers and others.

The Research Problem and Procedures

The data discussed in this article were drawn from a $2^1/_2$-year case study (1983–1986) of factors that contribute to changes in teachers' work perspectives over time. As an investigation of socialization effects in teachers, this research followed a tradition initiated by Waller (1932) in addressing the general question 'What does teaching do to teachers?'

The total study sample for the first two 1-year phases of the project consisted of between 75 to 80 (the number of teachers varied slightly over the years) male and female teachers in an urban, biracial high school in the southeastern United States. The mean number of years in teaching was 11. The teachers in the sample were, for the most part, highly educated, highly satisfied with the current school principal, and, at least in this researcher's view, seriously committed to their work. The school, whose enrolment was approximately 1,500 students, was also staffed by one principal, two assistant principals, and three counsellors.

Data were collected and coded according to qualitative research guidelines for grounded theory research. This approach to qualitative inquiry begins with open-ended questions rather than hypotheses. Data are generated and scrutinized concurrently, through an inductive process designed to product description and theoretical ideas. In essence, grounded theory research focuses on the discovery of substantive categories and hypotheses relevant to the phenomenon under investigation. This research methodology permits categories, themes, and theory to be constructed directly from the data (Bogdan & Biklin, 1982; Bogdan & Taylor, 1975; Glaser, 1978; Glaser & Strauss, 1967; LeCompte & Goetz, 1982; Miles & Huberman, 1984).

During the first year (1983), experienced teachers were asked to identify and discuss all personal and professional life factors that they believed contributed to significant changes in their work perspectives since beginning their careers (Blase, 1985, 1986). In effect, teacher work histories were created from data collected retrospectively (Stern, 1978) and analyzed through open coding procedures (Glaser, 1978; Glaser & Strauss, 1967). Analysis of these data—in-depth taped interviews (a series of three), questionnaires, and observations—suggested that, among other things, the leadership orientation of effective and ineffective school principals was a significant factor in shaping the teachers' work perspective as well as affecting significantly the sociocultural context (patterns of behaviour and norms) of the school.

In light of the importance of school principals to an understanding of socialization effects in teachers, as well as the fact that most of the teachers in the study had worked previously for several principals in other high schools and for other principals in the one high school under investigation (this school had had four principals since 1974), it was decided that the research setting provided an excellent opportunity to explore teachers' perceptions of leadership effectiveness and ineffectiveness (Glaser, 1978; Glaser & Strauss, 1967).

In accord with theoretical sampling guidelines for grounded theory inquiry, a second phase of the project (1985) was planned to probe more deeply the dimensions of school principals' effectiveness and ineffectiveness from the teachers' standpoint. A series of three interviews was conducted with 40 teachers in the research setting (total interview hours = 170). Research procedures were designed to produce the widest possible range of substantive categories and themes regarding the leadership phenomenon under investigation. (Connidis, 1983; Glaser, 1978; Glaser & Strauss, 1967). After completion of an initial set of interviews with 30 teachers selected randomly, these faculty were asked to review a list of teachers who had participated in this research and to recommend others who held perspectives not adequately represented. From these recommendations, 10 additional teachers were contacted and interviewed. Consensus that the interview participants represented a cross section of the school population was achieved.

These interviews focused on themes representing teachers' definitions of effective and ineffective school leadership specifically in the one research setting. In addition, teachers were asked to identify and describe fully the characteristics (behaviours/traits) of all effective and ineffective high school principals for whom they had worked (at the one high school as well as at other high schools) and how such principals affected them and their relationships with others—faculty, students, and parents. All interviews were tape-recorded and transcribed. In total, the 40 teachers interviewed described roughly 30 effective and 95 ineffective school principals in a variety of urban, suburban, and rural settings where they had been employed.

To ensure that the meanings teachers themselves associated with school principal effectiveness and ineffectiveness would be elicited, precautions were employed to minimize premature theoretical control over data collection, that is, directing the participants' responses (Lofland, 1971). Before discussing themes identified in the earlier interview, teachers were asked during second- and third-round interviews, to identify additional themes related to their perceptions of effective and ineffective principals. Subsequently, facilitative (nondirective) questioning techniques were employed to probe and validate themes that emerged during the interviews. For example, questions such as the following were used: 'Are there other characteristics of effective and ineffective principals that you have not mentioned?' and 'Last time you mentioned _____; can you tell me more about that?' Specific questions related to substantive themes analyzed from earlier interviews (e.g., accessibility) and theoretical ideas (e.g., that accessibility contributes to social cohesion among teachers) were pursued more directly with each research participant.

To develop alternative data sources (Glaser & Strauss, 1967), the researcher held informal interviews with other teachers throughout the school (Blum, 1970). Field notes describing the context of these interviews were written and systematically coded.

Constant comparative analysis was utilized to code the research data. This procedure refers to line-by-line inspection of all incoming data to determine 'fit' to emergent categories and hypotheses or to create new categories and hypotheses. The aim was to generate the maximum number of descriptive categories and their properties (e.g., types, dimensions, conditions, consequences, relations to other categories) directly from the data (Glaser, 1978; Glaser & Strauss, 1967). For instance, characteristics linked to leadership effectiveness (e.g., accessibility, decisiveness, goals/direction) and major hypotheses that describe the impact of these characteristics on teachers were examined. All major data lines were saturated; themes, relationships, and interpretations were sampled to the point of repetition (that is, no new categories or properties were produced).

This method of qualitative analysis, the aim of which is to achieve 'conceptual specification,' should not be confused with conceptual definition or formal techniques for conceptual analysis associated with certain schools of analytic philosophy. In grounded theory research, properties of a category (e.g., descriptive and theoretical elements) must earn their way into an emergent theory; criteria of necessity and sufficiency are not applicable to this type of analysis, because 'logical' elaboration of the universe of ideas related to a particular category is not the goal.

The researcher collected and analyzed all of the study data. Glaser and Strauss (1967) insist on the necessity of this, given the requirement of deep involvement and the complex and cyclic nature of data collection and analysis in grounded theory inquiry. A panel of four experts (two professors and two doctoral students) was consulted when questions arose about coding or interpretation of the data. Finally, 12 teachers were asked to critique the researcher's description of substantive categories and hypotheses derived from the raw data (see 'Results' section of this article) and the presentation format (Gruba, 1981). In five instances, teachers suggested that additional data (brief quotations) be included for purposes of clarification.

In total, more than 400 hours were spent in the school setting during the 2½-year period. It is believed that this amount of time and the rapport that developed between researcher and teachers served to increase the validity of the data produced. Moreover, throughout the interviewing process, teachers were asked to give detailed examples for all statements made (Becker, 1980; Bogdan & Taylor, 1975). Data were systematically examined for consistency within and between interviews (for the same individual) and between and among all formal and informal interviews (Connidis, 1983; Denzin, 1978). Given the length of time spent at the research site and the utilization of joint collection and coding procedures, the researcher was able to explore with teachers important ambiguities and questions that surfaced in the data. Data were also assessed in terms of whether they were solicited/unsolicited, stated/inferred, and subject to researcher influence (Bogdan & Taylor, 1975; Denzin, 1978; Erickson, 1986; Glaser, 1978; Glaser & Strauss, 1967).

The data sections of this article describe what teachers themselves perceived as the major dimensions of effective school leadership. Because of space limitations, only abbreviated excerpts (quotations) from the study data are included to illustrate selected ideas. A discussion of data related to ineffective principals and their impact on the school context (Blase, in press) is beyond the scope of this article. However, the concluding discussion reflects some of the implications of both data sets.

The Data: A Thematic Analysis

Two dimensions of leadership identified in the professional literature were used *as an organizing framework*. It should be stressed that this framework was selected as a logical way to organize and present the data *after* they have been collected; it was not used to control data collection. The first dimension of leadership is related to *task*-relevant competencies demonstrated in such activities as planning, defining, organizing, and evaluating the work of individuals. The second dimensions of leadership is determined by the social-emotional needs and expectations of workers. Activities that serve to recognize people and enhance their work satisfaction and self-esteem are examples of consideration (Bass, 1981). Therefore, themes describing school principal effectiveness were grounded according to meanings and their general correspondence to the two aforementioned leadership dimensions.

As mentioned earlier, it was found that effectiveness factors associated with both task and consideration dimensions of leadership were, in fact, tightly intertwined. For example, three categories—accessibility, goals/direction, and problem-solving orientation (placed in the task frame)—were, in the teachers' view, related to support/confrontation of conflict and participation/consultation (placed in the consideration frame). Because of space considerations, only the most salient links coded between and among themes in the data are identified. In addition, Tables 1 and 2 specify some of the major connections between leadership factors (task, consideration) and their impact on teachers.

Overview of Data

Nine prominent task-related themes (factors)—accessibility, consistency, knowledge/expertise, clear and reasonable expectations, decisiveness, goals/direction, follow-through, ability to manage time, and problem-solving orientation—were coded in the data. In addition, five prominent consideration-related themes (factors)—support in confrontations/conflict, participation/consultation, fairness/equitability, recognition (praise/reward), and willingness to delegate authority—were cited in the data.

In general, the study data implied that affective school principals contribute to the development of associative (cohesive), social (behavioural), and cultural (values, norms) patterns in schools. These factors and the hypotheses that delineate their impact represent major elements of the teachers' perspective on effective school leadership. Not surprisingly, it was discovered that each effective principal described tended to exhibit all of the task and consideration factors identified above (in varying degrees, of course). It was also found that factors were interrelated. Therefore, in addition to defining factors separately, the following descriptions also include some discussion of other factors that teachers indicated were strongly related to a particular factor. The impact of each factor on teachers and their relationships with others is also described.

Task Factors

Accessibility. Accessibility refers to availability and visibility. Principals who were available to teachers 'arrived at work early and stayed late,' 'worked hard and long hours,' 'circulated a lot,' and were 'involved in everything'—'you see them everywhere.' Teachers explained that such principals were prepared to deal with the large number of teacher- and student-related problems, issues, and questions that typically 'cropped up' during the school day. Principals who were visible spent significant amounts of time 'in the school . . . in the halls and cafeteria, where . . . trouble with students was likely to occur.' According to the study sample, such principals seemed to help control and stabilize teacher and student behaviour. To illustrate, teachers disclosed that the principal's presence prevented certain problems altogether: 'Kids are just better when the principal is around, and teachers are more willing to get involved.'

Accessible principals were also viewed as 'informed' and 'aware of what was going on in the school.' Thus, their decisions 'made sense' to teachers. Consequently, accessible principals were perceived as using impromptu opportunities to discuss and support teacher goal attainment. Generally, such principals made authoritative decisions, shared information, coached, advised, and provided support to teachers and students. In addition, visibility in the classroom, at athletic events, and at evening social activities seemed to carry important symbolic implications. The willingness of the principal to 'mix with . . . teacher and student' was, in the teachers' view, related to 'caring', 'guts,' empathy, dedication, and generally the kind of leadership involvement essential to individual and organizational improvement.

More broadly, attitudes and behaviours associated with accessible principals helped connect teachers to their schools as a whole ('I feel like a real part of the school') and appeared to strengthen teacher respect for and rapport with principals. Positive interactions initiated by these principals were described as precipitating reciprocal actions from teachers. The accessibility of principals and the positive interplay related to it seemed to enhance organizational cohesiveness by reducing the social and psychological distance commonly present in superordinate-subordinate relations.

Teachers associated accessibility with other categories—problem solving, time management, goals/direction, knowledge, ('principals with nothing to offer quickly retreat to the office') and

TABLE 1 Task-related leadership factors: Their impact on teachers and relationships with others

Principal leadership factor	Teacher (Self)	Teacher -Student	Teacher -Teacher	Teacher -Parent
Accessibility	Increase in feelings of confidence, patience, control	Increase in acceptance of advice and criticism Increase in involvement	NDE*	NDE
Consistency	Reduction in feelings of tension, frustration, and uncertainty	Decrease in student discipline problems Increase in ability to control students Increase in hopefulness about goal achievement Decrease in student misbehaviour Increase in time on task	Decrease in ambiguity, conflict, competitiveness Increase in predictability and stability of relationships	Decrease in tension associated with teacher role conflict
Knowledge/expertise	Increase in feelings of satisfaction Increase in sense of professionalism Increase in feelings of being understood, respected	Increase in problem-solving effectiveness Increase in rational decisionmaking Increase in integration (from symbolic leadership)	NDE	NDE
Clear and reasonable expectations	Decrease in feelings of frustration, anger, ambiguity	Decrease in uncertainty and conflict Increase in ability to predict program direction	Increase (slight) in cohesive-ness	NDE
Decisiveness	Decrease in feelings of uncertainty, confusion	Increase in ability to make timely decisions	NDE	NDE
Goals/direction	Decrease in feelings of uncertainty Increase in sense of commitment and involvement in the "school as a whole" Increase in optimism	Increase in teacher expectations for student achievement Increase in integration, decrease in social-psychological distance Increase in direction/focus	Increase in collaboration (related to sense of focus and ownership) Decrease in bases of nonproductive conflict	NDE
Follow-through	Decrease in feelings of frustration, anger, uncertainty Increase in sense of direction	Increase in success of program development and maintenance Increase in efficient use of time	NDE	NDE
Ability to manage time	Decrease in feelings of frustration	Decrease in time wasted	Increase in productive faculty-meeting interactions	NDE
Problem-solving orientation	Minimization of feelings of anger, frustration, and uncertainty	Increase in ability to identify and confront problems Decrease in intensity of problems	Increase in ability to identify and confront problems Increase in the basis for positive interactions (spill-over)	Increase in ability to identify and confront problems Increase in parental support and understanding

*NDE = No Discernible Effect

Note. Teachers frequently discussed 'effects' as decreases in negative feeling states. This may be due to the fact that, even in schools administered by effective principals, considerable tension exists.

TABLE 2 Consideration-related leadership factors: Their impact on teachers and relationships with others

Principal leadership factor	Teacher (Self)	Teacher -Student	Teacher -Teacher	Teacher -Parent
Support/confrontation of conflict	Increase in teacher efficiency	Increase in ability to solve problems	Increase in communication, trust	Increase in rational and productive interactions
	Increase in professional growth	Increase in control of students	Increase in group cohesiveness	Increase in parental support
	Increase in self-esteem	Increase in student respect	Increase in teacher cooperation	
	Increase in cognitive emotional and physical energy commitment	Increase in time for instruction		
		Increase in value of education		
		Increase in stabilization of relationships		
Participation/consultation	Increase in sense of professionalism	Increase in class and school goal consistency	Increase in collegiability, communication, collaboration, trust, respect	NDE*
	Increase in self-esteem	Increase in tolerance/compassion for students	Increase in team development	
	Increase in cognitive, emotional, and physical energy commitment		Increase in group problem solving	
	Increase in sense of commitment to the 'whole school'			
Fairness/equitability and decisions	Increase in sense of professionalism	NDE	Increase in faculty morale	Decrease in irrational interactions
	Decrease in ambiguity and unpredictability		Decrease in competition and conflict	
	Increase in self-esteem		Increase in cooperation	
	Increase in satisfaction		Decrease in defensive clique formation	
Recognition: praise and reward	Increase in self-esteem, confidence, pride	Increase in class instruction and program compatibility	Increase in faculty morale	Increase in interaction (if teacher is recognized for involvement with parents)
	Decrease in goal uncertainty	Increase in instructional and extracurricular involvement	Increase in faculty cohesiveness, cooperation	
	Increase in cognitive, emotional, and physical energy commitment		Decrease in nonproductive conflict (e.g., backbiting)	
Willingness to delegate authority	Increase in self-esteem	Increase in faculty morale		
	Increase in sense of professionalism	Increase in teacher efficiency	NDE	NDE

*NDE = No Discernible Effect.

personal traits such as authenticity, compassion, friendliness, security, trust, open-mindedness, and optimism.

Consistency. Consistency refers to the compatibility of principals' behaviour and decisions with existing policies, programs, rules, regulations, and norms. Consistency in the enforcement of rules regarding student discipline appeared to be most salient in this vein. To teachers, consistency was perceived to enhance their ability to control students in two ways: preventatively ('if [students] know what the teacher says goes . . . there will be fewer problems') and remedially ('a student is sent to the office . . . something happens . . . he is dealt with'). As with support (to be discussed), teachers indicated that consistency by principals also reduced the possibility that students would personalize punishments, blame the teacher, 'build up defensiveness and resentment,' and exacerbate social-emotional tensions. Clearly, the data suggest that consistency was inversely related to levels of classroom conflict and tension. Indirectly, consistency was perceived to increase teachers' abilities in curriculum planning and instruction ('when discipline is a problem, your lessons are geared for control . . . learning takes a back seat'). In general, teachers reported that principal consistency helped to maintain a 'rational' (understandable and fair) organization: 'Inconsistency ruins everything . . . the whole system is ruined.'

Consistent principals were seen as being adept at withstanding pressure to make decisions for 'political' reasons at the expense of sound educational practice. (For example, teachers believed that ineffective principals frequently 'caved in' to parental demands for preferential treatment of students.) Teachers indicated that consistent principals helped reduce the tension and conflict among individuals and groups, conflict that was viewed as salient under inconsistent principals.

According to the teachers, consistency was related to goals and direction, clear expectations, problem-solving orientation, knowledge/expertise, fairness/equitability, and personal traits such as honesty and security.

Knowledge/expertise. Although teachers associated effective administrators with a broad range of competencies, they emphasised formal knowledge of curriculum and research in the content areas. However, informal knowledge, 'awareness of teachers' problems and students needs,' was also indicated as important to effective administration. Knowledgeable principals were described as 'intelligent,' 'worldly,' 'experienced,' 'perceptive,' 'prudent,' 'analytical,' 'having substance,' 'well-rounded,' and 'well-educated.' One teacher remarked, 'He doesn't have to be an Einstein, but he can't be a big dumb jock . . . many are.' These sentiments were echoed by another, who stated: 'My suspicion is that many people in administration . . . their primary track has been athletics. This does not equip a person to be an effective principal over an entire school curriculum.'

Teachers pointed out that principals demonstrated knowledge by giving helpful advice, showing awareness of the school, and maintaining 'real involvement' (e.g., attending activities) in all aspects of the school. The latter point cannot be overstated. Broad and productive involvement 'in the whole school' was stressed repeatedly. From the teachers' standpoint, such involvement was seen to offset the forces of favouritism and limited what appeared to be a natural tendency toward fragmentation in the schools described by teachers. The data suggest that principals' knowledge was linked to levels of commitment, communication, and cohesiveness.

Knowledge and expertise were strongly correlated by teachers with accessibility, decisiveness, goals/direction, problem solving, participation, fairness, and personal factors such as compassion, friendliness, security, intelligence, and working long hours.

Clear and reasonable expectations. This category refers to the school administrators' success in creating policies, rules, goals, and standards, based on a 'realistic assessment' of teachers, and the ability to communicate the meaning of expectations to teachers. In the simplest sense, teachers linked clear expectations to skills in verbal and written communication. Clarity of expectations was also related to rationality in approach and interpretation ('he had a process of getting to the goals'), the ability to anticipate problems, and the use of evaluative standards to make judgments about goal achievement.

In the teachers' perspective, clear expectations were further demonstrated by the persistence of principals ('he doesn't move from one thing to another . . . that confuses us'). This category was also closely related to those of support ('stands behind us'), praise/recognition ('he recognizes our efforts . . . this helps me understand expectations'), follow-through ('provides materials, feedback'), fairness ('not showing favouritism . . . bending with the wind'), and goals/direction ('I am encouraged to set high goals'). Clear expectations were associated with reductions in teachers' ambiguity, conflict, and fragmentation ('doing your own thing'). Such expectations 'tied us [teachers] together . . . refined focus,' and, as far as teachers were concerned, resulted in more cooperative interaction in schools.

According to the data, clear expectations were also related to participation, working long hours, and such personal attributes as authenticity and security on the part of principals.

Decisiveness. This term refers to the principals' willingness to make decisions in a timely manner ('some of them won't make decisions,' 'they avoid decisions . . . decisions are postponed endlessly,' 'principals change their minds'). Decisiveness was positively related to clear expectations, goals/direction ('knows where we are going'), problem-solving orientation, knowledge/expertise ('aware of all the issues'), consistency ('doesn't play favourites') and the personal traits of authenticity, compassion, security, and working long hours.

Goals/direction. This category describes global and comprehensive goal structures (in contrast to clear expectations) associated with student discipline, curricular, and extracurricular areas. In terms of the curriculum, the goals teachers identified with effective principals tended to emphasize improvement. This was viewed by teachers as helping them focus their efforts with students ('it gives me something to strive toward . . . help focus on important parts').

For teachers, effective principals used goal-setting processes based on faculty participation. Roughly half of the teachers studied reported that effective principals tended to define overarching goals and to seek teacher input on the implementation of policies and plans related to these goals. Others described effective principals for whom they had worked as individuals who 'encouraged' teachers to become involved at all levels. Teachers reported that such administrators worked collaboratively with faculties, for example, in 'defining problems,' 'getting input on resources,' 'understand[ing] feelings . . . problems,' 'demanding higher goals,' 'listening to alternative views,' and 'organizing input from all sources.' As one teacher expressed it, 'he did more than just publish goals.'

Goal development processes, according to the findings, were perceived as a complex set of interactions 'which keeps the system moving' and, according to teachers, increased the probability for understanding, agreement, and commitment to common purposes. In the schools described by teachers, collaborative goal development (e.g., definition, evaluation, redefinition) seemed to contribute to the creation of common values and norms and to the integration of social and cultural patterns. That is, goal-setting processes were identified with increases in organizational cohesion and greater consistency between teacher values and teacher behaviour.

Teachers linked goal-related processes, as described, to clear expectations, problem solving, accessibility, participation, support, praise/recognition, knowledge/expertise, and such personal factors as authenticity, friendliness, intelligence, working long hours, open-mindedness, and optimism.

Follow-through. This category is associated with the principals' inclination to provide appropriate and timely resources (e.g., symbolic, material, technical) in support of routine work processes and programs designed for school improvement. Effective principals were perceived as assuming responsibility for the initiation of programs and for the continued supervision (when necessary) and material resources essential to maintain and enhance teacher work efforts. (Ineffective principals were often viewed as failing to provide resources for long-term maintenance of new programs.) Effective principals were considered 'proactive,' 'involved,' and 'facilitative' in terms of supplying resources ('she would get the process going . . . you could count on her help'). Teachers reported that their time and energy were utilized more efficiently as a result. Follow-through means 'that there's a serious effort to [help] you . . . to achieve your goals . . . no follow-through . . . it's all wasted.'

Many teachers also discussed follow-through with regard to receiving timely supervision ('he kept us informed'; 'you get a definite response to a concern you shared'; 'I knew how the situation was progressing'). Teachers explained that follow-through by principals worked to reduce uncertainty, assisted in the clarification and determination of real goals ('I watch to see if they are serious'), and allowed teachers opportunities to make plans and decisions consistent with those of principals.

According to the teachers, follow-through was directly related to support, goals/direction, clear expectations, decisiveness, accessibility, participation, and the personal factors of working long hours, compassion, and authenticity.

Ability to manage time. Effective principals were defined as individuals who managed time efficiently. This meant that much administrative and clerical work was completed on their own time. Although effective principals were 'constantly busy', they did not overschedule or overcommit themselves during the school day. Thus, according to teachers, such principals were accessible at various times and in various locations in their schools to talk, advise, and make decisions required by teachers and students.

In the most fundamental sense, the effective management of time on the principals' part was evidenced during faculty meetings. Effective principals prepared and followed agendas. They were also able to facilitate discussion and coordinate input in an efficient manner ('they solicit input . . . control the process . . . some teachers will talk forever'). All in all, teachers explained that effective principals respected teachers' time, 'don't run overtime,' or 'don't meet just because it's Wednesday.'

Efficient time management was linked by teachers to working long hours, accessibility, follow-through, goals/direction, clear expectations, and participation.

Problem-solving orientation. An effective problem-solving orientation was associated with the ability of principals to interpret and conceptualize problems in ways that make sense to teachers ('they understand the whole picture'). Principals who demonstrated such an orientation were perceived as 'thoughtful' and 'prudent' ('he doesn't shoot from the hip'). From the teachers' standpoint, competence in problem solving was judged largely in terms of the principals' ability to confront and reduce tensions associated with interpersonal conflicts. (The ineffective principals' approach to conflict, in contrast, was frequently defined as exacerbating problems.) In general, the data point out that effective principals had rational responses to problems. Such principals usually employed an incremental approach ('there was a step-by-step approach . . . a definite way of looking at things') which, according to the teachers, relied on skills in problem definition ('together we were able to construct a picture . . . '; 'questions she raised helped clarify . . . ') and problem solution.

In approaching problems, effective principals were seen as 'positive' and sensitive to the feeling of teachers ('I wasn't made to feel incompetent'; there were no put-downs'; 'she knew how to treat people'; 'I didn't feel useless . . . like I failed').

Clearly, the problem-solving orientation of effective principals was related to reducing barriers to teacher performance, which, in turn, seemed to reduce levels of stress and conflict ('the problems most stressful to teachers affect time and energy'). For teachers, effective problem solving meant elevated expectations ('I demand more from myself') and an increased capacity to attain a range of role-related goals. The data imply that, in many cases, the problem-solving process of effective principals was sufficiently pervasive to affect entire schools ('it's really a whole approach . . . the way you work with people day by day, which is good or bad'). Taken together, productive problem-solving processes appeared to enhance solidarity and cohesiveness in schools described by teachers ('we came together, we were partners').

Teachers associated principal effectiveness in problem solving with decisiveness, accessibility, knowledge (specifically about the problems of teachers and students), participation, follow-through, and support. Personal traits related directly to this category were authenticity, friendliness, compassion, and open-mindedness.

Consideration Factors

Support in confrontations/conflicts. Support refers to the willingness of principals to 'stand behind' teachers, especially in regard to confrontations with students and parents involving discipline and academic performance. In matters of student misbehaviour, the actions of effective principals were seen as reinforcing teacher decisions. Disciplinary referrals, for example, were followed by timely reprimands/punishments: 'students were not sent back 10 minutes later smiling . . . with a note saying that the student regrets the incident.' Although principals disagreed occasionally with teachers, such disagreements were approached 'positively,' 'discreetly,' and 'constructively.' Teachers indicated that the support of principals was related to decreases in classroom misbehaviour. Many problems were either 'siphoned off' or prevented altogether ('students know they will be punished . . . are less likely to test . . . to take chances'). In effect, the classroom's vulnerability to disruption and the displacement of teacher work effort seemed to be reduced.

It should be explained that although effective principals tended to support teachers in conflicts with students and their parents, this was by no means easy. Teachers explained that principals frequently had to respond to conflicting expectations regarding student control problems, educational considerations (e.g., program placement), and political factors (e.g., accommodating parents). Within the political realm, for example, teachers frequently required support from principals in confronting parents who demanded less homework and, occasionally, grade changes and who objected to the placement of their children. In many cases, effective principals were considered skilful at 'clearing up the communication problems' or 'convincing a parent that the school was trying to help their child.'

In essence, the data suggest that the actions of supportive principals increased the probability of productive interaction among teachers, students, and parents. Teachers reported that under effective principals, they were able to be more 'open' and straightforward' with students and parents. Hence, meetings, conferences, and telephone conversations tended to produce 'real' communication, that is, 'an understanding of a student's problem . . . on both sides.' Indeed, teachers reported that there was less suspicion and defensiveness, a greater consensus regarding decisions and goals, and an inclination in parents to 'cooperate with the school . . . for the child's sake.'

Finally, some teachers discussed support in terms of teacher development. For instance, teachers indicated that encouragement by principals to attend workshops and conferences and to take university course work facilitated professional growth and self-esteem ('she did everything she could to build us up . . . that's why I am what I am today').

Teachers related support to accessibility, follow-through, consistency, clear expectations, goal/direction, knowledge/expertise, praise/recognition, and personal factors such as compassion, open-mindedness, and security.

Participation/consultation. This category describes the principals' willingness to develop meaningful channels ('not for image building') for teachers to express their expertise, opinions, and feelings, especially with regard to programs and student discipline. The data point out that, although effective principals were perceived as generally more knowledgeable than their ineffective counterparts, teachers believed that even an effective principal's understanding of curriculum, the content areas, and the problems and needs of teachers and students was insufficient: 'The school is too complex for any one person'; 'some principals have been out of the classroom for 10 years.' Teachers argued that 'many problems could not be resolved without their help.' In this respect, teachers linked shared decisionmaking to the quality of decisions made by principals. The data indicate that the teachers' participation in decisionmaking was usually consultative ('the principal made decisions based on input') or shared (decisions seemed to evolve naturally from discussion with principals).

It was apparent that positive interactions between principals and teachers and among teachers increased under administrators with a participatory perspective. Without exception, teachers reported that effective principals encouraged teacher participation by developing open relationships. It was implied that the social and psychological distance between teachers and administrators, typically associated with ineffective principals, was reduced as a result.

A participatory orientation in principals was linked to trust and respect for teachers. This was further related to teachers' sense of professionalism ('I'm recognized for my professional knowledge') and the development of collegiality ('it's a partnership'; 'I work with him, not around him') between teachers and principals. Participation was viewed as helping connect teachers to the school processes, programs, and goals ('I'm a part of the whole'; 'you're on a team that's going somewhere'; 'you are important to others'). To be sure, teachers implied that principals who encouraged participation positively affected both quantitative (e.g., time, energy) and qualitative (e.g., caring) dimensions of their involvement in work.

Participation/consultation was linked by teachers to time management, problem-solving orientation, knowledge/expertise, accessibility, support, praise/recognition, and delegation of authority. Personal factors included authenticity, compassion, friendliness, trust, working long hours, and open-mindedness.

Fairness/equitability. Although consistency and fairness were strongly interrelated, fairness was more specifically associated with 'reasonable' recognition of the needs and problems of individuals teachers, students, parents, programs, and departments. Fairness extended to many dimensions of teachers' work. Generally, fairness in principals meant recognizing the personal and professional rights of all teachers; principals who were fair showed no favouritism. In displaying fairness, teachers explained that principals tended to maintain 'a broad interest in the entire program': 'Everyone was viewed in the same light.' Reasonable decisions regarding resource allocation ('the debate team was just as important as the football team'), the assignment of distasteful duties ('he didn't dump work on certain teachers . . . jobs were rotated'), the distribution of rewards and punishments ('the hotshot coach doesn't have special status'), and the handling of interpersonal conflict ('he listened to both sides . . . used a problem-solving approach') were related to teachers' perceptions of fairness.

According to the data, fairness by principals helped to develop positive personal and professional identities of teachers ('You grow . . . you are not slighted or put down'). Fairness seemed to contribute to reductions in ambiguity and unpredictability and to increases in faculty solidarity. This trait in principals worked to reduce informal status differences and barriers to communication and support among teachers ('they made everyone feel they are part of the team'). Fairness was further related to increased trust among faculties ('there's less jealousy here now . . . no reason to be suspicious') and better faculty morale ('we're a lot happier . . . as a group, teachers are treated equally . . . no backbiting as a result'). It seemed that cooperation and productive interactions were indirectly enhanced by principal fairness.

It should be noted that teachers demanded 'absolute equality' (versus equitability) of treatment only in areas that were easily quantifiable (e.g., monitoring assignments). Clearly, fair principals maintained a sensitivity to 'special needs' and 'legitimate reasons': 'A teacher should be given permission to leave early because of a sick child . . . if she comes and goes because she's the principal's friend, that's wrong.'

Fairness/equitability were clearly linked by teachers to consistency, problem solving, clear expectations, participation, praise/recognition, and personal qualities such as authenticity, compassion, security, and open-mindedness.

Recognition: Praise and reward. Recognition refers to praise and appreciation of both individual teachers and the faculty as a group. Face-to-face interaction was identified by teachers as the major means for the expression of both individual and group praise, although letters, notes, and intercom remarks were also cited in the data. It was implied that the willingness of principals to interact with teachers in this way was linked to their level of awareness and sincerity. (It should be mentioned that ineffective principals occasionally sent, for example, notes of praise to teachers. Since such actions were not defined as rewarding ['he sent a form letter'], they frequently precipitated negative forms of involvement.)

From the teachers' perspective, recognition of individual effort ('for little things . . . pats on the back') and group effort ('he is constantly celebrating our achievements as a faculty . . . we had a special luncheon') was perceived as rewarding. Additional responsibility ('it's got to be meaningful . . . something to be proud of'), allocation of needed resources (materials, room), and good assignments/schedules also indicated recognition. Teachers of both regular and slower students (as compared with teachers of the gifted) explained that recognition by principals was especially critical to their motivation: 'We don't have parents telling us how great we're doing.'

Examination of the data suggested that recognition by principals worked to reduce goal ambiguity ('I know where I stood . . . and what he wanted'; 'it helps you orient yourself toward the program') and confusion concerning performance effectiveness ('we knew we're doing well . . . she was pleased'). Awareness of 'what others were rewarded for' provided teachers with opportunities to correct problems and inconsistencies with program goals. Moreover, at both individual and group levels, teachers pointed out that principals' recognition reinforced existent teacher behaviour ('he notices I would call parents . . . I continued this practice') and stimulated new forms of involvement ('he recognized by participation . . . I wanted to do other things').

The data support the conclusion that recognition was related to teacher self-esteem, professional development ('I wanted to grow'), faculty morale ('there's less crabbing . . . pettiness'), group cohesion, and instructional and extracurricular work involvement ('if I don't receive recognition, I don't do it').

Teachers reported that praise was particularly meaningful because effective principals were considered knowledgeable ('it means something coming from him'). Principal accessibility, goals/direction, clear expectations, and personal qualities such as authenticity, compassion, and security were also related to recognition.

Willingness to delegate authority. Effective principals were willing to delegate authority ('discretion,' 'leeway,' 'use of one's own judgement') to teachers. (However, 'dumping' meaningless responsibilities and work, without extending resources or authority, was associated with ineffective principals.) As suggested earlier, teachers believed that extending authority to teachers was important to the school, since principals' time and relevant knowledge were limited. Thus, the willingness of principals to delegate authority meant timely decisions and more efficient work processes. As with participation, receiving authority from principals was correlated with trust, respect, self-concept ('you feel important working for a person like that'), and teacher job involvement.

Teachers associated principals' willingness to delegate authority with accessibility, goals/direction, participation, and personal factors such as compassion and open-mindedness.

Summary and Conclusions

Data from the research discussed above point out that nine task-related factors and five consideration-related factors represent, from the perspectives of the teachers studied, the major dimensions of effective high school leadership. In addition, the data indicate that such factors have, in varying degrees, dramatic effects on teachers and their relationships with significant others. Along these lines, it was discovered that leadership factors affected teacher motivation, involvement, and morale and, in general, enhanced the possibility of productive interactions between teachers and others. At a more abstract level, effective leadership was linked to the development of productive social and cultural structures in schools.

Throughout this article, it has been emphasized that the leadership factors described seemed to be highly interdependent. In their discussions of individual effective school principals, teachers voluntarily described (that is, without direct questioning by the researcher) all leadership factors identified here and did so in such a way as to suggest the interdependence of these factors. As one teacher explained, for example, 'They're not going to be available [accessibility] if they don't have skill and knowledge [knowledge] and truly care about helping teachers with problems [support].'

Data related to teachers' perception of ineffective school principals—who were viewed as being inaccessible, inconsistent, lacking knowledge, indecisive, lacking follow-through, unsupportive, authoritarian, political, and practicing favouritism—indirectly substantiates the importance of the factors discussed in this article. To be sure, the extent to which teachers consider each of the leadership factors identified as essential to effective, school-based leadership can be expected to vary from one school to another.

It has been suggested throughout this article that factors associated with effective school leadership influence the social (behavioural) and cultural (values, norms) structures of schools. In summarizing the impact of effective school principals, Tables 1 and 2 highlight this point. Beyond this, however, the study data point to the conclusion that dramatic changes in the sociocultural context of schools can be expected as a result of changes in leadership. This conclusion is supported by two dimensions of the research data. First, as teachers described responses to various principals at other schools in which they had worked, they explained that their attitudes and behaviours tended to change significantly in response to changes in leadership. Second, examination of data drawn from teachers regarding the high school that was the site for this research again indicated important changes in culture. When teachers' perspectives were compared for each of the four principals at the school since 1974, significant shifts in the teachers' perspective, and thus school culture, were apparent.

Broadly speaking, effective school principals appeared to contribute to school cultures viewed as associative; such cultures were described as cohesive: Interactions between principals and teachers and between teachers and others were defined as distant, uncaring, unsupportive, conflictive, inequitable, and in many ways nonproductive (Blase, in press). The terms *associative* and *dissociative* are used to capture the general impact of effective and ineffective leadership on the school. These terms are considered primitive concepts; their value is primarily heuristic and sensitizing (Bacharach & Lawler, 1982).

Implications

The overall pattern observed in the data stresses the importance of leadership competencies (related to working with people) in contrast to administrative competencies (associated with the technical aspects of work, e.g., scheduling, bookkeeping, budgeting). To illustrate, it was evident that personal qualities (e.g., honesty, security, compassion, respect for others) and competencies (e.g., listening skills, feedback skills, analytical and conceptual skills, problem-solving skills, and knowledge of curriculum) were perceived as essential to effective school leadership. Unfortunately, however, most university-level training programs tend to emphasize knowledge and skill in the administrative than the leadership dimensions. The present data suggest that such an emphasis may be misguided.

A broader training agenda, one that emphasizes those competencies directly affecting teachers' performance and the 'everyday' sociocultural dynamics of schools (some of which have been described in this report), would seem useful. Among other things, training in communication, conflict management, problem solving, team development, and interpersonal and group dynamics would be helpful. Training experiences designed to increase self-awareness of an individual's values, beliefs, and behaviour would also be relevant.

In addition, school officials should undoubtedly give much greater attention to 'people-related competencies' in the selection, placement, and ongoing evaluation of school principals. Clearly, the use of instruments that measure knowledge of the interpersonal dimensions (for example, the Relationship Inventory [Barrett-Lennard, 1962]) could provide useful data. The services of principals' assessment centers should also be investigated. Needless to say, regular and systematic feedback from teachers and others with whom principals work would be invaluable.

In terms of research, Sergiovanni & Corbally (1984) have written:

> The real value of leadership rests with the 'meanings' which actions import to others than in the actions themselves. A complete rendering of leadership requires that we move beyond the obvious to the subtle, beyond the immediate to the long range, beyond actions to meanings, beyond viewing organizations and groups within social systems to cultural entities. (p. 106)

The study reported here has attempted to understand meanings teachers have attributed to effective school leadership. This, of course, is only one perspective. Other qualitative studies focusing on how students, parents, superintendents, and school board members perceive effective principals would be helpful. Such studies would furnish data to help elaborate, interpret, and undoubtedly contradict some of the findings presented in this article.

References

Bacharach, S.B., & Lawler, E.J. (1982). *Power and politics in organizations: The sociol psychology of conflict, coalitions, and bargaining.* San Francisco: Jossey-Bass.

Barrett-Lennard, G.T. (1962). Dimensions of therapist response as casual factors in therapeutic change. *Psychological Monographs*, 76(43), 1–36.

Bass, B.M. (1981). *Stogdill's handbook of leadership: A survey of theory and research.* New York: Free Press.

Becker, H. (1980). *Role and career problems of the Chicago public school teacher.* New York: Arno.

Blase, J. (1985). The socialization of teachers: An ethnographic study of factors contributing to the rationalization of the teacher's perspective. *Urban Education*, 20(3), 235–56.

Blase, J. (1986). Socialization as humanization: One side of becoming a teacher. *Sociology of Education*, 59(2), 100–12.

Blase, J. (in press). Dimensions of ineffective school leadership: The teacher's perspective. *Journal of Educational Administration*.

Blum, F.H. (1970). Getting individuals to give information to the outsider. In W. J. Filsted (Ed.), *Qualitative methodology: Firsthand involvement in the social world* (pp. 83–90). Chicago: Rand McNally.

Blumberg, A., & Greenfield, W. (1980). *The effective principal: Perspectives on school leadership*. Boston: Allyn & Bacon.

Bogdan, R., & Biklin, S. (1982). *Qualitative research for education: An Introduction to theory and methods*. Boston: Allyn & Bacon.

Bogdan, R., & Taylor, S. (1975). *Introduction to qualitative research methods: A phenomenological approach to the social sciences*. New York: Wiley.

Connidis, I. (1983). Integrating qualitative and quantitative methods in survey research on aging: An assessment. *Qualitative Sociology*, 6(4), 334–52.

Cusick, P.A. (1983). *The equalitarian ideal and the American high school: Studies of three schools*. New York: Longman.

Denzin, N.K. (1978). The logic of naturalistic enquiry. In N.K. Denzin (Ed.), *Sociological methods: A sourcebook* (pp. 245–76). New York: McGraw-Hill.

Dwyer, D.C. (1985, April). *Contextual antecedents of instructional leadership*. Paper presented at the annual meeting of the American Educational Research Association, Chicago.

Erickson, F. (1986). Qualitative research on teaching. In M.C. Wittrock (Ed.), *Handbook of research on teaching* (3rd ed., pp. 119–61). New York: Macmillan.

Glaser, B. (1978). *Theoretical sensitivity: Advances in the methodology of grounded theory*. Mill Valley, CA: The Sociology Press.

Glaser, B., & M. Strauss, A. (1967). *The discovery of grounded theory: Strategies for qualitative research*. Chicago: Aldine.

Greenfield, W. (1984, April). *Sociological perspectives for research in educational administration*. Paper presented at the annual meeting of the American Educational Research Association, New Orleans.

Guba, E. (1981). Criteria for assessing the trustworthiness of naturalistic inquiries. *Educational Communication and Technology Journal*, 29(2), 75–91.

Hannay, L.M., & Stevens, K.W. (1985, April). *The indirect instructional leadership role of a principal*. Paper presented at the annual meeting of the American Educational Research Association, Chicago.

LeCompte, M.D., & Goetz, J.P. (1982). Problems of reliability and validity in enthnographic research. *Review of Educational Research*, 52(1), 31–60.

Lipham, J.A. (1981). *Effective principal, effective school*. Reston, VA: American Association of School Principals.

Lofland, J. (1971). *Analyzing social settings: A guide to qualitative observation and analysis*. Belmont, CA: Wadsworth.

March, J.D. (1984). How we talk and how we act: Administrative theory and administrative life. In T.J. Sergiovanni & J.E. Corbally (Eds.), *Leadership and organizational culture: New perspectives on administrative theory and practice* (pp. 18–35). Chicago: University of Illinois Press.

Martin, W.J., & Willower, D.J. (1981). The managerial behaviour of high school principals. *Educational Administration Quarterly*, 17(1), 69–90.

Metz, M.I. (1978). *Classrooms and corridors: The crisis of authority in desegregated schools*. Berkeley: University of California Press.

Miles, M.B., & Huberman, A.M. (1984). *Qualitative data analysis: A sourcebook of new methods*. Beverly Hills, CA: Sage Publications.

Peterson, K.D. (1977–1978). The principal's tasks. *Administrator's Notebook*, 26(8), 1–4.

Sergiovanni, T.J., & Corbally, J.E. (1984). *Leadership and organizational culture: New perspectives on administrative theory and practice*. Chicago: University of Illinois Press.

Silver, P., & Moyle, C. (1984, April). *School leadership in relation to school effectiveness*. Paper presented at the annual meeting of the American Educational Research Association, New Orleans.

Stern, P. (1978). *Evaluating social science research*. New York: Oxford University Press.

Waller, W. (1932). *The sociology of teaching*. New York: Wiley.

Wolcott, H.F. (1973). *The man in the principal's office: An ethnography*. New York: Holt, Rinehart & Winston.

Author

Joseph J. Blase, Associate Professor, Department of Educational Administration, College of Education, University of Georgia, Athens, GA 30602. *Specializations:* organizational theory, sociology of teaching.

Source: *American Educational Research Journal*, vol. 24, no. 24, pp. 589–610. Copyright 1997 by the American Educational Research Association. Reprinted by permission of the publisher.

PART 4

SURVEY METHODS

Even though emphasis has been laid on the striking differences between quantitative and qualitative approaches in the previous two parts of this text, in many research studies we find that elements of both approaches are employed. Few researchers are rigidly quantitative or qualitative, with most recognising the complementary nature of the methodologies and adopting particular techniques as appropriate in their work.

Additionally there are methods of data generation and analysis that span both approaches and which are sufficiently flexible to be adapted to meet the contingencies and needs of researchers whose major concern is 'What methods are appropriate for my particular study?' and not 'What methods congruent with my doctrinaire approach are appropriate for my use?'.

Survey methods, usually employing a range of interviewing, questionnaire and attitude scale procedures, are in the middle ground, capable of adoption, modification and translation into the kitbag of researchers who hold a variety of philosophical positions about research methods.

Attitude

surveys

29

twenty nine

Attitude surveys, questionnaires and structured interviews are three methods of obtaining research data used in both quantitative and qualitative research. In the latter mode, they figure strongly in triangulation processes. This chapter will focus on attitude surveys, while the next one will consider interviews and questionnaire surveys.

Attitude measurement

Introduction

Attitudes are evaluated beliefs which predispose the individual to respond in a preferential way. That is, attitudes are predispositions *to react positively or negatively to some social object.* Most definitions of attitudes suggest there are three major components: the cognitive, affective and behavioural components. The cognitive component involves what a person believes about the object, whether true or not; the affective component is the feelings about the attitude object which influences its evaluation; the behavioural component reflects the actual behaviour of the individual, though this is rather an unreliable indication of an attitude.

Attitude scales involve the application of standardised questionnaires to enable individuals to be placed on a dimension indicating degree of favourability towards the object in question. The assignment to a position on the dimension is based on the individual's agreement or disagreement with a number of statements relevant to the attitude object. Many hundreds of scales indexing attitudes to a wide range of objects exist. A valuable collection of scales can be perused in Shaw and Wright (1968).

Despite the existence of many reliable and valid published attitude scales, the researcher often finds that they wish to assess attitudes to a specific social object for which no scales exist, or for which scales produced and validated in another culture are not appropriate in our context. The construction of attitude scales is not difficult, but there are a number of differing methods of construction, of response mode and of score interpretation. These various approaches will be considered shortly.

The individual items of statements in an attitude scale are usually not of interest in themselves; the interest is usually located in the total score or subscores. An attitude scale usually consists of statements, i.e. the belief component of the theoretical attitude. These statements could all be preceded by 'I believe that . . . ' and are rated on a 3, 5, 7 (or even more) point scale. This rating provides an index of the emotive value of the affective component of each statement. Of course, the third element of an attitude, the behavioural act, is not assessed. This behavioural component may not be congruent with the expressed attitude as measured on the questionnaire, since other factors such as social convention, social constraints, expectation, etc., may prevent the act which should follow from being performed. For example, a student who manifests negative attitudes to ethnic groups other than their own may not display such prejudice in their overt behaviour because of fear of the law, consideration of what others would think, etc.

Methods of attitude scale construction

The following section briefly outlines the major types of attitude scales and their construction. A more thorough and detailed account can be consulted in Edwards (1957).

Differential scales (Thurstone type)

Their construction

The method Thurstone devised represents attempts to facilitate interval scale measurement.

STQ148

Write down now what you remember an interval scale to be, then check your answer with the material in chapter 8.

The approach commences with the researcher's selection of a large number of evaluatively tinged statements about a particular object or topic such as those listed below which could be culled from newspapers, conversations, and direct questioning of people whose education, professional training or life experience were relevant to the issue under consideration. The initial array of statements may come from any source, as long as they cover a full range of attitudes towards the object/topic in question and are brief and unambiguous.

Example of attitude items (Thurstone type)

Attitudes towards teaching

1 Teaching is merely a routine job.
2 Teaching requires more intelligence than other professions.
3 Teaching is a dull eventful life.
4 Teachers are the nation's leaders.
5 Teaching is a lazy person's job.
6 To strive to teach well is to pattern after Christ. There can be no higher calling.
7 Women make the best teachers.
8 The importance of teaching is overestimated.
9 Teaching offers few avenues for advancement.
10 Teaching furnishes a chance for self expression.
11 Teaching has more influence on a nation than any other profession.
12 Teaching depends too much on textbooks.

The next step is to ask a number of individuals to judge the degree to which each statement expresses a positive or negative attitude towards the object on an eleven-point scale. Thurstone originally used several hundred judges in developing each attitude scale, but a much smaller number is adequate, as long as they have some knowledge of the attitude object and are themselves not heavily biased either for or against it.

The task is essentially to sort out the small cards on which each statement is written into eleven piles so that they seem to be fairly evenly spaced or graded. Only the two ends and the middle pile are labelled. The middle pile is indicated for neutral opinions. The judge must decide for each statement which of five subjective degrees of affirmation or five subjective degrees of negation is implied in the statement, or whether it is a neutral opinion.

A calculation is then made of the median score for each item (the position on the eleven-point scale which equally divides the judges, with half ranking the item above that point and half below). This median score is subsequently used as the scale value for that item. Calculations are also made as to how ambiguous each item is, how widely judgments of it are spread out across the entire scale, as well as how 'irrelevant' it is, and how frequently subjects who agree with it also agree with items at other scale positions. Items high in ambiguity and/or irrelevance are discarded.

Finally, out of the satisfactory items remaining, twenty to forty are selected to constitute an attitude questionnaire, including items which cover the full range of median scores assigned by judges, and with the median score of every item approximately equidistant from that of its closest neighbours. The questionnaire can then be given to any group of subjects whose attitudes are to be measured, with the instructions that they indicate the three items with which they most strongly agree. An individual's score on the questionnaire is the average (mean) scale score on all the items with which they agree.

The scale values, of course, are not shown on the questionnaire, and the items are usually arranged in random order rather than in order of their scale value. The mean of the scale value of the items that the individual checks is interpreted as indicating their position on a scale of favourable to unfavourable attitude towards the object. It seems reasonable to assume that the subject will choose statements on either side of, but close to, their true position. So an average scale value will be a good estimate of this position.

STQ149

Using the sample attitude to teaching items listed on the previous page, which have already been screened to exclude ambiguous or irrelevant items, act as if you are one of Thurstone's judges. Assign to each item a number ranging anywhere between 0.0 and 11.0 on a scale in which a score of 0.0 is given to those items that are most unfavourable towards teaching; 5.0 is given to neutral items; and 11.0 to the items most strongly favourable. Do not assign numbers on the basis of how you feel about teaching, but on the basis of how strongly each item indicates favourability or unfavourability to teaching in general. When you have finished, compare your judgements with the average judgements made by the original judges shown at the end of this chapter (p. 564). If there are large discrepancies between your judgements and the averages, can you think of reasons why?

Theoretically, if a Thurstone-type scale is completely reliable and if the scale is measuring a single attitude rather than a complex of attitudes, an individual should check only items that are immediately contiguous in scale value. If the responses of an individual scatter widely over non-contiguous items, their attitude score is not likely to have the same meaning as a score with little scatter. The scattered responses may indicate that the subject has no attitude or that their attitude is not organised in the manner assumed by the scale.

Criticisms of Thurstone-type differential scales

1 Many have objected to the amount of work involved in constructing it. Undoubtedly, the procedure is cumbersome.

2 Do the attitudes and backgrounds of the judges affect the position of the various items on the scale? This obviously is a matter that is open to experimental inquiry.

   A number of early studies supported the view that the scale values assigned did not depend on the attitude of the judges.

   For example, Hinckley (1932), found a correlation of 0.98 between the scale positions assigned to 114 items measuring prejudice toward black Americans. The study involved a group of Southern white students in the United States who were prejudiced against black Americans and a group of unprejudiced Northern students.

3 The assumption that Thurstone-type scales are true interval scales seems dubious. They do constitute reasonably satisfactory ordinal scales, i.e. they provide a basis for saying that one individual is more favourable or less favourable than another. Thurstone, on the assumption that his scales were true interval scales, advocated the use of statistics appropriate to interval scales—the mean and the standard deviation. Other investigators, operating on the more cautious assumption that the intervals are not truly equal, have favoured the use of the median as appropriate to ordinal scales.

4 An obvious criticism of Thurstone's scales is that the subjects normally endorse only a small number of items and the score for a particular subject will be based on only the small number of statements he endorses. For this reason, Thurstone's scales need to be longer than Likert's scales to obtain the same reliability.

STQ150

Which statistical test of difference would you use if you assumed the data were:

a   interval

b   ordinal

and you wished to test for differences in attitude between two groups?

The Likert method

Soon after Thurstone's first scales were published, Likert (1932) proposed a simpler method of attitude measurement. The procedure involves the researcher selecting a set of attitude statements, to which subjects are asked to indicate their agreement or disagreement to each statement along a five-point (or sometimes longer) scale, ranging from 'strongly agree' to 'strongly disagree'. No judges are used to rank the scale statements: it is assumed that all subjects will perceive 'strongly agree' as being more favourable towards the attitude statement than 'moderately agree' and 'strongly disagree'. A subject's score is tabulated by assigning a numerical value to each of the answers, ranging from 1 for the alternative at one end of the scale to 5 (or whatever the total number of possible choices is) for the alternative at the other, and then summing the numerical values of the answers to all questions.

Example items of a Likert scale

We are interested in your feelings about the following statements. Read each statement carefully and decide how you feel about it. Please respond to each item whether or not you have had direct experience with a Teacher's Union.

- **If you strongly agree, circle 1**
- **If you agree, circle 2**
- **If you are undecided or uncertain, circle 3**
- **If you disagree, circle 4**
- **If you strongly disagree, circle 5**

	Strongly agree	Agree	?	Strongly disagree	Disagree
*1 Teachers' Unions hold back progress.	1	2	3	4	5
2 I regard my union subscription as a good investment.	1	2	3	4	5
3 Every teacher should be compelled by law to join the Teachers' Union.	1	2	3	4	5

* Reverse scoring on this item. Items worded in a reverse direction are placed at random to stop people filling in the scale carelessly by going down in one column. This is known as a response set; forcing people to read and judge the statements carefully increases reliability and validity.

As Likert noted, however, the items chosen by the researcher for inclusion in his or her questionnaire may not all be appropriate measures of the attitude in question, because of a lack of understanding of the cultural background of the group whose attitudes he or she is measuring, or for other reasons. Therefore, Likert strongly recommended two additional steps in questionnaire development: the presentation of the initial set of items to a sample of subjects similar to those to be studied later, and an item analysis based on these pilot subjects' responses. The item *analysis* may be performed either by statistically correlating the scores on each individual item with scores on the entire questionnaire and then discarding any items that yield low correlations with the total (biserial correlation), or by comparing the individual item responses (*t* test) of those subjects generally *most favourable* (top 25 per cent) to the attitude object with the responses of the *least favourable* subjects (bottom 25 per cent), and discarding items that show similar levels of agreement among both groups. In either case, the result is a revised questionnaire that more precisely measures a single attitude concept.

Advantages of Likert method

The advantages of the Likert method include:

1 greater ease of preparation;
2 the fact that the method is based entirely on empirical data regarding subjects' responses rather than subjective opinions of judges; and
3 the fact that this method produces more homogeneous scales and increases the probability that a unitary attitude is being measured, and therefore that validity (construct and concurrent) and reliability are reasonably high.

Because measures made with the two techniques are highly correlated, most attitude researchers have relied on some version of the more efficient Likert scaling procedure to measure attitudes.

Disadvantage of Likert scales

1 The Likert-type scale does not claim to be more than an ordinal scale, i.e. it makes possible the ranking of individuals in terms of the favourableness of their attitude toward a given object, but it does not provide a basis for saying how much more favourable one is than another, nor for measuring the amount of change after some experience. Whether it constitutes a disadvantage of the Likert scale in comparison with the Thurstone scale depends on one's judgement of whether Thurstone scales really meet the criteria for interval scales! Many researchers, of course, assume Likert scales provide interval data.
2 The total score of an individual has little clear meaning, since many patterns of response to the various items may produce the same score. We have already noted that Thurstone-type scales are also subject to this criticism, but it applies even more strongly to the Likert scales, since they provide a greater number of response possibilities.

The semantic differential

The semantic differential is based on research done in the 1950s by Osgood and several collaborators, who were concerned with the 'measurement of meaning' (Osgood, Suci & Tannenbaum 1957). Osgood asked thousands of people to rate an array of objects or concepts in terms of many different attributes, then compared these ratings through factor analysis (a complex statistical technique involving the intercorrelation of large arrays of data in such a way as to locate the major dimensions underlying the data). Three major rating factors (i.e. three main dimensions of judgement) were found: an *evaluative* factor, in which the object or concept is rated on a good-to-bad dimension or something similar, such as kind-to-cruel; a *potency* factor, involving ratings of strong-to-weak or such related qualities as hard-to-soft; and an *activity* factor, where the main concern is active-to-passive, but also includes such qualities as fast-to-slow and hot-to-cold.

The evaluative factor represents the most important of these judgemental dimensions, according to Osgood's statistical analyses. It also happens to be the dimension that most other kinds of attitude scales utilise, as you can see from our examples of Thurstone and Likert scales; and it is the dimension that many definitions of attitude stress as being the key distinction between attitude and simple belief.

The reliability and validity of the semantic differential is well documented (for example, Warr & Knapper 1968). Scales which are loaded on the evaluative dimension are, for instance: good–bad, successful–unsuccessful, beautiful–ugly, cruel–kind, clean–dirty, wise–foolish, honest–dishonest, happy–sad, nice–awful.

The same set of scales can be used to rate a variety of different objects, so that it is possible to make direct comparisons among a person's attitudes towards smoking, examinations, particular teachers, or toward any other set of items whose attitude ratings the researcher is interested in comparing. Different concepts may require slightly different sets of scales for maximum rating precision; 'kind-cruel', for example, would probably not work as well in measuring attitudes toward modern painting as 'beautiful–ugly'.

A typical layout and instructions for the semantic differential techniques is as follows.

Semantic differential scale

The purpose of this study is to measure the meanings which certain concepts have for you. This is done by having you judge them against a set of descriptive scales which consist of adjectives and their opposites. You are asked to make your judgments on the basis of what these things mean to you. On each page of this booklet, you will find a different concept to be judged and beneath it a set of scales. You are asked to rate the concept on each of the scales in order.

Important

1 Place your check-mark in the middle of the spaces, not at the boundaries.
2 Be sure you check every scale for every concept; do not omit any.
3 Never put more than one check-mark on a single scale.
4 Do not look back and forth through the items. Do not try to remember how you checked similar items earlier in the test. Make each item a separate and independent judgement.
5 Work fairly quickly through the items.

6 Do not worry or puzzle over individual items. It is your first impressions, the immediate 'feelings' about the items that are wanted. On the other hand, do not be careless, for it is your true impression that is wanted.

Concept—Myself

	7	6	5	4	3	2	1	
Good	____	____	____	____	X	____	____	bad
Rigid	____	____	____	____	____	X	____	flexible
Independent	____	____	X	____	____	____	____	submissive
Democratic	____	X	____	____	____	____	____	authoritarian
Disorganised	____	____	____	____	____	X	____	organised
Cooperative	____	____	____	X	____	____	____	uncooperative
Nonconforming	____	____	____	X	____	____	____	conforming

The particular scales included are those the investigator wishes to include—usually on the grounds of relevance to the attitude under investigation.

To prevent the acquiescence response, set-scale polarity is reversed for pairs in random order, and for these the scoring on the 1–7 range is reversed. For individuals, a total score reflecting level of self-evaluation can be obtained on the dubious assumption—as with most other instruments—that all items are equal in their contribution and that the data are of the interval type. With groups, such totals would be averaged or an average response could be computed for each scale. The semantic differential technique appears appropriate for use with children of 12 years of age and upwards.

Advantages

1 In most uses of the Thurstone and Likert techniques, measurement of an attitude's affective aspects is stressed, though cognitive and conative qualities are often intermingled with the affective judgment. The individual's beliefs about an object's potency, activity, and at times other less important dimensions of meaning, may also be crucial to their overall attitude, determining whether their behaviour toward an object is similar to or very different from the behaviour of other individuals whose evaluative ratings resemble their own. As an example, one subject might rate the concept PRINCIPAL as *unfavourable, strong and active*; another subject might rate PRINCIPAL as equally *unfavourable*, but also as *weak* and *passive*. The first subject might actively avoid or seek to placate their principal; the second might ignore or attempt to exploit their principal.
2 A semantic differential is relatively easy to construct.

Disadvantages

1 The assumption of equal interval data may not be sound, and, like the Likert approach, ordinal data is certainly a more valid assumption.
2 Scales weighted heavily on the evaluative dimension for one concept may not be strongly evaluative when applied to another concept. It would seem necessary for a factor analysis to be undertaken to ensure that presumed evaluative scales actually do index the evaluative dimension when referring to a particular attitude object. The

marker scale 'good–bad' which is consistently evaluative will help identify the other evaluative scales. The meaning of a scale may vary considerably depending on the concept being judged.

The reliability and validity of attitude scales

Reliability

The reliability of attitude scales is usually assessed via the test–retest method, or where occasionally there are two parallel forms of the scale, an alternative form of reliability can be obtained.

STQ151

1   What do you understand by the test–retest method? (Refer back to chapter 20 if in difficulty.)
2   Why should a split-half reliability not be used?

It would be impossible to split a Likert attitude scale or a semantic differential into two comparable halves. It would be feasible but difficult in a Thurstone scale, provided items of the same scale value were included in each half. This would be akin to parallel forms of the scale.

Measures of internal consistency are possible with Likert scales by correlating item 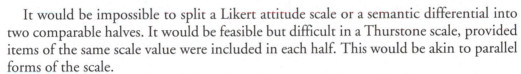 score to total score, the general principle being that item score should be congruent with total score. An item score that is not may well be measuring some other attitude. Refer to p. 348 on the use of Cronbach's alpha with SPSS.

Validity

The validity of attitude scales is often checked by concurrent validity using known criterion groups, i.e. sets of individuals who are known in advance to hold different attitudes to the relevant object. For example, random samples of ALP and Liberal Party members could act as criterion groups for the concurrent validation of an attitude scale towards private schools. If the scale differentiated statistically significantly between these two groups, then it could be said to have concurrent validity.

Predictive validity is also possible by selecting some criterion in the future such as voting behaviour. Content validity can be gauged by requesting judges to indicate whether the items are relevant to the assessment of that particular attitude. Finally, of course, construct validity using factor analysis of the inter-correlations of item responses will demonstrate homogeneity or heterogeneity of Likert and semantic differential scales. Many attitude scales are multifactorial or multidimensional, in that they do not measure one unitary attitude but groups of items, each measuring different dimensions of the attitude. Face validity can cause problems. In order to ensure motivation, the statements are often fairly obviously related to the attitude object in question. In fact, it is extremely difficult to disguise the purpose of the scale in most cases. However, because the manifest content of the statements usually makes clear the nature of the dimension being studied, it is possible for the individual, deliberately or unconsciously, to bias results in the direction thought to best suit his or her own purposes.

STQ152

What criterion would you select to check the concurrent validity of:
1   an attitude towards the wearing of seat-belts scale?
2   an attitude scale towards corporal punishment in schools?

General criticisms

The chief criticism that might be levelled at all attitude scales is concerned with the indirectness of measurement, i.e. verbal statements are used as a basis for inferences about 'real' attitudes. Moreover, attitude scales are easily faked. Although administering the scales anonymously may increase the validity of results, anonymity makes it difficult to correlate the findings with related data about the individuals, unless such data are obtained at the same time. It seems that we must limit our inferences from attitude-scale scores, recognising that such scores merely summarise the verbalised attitudes that the subjects are willing to express in a specific test situation.

Attitude scales are self-report measures and they suffer from the same problems as all other self-report techniques. What subjects are willing to reveal about themselves would seem to depend on such factors as willingness to cooperate, social expectancy, feelings of personal adequacy, feelings of freedom from threat, dishonesty, carelessness, ulterior motivation, interpretation of verbal stimuli, etc. The study of human emotions, feelings and values about objects in the environment is clouded by those very same variables.

Response sets too, such as acquiescence (the tendency to agree with items irrespective of their content) and social desirability (the tendency to agree to statements which social consensus would, it is believed, indicate are socially desirable and reject those that are socially undesirable) fog the data derived from attitude scales. The best way of eliminating acquiescence is to randomly order positive and negative items to prevent a subject ticking madly away down the same column.

Original judgements of statements in STQ149			
Item	**Scale value**	**Item**	**Scale value**
1	3.3	7	5.8
2	8.9	8	3.7
3	2.4	9	3.8
4	10.0	10	8.8
5	2.0	11	10.3
6	10.7	12	4.9

summary

Attitudes are evaluated beliefs which predispose the individual to respond in specific ways. Attitude scales measure the degree of favourability towards the subjects in question. The major types of attitude scales are the Likert, Thurstone, and the semantic differential. Attitude scales may often have low reliability and low validity as they are self-report measures and subjects may lie, give socially acceptable answers and misinterpret verbal stimuli.

References

Edwards, A.L. (1957), *Techniques of Attitude Scale Construction*, Appleton Century Crafts, New York.
Hinckley, E.D. (1963), 'The influence of individual opinion on construction of an attitude scale', *Journal of Abnormal and Social Psychology 67*, pp. 290–2.
Likert, R. (1932), 'A technique for the measurement of attitudes', *Arch. Psychology*, p. 140.
Osgood, C.E., Suci & Tannenbaum (1957), *The Measurement of Meaning*, University of Illinois Press, Illinois.
Warr, P. & Knapper, C. (1968), *Perception of People and Events*, Wiley, London.

Further reading

Shaw, M. & Wright, J. (1968), *Scales for the Measurement of Attitudes*, McGraw Hill, New York.
Thurstone, L.L. (1929), *The Measurement of Attitude*, University of Chicago, Illinois.

Structured interview and questionnaire surveys

30
thirty

The survey is the most commonly used descriptive method in educational research, and gathers data at a particular point in time.

Major forms of survey

- The *descriptive* survey aims to estimate as precisely as possible the nature of existing conditions, or the attributes of a population; for example, its demographic composition, its attitude to abortion, its religious beliefs, voting intentions, its child-rearing practices.
- The *explanatory* survey seeks to establish cause and effect relationships but without experimental manipulation; for example, the effects on teachers' motivation of merit schemes, the effects of social climate on adolescent values. Sometimes, of course, both descriptive and explanatory studies can be carried out in the same inquiry.

Thus, surveys may vary in their levels of complexity, from those which provide simple frequency counts to those which involve correlational analysis.

For descriptive surveys, representative sampling of the population is as crucial as in the experiment, since without representation estimates of population, statistics will be inaccurate. In explanatory studies, control is crucial, for failure to anticipate the necessity to control potentially confounding variables may invalidate the findings. All the problems inherent in the obtaining of reliable and valid measures are as important in surveys as in the experimental method.

The chief characteristics of the survey are:

- It requires a sample of respondents to reply to a number of standard questions under comparable conditions.
- It may be administered by an interviewer, by mailing the respondent a form for self-completion, or by telephone.
- The respondents represent a defined population. If less than 100 per cent of the defined population is sampled then a sample survey has been conducted; a 100 per cent survey is a census.
- The results of the sample survey can be generalised to the defined population.
- The use of standard questions enables comparisons of individuals to be made.

STQ153

Distinguish between a census and a sample survey.

The survey can be highly standardised with a schedule of questions which must be responded to in the same order, with the same wording and even the same voice tone in the interview to ensure each subject is responding to the same instrument. In less standardised surveys, there is only enough direction given to stimulate a respondent to cover the area of interest in depth while having freedom of expression. But the choice of method is affected by the following considerations, among others:

- Nature of population; for example, age, reading or writing skills, wide or localised geographical dispersal.
- Nature of information sought; for example, sensitive, emotive, boring.
- Complexity and length of questionnaires/interviews.
- Financial and other resources; for example, time.

The aim is to select an approach that will generate reliable and valid data from a high proportion of the sample within a reasonable time period at minimum cost.

An interviewer-administered survey is more accurate and obtains more returns than a postal self-completion survey.

Face-to-face interviewing is essential where:

- the population is inexperienced in filling in forms or poorly motivated to respond;
- the information required is complicated or highly sensitive; and
- the schedule is an open one, requiring individualised phrasing of questions in response to the respondent's answers.

The least expensive method, self-administered postal questionnaires, would be the obvious one to adopt if the opposite conditions held, especially if the population was highly scattered geographically.

The advantage of the survey is that it can elicit information from a respondent that covers a long period of time in a few minutes, and, with comparable information for a number of respondents, can go beyond description to looking for patterns in data. But the attempt to produce comparable information by standard questions can lead to the obscuring of subtle differences. Simplification of behaviour is the price paid to find patterns and regularities in behaviour by standard measures.

Interview schedules and postal questionnaires should be tried out in 'pilot studies' to remove ambiguity, test adequacy of response categories, and all the work involved in the administration.

Steps in survey research

1 Planning involves the determination of what topic is to be investigated and what population is to be studied. In this stage, one also decides on the methods and procedures that will be used to gather the data, and the resources needed.
2 Sampling involves decision-making about which people from the population of interest are to be included in the survey. The sampling procedure that is most likely to yield a representative sample is some form of random or stratified sample (chapter 6).
3 Construction of the data-gathering instrument involves writing the questions and planning the format of the instrument to be used.
4 Carrying out the survey includes pre-testing the instrument to determine whether it will obtain the desired data, training the users of the instrument (for example, interviewers), interviewing subjects or distributing questionnaires to them, and verifying the accuracy of the data gathered.
5 Processing data includes the coding of the data, computer processing of the data, interpreting the results, and reporting the findings.

The strength of the survey method would appear to be that:
- it is often the only way to obtain information about a subject's past life;
- it is one of the few techniques available to provide information on beliefs, attitudes and motives;
- it can be used on all normal human populations except young children;
- it is an efficient way of collecting data in large amounts at low cost in a short period of time; and
- structured surveys are amenable to statistical analysis.

Longitudinal and cross-sectional surveys

Some surveys involve multiple or repeated contact. 'Before-and-after' studies come into this category where there is an attempt to establish the effect of some event on the experimental group which has occurred between the two phases of the survey; for example, the effect of a television program on attitudes to free tertiary education.

There are two basic approaches in collecting survey data from large samples. The first of these is the *cross-sectional approach*. As the name implies, the method involves taking a cross-section of the population, selecting, for example, a particular age group, and measuring the value of one or more variables, such as height, reading ability, etc. These data can then be used to calculate norms for that particular age group. Cross-sections of other age groups can then be taken and the changes in norms from one cross-section to another can be used as an estimate of the development occurring between one age and another.

FIGURE 30.1 *Cross-sectional design—the number in each circle represents the subject number*

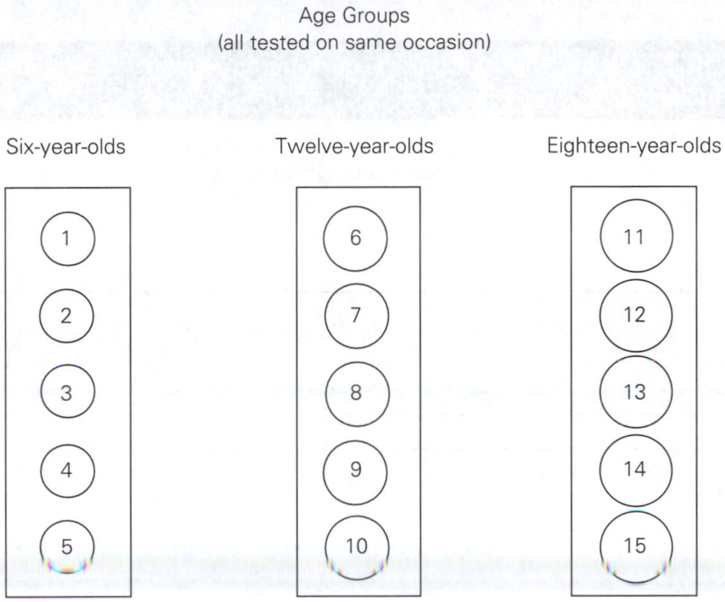

Age Groups
(all tested on same occasion)

Six-year-olds   Twelve-year-olds   Eighteen-year-olds

However, there are often difficulties in interpreting cross-sectional data. For one thing, there may be changes from year to year in the variable being studied. For example, if one were interested in using a cross-sectional approach to examine the development of number skills between the ages of four and six, one might assess these skills in two samples of 100 children at each of the two ages. It might then be found that the norms showed advances in some skills, no difference in others, and decrements in the rest between the two age groups. However, the actual sample of four-year-old children might, if followed up after two years, turn out to be much better in all skills than the original six-year-olds in the sample. The reason for this could be that environmental conditions relevant to the development of those number skills had changed during this period, though there are other equally likely explanations.

The cross-sectional method is most often used to produce developmental norms for different ages, thus allowing one to assess whether a particular child is ahead of or behind the norm, which is often an important diagnostic question. However, by concentrating on averages, this approach tells us very little about individual patterns of development, and may indeed give a false picture of growth. If some children develop very quickly between the ages of four and five, and others very slowly, this will be obscured in the cross-sectional data. The impression would be that all develop at a steady rate.

The final difficulty with a cross-section approach is that chronological age is by no means equivalent in terms of physical development for every individual. There are considerable differences in development status between children who are ostensibly the same 'age'.

The alternative approach for studying large samples of individuals is a *longitudinal study*. This avoids the pitfalls outlined above, by collecting observations and measurements through repeated contact with the same individuals over a period of years.

FIGURE 30.2 *The longitudinal study—each subject observed (tested) five times over the course of the study*

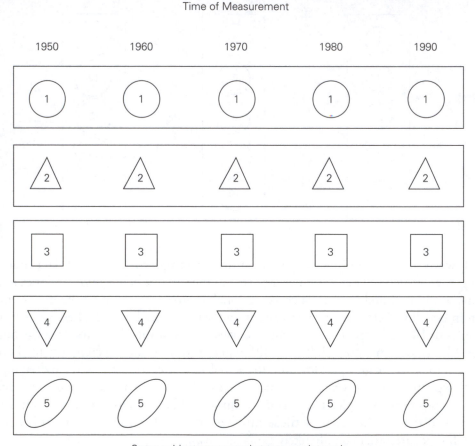

Time of Measurement

Same subjects measured at ten-year intervals

By collecting information in this way, one can interpret an individual's status in terms of their own past growth, and pick up many of the variations and individual differences in developmental progress.

A good example of a longitudinal approach is the UK National Child Development Study (Davie, Butler & Goldstein 1972) which followed up nearly 16 000 children from their birth, during one week in March 1958, for eleven years. A population followed up in this way in a longitudinal study is commonly called a cohort. The data from this particular study have been used to assess, for example, the long-term effects on children's attainment if their mother works.

Although it is a much more valuable way of studying development, the longitudinal approach is extremely time-consuming, costly, organisationally complex, and slow in producing results. Some indication of the difficulty of maintaining large-scale longitudinal surveys is given by the fact that only four British studies with samples of more than 1000 have been recorded. Particular care must be used in selecting the sample, because any initial errors are likely to have an increasing influence on the results as the study progresses. The study becomes increasingly difficult as the years go by, because families move and have to be followed up, and changes in research personnel may introduce error into the data collection. There is also a common tendency for the sample to become biased towards those who are more cooperative in informing the investigators of change of address, and, in addition, bias can occur because, for example, different social-class groups may be affected by differential illness and death rates.

STQ154

1 Briefly outline the relative merits of the longitudinal and cross-sectional survey methods.
2 What do you perceive to be the major factors which may lower reliability and validity indices in: (a) an interview (b) a questionnaire?

The questionnaire or interview schedule

Survey data are usually obtained by means of a questionnaire, a series of pre-determined questions that can be either self-administered, administered by mail, or asked by interviewers. When the questionnaire is to be administered by interview, it is often called an *interview schedule*. The use of questionnaires in research is based on one basic underlying assumption: that the respondent will be both willing and able to give truthful answers.

Three kinds of items generally are used in the construction of schedules and questionnaires: closed items, open-ended items, and scale items.

Closed items

The closed items usually allow the respondent to choose from two or more fixed alternatives. The most frequently used is the dichotomous item which offers two alternatives only: yes/no or agree/disagree, for instance. Sometimes a third alternative such as 'undecided' or 'don't know' is also offered. The alternatives offered must be exhaustive, i.e. cover every possibility.

Do you feel school uniforms should be compulsory?

❏ Yes

❏ No

❏ Don't know

Closed items have, for example, the advantage of achieving greater uniformity of measurement and therefore greater reliability; of making the respondents answer in a manner fitting the response category; and of being more easily coded. Disadvantages include their superficiality; the possibility of annoying respondents who find none of the alternatives suitable; or forcing responses that are inappropriate.

These weaknesses can be overcome, however, if the items are written with care, mixed with open-ended ones, and used in conjunction with probes if part of an interview.

Open-ended items

Open-ended items simply supply a frame of reference for respondents' answers, coupled with a minimum of restraint on their expression. Other than the subject of the question, there are no other restrictions on either the content or the manner of the respondent's reply, facilitating a richness and intensity of response. Open-ended items form the essential ingredient of unstructured interviewing (see chapter 24).

EXAMPLE

What aspects of this course do you most enjoy? ....

Open-ended questions are flexible. In interviews, they allow the interviewer to probe so that they may go into more depth if they choose, or clear up any misunderstandings; they enable the interviewer to test the limits of the respondent's knowledge; they encourage cooperation and help establish rapport; and they allow the interviewer to make a truer assessment of what the respondent really believes. Open-ended situations can also result in unexpected or unanticipated answers which may suggest hitherto unthought-of relationships or hypotheses. The major problem is coding or content analysing the responses.

A particular kind of open-ended question is the funnel. This starts with a broad question or statement and then narrows down to more specific ones. An example would run like this:

a Many school pupils smoke these days. Is this so at your school?

b Do any of your school friends smoke?

c Have you ever smoked?

STQ155

What are the advantages and disadvantages of open-ended questions compared with closed questions?

Scale items

The scale is a set of verbal items to which the respondent responds by indicating degrees of agreement or disagreement. The individual's response is thus located on a scale of fixed-alternatives.

EXAMPLE

How would you rate the teacher that you have this semester? (Circle number.)

1 Very poor
2 Less than adequate
3 Adequate
4 More than adequate
5 Excellent
6 Insufficient information

Ranking questions ask respondents to indicate the order of their preference among a number of options. Rankings should not involve more than five or six options because it becomes too difficult for respondents to make the comparisons. An example of a ranking item follows.

EXAMPLE

Which subjects do you find most interesting? Please rank the order of interest of the following subjects, with 1 being the most interesting and 5 the least interesting.

- History
- Maths
- English
- Science
- Geography

Ranked data can be analysed by adding up the rank of each response across the respondents, thus resulting in an overall rank order of alternatives.

A checklist response requires that the respondent selects one of the presented alternatives. In that they do not represent points on a continuum, they are nominal categories.

EXAMPLE

Which languages do you speak? (Tick as many as apply.)

❑ English
❑ French
❑ German
❑ Japanese
❑ Other (please specify)

This kind of response tends to yield less information than the other kinds considered.

Finally, the categorical response mode is similar to the checklist but simpler in that it offers respondents only two possibilities.

Paying for education increases motivation to study	True	False

Or

In the event of war, would you be prepared to give up your studies and fight for your country?	Yes	No

Summing the numbers of respondents for each response yields a nominal measure, suitable for chi square.

Questionnaire and schedule design

The appearance and arrangement of the survey form itself is vital to a successful study. A well-planned and carefully constructed questionnaire will increase the response rate and will also greatly facilitate the summarisation and analysis of the collected data.

The model questionnaire is designed in four parts: the introduction, warm-up questions, the body of the study, and demographic questions.

Alternatively, the introduction can be taken care of in a covering letter, and many researchers find it most suitable to place demographic questions concerned with the sex of the respondent, age, faculty, religion, socioeconomic status, and so on, first.

The reason for this is that one of the warm-up questions might offend and lead to the destroying of the questionnaire, whereas the demographic questions do not usually offend and lead the respondent well into the questionnaire, thereby making it more difficult to withdraw. One question which offends at the beginning may lead to a refusal to answer the whole schedule. Thus a broad scheme of (1) introduction, (2) demographic questions, (3) warm-up questions, (4) body of study, is advised.

Questionnaires used for mail surveys differ in many ways from those used for interviewing. For example, questions that ask people to rank ten things by assigning each of them a number from 1 to 10 work better in mail surveys because the respondent can see all ten items at once. They do not work as well in an interview because the respondent sees no list and would have to remember all ten items to be ranked. Also, some questions that read well in a mail survey can be tongue-twisters for interviewers.

The physical appearance of mail surveys is more important than that of interview forms because the respondent sees the actual questionnaire. Thinking up questions for a questionnaire is not a problem; coming up with the right questions is. Usually a literature review, preliminary interviews with potential respondents, and discussions with experts provide a multitude of possible questionnaire items. The difficult task is selecting only those items that are really needed in the questionnaire to accomplish the purpose of the study.

The following procedures should be followed in designing both mail and interview questionnaires:

1 Begin with a few interesting, 'non-threatening' questions because introductory questions that are either 'threatening' or 'dull' may reduce the likelihood of the subjects completing the questionnaire.

2 Group items into logically coherent sections; i.e. those that deal with a specific topic, or those that use the same response options should go together.

3 Make smooth transitions between sections, avoiding the appearance of a series of unrelated 'quiz' questions.

4 Do not put important items at the end of a questionnaire.

5 Number questionnaire items so that the respondent or interviewer will not become confused while completing the form.

6 Put an identifying mark on each page of the form so that if one page should get separated from the rest, it can be re-attached.

7 Put the study title in bold type on the first page of the questionnaire.

Because the response rate to mail questionnaires is affected by the visual appearance of the questionnaire, particular attention should be paid to the following format suggestions:

1 Make the questionnaire as 'appealing to the eye' and easy to complete as possible.

2 Include brief but clear instructions for completing the form. Construct questions so they do not require extensive instructions or examples. Print all instructions in bold type or italics.

3 If questions appear on both sides of a page, put the word 'over' on the bottom of the front side of that page.

4 Avoid constructing sections of the form to be answered only by a subset of respondents—such sections may lead respondents to believe the form is not appropriate for them, or it may cause frustration and result in fewer completed forms.

5 If you have sections that consist of long checklists, skip a line after every third item to help the respondent place answers in the appropriate places.

6 Avoid the temptation to overcrowd the pages of your questionnaire with too many questions. Many people squeeze every possible question onto a page, which can cause respondents to mark answers in the wrong place. Leave plenty of 'white space'.

7 Arrange the questionnaire so that the place where respondents mark their answers is close to the question. This encourages fewer mistakes.

8 Avoid using the words *questionnaire* or *checklist* on the form itself. Some people may be prejudiced against these words after receiving many forms not designed with the care of yours.

9 Put the name and address of the person to whom the form should be returned on the questionnaire, even if you include a self-addressed return envelope, since questionnaires are often separated from the cover letter and envelope.

The following are format considerations unique to interview schedules:

1 Print questions on only one side of each page of the questionnaire because it is cumbersome for interviewers to turn to the reverse side of pages during the interview.

2 Clearly distinguish between what the interviewer should read aloud and other things printed on the questionnaire that should not be read. Different type styles can be used to make this distinction unambiguous.

3 Provide clear instructions so that the interviewers will know exactly which questions to ask after each response is made. This means 'skip' patterns should be clearly indicated.

4 Arrange questions so that interviewers do not have to refer to earlier parts of the questionnaire.

5 Limit the number of response options so that respondents can remember them all.

6 Do not end an interview with an open-ended question because the interviewer will have a harder time controlling when the interview will end.

7 Leave enough space on each page so that interviewers can record any additional important information obtained from the respondent.

8 Anticipate responses to open-ended questions and provide a list of these on the interview form to help the interviewer mark responses. This will speed up the interview.

How do I ask a question?

Generally, the most effective questions are worded as simply as possible. Questions should communicate something specific, so do not try to impress respondents with fancy vocabulary at the risk of confusing your meaning. Use language that is familiar and appropriate to the population for whom the questions are intended. If the questions are designed for a specialised group, you may wish to use the language or jargon of that group.

Avoid using stuffy bureaucratic words or phrases (for example, *database* or *ad hoc*). These types of words bore respondents and detract from clarity of meaning.

Do not write loaded questions that suggest a response.

EXAMPLE

Is it desirable to have private schools?

VERSUS

Is it desirable or undesirable to have private schools?

The first suggests an affirmative answer. However, the second does not suggest an answer and gives the respondent a freer choice. Bias resulting from loaded questions is a particularly serious problem in interviews because respondents find it more difficult to disagree with an interviewer than with a self-complete questionnaire.

Furthermore, avoid asking questions that assume that a certain state of affairs existed in the past. For example, how would you answer the following questions?

a Have you stopped beating your children?
b Do you still design bad questionnaires?

Regardless of whether the respondent answers 'yes' or 'no', such questions imply previous participation in the activities about which the person has been asked.

The following are additional suggestions that should be considered when writing questionnaire items.

1 Before asking a question, be sure the respondent is capable of giving an accurate answer.

2 Avoid writing 'double' questions that ask for more than one piece of information per question. Trying to squeeze too much into an item may confuse the respondent or may actually make the question impossible to answer. Consider the following example: 'Do you like maths and English?' This question asks whether respondents like both. Suppose they like one but not the other? Ask two questions instead.

3 Furthermore, a question with more than one adverb or adjective is likely to be either a double question or an overly wordy question. Consider: 'Is the text informative and interesting?'. If *informative* and *interesting* are taken to mean the same thing they are redundant, and one of them should be eliminated. If their meanings are taken as different from each other, the question becomes a double question. When the data are analysed, it is impossible to know whether the answer given refers to both parts of the question or only one part.

4 Avoid using words with vaguely defined meanings. Such words as *country*, *population*, *environment* and *passive* have different conceptual meanings for different people. If a question asks, 'Do you believe the country's population should be less passive about maintaining the environment?', it certainly would be an ambiguous question. Whose country? How much of what population? How passive? What environment?

5 Avoid words that have more than one meaning (for example, *value*, *liberal*, or *conservative*). You will not know which meaning respondents had in mind when they answered.

6 Avoid using double negatives caused by joining a negative response to a question phrased in the negative. Instead of asking questions like (a) below, ask questions directly and concisely as shown in (b):

a Do you believe tertiary students should not pay tuition fees?
❑ Yes
❑ No

b Do you believe tertiary students should pay tuition fees?
❑ Yes
❑ No

7 Be careful if you use abbreviations. Be certain the people you ask will know what your abbreviations mean.

8 Avoid using, 'if yes, then . . .' questions on mail surveys. Usually these questions can be asked in an alternative manner. Consider the following example:

Are you married?
❑ Yes
❑ No

If yes, is your wife employed?
❑ Yes
❑ No

The same information can be obtained by asking the better question:

Is your wife employed?

❏ Yes
❏ No
❏ I'm not married

9 Do not be overly enthusiastic about asking people to rank various things by 'assigning a number from 1 to 10 with 1 being the most important and 10 being the least important'. This type of question assumes people do not feel the same about two or more of the things ranked, and this is usually not true. These questions also assume people can rank all the things listed, and often people cannot do so.

10 If you want general information from respondents, include an open-ended question at the end of the form. Although such questions are more difficult than objective questions to tabulate, they can be a useful supplement. Open-ended questions are useful in a pre-test to determine which response options to include in a later, more objective, item for the final questionnaire. Furthermore, the free-answer question provides quotable quotes which may add sparkle and credibility to the final report.

Response options

The response options offered to respondents can affect their answers. Confusing options lead to unreliable results and, usually, low response rates. The following suggestions will help you design appropriate response options for questionnaire items and ease coding into the computer:

1 Make certain one response category is listed for every conceivable answer. Omitting an option forces people either to answer in a way that does not accurately reflect reality or to answer not at all.

EXAMPLE

How many years have you taught at this school?

　0–6 years
　7–8 years

In this case, people who have over eight years' service are unable to answer the question.

2 Include a 'don't know' response option any time you ask a question to which people may not have the answer. When surveys find that many people do not know about a given issue, that information alone is often very valuable.

3 Balance all scales around a mid-point in the response answer:

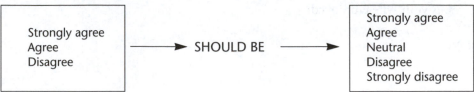

4 Use filter questions to ensure the respondent answers only questions which are relevant to him/her:

EXAMPLE

Section F

Q1 Do you have any children?
(Circle ONE
number)

	Yes	1	Go to Q2
	No	2	Go to Section G, Page 18

Q2 How many children do you have?
(Circle ONE
number)

	One	1
	Two	2
	Three	3
	Four	4
	Five or more	5

Notice that the respondent who answers 'No' to Q1 in Section F will move directly to Section G, omitting all questions which are not of relevance to them. As well as saving the respondent a lot of time, it will also enable you, at the time of the analysis, to easily identify those respondents who have children, and then perform certain analyses on this subset of the data.

5 Some writers believe that if the mid-point of an agree–disagree scale is labelled 'undecided', responses will differ from scales where the mid-point is labelled 'neutral'. Therefore, label the mid-point according to the 'exact' meaning the scale requires.

6 Arrange response options vertically:
❏ Yes
❏ No
rather than horizontally:
❏ Yes   ❏ No
This helps reduce errors that occur when people mark the blank after the intended response rather than before it.

7 Make certain the respondent knows exactly what information should be put in 'fill-in-the-blank' items.

EXAMPLE

Incorrect   What is your age? ....
Correct   What is your age?......years…....months

Pre-testing

By the time a study has journeyed through the planning stage and reached the stage when the questionnaire is constructed, much effort and money have already been invested. A pre-test of the questionnaire at this stage is useful to reveal confusing and other problematic questions that still exist in the questionnaire. Pre-testing involves administering the questionnaire to a sample of people as similar as possible to those who will ultimately be surveyed.

Finally, a brief note at the very end of the questionnaire can:

- ask respondents to check that no answer has been inadvertently missed out;
- solicit an early return of the completed schedule;
- thank respondents for their participation; and
- offer to send a short abstract of the major findings when the analysis is completed.

STQ156

In what ways can the accuracy of answers to questionnaire items be increased?

Obtaining a high return on a mailed questionnaire

Obtaining a high return on mailed questionnaires can be challenging. Some of the methods that have proven to be effective in increasing the rate of return are briefly presented:

1 The standard use of stamped, addressed, return envelopes for respondents to use for returning the completed questionnaires results in a higher return rate than a conventional business reply envelope and, of course, higher than providing nothing.
2 The use of follow-up cards or letters in which the investigator reminds the respondent of the need to cooperate, complete the questionnaire and return it.
3 A suggested deadline can be helpful if used skilfully. One should avoid creating the idea that if not returned by a certain date, it would be worthless to return the questionnaire. Perhaps a return date used as a guide would be better.
4 Personally typed or written letters with official letterhead are useful and tend to increase return.

An example of a covering letter is presented below.

This is a scientific study being conducted by the Education Department of the University of ....

We wish to find out what you and other students think about the subject of ....

Your viewpoint will be assisting the advance of knowledge in the area if you complete the questionnaire, fold it and place it in the included free postage-paid (or stamped) envelope and return by ...... [date] or 'as soon as possible'.

Please answer the following questions honestly. Your responses will remain strictly confidential.

Do not sign your name.

STQ157

List some suggestions for questionnaire construction that might increase the rate of returns for mailed questionnaires.

Advantages of a questionnaire

1 *Cost. Less expensive* to administer than face-to-face interviews, particularly when responses from a large, dispersed population are desired. In addition, funds are not required for the training of interviewers.

2 Useful when the instructions and questions asked are simple and the *purpose of the survey can be explained clearly in print.*

3 *Each respondent receives the identical set of questions, phrased in exactly the same way.* The absence of an interviewer, or third party, contributes to the standardisation of responses, as variations in voice inflections, word emphasis, or the use of probes, are eliminated. Better standardisation, particularly through the use of a structured instrument, means higher reliability.

4 *Errors resulting from the recording of responses by interviewers are reduced.*

5 *The respondent is free to answer in their own time and at their own pace.*

6 *Fear and embarrassment, which may result from direct contact, are avoided.*

7 *The problem of non-contact with the respondent* (i.e. the respondent is unavailable when the interviewer is available) *is overcome.*

8 When a questionnaire is designed for self-administration and mailed, it is *possible to include a larger number of subjects as well as subjects in more diverse locations* than is practical with the interview.

9 Another advantage is that a questionnaire that can guarantee *confidentiality* may elicit more *truthful responses* than would be obtained with a personal interview.

10 Furthermore, the interviewer, whose *personal appearance, mood or conduct* may influence the results of an interview, *is not present* when the questionnaire is completed.

Disadvantages of a questionnaire

1 *Difficulty of securing an adequate response.* Response rates tend to be much lower than when the interview method is used. While certain strategies, including follow-up mailings and careful attention to questionnaire design, may result in a response rate as high as 90–100 per cent, response rates to mail questionnaires seldom exceed 50 per cent and rates between 15–50 per cent are common.

2 *Sampling problems.* All questionnaires are not returned, so the likelihood of biased sampling exists as non-respondents may differ significantly from respondents. Usually, the investigator is unable to learn the reason for non-responses.

3 *Complex instruments, ambiguity or vagueness will cause poor responses.*

4 *The method is unsuitable when probing is desirable.*

5 *Ambiguous, incomplete or inaccurate information cannot be followed up.* Responses must be accepted as given.

6 *Non-flexibility.* Respondents may be limited from providing free expression of opinions as a result of instrument-design considerations. Alternatively, open-ended instruments may produce data that cannot be merged easily for systematic analysis.

7 *There is no opportunity to acquire supplementary observational data.*

8 *The respondent's motivation for answering the questionnaire is unknown.*

9 *Self-administered questionnaires are inappropriate for very young, illiterate or some disabled people.*

10 *Possibility of misinterpretation of the questions by the respondents.* It is extremely difficult to formulate a series of questions whose meanings are crystal clear to every reader. The investigator may know exactly what is meant by a question, but because of poor wording or differential meaning of terms, a significantly different interpretation is made by the respondent.

Conducting the interview

The interviewer's main job is to ask the questions in such a way as to obtain valid responses and to record the responses accurately and completely. The initial task for the interviewer is to create an atmosphere that will put the respondent at ease. After introducing themself in a friendly way, the interviewer should state briefly the purpose of the interview, but should avoid giving too much information about the study which could bias the respondent.

The interviewer also has the responsibility of keeping the respondent's attention focused on the task, and for keeping the interview moving along smoothly. This can best be done if the interviewer is thoroughly familiar with the questions and their sequence so that the questions can be asked in a conversational tone, without constantly pausing to find what question is coming next. Of course, the interviewer must refrain from expressing approval, surprise or shock at any of the respondent's answers.

If comparable data are to be obtained, it is important that the same questions be asked in the same order, and with the same wording for all respondents. If the respondent starts to hedge, digress or give an irrelevant response, or if he or she has obviously misinterpreted the question, then the interviewer may probe by saying, 'Explain your answer a little further', or 'Can you tell me a little more than that?'. Of course, the interviewer must be careful not to suggest or give hints about possible responses.

A complete and accurate recording of the respondent's answers must be made. On the open-ended questions, the respondent's exact words must be recorded verbatim while they are responding. This recording can be facilitated by abbreviating words and sentences, or by using a tape recorder. Taping has the obvious advantage of recording the subject's responses verbatim, along with the added advantage of freeing the interviewer up to participate in the dialogue, rather than having to concentrate on note-taking. However, many people feel uncomfortable about having their answers taped and may become inhibited and excessively cautious about what they say. Of course, ethics demand that the subject's permission be obtained before a tape recorder is used.

Advantages of interviews

1 *Flexibility.* One of the most important aspects of the interview is its flexibility. The interviewer has the opportunity to observe the subject and the total situation in which they are responding. Questions can be repeated or their meanings explained in case

they are not understood by the respondents. The interviewer can also press for additional information when a response seems incomplete or not entirely relevant.

2 *Response rate.* More people are more willing to talk and react verbally than to write responses to questions. A key benefit is therefore the high response rate, which makes the data more representative than data solicited through a mail questionnaire. Properly designed and executed interview surveys should yield response rates of at least 80–85 per cent. As fewer participants are needed than for a mail survey, this method is particularly suited to studies in which the size of the representative sample is small.

3 *A face-to-face interaction assists in the establishment of rapport and a higher level of motivation* among respondents.

4 *A useful method when extensive data is required on a small number of complex topics.*

5 *Probing may be used to elicit more complete responses* and the presence of the interviewer generally reduces the number of 'don't know' and non-responses to questions, as explanation and clarification are readily available.

6 *Observation of the respondent's non-verbal communication and environment are possible.* Such observations may provide added dimensions to data collection.

7 *Greater flexibility is afforded to the respondent* in an interview than when a written instrument is used.

8 *The interviewer is able to control the sequence of the items* as the respondent cannot look ahead and anticipate trends in the enquiries.

9 *This approach is useful in obtaining responses from people who would find a written response impossible*, such as very young children, the elderly, illiterate and some disabled groups.

10 Individualised appreciation can be shown to the respondents.

Disadvantages of interviews

1 The main disadvantage of interviews is that they are *more expensive and time-consuming* than questionnaires.

2 *Only a limited number of respondents may be interviewed due to time and financial considerations.* Scheduling of interviews may cause problems also.

3 *Finding skilled and trained interviewers with appropriate interpersonal skills may be difficult.* High inter-rater reliability is difficult to achieve.

4 *An interviewer effect may result from interaction between the interviewer and respondent.* Factors which may bias an interview include the personal characteristics of the interviewer (such as age, sex, educational level, race and experience at interviewing); the opinions and expectations of the interviewer; and a desire to be perceived as socially acceptable by the respondent. Variations in the use of interview techniques, including tone of voice and the inconsistent use of probes, also reduce standardisation. Validity and reliability are seriously affected by all these factors.

5 *Respondents may feel that they are being 'put on the spot'.*

6 *Flexibility afforded by unstructured interviews may generate* difficulties when attempts are made to categorise and evaluate responses.

TABLE 30.1 *Methods of data collection compared*

Mailed questionnaire	Telephone interview	Personal interview
Assumes the most of the respondent	Can reach the unreachable	Assumes the least of the respondent—least demands
Cheapest method of collecting data	More economical than personal interview	Most expensive method
Can reach widely distributed population	Speedy and efficient	Slowest method
Difficult to obtain adequate response rate	Response rate is generally high	Response rate is high
No interviewer bias/ no distribution bias	Interviewer's voice may be biasing	Interviewer's presence may be biasing
Difficult to maintain standardisation	Interviewer maintains standardisation	Interviewer maintains standardisation
Respondent is not always known	Can control participation of other household members	Difficult to control the participation of other household members
No third party bias	Monitoring presents biasing	Monitoring can be biasing
Questionnaire should be short	Questionnaire can be longer than mail	Longer questionnaire justifies the cost
Unlimited answer choices	Limited answer choices	Unlimited answer choices
Appearance of questionnaire is important	Appearance of the questionnaire is not important	Appearance of the questionnaire is not important
Questionnaire must be simple	Questionnaire can be more complex than mail but easy enough for interviewers	Questionnaire can be more complex than telephone
Informant cannot be observed	Informant cannot be observed	Informant can be observed
Difficult to get information to open-ended questions	Interviewer edits open-ended responses	Easier to ask open-ended question—behavioural cues

Anonymity and confidentiality

The issues of anonymity and confidentiality of respondents must be decided for all questionnaire studies. The decision you make regarding this issue may affect your response rate. An anonymous study is one in which nobody can identify who provided data on completed questionnaires. For interviews, anonymity is usually impossible, and for mail surveys, anonymity is not practical because of the need to send follow-ups to non-respondents.

It is usually possible to guarantee confidentiality to people in mail surveys and in interviews. A study is confidential when the project directors and interviewers know who has responded to each questionnaire and promise not to reveal this information. If you guarantee confidentiality, do not call it 'anonymity'.

It helps to use identifying numbers on questionnaires instead of using names or asking the subjects to fill in their names. In mail surveys, be sure to mention the fact that this number is being used and exactly why it is being used.

Validity and reliability

Some attention must be given to the validity question, i.e. whether the interview or questionnaire is really measuring what it is supposed to measure. The most obvious type of validity is *content validity*, which may be assessed by having some competent colleagues who are familiar with the purpose of the survey examine the items to judge whether they are adequate for measuring what they are supposed to measure, and whether they are a representative sample of the behaviour domain under investigation.

Some studies have used direct observation of behaviour to assess criterion-related validity of responses. After responses have been obtained, observations are made to see whether the actual behaviour of the subjects has agreed with their expressed attitudes, opinions, or other answers. Other data sources, such as third parties, may also be used as criteria.

Some variables that influence the validity of a questionnaire are as follows:

- How important is the topic to the respondent? We can assume more valid responses from individuals who are interested in the topic and/or are informed about it.
- Does the questionnaire protect the respondent's anonymity? It is reasonable to assume that greater truthfulness will be obtained if the respondents could remain anonymous, especially when sensitive or personal questions are asked.

Having two different interviewers interview the same individuals to check on the consistency of the results is one procedure for assessing reliability of questionnaires or interviews.

Internal consistency may be checked by building some redundancy into the instrument. That is, items on the same topic may be rephrased and repeated in the questionnaire or interview.

It is usually not possible to repeat a questionnaire or interview with the same individuals after a period of time, or to administer two different forms of the questionnaire to the same individuals. Another problem with this approach is that some answers to questions dealing with less stable aspects of behaviour may change legitimately over time.

Other factors influencing the reliability and validity of a subject's responses involve his or her personality, and where interviewers are concerned, the interaction of both of their personalities and social attributes. The sex, age, dress, race, social class and attractiveness of the interviewer are all known to influence the responses to and rapport with the interviewers.

STQ158

1 What are the major advantages of using mailed questionnaires instead of personal interviews?
2 What are the major advantages of using personal interviews instead of mailed questionnaires?

Data analysis

Data analysis in a descriptive survey may simply consist of determining the frequencies for the major variables involved in the study. For example, a survey of library resources may report the number of volumes of fiction, the number of volumes of non-fiction, and so on. A survey of people's attitudes on an issue may report the number of people falling in different response categories.

In an explanatory survey, however, there is interest in exploring the relationship between the variables of the study. That is, there is interest in knowing whether X and Y co-vary, or under what circumstances they co-vary. The relationship is generally explored by setting up frequency distributions of one variable against another variable by means of cross-tabulations. The simplest cross-tabulation contains two variables with two categories for each variable. More complex forms are possible, such as 2×3, 2×4, 3×4, and so on.

When both variables in the cross-tabulation are measured at a nominal level, the chi-square test may be used to determine whether a systematic relationship exists between the two variables (see chapter 15 for chi square).

Data preparation for computer analysis

With a large number of respondents, it has become popular to analyse the data by computer. This means that the questionnaire must be laid out so that responses can be easily coded.

Data have to be placed in categories for the purpose of analysis. If we wish to find out the frequency of, for instance, different opinions about education, or how opinions about education relate to, say, the age, sex and social class of an informant, then it is essential that we get our data into quantifiable form. This means, in practice, that all the answers to our survey questions must be allocated to categories identified by some symbol.

We see the following in Figure 30.3, overleaf:

1 Left of the vertical line is the interview record as completed by the interviewer; right of the line are the coding instructions as printed on the record form and as encircled, or otherwise completed by the researcher. In some circumstances, it would be possible to combine these two operations.

2 Each piece of information has its two reference numbers. Thus, the 'Life's ambition' of item VI is entered in Column 8 row 3.

3 Some pieces of information (example, I and VII) occupy more than one column. In a case such as I where reference numbers up to 999 are provided for but only two of the three spaces are used, a single-digit number should always be thought of as 003 (say) and a two-digit number as 079. This latter is the 079 which has been entered at the top of the coding column.

4 Provision has been made for:

a omissions: those items which the respondent or, in this case, the interviewer, has failed to complete; and

b additional entries uncategorised by the research worker and thus coded as other.

5 With the current introduction of Windows versions, variable names are placed at the head of each data column, with coded responses placed into the column directly from the questionnaire.

If the coding and column numbers or variable names are clear, it is possible for computer data input to be copied directly off the completed questionnaires.

FIGURE 30.3 *An example of an interview record*

Here is an example of part of an interview record:

I	Name	John Jones	Ref. No.	0 7 9	Col. 1, 2, 3.	079
II	Sex	Male		√	Col. 4	①
		Female				2
						omit 3
III	Age	20–24			Col. 5	1
		25–29				2
		30–34		√		③
		35–39				4
		40+				5
						omit 6
IV	First impression	Good		√	Col. 6	①
		Average				2
		Poor				3
						omit 4
V	Alertness	Alert			Col. 7	1
		Average		√		②
		Apathetic				3
						omit 4
VI	Reasons for applying for course				Col. 8	1
						2
		Interest in psychology				③
		Desires promotion				4
		Life's ambition		√		5
		Rigor mortis setting in				6
		Friend has applied				omit 7
		No particular reason				other 8
VII	Score on M.A.T.			2 5	Col. 9. 10	25
		etc.			etc.	

Suggestions to ease coding and input

1 It is not a good idea to ask a respondent to place a mark over the number he or she selects. The data preparation staff cannot then clearly read the responses. For example, the following should not be used:

(a) Sex? (Mark your response with a cross)   Column
   Male   1   (10)
   Female   ✗

(b) Do you think the refectory service is adequate?
(Tick one number)

Yes	No	Don't know	(11)
✓	2	3	

A better way to handle these two examples is as follows:

(a) Sex? (Circle *ONE* number)   Column

Male	1	(10)
Female	2	

(b) Do you think the refectory service is adequate?
(Circle *ONE* number)

Yes	No	Don't know	(11)
①	2	3	

2 Asking a respondent to *fill in* numbers is often unavoidable; for example, if you need to know the number of students, money values or some other quantity (usually continuous data).

However, if it is not necessary (depending on the data required), then avoid it because problems often arise with legibility of entries, entering only one digit per box, etc., and sometimes extensive editing of questionnaires is then required. Clear instructions may help overcome such problems.

Sometimes you can categorise such responses, but it depends on the analyses you require.

3 Avoid alphabetic coding where possible. Numeric coding is much quicker for the data preparation staff and is more economical in the processing (analysis) stage.

4 'Open-ended' questions require extensive work on the part of the coder (often yourself!) before the questionnaires can be handed in for data entry. For open-ended questions (Why did you choose this particular in-service course rather than XYX?), a coding frame has to be devised after the completion of the questionnaire. This is best done by taking a random sample of the questionnaires (10 per cent or more, time permitting) and generating a frequency tally of the range of responses as a preliminary to coding classification. Having devised the coding frame, the researcher can make a further check on its validity by using it to code up a further sample of the questionnaires. It is vital to get coding frames right from the outset—extending them or making alterations at a later point in the study is both expensive and wearisome.

5 Column numbers should preferably be located on the right-hand side of the page, and if possible, the answers should also be on the right-hand side. This is not always feasible and other layouts are acceptable as long as the coding and column numbers are clear and in a logical order.

STQ159

Practise coding by completing the 'Office Use Only' columns below.

Content analysis

Content analysis may be defined as the systematic quantification of certain characteristics the investigator may be interested in, in terms of their frequency of occurrence within a selected context.

The theme is the most useful unit of analysis. A theme is often a sentence, a proposition about something. Themes are combined into sets of themes. The letters of adolescents or college students may be studied for statements of self-reference. This would be the larger theme. The themes making this up might be defined as any sentences that use *I*, *me*, and other words indicating reference to the writer's self. Discipline is an interesting larger theme. Child training or control is another.

The use of software for content analysis is recommended and the list on pp. 436–9 should provide a suitable program, particularly NUD*IST.

STQ160

You may care to try some content coding of survey data for yourself. Below you will find some answers parents gave to a question in a pilot survey about the things parents talked to the teachers about when they visited their children's school. Construct a coding frame in terms of which the answers can be grouped or coded and compare this frame with the one actually produced for the main survey, which can be found on page 591.

When you have constructed the coding frame with numbers representing each of your categories, try to assign each of the answers to the appropriate category, writing the number of the appropriate category by the side of the verbatim answer. Then count up the frequency of each code and compare this with Table 30.2 on page 592.

Questions

Have you or your husband had a talk with any of X's class teachers or the head since she/he started at (present school)?

If YES, who have you seen? What did you talk to them about?

Responses given by parents (to be coded):

1 Invitation to see her teacher. Told me how X was getting on and asked me to tell him anything about X, whether she liked or disliked anything about school.
2 Future of child, what work he would have to do to catch up if he needed any particular subjects for future job. Trouble with his legs. To see R staying on for another year.
3 Progress, career.
4 Abilities; form master said to go and see him if any problems about child. Wrote also about his not getting on so well, and got reply.
5 Only a general talk to several parents about how school was run and to see head or teacher if any problem arose. Form master about X's work.
6 General progress (anything else discussed at PTA).
7 M's capabilities regarding getting job at Met Office. Progress and behaviour.
8 Progress.

FIGURE 30.4

OFFICE USE ONLY
Column

1. Please insert your Institution's code. [5] — Column 1
2. What is the nature of your current responsibilities? — Column 2

   [ ] Director/Dean of Institution/Faculty/School
   [ ] Assistant Director/Dean of Institution/Faculty/School
   [ ] Head of Department
   [√] Lecturer/Tutor, etc.
   [ ] Other (please specify) ____________

3. What is your current classification? — Column 3

   [ ] Professor/Principal Lecturer
   [ ] Senior Lecturer/Lecturer
   [√] Senior Tutor/Tutor
   [ ] Other (please specify) ____________

4. What is the nature of your current contract? — Column 4

   [ ] Tenurer/Tenure Track
   [√] Short-term contract

5. [√] Full-time — Column 5

   [ ] Part-time

6. What proportion (%) of your time is spent on each of the following?

	(%)	Column
Lecturing in Content Studies	___	6–7
Lecturing in Methodology Studies	30	8–9
Lecturing in Professional Education Studies	20	10–11
Practice Supervision	50	12–13
Administration	___	14–15
Student Advisor	___	16–17
Other (please specify) ____________	___	18–19
Total	100	

7. Are you a trained teacher? Yes [√] No [ ] — Column 20

9 Can't remember, just the general situation of his work.
10 To discuss what to take at Year 11. To see progress she was making.
11 General topics.
12 How she'd settled down. Scope of the work. Teaching methods as far as we could.
13 Maths if necessary to clarify a point.

14 To find out if she was of suitable standard in art and music to do Year 11.

15 Went frequently, regarding subjects P should take to study science.

16 When reports come before Parents' Evening, if she's gone down on anything, you just ask them. To discuss growing-up disturbances, crossing parents. Career.

17 To see Head because R away so much sick and when he went back, the teacher was very aggressive. To explain R was very nervous.

18 How settled in, what teachers thought of him.

19 Before report comes; all teachers are there and you can talk about progress (not PTA) in different subjects; also, after reports. Also, regarding choice of HSC subjects and if to stay on an extra year.

20 About her work and conduct.

21 How T is getting on, about subjects. How soon could leave school (not keen).

22 Progress.

Answer to STQ160
Actual coding frame from pilot survey

Code: Coding instruction:

What sort of things have you discussed with the head or any of the teachers (at present school)?

1 Educational progress at school—including teaching methods, examinations, homework, reports, extra tuition, attitude to work, how parents can help, concentration; staying on an extra year, when to leave, what courses/subjects to take, what class to go into; laziness; anything about curriculum; streaming; leaving school, quality of teaching staff.

   Use this code only for specific discussion/complaints, etc. about the selected child, not for general talks (5).

2 Further education after leaving school—including going to college ('leaving school' means leaving secondary school).

3 Further career—i.e. job, apprenticeship; in future.

4 Behaviour at school—including adjustment to school life, unhappiness, need for understanding, nervousness, relations with teachers, or with other children (including bullying), complaints about other children or about teachers; accusations of theft; discipline, being late.

5 General talk, or nothing in particular—including general matters about the school such as having a look around, the school facilities, class size in general, talk when first started (for example to a group of parents, or when introducing child), talk at Open Day (if not codeable elsewhere); school achievements and aims, school rules, uniform, or similar initial explanation.

   Note: Code 5 can be multi-coded with others. It deals with matters not directly relevant to the child, but also with any general or private introductory talks to parents (and child); if specifics are also mentioned, such as uniform, do not code these as well if they formed part of an introductory talk, but do code them if it was something the parent brought up/complained about later.

Code answers not falling within the above go into:

6 Medical defects or illnesses which can affect child's work (distinguish from code 9)—example, epilepsy, injury preventing sport, etc. (do not multi-code with work or sport), accidents.

7 Extra-school activities—including games, parties, holidays, camps, visits, outings, clubs, hobbies, music.

8 Administration matters such as clothing, attendance times (but coming late = 4); medical exams, notification of absence of medical or holiday reasons, etc.; transport to school; school dinners; school rules and procedures; change to comprehensive system (unless codeable as 1); loss of property; religion.

9 Going to secondary school (for primary school children).

10 Interviewer omitted to code.

TABLE 30.2 *Frequency distribution of content categories*

If _____ has had a talk with head or teacher:
**What sort of things have you discussed with the head or
any of the teacher/s? (at present school)**

	%
Educational progress at school	83
Further education after leaving school	0
Future career	15
Behaviour at school	34
General talk	13
Medical defect or illness	4
Extra-school activities	7
Administrative matters	4
Going to secondary school	0
Personal problems of parents	0
Others	1

With the tiny sample of parents' replies you have been coding, it is unlikely that the frequency counts you have obtained for the different categories will correspond closely to those above. Nevertheless, you should have found at least 'educational progress of child' and 'child's behaviour at school' had relatively high frequencies.

STQ161

1 What data-gathering techniques are used in surveys?
2 What are the major advantages of using mailed questionnaires instead of personal interviews?
3 What are the major advantages of using personal interviews instead of mailed questionnaires?
4 Under what conditions might a researcher want to use a telephone interview?
5 In what ways can the accuracy of answers to questionnaire items be increased?
6 List five suggestions for questionnaire construction that might increase the rate of returns for mailed questionnaires.

7 What are the advantages and disadvantages of open-ended questions compared with closed questions?
8 Distinguish between a census and a sample survey.

summary

Surveys are commonly used in educational and social science research. The descriptive survey provides information, while the explanatory survey seeks to establish cause and effect. Surveys can be face-to-face interviews, conducted by telephone, or mailed as a questionnaire. The interview is more reliable and valid, producing more useable returns than a telephone or mail survey. Longitudinal and cross-sectional surveys are undertaken to assess changes over time.

A variety of formats are used for survey questions and responses. These range from highly structured to open ended. Data analysis is mainly by computer and is facilitated by precoding the question items.

Reference

Davie, R. Butler, N. & Goldstein, M. (1972), *From Birth to Seven*, Longman, London.

Further reading

Beed, T.W. & Stimson, R.J. (eds) (1985), *Survey Interviewing: Theory and Techniques*, George Allen & Unwin, Sydney.
De Vaus, P. (1985), *Surveys for Social Planners*, Holt, Rinehart & Winston, Sydney.
Fink, A. & Kosecoff, J. (1998), *How to Conduct Surveys*, Sage, London.
Gahan, C. & Hannibal, M. (1998), *Doing Qualitative Research Using QSR NUD*IST*, Sage, London.
Kvale, S. (1996), *Interviews*, Sage, London.
Sapsford, R. (1999), *Survey Research*, Sage, London.
Stewart, C.J. & Cash, J.W.B. (1988), *Interviewing: Principles and Practices*, Wm.C. Brown Publishers, Dubuque, Iowa.

STQ answers

STQ11

1. a   M = 6; SD = 3.16
   b   M = 6; SD = 2.74
   c   M = 18; SD = 19.13
   d   Has a greater standard deviation because there is a greater dispersal of scores.
2. b is true. All scores are identical.
3. The standard deviation is 3.25.
   a   The standard deviation is still 3.25.
   b   SD = 6.50. The standard deviation has doubled.
4. The mean is a poor choice as a measure of central tendency when there are extremely large or small values in a distribution. An extreme score can exert a disproportionate effect on the mean.
5. If a distribution is substantially skewed, the median is usually preferred to the mean.
6. a   SS = 40; variance = 10; standard deviation = 3.16
   b   SS = 36; variance = 6; standard deviation = 2.45

STQ12

1. The student's score was equal to the mean.
2. John did better on maths.
   Hui did better on spelling.
   Rachel did equally well on both.
   Chris did better on maths.
   Zola did equally well on both.
3. Raw score = 91.
4. a   130
   b   85

c 122.5
d 90
e 100

5 It identifies a precise location on a distribution, the sign indicates whether location is above or below the mean and the magnitude indicates the number of standard deviations from the mean.

6 0.4, −1.2, +2.2, 50, 30, 59

7 Comparisons are possible because both distributions have the same M and standard deviation following a Z score transformation.

8 In distribution B.

9 80, 90, 100, 110, 120

10 25, 35, 45, 65, 80

STQ13

1 a 49.53%
  b 92.82%
  c 95%
  d 80%
  e The distribution is bilaterally symmetrical and bell-shaped.
  f 68.26%; 95 44%; 99.73%
2 a 34.13
  b 47.72
  c 72.13
3 a 9973
  b 3413
  c 13
  d 1587
  e 1587
4 a 74.95%
  b 67.30%
  c 9.34%
5 68 (approximately)
6 a ± 0.675
  b Scores between 54 and 66 (approximately)

STQ15

P < 0.01 means the probability of a chance occurrence of less than 1 in 100;
p < 0.001 indicates a probability of a chance occurrence of less than 1 in 1000.

STQ17

Level	Probability limits	Frequency of a chance occurrence	Significance levels	Odds against a chance occurrence
NS	$p > 0.05$	more than 5 in 100	> 5%	< 19 : 1
Low	$p < 0.05$	less than 5 in 100	< 5%	19 : 1
High	$p < 0.01$	less than 1 in 100	1%	99 : 1
High	$p < 0.001$	less than 1 in 1000	0.1%	999 : 1

STQ18

a   The mean ego strength level in the Gas Works High School sample.
b   The population consists of 12-year-old males in the city.
c   The sample consists of 12-year-old males at the Gas Works High School.
d   The parameter is the mean ego strength level of 12-year-old males in the whole city.

STQ26

1   a   Systematic sampling
    b   Opportunity sampling
    c   Stratified sampling
2   Obtain the registers and select students by some random technique—for example by using a random number table.
3   A random sample is defined as one in which every member of the population has an equal chance of being selected.
4   b
5   Because it ensures strata or groups will be represented.
6   Time and cost if interviewing is reduced when a population is highly dispersed.
7   No as not complete sampling frame.

STQ27

1   98–102; 99–101; and 99.33–100.66
2   For n = 4 the standard error is 8 points; for n = 64 the standard error is 2 points.

STQ28

107.41 and 112.59

STQ29

1   100
2   a   0.33

b 103.36 to 104.64
c 103.15 to 104.85

STQ34

3 It is easier to disprove a universal population statement than to prove one.
4 a The time taken to read non-rhyming words is significantly longer than the time taken to read rhyming words.
b The difference between the number of men and the number of women not walking under the ladder will be significant.
c Subjects will make significantly more errors on the sensorimotor task in front of an audience than when they are alone.

STQ35

1

p	t-value two-tailed	t-value one-tailed
0.05	1.96	1.65
0.01	2.58	2.33
0.001	3.29	3.09

2 a The advantage of a one-tailed test is that it is easier to obtain statistical significance, but you have increased the chance of making a Type I error.
b It is harder to obtain significance but there is less chance of making a Type I error.
3 Left-hand

STQ36

1 a nominal b nominal   c ordinal if considering birth order or interval if year considered d nominal e nominal f interval g ordinal h ordinal i interval j nominal k ordinal l ratio m nominal n ratio o ratio p interval
2 b and c

STQ38

1 *IV* attitudes towards education
  DV perceptions of effective teacher
2 *IV* height
  DV chosen as leaders' frequencies
3 *IV* test wiseness
  DV test performance
4 *IV* social class
  DV speed of learning

(continued)

5   IV   science/non-science course
    DV   aggression
6   IV   orientation
    DV   degree of illusion
7   IV   meaningfulness of items
    DV   items remembered
8   a   *IV* = noise and *DV* = work efficiency
    b   *IV* = time of day and *DV* = attention span
    c   *IV* = birth order and *DV* = individual personality
    d   *IV* = practice and *DV* = performance

STQ39

1   IV   brake light brightness
    DV   stopping time
    CV   could be all of speed, distance between cars, type of car, driving experience, etc.
2   IV   reinforcement
    DV   patient verbal behaviour
    CV   therapist
3   IV   sex
    DV   conformity
    CV   stop signs at crossroads
4   IV   amount of training
    DV   hand-eye coordination
    CV   IQ

STQ40

1   IV   teaching style
    DV   pupil preference
    MV   thinking style of pupils
2   IV   feedback source
    DV   teacher behaviour change
    MV   years of teaching experience
    CV   age of pupils; subject area of teacher, etc.
3   IV   behaviour modification treatment
    DV   physiological measure of test anxiety
    CV   initial level of test anxiety
4   IV   micro-teaching experience
    DV   questioning techniques
    CV   sex
    MV   experience
5   IV   perceptual motor training
    DV   coordination task performance

CV IQ
MV age

STQ51

This is because with an extreme level of significance like .001, even if the research hypothesis is true, the results have to be quite strong to be large enough to reject the null hypothesis. Alternatively, by setting the significance level at, say, 10, even if the null hypothesis is true, it is fairly easy to get a significant result just by accidentally getting a sample that is higher or lower than the general population before the study.

STQ52

a Increases power   b decreases power   c increases power
d decreases power   e decreases power

STQ53

Effect size = (Population 1 M – Population 2 M)/Population SD
a Effect size = (91 – 90)/4 = 1/4 = .25   b 0.5   c 1.0   d –1   e 0.5   f 1.0   g 2.0
h –2.0.

STQ54

a   Not affected. (That is what the significance level tests.)
b   Probably of small importance (due to small effect size)

STQ55

2    $t = 20.00$. Null hypothesis can be rejected at $p < 0.01$.
3    $t = 27.77$. No.

STQ56

1   a   That there is no statistically significant difference in empathy between the two groups.
    b   Two-tailed (using above H_0)
    c   ($t = 3.53$, $p < 0.05$)
2   a   That there is a statistically significant difference in comprehension skills (H_1). H_0 states that there is no statistically significant difference.

(continued)

b $t = 1.94$; retain null hypothesis.

c   Two-tail because no direction was stated in hypothesis.

STQ57

1   d t test for independent samples

b   A one-tailed test

2   There is no systematic bias in the rankings between each group.

3   There is a significant difference between scores at the 0.05 level, one tail.

4   a   Small samples; not normally distributed data; variances different

b   One-tailed

c   No

5   a   51 and 12

b   12

c   Yes, as equal to tabled value

6   For boys $U_1 = 31.5$; for girls $U2 = 4.5$. The critical value in the table is 4.0 so the null hypothesis cannot be rejected.

STQ58

1   Reject null hypothesis, $t = 5.52$, two-tailed

2   9 df

3   Reject null hypothesis.

4   No, retain null hypothesis.

5   Retain null hypothesis.

7   With $df = 4$ and critical value of $t = +/-2.776$ and calculated $t = -3.72$, we can reject the null hypothesis.

8   a   Mean D = −4

b $D_2 = 112$

c $t = -2.00$ and $df = 3$; we cannot reject null hypothesis

9   a $13 - 1 = 12$

b   6.289

c   3.055

d   Yes

10   a   Where there are few subjects and where changes across time are studied. It also reduces individual differences in a situation where these are large.

b   They are similar in that the role of individual differences is reduced.

c   The carryover effect is where after-effects of the first treatment influence performance on the second, e.g. fatigue, practice.

11   It decreases in value.

STQ59

1 a That there is no significant difference in attitudes to preschool education in mothers before and after their children have attended preschool. Reject null hypothesis.
2 c 3
   d 7
   e Retain
3 T = 4. N = 9. The critical value of T is 6; therefore we reject the null hypothesis.

STQ61

a and d

STQ68

1 No
2 Yes
3 18.467

STQ69

1 a The proportion who agree, disagree or are indifferent to the council's proposals will be equal.
   b $\chi^2 = 6$
   c 2
   d Yes
   e That the distribution of responses was not due to chance
2 No
3 Reject null hypothesis.
4 $\chi^2 = 4.79$, $df = 1$, $p < 0.05$ Since this is lower than the tabled value of 3.84 the null hypothesis is rejected.
5 $\chi^2 = 12.99$, $df = 3$, $p = 0.05$. Since the tabled value is 7.82, the null hypothesis is rejected.
6 b
7 Yes; $\chi^2 = 27.87$; $p < 0.05$
8 Yes; $\chi^2 = 20.00$

STQ74

1 $\chi^2 = 41.07$; $df = 3$, $p = 0.0001$
   Accept alternative hypothesis that there is a significant association between status and opinion.

(continued)

2 $\chi^2 = 4.59$; $df = 1$, $p = 0.03$
   There is a significant association.
3 a $\chi^2 = 9.58$; $df = 2$, $p = 0.05$, $\chi^2 = 5.99$ (tabled)
   b Hence null hypothesis rejected with boys showing significantly greater preference for basketball and girls for volleyball.
4 $\chi^2 = 3.85$; $df = 1$, $p = 0.049$
   Swimming and adjustment are associated.
5 $\chi^2 = 4.84$; $df = 2$, $p = 0.09$
   There is no significant association.
6 Significant $p < 0.002$; $\chi^2 = 9.21$; $df = 1$.
   There is a significant association.

STQ76

1 $r = +0.31$. This is a low positive correlation.
2 Hypothesis is two-tailed. $r = +0.747$; $p = 0.05$, $r = 0.707$ (tabled).
   $p = 0.01$, $r = 0.834$ (tabled).
   There is no statistically significant relationship between algebra and English. This null hypothesis is rejected at $p < 0.05$.
3 $r = 0.82$. Hypothesis is one-tailed. $p = 0.05$, $r = 0.521$ (tabled).
   $p = 0.01$, $r = 0.685$ (tabled).
   There is no relationship between spelling and English (H_0). This can be rejected at $p < 0.01$.
5 1 = positive; 2 = negative
6 $r = -0.80$
7 Yes as tabled value is 0.361
8 Correlation required is 0.444
9 The larger the sample the more accurately it represents the population.
10 a +93   b $N - 2 = 5$ c Yes

STQ80

1 rho = +0.86. With N = 12, f
   0r p = 0.01; rho = 0.777 (tabled). The null hypothesis that practice is not significantly related to efficiency is rejected at $p < 0.01$.
2 rho = −0.35. With N = 10 for p = 0.05, rho = 0.648 (tabled). The null hypothesis that teacher ratings and pupil ratings are not significantly related is retained.
3 rho = +0.624, not significant at p = 0.05.
4 That there is no significant relationship between grades and hours spent watching TV. rho = −0.89, p = 0.01. Reject null hypothesis. Those who watch most TV tend to have significantly poorer grades.
5 a −0.098
   b 0.786
   c No

STQ81

Tau = 0.62

STQ82

$r_{pbis} = -0.466$

STQ83

ad/bc = 12; $r_t = -.76$

STQ84

phi = +0.61; highly significant as chi square = 37.21 and tabled value is 6.63 at 1% level.

STQ85

a= vi; b = v; c = ii; d = i; e = iii; f = iv

STQ86

1   $r_{123} = 0.04$; not significant
2   Because age is related to both income and attendance; however the relationship does not entirely disappear.

STQ87

1   $b = 0.344$; $a = 4.28$
2   $Y = 7.72$

STQ88

The first situation because the correlation is stronger.

STQ89

Y = –5, –1, 3, 13
a = the intercept; b = the regression coefficient so for every year autonomy increases by 0.0623; c = 18.17 i.e. a score of 18.0; d = 13.19, i.e. a score of 13

STQ90

1   1.8 ; 23.0 – 29.6
2   20.9 – 32.3
3   The larger the correlation the smaller the standard error and therefore the smaller the confidence interval so that the prediction is more accurate.

STQ91

There are more than two conditions.

STQ92

1   Error or variance due to chance.
2   The F ratio will decrease.
3   It is measuring the same sources of variance as the error term.
4   1, because both parts of the ration are measuring the same variance.

STQ93

1 b   2 b   3 d   4 b   5 c   6 d   7 d

STQ95

1   a = 2; b = 0.209; c = 167.4; d = 6.2; e = 29
2   not significant

STQ96

1   86, 20, 66
2   29, 2, 27
3   3.35
4   4.09; yes

STQ98

1   Individual differences do not figure in the ratio of the repeated ANOVA, whereas it contributes to both numerator and denominator in the independent measures ANOVA.
2   a   Anxiety and meaningfulness
     b   4.02 with $df = 1$ and 56.
3   c

STQ99

Between method MS = 1.8; between language MS = 125.0: Interaction MS = 20; within groups MS = 7.25; only the between language F is significant at 17.241 as tabled F for 1,16 *df* at 0.05 level is 4.49.

STQ100

1   a = 13.5; b = 3.68; c = 73.5; d = 20; e = 10.2
2   Between treatments factor A, MS = 60, F = 12.0; between treatments factor B, MS = 0, F = 0; A X B interaction MS = 20, F = 4.0; within treatments MS = 5; tabled F (1,54) = 4.402 and tabled F (2,54) = 3.17. There is therefore a significant factor A treatment effect and a significant interaction effect.

STQ101

H = 4.625; *df* = 2; tabled value of chi square = 5.99 at 5% level. Cannot reject null hypothesis.

STQ102

Xr_2 = 14.72; *df* = 3; tabled value = 7.82 at 5% level; reject null hypothesis.

STQ103

a = iv; b = i; c = v; d = vi; f = iii; g = ii

STQ117

a   Negative
b   For *r* =.50, you find z =.549 at the intersection of the row labelled '.5' and the column labelled '.00.' For *r* = –31, the Fisher z is found at the intersection of the row labelled '.3' and the column labelled '.01 ' (where the value of z is shown as .321), which you note as –.321 because your result is in the 'wrong' direction.
c   Z = 2.22; p = .0132 one-tailed or .0264 two-tailed
d   The p value is small enough to convince you that your result differs significantly from the original one and therefore should not be combined with it without careful thought and comment. For example, in describing the results of both studies considered together we should report the differences between them and try to think of an explanation for their differences.

STQ118

a   Corresponding z's are .485 and .424, respectively.
b $Z = .47$
c   p associated with $Z = .47$ is .3192 one-tailed.
d   This is an example of two studies that do not disagree significantly in their estimates of the size of the relation between variables X and Y. They can now be routinely combined by means of a simple meta-analytic technique.

STQ119

a   z's are .485 and .424, respectively.
b   Mean $z = .45$
c   Combined effect size = .422

STQ120

a   Z's are 1.64 and 1.47.
b $Z = .12$
c $p = .4522$ one-tailed,
d   p value indicates a non-significant difference between the p-values, and thus shows clearly just how trivial the conventional line of demarcation between 'significant' and 'non-significant' results sometimes is.

Index